European Business

Pearson
Education

We work with leading authors to develop the
strongest educational materials in business,
bringing cutting-edge thinking and best learning
practice to a global market.

Under a range of well-known imprints, including
Financial Times Prentice Hall, we craft high quality
print and electronic publications which help readers to
understand and apply their content, whether studying or
at work.

To find out more about the complete range of our
publishing please visit us on the World Wide Web at:
www.pearsoneduc.com

European Business

Fourth Edition

Simon Mercado
Richard Welford
and
Kate Prescott

FINANCIAL TIMES
Prentice Hall

An imprint of **Pearson Education**

Harlow, England · London · New York · Reading, Massachusetts · San Francisco · Toronto · Don Mills, Ontario · Sydney
Tokyo · Singapore · Hong Kong · Seoul · Taipei · Cape Town · Madrid · Mexico City · Amsterdam · Munich · Paris · Milan

Pearson Education Limited
Edinburgh Gate
Harlow
Essex CM20 2JE
England

and Associated Companies throughout the world

Visit us on the World Wide Web at:
www.pearsoneduc.com

First published 1992
Second edition 1994
Third edition published under the Pitman Publishing imprint 1996
Fourth edition 2001

ISBN 0 273 64600 1

British Library Cataloguing-in-Publication Data
A catalogue record for this book can be obtained from the British Library

Library of Congress Cataloging-in-Publication Data

Mercado, Simon,
   European business/Simon Mercado, Richard Welford, and Kate Prescott. – 4th ed.
     p. cm.
   Rev. ed of: European business/Rochard Welford, Kate Prescott. 2nd ed. 1994.
   Includes bibliographical references and index.
   ISBN 0-273-64600-1 (pbk.)
   1. European Union countries – Economic policy. 2. Europe – Economic intergration. 3. Industrial management – European Union countries. I. Welford, Richard, 1960 – II. Prescott, Kate.

HC240 .M47 2000
650'.094 – dc21

                            00–064060

10 9 8 7 6 5 4 3 2
05 04 03 02 01

Typeset by 3 in 9.5/13pt Stone Serif
Printed by Ashford Colour Press Ltd, Gosport

Contents

Preface

The emerging European marketplace

The European marketplace is a continually changing and evolving entity. Eight years ago, when the first edition of this book was published, preoccupation was with the completion of the Single European Market and the dismantling of Communism in Eastern Europe. In 1996, when our last edition reached the shelves, the anticipation was of progress towards economic union in keeping with the Maastricht blueprint for European Economic and Monetary Union (EMU). Since that time, Europe's single currency has been launched and the EU has consolidated itself as one of the largest economic unions in the global marketplace. Laws and practices regulating commercial activity in Europe have become more harmonized and there has been a proliferation in the volume of supranational business regulation. The EU has further expanded its role in marketing and sales legislation, employment law, consumer protection and taxation. Events in East–Central Europe have also demonstrated radical change with transition economies deepening market reforms and taking further steps to harmonize domestic legislation with EU codes. To a lesser extent, change has also been witnessed on Europe's periphery (e.g. in the Mediterranean basin) with efforts directed at the liberalization of economies and the removal of barriers to international economic interaction.

Today, although plans for the consolidation and expansion of the EU are beset with uncertainty, the prospect is of an EU that, from an economic viewpoint, will look less like the fragmented EC market of old and more like the 'integrated' US economy. Open borders, harmonized business regulation and the adoption by some members of a single currency have carried the EU towards an advanced form of economic integration. The Single European Act (SEA) and Maastricht Treaty set the foundations for much of the new direction to be pursued. In their different ways, both of these Treaties have contributed to the creation of a new business, social and political environment for the people of Europe. The Amsterdam Treaty has cemented their achievements and has set out a framework for an enlarged union of more than twenty member states. Today, thirteen states including Turkey, Cyprus, Poland and Hungary are negotiating with the European Commission to become full EU members. The economies of Europe (East and West) will soon be considerably more integrated than the architects of the Single European Market ever envisaged.

In Europe 2000, business opportunities exist that were barely imagined a decade ago. Not only has the European marketplace become bigger but, as internal regulatory, fiscal and communications barriers have come down, so European enterprises have been able to tap new markets and to exploit location and scale economies with greater freedom. In many respects this wider European platform has proved a springboard for many firms to create global competitive advantage. Of course these freedoms have come at a price. The new European market is dominated by intense competition which raises the stakes for European firms to improve both their efficiency and effectiveness (their competitiveness). This intensification of competition in Europe is accompanied (or contextualized) by an increase in world-wide competition leading to new distributions of capital, production and labour. Thus European firms are competing not only in a more open European economy but in a more open (and competitive) global economy. As well as facing more open markets, companies and managers are also facing a technological revolution which is generating new forms of enterprise (e-commerce) and challenging established business structures. While the advance of digital and internet technologies means that many businesses are able to reach new customers and to slash their costs, so too firms are put under pressure to change and innovate.

It is inevitable that this new environment will encourage change in the way business is conducted and organized in Europe. Operational flexibility, innovation, market reach, and the depth and breadth of business networks are likely to be key to the future competitiveness of European companies. Many European companies may consider that they are already coping with these demands but for others, the challenges of the New Europe remain to be met.

The text and its intended market

No book on European business can seek to be prescriptive or to provide all the answers; the rapidity of change within the European environment (and in the world beyond) makes that impossible. Our aim, therefore, has been to raise the key issues facing European businesses today and to account for and to evaluate some of the strategic and operational responses to Europe's evolving environment. The book continues to provide a useful resource for introductory courses on European business and we would envisage its use on specific European business courses at under-graduate, postgraduate and MBA level. It should also be seen as a vital background resource for anyone studying the business disciplines. European political and eco-nomic integration will have an impact on all business activities, and any student of business who is unaware of the issues surrounding these processes will be less well-equipped to enter the modern business world.

The book itself is now organized into two main parts, preceded by a broad intro-duction. Part I (The 'new' European business environment) aims to present an understanding of the changing political, economic, legal, and labour environments of Europe and their implications for business. While concentration rests with the EU states, analysis extends to the study of Central and East European environments and to the emergence of a pan-European economic space at the start of the twenty-first century. The section begins in Chapter 2 with an overview of the development of the EU and of the role of the Community institutions in shaping the new leg-islative environment. No business can act in a vacuum, and the EU itself, via its institutions, policies and legislation, will have an impact on every firm and every individual in the EU states. Chapters 3 and 4 have a precise focus on the economics of EU integration. Chapter 3 provides an examination of the Single European Market (SEM), its history, aims and objectives. The chapter studies the philosophy of the Internal Market and its implications for business firms and markets. Chapter 4 considers the progress towards economic and monetary union in Europe, highlighting the advent of a single currency area. Again, while analysis works largely at the macro-level, the implications of EMU for business and competition in Europe are investigated and evaluated. The chapter also examines the debate over UK entry and over future fiscal harmonization in the EU. Chapter 5 examines some of the EU's 'business policies', that is, some of those policies of the European Union of direct and significant consequence to businesses in the EU. A focus on competition policy forms a body of knowledge on EU competition law vital to doing business in Europe. Concentrations on industrial policy, on state aid (controls) and on regional policy demonstrate the interlinkages between EU policies (and those of national authorities). Each of these policies plays a significant part in the shaping of Europe's competitive environment. Chapter 6 looks at EU social and employment policies, locating the analysis in a broad study of labour market dynamics and transitions in work. This chapter concludes an initial focus on the European Union although Chapter 7 encompasses an extended section on the EU's relations with Central and Eastern Europe and on the enlargement question. The critical purpose of Chapter 7 is to provide a thorough account of the deep-level changes in Central and East European business environments and to consider options and strategies for Western firms looking East.

In Part II ('The strategy and structure of European business') we discuss the different strategies that firms pursue when competing in the new Europe and focus on developments in European business organization. New directions in strategy are explored in Chapter 8, which focuses on the challenges ahead for firms operating on EU soil. Chapter 9, which focuses on marketing management in a European context, follows on directly from Chapter 8. Although marketing is an integral part of firms' strategy development, change in the marketing discipline as a whole, along with new challenges posed by integration, means that this topic is worthy of separate comment. It is not possible for firms to plan and to implement their strategies independent of the cultural environments they face. Failure to take account of cultural nuances between markets may potentially result in expensive mistakes and, while standardization may be possible in a variety of business functions, firms need to look closely at the markets of Europe to identify both commonalities and differences. These issues are discussed in Chapter 10 along with some prescriptions for managing cultural diversity and adopting new business practices. Companies are also faced with the challenge of integrating environmental considerations into their production and marketing plans. Apart from tougher standards (often emanating from EU directives), by incorporating the environmental dimension into their strategies and thinking, managers can reduce business costs and exploit the market opportunities offered by a growth in green consumerism. These issues are explored in Chapter 11 which shows how environmental management is becoming central to the strategic focus of many European firms. Although the above issues relate specifically to the operations of firms within Europe (principally within the EU), it is not possible to attain a comprehensive understanding of European business without insight into the international trade and investment framework and the changing global economy. Chapter 12 helps to provide such insight, exploring the causes and effects of globalization and examining the challenges and issues for European firms in achieving global presence and competitive advantage in increasingly global markets.

This division is one of several innovations marking our new edition. Each chapter now has an extensive list of references (providing a guide to further reading) and a mix of short and long case studies. Some of these case notes are carried forward from the previous edition and some are sourced from the *Financial Times*' global archive. Review questions at the end of each chapter have also been designed to assist students in testing their understanding of the material covered and may form the basis of class discussions. Each chapter also features a guide to subject-related web links. While every effort has been made to check the security and usefulness of these resources, the authors can take no responsibility for their content or argument. An updated list of web links will be maintained at our companion website: http://www.booksites.net/mercado. Overall, the work has been significantly revised and updated with an attempt made to achieve a more integrated progression of topics. Readers familiar with the third edition will identify changes in the titling and numbering of chapters, as well as in the material constituting the work. The edition features substantial contribution from a new team member, Dr Simon Mercado of Nottinghan Business School, who has led the process of updating the analysis and presentation. It is hoped that these changes make the text as up-to-date as possible and strengthen both its empirical and theoretical content.

Acknowledgements

Thanks go to all the staff at Pearson Education for their professional and technical assistance. Thanks go also to those of our colleagues who have provided helpful comments during the production of this work throughout its many stages. In particular, we are grateful to Dr Emil Helienek of Nottingham Business School for his review of the updated material on Central and Eastern Europe. We also owe a note of thanks to the many organizations and publishers that have given us permission to reproduce and/or to adapt models, tables and diagrams from external works and to the authors of incorporated notes and readings. In particular, our gratitude extends to the European Commission for its kind permission to reproduce many features from the europa web site. Every effort has been made to secure permission for the reproduction of material held under the protection of copyright and to ensure appropriate standards of attribution and referencing. Any shortcomings in the presentation and/or interpretation of such material is the responsibility of the authors.

The publishers are grateful to the following for permission to reproduce copyright material:

The Financial Times Limited for Case Study 2.1 from Prodi team gets down to work with Commission restructuring, © *Financial Times*, 20 September, 1999; Case Study 2.3 from Survey – UK Presidency of the EU: UK's view of Europe obscured by past glories, Philip Stephens, © *Financial Times*, 4 January, 1998; Case Study 3.5 from Brussels unveils financial services shake-up, © *Financial Times*, 12 May, 1999; Case Study 4.2 from European Economy Quarterly Review, from Front-runner in euro systems, Graham Bowley, © *Financial Times*; Case Study 4.3 edited and adapted from Volatile exchange rate poses dilemma for industry, Christopher Adams & Christopher Swann, © *Financial Times*, 1 July, 2000; Case Study 5.2 reproduced and amended from Brussels raids Coca-Cola offices, © *Financial Times*, 22 July, 1999; Case Study 5.5 from EU countries keen to maintain state aid, © *Financial Times*, 30 March, 1999; Case Study 6.1 from EU ministers agree to delay junior doctors' hours reform, © *Financial Times*, 26 May, 1999; Case Study 6.2 from National News: Most big companies back social chapter regulations, © *Financial Times*, 16 August, 1999; Case Study 6.3 from Europe's tiny dynamos: Robert Taylor, © *Financial Times*, 27 January, 2000; Case Study 7.1 from Survey – Central and Eastern Europe: Diverse routes to the region's riches: Entrepreneurs, Stefan Wagstyl, © *Financial Times*, 10 November, 1999; Case Study 7.2 from Survey – Central and Eastern Europe: Learning the hard way: Banking, Kevin Done, © *Financial Times*, 10 November, 1999; Case Study 7.3 from Survey – Bulgaria: Currency board is a boost to stability:

Economy, Kevin Done, © *Financial Times*, 8 March, 1999; Case Study 7.4 from Survey – Austria: Role at centre of wider region: Eastern Enlargement, Reinhard Engel, © *Financial Times*, 26 November, 1999; Case Study 7.5 from Comment & Analysis: Investors put their faith in Putin, © *Financial Times*, 4 April, 2000; Case Study 7.6 from Comment & Analysis: Into the east at full throttle, © *Financial Times*, 12 February, 1997; Case Study 9.4 from National News: Surge in shopping on the internet, © *Financial Times*, 2 October, 1999; Case Study 9.6 from Wind of change starts to blow, from FT Auto/Retail Survey, © *Financial Times*, 16 September, 1999; Case Study 10.2 from Taking on the world, © *Financial Times*, 3 April, 2000; Case Study 11.3 from World News: Trade: Commission to back trade in permits to pollute, © *Financial Times*, 7 March, 2000; Case Study 11.4 from World News – Europe: European car producers face big clean-up bill, © *Financial Times*, 4 February, 2000; Case Study 12.2 from Survey – World's most respected companies: At the forefront of innovation: Nokia, Christopher Brown-Humes, © *Financial Times*, 7 December, 1999.

Tables 1.1, 1.7, 1.8, 3.2, 3.3, 3.4, 3.5, 5.1, 5.2, 6.4, 6.5, 6.7, 6.9, 7.2, 7.6, 11.1, 11.3, 12.6 and 12.7 © European Communities. Reproduced from the europa.eu.int website by permission of the Publishers; Data for Tables 1.2, 1.3 and 12.8 from the www.fortune.com/fortune/global500 website, with the permission of Time, Inc; Tables 1.4, 6.1, 6.2, 6.6, 7.9, 11.2 and 11.4 reproduced with the permission of OECD; Figures 1.2, 4.1, 4.2, 4.3, 4.4, 5.3, 5.4, 6.1, and 7.1 © European Communities. Reproduced from the europa.eu.int website by permission of the Publishers; Figures 1.3 and 1.4 reproduced with the permission of the Office for National Statistics © Crown Copyright 2000; Table 1.10 © European Communities. Reproduced from the www.inforegio.cec.eu.int website by permission of the Publishers; Table 2.1 Adapted from one table concerning Treaties (pp 487–8) from *The Penguin Companion to European Union* by Timothy Bainbridge (Penguin Books 1995, Second edition 1998). First edition copyright © Timothy Bainbridge and Anthony Teasdale, 1995, 1996, 1997. Second edition Timothy Bainbridge, 1998. Reproduced by permission of Penguin Books Ltd; Figure 4.5 HM Treasury, 1998. Crown copyright is reproduced with the permission of the Controller of Her Majesty's Stationery Office; Table 6.3 reproduced and adapted with the permission of the Office for National Statistics © Crown Copyright 2000; Tables 7.3, 7.4, 7.5, 7.7, 7.8 and 7.10 reproduced from *Business Central Europe* Magazine Statistical Database (01.01.2000). Reproduced by permission of the Publisher © The Economist Newspaper Limited, 2000; Figure 7.2 from EBRD *Transition Report* 1998. Reproduced with the permission of the Publishers © EBRD; Table 8.3 reprinted from *European Management Journal*, Vol 12, No 1, Verdin, P. and Williamson, P., Successful Strategy: Stargazing or Self-Examination?, pages 10–19, 1994 with permission from Elsevier Science; Table 9.1 reproduced from the www.eto.org.uk website by permission of the publishers; Table 10.2 adapted from the www.webofculture.com website © The Web of Culture 2000 with permission from the Publisher; Table 10.6 and Figure 10.13 from *Riding the Waves of Culture*, Fons Trompenaars and Charles Hampden-Turner, Nicholas Brealey Publishing, London; Figures 11.1 and 11.2 from *Environment in the European Union at the turn of the century,* reproduced with the permission of the European Environment Agency; Figure 12.1 and Tables 12.1, 12.2 and 12.3 reproduced with the permission of the World Trade Organization.

Whilst every effort has been made to trace the owners of copyright material, in a few cases this has proved impossible and we take this opportunity to offer our apologies to any copyright holders whose rights we may have unwittingly infringed.

A Companion Web Site accompanies *European Business*, 4/e by Mercado, Welford & Prescott

Visit the *European Business* Companion Web Site at www.booksites.net/mercado to find valuable teaching and learning material including:

For Students:
- Study material designed to help you improve your results
- Links to valuable resources on the web
- Search for specific information on the site

For Lecturers:
- A secure, password protected site with teaching material
- A syllabus manager that will build and host a course web page

1 Introduction: business and economy in the 'new' Europe

Central themes

- Defining European business
- Types of European business
- The European business environment
- The 'new' European economy
- Features of the European economy
- Growth and development in the European economies
- Europe's regional economic groups

European business: an introduction

European business: definitions and terminology

European business is a generic term which describes different forms of enterprise within the European theatre. Sole-trader firms, family businesses and multinationals alike are engaged in European business if conducting any of their commercial activities within one or more European regions. Equally *a* European business can be described as any firm or undertaking engaged in profit-oriented economic activity in any part of Europe. Thus a European business may be as simple as a pig farm in North Wales or as complex as a multinational drugs firm, with assets and sales in several European countries. Activity need not be exclusive to Europe, nor Europe be its central part, but some form of value-creation activity (procurement, research, production, marketing or sales) must be carried out somewhere within its boundaries. Without this qualification, a firm is neither engaged in European business (business in Europe) nor can itself be properly counted as a European business.

Of course the term 'European business' is often applied to that commercial activity in Europe which extends across national boundaries. In other words the terminology of 'European business' is popularly adopted to describe forms of business interest and activity in Europe that have a cross-border character and which are distinct from purely domestic activities. While this is a more restrictive use of the term, it is the one that most of us will find familiar. Very often, the language of European business is attached to the notion of cross-frontier activity in an increasingly integrated European economy.

The approach taken in the present volume is a clear one. At one level, European business is recognized and employed as an umbrella term to describe commercial undertakings (and activity) in Europe of all kinds and form. A European business is just that: a business in Europe. It may be international in character or purely domestic in scope. It may be a local bakery in Florence, Italy or an international car company such as Volkswagen, with facilities and subsidiary operations in Germany, Spain and the Czech Republic. Even the subsidaries of American and Asian corporates, where located in Europe, constitute examples of European business. At the same time, our primary interest is in how businesses in Europe operate across national frontiers and achieve strategic position in international markets. In turn, the bulk of our analysis is directed towards the study of transactions taking place across national borders in Europe and towards those undertakings enagaged in such activity. Issues of strategy, marketing management and culture (amongst others) are explored primarily from the point of view of trans-national operation, with some guidance as to how to compete and manage successfully in the 'new' Europe.

The notion of a 'new' Europe itself requires some explanation. Whilst Europe's geographical identity is little changed, the continent itself has taken on new form since the collapse of the cold war with the emergence of newly independent states and a post cold war architecture. New pan-European trade links and investment flows, combined with the extension of EU law into new fields and territories, have brought radical change to Europe's commercial and political environments. A new community of European states is being created along with new opportunities and threats for economic actors throughout Europe. Much of the succeeding analysis gives character to these changes and to policy challenges for the new European environment.

Mapping European business

It should be clear, therefore, that there are many different forms and kinds of business in Europe: small and large, domestic and international, indigenous and 'foreign owned'. In the present section we aim to characterize the heterogeneous nature of business in Europe using five points of reference:

- size structure;
- market scope;
- sectoral focus;
- public or private ownership;
- legal form.

This approach is influenced by the analytical framework of Nugent and O'Donnell (1994), which provides three examples of variation in European business: size, sector and ownership. By profiling the nature and form of European business under these headings, we can gain insight into the diversity and varying scope of business and business activity in Europe. The reader may wish to note that, in 1998, the number of EU enterprises grew to just over 18 million, this figure excluding agricultural enterprises and those in non-market sectors. Estimates suggest a further 300,000 business firms in the rest of Western Europe and approximately 4 million in the emerging markets of Central and Eastern Europe. Eurostat, the EU's statistical arm, records a total of 3.4 million business registrations in the region's ten EU candidate countries prior to September 1995 (Eurostat, 1999).

The size structure of European business

Within the EU there is an imbalance between types of business in terms of their size and impact on the European economy. On the one hand there are a very large number of small and medium-sized enterprises (SMEs). On the other hand there is a much smaller number of very large organizations which are of considerable economic and political importance.

There is no single definition of SMEs within the EU and the thresholds for defining SMEs – number of employees, balance sheet totals etc. – are the subject of some debate. So as to determine the financial reporting obligations of SMEs in the European Union and their eligibility for EU R&TD Programmes, the European Commission applies three basic tests:

1. that a firm should not employ more than 250 persons,
2. that a firm should not be more than 25% owned, either singly or jointly, by a larger company and
3. that it should not have an annual turnover of more than €40 million.

It should be noted that member states have the option of granting SMEs certain exemptions from the financial reporting and disclosure requirements imposed on limited-liability companies.

The Commission's suggestion that SMEs employ 250 persons or fewer provides the basis of a 'common definition' and a profile of Europe's SMEs. On this basis, figures suggest that SMEs constitute 99.8% of all enterprises in the EU, employ 66% of the EU labour force and are responsible for 55% of turnover. These figures show how Europe's group of small and middle-tier firms (which are often family-owned) play a critical role in the EU economy, making a major contribution to growth and employment. In recent years, SMEs in Europe have shown great dynamism (not least in the UK) and have provided a real impetus to economic growth. Although often suffering from limited resources and from inefficient management methods, Europe's SMEs have proved to be innovative, flexible and market responsive. In many areas, SMEs have offered high-quality products and services to their customers and have come to achieve high levels of domestic market share. While few are international in their outlook – most SMEs are very small firms concentrated on local markets – many are proving successful in achieving international expansion and in securing global market share in their chosen niches. This is especially true of SMEs in the more advanced EU states, including Germany's 3 million medium-tier manufacturing companies ('De Mittelstand') and France's substantial community of Petites et Moyennes Enterprises (PMEs).

In detail, and according to the European Commission's Recommendation concerning the definition of SMEs, the SME community is made up of three categories of firm. These categories are:

- micro-enterprises (maximum of 10 employees);
- small enterprises (maximum of 50 employees);
- medium-sized enterprises (maximum of 250 employees).

In France and Germany, the employee ceiling for medium-sized businesses is higher, set at a maximum of 499 persons.

On the basis of the Commission's 'definitions', over 90% of all SMEs in the European Union are micro-enterprises, over half of which are a 'one-man (or woman) band' (Eurostat, 1999). Comparisons with the US and Japan are complicated by varying classifications. In US data, SMEs are generally classified as employing up to 500 persons. In Japan, the equivalent figure is typically 300.

There are many issues facing SMEs in the region – finance, market consolidation, and regulatory red tape, to name but a few. These issues are not unique to SMEs; they affect large firms as well, although to differing degrees. Equally, while many SMEs operate only within their national market they are no less subject to change in EU law than their larger rivals, many of whom will have acquired an international dimension. With respect to competition policy, social policy, regional policy, labour law and taxation, location within the EU means coverage by legal frameworks strongly influenced by EU-wide codes and regulations. Nevertheless, some of the barriers which have beset the free movement of goods and services across the EU may be felt more acutely by these institutions who lack the 'deep-pocket' advantages of larger firms.

Europe's larger (private) businesses constitute a numerical minority, just 36,000. Despite this, they account for about one-third of total EU employment (excluding agriculture) and nearly half of all output in the EU economy. In general terms, these firms are better known to their domestic constituencies and, in many cases, will have developed international activities and brand recognition. Sectors such as energy, automotives, construction and telecommunications play host to a relatively high proportion of larger firms (250+ workers).

Market scope

Many European firms pursue a strategy which is either national or subnational in its market scope. In other words, they operate within and service markets strictly within the confines of their national economy. According to Ellis and Williams

(1995) a distinction can be drawn between 'local companies' (highly localized and based on a small local area), '(sub-) national regional companies' (whose market scope extends to a number of local markets but without coverage across the home country) and 'national companies' (seeking to cover the national market comprehensively). Extending an organization's business scope from local, to regional, to national may be a sequential process designed to achieve business growth. If such companies source all of their raw materials from inside the home market then they may be described as 'purely domestic'.

Many European businesses of course have an international character and market scope. Familiar businesses such as Siemens, British Telecom and Unilever are involved in competitive interactions in many different markets and have a broad spectrum of activities and interests that transcend national frontiers. Their strategies are focused on multiple national markets, often with a high degree of integration. Such businesses can be accurately described as multinational corporations (MNCs) given that they engage in foreign direct investment (FDI) and own or control value-adding activities in more than one country (see Dunning, 1993, p. 3). There are many other businesses in Europe that may be judged as 'international' even allowing for the absence of foreign direct investments and/or control of foreign assets. As noted by Bartlett and Ghoshal (2000, p. 2):

> companies that source their raw materials offshore, license their technologies abroad, export their products into foreign markets, or even hold minority equity positions in overseas ventures without any management involvement may regard themselves as 'international'.

While these businesses are not MNCs as defined above, they are nonetheless engaged in some form of international business activity. Thus, international businesses may vary from those companies that remain centred on their home markets but sell and/or license their products overseas to genuinely multinational companies with direct investments in two or more countries.

International firms are considered throughout this book in terms of their forms, environments and strategic objectives. However, it may be noted here that the power of many international firms, especially those which can be characterized accurately as multinational enterprises (MNEs), means that many international institutions are intent on providing regulations on production, trade, pricing and investment actions on a worldwide scale. The OECD, for example, operates a code of practice, based on voluntary acceptance, designed to influence the activities of MNEs, three-quarters of which are carried out within the OECD area. While it is not the Commission's intention to discriminate against MNEs, many of its proposals and EU laws have more impact on this sector than others. Although there is no specific provision in the Treaties on the control of MNEs, there is scope though the implementation of labour laws, fiscal, company and competition legislation to influence and to regulate the conduct of these organizations within the EU (see Chapters 5 and 6 especially).

There is no statistical profile of the number of 'international' businesses in Europe, but there is clear evidence of a growing trend towards enterprise internationalization. Barriers to exports, imports and investment are coming down on a worldwide basis (see Chapter 12) and, in Europe, international business activities have been greatly facilitated by the integration of national economies and the elimination of technical, physical and fiscal barriers (see Chapters 3 and 4).

Sectoral focus

The service sector accounts for 68% of EU GDP and for 66% of EU employment. According to estimates provided by Eurostat (the European Communities Statistical Office), it is also home to most of the European Union's businesses. There are 5.5 million firms alone that apply their trade in the retail and distribution sector, adding to a further 1.3 million in the hotels, restaurants and cafes sector ('horeca'). Table 1.1 provides a breakdown by sector of activity and shows that, together, the distributive and horeca trades account for over a third of all EU enterprises. The table also shows that there are just short of 1 million enterprises involved in transport and communication services in the EU and just over 2 million in other 'business services'. This category encompasses a wide variety of service-oriented activities including legal, fiscal and management consultancy, computer and technical services, staff recruitment, cleaning; maintenance services and advertising. Enterprise growth is particularly rapid in these sectors. The table also highlights that excluding the construction sector, industry accounts for just 11.3% of all non-agricultural enterprises in the European Union. These figures reflect the mature service sector economies in most of the EU states and the tendency towards fewer, larger enterprises in the industrial sectors. Data for Central and Eastern Europe (not covered in Table 1.1) show a similar, if less exaggerated bias towards services. In 1995, just 16.9% of all non-agricultural enterprises in the Central and East European Countries (CEECs) were engaged in industrial activities.

Table 1.1 Enterprises in the European Union, 1995 (breakdown by sector of activity)

	Enterprises		Employment		Turnover		Employment share of SMEs
	Thousands	%	Million	%	ECU billions	%	%
Industry and energy	2,043	11.3	33.24	29.7	4,454	26.0	52.6
Construction	2,408	13.3	10.14	9.1	905	5.3	87.7
Trade and Horeca	6,804	37.7	29.82	26.7	4,787	28.0	78.8
Transport and communication	930	5.2	8.16	7.3	715	4.2	46.6
Financial intermediation	326	1.8	4.70	4.2	4,347	25.4	28.3
Other business activities	2,062	11.4	10.25	9.2	795	4.6	68.9
Other services	3,477	19.3	15.46	13.8	1,107	6.5	73.2
Total	18,050	100.0	111.76	100.0	17,109	100.0	65.7

Note: Excludes enterprises in agricultural and non-market sectors
Source: Eurostat, 1999

Public versus private ownership

Despite the dominance of private sector businesses, public sector organizations can be found in all EU countries often in key sectors of the economy (e.g. in defence, transport and the utilities). Public ownership can involve national (or federal) governments and subnational authorities, such as the regional governments in Germany. There is a distinction to be drawn between publicly owned organizations (in which state authorities have full or clear majority ownership) and the many thousands of 'private sector' businesses in which such authorities have a residual or minority share. Governments will often retain (or purchase) non-controlling shares in a private or privatized firm, 'whether as an investment and/or future source of revenue, or as a means of exerting influence in a particular industry or sector' (Worthington and Britton, 1997, p. 182).

The last decade in Europe has seen a dramatic move away from public ownership control in Europe. While Central and Eastern European economies have been engaged in wholesale privatization as a part of the transition to the market (see Chapter 7), governments in the EU states have continued the privatization of state-owned enterprises. Whereas state-run companies accounted for approximately 15% of economic activity in the EU at the start of the 1990s, this figure has now been reduced to below 10%. Between 1985 and 1995, France alone privatized $38 billion worth of public assets. In the late 1990s, its government was selling off significant public holdings in companies such as France Telecom and Air France. Throughout Europe, governments have brought new companies to the market through initial public offerings and have continued the tranche-based privatizations of their former state champions. While governments in France, Spain, Italy, Portugal, Germany and Austria retain significant holdings in a good number of 'privatized' companies, the number of enterprises whose majority share remains in state hands has been massively reduced.

Legal form

Through a taxonomy of legal forms, we can also differentiate between different types of European business.

Sole-trader companies

Sole trader is the term used for a 'single-owner' business with or without employees. There is no need to register this type of business and the sole proprietor (as the owner of the business) has total claim on all the business's earnings which are taxed as personal earnings. As Harris (1999) notes, sole-trader or sole-proprietor businesses:

> comprise the bulk of European businesses ... Typical examples might be a builder working in Barcelona, or a person renting out holiday villas in the Algarve, Portugal, or a person running a computer repair business in Gothenburg.

This is an unincorporated form of business and the sole trader has unlimited liability. Unlimited liability implies that the owner–proprietor is personably responsible for any business debts incurred up to the full value of personal assets. Although the business is legally inseparable from the proprietor, sole-trader companies may use a trade name. Where such a trade name is utilized, the business must show evidence of the name and address of the proprietor.

Partnerships

Like a sole-tradership, a general partnership firm has no legal independence separate from its owners and is not a separate tax entity. The owners of partnership firms also have personal liability for the debts of the business. In other words, a (general) partnership is legally equivalent to a sole-tradership but is distinguished by the fact that two or more people are in the position of proprietors who share joint liability for the debts of the business. Some confusion is brought to the characterization of partnerships by the scope for limited as opposed to general partnerships. The major difference here is that a limited partner gets the benefit of a cap on personal liability. The advantage of a limited partnership as a business structure is that it provides a way for a business owner to bring in a passive partner so as to raise capital for the business. The legal detail surrounding partnerships (and the rules on liability) varies from country to country as do the titles afforded to partnership agreements. For example, in Germany, the main type of general partnership is the OHG (Offene Handelsgesellschaft) and the main type of limited partnership the KG (Kommanditgesellschaft).

Private limited companies

A private limited company is a separate entity from the individuals who own or operate it. In other words, it has a legal identity for the purpose of contracts, financing, taxation of business earnings etc. A private limited company is an incorporated organization registered with the authorities, entailing shares (held by private individuals) and limited liability. Owners (stockholders) share financial risk according to their company stake. If a business fails or incurs large losses, the investors will not be liable for anything other than the value of their investment. Consequently, limited liability allows an organization to grow without the constraint of unlimited personal liability. Incorporation will be dependent on several conditions. In Ireland, for example, limited companies must be fully registered under the Companies Act, must have at least two directors, formal company rules (which must be published) and lodge audited accounts each year with the Companies Registration Office (CRO). Private limited companies in Ireland (as in the UK) are identified by the term 'limited' or *Ltd*. In Germany, the main form of private limited company is the GmbH (Gesellschaft mit beschrankter Haftung). This legal form is adopted by many Mittelstand companies (medium-tier companies) where the owners wish to limit their liability to the amount of the capital invested (Greiling, 1997, pp. 86–7). Founding capital must be at least DM5,000. Large numbers of GmbHs are owned and run by German families. In France, the principal form of private limited company is the SARL (Société à responsabilité limitée). The minimum capital for an

SARL is FF50,000. SARLs cannot issue shares to the general public. The Société Anonyme (SA) is the legal form chosen by larger companies in France. The minimum capital requirement is FF250,000. Unlike its junior the SARL, the SA can issue shares to the general public (and become publicly owned) if meeting a higher minimum capital requirement (see below). It should be noted that most European states have minimum capital requirements for incorporated limited companies.

Public limited companies

A public limited company is a company which is entitled to offer its shares for sale to the public through a recognized stock exchange (e.g. London or Frankfurt). Major European corporations such as British Telecommunications (BT), Ericsson and Nokia Corporation are good examples of publicly listed European Corporations which enjoy great revenue-raising capacity. In the UK, before a business can become a public limited company (plc) it must have allotted shares to the value of at least £50,000, a quarter of which, £12,500, must be paid up in cash. In Germany, the only company whose shares may be traded on the stock market is the AG (Aktiengesellschaft). Siemens, Preussag and other German AGs must have a minimum nominal capital of DM100,000. In France, the equivalent is the SA (Société Anonyme), although many SAs remain privately owned companies (see above). If publicly owned, the minimum capital requirement for an SA is FF1.5 million.

There are other legal forms of business in Europe – co-operatives, consortia and joint venture companies – that underline the diversity in legal forms of European business. Many of these will be addressed in later chapters.

Europe's best

At an industry level, banking and insurance, chemicals, pharmaceuticals, electrical engineering, IT, telecoms (hardware and communications services), food and beverages, metals, motor vehicles, transport and tourism services have emerged as Europe's strongest business sectors and as markets where European firms enjoy revealed competitive advantage. Global industry top tens for these sectors include some of Europe's largest and most successful corporations. At the enterprise level, seventy-six European corporations make into the global top 200 based on global revenue in 1998 (twenty-three from Germany, nineteen from France and thirteen from the UK). This performance is evaluated at various points in the present work including Chapter 12 which assesses the global presence of European business.

Measuring 'best performance' brings a series of complications. Not least, is that there is a range of possible measures including sales revenue, profitability, market capitalization and number of employees. Some of these indicators form the basis of published European rankings. Tables 1.2 and 1.3, based on the Fortune 500 rankings, provide a listing of Europe's top ten corporations by two different indicators. Table 1.2 uses revenue (calculated on a global basis) and Table 1.3 uses number of employees. Both of these rankings should be approached with care and look very

Table 1.2 Europe's top ten companies by global revenue (2000)

Rank (global)	Company	Nationality	Revenue ($ million)	Industry
1 (5)	Daimler-Chrysler	GER	159,986	Motor vehicles & parts
2 (11)	Royal Dutch/Shell Group	UK/NED	105,366	Petroleum
3 (15)	Axa	FRA	87,645	Insurance
4 (17)	BP Amoco	UK	83,566	Petroleum
5 (19)	Volkswagen	GER	80,072	Motor vehicles & parts
6 (21)	Siemens	GER	75,337	Elect./eng.
7 (22)	Allianz	GER	74,178	Insurance
8 (27)	ING Group	NED	62,492	Insurance
9 (31)	Deutsche Bank	GER	58,585	Banking
10 (35)	Assicurazioni Generali	ITA	53,723	Insurance

Source: Fortune Magazine

Table 1.3 Europe's top ten companies by number of employees (2000)

Rank (global)	Company	Nationality	Employees	Industry
1 (8)	Daimler-Chrysler	GER	466,938	Motor vehicles & parts
2 (9)	Siemens	GER	443,000	Elect./eng.
3 (12)	OAO Gazprom	RUS	368,900	Energy
4 (19)	Volkswagen	GER	306,275	Motor vehicles & parts
5 (20)	La Poste	FRA	306,000	Mail
6 (22)	Carrefour	FRA	297,290	Retail
7 (22)	Vivendi	FRA	275,000	Engineering & construction
8 (26)	Sodexho Alliance	FRA	269,973	Food & personal care
9 (27)	Deutsche Post	GER	264,424	Mail
10 (29)	Unilever	UK/NED	255,000	Food & personal care

Source: Fortune Magazine

different from those based on alternative measures such as market capitalization or profitability. Rankings based on market capitalization provide the clearest sense of companies' worth but are extremely volatile. Business combinations and demergers ensure regular changes in such listings while foreign exchange movements can also exert an influence. Extended and updated listings of Europe's leading competitors can be accessed by using the web links featured at the end of this chapter.

There is some evidence to suggest a recent strengthening of Europe's corporate performance. Higher investor returns, improved profitability, and market gains in many sectors, suggest that European companies are narrowing the productivity and innovation gaps with competitors in Japan and the United States. In high-technology sectors such as the information technology hardware sector and telecommunications services, Europe is also producing champions (such as Nokia and the Vodafone Group) after decades of eclipse by Japanese and East Asian rivals.

What stands out, however, is that a climate for entrepreneurship is not yet fully established in Europe, with impediments both to business creation and to venture financing. Relatively speaking, European industry is also burdened by heavier taxation and higher production costs and relatively sluggish domestic growth (compared with the US economy at least). All of these issues attract our attention in later chapters as we explore the context and strategies of European business.

The evolving European business environment

The context or the environment in which business is conducted is subject to constant change. Business environments are fluid and dynamic and, potentially, quite volatile. A characterization of the European business environment on the verge of the third millennium highlights an environment subject to rapid change. A central feature to this change, arguably the central feature, is the rapid integration or *'Europeanization'* of market and economic structures in Europe. As Nugent and O'Donnell describe it (1994, p. 1):

> At the heart of this emerging European business environment is a fledgling European economy, in which national economies are increasingly interconnected and inter-dependent, in which national economic policies and policy approaches are increasingly co-ordinated, and in which the regulatory regime to which business is subject is increasingly European wide.

This view of a changing European business environment is as valid today as it was in the early and mid-1990s. While we may no longer regard the Single European Market (SEM) as 'fledgling', the SEM continues to develop its character and to acquire the attributes of a fully integrated marketplace. Most obviously, the extension of Single Market rules to new issue areas (such as electronic commerce) and the introduction of a 'unified' currency regime are creating a deeper, more encompassing Single Market. The SEM itself now stands as the centre-piece of an emerging pan-European economic space, linking the EU to clusters of associate and non-member economies throughout the European region. Meanwhile, member governments are co-operating ever more extensively in such areas as employment strategy, and the trend towards supranational business regulation continues with further reach into the areas of company law and taxation. Progress is being made, for example, towards a European company statute and a definitive VAT regime based entirely on origin. At the same time, processes of corporate integration through cross-border mergers and acquisitions, along with new models of international business co-operation, are ensuring that Europe's business firms are becoming more transnational in character. It is not only the markets of European firms that are becoming Europeanized (if not globalized) but their structures themselves. None of this is to suggest that Europe or the EU has become a homogenized, denationalized theatre, devoid of variety or national preferences – nothing could be further from the truth. Rather, what is laid bare is the pace and progress of Europeanization in recent years, which is itself profoundly affected by the wider trend towards globalization.

Part I of this book ('The "New" European business environment') concerns itself explicitly with these changes. Beginning with the role of the European Union in the modern European business environment (EBE), it identifies and accounts for key features of a developing European political economy including:

- the Europeanization of economic and political decision-making;

- the consolidation and extension of a maturing Single European Market;

- a continuing process of monetary unification (and evolving forms of fiscal federalism);

- the laying down of European and global specifications on goods and products in international standards;

- the strengthening of domestic and international competition rules;

- the intensification of competition in industrial and services markets;

- the development of pan-EU labour markets and Europe-wide employment practices;

- the liberalization and deregulation of multiple European markets, including those of former Communist societies.

The second half of the book, in a more specific focus on contemporary issues in European (and international) strategic management, gives further highlight to:

- emerging forms of trade and distribution (such as the Internet);

- convergence in consumer tastes and the emergence of pan-European consumer segments;

- expansions in the volume and value of cross-border trade and investment;

- the globalization of markets and competition, shaping a wide variety of forces in Europe;

- a strengthening of 'green' thinking among businesses and their customers.

Each of the above can be regarded as a significant 'external' factor in the environment of European business. Not all firms will be affected in the same way or to the same degree by these environmental influences, but many will have meaning and consequence for firms at all levels of the European economy. A good number of European firms will see their competitive and contextual environments marked profoundly by these changes. Indeed, the increasing European–international orientation of many firms in Europe is itself a direct response to the threats and opportunities created by many of these changes.

This provides an important clue as to how we might approach and conceptualise the business environment, a point extended in Chapter 8. The idea of a set of external factors impinging on the business organization suggests immediately that the business organization is in some form of interaction with its external environment. In short, the business firm can be usefully viewed as an open system made up of interrelated parts (its 'internal environment') which are intertwined and interactive with the outside world (its 'external environment'). While we may refer in general terms to the external environment, it may be more helpful to consider two levels to this 'outer world': (i) the immediate, task or competitive environment, and (ii) the general, remote or contextual environment.

The distinction between these two levels can be explained in the following terms. The 'immediate', 'task' or 'competitive' environment is made up of those external factors and influences which are more or less immediate in their effect and which directly influence the capability of an organization to position itself against its rivals. Thus attention is drawn to suppliers, buyers, rivals or competitors (potential or actual) and to the features of the firm's market–operational environment. By contrast, the 'general' or 'contextual' environment is made up of those remote influences on business activity and competition such as cultural, demographic, political, legal and technological developments. These influences provide the overarching framework within which any organization or industry operates and filter through the permeable boundaries of the competitive and internal environment (see Figure 1.1). In Chapter 8 we show how managers need to work at both of these levels of analysis, to audit those environmental influences important to (or potentially important to) their organizations. Techniques such as PEST analysis and models based around the work of Porter and Ansoff are profiled and evaluated.

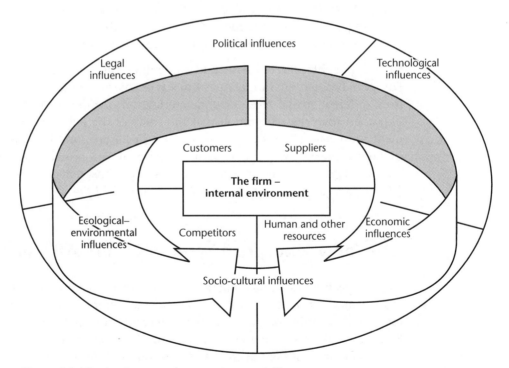

Figure 1.1 The business environment: a modelling

It should be noted that many of the major influences identified in the contemporary EBE may be organized or profiled under some of the headings featured in Figure 1.1. For example, the trend towards political union and the growth in EU-level decision-making are important aspects of the evolving political environment in EU-Europe. The proliferation of supranational business regulations and the continued development of the body of EU law (the acquis communautaire) are important elements of the legal environment in Europe. Other developments, such as the emergence of a new Internal Market Directive, may fit just as well under any one of a number of headings, e.g. economic, political or legal.

It is also clear that the many dimensions of the European business environment – political, economic, technological, cultural etc. (preserving their boundaries for a moment) – are themselves multilevelled with changes in each (or across each) stemming from different spatial levels. For example, Johnson and Turner (2000, p. 1) point to possible changes (and interactions) in the business environment of European firms at three different levels:

- *the national level*, 'where the discretionary actions of policy-makers are increasingly constrained by European integration and the internationalisation of markets';

- *the European level*, 'where previously fragmented markets are being integrated into a single unit' and where processes of business and political decision-making are being strengthened;

- *the international level*, 'where freer global trade is stimulating greater international interdependence' and where other developments outside Europe's borders are having 'a significant and increasing impact on the formulation of EU policy and on the strategies of European firms' (Johnson and Turner, 2000, p. 12).

Such a presentation is useful and underlines the real quality of the modern European business environment as a nexus of environmental influences emanating from different spatial levels. The determination or number of such levels is less important than the recognition that the study of the European business environment must reflect the reality that business in Europe (and the EBE itself) is profoundly affected by what happens at the national, European and global levels. This point is made clearly in the separate analyses of Johnson and Turner (2000), Harris (1999), El-Kahal (1998) and Nugent and O'Donnell (1994).

The 'new' European economy – an introduction

The European states are predominantly free-market capitalist systems, meaning that most economic activity is located in the private sector with prices set under market forces and governments limiting their intervention in the marketplace. The West European states have long been characterized by such systems, whereas the transition economies of Central and Eastern Europe are engaged in the construction (in some cases reconstruction) of market-based systems. Throughout Europe, the size of the public sectors has declined markedly. While technically all remain 'mixed economies' – characterized by active public and private sectors – the growth of private sectors is relentless. In many cases, e.g. in the UK, the Netherlands and Denmark, approximately 90% of national economic output is now attributable to the private sector, a trend encouraged by sustained efforts at privatization and by rapid rates of private sector business growth.

Post-industrial Europe

The European economy has, to a large extent, become a service-dominated or 'post-industrial' economy. Nowhere is this more true than in Western Europe where services are responsible for about two-thirds of total employment and for two-thirds of total output. The service economy is composed of two main elements: market and non-market services (such as public government and administration, health and education). The number of market-based services is considerable with examples including banking and insurance, the retail and distributive trades, transport, communications services, real estate, cleaning, personal services, and business services (previously disaggregated).

Table 1.4 provides data on sectoral contributions to employment for the EU-15 and for select economies. The table highlights that in 1997, the sectoral contributions to EU-15 employment were as follows: agriculture, forestry and fisheries (5.0%), industry – encompassing manufacturing, energy and construction – (29.8%) and services (65.2%). The Northern EU states have the highest shares of service sector employment, averaging out at 70%+. At the other end of the scale, Greece and Portugal have service sector shares of total employment which remain below 60% and have not yet attained the large service sector typical of highly developed economies. In these countries, the agricultural sector still contributes a major share to national output and employment. The Fisher–Clark hypothesis establishes an expectation that capitalist economies will progress from a reliance on primary sector activity, to manufacturing, to tertiary (or service) economy, with increasing levels of per capita wealth. The data on Western Europe tends to support this hypothesis, even though the pace of development across the member states is inconsistent. However, it is often argued that only a manufacturing sector, where raw materials and semi-finished products have value added to them in their processing, can generate significant wealth in an economy.

To a large extent, this post-industrial economy is a 'knowledge economy'. This rather nebulous concept highlights the growth of industries that are either major producers or intensive users of information technology products and services. By 2010, it is estimated that half of all jobs in the EU (current membership only) will be in such sectors. Among those industries whose major product is knowledge itself, we may count software, biotechnology and information technology. Among those industries that manage or convey knowledge (or information), we may count media, telecommunications, advertising, law, medicine, financial services and public administration. In these industries, effective handling and managing of information, rather than knowledge generation, are the keys to competitive success.

Table 1.4 Sectoral contributions to civilian employment, 1997 (EU-15 and select economies)

Country	Agriculture, forestry and fisheries	Industry	Services
Austria	5.9	30.3	63.8
Belgium	2.6	26.0	71.4
Denmark	3.7	26.8	69.5
Finland	7.0	27.5	65.5
France	4.5	25.6	69.9
Germany	3.3	36.5	60.2
Greece	20.2	22.9	56.9
Ireland	9.9	28.4	61.7
Italy	6.8	32.0	61.2
Luxembourg	2.6	25.6	71.8
Netherlands	3.7	22.2	74.1
Portugal	13.7	31.5	54.8
Spain	8.3	30.0	61.7
Sweden	2.7	26.0	71.3
United Kingdom	1.8	26.9	71.3
EU-15	**5.0**	**29.8**	**65.2**
Iceland	9.1	25.4	65.5
Norway	4.7	23.7	71.6
Switzerland	4.6	26.8	68.6
Czech Republic	5.9	41.6	52.5
Hungary	9.6	33.4	57.0
Poland	20.6	31.9	47.5
US	2.7	23.9	73.4
Japan	5.3	33.1	61.6
OECD Total	**8.2**	**27.7**	**64.1**

Source: Labour Force Statistics: 1977–1997, 1998 edition. © OECD 1999

The European Commission has launched a strategy to promote employment and skills for the new knowledge economy, in an attempt to overcome a perceived gap with the US. It has also set itself the challenge of ensuring a stable and conducive economic and legal environment for continuing innovation in information technologies and electronic commerce.

One crude measure of the growth of the knowledge economy rests with levels of electronic commerce (e-commerce), which refers to business and trading conducted though electronic networks such as the Internet and world wide web. In Europe, e-commerce is already worth €17 billion (based on Commission estimates for 1998) and is expected to reach €340 billion by 2003. Despite this, e-commerce in the United States alone is worth an estimated $37.4 billion and is expected to top the $400 billion mark by the end of 2002 (source: International Data Corp.). Net access in Europe is also below that in the US and is highly concentrated among middle and higher income groups in northern Europe. European Internet users also spend much less time on the web and less money (see Chapter 9).

Size and development

While the national economic systems of Europe (Western Europe at least) are similar in principle, the size and levels of development of national economies vary quite considerably (see Table 1.5). The big four West European states (Germany, France, Britain and Italy) account for approximately three-quarters of the gross domestic product of the EU and for over 60% of the GDP of Europe as a whole. GDP measures the net output or value added of an economy by measuring goods and services purchased with money. While all are overshadowed by the physical and human magnitude of the Russian Federation, these countries are also among the largest European states in terms of their populations and physical size (see Table 1.6). It might be recorded that the decisions of the 'big four' have dominated policy in the EU since the 1970s: earlier in the case of France, Germany and Italy. Spain, with its

Table 1.5 GDP/GDP per capita 1998 in PPP ($) – EU-15 and select economies

Country	Total GDP ($bn)	GDP per capita
Austria	184.5	22,700
Belgium	236.0	23,400
Denmark	124.4	23,300
Finland	103.6	20,100
France	1,320.0	22,600
Germany	1,813.0	22,100
Greece	143.0	13,400
Ireland	67.1	18,600
Italy	1,181.0	20,800
Luxembourg	13.9	32,700
Netherlands	348.0	22,200
Portugal	144.8	14,600
Spain	645.6	16,500
Sweden	175.0	19,700
United Kingdom	1,252.0	21,200
EU-15	**7,752.5**	**19,970**
Iceland	6.1	22,400
Norway	109.0	24,700
Switzerland	191.8	26,400
Czech Republic	116.7	11,300
Hungary	75.4	7,400
Poland	263.0	6,800
Russia	593.4	4,000
Turkey	425.4	6,600
US	8,511.0	31,500
Japan	2,903.0	23,100

Note: GDP dollar estimates for all countries are derived from purchasing power parity (PPP) calculations rather than from conversions at official currency exchange rates. PPP is a unit of measurement which cancels out differences in price levels and can be used to make comparisons in real terms.
Source: CIA World Factbook 1999

Table 1.6 Area and population, 1998 (EU-15 and select economies)

Country	Population (million)	Area (square km)
Austria	8.14	83,858
Belgium	10.18	30,510
Denmark	5.35	43,094
Finland	5.16	337,030
France	58.98	547,030
Germany	82.08	356,910
Greece	10.71	131,940
Ireland	3.63	70,280
Italy	56.73	301,230
Luxembourg	0.43	2,586
Netherlands	15.81	41,532
Portugal	9.92	92,391
Spain	39.17	504,750
Sweden	8.91	449,964
United Kingdom	59.11	244,820
EU-15	**374.58**	**3,191,000**
Iceland	0.27	103,000
Norway	4.44	324,220
Switzerland	7.27	41,290
Czech Republic	10.28	78,703
Hungary	10.19	93,030
Poland	38.61	312,683
Russia	146.39	17,075,200
Turkey	65.60	780,580
US	272.64	9,629,091
Japan	126.18	377,835

Note: Commission estimates suggest EU population currently 376 million
Source: CIA World Factbook 1999

large population and developing economy, is also increasingly important and its overall economic growth has been significant since joining the EU. A number of smaller European countries such as Switzerland, Norway, Luxembourg, Sweden, Denmark, the Netherlands, Finland and Austria, emerge as wealthy European economies. Per capita incomes in these states are among the very highest in European (and global) terms and the level of industrial development in these economies is high. Each is characterized by a sizeable service economy. A number of these states such as Belgium and the Netherlands are characterized by very dense populations. Such density often leads to land shortages and to relatively high land prices. With a purchasing power standard measurement of GDP per head significantly lower than the average, Greece and Portugal demonstrate their relative underdevelopment *vis-à-vis* their EU–EEA partners. In a short period of time, per capita incomes in the wealthier Central European countries may overtake the real income levels in these societies.

Table 1.5 shows the dominance of Germany, producing around one-quarter of the EU's total GDP. Not only has this resulted in higher standards of living for the population but it has also led to the strengthening of German enterprises. As the EU has developed it has often been German firms which, helped by their profitability and a relatively strong Deutschmark, have been most 'bullish', seizing opportunities for new investment, mergers and takeovers. This has led to accusations of German domination over the EU economy which, on the one hand, is tautologous but is also a product of relative efficiency. Ultimately, it is argued that the spread of this efficiency can only be to the good of the EU as a whole so long as it is not environmentally damaging (see Chapter 11).

Growth

Over the last ten years, the overall pattern of EU growth has been inconsistent. While strong growth marked both the start and end of the 1990s, the EU experienced a deep recessionary period between 1992 and 1993 which is well illustrated in Figure 1.2. By the end of the decade, the EU economy was growing steadily and, at time of writing (spring 2000), real GDP growth for 2000 was forecast to reach 3.4%. The Commission's forecast for the period until 2006 is for an average annual growth rate of 2.5% for the EU-15 against a background of favourable demand conditions and improving economic fundamentals. Based on the experience of the 1990s, this forecast for EU growth leans on the optimistic side, although it may not be completely unrealistic. As reported in the Presidency Conclusions of the Lisbon European Council (23–24 March 2000):

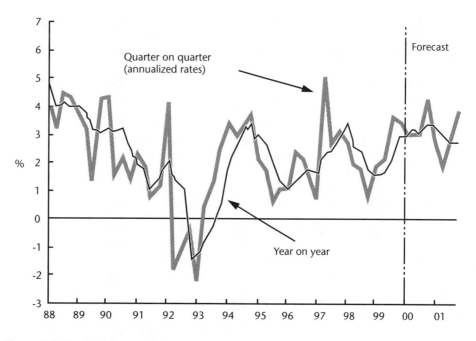

Figure 1.2 Real GDP growth in EU-15
Source: European Commission (2000)

The Union is experiencing its best macro-economic outlook for a generation. As a result of stability-oriented monetary policy supported by sound fiscal policies in a context of wage moderation, inflation and interest rates are low, public sector deficits have been reduced remarkably and the EU's balance of payments is healthy.

Although structural changes remain necessary to strengthen employment and to prepare the transition to a knowledge-based economy, growth prospects are favourable. The economic benefits of the euro and the forthcoming enlargement of the Union can both be expected to create new opportunities for trade and investment. The shift to a digital, knowledge-based economy should also prove a powerful engine for growth, competitiveness and jobs.

Projections for the EU's applicant countries are for average annual growth rates over this period (2000–06) of some 4%. The reader may wish to note that a macroeconomic profile for these countries is provided in Chapter 7 and that the succeeding sections concentrate on the West European economies, in particular those of the European Union (EU).

At the national level, rapid growth is forecast for the Southern EU states and for a number of the smaller EU economies including Luxembourg, Finland and the Netherlands. These same economies have registered some of the highest growth rates in EU–Europe in recent years, with the Irish economy growing at the single fastest pace (see Table 1.7). All of these countries (with the exception of

Table 1.7 GDP at constant prices – annual percentage change since 1961 (EU-15, Japan and US)

	1961–1973	1974–1985	1986–1990	1991–1995	1996–2001	1997	1998	Estimates 1999	Forecasts 2000	Scenario: unchanged policies 2001
B	4.9	1.8	3.0	1.5	2.7	3.5	2.7	2.3	3.5	3.3
DK	4.3	2.0	1.3	2.6	2.4	3.1	2.7	1.4	2.0	2.1
D	4.3	1.7	3.4	2.0	1.9	1.5	2.2	1.5	2.9	2.9
EL	8.5	1.7	1.2	1.2	3.5	3.4	3.7	3.5	3.9	4.0
E	7.2	1.9	4.5	1.3	3.5	3.8	4.0	3.7	3.8	3.4
F	5.4	2.2	3.1	1.1	2.7	2.0	3.2	2.8	3.7	3.2
IRL	4.4	3.8	4.6	4.6	8.2	10.7	8.9	8.3	7.5	6.2
I	5.3	2.7	2.9	1.3	1.9	1.8	1.5	1.4	2.7	2.7
L	4.0	1.8	6.4	5.4	5.2	7.3	5.0	5.0	5.6	5.7
NL	4.9	1.9	3.1	2.1	3.6	3.8	3.7	3.5	4.1	3.7
A	4.9	2.3	3.2	1.9	2.4	1.2	2.9	2.3	3.2	3.0
P	6.9	2.2	5.5	1.8	3.4	3.5	3.5	2.9	3.6	3.5
FIN	5.0	2.7	3.3	−0.7	4.7	6.3	5.0	3.5	4.9	4.2
S	4.1	1.8	2.3	0.6	2.8	2.0	3.0	3.8	3.9	3.3
UK	3.2	1.4	3.3	1.6	2.8	3.5	2.2	2.0	3.3	3.0
EU-15	4.8	2.0	3.2	1.5	2.6	2.5	2.7	2.3	3.4	3.1
EUR-11	5.2	2.1	3.3	1.5	2.6	2.3	2.7	2.3	3.4	3.1
USA	4.4	2.8	3.3	2.4	3.9	4.5	4.3	4.1	3.6	3.0
JAP	9.4	3.4	4.6	1.4	1.2	1.6	−2.5	0.3	1.1	1.8

Source: European Commission (2000)

Luxembourg) have come relatively late to EU membership with Greece, Ireland, Spain and Portugal benefiting signficantly from inflows of EU capital directed under the CAP and the EU's Structural Programmes. Along with record levels of inward investment, these capital transfers from the EU's own resources have been central to modernization efforts in Southern Europe and to processes of deep-level structural reform.

Inflation

During the last years of economic growth, there has been a significant improvement in the inflation record of the EU economies (see Figure 1.3). In large part, this improved performance can be explained by the monetarist policies introduced throughout the EU in the context of preparation for European Economic and Monetary Union and by the fiscal restraints imposed by the EMU Growth and Stability Pact (see Chapter 4). In wider view, increased competition and deregulation are helping to keep a lid on inflation in the EU and wage claims have remained moderate with a general reduction in tax pressures on personal income.

Figure 1.3 EU-15 consumer price index 1990–2000 (year on year percentage change, months)
Source: Economic Trends, March 2000, National Statistics © Crown Copyright 2000

At the time of writing (spring 2000) inflationary pressures in the EU economy were building, with higher oil prices and the depreciation of the Euro against the dollar and other currencies, contributing to a modest increase in EU-wide inflation. In January 2000 the EU's harmonized consumer price index stood at 1.8%, up somewhat on levels for 1999. It may be recorded that the European Central Bank operates a target range for EU-11 (Eurozone) inflation of 0–2% and that many independent national authorities (e.g. the Bank of England) operate similar targets. Thus any significant increase in inflationary pressures in the EU or in the Eurozone economy (say from rising oil prices or from dearer imports) will result in an increase

21

in interest rates. At the start of 2000, short-term interest rates were at relatively low levels with the ECB's main re-financing rate set at 3.5%.

The overall rate for EU inflation – as measured by the Commission's Harmonized Index for Consumer Price increases (HICP) – has now remained between 1.0% and 3.0% since early 1996. However, one of the ways in which we may continue to categorize (EU) countries is by domestic inflation rates. As seen in Table 1.8, inflation differentials between the member states remain significant. Based on figures for 1999 (which show an overall EU rate of just 1.2%), highest annual rates in the EU were in Ireland (2.5%) – where the economy began to show signs of overheating – Spain (2.2%), Portugal (2.2%) and Greece (2.1%). Lowest rates were in Sweden (0.6%), Austria (0.5%), Germany (0.5%) and France (0.6%). Note that these twelve-month averages are calculated and compared using the EU's harmonized measure and may therefore vary from official inflation figures published in the member states themselves.

The higher-inflation countries – Spain, Portugal, Greece and Ireland – are part of a group of EU states including Italy which have had a traditional inflation problem. This fact can be explained by several factors including the relative ineffectiveness of past government macroeconomic policy-making, (until recently) the loose management of the money supply and fiscal policy, the size and number of parallel (black) markets, and the lesser-developed nature of economic structures. EMU mem-

Table 1.8 Consumer prices – annual percentage change since 1961 (EU-15, Japan and US)

	1961–1973	1974–1985	1986–1990	1991–1995	1996–2001	1997	1998	Estimates 1999	Forecasts 2000	Scenario: unchanged policies 2001
B	3.7	7.4	2.2	2.3	1.3	1.5	0.9	1.1	1.3	1.4
DK	6.6	9.6	3.8	1.6	1.9	1.9	1.3	2.1	2.4	1.7
D	3.4	4.3	1.4	3.3	1.2	1.5	0.6	0.6	1.6	1.6
EL	3.6	18.2	17.6	13.8	4.1	5.4	4.5	2.1	2.3	2.3
E	6.5	15.4	6.6	5.6	2.4	1.9	1.8	2.2	2.5	2.2
F	4.7	10.6	3.1	2.5	1.2	1.3	0.7	0.6	1.1	1.2
IRL	6.3	13.8	3.2	2.6	2.5	1.2	2.1	2.5	3.7	3.0
I	4.9	15.9	6.1	5.8	2.3	1.9	2.0	1.7	2.1	1.9
L	3.0	7.4	2.4	3.0	1.4	1.4	1.0	1.0	2.0	1.8
NL	5.1	5.7	0.9	2.5	2.2	1.9	1.8	2.0	2.4	3.4
A	4.1	5.8	2.0	3.0	1.1	1.2	0.8	0.5	1.3	1.0
P	3.9	22.2	12.2	7.7	2.3	1.9	2.2	2.2	2.2	2.1
FIN	5.7	10.7	4.3	3.0	1.5	1.2	1.4	1.3	2.3	2.0
S	4.8	10.3	6.7	4.7	1.3	1.8	1.0	0.6	1.6	2.0
UK	4.8	11.9	5.4	4.2	1.7	1.8	1.6	1.3	1.4	1.6
EU-15	4.6	10.9	4.4	4.2	1.7	1.7	1.3	1.2	1.8	1.7
EUR-11	4.6	10.4	3.8	3.9	1.6	1.6	1.1	1.1	1.8	1.8
USA	2.9	6.8	3.8	2.6	–	–	–	–	–	–
JAP	6.1	6.5	1.2	1.1	–	–	–	–	–	–

Note: Harmonized measure from 1996 onwards
Source: European Commission (2000)

bership and disciplines makes these factors more an explanation of past inflation difficulties, although the tendency towards relatively fast rates of growth and (in some cases) continuing weaknesses in the domestic economy means that these countries continue to experience inflation higher than most of their EU counter-parts. It has already been commented that Southern European economies have experienced significant growth since joining the EU and fast growth and conse-quential increases in aggregate demand do cause prices to rise.

General government balances

With respect to government deficits, member states are approaching the close-to-balance objective of the Stability and Growth Pact linked to European Economic and Monetary Union (see Chapter 4). In 1999, budgetary surpluses were recorded in seven member states, with the others recording relatively small deficits (at or under 3% of GDP). EU-wide, the net borrowing of government as a percentage of GDP fell to 0.6%, i.e. a position very close to balance (see Table 1.9). Since the launch of EMU in 1999, the EU states have made good progress in further improv-ing their financial positions, in most cases benefiting from lower interest rates and from a period of good economic growth. Cumulative public debt has also fallen throughout the EU. In 1999 the debt to GDP ratio in the EU as a whole stood at below 70% (67.6%), with the original Maastricht reference value of 60% soon to be approached (see Table 1.9). The EU states with the highest levels of public debt (rela-tive to their GDPs) are Belgium, Greece and Italy. These states still have debt/GDP ratios close to or above 100% (European Commission, 2000).

Table 1.9 EU-15 – general government balances (% of gross domestic product)

	1997	1998	1999	2000 (estimate)	2001 (estimate)
Total government receipts	46.3	46.1	46.6	45.9	45.2
Total government expenditure	48.7	47.6	47.2	46.3	45.5
Actual government balances	−2.4	−1.5	−0.6	−0.4	−0.3
Gross debt	71.0	69.0	67.6	65.1	62.6

Source: European Commission (2000)

Employment

In a context of steady growth, low inflation and reduced public sector deficits, Europe's employment position has shown signs of improvement (see Figure 1.4). The EU-15 unemployment rate fell to just under 9.0% during the second half of 1999 from a peak of 11.3% (17.8 million persons) at the end of 1993. The European Commission estimates that employment growth will lower the number of unem-ployed to 8.5% of the total workforce in 2000 and to a percentage rate of 7.9 in 2001 (14.4 million workers). Employment patterns and issues are examined extensively in Chapter 6 of this volume where the reader will find various employment-related data sets. Chapter 7 also covers the employment situation in Central and Eastern

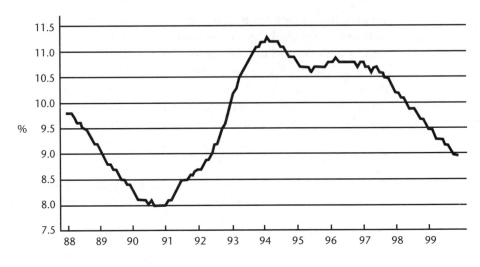

Figure 1.4 Annual unemployment rate (EU-15)
Source: *Economic Trends, February 2000*, National Statistics © Crown Copyright 2000

Europe. At this point, it is suffice to say that more than 15 million EU citizens are still out of work and that the EU's employment rate is below those of the US and Japan. The EU economies are characterized by insufficient participation in their labour markets (especially by women and older workers) and long-term structural unemployment. It is also the case that marked regional unemployment imbalances remain endemic in parts of the Union, a point covered more thoroughly in the section that follows.

A picture of diversity – core and periphery in the European economy

As well as finding significant differences between countries in the EU, we can also identify regional differences within those countries. Many regions, even within the wealthiest countries, have local GDPs well below the EU average and relatively high levels of unemployment. With respect to gross domestic product (GDP) per capita, published data from the European Commission show that in 1996 (excluding overseas territories) income levels amongst the EU's 208 NUTS II regions, range from Ipeiros, Greece at 44% of the EU-15 average, to Hamburg at 192% of the average. In fact, GDP per capita in the EU's ten richest regions is over three times that in the EU's ten very poorest regions. Regional economic disparities were reduced during the boom years of the 1960s and early 1970s but widened in the 1980s with the introduction of some very poor regions in Greece, Spain, and Portugal. Although high growth in these economies led to a narrowing of regional income gaps in the late 1980s and early 1990s, German re-unification and the further enlargement of the EU (to include the wealthy regions of Sweden, Austria and Finland) have meant that the disparities between the EU regions as a whole remain considerable. While figures suggest the convergence of a greater number of regions around average levels of income, at the extremes the gap between rich and poor has barely narrowed. Relative GDP per head in the ten richest regions has, since 1986, declined from 3.7 times to only 3.1 times the level in the ten poorest ones (European Commission, 1999). Even within individual countries the gap between the very richest and the very poorest remains substantial. For example, Hamburg, the richest EU region in 1996, is 3.5 times better off in terms of GDP per capita than Germany's poorest regions Thüringen and Mecklenburg (see Table 1.10).

The highest degree of economic activity (and wealth) is found in a number of regions in the economic heartland of the EU economy, particularly in the 'hot banana' stretching from the South-East of England, across much of France and the Rhineland, into Northern Italy and Northern Spain. In contrast, regions formerly dependent on traditional industries such as coal, steel and shipbuilding have found themselves marginalised along with the 'lagging' and underdeveloped regions dominating the rural parts of Greece, Italy, Spain, Portugal and Ireland. Based on averages for the period 1994–96, fifty of the EU's 208 regions (concentrated in these countries) remain below 75% of the EU average including all thirteen Greek regions and six of Portugal's seven. As discussed in Chapter 7, seventy-seven of the eighty-nine Central and East European regions fall below 50% of average EU per capita GDP (source: Eurostat).

The scenario is similar to that which has created a core of activity in the South-East of England and relatively depressed areas in the North. Firms see advantages of being near to other firms and close to the more affluent consumer markets created by higher levels of employment and higher wage rates. The consequence of a core of activity and the relocation of companies into that core is to leave some areas in a state of peripherality and decline. However, the 'regional problem' is multidimensional and is very much tied up with four fundamental characteristics of a modern capitalist economy:

- First, there is a declining use of labour relative to capital in agriculture and a corresponding urbanization process. This has led to the continuing depopulation of peripheral regions.

- Second, there is a declining reliance of manufacturing industry on natural materials and the consequence is that the location decision often has to be to establish enterprises near to final markets. This, again, has reinforced urbanization trends and left regions rich in natural resources nevertheless underdeveloped.

- Third, service activities continue to be important and they tend to serve large urbanized populations, further increasing the pull to a centre.

- Fourth, there is fierce competition from lesser developed economies for labour-intensive production leaving some traditional industries unable to compete and in decline. Where these industries have previously been regionally based, they disappear and there is nothing to replace them. Such regions exist in many member states, including Belgium, Spain, France, Italy and the United Kingdom.

It is also the case that the European Single Market and European Monetary Union

Table 1.10 GDP per head (PPS) in richest and poorest regions in the Union, 1986 and 1996

1986			1996		
Regions	GDP/head EUR-15 = 100		Regions	GDP/head EUR-15 = 100	
Hamburg (D)	185	1	Hamburg (D)	192	1
Reg. Bruxelles-Cap./Brussels Hfdst. Gew. (B)	163	2	Reg. Bruxelles-Cap./Brussels Hfdst. Gew. (B)	173	2
Île de France (F)	162	3	Darmstadt (D)	171	3
Darmstadt (D)	152	4	Luxembourg (Grand-Duché) (L)	169	4
Wien (A)	148	5	Wien (A)	167	5
Greater London (UK)	145	6	Île de France (F)	160	6
Bremen (D)	144	7	Oberbayern (D)	156	7
Stuttgart (D)	143	8	Bremen (D)	149	8
Oberbayern (D)	141	9	Greater London (UK)	140	9
Luxembourg (Grand-Duché) (L)	137	10	Antwerpen (B)	137	10
Top 10	**153**		**Top 10**	**158**	
Stockholm(S)	133	11	Stuttgart (D)	135	11
Ahvenanmaa/Aland (FIN)	132	12	Groningen (NL)	134	12
Lombardia (I)	132	13	Emilia-Romagna (I)	133	13
Uusimaa (FIN)	129	14	Lombardia (I)	132	14
Valle d'Aosta (I)	129	15	Valle d'Aosta (I)	131	15
Berlin (D)	128	16	Uusimaa (FIN)	129	16
Emilia-Romagna (I)	125	17	Trentino-Alto Adige (I)	128	17
Mittelfranken (D)	124	18	Grampian (UK)	128	18
Antwerpen (B)	124	19	Friuli-Venezia Giulia (I)	126	19
Karlsruhe (D)	123	20	Karlsruhe (D)	126	20
Düsseldorf (D)	122	21	Veneto (I)	124	21
Grampian (UK)	122	22	Berkshire, Buckinghamshire, Oxfordshire (UK)	124	22
Noord-Holland (NL)	117	23	Mittelfranken (D)	123	23
Köln (D)	117	24	Stockholm(S)	123	24
Piemonte (I)	117	25	Salzburg (A)	121	25
Top 25	**138**		**Top 25**	**143**	
Guyane (F)	37	1	Guadeloupe (F)	40	1
Guadeloupe (F)	37	2	Ipeiros (EL)	44	2
Alentajo (P)	37	3	Réunion (F)	46	3
Apores (P)	40	4	Guyane (F)	48	4
Madeira (P)	40	5	Apores (P)	50	5
Réunion (F)	40	6	Voreio Aigaio (EL)	52	6
Centro (P)	42	7	Martinique (F)	54	7
Voreio Aigaio (EL)	44	8	Madeira (P)	54	8
Extremadura (E)	44	9	Extremadura (E)	55	9
Algarve (P)	44	10	Dessau (D)	55	10
Bottom 10	**41**		**Bottom 10**	**50**	
Ipeiros (EL)	47	11	Andalucia (E)	57	11
Martinique (F)	49	12	Dytiki Eliada (EL)	58	12
Dytiki Eliada (EL)	49	13	Magdeburg (D)	58	13
Norte (P)	51	14	Peloponnisos (EL)	58	14
Ionia Nisia (EL)	52	15	Calabria (I)	59	15
Andalucia (E)	53	16	Alentajo (P)	60	16
Castilla-La Mancha (E)	54	17	Centro (P)	61	17
Galicia (E)	55	18	Anatolki Makedonia, Thraki (EL)	61	18
Thessalia (EL)	55	19	Thüringen (D)	61	19
Anatolki Makedonia, Thraki (EL)	56	20	Mecklenburg-Vorpommern (D)	61	20
Kriti (EL)	57	21	Dytiki Makedonia (EL)	62	21
Dytiki Makedonia (EL)	58	22	Ionia Nisia (EL)	62	22
Kentriki Makedonia (EL)	58	23	Norte (P)	62	23
Calabria (I)	59	24	Thessalia (EL)	63	24
Peloponnisos (EL)	61	25	Galicia (E)	63	25
Bottom 25	**52**		**Bottom 25**	**59**	

Source: European Commission (1999)

have exacerbated the problem by promoting cross-frontier competition and the freedom of movement of capital.

Free market theory would suggest that in time the core will become an expensive area in which to locate and that there will be profitable opportunities associated with locating in peripheral areas where land prices will be cheaper and wage rates lower. A free functioning market would therefore cause factors of production to move out of high cost regions into low cost regions until cost differences are minimized and profits roughly equalized. Even if one accepts the free market argument, there may still be a role for intervention by governments for three reasons:

1. The relocation response may be very slow and there may be a role for speeding up the process via additional relocation incentives.

2. The movement of capital and labour to new locations will be based on private cost assessments and not on social cost. Thus costs associated with congestion, pollution and personal utility will not be taken into account. There may therefore be a role for government in discouraging movement towards a core and promoting peripheral development. This is likely to be achieved with appropriate taxes, subsidies and grants.

3. The mobility of labour is not equal within any workforce. It is generally younger, more able and more enterprising individuals without strong family ties who are able to move. This can result in a population being left behind in a peripheral location which is not only reduced in size but also in competitive ability.

Trends in technology and communications have made the dispersal of economic activity technologically easier. Because of the existence of electronic communications links, remote monitoring processes, computerized stock control and the speed and reliability of such electronic systems, it is possible for the management function to be physically separate from the manufacturing function. Thus, there may be an incentive for firms to establish manufacturing bases where wages are lower and where land prices are cheaper while maintaining links with the core at the management level. However, there is a more worrying aspect to this, which is that if firms can locate their manufacturing plants in lower-cost areas then why should they choose areas within the EU at all? Why not, for example, choose Eastern European locations which have even lower costs but retain their locational advantages with respect to Western Europe? If costs are substantially lower and can even make large transportation costs viable then there may be an incentive to locate to the Third World as well. Such scenarios will do little to cure a potential peripheral problem.

The service and information sectors of an economy may also become decentralized over time as providers of services and information have more and more electronically generated information available to them and where electronic communications become the norm. Already large databases of information with remote access to them via the telecommunications network have meant that firms no longer have to be near to the centre of economic activity. It remains to be seen which forces in the core–periphery debate will dominate in the long run and in any case there will be significant governmental pressure to avoid the creation of a periphery. Nevertheless, this is a major issue which has to be addressed in a regional context and the EU has developed a number of instruments aimed at alleviating current and potential regional problems (see Chapter 5).

An interdependent Europe

Interdependence and regionalization

One of the principal characteristics of the 'New' European economy is the high level of economic interdependence between national and regional economies and the evidence of dynamic regionalism. Among the EU states, for example, an average EU member conducts nearly 70% of its 'foreign' trade with other EU economies. In the EU, the Internal Market Programme has not only strengthened economic ties between 'sovereign' economies but has also contributed to a new 'European regulatory structure'. As Tsoukalis (1997) notes, new regimes on banking and financial services and on technical standards (not to mention competition policy) have emerged as a response to heightened links and interdependence between the EU states. These regimes are being progressively extended to the EU's associates (and aspirant members) establishing the EU as the hub of a 'new European political economy' (Tsoukalis 1993). EMU, redistributive instruments at the supranational level and the rapidly increased mobility of capital throughout Europe also demonstrate the financial and capital interdependencies of the modern European states. EMU alone introduces a single-currency regime in eleven countries and for 290 million European citizens with the likelihood of future additions.

The regionalization of the European economy is of course evident in the existence and function of communities such as the European Union. Europe now houses four major regional economic groupings: the European Union (EU), the European Free Trade Association (EFTA), the Central European Free Trade Area (CEFTA) and the Commonwealth of Independent States (CIS), each of which represents a response to economic (and political) interlinkages between their members. Apart from the extensive internal links characterizing each of these groupings, there are also developed (or developing) links between each. In illustration, the EU is linked closely with the EFTA group through the European Economic Area (EEA) Agreement and with the CEFTA states through a series of 'uniform' association agreements. Ties with the CIS economies are also being developed through Partnership and Co-operation Agreements (PCAs) which, although concluded on a bilateral basis, are also marked by a rough uniformity (see Chapter 7). Beyond this, the Union is establishing itself at the heart of an evolving Euro-Mediterranean economic area (EMEA) extending to such distant markets as Israel, Jordan, Morocco and Tunisia (see Chapter 12).

In the sections that follow, we provide a brief profile of the four existing groupings – EU, EFTA, CEFTA and CIS – all of which attract discussion in the later stages of this work. Each of these regional communities represents a different form and level of economic integration, the theory of which is discussed in Chapter 3.

Main economic groupings

The European Union

The EU is the most advanced of all of Europe's regional economic groupings. At the start of the year 2000, it had fifteen member states – Austria, Belgium, Denmark, Finland, France, Germany, Greece, Ireland, Italy, Luxembourg, the Netherlands, Portugal, Spain, Sweden, and the United Kingdom – and a population of nearly 376 million. Based on estimates for 1998, at purchasing power parity, the EU-15 have a combined gross domestic product of some $7,752 billion.

The original communities – the European Coal and Steel Community, European Atomic Energy Community, and European Economic Community – were created in the 1950s (by just six states), both as a means of uniting the nations of Europe economically and as a step towards closer union among the peoples of Europe (see Chapter 2). The consolidation of these communities since the 1950s reached a high point in 1993 with the completion of a Single European Market (SEM) between an enlarged total of twelve member states (see Chapter 3). The SEM now provides for the freedom of movement of goods, services, capital and labour throughout the present membership of fifteen EU member states and the wider European Economic Area (see subsequently). In 1993, the Communities also formally adopted the title of the European Union following ratification of the Maastricht Treaty. This Treaty has laid the foundation for the strengthening of the EU and of its common institutional framework. This has taken clearest form in the continued development of economic policy co-operation (which in many fields is now at an advanced level) and in the steps towards Economic and Monetary Union (see Chapters 4–6). In January 1999, eleven of the EU-15 entered into the final stage of monetary union, adopting a single currency (the Euro) and a unified monetary policy regime. At the start of the twenty-first century, the EU is faced again with familiar tensions between the deepening of the union and the widening of its membership, some of which were addressed in the last major Treaty revison, the Amsterdam Treaty (1997). Thirteen applications for EU membership are currently being managed by the European Commission (the EU's executive arm), raising the prospect of a larger, pan-European Union.

The European Free Trade Association

In 1959, seven West European countries that were not members of the European Economic Community (Austria, Denmark, Norway, Portugal, Sweden, Switzerland and the United Kingdom) established EFTA. The Association's goal was to remove all mutual import duties, quotas and other obstacles to trade in industrial products and to uphold liberal, non-discriminatory practices in world trade. Iceland, Finland and Liechtenstein became later members of EFTA, but the Association's membership has been progressively reduced by the loss of members to the EC–EU. At the start of the year 2000, only Norway, Switzerland, Iceland and Liechtenstein remained as full members.

As well as providing for an industrial FTA between its members, EFTA also constitutes a platform for three of its members, namely Iceland, Norway, and

Liechtenstein, to participate in the *European Economic Area* with the fifteen EU economies. The EEA Treaty was signed between the EU and EFTA countries in 1991. The agreement amounted to the EFTA countries accepting the fundamental principles of the Community's internal market programme, namely free movement of goods, services, people and capital. The EFTA member states do not, however, adhere to the EU's common external tariff nor to the rules and requirements of the EU's common agricultural and fisheries policies. In 1992, Switzerland declared its intention not to join the European Economic Area.

The Central European Free Trade Area

The Central European Free Trade Agreement was signed in December 1992 in Krakow by Czechoslovakia, Hungary and Poland. It became effective in March 1993. Following the split between the Czech and Slovak Republics in 1993, membership increased to four countries. Since 1994, CEFTA has been expanded to include Slovenia, Romania and Bulgaria. The elimination of customs duties on most industrial goods means that most products manufactured or processed within one member country can be exported to another duty free. Trade in industrial products will be completely liberalized by 1 January 2001 (except for the export of cars to Poland, which will be liberalised by 1 January 2002). The CEFTA agreement also provides for mutual concessions on agricultural products. The CEFTA market consists of approximately 100 million consumers.

The Commonwealth of Independent States

Founded in December 1991, the CIS originally consisted of three members – Belarus, Ukraine and Russia. Two weeks after its establishment, eight other former Soviet republics – Armenia, Azerbaijan, Kazakhstan, Kyrgyzstan, Moldova, Tajikistan, Turkmenistan, and Uzbekistan – were also admitted as members. Georgia joined in 1993. Today, the CIS provides a framework for broad economic co-operation between these former Soviet Republics, with members functioning as 'fully independent states'. The only exception to this rule is provided by the newly formed Russian–Belarussian Union which signals an effective diminishment in the sovereign independence of Belarus. Members are highly dependent on one another for trade and co-ordinate many aspects of their economic and foreign policies through a central council. Co-operation is also pursued on defence, law enforcement, immigration and environmental protection.

Conclusion

The European business environment is a dynamic environment marked by rapid change. In this context, the structures and forms of European business will continue to evolve and the European economy itself will continue to develop. In the chapters that follow we provide analysis of these dynamic processes, giving further definition to the new EBE and to the direction of European business. The present chapter has offered only the briefest of glimpses into business and economy in the 'New' Europe and with some considerable bias towards the West European states. In what follows, we provide detail on the economic, political, social, technological and legal environments of businesses throughout the European region. Progressively, we investigate the changing strategies and structures of businesses operating in and across this theatre and look towards the challenges of competing in a 'global' marketplace. A profile of the book's organization is provided in the Preface. At each stage the reader will observe some common features. Each of the forthcoming chapters attempts to achieve a balance of theory, evidence and case study and each boasts a set of discussion questions as well as numerous references.

Review questions for Chapter 1

1. How would you define a European business?

2. How might the term 'European business' be employed?

3. Discuss the role of small and medium-sized enterprises in the contemporary European economy. How might we define SMEs?

4. How might a business be considered 'international'?

5. What are the defining characteristics of multinational enterprises? Can you provide examples?

6. How do we measure which are the most successful firms in Europe?

7. List the sectors where Europe has a large number of internationally competitive firms. Why do you think Europe has strength in these sectors?

8. Explain the difference between a sole-tradership and a partnership.

9. Explain the difference between a private limited company and a public limited company.

10. Which European countries have the largest economies (by gross domestic product) and the highest living standards?

11. In what sense are terms such as 'post-industrial' and 'knowledge-based economy' relevant to these countries?

12. Among the EU states, which countries have the smallest economies (by gross domestic product) and the lowest living standards?

13. To what extent do differences in prosperity and economic development exist within individual states?

14. How far is it fair to say that the European economies are 'interdependent'?

15. Contrast and compare Europe's main regional economic groupings.

Web guide

Information on the European economies (including macroeconomic data)

EUROSTAT @ http://europa.eu.int/comm/eurostat/

European Commission: Economic and Financial Affairs @ http://europa.eu.int/comm/economy_finance/

OECD @ http://www.oecd.org/publications/figures/index.htm

The CIA World Factbook (basic country–market information) @ http://www.odci.gov/cia/publications/factbook

UN/ECE Statistical Yearbook Europe (basic country–market information) @ http://www.unece.org/stats/trend/trend_h.htm

The Library of Congress Country Studies @ http://lcweb2.loc.gov/frd/cs/cshome.html

Newswire

BBC News (Europe) @ http://news.bbc.co.uk/hi/english/world/europe/

EUBusinessNews @ http://www.eubusiness.com/

Europe Online international (top news stories and bulletins) @ http://www.europeonline.com

European newspapers and business press titles @ http://ihr.sas.ac.uk/ihr/newspapers/europe.html

Bloomberg's News-Service (UK and Europe) @ http://www.bloomberg.com/uk/

European Voice (EU affairs newspaper) @ http://www.european-voice.com

International Herald Tribune (Europe bureau) @ http://www.iht.com/IHT/JV/00/index.html

PriceWaterhouseCoopers (European economic outlook) @ http://www.pwcglobal.com/gx/eng/ins-sol/spec-int/eeo/index.html

Companies: profiles and performance ratings

Biz/ed company facts @ http://www.bized.ac.uk/compfact/comphome.htm

Hoover's online: company and industry information @ http://www.hoovers.com/

FactMerchant BusinessNews @ http://www.factmerchant.com

Financial Times: European performance league @ http://www.ft.com/euroleague/

FT 500 @ http://www.ft.com/FT500/

References

Bartlett, C.A. and Ghoshal, S. (2000) *Transnational Management: Text, Cases and Readings in Cross-Border Management,* 3rd edition, McGraw-Hill.

Dunning, J.H. (1993) *Multinational Enterprises and the Global Economy*, Addison-Wesley.

El-Kahal, S. (1998) *Business in Europe*, McGraw-Hill.

Ellis, J. and Williams, D. (1995) *International Business Strategy*, Pitman Publishing.

European Commission (1999) *Sixth Periodic Report on the Social and Economic Situation and Development of the Regions of the European Union*, Office for Official Publications of the EC, Luxembourg.

European Commission (2000*) European Economy Supplement A. Economic Trends*, no. 1/2, April, Office for Official Publications of the EC, Luxembourg.

Eurostat (1999*) Enterprises in Europe, 5th Report*, Statistical Office of the European Communities, Luxembourg.

Greiling, D. (1997) The legal framework: company and labour law, in Reeves, N. and Kelly-Holmes, H. (eds), *The European Business Environment: Germany*, International Thomson Business Press.

Harris, N. (1999) *European Business*, 2nd edition, Macmillan Business.

Johnson, D. and Turner, C. (2000) *European Business: Policy Challenges for the New Commercial Environment*, Routledge.

Nugent, N. and O'Donnell, R. (eds) (1994*) European Business Environment*, Macmillan.

Tsoukalis, L. (1993) *The New European Economy: The Politics and Economics of Integration*, Oxford University Press.

Tsoukalis, L. (1997) *The New European Economy Revisited*, Oxford: Oxford University Press.

Worthington, I. and Britton, C. (1997) *The Business Environment*, 2nd edition, Pitman.

The 'new' European business environment

2 Understanding the European Union

Introduction

The idea of creating a political and economic union in Europe is not a new one. Even before the beginnings of the twentieth century there were those, like the great intellectual Victor Hugo, who thought of European unification as the answer to national rivalries and as a way of controlling divisions of interest between competing European powers. In the interwar years (1918–39) proposals for greater co-operation between European states were also formally advanced including those tabled at the League of Nations (in 1929) by the then French Foreign Minister, Aristide Briand. While Briand's plans were clearly driven by the target of preserving the Versailles peace settlement (1919), they were nonetheless explicit in prescribing 'a system of European Federal Union' and 'a permanent regime' in Europe based on international treaty agreements. Although not endorsed, the interest in European co-operation suggested in these proposals remained a genuine feature of European politics up to and including the period of the Second World War. Indeed, although rampant nationalism fragmented the continent into warring powers, one legacy of

37

war (1939–45) was the resulting need to transform the relations between the states of Western Europe and to develop a new model of international relations. Although thoughts of pan-European integration were now shattered – the terms of post-war settlement imposed a Manichean division between Europe's West and East – the post-war needs of the Europeans were such that interstate co-operation would now be ensured.

Today, and through the present and antecedent structures of the European Union (EU), Western European integration has reached an advanced stage. Member states have decided not only to co-operate in a great number of areas, ranging from trade in goods to foreign policy, but also to create communities of shared interest and authority. Three 'communities':

- the European Coal and Steel Community (ECSC),

- the European Community (EC) – formerly the European Economic Community, and

- the European Atomic Energy Community (EAEC)

have been progressively deepened and supplemented so as to heighten the economic, political and legal dimensions of Union. Moreover, the EU, already covering fifteen European nation-states and some 376 million persons, is now the foundation stone of wider processes of European integration and co-operation extending into Eastern Europe and the Mediterranean basin. Through a combination of the EU's own extraordinary growth (and appeal) and of circumstances confronting developing and transition economies in the 'wider Europe', the prospect is raised of a genuinely pan-European construct (built around the existing EU) sometime early in this new century. Already, large parts of the EC 'acquis' are being extended to candidate countries in Central and Eastern Europe, to customs union partners (Turkey) and to other West European nations (e.g. Norway and Iceland). These states have either targeted future EU membership (see Figure 2.1) or settled on a form of coexistence that sees them closely linked to the EU and to the rules of its internal market.

Furthermore, while the EU remains far removed from the united order of its great rival (the United States of America), it has moved ever closer to its design and federal aspect. At the close of the twentieth century, it had an array of legislative competencies, a number of powerful central institutions and extensive majoritarian decision-making within those institutions. Its body of law – the 'acquis communautaire' – and single-market framework establish it firmly as the anchor of a process of deep regional market integration combining the bulk of the West European nations. In short, although the continent remains the home of independent nation-states and of diverse cultural values, it has emerged as the theatre for the growth and consolidation of a new supranational civilian and regulatory power (the EU). The fact that this power encompasses four separate members of the G-8 grouping of industrial heavyweights (France, the UK, Germany and Italy) and a combined domestic product of €7,495 billion (over $7 trillion) underlines its significance in global as well as in regional terms. A fledgling currency union underscores its weight and unity.

Figure 2.1 Map of the European Union (1999) and of candidate countries
Note: Candidate countries are shaded

Of course the real quality of the European Union is its unique nature. The European Union is unlike any other international organization – e.g. the UN, OECD or WTO – in the sense that participating governments have transferred a large measure of their political sovereignty to supranational structures. Indeed, the inherent process of fusing supranational layers of authority onto existing sovereign entities is, in its form and timing, a process without precedent or parallel. Thus, while comparisons are sometimes struck between the EU and such bodies, in no sense do those fellow organizations represent such innovation in the means of organizing relations between established nations.

The development of the European Communities

As noted, the history of modern European integration was launched in the late 1940s in the wake of the Second World War. Six years of conflict had left a demand for politico-economic reconstruction as a devastated Western Europe sought ways to rebuild its economy and to prevent future wars. Much of Europe lay in ruins, communications were broken, food and fuel were in short supply and industry was geared to the needs of war. The continent also faced a future between the superpowers, a developing 'Cold War' creating a dividing line between Europe's war-ravaged nations. As expressed by Young (1991, p. xiv):

> [T]he 'iron curtain' which split the continent after 1945 was unprecedented in effect on all levels – ideological, military, economic, social and cultural. In the East the Soviet Union asserted its dominance, Communist policies were enforced by a police-state, and rigid methods of central planning were used to create heavy industries under state ownership. In the West the US provided economic aid (the Marshall Plan) and led a military alliance (NATO), liberal democracy was generally fostered, and capitalist measures were used to achieve growth.

The completion of a European Recovery Programme in 1948 (as the Marshall Plan had become) quickly forced the West Europeans to work together in overcoming their problems. The programme required an appropriate structure for the implied economic co-operation (the OEEC) and the logic of co-ordinated action was taken further by the formation of a small-scale customs union between Belgium, the Netherlands and Luxembourg. However, although these initiatives were significant, neither provided the necessary impetus for effective regional co-operation or a framework to challenge the competition of European state interests. Anyone could be exempt from a decision in the OEEC and the Benelux arrangement was limited to the 'Low Countries', thereby doing little to bring the fuller set of continental markets into closer relationship. Finally, in 1950, co-operation was moved dramatically forward with a French-sponsored plan to pool European coal and steel production under a common high authority and to achieve a unified market within this controlling area of economic effort. Common decisions would be binding on all participants, consistent with the achievement of a supranational regime, albeit one within a limited field.

The architects of this proposal, French Foreign Minister Robert Schuman and Jean Monnet (the man responsible for the post-war French industrial modernization plan), were quite explicit that the proposals were intended to be but the first step in the realization of a future (and much wider) European union. When announcing the plan in 1950, Schuman was entirely clear that the coal and steel project provided only 'a basis for the building of a new Europe', declaring '. . . this proposal will be the first concrete foundation of a European federation which is indispensable to the preservation of peace'. In this respect, while it was important that other European states were to join, the basis of the plan was that of a new form of relationship between France and Germany, with the implied sectoral arrangements providing a European roof for the industrial reconstruction of post-war Germany. Indeed, while not all of the other eventual members – Italy, Belgium, the Netherlands and Luxembourg – shared France's post-war visions, all were united with Paris in seeking to monitor the control and employment of (then) strategically important resources in the post-war German territories. A formal treaty – the European Coal and Steel Community Treaty – was concluded between the six parties in Paris on 18 April 1951. Four central institutions, a High Authority, Council of Ministers, Common Assembly and Court of Justice, were established with member states transferring many sovereign powers to this set of central institutions. As explained by Nugent (1999, p. 37), between them, these institutions had the authority to:

> see to the abolition and prohibition of internal tariff barriers, state subsidies and special charges, and restrictive practices; fix prices under certain conditions; harmonize exter-

nal commercial policy, for example by setting minimum and maximum customs duties on coal and steel imports from third countries; and impose levies on coal and steel production to finance the ECSC's activities.

Encouraged by the success of the ECSC – the plan was so successful that coal and steel trade between the Six increased by 129% in the first five years – the Six attempted to pursue integration in the military and political fields. However, when ambitious plans for European political and defence communities were derailed in the French Parliament in 1954, European leaders returned to the process of European market integration. In June 1955, foreign affairs ministers of the six ECSC member countries met in Messina, Sicily, to investigate the possibilities of progress towards a broader economic and market arrangement. The UK left these negotiations denouncing their intent and decrying the possibilities of serious agreed outcomes. Despite this, a committee under the chairmanship of the Belgian Foreign Affairs Minister Paul-Henri Spaak was formally established at Messina and culminated its work with production of concrete proposals for the formation of a broad economic community. Based on a customs union arrangement and a set of common economic policies, this became a reality in 1958 following the conclusion of the European Economic Community (EEC) Treaty of Rome. The EEC Treaty (actually signed in 1957) provided detailed plans for the creation of a common market among its signatories, including the removal of customs duties between member states, the establishment of a common external tariff and the elimination of mutual quantitative restrictions (quotas) and measures having equivalent effect. Article 2 of the Treaty laid down the following broad objectives:

> The Community shall have as its task, by establishing a common market and progressively approximating the economic policies of member states, to promote throughout the Community a harmonious development of economic activities, a continuous and balanced expansion, an increase in stability, an accelerated raising of the standard of living, and closer relations between the states belonging to it.

While the EEC Treaty was of greater significance (and profile) to 'the Six', it is also important to record that the 'member states' concluded a second treaty at Rome, one on atomic energy co-operation. The European Atomic Energy Community Treaty (EAEC Treaty) established a third 'community' of the member states to be known as Euratom. As with the new EEC, institutional arrangements would be modelled broadly on those of the ECSC, with four principal institutions: a Court of Justice, Commission, Council of Ministers, and a representative (although non-elected) Assembly. In the case of the new EEC, member states would work through these structures to ensure the successful operation of the common market and to pursue a series of common policies in the areas of transport, agriculture and trade. In the case of Euratom, objectives would be pursued in relation to atomic energy co-operation for peaceful means, treaty provisions aimed at a pooling and sharing of technical information and knowledge.

The UK's opt-out from the EEC and EAEC negotiations effectively eliminated countries such as Ireland and the Scandinavian nations from the early years of 'Community co-operation'. At this time, the UK was a much more important trading partner for these countries and Austria, Sweden and Switzerland also regarded the Community Treaties as having political overtones incompatible with their status as independent, politically neutral countries. Elsewhere, Spain, Greece and Portugal were ruled out of membership as a consequence of their undemocratic governments. Nonetheless, early success in the operation of the Common Market gave inevitability to a longer-term process of Community enlargement. The first round of enlargement followed in 1973 when the UK, Ireland and Denmark joined the original six. For the UK in particular, this was a significant change of policy although the change was not brought about by any ideological commitment but by some harsh economic facts. Industries within the EEC were expanding at twice the rate of British industry, and, as a single entity, the UK was lacking its former influence over world affairs. The view among many politicians within the UK, therefore, was that outside of the EEC the UK would become weak and isolated. In 1981, Greece – now under democratic government – joined the Community (the second enlargement), followed by Spain and Portugal in 1986 (the third or 'Iberian' enlargement). By this time the nature of Community-based co-operation was being re-evaluated and the process of revision of the founding treaties was firmly underway.

Re-launching the Community: the Single European Act

Despite the European Community's success in expanding its membership, by the early to mid-1980s, the competitiveness of the Community group had been continually falling behind that of Japan and the USA, the world's leading trading nations. This manifested itself in a slow-down in absolute output, in high rates of inflation and unemployment, and slow growth in investment and productivity. Unlike their Japanese and American counterparts, European firms were constrained to competition in small national markets. Any attempt to broaden their competitive scope by expanding into other Community nations was hampered by a broad array of barriers, which raised costs and undermined efficiency. Although the Community project had successfully eliminated internal (mutual) tariff barriers, new non-tariff barriers were now a genuine and more insidious impediment to the effective functioning of the internal market. Technical and legislative differences hindered competition and were being exploited by firms and governments in order to sustain differential advantages between markets. This meant limiting cross-border expansion by biasing business towards indigenous firms and effectively discriminating against foreign entrants. Problems did not stop there. Broader restrictions on the free movement of goods, people and capital added further to the fragmentation and segmentation of the EC market. The entire customs union project, and with it much of the enthusiasm for the Community itself, was being frustrated.

In truth, successive efforts to strengthen the political and economic role of the EC had proved difficult to realize at a time when member states looked first to protect short-term national interest. In a recessionary climate (the 1970s were marked by a slow-down in European growth rates and by escalating mass unemployment), failure to make the Common Market 'work' had been joined by a lack of progress towards economic and monetary union. In the political sphere, although an elected assembly had been established in 1979, this only went part way to correcting the democratic deficit in the institutional machinery of the Communities. The member states also proved unable to streamline their decision-making procedures. Thus, as Young (1991) expresses: 'activity on political union in the 1970s and early 1980s involved words rather than deeds, and the power of national governments remained paramount' (see Young, 1991, p. 50).

In order to achieve the twin objectives of re-launching the Community and of improving member states' economic performance, it was necessary for the Commission to set specific targets for the creation of a genuinely integrated Single Market and to propose a series of decision-making reforms. Progress followed in 1985 with the launch of the Commission's White Paper on 'Completing the Internal Market', drawn up under the guidance of British Commissioner Lord Cockfield. This included a seven-year time frame for Single Market completion – setting a precise deadline of 31 December 1992 – a period that was to see just under 300 legislative proposals introduced. These measures, which would achieve smoother legislative passage with the extension of majority voting in the Council of Ministers, were formally grouped under three main objectives:

■ the elimination of physical frontiers, by abolishing checks on goods and persons at internal frontiers;

■ the elimination of technical frontiers – breaking down the barriers of national regulations on products and services by harmonization or mutual recognition;

■ the elimination of tax frontiers – overcoming the obstacles created by differences in indirect taxes by harmonization or approximation of VAT rates and excise duty.

On the basis of the Cockfield Report, the Single European Act came into force in July 1987. Formal treaty provisions set out the objective of 'an area without internal frontiers' in which the free movement of goods, persons, services and capital would be ensured. New powers were defined in the areas of regional development, health and safety, research and the environment. Changes to the Community legislative system were also realized so as to encourage the swift adoption of market reform measures. Specifically, a new article (Article 100a EEC) was added to the Treaty of Rome to allow Single Market measures to be agreed not by unanimity (as under the original Article 100) but by qualified majority vote (QMV). Exceptions would apply to fiscal provisions, the free movement of persons, and the rights and interests of employed persons (Article 100a.2 EEC). Here, as previously, unanimity would continue to apply and the European Parliament's role would be confined to consultation. Elsewhere, greater co-operation with the European Parliament would be a requisite of a new 'co-operation' procedure applying to those matters determined by qualified vote.

The SEA provided the first substantial revision of the treaties. Although many of its changes have since been modified or superseded by the Maastricht and Amsterdam Treaties, it was this Act that 're-launched' the Community at a time of some malaise. Firms and governments in Europe, many of whom had lobbied hard for just such an initiative, were forced to wake up quickly both to new procedures and policies at Community level and to the beginnings of a new market order in Europe.

From Community to Union: the Maastricht Treaty

Having set the wheels in motion for economic and social change within the EC, the SEA gave rise to an agenda of momentous change. Before the end of the 1980s, an emboldened European Commission sought member state agreement on ambitious plans for the strengthening of Community co-operation. Targets included the establishment of a social dimension to the Single Market, the achievement of Economic and Monetary Union (EMU), and the assertion of European identity on the international scene. In 1993, with the entry into force of the Treaty on European Union (signed at Maastricht on 7 February 1992) the Commission claimed success. The European Community had become the European Union, a reflection of agreed moves toward a broader platform of economic, political, security and judicial co-operation.

In achieving this feat, Maastricht marked a new stage in the process of creating what Monnet had described as 'the greatest common interest managed by common democratic institutions' (Monnet, 1976, p. 786). The established European Community – based on the ECSC, EEC and EAEC Treaties – had become supplemented by a common foreign and security policy (CFSP) and a common justice and home affairs policy (JHA). Although the member states would continue to be served by a single, united institutional framework, three domains or 'pillars' to member state co-operation had been established (see Figure 2.2). These would be managed simultaneously with variance in decision-making procedures and institutional apparatus according to specific Treaty provisions. Titles I–IV of the Treaty defined common provisions and the function and aims of the EC pillar, while separate titles covered the CFSP and JHA pillars. Though a new and 'consolidated' version of the TEU now exists (post-Amsterdam) this basic division continues to hold with Title V containing provisions on a Common Foreign and Security Policy, and Title VI on police and judicial co-operation.

Most of the provisions of the TEU were concerned with the three pillars, which in the case of pillar one meant amending, and in key respects extending, the provisions of the Rome Treaty. In the cases of pillars two and three, the TEU effectively provided a statement of guiding principles and operational rules.

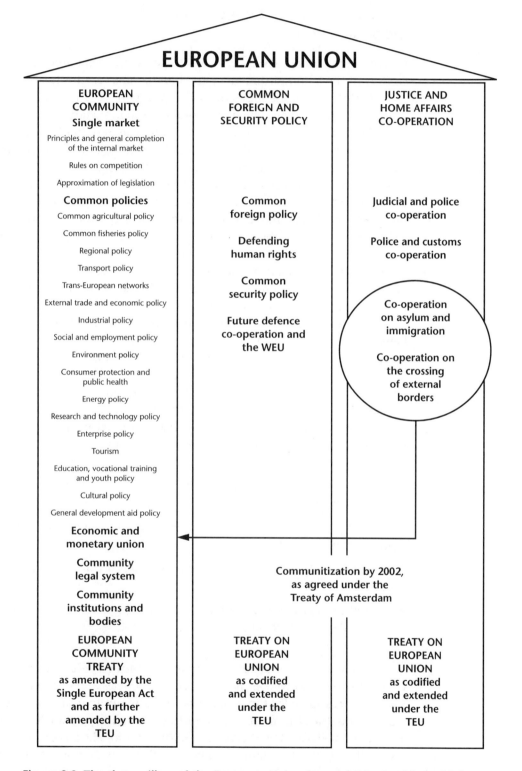

Figure 2.2 **The three pillars of the European Union (as established at Maastricht)**

Pillar one: internal common policies and economic and monetary union

In terms of the strengthening of an area of social and economic cohesion within the context of the accomplishment of the internal market, the Treaty outlined several important steps. Among these, the most important was the definition of three clear stages towards the achievement of economic and monetary union by the 1 January 1999. Plans included the setting up of a European System of Central Banks (ESCB) comprising a European Central Bank (ECB) and its national counterparts, so as to ensure an institutional framework for the management of a common European monetary policy. Monetary union had been a discreet objective of the SEA – defined in the preamble to the Act – and of historical plans throughout the Community's history. Now Maastricht delivered an irrevocable commitment to EMU before the century's end, minus the agreement of Denmark and the United Kingdom who reserved the right of 'opt-out' (see Chapter 4).

The Treaty also established the basis of a new EU Agreement on Social Policy (see Chapter 6). This was designed so as to enable the member governments (with the exception of the United Kingdom) to more fully implement the principles of the 1989 Charter on Fundamental Working Rights. The UK's opt-out served to widen the gap between UK and continental job laws before a new Labour government in the UK reversed the social policy 'opt-out' in the summer of 1997.

The emphasis on the rights of nationals of member states was also continued with the introduction of citizenship of the Union under Article 8 of the TEU (now Article 17 of the newly consolidated version of the EC Treaty). Citizenship of the Union was not intended to weaken existing national identities, but to bring new rights and benefits to the people of the Union. These included:

- the right to move and reside freely within the territory of the member states (Article 18, ex Article 8a);
- the right to vote and stand as a candidate at municipal and European elections (Article 19, ex Article 8b);
- the right to diplomatic or consular protection in third countries (Article 20, ex Article 8c);
- the right to petition the European Parliament and to apply to the Ombudsman (Article 21, ex Article 8d).

For these and other areas of Community business, Maastricht outlined such a comprehensive and wide-ranging package of policies and decision-making reforms that there was some legitimate fear that this attempt to unify the member states of Europe would lead to the break-up of the Community. Apart from the inclusions and amendments already described, and the additional transfer of responsibility for visa policy to the Community Pillar, reluctant integrationists were uneasy with changes to legislative procedure and to the balance of power between the institutions. Critically here, qualified majority voting had been widely extended to most of the areas that were either wholly new (such as trans-European networks, education and public health) or subject to more extensive provisions (such as the environment). These areas would be added to the set of Single-Market-based issues already determined under majority voting, with the European Parliament afforded new powers of co-decision (and the right to reject proposals) in several such matters.

Although these fears have proved exaggerated, it is clear that the results of the Danish and French referenda on Maastricht came perilously close to scuppering the TEU and rocked the foundations of the EU monolith. At very least, the initial 'no' vote in Denmark (subsequently reversed) forced EU legislators to re-examine Treaty terms (with particular concern to the position of Denmark) and to reaffirm that decisions should be taken at the lowest level consistent with effective action within a political system. This is the so-called subsidiarity rule and the insertion of a related clause into the Community Treaty was seen as an important step. Political, if not judicial, recognition was provided that some decisions should remain within the hands of national and subnational authorities, offering possible protection against the movement of Union institutions into new issue-areas. The insertion (now EC Treaty Article 5, ex Article 3b) declares:

> The Community shall act within the limits of the powers conferred upon it by the Treaty and of the objectives assigned to it therein. In the areas which do not fall within its exclusive competence, the Community shall take action, in accordance with the principle of subsidiarity, only if and in so far as the objectives for the proposed action cannot be sufficiently achieved by the member states and can therefore, by reason of scale or effects of the proposed action, be better achieved by the Community. Any action by the Community shall not go beyond what is necessary to achieve the objectives of this Treaty.

Pillar two: common foreign and security policy

According to union officials, it is not the purpose of the CFSP 'to make independent foreign policies disappear' or to 'threaten the defence system of each individual member state'. Rather, the introduction of a new common and foreign security policy should better enable the member states to reach agreement on certain international issues and to assert their collective identity on the international scene (http://ue.eu.int).

Going in to Maastricht, the member states had established their determination, where possible, to speak more clearly with one voice in international affairs, and Titles of the TEU were therefore designed so as to build on the foundations for European political co-operation put down by the Single European Act. These Titles now establish that, in acting together in the foreign policy field, the member states shall support the Union's external and security policy actively and unreservedly in a spirit of loyalty and mutual solidarity. They shall refrain from any action which is contrary to the interests of the Union or likely to impair its effectiveness as a cohesive force in international relations. Specific objectives include those of:

- safeguarding the independence of the EU;
- strengthening regional security;
- promoting international co-operation;
- preserving peace in line with the United Nations Charter;
- working together with respect to disarmament and arms control.

Treaty terms also enable 'the Fifteen' to work together towards a common defence policy so as to strengthen European security. What the French and British now hope to do is to drive forward a set of arrangements that will create a form of European defence identity that will not prejudice national defence and that will be developed within NATO obligations. It is envisaged that such an arrangement would be able to call on NATO assets to deal with limited crisis situations in Europe, by implication, in circumstances where the US was not inclined to act. British and French forces have already been working together in Mostar (Bosnia) and Kosovo during the recent period of Balkan instability and see such a development as a logical step towards improved co-ordination.

Although the CFSP framework is intergovernmental in character (limiting the powers of the Commission and Parliament), the new articles of the TEU demanded greater transparency of information between the member states on all issues related to security so that the Council 'may define a common position'. Member states will, in future, find that joint decisions made at an EU level are binding (pursuant on a unanimous decision by the Council). Relevant Treaty provisions are now to be found in Articles 11–28 of the consolidated version (the post-Amsterdam version) of the Treaty on European Union.

Pillar three: justice and home affairs

For the first time, Maastricht made justice and home affairs a matter for intergovernmental co-operation between the member states. Co-operation in the field of justice and home affairs brings together the ministries of justice and of the interior, and their departments, of the fifteen member states of the European Union. It enables 'dialogue, mutual assistance, work and cooperation between the police, customs and justice departments of The Fifteen' (http://ue.eu.int). There are two aspects to co-operation between justice administrations: co-operation in civil matters and co-operation in criminal matters, the latter concerning such matters as extradition. Judicial co-operation is now wide-ranging and is backed by the so-called Grotius programme. Customs co-operation is now also established with the TEU providing for the customs administrations of the member states to provide each other with mutual assistance and to co-operate in ensuring compliance with national and Community legislation. One aspect of this work is to combat illicit trafficking in drugs, arms, cultural goods, dangerous waste and nuclear materials. The TEU establishes clearly that co-ordinated action should also be undertaken by police authorities in order to help cope with these threats and to combat international terrorism and criminal activity. Europol, the European police office, will play an important role in assisting this co-operation. EU governments and the European Commission are expected to report annually to the European Parliament on their activities in this area. Relevant Treaty provisions are now to be found in Articles 29–42 of the consolidated version of the Treaty on European Union.

The Amsterdam Treaty

It is thus that when the next countries to join the European juggernaut (Finland, Austria and Sweden) did so in 1995, they became members of a new wider and more encompassing European Union (EU-15). The Maastricht Treaty had initiated a new momentum for economic union and had taken the then EC-12 a step towards greater political union. However, despite the importance of Maastricht in the history of EC–EU development, some interpreted this treaty as 'a fudge' and as a compromise, with opt-outs and special protocols applying to numerous fields and a lack of address of serious policy reform. The seismic changes in Central and Eastern Europe cast these limitations in clearer light and, by the end-point of treaty ratification (November 1993) the EU already had to look ahead at a 'wider' as well as 'deeper' future. In the summer months of 1993, the EU had determined that its new associate partners in Central and Eastern Europe could 'expect' to become future EU members and faced several applications for membership as well as requests for improved terms of association (see Chapter 7).

Launching an intergovernmental conference (IGC) in 1996, the member states set out to deal with this issue as a part of a broader exercise designed to review EU operations and to confront some of the anomolies of the Maastricht agreement (e.g. the Protocol-based Schengen and Social Policy Agreements). This initiative, managed first in the UK by the Conservative government of John Major, concluded in the summer of 1997 with the most recent of the major EU Treaties, the Amsterdam Treaty (see Table 2.1). The Treaty makes substantial changes to the TEU, comprising thirteen protocols, fifty-one declarations adopted by the conference and eight declarations by member states plus amendments to the existing treaties set out in fifteen articles. The combined effect is to begin the process of institutional reform in the run-up to enlargement, to strengthen foreign and security policy co-operation, and to deliver a Community area of fundamental rights, security, freedom and justice. The Treaty entered into effect on 1 May 1999. The Amsterdam Treaty represents a major advance towards economic and political union in several respects:

■ It simplifies the Community texts, incorporating past protocols into the main body of the treaties, deleting more than fifty-six obsolete articles and renumbering the rest in order to make the whole more legible. The reader will have noticed indication of 'new' article numbers in earlier outlines of treaty provisions.

Table 2.1 Treaty agreements establishing the European Union

Treaty	In force	Summary
European Coal and Steel (ECSC) Treaty (Treaty of Paris, 1951)	1952	A sector-specific Treaty of limited application. First of the founding Treaties
European Economic Community (EEC) Treaty (Treaty of Rome, 1957)	1958	Concluded on the model of the ECSC Treaty but with a broader range of objectives
European Atomic Energy Community (EAEC) Treaty (Rome, 1957)	1958	A sector-specific Treaty of limited application
Treaty establishing a Single Council and a Single Commission of the European Communities (Merger Treaty, 1965)	1967	Created a single institutional framework serving all three Communities
European Elections Act (1976)	1978	The basis for the first (1979) and subsequent European Parliamentary elections
Single European Act (1986)	1987	Amended and expanded the EEC Treaty. Introduced measures for the completion of the Internal Market and extended the scope of qualified majority voting
Treaty on European Union (Maastricht Treaty, 1992)	1993	Established the European Union; amended and expanded the EEC Treaty; created the co-decision procedure; codified the EC, CFSP and JHA 'pillars'
Treaty of Amsterdam (1997)	1999	Amended the Maastricht and EEC Treaties. Extended co-decision; added new employment title to Treaties and incorporated the Schengen accord into the EEC Treaty

Source: Adapted from one table concerning Treaties (in Bainbridge, 1998, (pp. 487–8))

■ It places a new emphasis on 'flexibility' in member state co-operation with multispeed integration made possible in a limited number of areas. Minilateral co-operation (that between a subset of EU members) is permitted where it aims at furthering the objectives of the Union and at protecting and serving its interests. There is a requirement that the co-operation concerns at least a majority of member states and that it does not affect the competences, rights, obligations and interests of those member states which do not participate.

■ Rights of citizens to have access to the documents of the Council of Ministers have been established under conditions of control defined by the member states, and national parliaments are encouraged to take a closer interest in Union affairs. The Union is thereby committed to a greater level of transparency in its essential operations.

■ Policies on sustainable development, human health protection and consumer protection were made formal objectives of the EU, and matters relating to internal cross-border movements and to employment and social policies were made subject to EU rules and procedures by formal incorporation of past agreements.

■ It timetables the full communitization of certain aspects of JHA co-operation –

co-operation on visas, asylum and immigration. Communitization is to be achieved over a period of five years, with some exemptions applying to Denmark, Britain and Ireland.

Despite these successes and innovations Amsterdam was a failure with respect to institutional reform and preparation for future enlargement. Indeed, the restructuring of the EU institutions and procedures, a primary task of the 1996–97 IGC, was all but shelved. Proposals to extend the use of qualified majority voting and to amend voting procedures in the Council, as well as to reduce the future size of the Commission, were either fudged or delayed. In practice, after two years of the Intergovernmental Conference, the member states could agree only that future Council votes would be reweighted, coterminous with a reduction in the size of the college of the Commission. Article 1 of the 'Protocol on the Institutions' (Treaty of Amsterdam) reads:

> At the date of entry into force of the first enlargement of the Union the Commission shall comprise one national of each of the member states, provided that, by that date, the weighting of the votes in the Council has been modified, whether by reweighting of the votes or by dual majority, in a manner acceptable to all Member States, taking into account all relevant elements, notably compensating those Member States which give up the possibility of nominating a second member of the Commission.

Therefore, though the principle has been established that the five countries with two commissioners will eventually surrender one apiece to five new EU members, it is also clear that the details of reform will only be hammered out in the IGC expected to run between February and December 2000. Effective progress at Amsterdam was limited to a redefinition of the powers and legislative role of the European Parliament where the member states could fall back on a greater level of consensus. The Treaty signals that the European Parliament will gain joint legislative powers with EU governments in additional areas of member co-operation, with a streamlined co-decision procedure established as the principal mode of adopting Community legislation. Exceptions to this rule are now limited to constitutional, agricultural and budgetary issues and to decisions relating to EMU and Community enlargement. The European Parliament will now also have the formal authority to reject the President of the European Commission when nominated by the member governments and, thereafter, to reject 'as a body' the President and the other nominated members of the Commission before their formal appointment.

Theories of integration

It is tempting to see this history of EU development as the product of a series of purposeful and forward steps towards a particular end-goal. Despite this temptation, it is more accurate to record that the task of creating a secure union of countries in Europe has enjoyed moments of successful forward movement and nadirs of frustration, hesitation and sclerosis. Throughout a fifty-year history there have been fundamental uncertainties as to the appropriate path for European co-operation and a lack of consensus as to what 'Union' should mean and entail. Even today, there is little unity as to the nature of necessary reform plans or of visions of the new Europe. Much of the debate at Amsterdam focused on differing French and German perceptions of future EU integration.

Several theories of political integration have emerged to try to explain the history of the European Union's integration process and to present a model from which to predict what the European Union of the future will be (see Cram, 1996, for a comprehensive review). Drawing on devices rooted in international relations theory, analysts of the European Communities have associated different phases of their evolution with particular approaches to the study of European integration. According to Lodge (1983, p. xvi), a 'loosely linear development' can be identified. In this, the 1950s and 1960s may be characterized as a period of functionalism or neo-functionalism, the 1970s–early 1980s as a period of ascendant confederalism and intergovernmentalism, and the late 1980s and 1990s as a time of resurgent federalism or neo-federalism. This establishes separate theories of political integration that fall into a number of categories.

Functionalism

Functionalist theory (see Mitrany, 1966) suggests that states may co-operate in certain areas with a minimum of institutional apparatus – initially where no vital state interests are threatened. In short, common authority may apply to specific activities with the creation of new bodies and agencies to oversee the very processes of 'technical–functional' co-operation. This process of integration may have its own dynamic. Interstate co-operation will move on to new areas through a kind of invisible hand (functionalist spill-over) where positive experience provides a template and incentive for the creation of further functionally specific organizations. This will foster demands for democratic control in those areas to be exercised by new supranational institutions but technical 'self-determination' would mean that there would be 'no need for any fixed constitutional division of authority and power, prescribed in advance' (Mitrany, 1966, p. 73). Therefore, as explained by Bainbridge (1998, p. 278):

> By contrast with federalism, functionalism is driven by economic, social and technical imperatives rather than by political forces ... Applied to European integration, functionalism has always had an attraction for the British and the Scandinavians as being both more 'pragmatic' and less likely, at least in the short term, to raise sensitive issues of sovereignty.

Functionalism dominated the debates about European political integration for many years, taking revised expression in the theory of neo-functionalism (see Haas, 1958; Lindberg and Scheingold, 1970). In the context of European integration it remains primarily important for its influence on the architects of the European Coal and Steel Community, Monnet and Schuman. Although these men were of federalist leanings, in creating the ECSC they borrowed key aspects of what might be termed the functionalist method (see McCormick, 1999, p. 19; Cram, 1996, p. 43).

Neo-functionalism

Neo-functionalist theory extends and expands on the theory of spillover and re-assesses the nature of involvement of social actors and political elites in the integration process. Whereas functionalists identified the construction of joint agencies with rationalist technocratic administration and viewed the integration process as essentially non-political (a view met with many criticisms), neo-functionalists argued that the process was inherently 'political' and that socio-political elites were key drivers of the European integration process. Integration for the neo-functionalists is 'the process whereby political actors in several distinct national settings, are persuaded to shift their loyalties, expectations and political activities towards a new centre'. Here, 'institutions possess and demand jurisdiction over the pre-existing national states' (Haas, 1958, p. 16). Supranational institutions are able to secure such jurisdiction as the efficiency of collaborative action is demonstrated. Spill-over may take place from initially non-controversial technical sectors to other sectors–areas of greater political sensitivity. The end result is a new political community superimposed on the pre-existing state system. Within this, the supra-national institutions are allotted a key role as 'agents of integration' and as 'brokers' of competing national interests in multilevelled authority systems.

The degree to which 'authority–legitimacy' transfers have taken place provides a measurable indicator of progress towards a new European political community (Haas, 1970; Lindberg and Scheingold, 1970). Those that use the neo-functionalist literature to explain the EU thus highlight the lineal construction of the European Communities, exponential growth in EU policy competences and the progressive deepening of the EU's institutional authority. Analysis of the passage of succeeding treaties (and especially that of the Treaty on European Union) may also find relevance in the early neo-functionalist claim that 'integration is an elite process that proceeds in a situation of permissive consensus where publics acquiesce to decisions reached by elite coalitions'. Critics have argued, however, that the linear logic of neo-functionalism (that there will be a gradual move from one policy activity to another) has been frustrated and that 'a more multivariate form of analysis should be employed' (see Lodge, 1983, p. xxi). Sharing some of the reference points of functionalist theories, European integration has become seen in terms of managed interdependence or 'concordance' (Puchala, 1972), 'preference–convergence' (Keohane and Hoffman, 1990, 1991) and 'elite coalitionism' (Sandholtz and Zysman, 1989).

Federalism

Outside of these more eclectic theories of political integration in Europe, a prominent and traditional theory remains that of *federalism*. Federalism is a way of forming political union among states (at regional or alternative levels) in which a central (here European) and local (national and subnational) administrative units coexist with shared and independent powers. Among the areas usually reserved to the central federal authority – witness the USA – are defence, foreign trade, monetary policy, external representation and border control. As Barnes and Barnes put it (1995, p. 5):

> For the proponent of federalism the establishment of a constitution that allocates the roles of the government is a crucial initial stage in the integration process. This is in direct contrast to the functionalist approach to integration, which avoids a formal constitution-drafting procedure.

Federalism was the main focus of the debates over the future of the European Communities concluding in the political agreement at the Maastricht Conference. Consistently its implied division of powers and constitutional aspect, when taken with the implications of extended central (supranational) authority, have engendered deep concern among many member governments and European political leaders. Although explicit use of the term has been avoided in the treaties of the late 1980s and 1990s, those same agreements have revived the concept which 'enjoyed a powerful influence upon many of the pioneers of European integration' (Bainbridge, 1998, p. 259). Institutional reforms introduced in the SEA were, in part, inspired by the federalist plan embodied in the European Parliament's 1984 Draft Treaty establishing a 'European Union'. The TEU was widely interpreted as a federal blueprint for a European Union, intact with a common currency and foreign–security policy, and the Amsterdam Treaty appears to have taken the EU closer to a supreme constitution with its consolidation of the treaties. Although these treaties do not leave the EU specifically described as a 'federal entity' – reference to the federal term was deleted from the Draft Treaty on European Union – there can be no question that the EU has a quasi-federal character. The doctrine of direct effect in EC law is a federal principle and a core of constitutionalism lies at the heart of the EC pillar.

Intergovernmentalism and confederalism

The federalist vision has rarely passed without direct challenge in the histories of the European Communities. First, through a Gaullist vision of Europe – 'L'Europe des Patries', and in the later form of a Thatcherite critique of 'Brussels centralism', the importance of the nation-state as 'building block' has been powerfully asserted. Although these different visions of European co-operation were not explicitly tied to singular theories, as state-centred approaches to the construction of Europe they may be associated respectively with confederalist and intergovernmentalist theories of action and change.

Within de Gaulle's pluralistic vision of the 1960s, we find clear distinction between an underlying federalist theory and a co-operative *confederalist* method of interstate co-operation. This is premised on the establishment of a European political community – 'a Community of states' – in which there is a large measure of independence for constituents and limited supranational authority. The influence of this theory may be seen in the history and pattern of EU governance. As Armstrong and Bulmer advance (1998, p. 67), there has been a 'creeping confeder-alisation, based on efficiency grounds' with 'a tendency on the part of the member states to seek supranational policy solutions to problems which are less efficiently resolved at the national level'. Within this process, there has been a tension between finding joint policy solutions and meeting the demands of states to pre-serve their sovereignty and to protect the principle of subsidiarity. Attempts to clearly catalogue competences – national and supranational – have been largely resisted.

In terms of the theorization of European political integration, proponents of *intergovernmentalist* (and *domestic-politics*) approaches have directed attention to the contingent nature of transnational co-operation in Europe (Hoffman, 1966) and to the continued relevance of (internal) national politics to domestic–EC linkages (Bulmer, 1983). Centrally, intergovernmentalist theory has asserted the primacy of interstate politics and of the formation of national preferences within member states. This is clearest in the evolution of the work of Moravcsik (1991, 1993). Moravcsik starts with a simple premise that intergovernmental bargaining remains the driving force of European integration. Concentrating on the evolution of the SEA, he advances an intergovernmental interpretation that is based on three key elements: the important role of the leading member states in EC bargaining; lowest common denominator bargaining; and the protection of national sovereignty. Attention to the domestic dimension of the shaping of the SEM–SEA package is then addressed in Moravcsik's 1993 work. This 'liberal intergovernmentalist' theory preserves his account of rationally-constructed state interests but uses liberal theory to account for the formation of domestic preferences ('lower-tier' bargaining processes).

Although intergovernmentalist accounts are attractive in their assertion of state-led processes, where they are weakened is in their failure to capture the complex multi-actor character of modern Community politics and the expanse and influ-ence of powerful supranational institutions such as the European Commission. Arguably, they distort or overlook elements of bargaining and consensus-building which set the European model apart from other international organizations.

The governing institutions

Having considered a brief history of European integration and the role of inte-gration theories in helping us to understand pathways and progress, attention should now be turned to the organization of the European Union and to the insti-tutional arrangements of the Community pillar. Much recent attention has been paid to the EU as a governance system and an understanding of its basic elements is a fundamental requirement for European businesses. Those firms hoping to influ-ence the decision-making process (e.g. through lobbying) require a detailed under-standing of the openings for dialogue and of the centres of executive and legislative authority. Those firms operational in the European business environment should at least understand how European Union rules, regulations and directives, many of which govern their activity and behaviour, are issued and from which centres of power. In order to understand the workings of the EU it is necessary to outline the role and activities of each of four governing institutions with a role in the initiation, enactment, interpretation and application of Union law:

- the European Commission,
- the Council of the European Union (or 'the Council of Ministers'),
- the European Parliament, and
- the European Court of Justice.

In reality, these four governing institutions form a central loop for decision-making and legislative action within a crowded, multi-actor EU system. The full cast list of official organs is much more extensive encompassing various banks, courts and advisory committees. In the succeeding analyses, an attempt is made to provide outlines of the organization, function and influence of these key institutions and to examine their place in the European policy process. Subsequent to these outlines, brief attention will be paid to the 'principals' from among that wider cast of advisory and specialist institutions helping to constitute the broader EU polity.

The European Commission

The role and responsibilities of the European Commission place it firmly at the heart of the European Union's policy-making process. As an institution it is headed by twenty civil servants representing the fifteen member states who are chosen to represent the interests of the EU rather than individual countries. On appointment, Commissioners are compelled to swear an oath of allegiance to the EU promising to put EU interests before national objectives. Theoretically, this impartiality enables the Commission to function as 'an honest broker', mediating conflicts of interest between member states when needed. Although practice may vary from this norm, in most respects the Commission is independent of national governments.

Although not controlled by the member states, the Commission is at least appointed by them. Each member state must be represented by at least one Commissioner, but no member state may have more than two nationals. Prior to the next enlargement, the largest nations – Germany, France, Italy, the UK and Spain – send two Commissioners and the smaller states one each. Commission members are appointed by common agreement of the member states to serve a five-year term, which is renewable. There is a President of the Commission and he or she is appointed by agreement among the member heads of state and is subject to the approval of the European Parliament. Prior to the recent appointment of Italian, Romano Prodi, two men occupied this senior position in the 1990s. The most recent was the former Prime Minister of Luxembourg, Jacques Santer (1995–99), whose predecessor was the former French Finance Minister, Jacques Delors (1985–95).

The President and the full 'College' of Commissioners are assisted by a group of political officials known as a 'cabinet' who have traditionally numbered between six and seven (except for the President's cabinet which is larger and numbers around twelve). These senior-ranking officials have traditionally been fellow nationals of the Commissioner in question and have been seconded or recruited from national or EU administrations. Beneath this executive level, the Commission employs around 20,000 permanent staff, two-thirds of which are in administration.

At the start of 1999, the Commission was organized into twenty-four directorates-general (divisions) and a number of specialist units and support services. These are outlined in Table 2.2. Under this structure, single Commissioners

Table 2.2 Directorates-General, Services and Special Units of the European Commission (at January 99)

Directorates-General

DGI	External Relations: Commercial policy & relations with North America, the Far East, Australia and NZ
DGIA	External Relations: Europe and the New Independent States, CFSP and External Missions
DGIB	External Relations: Southern Mediterranean, TOP and Near East, Latin America, South and South-East Asia and North–South Co-operation
DGII	Economic and Financial Affairs
DGIII	Industry
DGIV	Competition
DGV	Employment, Industrial Relations and Social Affairs
DGVI	Agriculture
DGVII	Transport
DGVIII	Development
DGIX	Personnel and Administration
DGX	Information, Communication, Culture and Audiovisual
DGXI	Environment, Nuclear Safety and Civil Protection
DGXII	Science, Research and Development
DGXIII	Telecommunications, Information Market and Exploitation of Research
DGXIV	Fisheries
DGXV	Internal Market and Financial Services
DGXVI	Regional Policies and Cohesion
DGXVII	Energy
DGXVIII	Credit and Investments
DGXIX	Budgets
DGXX	Financial Control
DGXXI	Customs and Indirect Taxation
DGXXII	Education, Training and Youth
DGXXIII	Enterprise Policy, Distributive Trades and Tourism
DGXXIV	Consumer Policy and Consumer Health Protection

Services and Special Units

Secretariat-General	Legal Service
Forward Studies Unit	Inspectorate-General
Spokesman's Service	Conference Service
Statistical Office	Translation Service
Informatics Directorate	Publications Office
Humanitarian Office	EAEC Agency
Accession Task Force	

straddled separate directorates and a number of different policy areas. For example, in the five years 1995–99, a single Commissioner, Emma Bonino, enjoyed responsibility for fisheries (DG XIV), consumer affairs (DG XXIV) and humanitarian aid (the Community Humanitarian Office). However, the number and definition of Commission departments have now been re-examined as a part of the process of installing a new Commission team (see Table 2.3). On 15 September 1999, the European Parliament approved all twenty designate Commissioners (and their portfolios) and a new Commission held its first official meeting on 18 September 1999. The Commission is now headed by Romano Prodi, whose nomination as President Designate was confirmed in May 1999. This followed the collective resignation of the incumbent Commission team following charges of fraud, nepotism and financial mismanagement in early 1999.

The new Commission structure suggests a clear attempt to simplify and to streamline the structure of the Union's executive service. Portfolios have been regrouped so as to establish more logical connections (for instance, between health and consumer protection) and the external relations portfolios have been shared out on a new basis, with the abandonment of the previous geographic divisions. Although not explicit in Table 2.3 it is also clear that the new Commission will make greater use of inter-functional working groups (at senior level) with the new President co-ordinating inter-directorate action on major issues such as Balkan reconstruction. These and other aspects of the new Commission structure are considered further in Case Study 2.1.

Table 2.3 The new Directorates-General and their Commissioners (as of 15 September 1999)

Commissioner	Portfolio
Romano Prodi	President
Neil Kinnock	Vice-president Administrative Reform
Loyola de Palacio	Vice-president Parliamentary Relations *plus* Transport and Energy
Mario Monti	Competition
Franz Fischler	Agriculture and Fisheries
Erkki Liikanen	Enterprise and Information Society
Frits Bolkestein	Internal Market
Philippe Busquin	Research
Pedro Solbes Mira	Economic and Monetary Affairs
Poul Nielson	Development and Humanitarian Aid
Gunter Verheugen	Enlargement
Chris Patten	External Relations
Pascal Lamy	Trade
David Byrne	Health and Consumer Protection
Michel Barnier	Regional Policy
Viviane Reding	Education and Culture
Michaele Schreyer	Budget
Margot Wallström	Environment
Antonio Vitorino	Justice and Home Affairs
Anna Diamantopoulou	Employment and Social Affairs

CASE STUDY 2.1 **Prodi Commission gets down to work**

The new European Commission team led by Romano Prodi began work in decisive style on 18 September 1999, agreeing the biggest restructuring of the European Union's Brussels-based administration in recent years.

Holding their first working meeting, the twenty commissioners authorized the creation of a new Commission department, or directorate-general, responsible for enlargement of EU. That policy had been previously handled by a 'task force' within another department. The move reflects the desire that Mr Prodi has already made clear to give a new impetus to EU expansion into southern Europe and the former communist economies of the East. Justice and home affairs policy also gets its own directorate-general for the first time, reflecting the importance being attached to creating a single EU legal area and co-ordinating efforts to fight cross-border crime and terrorism.

The twenty-four directorates-general, previously identified only by numbers apt to confuse even Brussels insiders, were renamed according to their policy area – such as competition, trade, external relations, and agriculture and fisheries. The commissioners, instead of being grouped together in a single headquarters building, will now work from offices in the directorates for which they are responsible, as part of a move to create 'ministries' in what

Mr Prodi has compared to an embryonic EU 'government'.

The total number of Commission departments and services will be reduced from forty-two to thirty-six. Neil Kinnock, Commission vice-president responsible for reform, said the coming structural changes would be followed by publication of a comprehensive reform strategy in February 2000.

The commissioners are pledged to carry out a far-reaching shake-up of the EU executive after their predecessors, headed by Jacques Santer, resigned in March 1999 over a damning report on nepotism and maladministration. The new Prodi team has adopted fresh codes of conduct agreed at informal meetings in July 1999. These go further than codes introduced in the closing days of the Santer Commission, requiring commissioners 'to act in accordance with the highest standards of public life'.

Commissioners will now be subject to a one-year 'cooling-off period' after leaving office in which their prospective jobs could be vetoed by a special ethics committee. This aims to avoid any repeat of the potential conflict of interest created when Martin Bangemann, industry and telecommunications commissioner in the Santer team, this summer accepted a post with Telefonica, the Spanish telecoms group he used to regulate.

Source: Financial Times, 20 September 1999

The Commission's role and function

The European Commission may be regarded as having a multiplicity of roles. Its three basic tasks are to initiate EU action, to act as guardian of the treaties and to operate as manager and executor of the Union's policies.

Initiator

In the EC pillar, the legislative process begins with a Commission proposal. Community law cannot be made without one, the Council and the European Parliament needing a proposal from the Commission before they can pass legislation. This right of initiative gives the Commission great influence which it uses by passing between 700 and 800 proposals, recommendations and drafts to the Council each year. However, its proposals are often a response to invitations made by member governments and the exclusive right of initiative enjoyed within the

Community pillar is lost in the two areas of intergovernmental co-operation covered by the Treaty on European Union. Here, in CFSP and in JHA, the Commission is able to submit proposals in the same way as national governments but its powers are significantly reduced.

In devising its proposals, the Commission has three constant objectives: to identify the European interest, to consult as widely as is necessary and to respect the principle of subsidiarity. With respect to consultation, a series of working groups bring Commission officials into regular contact with the Council's Committee of Permanent Representatives (COREPER) and a variety of advisory committees and consultative bodies provide a sounding board for new policy initiative. Different types of committee exist, each reflecting a different mix between Commission- and national-level officials. It is fair to say that Commission officials are largely dependent on such dialogue and on outside advice. Indeed, for many issue areas, there exists what may be descrbed as a 'resource interdependence' between Community and national officials, technical experts, interest and pressure group representatives.

Guardian

Acting as guardian to the treaties, the Commission is responsible for ensuring that obligations are met and that infringements of Community law are investigated. In certain circumstances, the Commission can levy fines and issue legal 'decisions' in application to a government, EU business or citizen. Such powers exist with respect to the control of anti-competitive practices and in regulation of state aid. Generally, however, the Commission has to rely on the enforcement powers of the European Court of Justice, to which it refers many cases, and on the goodwill and adherence of member governments and private parties. A number of obstacles also exist which deny the Commission total freedom to exercise its legal obligations of guardian:

■ limited resources mean that not all allegations of infringement can be investigated;

■ problems of collecting information which either does not exist or is deliberately hidden; and

■ political sensitivity which may result in the Commission being lenient in certain instances.

Manager and executor

The Commission manages the Union's annual budget (€92.453 billion in 1999) which is dominated by farm spending (under the Common Agricultural Policy) and by the Structural Funds, designed to even out the economic disparities between the richer and poorer EU areas. Its executive responsibilities are wide. As described by its own officials:

> [I]t has delegated powers to make rules which fill in the details of Council legislation; it can introduce preventive measures for a limited period to protect the Community market from dumping by third countries; it can regulate mergers and acquisitions above a certain size; and must also maintain a close scrutiny over government subsidies to industry. (http://europa.eu.int/inst/en/com.htm)

The Commission also has an especially important function to play in external representation. It negotiates with key institutions, principally the United Nations, the World Trade Organization (WTO), the Council of Europe and the Organization for Economic Co-operation and Development (OECD), as well as bilaterally with the likes of Japan and the United States. The latter role includes the determination and implementation of the EU's external trade policy (see Chapter 12) with agreements being passed on to the Council after consultation with Parliament. More than 100 such agreements are in place including those with the developing countries of Africa, the Caribbean and Pacific (covered by the EU–ACP Agreement) and those with countries in Central and Eastern Europe and the former Soviet Union. The Commission also has managerial responsibility for a series of externally targeted European development aid efforts and for the European Investment Bank. The latter institution (discussed at a later stage in this chapter) has an important role to play in its own right in shaping the internal development of the EU by making long-term loans to help finance specific investment projects in less privileged regions.

Summary

For all of these powers, the Commission's proposals, actions and rulings are in various ways scrutinized, checked and judged by all of the other institutions. The legal effects of its 'decisions' are subject to the right of appeal to the European Court, and its proposals have to be acted on by some combination of the other governing institutions. As an institution, it remains accountable to the member states who continue to take the main decisions on Union policies through the structures of the Council of the European Union, independently or in conjunction with the European Parliament. The Commission also faces a crisis of legitimacy. It is popularly decried as the non-elected and unaccountable face of the EU (especially in the UK and in France) and its staff and senior administrators are now publicly associated with evidence of fraud, nepotism and financial mismanagement in the conduct of EU affairs (see Case Study 2.2). The appointment of a new Commission team may go some way to repairing this tarnished image but the Commission will have to work hard to restore faith in its own role and reputation and to manage looming challenges such as enlargement and institutional reform.

CASE STUDY 2.2 'Commission in the dock'

On 15 March 1999 the business of the European Union was thrown into turmoil. The publication of a scathing independent report ('First Report of the Independent Committee of Experts') suggested widespread corruption, nepotism and financial mismanagement in the institution of the European Commission. This followed early claims and protestations from political groups within the European Parliament and the establishment of an investigatory committee into alleged fraud and malpractice within the Commission institution.

In the aftermath of this 'First Report' – the Committee restricted its initial evaluations and provided its Second Report on 13 September 1999 – all twenty incumbent Commissioners, including the Commission President Jacques Santer, were forced to step down. Few had been personally blamed for any serious wrongdoing, but the institution as a whole (and its most senior officials) had been subjected to wounding criticism. With the European Parliament positioned to censure the Commission, and to dismiss them en masse, the twenty 'bailed out' before the ultimate humiliation. Many, such as British Commissioner Neil Kinnock, were eventually to be re-appointed by their member states. In so doing, the Commissioners took collective responsibility for what the Expert Committee had identified as 'serious or persistent infringements of the principles of sound administration and acts or omissions allowing or encouraging fraud or irregularities to occur or persist'.

The Committee did not encounter cases where an individual Commissioner was directly and personally involved in fraudulent activities but found several instances where Commissioners had acted irresponsibly or where the Commission as a whole bore responsibility for instances of fraud or mismanagement. One specific charge was that an established female Commissioner had, in her services or areas of special responsibility, failed to act in response to known serious and continuing financial irregularities over several years associated with the running of a Community training programme. The same Gallic Commissioner, Mme Cresson, was also accused of inappropriately appointing a close friend (and local dentist) to head up an EU AIDS research project.

As the resignation of the Commission became inevitable, the member states quickly scrambled to restore public confidence in the assailed institution. Formally backing the resignation action at the Berlin Council in late March, the European Council pledged a root-and-branch review of Commission practice and nominated a new Commission President. In practice, the crisis had brought forwards the process of electing and installing a new Commission team (originally scheduled for the year 2000) under a respected and unsullied figure and had instigated a wide-reaching reform process that many critics had said was long overdue.

The Council of the European Union

The Council of the European Union represents the interests of the fifteen member states and remains the key decision-making body of the European Union. Its present title was afforded as an outcome of the TEU but the institution is still widely referred to as the Council of Ministers. It has four main elements: the Councils of Ministers themselves, the Permanent Representatives (COREPER), the Presidency and the Secretariat General.

Function and organization

The Council enacts all major laws under the Community pillar (freely or in conjunction with the European Parliament) and is responsible for the co-ordination of intergovernmental co-operation in the second and third pillars. The institution also acts as an important initiator of policy. In this regard, rotating presidencies, held by single Council members on a half-yearly basis, can impart broad direction to the EU's activities. Additionally, and under the chairmanship of these presidencies, heads of state and government meet formally in the shape of the 'European Council'. During council summits, the national governments decide main issues of policy (adopting specific legislative proposals and treaty amendments) and lay out their future priorities. The Commission is often charged with future action in order to satisfy established interests.

The European Council, therefore, although technically a separate institution, can be viewed as the top 'level' or 'tier' of the Council of the European Union. Below this, the Council is composed of one representative at ministerial level from each member state with several different councils operational (e.g. councils for agriculture, transport and employment). By meeting on a subject matter basis, or by policy area, it is ensured that the appropriate ministers from the government of each member state address those policy proposals that would naturally and necessarily come under their ministries' consideration. Foreign secretaries and economic and financial ministers meet respectively in the so-called 'General Affairs' (GAC) and Economics and Finance (ECOFIN) Councils. Meetings of the GAC and ECOFIN are generally believed to hold highest status and take place once a month. Other ministers meet in such councils as transport, environment and agriculture, which meet only two to four times a year.

As Council membership varies, and as members continue to hold down full-time posts within their own national governments, most of the actual work of the institution is conducted by a Committee of Permanent Representatives and a multitude of working groups. It is their function to filter through the proposals before passing them on to the Council or to make low-level decisions directly. COREPER and its specialist working groups (set up to study the law or policy under discussion) are not to be confused with the Secretariat General of the Council. Whereas COREPER consists of national delegations and professional diplomats sent on behalf of individual member governments to assist with Council business, the Secretariat General is the working bureaucracy of the institution. This Secretariat consists of approximately 2,000 administrators, translators, service staff etc.

Decision-making in the Council

In the Community pillar of course, the main function of the Council of the European Union is to formulate law. The Council receives legislative proposals from the Commission and may turn those proposals into legal Acts. Once the Commission has proposed a new measure, it is considered and amended by the European Parliament and the Council of the European Union together, with the two bodies now acting (in most cases) as 'co-legislators'. Critically, a proposal cannot become law without the approval of the Council, an enduring fact that continues to establish the Council as the main decision-making branch of the EU. Depending on the subject matter of proposals, decisions are taken either by unanimity or on the basis of majority voting. This is predetermined by treaty provision.

The *unanimity* reqirement now applies to a limited number of areas in the EC pillar, to those of a constitutional, monetary or budgetary nature. It does, however, remain the general rule in respect of the CFSP and JHA pillars. Only measures designed to implement joint actions in these areas of intergovernmental co-operation can be agreed on a majority basis. Decisions taken by common accord between the governments, for example, in appointment of members of the European Commission, also require unanimity. Elsewhere, decisions will be taken either by simple or, more typically, by qualified majority vote. Once the unanimity rule is abandoned, states lose an effective national veto over policy proposals. It is worth recalling that 'unanimity used to be the normal requirement when a new policy was being initiated or an existing policy framework was being modified or further developed' (Nugent, 1999, p. 166).

A *simple majority* is established by eight members out of fifteen voting in favour of a proposal. This is a simple numerical majority and all states have one vote each. It has limited application on procedural points, in areas of single market co-operation, and for anti-dumping and anti-subsidy actions within the context of the Common Commercial Policy (CCP).

Qualified majority voting (QMV) has been widely extended in recent years. The SEA introduced QMV as a means of lubricating decision-making on single market proposals and it now applies to most types of decision under the EC pillar. In practice, the vote of each member state is given weighting ranging from ten in the case of the larger states to two in the case of the very smallest (Luxembourg). The division of votes, which is roughly in proportion to the size of national populations, can be seen in Figure 2.3. A total of eighty-seven votes are cast on a legislative proposal with set thresholds for determining the passage or blocking of a measure. Member states cannot disaggregate their own blocks of votes and an abstention has the same effect as a negative vote. The procedure may also apply to a limited number of decisions under the Union's other pillars. At the time of writing, a qualified majority of sixty-two votes or more would give passage to a proposal (that is 71.3% of the total), with the blocking minority set formally at twenty-six. This means that the five larger states cannot carry a vote alone and that two

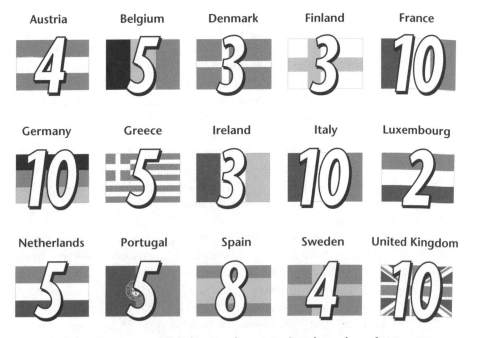

Figure 2.3 Council representation by member state (total number of votes: 87)

large states cannot constitute a blocking minority. If, however, twenty-three to twenty-five votes are cast against a proposal, the Council's verdict is deemed to be 'inconclusive' and a satisfactory solution will have to be found within a reasonable timeframe. This complication, to what is otherwise a quite simple rule, is based on an agreement reached by the foreign ministers of the European Union in Ioannoni (northern Greece) in March 1994.

As QMV has become the norm for Council decision-making, so galvanizing decisional speed in the institution, political pressure has been growing for a redistribution of votes and/or new majority tests. Germany, France, Italy and the UK have been in broad favour of a form of 'double majority' system in the Council – so as to reinforce their influence – but have been opposed on this front by the smaller member states. The concept means that a proposal would have to command the support of a majority of member states as well as a 'qualified' majority of votes. Conspicuously, no final agreement was reached on this issue in the 1996–97 Intergovernmental Conference.

Summary

Whereas the Commission remains a neutral agent in orchestrating EU policy, the same cannot be said for the Council. Individual representatives are intent on getting the best deals for their own state and the Council is the primary EU arena for inter-state bargaining and for the mediation of competing national interests. This does not mean that the Council's aim is not to realize collective solutions but it does ensure that negotiations can be difficult and that many solutions to collective problems are of the lowest common denominator. The process of effective decision-making has been greatly enabled by the introduction and extension of qualified majority voting, but the member states have been careful to protect their sovereign powers in sensitive areas. Although properly identified as the EU's primary decision-making body, current procedure is such that many legislative acts are passed jointly with the European Parliament.

The European Parliament

The Parliament sees itself as 'the guardian of the European interest and the defender of citizens' rights'. The legitimacy of this claim rests with its supervisory and legislative roles and with the fact that it is the EU's main (and only elected) public forum. The most recent elections have been in 1994 and 1999. In the 1994 elections, the number of people in the Parliament was raised from 518 to 572. Following the accession of Finland, Austria and Sweden this was raised to 626 with the addition of new MEPs for these three countries. These 626 seats were contested in the June 1999 elections, which were marked by historically low turn-outs.

The breakdown of the European Parliament by national representation is shown in Figure 2.4 but most activity in the European Parliament is channelled via indi-

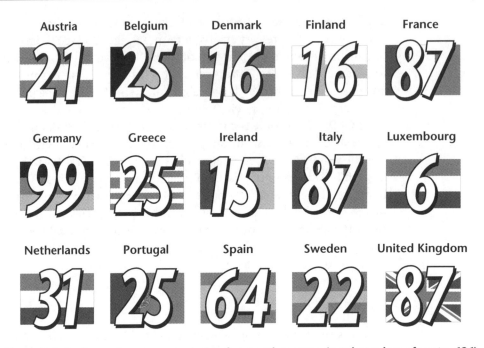

Figure 2.4 Parliamentary representation by member state (total number of seats: 626)

vidual political groups which are transnational in character and which receive and administer political funds. From July 1999, these can be established with a minimum of twenty-three MEPs if originating from two member states, eighteen if from three and fourteen if from four or more. Eight such groups were active in the 1994 Parliament and seven groups have formed for the new Parliament which will run until 2004. These groups are as follows:

EPP	The European People's Party/European Democrats
PES	The Party of European Socialists
ELDR	The Liberal, Democrat and Reform Party
Verts/ALE	The Greens/European Free Alliance
GUE/NGL	The European United Left/Nordic Green Left
UEN	The Union for a Europe of Nations
EDD	The Europe of Democracies and Diversities

In the 1994–99 Parliament, the groups of the Party of European Socialists, with 217 members, were the largest single cohort. However, in the new Parliament (which began its work in July 1999) the largest political group is the EPP with 233 members drawn from across the member states. The PES's presence has been reduced to 180 members from nineteen national Socialist parties. This reversal in fortune for the two major groups follows the disappointing performance of ruling Socialist and Social Democrat parties in the 1999 elections. While Socialists maintained their position in France, Portugal and Sweden, losses in key member states (including the UK and Germany) tilted the balance of power back to the centre-right parties of the EPP and to the 'centrist' ELDR grouping.

The powers of the European Parliament

The most important powers of the European Parliament fall into three categories: legislative power, supervision of the executive and powers over the budget. Operationally, these powers are exercised through a complex of plenary sessions, committees, subcommittees, working parties and delegations. Although the Strasbourg sessions represent the public image of the Parliamentary process (a new Parliamentary building will shortly showcase this work), much of the effective work of the institution is conducted at committee level. EP committees cover all areas of the Union's activities, ranging from agriculture to common foreign and security policy, from legal affairs and citizens' rights to overseas co-operation and development.

Legislative power

The European Parliament started out as a purely consultative body composed of representatives delegated from the national parliaments and has often been regarded as the weakest of the main policy-making institutions. Over the last decades, however, it has seen its powers extended with each major treaty reform and the image of a weak and ineffective institution has been seriously challenged. Originally, under the Rome Treaty, the European Parliament was afforded the right of participation in the legislative process – giving an opinion on legislation by the Commission – but enjoying no powers of amendment or veto. Today its influence is felt more greatly.

First, the new *'assent'* procedure – introduced under the SEA and confirmed by subsequent treaties – ensures that Parliament's backing is required for important international agreements such as the accession of new member states and the conclusion of association agreements with third countries.

Second, as a consequence of both the TEU and Amsterdam Treaties, the *'co-decision'* procedure has been firmly established as the principal mode of collaboration between Parliament and Council in the legislative field. Under its terms, decision-making powers are shared equally between the Parliament and the Council in most areas where the member states act in a legislative capacity. Legislation processed is formally the 'common act' of Council and Parliament.

In procedural terms, the EP is presented first with opportunity to review and to amend Commission proposals and the Council's preliminary position on that proposal. If it does not amend the Commission's proposal, or if the Council accepts the Parliament's amendments, the measure can be adopted after this 'first reading'. If neither is the case, the Council draws up a common position which on second Parliamentary reading can be accepted, amended or rejected. Given continued disagreement between the two institutions (i.e. Parliamentary rejection of the Council's 'common position' or Council objection to Parliamentary amendments), a conciliation committee – made up of equal numbers from the two houses – may assist the construction of a text on which the Council and Parliament can finally agree. However, if at this final stage there is no agreement, Parliament can reject the proposal outright. In short, by an absolute majority of its total membership, a legislative measure on which agreement cannot be reached with the Council of Ministers can now be voted down.

Yet while these procedures have given the EP real legislative power, reforms agreed as an outcome of the 1996–97 intergovernmental conference have not eliminated the use of alternative procedures under which Parliamentary powers are seriously curtailed, failing to extend co-decision to all legislative areas. Completing an enduring patchwork of decision-making procedures, the *'consultation'* and *'co-operation'* procedures, previously the basis of Parliamentary–Council collaboration, continue to enjoy a legislative root. *Co-operation*, in which Parliament only enjoys the right to propose amendments to Commission proposals, continues to apply in respect of economic and monetary union. Further, in some central issues where the Amsterdam Treaty introduces new provisions or amends existing ones, there is still only *consultation* of the EP. This concerns measures against discrimination, most decisions on asylum–immigration, and parts of the social, agricultural and research and development policies.

Supervision

The basic mechanism for supervision rests on addressing questions to the Commission and the Council. Ministers and Commissioners must respond to written questions and attend plenary sessions where they may take part in Question Time and respond to oral questions in important debates. Members and senior officials of the Commission are also often present at the European Parliament's committee meetings. Parliament also has the right to take the Commission or the Council to the ECJ and exercises detailed scrutiny of Commission programmes through a close examination of the many monthly and annual reports which the Commission is obliged to submit. Parliament also has an important role every five years in appointing the President and members of the Commission. Its ultimate power of sanction over the Commission is that it may – with a two-thirds majority – force the resignation of the entire College of Commissioners through a vote of censure. In such an event, as witnessed in the spring of 1999, the Commission would be compelled to resign as a body.

Powers over the budget

The European Parliament is the second arm of a joint budgetary authority, acting with the Council to fix the EU budget (see Box 2.1). The budgetary procedure allows Parliament to propose modifications and amendments to the Commission's initial proposals and to the position taken by the member states in Council. The Council has the final say over what is termed 'compulsory expenditure' – that arising from the treaties – but Parliament has the final say over 'non-compulsory' expenditure. Each accounts for around 50% of the total budget for payments. As a consequence, Parliament has a veto right (used for the first time over the 1980 budget proposals)

BOX 2.1

The General Budget of the European Union

The EU is endowed with revenues which it is empowered to discharge for certain specified functions, including institutional administration and policy-related expenditure. These revenues (capped at a limit of 1.27% of EU GNP) are generally referred to as the General Budget of the European Union. The pattern of the EU's budgetary revenues and expenditures has changed over time. For the first decade expenditures were modest – less than 0.1% of EU GDP. It was roughly evenly distributed among administration, agriculture, research and energy and aid for developing countries. The introduction of the Common Agricultural Policy in 1968, whereby a guaranteed price system for farm products was established, transformed this situation. Not only did total expenditure rise dramatically, the great bulk of that expenditure was absorbed by agricultural policy. Today, the EU budget totals nearly €100 billion with commitment appropriations of €96.93 billion in 1999. This now represents 1.11% of EU GDP and about 2.5% of the total expenditure of the EU member states.

These budgetary funds (which are of the same order of magnitude as a large UK government department) emanate from three sources. First, the duties that member states collect on imports into the EU are paid centrally. These consist principally of general customs duties, agricultural tariffs and levies on sugar imports. Second, a proportion of VAT receipts levied by member states is paid over to the EU. Between 1986 and 1994 this was equivalent to 1.4% of VAT revenues raised on 55% of GNP at market prices. Since 1995 (and until 2002), the proportion of VAT receipts paid over has been reduced to 1.0% raised on a lower total of 50% of GNP. Third, since 1988, the difference between what is raised from the first two revenue sources and what is required to meet EU expenditure is raised from member states in proportion to their national income. In 1999 the projected proportions from these three resources were as follows: VAT, agricultural and sugar levies (38%); customs duties (15.5%); and GNP resources (46.5%).

Since 1988 expenditure has been divided into six broad categories:

1. agriculture;

2. structural operations;

3. internal policies (with multi-annual allocations);

4. external (or other) policies;

5. repayments and administration;

6. monetary reserves.

The annual increases of expenditure on each category have to be contained within an agreed rate of increase. Political priorities have been reflected in allowing the rates of increase to differ between categories. For example, since 1988 Categories 2, 3 and 4 have been allowed to expand more rapidly than others. Nonetheless, European Union expenditure is still dominated by agriculture and, in particular, for price guarantee purposes. While the amount spent on agriculture (including the Agricultural Guidance Fund) had been reduced to 45.6% of total commitment appropriations by 1999, this is only approached by spending on structural operations (excluding the EAGGF) which accounted for 34.8% of total spending in 1999. Key areas such as education and the environment and other internal policies such as research claim only 5.9%

▶

of the budget, and external policies (and action) a comparable 6.0%. Equally, while it is often argued that the EU is excessively bureaucratic, it should be noted that only 4.5% of the EU budget is spent on administration, which is probably not excessive for any organization of its size. Two-thirds of this expenditure goes to the European Commission. In 1999, 1.2% of the EU's budget was directed towards category 6 (monetary reserves). These reserves are used for a variety of purposes, including emergency aid.

and it is the President of the Parliament who signs a final budget into law. Monitoring of expenditure is the continuous work of the Parliament's Committee on Budgetary Control. This committee forms 'the central column of the Parliament's entire budgetary process' (Laffan, 1997, p. 74).

Summary

Despite these powers and supervisory functions, it is quite clear that the Parliament remains at some distance from genuine co-legislator status. The now equal position of both institutions (under co-decision) is limited to the EC pillar and applies to only the majority of its business. It is fundamentally unlikely that the EP will ever acquire predominance over the Council and it is clear that the institution still has limited constitutional power *vis-à-vis* established national legislators (see Nentwich and Falkner, 1997). Unlike national Parliaments, it does not elect a government (no 'traditional' government existing at Community level) or hold it effectively to account. Nonetheless, the EP continues to play an important role in the EU political process and with ever greater care and influence. Although the European public is sceptical as to whether or not it is an appropriate agency for the proper exercise of supervisory and legislative tasks, its credibility has been enhanced by its role in exposing the Commission's poorer internal practices. Whether this credibility is to last or not, its newly elected assembly will be looking to flex its muscles at each and every opportunity presented.

The European Court of Justice (and Community law)

The Court of Justice, based in Luxembourg, is the final arbiter in disputes arising from the Community Treaties or the legislation based on them. It is made up of fifteen judges – one from each member state – and of nine advocates-general. The latter are responsible for investigating cases and for submitting reasoned submissions in open court on those cases on which the Court is required to adjudicate. Both the judges and advocates-general are appointed by common accord of the member state governments for a term of six years, the judges themselves selecting one of their number to be President of the Court.

Nearly 10,000 cases have been brought before the Court since its inception. Since 1989, it has been assisted in its work by a supplementary judicial body, the Court of First Instance, the two institutions disposing of 768 cases between them in 1998 alone. This innovation – the Court of First Instance has jurisdiction to rule at first instance on many matters – combined with amendments to rules of procedure, has allowed the ECJ to deal with cases more rapidly and to better concentrate on its essential tasks.

Function and powers

Article 220 (ex Article 164) of the EC Treaty asserts that the European Court of Justice 'shall ensure that in the interpretation and application of this Treaty [the EC Treaty] the law is observed'. Within this remit, the Court's main responsibilities are to:

- settle disputes of a legal nature between the member states,
- settle disputes of a legal nature between the EU and member states,
- settle disputes of a legal nature between Community institutions,
- settle legal disputes between individuals and the EU,
- give opinions and recommendations on international rulings, and
- give preliminary rulings on disputes which are referred to the European Court of Justice by national courts.

In practice, the work of the Court falls under two main headings:

1. *'direct actions'* and
2. *'preliminary rulings'*.

Direct actions are where the ECJ acts directly and gives judgments after an individual, company, member state or EU institution brings proceedings before it rather than before a national court. Direct actions take several forms: action for failure to fulfil Treaty obligations (against a member state); action for annulment (judicial review of the legality of Community acts); action for failure to act (against the Parliament, Council or Commission); and actions for damages (against Community institutions or servants). In upholding its rulings the ECJ lacks many effective powers of sanction but one privilege it does enjoy is to 'impose a lump sum or penalty payment on a member state found to have failed to fulfil a treaty obligation'. The amount of the lump sum or penalty payment to be paid by the member state concerned must be appropriate to the circumstances and is specified by the European Commission.

References for *preliminary rulings* are quite different. They do not involve the Court itself giving judgments in cases but require the European Court to give interpretations on points of EU law as requested by national courts in order to clarify the effect, coverage and validity of an EU law. This constitutes the bulk of the Court's work and caseload. At any stage in their business, national courts may seek from the Court of Justice answers to the problems encountered by them in applying Community law. Interpretations by the Court following such request (the ECJ is obliged to respond) must then be accepted and applied by the national court behind the referral. Therefore, as Nugent puts it (1999, p. 270), preliminary rulings:

help to ensure that national courts make legally correct judgments, promote the uniform interpretation and application of EU law in the member states . . . [and] provide a valuable source of access to the Court for private individuals and undertakings who cannot directly appeal to it.

Role and contribution

In carrying out this work – and in the volume of case-law established under its operation – the Court of Justice has decisively contributed 'to defining the European Community as a community governed by the rule of law' (http://curia.eu.int/en/pres/cjieu.htm). This does not imply that national frameworks fail to provide the guarantee of rule of law, but that the Court has contributed to legal frameworks in the Union in important respect. Indeed, in the hierarchy of things, a series of case rulings – *van Gend en Loos* (1963), *Costa* v. *ENEL* (1964) and *Simmenthal* (1978) – have established the 'direct effect' of Community law in the member states and its 'primacy' over many national codes. Both of these rules represent a fundamental challenge to the principle of (legal) sovereign authority at state level and merit careful definition. 'Direct effect' refers to the principle whereby certain provisions of EU law may confer rights or impose obligations on individuals, that national courts are bound to recognize and to enforce. 'Primacy' implies that Community law has precedence over national law with the authority and nature of EU law to be fully respected by courts and legal authorities in the individual member states.

By forging new laws and by interpreting Treaty provisions (usually in a way which promotes further integration), the ECJ also functions as a forceful 'motor' for the legal and economic unification of Europe. Indeed, the judgments of the Court have had a pervasive effect on shaping Community integration, with EU policy competence often strengthened and extended by Court judgments (see Wincott, 1996, for an interesting summary). This has been most clearly the case with respect to the Internal Market, enabling or forcing the Commission to pursue market deregulation and establishing important legal principles in existing areas of competence. Foremost here has been the *Cassis de Dijon* Ruling 120/78 [1979] ECR 649 examined further in Chapter 3. This was a particularly influential decision in determining a new approach to standards harmonization in the EU subsequent to the agreement on the 1985 Single Market White Paper. More recent Court decisions have served to strengthen individual rights and to promote the free movement of workers across the Union. In one high-profile case – the so-called Bosman ruling – the ECJ managed to turn the European football industry on its head by establishing the incompatibility of European football federation rules with the legal principle of freedom of movement for workers. Applying well-established case-law, the Court held that sport at professional level constitutes an economic activity, the exercise of which may not be limited either by rules on the cross-border transfer of players out of contract or by limits on the number of players from other member states.

EU legislation: a quick guide

It is opportune here to make brief note on the principal forms of EU legislation. Those parts of the treaties that are subject to the jurisdiction of the Court constitute the so-called primary law of the EU, but the governing institutions are of course involved in generating forms of secondary legislation (encompassing directives, regulations and decisions) and in issuing recommendations and opinions. In accordance with defined procedures, these are adopted by the Council, by the Council in conjunction with the Parliament, or by the European Commission. The ECJ may be led to rule on their range, interpretation and implementation.

Regulations are automatically applicable from the moment they are published. They are mandatory, take precedent over national law and are effective as law without any intervention or action on the part of member states. Some analysts have compared them with legal statutes, highlighting their binding nature and immediate effect. Most regulations are adopted by the Commission and concern adjustments to established regimes, e.g. the CAP (Common Agricultural Policy), the CCP (Common Commercial Policy), and the EU's competition rules. Some 975 different regulations were enacted in 1998 alone.

Directives are binding as to the result to be achieved – i.e. they should state the goal or outcome that is aimed at. Unlike regulations, however, the form and methods of their transposition into national codes are left up to the individual state. In this sense, directives need to be introduced into national law by action on the part of the member states themselves, something which gives the member states a certain measure of discretion. A time limit is included in the directive by which time it must be fully implemented. Directives are frequently concerned with the harmonization or approximation of laws and practices in fields of EU activity. The Commission, the Council and the Council in conjunction with the European Parliament may all be enacting institution(s). Some 97 directives were enacted in 1998 alone.

Decisions are specifically targeted. They may be addressed to any or all of the member states, to undertakings (firms) or to individuals. A decision is mandatory for the party to whom it is addressed. A total of 733 were enacted in 1998, well over half by the European Commission.

Recommendations and *opinions* issued by the Council and the Commission are in no sense binding. Their legal status is confused. Although they do not constitute secondary legislation, they may be referred to in rulings and interpretations. The Council and the Commission issued 23 recommendations between them in 1998.

Other EU organs and autonomous bodies

In the conduct of their work and responsibilities, the four governing institutions – the Court of Justice, Parliament, Commission and Council – enjoy a wider relationship with other EU organs and with a number of autonomous EU agencies. At the heart of this grouping are the so-called advisory committees – the Committee of the

Regions (CoR) and the Economic and Social Committee (ESC or EcoSoc) – along with the Court of Auditors and European Investment Bank (EIB). In their own right, these are important EU bodies with a specific and functional role to play. The governing institutions also have an important relationship with a further institution, the European Central Bank (ECB), the role of which is examined in Chapter 4.

The Economic and Social Committee: membership, 222; location, Brussels

In accordance with the treaties, this Committee advises the Commission, the Council and the Parliament on matters associated with the operation of Community policies and on draft legislation. Its membership is drawn from all levels of industry, society and the professions such that its advice represents informed and balanced opinion from those directly affected by EU legislation. Its 'opinions', which are delivered either in response to a referral or on its own initiative, are published formally in the EU's *Official Journal*. Although the governing institutions are under no obligation to accept or to endorse these declarations, it is widely viewed that these may be helpful to the Council in the sense that they represent a form of consensus among important stakeholders. Outside of the forum, these stakeholders may belong to lobbies with differing views, but inside the ESC they know that their responsibility is to look for mutually acceptable solutions and for common positions. As such, the committee continues to provide an important forum in which employers, employees and other interests can thrash out their differences and explore issues of mutual relevance.

The Committee of the Regions: membership, 222; location, Brussels

As the elected representatives or chief officers of local, district and regional authorities, the 222 members of the CoR provide the first guarantee that the interests of local and regional authorities are officially represented within the European Union. The TEU specifies that the Council or the Commission must consult the CoR in several spheres – education and youth, culture, public health, TENS, economic and social cohesion, and the structural policies. In these areas, the role of the CoR is to represent the interests of local and regional communities. Thanks to their representatives on the CoR, regional, local and district authorities are also kept posted on all EU legislation.

The European Investment Bank: membership, EU-15; location, Luxembourg

The EIB was set up in Luxembourg in 1958. Currently, the bank grants loans and guarantees so as to assist in the economic development of less-privileged European regions (internal loans) and so as to help in the development or reconstruction of industry and infrastructure in regions covered by the EU's external co-operation agreements (external loans). Its €20 billion volume of annual lending makes it the largest international financing institution in the world. Its projects are designed to help poorer and peripheral areas by supporting industrial modernization efforts and by improving communications (including transport and telecommunications links) and industrial competitiveness. For internal loans, projects are assessed in terms of their 'economic and environmental justification' as well as with mind to their 'financial and technical viability'. The EIB's financing for development projects often goes 'hand in hand' with grants from the EU's Structural and Cohesion Funds and typically carries 'the lightest possible interest rate burden' (http://www.eib.org).

The Court of Auditors: membership, fifteen (one from each member state); location, Luxembourg

The Court of Auditors is the EU's financial watchdog. Its fifteen auditors (one from each member state) and 500 staff members carry out annual audits of the EU institutions to ensure proper and accountable expenditure. Often seen as the taxpayers' representative, the institution has a low external profile but plays a critical role in ensuring that the European Union spends its money according to budgetary rules and in an efficient and cost-effective manner. The continued increase in EU expenditure ensures the importance of this role.

The autonomous institutions

Outside of those influential bodies listed above, there are also a number of important agencies, foundations and centres that play an important part in the execution and/or framing of European policies (see http://europa.eu.int/en/agencies.html). Among these we would count the European Environment Agency (based in Copenhagen) and the European Agency for the Evaluation of Medicinal Products (based in London). These and other agencies are significant players in sector- or issue-based 'networks' underpinning EU policy deliberations. Their shared characteristic is that they have been set up by a European Commission or a European Council decision but work entirely as autonomous bodies. Some of their work is addressed in later chapters.

Institutional reform: future challenges

The recent pace of institutional development has been dizzying even by the standards of the 1950s. Despite this, important changes still need to be brought to the organization of individual institutions and to procedures of interinstitutional co-operation. Given the failings of the Amsterdam Treaty, questions of institutional reform are set to dominate the new IGC, launched in February 2000. The Helsinki European Council (10 and 11 December 1999) confirmed that the new IGC will consider the size and composition of the European Commission, the weighting of the member states' votes and the possible extension of qualified-majority voting within the Council. If this proves unsuccessful, it seems obvious that negotiation and decision-making will be even more complicated at point of enlargement than they are at present or that enlargement will be further stalled. Already, a Community of fifteen member states and of several EU institutions is working within a structure of organization designed nearly fifty years ago for a Community of just six member states. This structure will come under unparallelled strain with Community enlargement and yet success in reforming 'the grand design' cannot be taken for granted. The present scheme represents a delicate balance of power among the major institutions and between them and the governments of the member states. As a consequence, any major reforms will remain difficult to achieve, witness the disappointing results of the Amsterdam Treaty.

The European Union: the business impact

It should now be clear to the reader that the European Union has developed a substantial body of governing institutions to make broad policy decisions (in a number of areas) and to develop and to adopt laws on behalf of its member states. Equally, analysis has shown that the European Union has brought together fifteen nation-states in order to form the largest and one of the richest economic zones in the world with an integrated consumer base of some 376 million consumers.

The business impact of this situation is immense. The EU can almost be regarded as one market and has a reputation for proliferating regulation and control. There are now few areas of economic or commercial policy-making where the EU does not enjoy at least a measure of involvement and several areas where its supranational institutions have established exclusive competence. A mass of legislation has come from the EU, which has been enacted into national law. In areas such as competition policy, technical harmonization, environmental standards, consumer rights and social policy, business in Europe has adjusted to the reality of EU policies backed by substantial funds and culminating in supranational controls. Of course, the EU is also in the throes of two huge changes, monetary union and eastward enlargement. These will also have dramatic consequences for future European markets and for the basis of competition in manufacturing, primary and tertiary sectors.

For all of these reasons, business in Europe operates in a context in which the EU makes powerful contribution. Not least, this is registered in:

- the structure and organization of European markets,
- the freedom of movement of goods, services, capital and labour (throughout the EU-15),
- the control and regulation of business activity,
- the structure and format of commercial law,
- the (public) financing of business ventures,
- the issue of substantial commercial contracts (under Community programmes),
- the negotiation of (external) trading terms and freedoms,
- the nature and operation of product standards, and
- the conduct of monetary co-ordination and joint monetary actions.

In effect, the EU has consolidated itself as a powerful regional authority at the heart of the 'New' Europe. At the end of the twentieth century, companies and business-men in Europe, like consumers and citizens in turn, must be as much concerned with what happens in Brussels (the new regional epicentre) as they are with devel-opments in their own national capitals. In particular, the provisions, stipulations and legal requirements attaching to the different EU policy areas (see Figure 2.5) require a careful audit on the part of European firms. These need to identify which pieces of current or proposed legislation are likely to have effect on the organization and to assess their business systems and strategies in light of any impacts (Piggott and Cook, 1999, pp. 45–6). Policy development may be quite rapid and the absence of effective monitoring may lead to competitive disadvantage and to legal embar-rassment. Moreover, companies should also monitor the expansion of the EU and the effects of trade and co-operation agreements with neighbouring and rival economies as well as the major impact on business arising from EMU.

In the chapters that follow, concentration falls on some of the main areas of EU co-operation impacting on European business organization and strategy. In Chapter

BUSINESS IN EUROPE

1: On the free movement of persons, capital, services and labour
*2: On the approximation of national laws, regulations or administrative provisions
directly affecting the establishment or functioning of the common market*

Figure 2.5 EU policies: an environmental audit

3, focus is provided on the EU's Single European Market (SEM) and, in Chapter 4, on the emerging process of economic and monetary union (EMU). The function of these two chapters is to provide a basic grounding in the organization of European markets and to address the various processes surrounding SEM completion and the introduction of the Euro. In completing an initial focus on the EU's competitive environment, Chapter 5 addresses the EU's policies on competition, aid and industry. These policies are instrumental in defending and facilitating the Single Market and provide some opportunity for address of EU regulatory action and supranational policy-making. Although this provides a far from exhaustive sweep of the EU's various business policies, it is to be noted that later chapters provide windows through which to examine other examples of EU policy action. These include the Common Commercial Policy and the EU's growing involvement in social, employment and environmental issues. In these and other areas, policy and regulation has emerged as a consequence of collective interests (e.g. sustainable development) and of the liberalization essential to the internal market.

CASE STUDY 2.3 Britain and the European Union – a history

Survey – UK's view of Europe obscured by past glories: Politicians are shy of admitting Britain's place in the modern world, writes Philip Stephens

Britain lives with its history. The post-war relationship with its European neighbours has been one infused with misery and missed opportunities. To come to terms with what is now the European Union is to come to terms with the retreat from past glory. The nation's leaders have shunned the challenge.

From that refusal all else has followed: the initial belief that they could stand aloof from Franco-German rapprochement, a fatal hesitation in recognizing that decisions taken on the continent of Europe would inevitably shape Britain's destiny and, when it eventually joined, an approach which has been at once indecisive and self-consciously superior. A perceptive American anticipated the agonies even before the fall of Berlin. In 1944, Edward Stettinius, the secretary of state, reminded President Roosevelt of 'the emotional difficulty which anyone, particularly an Englishman, has in adjusting himself to a secondary role after always having accepted a leading role as his national right'.

Just so. Germany, France and their continental neighbours had been defeated and invaded in the conflagration. Britain had suffered neither indignity. It saw itself in 1945 as a victor and a world power. Its outlook was global, built on a special relationship with the the US and its ties to the Commonwealth as much as its view of its own continent.

Politicians in Washington might want to see Britain at the heart of the new Europe but, as Winston Churchill observed in cabinet in 1951, 'I should resist any American pressure to treat Britain on the same footing as the European states, none of whom have the advantages of the channel and who were consequently conquered'.

Five years earlier, Churchill had spoken in Zurich of a united states of Europe. Now he added 'I never thought that Britain, or the British Commonwealth should, either individually or collectively, become an integral part'. This conviction that Britain's role lay on the world stage is embedded still in the nation's psyche. It has permeated the relationship ever since.

Thus, during the early 1970s, Harold Wilson could accuse the Brussels bureaucrats of seeking to rob Britain of its traditions. There would be no 'Euroloaf' nor 'Eurobeer', he promised, on the English side of the Channel.

A few years later Margaret Thatcher would demand 'her' money back from Europe. John Major would try and fail to build bridges. By the time sterling had been forced from the European exchange-rate mechanism, he would dismiss plans for a single currency as carrying 'all the quaintness of a rain dance and about the same potency'.

The convulsions within the Tory party over the Maastricht treaty were born of the same delusion that Britain could prosper alongside an integrated Europe while standing aside from its obligations. As Lionel Jospin, France's prime minister, has remarked, the British invented clubs. Yet, in Europe, they have always resented the rules.

Uniquely, Edward Heath, the prime minister who took Britain into the European Community in 1973, understood the ambitions of its partners. Of Tony Blair, it is too early to say.

Alongside the hauteur of past empire has been a refusal to face up to the fact that the Franco-German construction of Europe has always been a political rather than an economic enterprise. The British have pretended they joined a 'common market' – and then cried foul each time the founding members reasserted its political ambition.

The customs union argument does not withstand scrutiny. If one looks carefully enough, it is exploded by the words of the British leaders who have so often hid behind the pretence. Even Mrs Thatcher, who still calls it a common market, is on record admitting Europe's essentially political character.

When Robert Schuman, the French foreign minister, proposed the creation of the European Coal and Steel Community in 1950, as the precursor of the European Community, he could not have been clearer about its purpose. The pooling of Franco-German industrial might was 'the first step in the federation of Europe'. Germany's Konrad Adenauer concurred: 'The purpose of the French proposal is to create a European federation. On this I am in total agreement'.

France and Germany had fought three wars during the previous century. By sharing sovereignty they would avoid a fourth conflagration. The chosen means might be economic but the all-

important end – peaceful coexistence and enhanced security – was always political.

By 1961, when Harold Macmillan sought membership – only to have the application vetoed by General de Gaulle – the British government privately acknowledged as much. The Suez debacle and the winds of change blowing through its fast-shrinking empire had persuaded it that, without influence in Europe, its voice would not be heard elsewhere.

A cabinet minute saw the risk that a flourishing European Community would see Britain 'replaced as the second member of the Atlantic Alliance and our relative influence with the US in all fields would diminish.' Macmillan echoed this view. Setting out the case for membership a year later, he said his aim was to gain 'a new stature in Europe and increased standing in the counsels of the world'.

The then Mrs Thatcher said much the same during the 1975 referendum campaign. 'The paramount case for being in is the political case for peace and security', she told the House of Commons. 'The Community opens windows on the world for us that since the war have been closing.'

These were rare moments of honesty. Even Mr Heath found it convenient to forget that the price of entry to the European club was a partial surrender of sovereignty. Thus his 1971 White Paper declared 'There is no question of any erosion of essential national sovereignty; what is proposed is a sharing and an enlargement of individual national sovereignties in the general interest.' As far as the people were concerned, Britain was joining a common market.

It is the fiction that it can prosper in Europe without commitment or compromise, and that the sovereignty of the House of Commons is inviolate, which has haunted Britain's role. Politicians of all colours have admitted behind cupped hands that Britain cannot deny itself a voice in a group whose decisions have a profound impact on its security and prosperity. But they have refused to spell out the whole truth to their electorates.

To admit that others mould the nation's future is to acknowledge its diminished role in world affairs. So each time its partners have taken another step towards closer integration, there has been a noisy fight. The subsequent retreats (it was after all Mrs

Thatcher who signed the Single European Act) have followed under cover of darkness.

From time to time the rhetoric has changed. Instead of resistance, governments have declared their intention to lead in Europe, to shape the continent in their own likeness. It is not an absurd proposition. Britain's military strength, its global reach and, in spite of its relative decline, its place as one of the biggest economies make it a powerful player. But influence requires a consistency of purpose which has eluded its leaders. It demands an understanding that nineteenth-century balance-of-power diplomacy will not break the Franco-German alliance.

It is a background against which the British people have proved remarkably sanguine. True, there is no great enthusiasm for the European enterprise. And there is ample evidence of resentment at its intrusions into what Douglas Hurd once called 'the nooks and crannies' of national life. Against that there has been a strikingly constant majority in favour of continued membership of the club.

The British may not much like Europe but they sense, better perhaps than their politicians, that they cannot escape its consequences. In 1975, two-thirds voted in favour of continued membership in a referendum. For all the battles since fought in their name in Brussels, polls suggest that majority would be the same were the vote repeated today.

Mr Blair has said he wants to do better, to persuade the voters that Europe is more than a tiresome insurance policy. But he frets about the saloon-bar xenophobia of the tabloid press. And the Tories, anti-federalist under Mr Major, are fast becoming anti-European under William Hague.

A decision on participation in the single currency has been deferred until after the next election. Mr Blair thus has a breathing space in which to deploy his huge parliamentary majority in support of the European cause. But to do so means being honest about Britain's place in the world – admitting that, for all its talents, it is a middle-ranking rather than a great power. I wonder whether he is confident enough a leader to grasp the nettle.

Source: Financial Times, 4 January 1998

Review questions for Chapter 2

1. What does it mean to say that the European Union (EU) is a treaty-based framework?

2. Which were the original 'Communities' and what were the economic and political motives behind their creation?

3. How did the Single European Act 're-launch' the Community project?

4. Which treaty established the European Union (EU)? What were its central elements?

5. What were the central objectives of the Treaty of Amsterdam? Critically evaluate the achievements of this agreement.

6. What does it mean to say that the EU governing system differs from other national and international models?

7. What role can integration theory play in explaining the history and form of EU development?

8. What role does the European Commission play in the integration process?

9. What major challenges are faced in the construction of a new Commission team?

10. How has the legislative role of the European Parliament been strengthened?

11. What different procedures exist to govern the process of Council decision-making? How important is the Council of the European Union in the legislative process?

12. What is the 'acquis communautaire'? What is the meaning of Community law for the member states and for the citizens of the European Union?

13. What are the main forms of EU legislation?

14. How has the growth of EU legislation affected business in Europe?

15. Why have many characterized the UK as a 'reluctant partner' in the project of European integration?

Web guide

The institutions

EUROPA (integrated server of the EU institutions) @ http://europa.eu.int/

The Committee of the Regions of the European Union @ http://www.cor.eu.int

The Council of the European Union @ http://ue.eu.int/

The Economic and Social Committee of the European Union @ http://www.esc.eu.int

The European Commission @ http://europa.eu.int/comm/

The European Court of Justice @ http://curia.eu.int/

The European Investment Bank @ http://www.eib.org

The European Parliament @ http://www.europarl.eu.int/

Resource banks and listings of EU information sources

The EU Insiders Game (simulation based learning materials for multi-party game-play) @ http://eu15ue.europa.eu.int/

University of Mannheim (Electronic) European Documentation Centre @ http://www.uni-mannheim.de/users/ddz/edz/doku/especial.htm

Glossary of EU terminology – SCADPLUS Database @ http://europa.eu.int/scadplus/

European Access Plus @ http://www.europeanaccess.co.uk/

Legislative information

EUR-Lex (full-text legislative information) @ http://europa.eu.int/eur-lex

References

Armstrong, K. and Bulmer, S. (1998) *The Governance of the Single European Market*, Manchester University Press.

Bainbridge, T. (1998) *The Penguin Companion to European Union*, 2nd edition, Penguin Books.

Barnes, I. and Barnes, P. (1995) *The Enlarged European Union*, Longman.

Bulmer, S. (1983) Domestic politics and European Community policy-making, *Journal of Common Market Studies*, **21**.

Cram, L. (1996) Integration theory and the study of the European policy process, in Richardson, J. (ed.), *European Union: Power and Policy-Making*, Routledge.

Haas, E. (1958) *The Uniting of Europe*, Stanford University Press.

Haas, E. (1964) *Beyond the Nation-State: Functionalism and International Organization*, Stanford University Press.

Haas, E. (1970) The study of regional integration: reflections on the joys and anguish of pre-theorising, *International Organisation*, **4**, 607–46.

Hoffman, S. (1966) Obstinate or obsolete? The fate of the nation-state and the case of Western Europe, *Daedalus*, **95**, 892–908.

Keohane, R. and Hoffman, S. (1990) Conclusions: Community politics and institutional change, in Wallace, W. (ed.), *The Dynamics of European Integration*, Royal Institute of International Affairs.

Keohane, R. and Hoffman, S. (1991) *The New European Community: Decision-Making and Institutional Change*, Westview Press.

Keohane, R. and Nye, J. (1977) *Power and Interdependence: World Politics in Transition*, Little, Brown.

Laffan, B. (1997) *The Finances of the European Union*, Macmillan.

Lindberg, L. and Scheingold, S. (1970) *Europe's Would-Be Polity: Patterns of Change in the European Community*, Prentice-Hall.

Lodge, J. (1983) *The European Community and the Challenge of the Future*, Pinter Publishers.

McCormick, J. (1999) *Understanding the European Union*, St. Martin's Press.

Mitrany, D. (1966) *A Working Peace System*, Quadrangle.

Monnet, J. (1976) *Memoires*, Favard.

Moravcsik, A. (1991) Negotiating the Single European Act: national interests and conventional statecraft in the European Community, *International Organisation*, **45**, 19–56.

Moravcsik, A. (1993) Preferences and power in the European Community: a liberal intergovernmentalist approach, *Journal of Common Market Studies*, **31**(4), 473–524.

Nentwich, M. and Falkner, G. (1997) The Treaty of Amsterdam: towards a new institutional balance, *European Integration Online Papers*, **1**(15) (http://eiop.or.at/eiop/texte/1997-015a.htm).

Nugent, N. (1999) *The Government and Politics of the European Union*, 4th edition, Macmillan.

Piggott, J. and Cook, M. (1999) *International Business Economics: A European Perspective*, Longman.

Puchala, D.J. (1972) Of blind men, elephants and international integration, *Journal of Common Market Studies*, **10**.

Sandholtz, W. and Zysman, J. (1989) 1992: recasting the European bargain, *World Politics*, **42**(1), 95–128.

Wincott, D. (1996) The Court of Justice and the European policy process, in Richardson, J. (ed.), *European Union: Power and Policy-Making*, Routledge.

Young, J.W. (1991) *Cold War Europe, 1945–1989*, Edward Arnold.

3 The Internal Market

Introduction

The creation of the Single European Market (SEM) represents one of the principal achievements of post-war Western European integration. Much of the institutional process considered in Chapter 2 concerns the governance of this integrated market and, in a genuine sense, the SEM is the very axis and reference point of the Union itself. All European Union (EU) members have to abide by its rules (although their terms are not always applied correctly) and, while operational issues continue to irk governments and the business community alike, nearly all stakeholders are united in support of the SEM and of the notion of a frontier-free Community market. At 376 million persons (389 million when taking into account the wider coverage of the European Economic Area), this market outsizes the 272 million US economy and offers a domestic 'European' market nearly five times as large as that of its biggest member state, Germany. Even successive British governments, which in other respects have appeared hesitant to subscribe to large-scale integrationist projects, have welcomed the Single Market as a victory for supply side economics and as contribution to a more open and competitive European economy.

As a consequence of the rules and policies establishing the Single European Market, businesses can trade across national borders with the minimum of impediment, exploiting economies of scale and new market opportunities in a large 'barrier-free' trading area. Further, elimination of internal barriers combined with effective competition rules is expected to create a 'level playing-field'. Theoretically, players from any member state can compete on equal terms with 'home' firms in other EU markets. The principle of freedom of establishment ensures their right to set up branches or subsidiaries anywhere in the Community and/or to operate on an EU-wide basis. Simultaneously, the freedom of movement of 'persons', to go with those of 'capital', 'services' and 'goods' (the so-called 'four freedoms'), ensures that EU citizens are free to move around to live, shop and work anywhere in the EU with the minimum of interference. As consumers, these people profit from an increased choice of goods and from keener prices. Thus, although the Single Market is neither perfect nor complete, it has played a dramatic part in bringing the concept of Europe to the European (EU) public and in changing many of the rules of engagement for businesses in Europe. Its completion and consolidation under the Internal Market Programme (and continuing initiatives) has also led to an altered perception of the EU economy as a rejuvenated trading area united by a common set of rules, tariffs and operational requirements.

In this chapter the objectives are to explain how this Single European Market works and the role that it plays at the heart of the new European business environment. With European market integration (and related legislation) having a major impact on organizational environments, it has never been more necessary for firms and students of the European economy to understand the nature and meaning of the Single Market. The initial focus of this chapter is to examine the history of market integration in the EU, drawing on relevant theory. Thereafter, attention is turned to the mechanics and operation of the SEM and to the many implications of European market integration for economic agents in the EU–EEA theatre. Examination is also made of the challenges involved in extending the benefits of the SEM into previously protected sectors and of the many thrusts of Single Market action at the start of the new millennium. Although the important issue of strategic planning for the Single Market is considered at length in the later stages of this text (see Chapter 8), analysis starts here with the premise that any global business strategy must take account of this enormous economic area.

Regional economic integration: the case of Europe

For half a century, Europe has been the home and testing ground of developed processes of regional economic integration, a term encompassing different forms of economic co-operation between the independent nations of a particular region. Various regional economic groupings now exist worldwide – NAFTA (the North American Free Trade Agreement) and MERCOSUR in the Americas, ASEAN (the Association of South East Asian Nations) in Asia – but the elimination of trade restrictions between neighbouring countries is nowhere more developed than in Europe and in the case of the EU.

Integration theory

The eagerness of countries to affiliate themselves to a regional economic grouping (REG) stems from the various benefits offered by economic integration including opportunities for gaining economies of scale (in an enlarged trading market) and the promotion of trade and welfare through increased specialization of production. Although specific incentives may vary over time and by case – political and security dimensions may also be relevant in the formation of regional economic groupings – REGs are expected to be at their most attractive when the level of economic and commercial interdependency between 'members' is at its greatest. This provides conditions for net trade creation. In this context, it is worth noting that the European situation is unique. The high level of trade conducted within the continental region between European states makes trade with other parts of the world less significant than for countries in other regions. The US relies on the north and south American region for just 35% of its exports and Japan sells only an equivalent percentage of its exports in the Asia–Pacific area. In contrast, since the 1960s, the average EC/EU member state has relied on Community markets for over 50% of total export sales. Since 1995, the average share of intra-EU trade has been somewhere between 63% and 69% of total foreign trade and the average share of regional trade (taking account of other European market sales) in excess of 70%. Therefore, the extension and development of regional market integration in Western Europe at least makes a great deal of commercial sense.

The study of economic integration is the study of arrangements between two or more sovereign states as a result of which trade and economic transactions between them are conducted on a basis more favourable to them than to states outside the agreement. Agreements of this kind can range from preferential tariff arrangements to full economic union and different models involving an ascending order of degrees of integration can be characterized on a five-point scale:

1. One of the most basic forms of integration or co-operation is that of a *preferential agreement* wherein preferential tariffs are applied mutually or by one party on another. Preferences will be limited to a particular good or range of goods. In the case of mutual preferences, participating countries agree to levy a lower rate of taxation on imports from each other than that levied on countries outside the agreement. Such an agreement is common among countries which have close political links, for example between the UK and members of the Commonwealth prior to the UK's EEC entry (1973).

2. A form of integration extends the preferential tariff to cover all imports between the countries involved in the agreement. Commonly all imports from one country party to the agreement will be at a zero tariff while comparable imports from countries outside the agreement will be subject to a tariff barrier. This sort of arrangement is often referred to as a *free trade area* and characterizes the

arrangement for industrial products made between the countries of EFTA (the European Free Trade Association), NAFTA and ASEAN. Tariffs levied on products imported from non-participating countries are levied at whatever rate the individual country chooses.

3. There is a type of arrangement known as a *customs union*. Here there is completely free trade in all products between the members of the union and a common external tariff levied on imports from non-member states. Tariff revenues become common property and are subsequently shared out according to some agreed set of rules. Examples include the Central African Customs and Economic Union and the MERCOSUR grouping in Latin America.

4. There is another level of integration which carries this process one step further and leads to the creation of a single or *common market*. Free trade between member countries is ensured not only by the elimination of tariffs but also by the removal of all other obstacles (non-tariff barriers) to free trade in goods and services. Thus licences, foreign exchange controls, customs procedures, standards and indirect taxes other than tariffs have to be harmonized or eliminated. An internal market also operates with respect to production as well as exchange and therefore freedom of mobility for labour and capital is also required. The EC, at the end of 1992, provided an example of an integrated group of countries with common market policies and principles.

5. The ultimate level of economic integration is complete *economic union*. This implies a high degree of co-operation between members of the union and will include the co-ordination of monetary and fiscal policies and macroeconomic planning across all member countries. This would usually result in a single currency being used. When this is achieved, while countries may remain individual political units, they cease to be independent economic units. In time, many argue, it is likely that their political independence will be reduced and political and economic decisions will be made at the centre, although a degree of devolvement to regions is likely. The USA is a collection of separate states, and, while a degree of political and legal sovereignty is maintained by each state, they share a single monetary system and are subservient to a federal government with control over most, though not all, taxation and public expenditure. With the realization of the single currency in Europe (the Euro), the EUR-11 grouping of EMU participants (the 'Eurozone') exhibits many of these traits. The further extension of fiscal and tax harmonization would go some way to realizing a full economic union amongst these economies.

West European integration (–1985)

As addressed in Chapter 2, the original members of today's European Union set out with the specific goal of co-operating on coal and steel production. Buoyed by the success of this arrangement, and in line with their broader objectives for economic integration, progress was made towards a customs union arrangement under the terms of the Rome Treaty (1957). Customs union co-operation was established in

1968 (ahead of schedule) along with developed co-operation in external trade, agriculture and competition. In the 1970s, however, there was little progress towards ensuring the free movement of the factors of production, a basis for common market co-operation. Community states preserved a series of import restrictions between themselves including frontier controls and a patchwork of national standards for goods and services. Therefore, at the start of the 1970s, the EEC market continued to be fragmented by internal (non-tariff) restrictions on trade and cross-border movements. In turn, the Community could still not accurately be described as a 'common market' despite the popularity of this label among politicians and industrialists.

The Community states were conscious that these barriers contributed to a loss of trading opportunities and to substantial costs for their own governments and businesses. Despite this, their efforts to eliminate them, or at least to minimize their inconvenience, were largely disappointing. The requirement to achieve unanimity in the Council of Ministers meant that any remedial proposals put forward by the Commission were frequently blocked. For example, the Commission's attempts to universalize product regulations, design and safety standards etc. ('old approach harmonization') were discouraged and impeded by disagreement between the national governments. Community historians now locate this inaction in a context of preoccupation with high levels of domestic inflation and unemployment. The economic climate in Europe deteriorated in the face of global monetary instability and slid further downhill under the effects of the 1973 oil crisis. These conditions provided little obvious incentive to eliminate differential standards, border formalities etc., and actually encouraged the abuse of national regulations in order to provide short-term protection to indigenous firms.

By the early 1980s, the European Commission had reached clear conclusions as to the relationship between these internal barriers and Europe's economic malaise. Physical, administrative, legal, technical and fiscal impediments to intra-Community trade were viewed as discouraging the freedom of movement of products and services and as an impediment to European-scale operation. The Community was paying the price of these barriers – which also distorted patterns of production – and of its failures to free up the supply side of its economies. As a consequence, its firms and industries were slipping behind those of the United States and Japan where greater scale economies and competition contributed to more competitive global performance. The Commission had also determined that detailed legislative harmonization (as a method of removing technical barriers to cross-border trade) was largely ineffective and that several necessary components to the Common Market were outstanding. Problems were compounded by the adverse (and unanticipated) consequences of external border protectionism and by the market distortions associated with state patronage and subsidies. Cosseted European producers were becoming less competitive in many sectors.

Under persuasion from senior Community officials and from leading European industrialists, the member states slowly began to address the problem. As recalled in one leading commentary on the genesis of the Single Market Programme:

As early as the June 1981 meeting of the European Council in Luxembourg, the government heads expressed concern that the intentional or unintentional erection of trade barriers, along with excessive state subsidies, was undermining the internal market. In consequence, the European Council agreed that concerted efforts should be undertaken to develop a free internal market for goods and services . . .[E]xamination of the conclusions of summit meetings shows that such statements were made on the occasion of nine out of thirteen European Council meetings between June 1981 and June 1985. (See Armstrong and Bulmer, 1998, p. 17)

The Internal Market Programme

At the Milan Council of June 1985, the member states finally and formally endorsed a concrete plan of action proposed by the European Commission. This plan, presented in the form of a White Paper, *Completing the Internal Market* (European Commission, 1985), was the end-point of five years of intense Commission study of the caveats and deficiencies of the Community's trading order. Under the 'authorship' of British Commissioner Lord Cockfield, it outlined three different types of barrier to the completion of the internal market *(physical, technical and fiscal)* and a deadline of 31 December 1992 for the implementation of a series of liberalizing measures. Eventually, these were to be whittled down from over 300 in number to just over 270. Physical barriers were identified as those hindering the free movement of people, goods and capital, and technical barriers as those extending from different national standards, legal and administrative requirements across the Community states. Fiscal barriers were described as a consequence of diverse fiscal arrangements in Community territories, including divergent sales taxes, excise duties and varying payment collection systems.

The basis of the Milan agreement was quickly embodied in Community law by the Single European Act (SEA). This was signed in February 1986 and entered into force on 1 July 1987. The SEA also introduced changes in the Community legislative system (designed to encourage the adoption of internal market measures by majority voting) and revised the terms of the third article of the Rome Treaty. This was necessary so as to ensure that the concept of the Internal Market would be placed formally within the Treaty's headline listing of fundamental Community activities. Between the passing of the SEA and '1992', successive directives were agreed to facilitate 'the four freedoms' envisaged in the (revised) Community Treaty, completing 90% of the projects listed in the original White Paper. Omissions in the White Paper such as energy market reform, were to be addressed by later proposals.

Analysis now proceeds with examination of those three categories of Internal Market barriers identified in the Cockfield Report with consideration of the Community's subsequent actions in each of those areas. This establishes a basis on which the current state and condition of the Single Market can be more fully explored, with attention to those recent attempts to close enduring loopholes. Therefore, much of the analysis that follows here turns our attention back to the essential targets of the IMP and to the conditions applying in Europe prior to SEM completion.

The removal of physical barriers

The Cockfield Report highlighted significant physical barriers to trade and to the movement of persons and capital throughout the EC (pre-SEM). As a point to check compliance with national rules on indirect taxation and as a method of monitoring and controlling the movement of persons throughout the Community, internal customs posts frustrated companies' attempts to move goods and services across national boundaries with speed and efficiency. Practical difficulties associated with these frontier controls (including paperwork and stoppages) were estimated to cost EC industry the equivalent of 12 billion ECU per annum. Carriers of UK exports bound for other EC countries used to present an estimated thirty or so documents when crossing a Community border and would find themselves repeatedly delayed by bottlenecks at customs posts at ports or other border crossings. Whereas today fresh food can be collected from UK production points and sold in French super-markets within twelve hours (and with little interference), such trading would then have been impossible. UK producers of perishable products (like any others) faced costly delays as a consequence of hold-ups at customs points accounting for up to one-third of total journey times. This frustrated the whole exercise of cross-border trade adding substantial costs (estimated at up to 2.0% of average consignment value) and providing a strong psychological barrier to cross-border business for many smaller firms.

A central aim of the White Paper was to ease these border formalities and to move inland tasks relating to national customs, taxation, veterinary and phytosan-itary controls. In the Commission's view, the removal of a frontier-controlled VAT and excise system would significantly reduce waiting times at borders and associ-ated costs. The balance of customs-related administrative activities could be shifted to more efficient points within the Community system and, in the process, some 60 million tax forms could be abolished. Further, seventy different administrative forms could be consolidated into a Single Administrative Document, the require-ment for which would pass with internal market completion. Checks arising from health protection, for example of animals, foodstuffs and flora, could also be moved away from the border to the place either of departure or destination. This would further alleviate the burden at border points and enable the introduction of a tougher and more humane supervisory regime for livestock trade.

Elsewhere, passport checks for internal EC flights would be 'lifted' (the Commission would seek their removal with the co-operation of the member states) and residual capital controls would be terminated. Although the process of ensur-ing free movement of persons would be complicated, capital would be allowed to move freely out of national jurisdictions as a part of a basic deregulation under a new 'Capital Movements' Directive. Although countries including Germany, the UK and the Netherlands had removed controls or taxes on capital movements, such restrictions endured in a number of southern EC member states, for example in

Greece and Portugal. One effect of this deregulation would be to facilitate the cross-border selling of financial products and to assist processes of cross-border capital investment.

The removal of technical barriers

The importance of removing technical barriers was underlined for the Commission by the inhibited nature of cross-border competition in several markets (goods and services) and by the dwindling international competitiveness of European firms in 'strategic' high-tech markets. In several sectors, Europe's leading firms were confronted with different national product regulations, national industry standards, national testing and certification procedures, and other state laws and provisions that fragmented and segmented the EC market (see Table 3.1). These barriers – which had been adopted over several years – prevented European businesses from reaping the full benefit of economies of scale in relation to production, research and development, and imposed serious restrictions in efforts at pan-European marketing and distribution. Their existence, say as affecting the design, building and marketing of audio-visual equipment, cars and televisions, encouraged many firms to produce their various products in plants based in end-user markets. This kind of duplication often resulted in sub-optimal plants and supported company inefficiency. Equally, firms wishing to export their products throughout the EC from a single production point (and around a basic standard) were heavily penalized. As put by the European Commission (1995a, p. 21), 'Not only did they have to forego natural scale economies (through often minor product modifications) but they also had to pay for the inconvenience by having their products type-approved by the authorities in each importing country'.

Table 3.1 A typology of costs resulting from divergent standards and regulations

For companies
- duplication of product development
- loss of potential economies of manufacturing scale
- competitive weakness on world markets and vulnerability on European markets as companies operate from a narrow national base

For public authorities
- duplication of certification and testing costs
- not getting value for money in public purchasing whose non-competitive nature is often reinforced by national standards and certification

For consumers
- direct costs borne by companies and governments means higher prices
- direct and larger losses due to industry's competitive weakness and inefficiency structure

Source: Adapted from Cecchini (1988)

As with the physical barriers already discussed, the Internal Market paper proposed to tackle these barriers by pursuing a strategy of convergence. Specifically, it proposed a three-tier approach based on:

- mutual recognition,
- the select approximation of standards, and
- the strengthening of common reporting and notification procedures.

This approach, which is now firmly established, was to displace a traditional method of wholesale (product-by-product) legislative harmonization. While holding out the attraction of uniform product regulations, this approach had proven inefficient for two central reasons. First, the legislation was becoming highly technical (and extraordinarily complex) as it looked to meet the individual requirements of each product category. Second, the adoption of technical harmonization directives was based on unanimity in the Council. This was a recipe for extended argument and discussion, for frequent failure to agree on proposed standards and for standards that were often obsolete before their formal approval.

Mutual recognition

In order to facilitate the right of firms to sell and market their goods across the Community, mutual recognition of standards has been introduced. This means that, in principle, each member state must give access to goods accepted as fit for sale in another EU market. In effect, this ruling reduces the need for the Commission to make undertakings on an individual product basis. The effect and meaning of this principle was clarified in the 1979 'Cassis de Dijon' ruling of the European Court of Justice. The ruling emerged out of ECJ case 120/78 relating to German attempts to block French (blackcurrant) liqueur imports on the grounds of low alcohol content.

Nevertheless, there remain two key issues which mean that mutual recognition alone is insufficient to eliminate all of Europe's technical barriers:

1. Countries are still able to restrict access to those goods which do not meet their 'essential requirements'. This means that products can be barred access on the grounds that they infringe local rules (essential requirements) on health, safety, consumer and environmental protection.
2. Historically, standards have been different and goods are often required which are compatible with existing equipment and systems.

Standardization of essential requirements

The Commission has undertaken to standardize the essential requirements rulings in a number of areas where a close approximation of technical requirements is beneficial. In areas such as chemicals, foodstuffs and pharmaceuticals, a wide range of products (and product risks) may be sufficiently homogenous to allow for the identification of 'common essential requirements'. While this does not provide exacting standards for individual products, this approach permits a degree of harmonization to be achieved at a relatively quick pace. The technical specifications of products meeting essential requirements are laid down in harmonized standards agreed by common professional organizations such as the European Standardization

Committee (CEN) and the European Electrotechnical Standardization Committee (CENELEC). The specifications being adopted by these organizations for repeated or continuous application are being transposed at national level by local standards authorities such as AFNOR in France and DIN in Germany.

While these standards are not legally enforceable (they remain voluntary), products manufactured in conformity with a national standard which itself transposes a published harmonized standard benefit from a presumption of conformity with essential requirements throughout and across the EU. In this sense, there is now a clear incentive for producer firms to adapt their products so as to comply with EU-wide standards.

Mutual information–notification procedures

Finally, the Commission has introduced mutual information–notification procedures, which require national authorities to inform the Commission of any changes in regulations and standards. Although this chapter will later highlight the continued failure of member states to do this, this is an important element of the new approach to standards in the EU. The Commission is empowered to block changes in national regulations if they are deemed to raise barriers to market entry and to competition.

Sectoral action

In addition to these across-the-board provisions, the Community has also introduced new legislation for specific industries seriously hampered by continued technical and regulatory barriers. The cases of energy and financial services are addressed at later stages in this chapter, but the example of pharmaceuticals is discussed in Case Study 3.1. This case highlights the specific nature of action which may be necessary to liberalize individual sectors and draws attention to the mix of approaches underpinning the Community's efforts to encourage open, EU-wide competition in heavily regulated sectors.

CASE STUDY 3.1 **Action on internal barriers: the case of pharmaceuticals**

The pharmaceutical industry was, for decades, seriously hampered by protracted testing and registration procedures in the various member states. These could take as long as three years and seriously curtailed the effective market life of the product, thus impacting on profit. This has sometimes been referred to as the 'drug-lag'. In an attempt to overcome these problems, the Commission introduced a number of measures designed to promote a single market in medicinal products and to speed up product authorization. By 1995, the following were in place:

1. A new centralized procedure for drug authorization across all member states (compulsory for medicinal products derived from biotechnology and optional for other new products or medicines). Applications are made directly to the European Agency for the Evaluation of Medicinal Products (EMEA), leading to the granting of a European marketing authorization.

2. A new decentralized procedure, applying to the majority of conventional medicinal products. Applications for authorization are lodged in one particular state, with a marketing authori-

▶

93

zation granted by one national authority enabling marketing of the same product in any other EU state under the mutual recognition principle.

3. A centralized regulatory body – the European Agency for the Evaluation of Medicinal Products.

Based on this formulation, producers of medicines and pharmaceuticals can either (a) apply for registration in any EU country (and then market their drugs EU wide) or (b) turn to a one-stop registration and drug approval procedure. Opinions adopted by the scientific committee of the EMEA (either on applications made under the centralized procedure or in cases of arbitration) lead to binding decisions adopted by the European Commission. The progress of both of these procedures has been good, with Community, industry and health officials all reporting speedier EU-wide product registration and improved patent protection. Most analysts accept that the new system has improved the circulation of medicines and drugs throughout the Single Market (a key aim) and that it has helped new and better medicines to arrive on the EU market more quickly. It is clear that gaps can be further narrowed between product authorization and market placement but the measures taken to date have greatly facilitated the development of a European Single Market in this sector.

Liberalizing public procurement

Under the category of technical barriers, the White Paper on the Internal Market also addressed the situation in the European market for contracts concluded by public authorities and by public sector firms. This is generally referred to as the 'public procurement' market. The cost savings to be derived from opening up public purchasing were deemed to be substantial and the Commission promoted a number of benefits including:

1. the static trade effect – which involves cost savings for buyers as they purchase from the cheapest source;

2. the dynamic trade effect – sometimes referred to as the competition effect – wherein there is a downward pressure on prices as a result of competitive bidding by numerous firms for tendered contracts;

3. the restructuring effect – which, in the longer term, will allow economies of scale, particularly in specific high-technology sectors such as computers, telecommunications and aerospace;

4. the savings to be made by private sector buyers who benefit from the lowering of prices by firms serving the public sector;

5. the greater innovation and investment of firms operating in a competitive environment.

These gains were of the clearest importance given estimations of the sheer size of the EC procurement market. At the time of the White Paper, this was estimated at somewhere between 10% and 15% of Community GDP although subsequent analysis has estimated a current contribution to Union GDP of some 11% (£500 billion). The Commission evidenced that less than 5% of contracts were awarded to companies from other EU countries and highlighted closed bidding and exclusive trading in favour of national suppliers. Such practices – encouraged by the social and political benefits of supporting local profit and employment – worked against the spirit of EU competition and fragmented the European market. National government purchasers were also paying the price of 'staying local', by facing higher prices and limited choice.

After an initial upgrading of Community texts on public contracts and the extension of rules to formerly excluded sectors, the various texts in this area were consolidated in 1993. Directives 93/36 for public supply, 93/37 for public works and 93/38 for the formerly excluded sectors (energy, transport, telecommunications and water) tightened the obligations on member states and established the principle that equal opportunities shall apply for national and non-national undertakings. This principle is implemented through the central requirement that contracting authorities shall publish all contract notices (on the basis of a model notice) and a periodical notice summarizing the most important information on the contracts planned for the twelve months ahead. 'Publication' must be in the Official Journal of the EU and requirements shall apply above the following minimum thresholds:

- supplies and services (€200,000),
- works (€5 million),
- telecommunications supplies and services (€600,000),
- supplies and services of other public service sectors (€400,000).

However, although the opening up of public sector contracts to competitive bidding has been encouraged, certain restrictions continue. EU public authorities can sometimes limit the bidding ('restricted tender') to satisfy conditions set by the purchaser (e.g. essential financial requirements) or may turn to 'negotiated procedures'. These involve a 'closed' short-list of suppliers and may apply only where tenders are not received under open tendering or where exceptional circumstances apply. Purchasers can be forced to justify a decision to use negotiated procedures to the European Commission. The use of this negotiated procedure is just one of a number of problems with current legislation. Other weaknesses include excessively high thresholds, deficient transposition into national law and flawed application of the rules by the contracting authorities.

The removal of fiscal barriers

The target of removing fiscal barriers related to the impact of divergent excise duties and indirect taxation regimes on cross-border trade in the EC. In theory at least, fiscal harmonization is required to ensure a single market. Although rates may not have to be completely equalized, research from the United States suggests that contiguous states can maintain differentials in sales taxes of only up to 5% without the tax leakage becoming unbearable (El-Agraa, 1990). The existence of differential sales taxes and excise duties between the units of an integrated economy, and in income and corporation taxes, can therefore provide major market distortions. Significant variations in comparable tax rates can interfere with the optimal allocation of resources and distort otherwise normal trading relationships. In addressing this problem, the White Paper made several proposals, further elaborated by the European Commission in 1987.

With respect to the harmonization of sales taxes, the European Commission proposed moving towards a system which established two VAT rate bands. The lower or reduced rate was to be set at between 4% and 9% and the upper or standard rate set at between 14% and 20%. The lower rate would cover foodstuffs, energy products, water supplies, pharmaceuticals, books, newspapers, periodicals and passenger transport. This proposal was rejected by the member states, who saw it as too constraining, and was subsequently modified. From 1 January 1993 a more flexible approach was introduced involving an all-party pledge to keep standard VAT rates at between 15% and 25%. Under the agreement of EU Finance Ministers, some scope is also provided for the application of reduced and super-reduced rates and for the zero-rating of specific items. Table 3.2 presents the standard, reduced and super-reduced rates applying in the EU-15 in May 2000. The White Paper on the Internal Market also proposed a new payment and collection regime based on the collection of VAT in the country of production or origin and the redistribution of revenues to the country where the good or service would be consumed. While a transitional VAT system was introduced in 1993, there has been little progress towards a definitive origin-based system despite successive Commission proposals.

On excise duties, as applying to mineral oils (e.g. petrol), alcoholic beverages and tobacco-based products, the Commission's original proposal was for absolute harmonization. As example, its proposed harmonized rate for cigarettes was calculated as an arithmetic average of national duty rates, at the time 53% of the tax-included retail price. This plan was rejected by the member states because it implied too radical an attack on existing excise discrepancies. In many cases, these discrepancies afforded a degree of protectionism for domestic producers. Wine for example was not

Table 3.2 VAT rates in EU member states, 1 May 2000

Member states	Super-reduced rate	Reduced rate	Standard rate
Belgium	–	6	21
Denmark	–	–	25
Germany	–	7	16
Greece	4	8	18
Spain	4	7	16
France	2.1	5.5	19.6
Ireland	4.2	12.5	21
Italy	4	10	20
Luxembourg	3	6	15
Netherlands	–	6	17.5
Austria	–	10 or 12	20
Portugal	–	5 or 12	17
Finland	–	8 or 17	22
Sweden	–	6 or 12	25
UK	–	5	17.5

Source: European Commission

taxed in large-scale producer countries such as Greece, Italy, Portugal and Spain, while extremely high rates applied in Denmark, Sweden and the UK. In the end, minimum excise duty rates were established through directives on cigarettes (92/79/EEC), on other tobacco products (92/80/EEC), on alcoholic products (92/84/EEC) and on petrol. The minimum EC rate for cigarettes was set at 57% of the tax-included retail price and, in 1993, a minimum tax of €0.3337 was required per litre of petrol.

Divergence with respect to excise duties (like sales tax) has narrowed as a consequence of the agreed convergence measures but remains sufficient to maintain major price differentials between countries. One consequence of this is a growing trend towards targeted cross-border shopping. For example, the 'booze cruise' phenomenon (familiar to British readers of this title) sees UK-based consumers exploit the lower duties on beer and wine in France and a sizeable duty-paid allowance for personal consumption. Analysts suggest that the elimination of the duty-free internal market on 30 June 1999 will add further stimulus to such cross-border shopping, with travel companies encouraged to expand their presence in the duty-paid market (see Case Study 3.2).

CASE STUDY 3.2 'No end to the booze cruise'

Eurostar, which operates high-speed train services through the Channel tunnel, plans to promote shopping trips to Calais and Lille to meet demand from travellers following the abolition on 30 June 1999 of duty-free sales within Europe. The company expects a huge market for rapid cross-border shopping excursions fuelled by the loss of duty-free bargains and by the lower taxes and duty rates in France and Belgium. The company has been seeing a steady rise in its number of passengers and is now in talks with retailers in Calais about arranging bus services between the Eurostar station at Fréthun and the town centre (Batchelor, 1999). Eurotunnel, the Anglo-French tunnel operator, also expects a positive impact on business in the medium term with an increase in passenger and freight traffic across the Chunnel.

Elsewhere, ferry companies such as P&O Stena Lines are preparing for reduced profit margins as a consequence of the ending of duty free. Ferry companies have been taking margins of up to 80% on duty-free sales, which had enjoyed a stay of execution since 1991. Despite this, the company, like many other cross-channel travel operators, recognizes future opportunity in high-volume, low-margin duty-paid sales. New customs and excise guidelines provide for 800 cigarettes, ninety litres of wine and 110 litres of beer per person. Previous duty-free levels were far more restrictive, limiting passengers to 200 cigarettes, two litres of wine and one litre of spirits. P&O aims to take advantage of lower French duties for on-board sales (these duties will apply when ferries are in French waters).

Meanwhile, operators on a Finnish–Swedish route are considering ways to exploit the tax-free status of the Aland Islands in the Baltic Sea. These enjoy a form of autonomy from Finland and fall outside of the EU tax area. Duty-free shopping has been a popular perk in this Nordic region owing to high levels of tax and excise duty.

The costs of 'non-Europe'

Although the costs of those barriers were only calculated retrospectively, the *Cecchini Report* published in 1988 estimated the potential gains of Single Market completion at a staggering €216 billion (then approximately £140 billion at 1988 market prices). There would be immediate savings due to the removal of barriers and savings spread over time due to the exploitation of economies of large-scale production. The net welfare gain would be between 5% and 7% of the EC's GDP, with benefits accruing fully with appropriate and co-ordinated macroeconomic policies on the part of member states. Additional gains in terms of jobs, prices, trade and budgetary balances were projected by use of a variety of methods. Projections included:

■ price deflation of an average 6.1%,

■ an improvement in the EC's external trade by about 1%,

■ an improvement in budget balances of about 2.2%, and

■ as many as 1.8 million new jobs (equivalent to a reduction in unemployment of around 1.5%).

According to the Report, by attacking non-tariff barriers and by introducing market forces into sectors previously shielded from competition, the SEM was to be a spur to greater efficiency at unit and industry level and would lead to growth and enhanced welfare throughout the EC. By removing non-tariff barriers, Europe would benefit from greater competition in product markets and from reduced production costs. Falling prices (coupled with reduced x-inefficiency) would act as a natural stimulus to demand and investment, which, in turn, would contribute towards increased output, better resource exploitation and increasing economies of scale. As phrased by Johnson (1995, p. 12), in macroeconomic terms, 'this should manifest itself in an improved European trade performance and in additional growth and jobs'.

Subsequent Commission research has downgraded claims in relation to the yield of real and actual savings (see the next section in this chapter). Despite this, the Cecchini Report was entirely accurate in identifying welfare-generating and deflationary consequences of SEM completion and in associating EC market fragmentation with real economic cost – the 'costs of non-Europe'. Yip (1991), for example, in focusing on European business performance prior to SEM completion, found that continental-scale businesses in Europe performed less efficiently in financial terms than continental-scale businesses in the United States. The same European firms also fared poorly compared with those focused on individual country markets or on micro-regions. This weaker relative performance (in terms of financial returns on investment) was a broad consequence of diseconomies of scale in production, distribution and administration, high co-ordination costs, and an inability to take advantage of economies of scale in development and marketing. Yip's results, like those of the Cecchini Report before them, were evidence of a well-known fact that such barriers segmented the EC market with companies having separate production lines for different markets or having to modify their product to suit the standards of other markets. Given such fragmentation, in many European industries 'the incentives for managers to invest in continental-scale businesses during the 1970s and 1980s were missing, or even negative' (see Clayton, 1999).

The impact of the SEM

Whatever the debates over the 'costs of non-Europe', it is clear that the Single European Market *has* realized dramatic and positive changes to the European business environment. Technical and regulatory barriers have been reduced with the principle of mutual recognition of standards meaning that manufacturers can sell their products all over the EU, eliminating expensive re-testing and maximizing scale economies. Businesses can bid for public sector contracts outside their home state and operate more freely in internal EU markets, many of which (e.g. telecommunications and air transport services) have been significantly liberalized. Most of the physical and administrative restrictions on goods crossing borders within the EU have been removed, free movement of capital has stimulated cross-border investments, and there is now much greater freedom to provide many services across internal frontiers. Although only 2% of EU workers work 'permanently' in a foreign member state, individuals can move more freely (with residency rights attached) and with mutual recognition of their professional and higher education qualifications in the vast majority of cases. As consumers, there is some evidence of these ordinary people enjoying keener prices as a consequence of Single Market liberalization including an average 10–24% reduction in airfares and an estimated 3% reduction in the price of the average basket of groceries.

Macroeconomic effects

The abolition of customs and fiscal formalities and the gradual elimination of technical barriers have been a catalyst for greater competition in Community markets, for increased cross-border trade and for improved technological performance. The effect has been a stimulus to economic growth, to investment and to employment creation. It is difficult to put a figure on these gains, but succeeding Commission reports have estimated that the IMP has achieved measurable gains with respect to GDP growth, net employment creation, inflation and private investment. In the terms of the Monti Report of 1997, these include a number of measured results that would not have been experienced without internal market completion. The following estimates have been provided for the EU as a whole:

- a 1.1–1.5% hike to aggregate EU GDP (1987–93);
- a 1% increase in internal investment;
- the creation of 900,000 extra jobs (albeit just half of the initial prediction);
- a reduction in EU average price inflation by at least 1%.

On trade, the SEM appears to have boosted both the EU's external trade performance and the volume of intra-Community (or internal Community) trade. The percentage of total merchandise trade constituted by intra-EU dispatches has accelerated from 61.2% in 1985 to 67.9% in 1998. In terms of external trade performance, the EU has moved from an external trade deficit in 1992 to a €19.21 billion trade surplus in merchandise goods in 1998 (Eurostat-Comext database).

Internal as well as external trade in services has also expanded rapidly. The EU-15 enjoyed an external trade surplus in services of €8.2 billion in 1998, benefiting from a general pattern of sectoral change, deregulation and technical progress. Patterns of EU trade are discussed at length in Chapter 12.

On investment, the period of the SEM has been associated with an increase in internal (intra-EU) and external (inward) investment. With respect to intra-Community investment flows, gains have been most clearly felt in the UK and Holland. During the period 1993–97, these two member states sucked in about 30% of all intra-EU cross-border investments. With respect to inward investment, FDI assets held in the EU by foreign investors have steadily increased since the first efforts to complete the Single Market. In 1998 alone, the EU attracted €94.3 billion of inward investment (mainly from North America), with the UK benefiting from €49 billion of this total. At the end of 1996, the EU countries hosted FDI liabilities worth an estimated €422 billion. Much of this investment has been stimulated by concerns over future access to the EU market, although in recent years fears of a 'fortress Europe' have greatly dissipated. Today, foreign investors are less concerned with EU market barriers and are more concerned with the advantages offered by the Single European Market (see subsequently) and with insider advantages. These insider advantages can be said to include:

- Closeness to the market – this involves not only geographic proximity which makes delivery easier but also closeness in the sense of shortening the communication links between the market and the manufacturer for the diffusion of information.

- Better market information – related to the above point, gathering market information on which marketing strategies are based is easier at first hand. In turn, this also helps firms adapt more quickly to changes in market conditions (demand, consumer behaviour, competition) and adapt products and strategies accordingly.

- Stimulating demand – there is often assumed to be a presence effect in foreign investment where the introduction of new competition into the market serves to raise overall levels of market demand.

- Raises image and local identity – one of the major problems for firms doing business abroad, particularly in highly nationalistic countries, is their 'foreignness'. This manifests itself in a lack of understanding of the local culture (see Chapter 10) and also the image of the company held by local customers. Firms with a local manufacturing presence often come to be considered as 'local firms'.

- Access to public procurement – similarly to the way that barriers to competition between the fifteen member states within the EU made it difficult (or nigh impossible) for non-indigenous firms to gain access to public procurement, non-EU firms may only win contracts if they have a local market presence.

The SEM also appears to have provided a spur to innovative activity in the EU and to technological development. Eurostat records that in 1996, 36,469 patent applications were filed in EU countries. This figure represents a 22% increase on that for

1989 (29,897). Patents are a means of protecting inventions which have been developed by enterprises, institutions or organizations in order to benefit from an invention or innovation. Member states with positive annual R&D expenditure growth – such as Ireland, Spain, Sweden, Denmark and Finland – had the highest growth of patent applications in the seven years to 1996. In contrast, countries with negative R&D expenditure growth – such as Germany, France and UK – had the lowest growth. Patent data has long been used for international comparison of technological innovation and growth.

The impact on market structures

The effect of the SEM on market structures in Europe is considered in greater detail elsewhere in this book. On balance, it does appear that the IMP has led to substantial restructuring of industry, facilitating deregulation and market liberalization in many sectors, encouraging greater competition in a wide range of markets, and accelerating market concentration. Benefits of the Single Market are seen as being particularly pertinent in the sectors of telecommunications, automobiles, foodstuffs, energy, construction and building materials, financial services, transport services, textiles, clothing and pharmaceuticals. Deregulation has dramatically affected a number of these sectors and may yet be further realized under detailed timetables for specific industries (see Case Study 3.3). Consequently, previously regulated and protected national markets have become more international in character, with the establishment of new market entrants, lower prices and a greater level of competition.

The trend towards industrial market concentration in Europe deserves particular comment. This is the process wherein the market share of the largest N firms in a given industry is increased. Largely in anticipation of the advent of the SEM, EU manufacturing and service sectors underwent a substantial amount of consolidation with significant increases in the volume of domestic and cross-border mergers and acquisitions. By 1996, the European M&A market had grown to a staggering £256 billion, about two-thirds of the size of the M&A market in the US economy. Such trends have led to an increase in the concentration within industries related to public procurement, telecommunications, transportation (aerospace and rail stock), food, finance and banking, electrical machinery and domestic electrical appliances. Right across the manufacturing sector, the C-4 concentration ratio (the market share of the top four firms) increased from 20.5% to 22.8% between 1987 and 1993. The arrival of the Euro has provided further impetus to such concentrations (see Chapter 4), the regulation of which is considered at some length in the context of Chapter 5.

Implications for business firms

The SEM was of course heralded as a form of 'deliverance' for cross-border business and for firms previously excluded from competition in closed and heavily regulated markets. Indeed, much as Europe's corporate powerhouses have been the fiercest

> **CASE STUDY 3.3** **Slow burn to energy market liberalization**
>
> One industry clearly affected by the Single Market is the energy industry. Although liberalization has been slow in coming, the EU's Energy Council has made notable breakthroughs in the 1990s to finally deliver on the hopes raised for wider industry competition in the 1980s.
>
> The Internal Market for Electricity Directive (1996) provides a step towards an open and competitive electricity market in Europe. The level and degree of deregulation provided for are modest but the effect should be to introduce a measure of competition to the market and to bring lower electricity prices to European consumers. The Directive establishes common rules for the generation, transmission and distribution of electricity, a number of basic public service obligations and a series of timetables for Europe-wide market opening. This is to be achieved in three steps between 1999 and 2003 with an initial and minimum market opening by February 1999 equivalent to 26% of the national market, moving to 33% by 2003. Member states are allowed to go for further deregulation and/or to achieve complete liberalization. Evidence suggests, however, that it is only in the UK, Spanish, Dutch, Nordic and German markets that liberalization will
>
> go beyond this minimum expectation. These countries have already been pushing ahead with market deregulation and with associated privatizations. Companies and governments in France, Italy and Greece, meanwhile, have shown little inclination to deregulate since their reluctant agreement to approve the Directive in 1996 (*The European*, 29 June 1998, p. 22). In these countries, markets remain dominated by single producers.
>
> The Internal Market for Gas Directive has followed the 1996 directive on electricity, with the European Parliament and the Council adopting the Directive in June 1998. Like its predecessor for the European electricity sector, the Directive, which entered into force on 10 August 1998, establishes common rules for transmission, distribution, supply and storage. It also lays down a timetable for market liberalization requiring member states to initially open up a share of the market (by August 2000) equal to at least 20% of total annual gas consumption. The share will increase to 28% by August 2003 and to 33% of total annual consumption by August 2008. Again, then, the Directive provides for significant if partial deregulation.

supporters of European monetary integration, the Single European Market initiative was widely called for among leading European industrial firms. Effective lobbying was undertaken by the so-called European Round Table (ERT) and by a coalition of information technology firms frustrated by inadequate standardization across the Community market (see Sandholtz and Zysman, 1989; Cowles, 1995). But has the SEM delivered its expected fruit for these and other European businesses? Analysis follows within the framework of a simple cost–benefit analysis. This proceeds at a broad level of examination and without specification of firm, commercial scale or category.

Benefits for the individual business

- The removal of barriers to intra-EU trade has allowed firms to operate more freely in a community market of some 376 million consumers. As they take up the opportunities of expanding their European coverage and of increasing their output, they are better placed to raise the scale of their manufacturing units, to reduce their costs and to gain from economies of scale.

- The mutual recognition of standards means that manufacturers can, subject to few restrictions, sell their products all over the EU. Given compliance with 'essential requirements', opportunities exist for the sale of a standardized product across Europe.

■ By no longer having to adapt production and operations to national standards, firms may expect to rationalize their production and operations. Unilever once had factories producing soap in every European country; now toilet soap for the whole of the Continent is produced at a single facility in Merseyside. The Dutch consumer electronics firm Philips now sources the European market for audio hi-fi equipment from a small number of production points having previously had production sites in nearly all Community markets.

■ The Single Market has led to the scrapping of customs forms and paperwork associated with internal frontier checks and with cross-border passage. This has led to shorter border waiting times, reduced transport costs and simplified border formalities. Taking the UK as example, some 10 million customs forms have been dispensed with, saving UK business around £135 million per year.

■ Lower transport costs combined with the free movement of goods have enabled companies to relocate production from their domestic market to areas where production is cheaper or for other targeted benefits.

■ The internal market regime has also provided new incentives for innovation and to develop new technologies as a way of sustaining long-term advantage.

■ The SEM has contributed to a reduction in input costs for many firms. Among other things, the four freedoms of the SEM provide improved access to other member states for the purpose of acquiring cheaper raw materials and component parts.

■ Closer market integration has provided freer access to insurers and financiers across the EU's economic space. This has provided potential for reductions in costs of credit and insurance although advantages here will only be maximized with the elimination of exchange rate risk exposure under EMU.

■ Collaborative arrangements are encouraged within the Single Market, permitting companies to gain from an exchange of ideas and expertise, to burden share and/or to penetrate new markets at lower risk and shared cost.

■ Expansionary strategies are encouraged by several factors including new rights of establishment, market access freedoms and the removal of restrictions on cross-border investments and capital movement.

Threats and challenges

Despite these 'gains', European businesses (large and small) have been forced to confront threats to their operations and to respond to the challenges of enhanced competition. Underpinning the following 'concerns' is an assumption that powerful Asian and US companies will tend to produce/manufacture locally in order to take advantage of SEM freedoms and to avoid paying import tariffs. This assumption has been validated by an upward trend in inward investment since the advent of the SEM.

- Increased competition in consequence of any EU firm being able to sell freely in any EU market may imply reductions in market share for company X.

- Profits and margins in established markets may be squeezed as a result of increased market entry. Heightened competition will tend to encourage a downward movement of prices.

- With domestic protection from external competition largely removed, and with downward pressure on prices, business closure rates will accelerate among least efficient firms and sectors.

- State assistance of competitors from other member states (state aid) may threaten an ability to compete in specific markets along with the potentially uneven enforcement of internal market rules and regulations.

- Smaller operators will be more vulnerable to take-over as market integration stimulates domestic (national) and cross-border mergers and acquisitions.

Whatever the actual or perceived threat for individual businesses, the removal of barriers between the fifteen member states of the EU has, in theory at least, raised the opportunity for European players to consider the whole market as their 'domestic back yard'. Although the balance sheet may be mixed, the SEM has created opportunities previously denied to European firms to penetrate and to capture foreign markets and to realize significant efficiency gains. However, in looking to take advantage of those opportunities, a number of strategic choices are presented to which there is no easy or obvious answer. In constructing appropriate and efficient strategies for Europe, firms will have to weigh up several factors including company resources, product traits and life cycles, market conditions, cultural and regulatory practices. A detailed discussion of strategies for the Single Market is presented in Chapters 8 and 9, with these chapters providing many case studies. For the moment, and in illustration of the stimulus provided by the SEM towards pan-European strategies and operation, the reader may like to consider Case Study 3.4.

Field or fortress?

A key question of course is whether or not the completion of the Single Market has led to more or less protection for indigenous firms. This issue is bound up with outsiders' concerns that the creation of the Single European Market might lead to a 'fortress Europe'. Early action against many industrial imports, particularly Japanese exports in high-technology sectors, suggested that the new Europe was not going to welcome further encroachment by competitive foreign imports. Added to this belief were reports emanating from member capitals (and from Brussels) which seemed to suggest that, along with the new internal freedoms from competition across the EU, external trade policies, in the short term at least, would be designed to protect the EU from external pressures in an effort to allow firms and industries alike to strengthen their position in the new Europe. The Cockfield Report on the EC Single Market (1985), which launched the Single Market project, even threatened that 'the

---

CASE STUDY 3.4   'Kwik-Fit drives a swathe through European market'

The creation of the Single European Market has created the opportunity and incentive for several British firms to make inroads into continental European markets. Kwik-Fit Holdings plc, the Edinburgh-based tyres, exhausts and brakes group established in 1971, provides one example of a UK-based firm taking advantage of the new European market opportunities. Kwik-Fit had already opened repair centres in Ireland, Holland and the northern part of Belgium prior to completion of the SEM but has massively developed its European operations since 1993. An expansion of services in the Benelux markets has been followed by acquisition of the 'Speedy Europe' group of service and repair centres trading in France, Spain, Belgium, Switzerland and Germany (under the Pit Stop name and logo). The company is now also expanding its operations in Northern Europe, concentrating on Scandinavia where it hopes to make future small-scale acquisitions.

Strategically, Kwik-Fit has looked to take advantage of the steady growth and rich pickings in the European fast-fit market. Its European retail services – which see company divisions lead the market in four out of seven countries of operation – are complemented by a developed network of trade distribution centres ('Centuri') and an import and wholesale supply service, Uitlaatservice Nederland (USN). Business in Holland and Belgium has shown consistent growth over the last ten years. For the twelve months ending 28 February 1999, European operations recorded operating profits of £7.0 million from a turnover of £92.5 million. Kwik-Fit chairman and chief executive Tom Farmer highlights the fact that the aggregate European market is more than four times the size of the UK market (where Kwik-Fit is a clear market leader) and is less developed in terms of the fast-fit share of the total aftermarket. This underlies the Ford Motor Group's intentions to buy Kwik-Fit as a vehicle to develop an international fast-fit parts business. Ford plans considerable further investment in the brand in Europe to make Kwik-Fit a pan-European operator and wants the Kwik-Fit board to take the business beyond the SEM and into the Far East.

commercial identity of the Community must be consolidated so that our trading partners will not be given the benefit of a wider market without themselves making similar concessions' (quoted in Hanson, 1998). In the late 1980s, many foreign firms invested heavily in the EU as a means of bypassing the trade restrictions being levelled against them and/or of managing concerns over future barriers. Japanese firms in particular decided to locate their production within the EU and bypass the barriers altogether or enter into collaborative arrangements with EU firms as a way of securing a market presence and local involvement. By the early 1990s for example, Sony Corporation had established a number of dedicated manufacturing facilities throughout the EU and Matsushita Electric had set up a network of subsidiaries to manufacture and supply components as well as entering into a number of joint ventures with EU competitors. These and other Japanese firms augmented their European investment so as to ensure that they had a strong position inside the SEM before barriers were strengthened. Sony Corporation's founder, Akio Morita, is reported as saying in the run-up to 1992 'Japanese are not fools. Japanese industry will move technology to Europe'.

As the SEM took its final shape in the early–mid-1990s, fears of a 'fortress Europe' began to dissipate. In practice, the completion of the internal market undermined the ability of the member states to use national tools of protection and it became clear that those countries that favoured protection (such as France) faced a strengthened liberal coalition in the form of the Commission's external relations directorate (DG-1) and a cluster of 'liberal' states (the UK, Denmark, Germany and the Netherlands). While the EU emphasized reciprocity on market opening, very few national restrictions (quotas, voluntary export restraints etc.) were replaced with EU-level trade restrictions and the number of EU anti-dumping measures stabilized at around 150 a year. The completion of the SEM also coincided with the completion of the Uruguay Round GATT trade talks, which committed the EU to various market-opening measures even in its most sensitive sectors (see Chapter 12).

While EU trade defences remain significant, there is now a strong consensus that the formation of the SEM has not led to an increase in European trade barriers or to a picture of aggressively competitive inward-looking regional trade blocs. The WTO's Trade Policy Review Board has concluded that:

> the deepening of European integration, with single market completion ... has not reduced the EU's involvement in the multilateral system nor increased its levels of overall protection. (WTO PRESS/TPRB/66, 27 November 1997)

In a growing number of areas, the interface between the single market and the international trading system now appears to be working together to the benefit of both the Union and its trading partners. This points to the extent to which the Community has succeeded in negotiating an extension of some of its own regulatory practices (e.g. for commercial services) into WTO codes.

The state of play

Business confidence

Business confidence in the Internal Market is generally high. Results from the Commission's Single Market Scoreboard survey of 4,000 European businesses (September 1999) show a continuing improvement in the functioning of the Internal Market and a recognition of significant reductions in barriers to doing business in other countries of the Union. In rating the current openness and functioning of the SEM, businesses awarded it 61.8 points out of 100. Despite this the survey found that an effort is still required to remove remaining obstacles. Firms identified a wide range of problems including barriers related to technical standards for goods and services, problems with VAT obligations, state aids favouring competitors, and restrictions in accessing markets related to licences, rights or exclusive distribution networks (see Table 3.3). This draws our attention to the continuing imperfections in the Single Market and to the question 'just how single is Europe's Single Market?'

Table 3.3 Most frequent obstacles in the Internal Market (Single Market Scoreboard Survey, September 1999)

	SME (2893)	Majors (502)	Total (3395)
Additional costs to render products or services compatible with national specifications	36%	41%	37%
Unusual testing, certification or approval procedures	31%	34%	31%
State aids favouring competitors	28%	36%	29%
Difficulties related to the VAT system and VAT procedures	27%	30%	27%
Restrictions on market access; existence of exclusive networks	22%	29%	23%
Costly financing arrangements for cross-border transactions	18%	20%	18%
Insufficient action against piracy and counterfeiting	18%	13%	18%
Discriminatory tax treatment of your operations	17%	20%	17%
Lack of legal security of cross-border contracts/transactions	17%	14%	17%
Requirement to establish branch in another MS	15%	20%	15%
Requested rights or licences in hands of local competitors	14%	20%	15%
Other legislative or regulatory obstacles	14%	21%	15%
Discriminatory practices of awarding authorities in public procurement markets	14%	19%	15%
Outright refusal of permission to market products or services legally marketed in another MS	9%	11%	9%
Double payments in social security for personnel posted abroad	8%	12%	8%

The numerals in parentheses indicate the number of interviews.
Source: European Commission

Technical and legal barriers to the free movement of goods

Throughout the EU, the huge number of different technical standards has been massively reduced. Nonetheless, significant problems remain and, with countries continuing to operate their own standards against 'essential requirements' prescribed in EU legislation, there remains much potential for argument and confusion. Several operators have reported delayed acceptance of standards and expensive 're-testing procedures' for their products. In addition, although procedures exist requiring member states to notify new technical regulations to ensure that no new technical barriers to trade arise in the Single Market, member states are still putting in place an increasing number of technical rules without proper notification and approval. Not all national specifications pose problems for cross-border business, but, in 1997, doubts concerning the compatibility of national technical rules with the Single Market were raised in 240 instances.

In short, the patchwork of national product standards, the vagaries of notification, and the ambiguities of mutual recognition, continue to trouble intra-EU exporters–importers. In one recent case, French authorities blocked the sale of imported disposable barbecues, rejecting the standard of the product on the grounds of unacceptable fire risk. Despite product modifications by the exporting company and improvements to the instructions for use, the Commission reports that French authorities continue to refuse sales authorization. The Commission's reasoned opinion of May 1998 stresses that, in its modified form, the product comfortably meets the requirements invoked by the French authorities. The case is now in the hands of the ECJ (European Commission, 1999a).

Although against the spirit of the Single Market, there is also continuing evidence of individual member states improperly restraining imports through prior national (legal) codes. For example, the Commission is to bring an action before the Court of Justice in connection with an item of French legislation that unjustifiably restricts the sale of pasta legally manufactured in another member state from wheat other than durum wheat. These restrictions are based on a French Law of 3 July 1934, which stipulates that all pasta produced or sold in France must be made from durum wheat and that French authorities are entitled to lay down strict rules for the manufacture of pasta in France. However, the Commission thinks that extending a ban on pasta made from soft wheat or from a mixture of soft and durum wheat violates provisions of the Treaty on the free movement of goods. The Commission won a similar case against comparable legislation in Italy (European Commission, 1999a).

The non-implementation of Single Market Directives

In light of the above, it is worth noting that the number of formal infringement procedures opened by the Commission against member states for failure to apply Single Market rules and for incorrect application has continued to be high. Yet these statistics on 'infringement' do not include the simple failure on the part of member states to actually 'implement' directives. Incomplete implementation of the rules is a serious problem for citizens and businesses that wish to take full advantage of the Single Market.

In setting directives in relation to the Internal Market, the EU sets rules but then requires the member states to transpose them into national law, something that is not always done quickly or completely (see Chapter 2). Although the Commission's Single Market Scoreboard shows that member states have made significant progress in tackling this implementation deficit, the fragmentation factor concerning those directives not yet implemented in one or more member country still holds at around 12.8%. Recent progress has been made by the likes of Belgium and Germany, but the implementation record of a number of member states (notably Portugal, Italy and Greece) remains poor. Table 3.4 shows the performance of each of the member states in this regard and highlights the credibility of Finland and Denmark as the most efficient implementers of Single Market directives.

Table 3.4 Percentage of Single Market Directives not yet notified to the Commission (Single Market Scoreboard, June 1999)

	P	I	EL	L	F	A	IRL	B	UK	D	NL	S	E	DK	FIN
May 1999	5.7	5.5	5.2	4.8	4.8	4.5	3.9	3.5	3.3	2.4	2.4	2.1	1.8	1.4	1.3
Nov 1998	5.6	5.7	5.2	6.2	5.5	4.2	5.8	5.2	3.8	2.7	2.1	1.5	2.7	1.5	0.9
May 1998	5.9	6.4	5.5	5.6	5.6	5.2	5.4	7.1	3.8	5.4	2.2	2.0	3.3	2.2	1.2

Source: European Commission

The Commission's Single Market Scoreboard also provides interesting presentation of how the implementation of internal market directives remains uneven across sectors and within member states. Its most recent evidence (see Table 3.5) shows that, although competition among utilities has increased, particularly in the telecommunications field, 'gaps still remain in the implementation of the relevant EU legislation' (European Commission, 1999b). Other sectors with the highest rates of non-implementation include transport, public procurement and intellectual property.

Table 3.5 Non-implemented Directives by area (Single Market Scoreboard, June 1999)

Sector (number of Directives concerned in parentheses)	%	B	DK	D	EL	E	F	IRL	I	L	NL	A	P	FIN	S	UK
Telecommunications (16)	56.2	6	–	–	6	–	2	1	3	2	–	–	4	–	3	1
Transport (60)	51.7	11	2	5	10	9	9	10	15	18	9	11	17	5	8	10
Intellectual and industrial property (8)	50.0	–	1	1	1	1	1	4	1	2	2	1	1	1	–	1
Public procurement (11)	36.4	–	–	2	3	1	2	–	1	2	–	2	2	–	–	2
Social policy (39)	28.2	3	–	–	3	–	3	2	8	9	–	3	2	–	–	–
Veterinary checks (198)	17.2	3	3	3	17	2	20	12	15	9	4	14	15	6	7	13
Chemical products (78)	16.7	1	–	3	3	–	4	1	1	1	2	5	5	1	2	2
Energy (12)	16.7	–	2	1	1	–	2	1	1	2	–	–	1	1	1	–
Environment (91)	14.3	6	2	4	7	5	4	6	8	3	2	3	5	1	1	5
Food legislation (103)	13.6	2	–	4	3	2	2	5	5	–	–	2	9	–	–	1
Cosmetic products (38)	10.5	1	–	1	–	–	3	–	–	–	–	1	1	–	1	–

Source: European Commission

The free movement of persons

Another enduring problem, although not one emphasized in the stated survey, is the continued failure to ensure the free movement of persons throughout the Community. Although customs formalities for the movement of goods were simplified during the period 1985–92 and then abolished on 1 January 1993, border controls on the movement of persons remain. As a consequence of this and of factors tied to cultural diversity and to restricted rights of residence, the free movement of people throughout the EU remains no more than an aspiration. In fact, labour mobility between European nation-states is barely one-third the level found in the USA and a Commission survey has found that more than 80% of French and German workers would never seek work elsewhere in the EU.

The Schengen Agreement on frontier controls, now integrated into Community law, is supposed to allow EU citizens to travel without a passport within EU countries, with non-EU citizens requiring only one visa to enter any EU nation. Despite this, passport-free movement is a reality only for EU citizens moving between the thirteen member states that have presently signed the accord – the UK and Ireland have refused to do so – or within the Anglo-Irish common travel area. Even within the expanded circle of the Schengen Group, certain restrictions on freedom of movement continue to exist. Despite the relaxation of internal border controls since 1995, Schengen nationals and nationals of other EU member states need a European identity card (or valid passport) for the purpose of their identification when travelling throughout the Union.

Aside from this impediment to the free circulation of EU citizens, for the SEM to work properly, people must also have the right to live and work where they can find suitable employment and businesses must be allowed to recruit and to post workers according to their requirements. According to Article 39 (ex Article 48) of the Community Treaty, any European Union citizen has the right to enter the territory of any member state in order to work or to look for work. According to EU rules, this is with the legal guarantee of equal treatment in the host country (e.g. access to jobs, pay and unemployment rights) and of full integration of the 'worker' and his or her family. In other words, EU rules are supposed to make sure that individuals from other member states, whether employed or self-employed, are treated on the same terms as nationals of the host country and to provide rights of residence where a job is secured. Despite this, 'worker freedoms' remain frustrated by three factors:

1. There is still significant evidence that many countries refuse to accept the educational, technical and vocational qualifications of other member states. In a widely reported case, French authorities were exposed as barring British and Danish ski instructors from giving ski lessons in the Alps on the grounds that there were 'substantial differences' between their's and national qualifications. This form of non-recognition of national certificates flies in the face of EU rules underwritten by the 1992 Directive on European Mutual Recognition of Sports Diplomas. In another reported case, a British art restorer's attempts to secure a job at the Royal Institute of Artistic Heritage in Belgium were initially frustrated by the relevant Belgian authority's refusal to certify the equivalence of her Master's qualification (European Commission, 1999a). Only after direct intervention by the European Commission did Belgian authorities recognize the British degree in accordance with the terms of a Directive concerning a general system of recognition of higher education diplomas (89/48/EEC).

2. Big differences in employee benefits across the member states and the absence of a Single Market for pensions (with restrictions on transfers) are also a serious

problem for the functioning of the Single Market. Supplementary pension schemes continue to operate largely on a national basis and workers wishing to exercise their right to move to another member state risk losing some or all of their supplementary pension rights in the process. The Commission's 1997 Single Market Action Plan was targeting this very problem before its expiry in mid-1998 (see succeeding analysis).

3. The very definition of freedom of movement for the purposes of work and establishment remains limited. There is a confusion of rights for those working under a series of short- and fixed-term contracts, for those 'seeking work' over extended periods and for those looking for vocational training in other EU states. Confusion also surrounds rights of residence for worker families and dependents. For example, existing legislation only enables a worker's descendants who are under the age of 21 and who are dependent (and their ascendants who are dependent) to take up residence with workers once they are employed in another member state. Despite this, ECJ case rulings appear to contest age and dependency criteria and the Commission's specialist working group suggests future non-application.

Enhancements and improvements

The Commission has naturally targeted the elimination of these remaining barriers and of the operational problems reported by Single Market operatives. Along with the member governments, it is looking to:

1. further enhance the coverage and impact of the Single Market (examining enduring barriers and market distortions),
2. improve the application of internal market rules,
3. make the existing rules more effective and more transparent,
4. achieve a closer approximation of (national) market legislation, and
5. deliver a single market for the benefit of all citizens.

This applies both to the fifteen member states and to those territories (Iceland, Norway and Liechtenstein) committed to operating by the full set of Single Market rules under the European Economic Area Agreement (see Chapter 1).

Action programmes and initiatives

As a means of realizing these objectives, the Commission has proposed a number of initiatives, encompassing legislative and non-legislative actions. Many of these initiatives are discussed in the following section, which highlights the development of a new 'Single Market Action Plan'. This plan (developed in 1997) has required all of the member states to renew their commitment to the SEM and brings together a range of measures in a coherent action framework.

SLIM (The simpler legislation for the internal market initiative)

This has been introduced as a way to simplify EU legislation for governments, operators and consumers alike. Many member authorities and businesses in the EU complain that Internal Market rules are unnecessarily complex or that their requirements are unfathomable. Currently targeted areas include dangerous substances and pre-packaging legislation. Small groups of experts and users meet in an informal framework to look at particular legislation (one or more legal texts concerning a particular subject). These groups identify existing problems and make recommendations to the Commission on how to simplify and improve the existing legislation.

The Single Market Scoreboard scheme

This initiative has been operationalized as a means of monitoring progress on implementation and enforcement of internal market rules by member governments. The results of the scoreboard (covering infringement of rules, non-implementation and enforcement) have been presented at an earlier stage in this chapter. The scoreboard also features results from the various dialogue schemes – including 'Citizen's Signpost' and 'Business Dialogue' – set up under the Single Market Action Plan. These schemes are being expanded so as to ensure that more citizens and businesses are aware of basic SEM rights and have assorted contact points throughout the regions. Evidence suggests that enquiries by individual EU citizens are dominated by uncertainties over working in another EU country, living in another EU country and buying goods and services abroad. A large number of enquiries is received in relation to studying, training and doing research in another EU country.

The communication on improved mutual recognition

The Commission has also presented a recent communication on how to facilitate and improve the application of the principle of mutual recognition in the Single Market, an area again singled out for attention in the Single Market Action Plan. Recalling that mutual recognition is a key principle for the functioning of the internal market in all the sectors which have not been the subject of harmonization measures at Community level, the Commission's present attempt is to address weaknesses in the application of this principle. Four lines of action include:

1. improving the monitoring of mutual recognition,
2. making citizens and economic operators more aware of it,
3. improving the application of the principle by the national authorities, and
4. improving the management of individual complaints.

The Green Paper on Combating Counterfeiting and Piracy in the Single Market

According to this paper (presented in 1998), problems with counterfeiting and piracy affect a wide variety of sectors including textiles, pharmaceuticals, entertainment and computing. Moreover, the levels of counterfeiting and piracy in relation to the turnover of the sectors concerned are considerable. Estimates put the figure at 35% in the software industry and at 12% in the toy industry. The former Single Market Commissioner, Mario Monti described counterfeiting and piracy as 'prejudicial to the development of all forms of creativity and to the growth and competitiveness of European industry'. It is estimated that these practices cost up to 100,000 EU jobs per year (European Commission, 1998).

The lines of approach explored in the Green Paper include monitoring by the private sector, the use of technical devices, and tougher sanctions and enforcement of intellectual property rights. Initiatives on intellectual property rights have previously focused on harmonizing national legislation (for example trademarks, biotechnology inventions) and on creating unitary rights at Community level (for example, the Community trademark).

The financial services action plan

With limited progress to date in financial services liberalization, the European Commission continues to lay great stress on creating an integrated European financial environment. It has recently adopted a five-year Financial Services Action Plan (COM (99) 232 final) which is discussed further in Case Study 3.5. This plan suggests time-scales for legislative and other measures to tackle three strategic objectives:

1. ensuring a Single Market for wholesale financial services;
2. achieving open and secure retail markets;
3. providing modern and harmonized prudential supervision.

The overarching aim here is to build on existing achievements and to ensure that the Single Market for financial services 'delivers its full potential' for consumers and providers alike. Initiative should complement and further secure the single-passport principle that once a home country authorizes a bank to operate within its domestic territories the operator is then free to provide services in other EC markets. This principle is elaborated in the Second Banking Directive (89/646/EEC) on the provision of financial services, which figures at the heart of the various legislative acts providing a framework for cross-border financial services in the EU. The Commission has also proposed new legislation on the distance selling of financial services. Financial services were excluded from an earlier EC directive which gave consumers the right to return mail order goods. The explosion of distance selling, of electronic commerce and the introduction of the Euro (eliminating exchange rate risk exposure), makes such action an imperative and an important part of the current action plan.

Pending legislation

Several directives have been proposed to complete outstanding projects and to respond to emerging challenges. While the problem of fragmentation in European

---

CASE STUDY 3.5 **Community invests in financial services liberalization**

The European Commission has set a five-year deadline for shaking up Europe's financial services sector and updating supervision and prudential rules. The double-pronged attack on Europe's financial services sector, still largely carved along national lines, sets out a number of proposals to be taken up by the new Prodi Commission. The Commission's outgoing financial services chief, Mr Monti, indicated that failure to pursue reform would stop Europe reaping the benefits of its single currency, launched at the beginning of the year. 'It is crucial that the single market for financial services delivers its full potential for consumers, in terms of a broad range of safe, competitive products, and for industry in terms inter alia of easier access to a single deep and liquid market for investment capital', he said.

The incoming Commission will be expected to draft legislation to liberalize supplementary pensions. This should stand a better chance of becoming law than previous initiatives, thrown out after some member states balked at giving up their right to dictate the terms of pension fund investment. Mr Monti also said that while many national limi-

tations on asset management were described as prudential, '... there is also a fairly hefty dose of protecting national markets'. 'This is a relic of the past', he said.

For wholesale markets, the Financial Services Action Plan calls for the removal of outstanding barriers to raising capital on an EU-wide basis, a common legal framework for integrated securities and derivatives markets (including possible amendments to the investment services directive) and a proposal for a directive on cross-border use of collateral. The paper steers clear of proposals for a pan-European regulatory body, but to ensure the stability of EU financial markets it suggests moves to bring banking, insurance and securities prudential legislation up to the highest standards in all member states. It also proposes legislation for the prudential supervision of financial conglomerates and calls for greater co-operation between authorities through the setting up of a Securities Advisory Body. Mr Monti reiterated the need to eliminate tax obstacles and distortions.

Source: Financial Times, 12 May 1999

---

company law continues to demand the EU's attention, there is also a real test in the development of digital technologies and of electronic commerce. The latter trend opens up new opportunities for buying and selling goods and services across frontiers but exposes current limitations in present EU frameworks relating to such matters as the protection of personal data. The following EC directives were under consideration at time of writing. The summaries that follow are heavily indebted to those provided in the press release of the 2,193rd Internal Market Council Meeting, Luxembourg, 21 June 1999. The reader can monitor the member states' progress with these and other relevant directives by using the web links highlighted at the end of this chapter.

The Thirteenth Company Law Directive

This directive, if agreed upon by the member states, will harmonize the essentials of national take-over regulations in the EU. Member states will be left some scope to adopt more stringent rules. At a minimum, the protection of shareholders is to be ensured by obliging the person who acquires the control of a company to make a bid to all holders of securities for all their holdings. The directive clarifies which is the competent authority for regulating a cross-border takeover and which law is applicable. Under the terms of the draft directive, member states will have a four-year transposition period. The legislation would require several member states to adapt their laws on take-overs substantially. This is one of several areas where company law is fragmented throughout the European Union.

Directive on Copyright and Related Rights in the Information Society

The objective of the proposal is to adapt existing legislation concerning the rights of authors and of holders of related rights with regard to reproduction, communication to the public and distribution of their works. This is to take into full account the threats and possibilities offered by new technologies (digital copying and transmission, e.g. via the Internet). One aim shall be to ensure that in the 'digital era' material protected by copyright does not encounter obstacles when transmitted from one EU country to another. The proposal covers not only performers but also producers of CDs and CD-ROMs as well as broadcasters. It seeks to maintain a balance between the interests of these rights holders (who are worried about piracy of digitally transmitted material) and those of the distributors (such as telecoms operators or Internet access providers).

Draft Directive on Certain Legal Aspects of Electronic Commerce in the Internal Market

The proposal aims at establishing a coherent legal framework for the development of electronic commerce within the Single Market. It builds on and completes a number of other initiatives (regulatory transparency, protection of personal data, legal protection of conditional access services, electronic signatures) that together will eliminate the remaining legal obstacles to the on-line provision of services. The target is to optimize the benefits of electronic commerce for both citizens and industry in the European Union and to improve the coherence of the legal framework for electronic commerce in the European Union.

An enlarged Single Market?

The Commission is also managing a rolling programme designed to assist the Central European Candidate Countries (CECCs) to prepare for life inside the Internal Market. This follows member state agreement on a White Paper on Preparation for the Internal Market (COM (95) 163 final) proposed by the European Commission in July 1994. This lays out a clear programme for each associated country so that it can meet the obligations of the Internal Market (European Commission, 1995b). Here, and in subsequent communications, the Commission has stressed the magnitude of the task of approximation and the need for close co-ordination and for technical assistance. This issue of legislative alignment between the EU and the CECCs is given further consideration in Chapter 7 on the transition economies.

Conclusions

The present chapter has provided extensive detail on the mechanics of the Single European Market and on those policies helping to establish it. Its purpose has been to introduce the reader to the basic detail of the 'European home market' and to establish the history and future direction of this unique regime. What is clear is that the SEM has been a huge success. Before its completion, goods destined for other Community markets were stopped and subjected to frontier controls, products had to comply with different sets of national requirements and the EC market was strictly segmented. The SEM programme has realized dramatic change. Goods can now move across internal borders without frontier checks and a combination of standards approximation and mutual recognition has greatly facilitated the cross-border movement of goods, services and labour. Capital controls have been removed and previously pervasive fiscal barriers have been much diminished.

Despite this, the goal of the Single Market itself requires perpetual action and initiative. As Johnson (1995) explains, 'the single market is not a static concept but an ongoing process'. In this context, analysis has highlighted both poor observation of Internal Market rules and areas of business as yet little touched by the Single Market Programme. In particular, efforts need to be directed at key market distortions (most notably those related to significant tax differentials), to removing sectoral obstacles to market integration and to the confused picture of European company law. In this respect, the EU faces up to its present and future challenges conscious that all of its efforts to reduce trade and fiscal barriers can do nothing to counter the market fragmentation arising from the cultural diversity that is its very hallmark (see Chapter 10).

Of course, the internal market is closely linked with other policy areas. First, the internal market could not have been created without the provisions in the Community treaties for an effective European competition policy. Indeed, Article 3 of TEC recognizes a system ensuring fair competition as a component part of the internal market. Second, policies tied to industry, trade and the environment, as well as those designed to strengthen the EU's economic and social cohesion, enjoy an important relationship with those examined in the present chapter. Such policies help to deliver on many of the Single Market's objectives and ensure that Community concentration does not rest exclusively with the economic or market aspects of integration. Many of these different policy areas (including competition policy) are discussed in Chapter 5. Before this, however, Chapter 4 examines the progression made by the EU towards monetary union. As we shall see, the elimination of the quasi-tariff of competing national currencies may be seen as a major contribution to the completion of Europe's Single Market. Among other things, it gives firms further impetus to respond proactively to the challenges of the Single Market and consumers clearer information as to the cheapest sources of goods and services throughout the Community.

Review questions for Chapter 3

1. What do we mean by economic integration? Identify different levels of co-operation within regional economic groupings.

2. How quickly did the Europeans establish their customs union? What did this imply for tariff barriers between EC members as well as for their external tariffs?

3. What were some of the non-tariff barriers that bedevilled the EC market up to the mid-1980s?

4. Why was the European Commission anxious to harmonize technical standards across the EC?

5. What did the 1985 White Paper propose on standards harmonization?

6. What were the other main objectives of the Internal Market Programme (IMP)?

7. Account for the relationship between the Single European Act and the IMP.

8. In what ways did SEM completion raise fears of a 'fortress Europe'?

9. What is the Schengen Agreement? Account for the evidence that certain member states have been reluctant to sign up to its terms.

10. In what sense was the SEM 'enlarged' by the conclusion of the European Economic Area Agreement?

11. How far would you consider the Single Market a true success?

12. List five examples of how businesses have benefited from an integrated internal market.

13. Where do you expect future action to further the aims and objectives of the Single Market?

14. What are some of the implications of different levels of excise duties and VAT throughout the EU?

15. Why do you think there is concern about continued fragmentation of EU financial markets? What is the Commission doing to address this?

Web guide

See also Web guide for Chapter 2.

European Parliament: Single Market Fact Sheet @
http://www.europarl.eu.int/dg4/factsheets/en/default.htm#3

EUROPA: Internal Market index @ http://europa.eu.int/pol/singl/index_en.htm

EU Business News: Economy (EU market news and related stories) @
http://www.eubusiness.com/

The European Commission: Internal Market Directorate General @
http://europa.eu.int/comm/dgs/internal_market/index_en.htm

European Commission: 'Single Market Scoreboard' @
http://europa.eu.int/comm/internal_market/en/update/score/index.htm

European Commission: 'Dialogue With Business' @
http://europa.eu.int/business/en/index.html

Green and White Papers (Internal Market) @
http://www.uni-mannheim.de/users/ddz/edz/doku/wirte.html#publi

New Approach to Standardization in the European Internal Market @
http://www.NewApproach.org/

References

Armstrong, K. and Bulmer, S. (1998) *The Governance of the Single European Market*, Manchester University Press.

Batchelor, C. (1999) 'Booze Cruise' to Calais to be promoted, *Financial Times*, Wednesday 7 July 1999.

Begg, I. (1998) Commentary: the Single Market (Internal Market Programme in Europe), *National Institute Economic Review*, April, (164).

Begg, I. and Maher, I. (1998) The inconsistent Single European Market, *European Business Journal*, **10**(2).

Cecchini, P. (1988) *The European Challenge 1992: The Benefits of a Single Market*, Wildwood House.

Clayton, T. (1999) The performance of Europe-wide businesses: has the Single Market led to scale economies?, *Business Strategy Review*, **10**(1).

Cowles, M.G. (1995) Setting the agenda for a New Europe: the European Round Table and EC 1992, *Journal of Common Market Studies*, **33**(4).

Dudley, J.W. and Martens, H. (1993) *1993 and Beyond: New Strategies for the Enlarged Single Market*, Kogan Page.

El-Agraa, A.M. (1990) *The Economics of the European Community*, 3rd edition, Philip Allan.

European Commission (1985) *White Paper: Completing the Internal Market*, COM(85) 310 final, Commission of the European Communities, Brussels.

European Commission (1995a) *The Single Market: Europe on the Move*, Office for Official Publications of the European Communities, Luxembourg.

European Commission (1995b) *White Paper: Preparation of the Associated Countries of Central and Eastern Europe for Integration into the Internal Market of the Union*, COM(95) 163 final, Commission of the European Communities, Brussels.

European Commission (1998) The Commission adopts a Green Paper on tackling the problem of counterfeiting and piracy in the Single Market (online) (http://europa.eu.int/comm/dg15/en/intprop/indprop/922.htm).

European Commission (1999a) Barriers to trade: infringement proceedings against France, Belgium and Germany (online) (http://europa.eu.int/comm/dg15/en/goods/infr/1124.htm#2).

European Commission (1999b) June 1999 Single Market scoreboard underlines further efforts required by member states (online) (http://europa.eu.int/comm/dg15/en/update/score/score4.htm).

Hanson, B.T. (1998) What happened to fortress Europe? External trade policy liberalization in the European Union, *International Organization*, **52**(1), 55–85.

Johnson, D. (1995) The Single Market: competition in context, in Davison, L. and Fitzpatrick, E. (eds), *The European Competitive Environment: Texts and Cases*, Butterworth-Heinemann.

Monti, M. (1997) *The Single Market and Tomorrow's Europe (Monti Report)*, Kogan Page.

Monti, M. (1999) Britain and the Single Market: a longer-term view, Reception Europe 21 (speech), London 12 May 1999 (online) (http://europa.eu.int/comm/dg15/en/speeches/spch76.htm).

Sandholtz, W. and Zysman, J. (1989) 1992: recasting the European bargain, *World Politics*, **42**(1), 95–128.

Yip, G.S. (1991) A performance comparison of continental and national businesses in Europe, *International Marketing Review*, **8**(2).

4 The Euro – a currency for Europe

Introduction

On 1 January 1999, eleven EU countries – Austria, Belgium, Finland, France, Germany, Ireland, Italy, Luxembourg, the Netherlands, Portugal and Spain – irrevocably locked their currencies to form a new European currency union. Until 2002, the 'Euro' (although not yet in physical form) will gradually be used across these nations in a variety of financial and market transactions with national currencies reduced to mere subdivisions of the Euro. From the first half of 2002, Euro notes and coins will be physically circulated and the national denominations removed from circulation. By July 2002, this new money will have acquired sole legal tender status in the Eurozone economies, covering some 290 million persons. Behind the physical evidence of this 'new money' will lie first experience of a unified European monetary policy. As of January 1999, Eurozone decisions in the key area of monetary policy are being taken by the Governing Council of an independent European

Central Bank (the ECB). This means a unified exchange rate for the Eurozone participants and a single interest rate set by the 'federal' anchor of a new European System of Central Banks (ESCB). According to the EU's former Monetary Commissioner, Yves Thibault de Silguy, this is not just a radical departure for Europe's economies but 'the threshold of an exciting new era'. After decades of doubts, maybes and possibilities, '... Europe [will have] a single currency for the first time since the fall of the Roman Empire' (de Silguy, 1998a).

Discussion on the European business environment in recent years has been much dominated by this venture. The movement towards the Euro has massive political, economic and commercial implications and both public and private actors have had to prepare extensively for the process of economic and monetary unification. As governments in the Eurozone adapt to the currency and to a loss of independent monetary controls, so thousands of companies throughout Europe are calculating and responding to its effects. Those who want to work in Euros before they are compelled to do so have been busy changing their systems and their business strategies. Others, including many small firms outside the Eurozone, are witnessing the reach of Europe's new currency, with some facing demands from larger enterprises for Euro-based billing and invoicing. Citizens on the continent are also seeing prices quoted simultaneously in Euros and familiar denominations (e.g. francs, D-marks, pesetas) with national currencies rendered mere expressions of the Euro.

In the present chapter, efforts are made to examine these changes and to understand the profound political, economic and commercial effects of European Monetary Union. Analysis extends from a chronicle of the EU's journey towards economic union to an assessment of the major implications of EMU for the strategies and operations of commercial enterprises throughout the European economy. While Chapters 8 and 9 provide some amplification of the strategic issues arising from the Euro, this chapter represents the sole dedicated concentration on EMU in this book. The reader is advised that the chapter is best explored following a reading of the preceding chapter on the EU's internal market regime. The positive and negative aspects of EMU (including its implications for business and competition in Europe) are best understood with a basic appreciation of the EU's internal market regime.

European monetary co-operation: a history

The EU's history of monetary integration begins with the establishment, in the 1970s, of a series of formal mechanisms designed to limit exchange rate volatility in the then EEC markets. The advantages of stable exchange rates were identified by European leaders as early as the 1950s but for many years European leaders were happy to participate in the international post-war system of exchange rate co-ordination known as Bretton Woods. This involved a system of cross-rate parities against the US dollar. It was only as this system began to show terminal signs in the late 1960s that European leaders paid attention to the benefits of regional (European) schemes of exchange rate co-ordination and to seriously explore the possibilities of monetary union. There had been no mention of a unified monetary system within the original Rome Treaty but the idea had long circulated among European leaders and technocrats. In March 1970, the ECOFIN Council established the so-called Werner Committee which formalized a number of proposals concerning macroeconomic policy co-operation following on from the so-called Barre Plan of 1969. The Werner Committee Report of October 1970 proposed a managed currency arrangement as a part of a three-staged move to full EMU within ten years. Although this principle was subsequently agreed by the ECOFIN Council in March 1971, the collapse of the Bretton Woods system and the decision of the US Government to float the dollar in August 1971 produced a wave of instability on foreign exchanges. This instability, coupled with internal Community tensions, ended hopes of realizing monetary union according to the Werner Plan. This left in place only the agreed mechanism for exchange rate co-ordination which had originally been perceived as an experimental arrangement. In its first incarnation ('the snake' of 1971) and then as 'the snake in the tunnel' (1972–76) a mechanism was provided for the managed floating of EEC currencies (the 'snake') within narrow margins of fluctuation against the dollar (the 'tunnel'). Although these arrangements promised some exchange rate stability in a turbulent period, weak mutual support mechanisms, continued dollar instability and a rolling oil crisis all contributed to system failures.

The European Monetary System and the birth of the ERM

In 1977, Roy Jenkins, the President of the European Commission, once again raised the issue of macroeconomic policy integration with the EEC Council and called for a zone of monetary stability in Europe. With the backing of German Chancellor Schmidt and French President Giscard d'Estaing, the Commission pushed through complex proposals for exchange rate co-operation based on four assumptions:

1. That currency movements had a destabilizing effect on the economies of member states and that exchange rate volatility was inherently damaging.

2. That the linkage of exchange rates would be beneficial for business confidence and make trade between countries more likely. This would fuel growth and ensure a high level of employment.

3. That a strictly European system was both feasible and preferrable (recalling failed links with the US dollar).

4. That a European exchange rate mechanism (and broader monetary system) had independent merits and did not depend on the ability or choice of the member states to move towards EMU, the idea of which was at least revived.

Consequently, the EMS was set-up with three main elements.

The Ecu

The Ecu (a basket of all the member states' currencies) was introduced as the denominator used for fixing exchange rates and for operations within the system.

It was to be revised from time to time in line with underlying economic criteria on the consent of all the members. Although the Ecu did not exist in note and coin form, Ecu bank accounts were available and the Ecu could therefore be used as an instrument of settlement between monetary authorities, institutions, firms and even individuals. Note that the market values of the Ecu were adopted as the basis of Euro values in 1999 under a simple one-for-one rule.

The Exchange Rate Mechanism (ERM)

The central element of the EMS was to be the ERM. Within this system, each member state's currency enjoyed an exchange rate against the Ecu, called the central rate. A complete grid of bilateral rates was calculated on the basis of these central rates and fluctuations against these had to be contained within tight margins. Prior to August 1993 (when bands were widened to ± 15%), the permitted limits of fluctuation were set at up to ± 2.25% or at ± 6% for high inflation states such as Italy and Spain. Member states were committed to supporting their own currencies within these bands and intervention points would be reached before currencies attained their maximum permissable spreads. The system was thus fairly described as a semi-fixed exchange rate system. The possibility of fluctuations and of formal re-alignments meant that some exchange rate uncertainty remained.

Financial support mechanisms

The EMS also included short- and medium-term credit or financial support mechanisms designed to assist member states with balance of payments difficulties.

The ERM: life and times

For several years, the European monetary system contributed powerfully to exchange rate stability in Europe. Harrison (1995, p. 108) recalls 'a good first decade of existence' with the ERM/EMS largely succeeding 'in establishing (or re-establishing) an island of comparative internal exchange rate stability in a world of currency turmoil'. Equally, there is evidence to suggest that the ERM/EMS provided a framework whereby member states were able to pursue counter-inflationary policies contributory to a sustained period of economic growth. Exchange rate realignments were infrequent and, prior to 1989, inflationary pressures were cooled by the alignment of other member states' monetary policies on those of the Bundesbank (in itself committed to price stability). The Ecu also became established as a significant currency of denomination.

Despite this, the experiences of 1992 and 1993 when speculators 'ram raided' one currency after another, leading to an abandonment of ERM disciplines (see Case Study 4.1), have led to strong criticism of the operation of the ERM. For example, when the system came under its greatest pressure, the assumption that co-ordinated efforts on the part of all member states would be made in order to prevent the 'breaking' of individual currencies proved false with exits for the lira and sterling. In the realignments of 1992 and 1993 very little co-operation and co-ordination was evident. Despite the countries of currencies under attack pushing up interest

---

CASE STUDY 4.1 **The United Kingdom and the Exchange Rate Mechanism: sterling under pressure**

One of the consequences of the derestricted capital movements which accompanied the development of the EMS was that speculators found it easier to put pressure on currencies which they expected to depreciate. The poor performance of the UK (and other countries) during the recession of the early 1990s was the underlying reason why, despite the commitment to stable currencies implied by membership of the ERM, the speculators did not believe that those exchange rate levels were appropriate. Thus, on the days leading up to 16 September 1992, later known as 'Black Wednesday', despite the UK government's attempts to express its commitment to no realignments within the ERM, the speculators continued their relentless selling of sterling. On Wednesday 16 September, UK domestic interest rates were increased by 5% in an attempt to keep sterling within its ERM bands. But, by the end of the day, sterling's ERM membership had been suspended and the value of the currency allowed to float downwards. Over the coming weeks the devaluation of sterling amounted to 20% against the Deutschmark and it emerged that the UK had spent £16 billion in its efforts to 'back the pound'.

Why did the United Kingdom leave the Exchange Rate Mechanism? The power of the speculators and the weakness of the UK government in a new era of derestricted capital movements were the direct triggers for the exit of sterling from the ERM. However, the underlying reasons for that departure were threefold:

1. Undoubtedly, with hindsight, the entry rate of sterling into the ERM in October 1990 (£1.00=DM2.95) was too high. DM2.95 was the market rate at point of entry but this was artificially high because of high domestic interest rates (pulling in foreign investors) as well as the prospect of higher oil prices, because of the Gulf conflict in the second half of 1990.

2. The underlying performance of the UK during the recession had been poor with domestic output falling dramatically, unemployment soaring and UK inflation running at a 5% differential with the average EU rate. Speculators clearly felt that the UK's economic performance would continue to be poor relative to other member states.

3. German interest rates were high as a result of the costs of reunification and, when it came to a decision about whether to lower those interest rates to help maintain the value of sterling and the other currencies under threat, the Bundesbank clearly put domestic considerations before European ones.

After the UK left, interest rates in the UK fell and, by May 1993, the recession had been declared at an end. At that time, there seemed little prospect of the UK rejoining the ERM and the UK government had opted out of signing the Maastricht Chapter on Monetary Union. To this day, the UK has remained distanced from the ERM and uncertain about monetary union.

rates, speculators often pursued their relentless attack on the chosen currency in the certain knowledge that realignment would follow and a large profit would be made. For some, these speculative attacks were assisted by the EU's relaxation of capital controls as a part of the IMP although, in practice, capital markets were already largely derestricted. It is also clear that the relatively poor economic performance of countries such as the UK, Spain, Portugal and Italy meant that a number of central rates were barely sustainable. Were these currencies not overvalued (against the Ecu and D-mark), there would have been no motive for a speculative attack, since the equilibrium value of the exchange rate would not have been outside the ERM bands.

It must be recognized, however, that these experiences cannot be separated from the recession of the early 1990s which affected different member states in different ways, leading to a period of divergence rather than convergence of macroeconomic indicators. Above all else, we should not ignore the way in which the Deutschmark and not the Ecu had become the 'real core of the system', placing undue weight on domestic German monetary policy decisions such as interest rate changes. As Harrison further explains (1995, p. 114):

> While this arrangement provided benefits to the other members in terms of exporting German monetary virtues it did, of course, also have the risk that any German monetary troubles would be exported too. The massive shocks to the German economy resulting from the unification of East and West Germany in 1990 were bound to produce shocks for the European economy as a whole. Specifically, the inflationary effects of German unification led the Bundesbank to raise German interest rates higher . . . simultaneously making the DM a more attractive currency to hold and forcing other European currencies linked through the EMS to maintain the value of their own currencies (at enormous costs to official reserves).

In the autumn of 1993, a more flexible ERM was adopted which involved the introduction of wider bands (± 15%) for all remaining currencies except the German and Dutch currencies which retained a 2.25% margin. Although this meant a serious departure from the principle of fixity of exchange rates, a complete abandonment of the ERM was successfully avoided. Given the ERM's central position in the European Monetary System, this would have placed serious doubts on the ability of Europe to move forward on a now agreed timetable for EMU. The new more flexible ERM also allowed countries to pursue monetary policies which, although less co-ordinated, were, at the same time, better suited to the domestic situations left as a result of the recession in the early 1990s. With the freedom to appreciate and depreciate by as much as 15% either side of the old parities (or, as in the UK, to float freely outside of the mechanism), national banks enjoyed much more discretion to cut interest rates below those of Germany, thus boosting their own domestic economies.

The Italian lira re-entered the Exchange Rate Mechanism in November 1996, following the first arrival into the mechanism of the Finnish markka (October 1996). By the start of 1997 this left only the British, Greek and Swedish currencies still outside of the mechanism. At the Amsterdam Summit of 1997 (16–17 June), the European Council drew up the principal features of a new exchange rate mechanism (ERM II) linking the new 'Euro' to EU currencies not participating in the single currency. This system is now established with central rates set exclusively in terms of the Euro. A relatively wide standard fluctuation band is again in place and unlimited intervention by the ECB is to be available when a currency reaches its floor. However, the ECB reserves the right to suspend intervention when this conflicts with its monetary objectives and to initiate discussions on a re-alignment of a country's central rate. Greece has been a member of the ERM since March 1998 but, at the time of writing, the pound sterling and the Swedish krona remain outside of the system.

Launching EMU: Maastricht and the Delors Plan

Before the tumult in the ERM in 1992–93, the Community's interest in wider monetary policy links had been revived. A plan constructed by Commission President Jacques Delors (the Delors Plan) was unveiled in 1989 in the aftermath of the Single European Act which had itself discreetly recognized some form of monetary unification as being advantageous. This plan, contained in a Commission *Report on Economic and Monetary Union in the European Community* (known as the Delors Report), satisfied all the requirements of a true economic and monetary union for the EU. It led directly to an Intergovernmental Conference (IGC) on monetary union and, eventually, to the EMU provisions of the Treaty on European Union (TEU). In its detail, it outlined a three-stage transition to full EMU with the indissoluble locking of exchange rates leading to the introduction of a common currency. A European Central Bank would make monetary policy for the whole of the EU. This institution would be independent of member governments and would be charged with a statutory obligation to pursue price stability.

The description of the three stages below represents the essential prescriptions of the Delors Report as adopted by the European Council at the Maastricht Summit in December 1991. The date insertions (in parentheses) reflect the actual transition periods to be associated with each of the three EMU stages according to the Maastricht Treaty. On the basis of the Delors Plan, the Maastricht Treaty provided the first effective timetable for European Monetary Union.

EMU Stage 1 (July 1990–31 December 1994)

This required completion of the Internal Market (before 31 December 1992), including the derestriction of capital movements and convergence of economic performance within the member states. Convergence would be fostered by the provision of greater co-ordination of monetary policy between nations and by wholesale participation in the ERM under its narrow bands. The convergence criteria set out in the TEU (Articles 109j and 104c) were as follows:

- Public deficits: budget deficits must be less than 3% of GDP unless higher deficits are temporary or exceptional.
- National debt: public debts must be less than 60% of GDP or should be approaching this reference value at satisfactory speed.
- Price stability: a rate of inflation no more than 1.5% above the average of the three best-performing member states.
- Interest rates: for the previous year, nominal long-term interest rates should be no more than 2.0 percentage points above the average of those of the three best-performing member states in terms of price stability.
- Exchange rates: domestic currency values must have been within the narrow bands of the ERM for two years.

EMU Stage 2 (January 1994– between 1997 and 1999)

In Stage 2, the structure of future EMU would be established in a transitional stage which left macroeconomic policy decisions still with national governments. In the monetary field, a European System of Central Banks would be established (by the end of 1996) to consist of a committee of national central banks and a European Central Bank, the latter being responsible for the future implementation of joint monetary policy. A new European Monetary Institute (EMI) would start the transition to EMU by beginning to co-ordinate independent monetary policies and by preparing for ECB–ESCB set-up. This institution would have to specify the regulatory, organizational and logistical framework for the future ECB and, in conjunction with the Commission and Council, prepare all legislation in relation to the ECB–ESCB and the introduction of the single currency.

Throughout the stage, national monetary policies should be executed in accordance with the general monetary orientations set up for the EU as a whole, and member states should seek to achieve nominal convergence according to the established criteria. A proportion of all foreign exchange reserves would also be pooled and the EMS would be carefully monitored with further facilitation of the use of the Ecu. Technical studies would be conducted into the difficulties involved in replacing domestic currencies with a European currency unit and annual reports would be provided on convergence. During Stage 2, a date would also be set for the beginning of the third stage. If the start date for Stage 3 were not set at a time before the end of 1997 (and this would require a majority of EU states to be ready), then EMU would begin automatically for those countries fulfilling the convergence criteria on 1 January 1999.

EMU Stage 3 (commencing 1999 at latest)

In the final stage of the plan, the ESCB–ECB would take over the control of monetary instruments and manage the technical and regulatory preparations for final transition to a single currency. During this stage we would initially see:

- the irrevocable fixing of conversion rates,
- entry into force of key legislation relating to the common currency unit,
- the definition and execution of common monetary policy *by the ESCB–ECB*, including a new single interest rate,
- the establishment of binding macroeconomic policy rules at EU level,
- conduction of foreign exchange operations in the common currency unit *by the ESCB–ECB*,
- the issue of new public debt in the common currency unit, and
- the pooling of foreign exchange reserves.

Before the conclusion of Stage 3, there would be:

- a complete changeover to the common currency in public administration, and
- a period of dual circulation of the common currency and national notes and coins.

The process should culminate in:

- the final withdrawal of national banknotes and coins, and
- the ascription of sole legal tender status to the new European currency unit (to be later christened the 'Euro').

It should be recorded here that neither the Delors Report nor the Treaty on European Union laid down the practical arrangements for this changeover but merely established the principles and contents of Stages 1–3 along with the overarching aims of monetary union. In this sense, EMU was justified in terms of enhancing the effects of the SEM (and smoothing its operation), delivering lower inflation and greater price stability across the EU, stimulating higher levels of investment and economic growth, and creating a new international currency to represent the EU's combined economic weight.

The changeover to the single currency

Although Stage 3 could have started as early as 1997, this opportunity was passed up by the member states. By the end of 1994, there was no single country which met all the convergence criteria and, with the effects of recession biting hard in borrowing requirements and other poor economic indicators, targets appeared distant. Germany, seen as the cornerstone of the single currency, had no realistic chance of meeting the convergence criteria before 1996 because of the soaring costs of reunification and relatively high inflation. Either serious relaxation of entry tests would be needed or, short of suspending the whole EMU project, the Treaty's provision of a later start date, 1 January 1999, would have to be relied upon. At the Madrid meeting of the European Council (15–16 December 1995) the European Council bowed to the inevitable. The launch of the Euro would be delayed until January 1999 subject to a majority of states meeting the Treaty requirements on economic convergence.

Economic conditions in Greece and policies of self-exclusion (in Denmark, Sweden and the UK) also made it clear that membership would be limited initially to a core of EU states. As early as the Maastricht Summit, Denmark and Britain had signalled their reservations about Stage 3, securing 'opt-outs' in the final terms of the Treaty on European Union.

Readers of this text will be fully aware that Stage 3 of EMU is now well underway and that a series of new dates and timetables apply to the practical introduction of the single currency. In the following analysis, the aim is to highlight these current schedules and to cast further light on those developments leading up to 1 January 1999.

Convergence paths

A number of countries moved closer to the various convergence targets in 1996 and 1997. Fear of exclusion from EMU in January 1999 meant that several member governments redoubled their efforts and help was provided in the form of improved economic conditions throughout the EU. It is also clear that several governments undertook dubious measures or 'accountancy tricks' to satisfy the convergence demands connected to public finances. France Telecom for example handed over future pensions liabilities to state authorities for a one-off payment to government of £4.5 billion. This represented a sizeable reduction in the French government deficit. When decisions were reached on first wave entry in March 1998 (as consistent with the timetable established at Madrid) the situation in eleven member states could be regarded as compatible with the Treaty requirements for Stage 3 entry. On 25 March, the European Commission published a Convergence Report which recommended that these eleven states – Belgium, Germany, Ireland, Italy, the Netherlands, Portugal, Spain, France, Luxembourg, Austria and Finland – should progress to EMU Stage 3 in accordance with the Madrid timetable. On the basis of this recommendation, and that of the EMI, the Council agreed formally that these eleven countries would commence EMU Stage 3 on 1 January 1999. Because they were exercising their opt-outs, it was not necessary for the Commission to assess whether Denmark and the United Kingdom had fulfilled the necessary conditions for the adoption of a single currency. It is nonetheless noteworthy that, given the possible impediment of Britain's earlier ERM exit, both would have done so. By this time too, Sweden had also signalled that it would not be looking to join EMU, the Swedish Krona remaining outside of the ERM.

Figures 4.1–4.4 provide a summary of member state convergence as of 1998 according to the four central criteria on interest rates, price stability, government deficits and public debts. All of the eleven member states eligible for Stage 3 participation on the basis of these criteria had demonstrated reasonable exchange rate

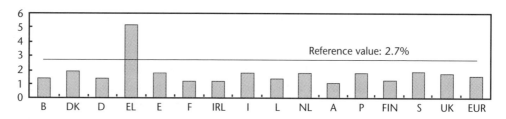

Figure 4.1 Average inflation rate (%), January 1998
Source: European Commission (1998)

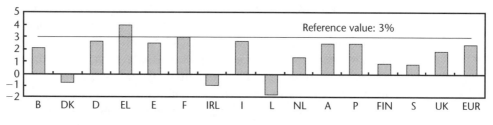

Figure 4.2 Government deficits (% of GDP), 1997
Source: European Commission (1998)

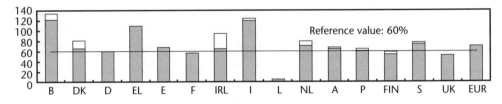

Figure 4.3 Government debt and peak value since 1993 (% of GDP), 1997
Source: European Commission (1998)

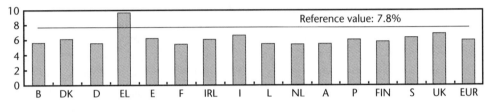

Figure 4.4 Average long-term interest rate (%), January 1998
Source: European Commission (1998)

stability over a two-year reference period and had (with the exception of Finland and Italy) been members of the ERM for at least two years. The performance of the Italian and Finnish currencies since their ERM entries in October–November 1996 inclined the Commission to recommend that any shortfall in months be disregarded. What should be clear from these tables is that the Commission's ability to declare eleven member states 'fit' for Stage 3 required a generous interpretation of EMU's public debt requirement. Only four of the Stage 3 candidates registered public debt ratios at or below the reference value of 60% of GDP (France, Germany, Luxembourg and Finland) and the Commission was therefore led to recommend abrogations for the remaining candidates. The security of this course of action had been provided both by evidence of improved budgetary performance in these countries (levels were approaching the target value) and by the greater concern with convergence and financial discipline over the long term. In this respect, an important step had already been taken at the Dublin Council in December 1996 when the member states agreed the so-called 'Stability and Growth Pact' on post-EMU disciplines. Here, agreement had been established that government debt and deficit levels would have to be preserved over the long term at or below the EMU ratios (60% and 3% of GDP respectively). Failure to do so would open up member governments to the possibility of financial penalties. Moreover, the Maastricht Treaty had always made provision for political judgement about the application of the convergence rules. This, for example, would allow for judgement relating to financial deficits and for excuse of failures to reach target values where temporary or exceptional circumstances applied or where rates were approaching values at reasonable speed.

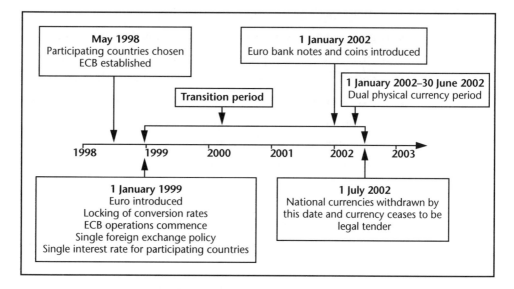

Figure 4.5 Timetable for participating countries
Source: HM Treasury, 1998

The Madrid scenario: practical arrangements

The Madrid Council of December 1995 has already been considered as important for its decision that the third stage of Economic and Monetary Union would commence on 1 January 1999. It was also at this summit that the member states agreed on the title of 'the Euro' for the new European Currency Unit and on a detailed calendar for the completion of EMU. The Madrid changeover scenario envisages a staged transition through three phases (A, B and C) running through May 1998–July 2002 (see Figure 4.5).

Phase A

Preparation (2 May 1998 – 31 December 1998):

■ European Council of Heads of State and Government designate member states to participate in EMU Stage 3

■ the European Central Bank and the network of national central banks are finally established

■ financial and banking sectors finalize changeover preparations

■ businesses accelerate preparation efforts

Phase B

Launch (1 January 1999 – 31 December 2001):

■ conversion rates of participating countries are permanently fixed on 1 January 1999

- establishment of the Euro as EMU currency
- definition and execution of the single monetary policy in Euros
- monetary, capital, foreign exchange and interbank markets converted to Euros
- economic agents may choose to operate either in the Euro or in national currency
- conversion of currencies in and out of the Euro on the basis of triangulation
- voluntary Euro price referencing
- issue of new government debt in Euros
- most consumers continue to deal in national currencies

Phase C

Completion (1 January 2002 – 1 July 2002):

- introduction of Euro notes and coins on 1 January 2002 leading to dual circulation
- withdrawal of national currencies no later than 1 July 2002
- Euro becomes sole legal tender on 1 July 2002
- all participants complete the changeover
- all assets are converted into Euro

It is worth noting here that in phase C (see above) the length of the period of 'dual circulation' will be limited to a maximum of six months. In practice, it will be up to each member state to decide on the exact length of this period within their own country. Germany has already decided that its dual circulation shall be limited to two months.

The Dublin Agreement: towards a legal framework

As a complement to the transition process, the European Council of December 1996 (in Dublin) established a legal framework for the changeover to the Euro. This framework has now been introduced under Council Regulations 1103/97 and 974/98. It is now clear that a 'no compulsion – no prohibition' rule will govern the use of the Euro during phase B of the transition period (1 January 1999–1 January 2002). The 'no prohibition' principle requires that there should be no legal barrier to the use of the Euro unit when all parties to an agreement so decide. At the sime time, the 'no compulsion' principle implies that one party to an agreement cannot unilaterally insist on the use of the Euro unit. With regard to contractual relationships, it is established too that the introduction of the Euro will not have the effect of altering the terms of any legal contract. In other words, there will be continuity of contract with no single party permitted to terminate or to alter a contract on the basis of the shift to the Euro. After 1 January 2002, the performance of contracts denominated in national currency units will be carried out in Euro units using conversion at the official rate (see Box 4.1). It is also established that, during the transitional period, defined legal conversion formulae have to be followed when a company converts monetary amounts from a national currency to the Euro (and vice versa) or from one national currency into another. For example, in transactions involving conversion between more than one national currency, the 'triangulation method' shall apply. This means that in order to convert from French francs to Dutch guilders, you must first convert the francs to Euros and then convert the Euro amount to guilders, all according to precise rounding rules. These issues will be examined further when we address the question of how businesses might prepare for EMU, including that three-year gap between the launch of the Euro (January 1999) and the time when existing banknotes and coins are withdrawn (2002).

BOX 4.1 **Official conversion rates – a primer**

Prior to the launch of phase B (I January 1999) the Commission was obliged to make proposals to the Council for the irrevocable fixing of conversion rates between the Euro and the currencies of the eleven participating member states. These rates were published in the Official Journal on 31 December 1998. For example, 1 Euro was fixed at a value of DEM1.95583 (German marks) and at FRF6.55957 (French francs). The full list of bilateral conversions is as follows:

Currency	Euro rate
Austrian schilling	13.7603
Belgium franc	40.3399
Dutch guilder	2.20371
German mark	1.95583
Finnish markka	5.94573
French franc	6.55957
Irish punt	0.78756
Italian lira	1936.27
Luxembourg franc	40.3399
Portuguese escudo	200.482
Spanish peseta	166.386

All conversions are to six significant digits. Very simply, these values are precisely equivalent and are permanently fixed.

This situation can be contrasted to that prevailing in the UK, Greece, Denmark and Sweden or, for that matter, in any other country outside of the Eurozone. In such cases, bilateral rates against the Euro will continue to appreciate and depreciate. In this sense, the Euro is just another foreign currency. This begs the question as to how these rates were determined. On 2 May 1998, participating member states announced that their currencies' central rates against the Ecu would be the basis for fixing their irrevocable conversion rates against the Euro. In other words, the Euro would replace the Ecu on a one-for-one basis (i.e. 1 Ecu = 1 Euro). It should be clear, however, that the Euro is a true currency in its own right (unlike the earlier Ecu) and that its value depends on no other constituent currency. Its introduction will be completed with the issuing on 1 January 2002 of Euro banknotes and coins. There will be seven Euro-denominated notes (5, 10, 20, 50, 100, 200 and 500 Euro) and eight coins (1, 2, 5, 10, 20 and 50 Euro cents and 1 and 2 Euro coins).

EMU impacts

Economic management

The move towards EMU requires that national governments give up independent control of a separate national currency, exchange rate and interest rate. In practice, each participating state takes a stake in the joint exercise of monetary policy authority (including the fixing of a single interest rate) and adopts a common unit (the Euro) as its official currency. Therefore, nations will lose much of what remains of their economic independence, including important instruments of monetary policy-making. Individual states will no longer be able to use competitive devaluations as a way of enhancing national export performance or lower or raise their own interest rates as and when local conditions require it. For example, when a national economy goes into a recession or inflationary boom not shared by other countries in the EMU zone, its response will rest largely with various fiscal policy tools. Although the single interest rate regime is managed within a European System of Central Banks in which the member state has representation, this rate cannot and will not be set according to the specific demands or requirements of any one member (see Currie, 1997). Moreover, under the combined effects of EMU and the Stability and Growth Pact, the 'independent' fiscal policy powers of individual EMU members will be much diminished. In particular, the Stability and Growth Pact constrains fiscal policy freedoms by setting out fines for deficits in excess of 3% of GDP. Without such a stability pact loose financial discipline in a single member state could force interest rates up for all other members.

These massive implications for economic policy management (and for economic sovereignty) are at the very heart of continuing debate over EMU. However, any assessment of these implications must be considered in the light of the main benefits associated with the move towards EMU and with the exercise of joint monetary authority. It can be argued that common European monetary authority, and a single currency, will make a contribution to a healthier economic environment that inspires greater confidence, growth and wealth creation. A common, sound and independent monetary policy may also contribute to a stable low-inflation environment and facilitate the emergence of conditions necessary for sustained non-inflationary growth throughout the EU. Clearly, the independent policy records of individual member states have been less than impressive and, through EMU, disinflation benefits will be felt in countries that hitherto have not enjoyed the benefits of price stability. A common interest rate regime characterized by low rates of interest will, for many participants, also lead to significant reductions in the traditional costs associated with credit-financing and debt-servicing in the domestic economy. Under the combined effects of EMU and the Stability Pact, pressures are also exerted for fiscal responsibility on the part of member authorities. In turn, progress towards sounder public finances should create scope for tax reductions and should stimulate investment. Reducing government deficits by 1 percentage point in Europe releases an estimated €60 billion a year for investment and consumption (de Silguy, 1998b).

Business operations and functions

In this section, an attempt is made to develop an overview of the main issues for businesses and for business functions as a result of the changeover to the single currency. While this can give us some sense of how enterprises will be effected by the switch to the single currency, it should be recorded that effects will be felt to a greater or lesser degree depending on the size, sector and location of businesses and on the extent of cross-border operations. The greatest impact will be on those enterprises which operate on a transnational basis, which are engaged in commercial relations with such enterprises and/or which have a high export focus. Such firms are also likely to see the clearest benefits in EMU and to find good compensation for their conversion bills.

Main impacts

Foreign exchange

As a consequence of a common currency, Eurozone firms are able to avoid the risk that exchange rate changes might reduce or wipe out the value of their future profits. Exchange rate movements do not necessarily impose a penalty but volatility in exchange markets and/or the unpredictability of rates can play a disruptive and costly role in multi-currency transactions. Many firms have opted to hedge these exchange risks for long-dated transactions and/or have included a margin in their prices to cover adverse exchange rate movements. The costs of hedging alone are estimated to be between 1% and 2% of the sales and purchases of small companies in Europe (AMUE, 1998). Under a single-currency regime, foreign exchange transaction costs are also eliminated on all internal (intra-Eurozone) dealings. Putting these 'gains' together, the suggested benefits are predicted at as much as 8% on the total price of industrial goods (Floyd, 1999, p. 5).

Bigger, more competitive markets

The Euro, by providing a common unit of account for commercial activities, ensures that companies will face a more integrated European market. Cross-border trade and investment will be stimulated and, as such, the forces of competition will be strengthened in many product markets. In particular, businesses who currently see foreign exchange risk and transaction costs as major barriers to cross-border trade are more likely to move into new markets once these 'barriers' are removed. New business start-ups may also be encouraged.

Transparent price differences

With the Euro it will be possible to directly compare prices for the same goods and services in different EUR-11 countries and to spot the best prices. Despite the SEM, substantial price disparities persist as a result of differential pricing policies, differences in tax rates, the costs of transporting products from factories, national market structures, and perceived product values. For example, anyone shopping for an excavator in the EU can end up paying 40% more, depending on where the product is sold (see Marsh, 1999). The ability of consumers to compare prices more easily will tend to move prices towards the lowest market level and it will become harder for businesses to maintain differential pricing policies by country and currency. 'The pressure will be greatest in border regions and for high value goods which are easily transportable' (European Commission, 1997, pp. 20–1).

Lower borrowing costs

As Connor explains (1998, p. 46) 'It is axiomatic that with a single currency and a single central bank that there will be a single interest rate regime across the Community'. In turn, banks will be able to lend in Euros throughout the Community and enterprises will be able to borrow from outside their home countries without incurring the risk of exchange rate exposure. This may provide scope for a reduction in total borrowing costs. Cost savings may be greatest in countries where Euro interest rates fall below previous rates. The introduction of the Euro should also favour the development of new financing methods. Overall, firms should have more choice and flexibility in raising finance and, in many cases, will face lower costs.

Wage transparency

It will now be easier for employees to calculate whether like workers in other countries are offered higher wages and to compare wages with payments made to other employees in different countries but within the same company. This is referred to as 'wage transparency', cutting out the need to convert currencies when comparing wages across markets. Transparency of wage and salary differentials will probably bring salary convergence closer to reality and should, in theory, result in increased labour mobility. However, just as intra-national variations in salary and remuneration exist today, international variations are likely to persist. Although people will ask 'Why are they paid that much over there when I'm paid this much here?', firms can usually demonstrate differences in taxation, benefits, purchasing power etc. by country and currency. Fundamentally, organizations will need to consider how to set fair and competitive remuneration packages in a Euro-denominated environment. Salary denomination issues will also surface during the transition perod.

Treasury and finance

While the complexity of treasury and financial activities may be heightened during the period of transition, for many European businesses the Euro will present opportunities for long-term savings. The Euro will alter balance sheeets, cash flow management, currency management and corporate finance. Among other things, businesses with units operating in different corporate currencies (that is, those different national currencies used for book-keeping and reporting) will eventually be able to record and to compare all accounting values, margins, costs, expenditures etc. in one currency. Such transparency may greatly assist in processes of internal planning, accounting and benchmarking.

Purchasing–procurement

For many firms, the changeover to the Euro will provide significant opportunities in terms of procurement. With the Euro it will be easier to work with suppliers outside of the home market and to identify best options. This raises the prospect of real business savings for those prepared to source on a pan-European basis.

Information technology systems

To be Euro compliant, several systems may need to be adjusted or upgraded. This includes electronic payment systems, budgeting and costing systems, databases and other commercial software packages containing references to financial information. While some systems will have multi-currency capabilities (facilitating the use of two denominations during the transitional period), Euro functionality is unlikely without major changes. Systems and software packages must also conform to EU rules on rounding, conversion and triangulation. IBM Europe has reported changes to over 700 different software applications in its drive towards full Euro compliance (Vowle, 1999, p. 50). This represents over half ($150 billion) of its total Euro conversion budget with over 80% of IT applications affected. The BBC's Euro case study of electronics giant Siemens quotes the company's IT–IS conversion bill at DM100 million ($60 million). With respect to SMEs in a country like Spain, Pardo has estimated that the costs associated with the information systems challenge for firms may be between 0.25% and 1.25% of company turnover.

Extending our analysis here, we may separate the unit-level impact of the Euro into two broad categories (see Figure 4.6). The first such category refers to those effects which will impact on business and marketing environments and will therefore raise a series of *strategic* questions. This directs attention to overarching management strategies and to key business functions such as marketing and procurement. The second class is of those effects at organizational level which raise more practical concerns and which impact upon internal business processes and/or *technical* systems. Alternatively, this directs attention to the Euro's effects on business accounting procedures, contract and payroll arrangements, IT and information systems etc. (see Connor, 1998; FEE, 1998; AMUE, 1998). However, while it is analytically convenient to think in terms of strategic versus practical issues, the effects of the Euro on major business functions will be both strategic and operational in nature. In terms of business and functional strategies, a company must prepare with internal and external focus in order to capitalize on new opportunities and to ensure support of essential business processes. This point is clearly demonstrated in the subsequent focus on the marketing function and on the implications of the Euro for commercial and marketing departments. This concentration should be considered in light of the earlier statements made about the contribution of EMU to the stimulation of trade and competition in many market sectors.

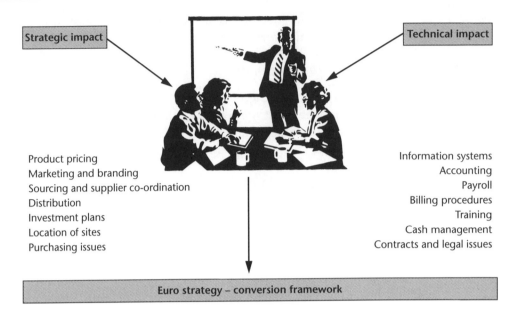

Strategic impact

Technical impact

Product pricing
Marketing and branding
Sourcing and supplier co-ordination
Distribution
Investment plans
Location of sites
Purchasing issues

Information systems
Accounting
Payroll
Billing procedures
Training
Cash management
Contracts and legal issues

Euro strategy – conversion framework

Figure 4.6 The organizational impact of the Euro

The marketing function: implications of the Euro

By eliminating foreign exchange risks and by bringing about price transparency throughout the Eurozone, the Euro will encourage companies to review their marketing and pricing strategies. Strategically, the increase in price transparency between different countries that arises with the Euro is likely to have a significant impact on the prices charged by a business for its goods and services in different markets. With the new currency regime, prices from different companies in different countries will now be transparently comparable in terms of a common unit. This may discourage differential pricing strategies on the part of a single business with a presence in different Euro markets or, in other circumstances, may demand serious pricing action in order to preserve competitiveness. For example, although a PC priced in Deutschmarks and retailed in Stuttgart (Germany) may have always been dearer than its like in Strasbourg (France), short of a price change it is now transparently so. With both the Stuttgart and the Strasbourg outlets marking up their goods in Euros, and with exchange rate risk eliminated, there may be a genuine stimulus for a small business in Baden (Germany) to purchase a stock of computers over the border at the lower market price. There will be no disincentive arising from delivery costs – Baden is only a little nearer to Stuttgart than it is to Strasbourg – and, even where such costs become a factor, the disparity in prices may be so great as to preserve real advantage.

As a general rule, the pressure of price comparability will be to move prices towards the lowest market level and/or to encourage firms to emphasize product differentiation. '[C]ompanies will need to consider the impact of this on their cash flow and profit and loss account' (FEE, 1998, p. 9). Of course, the advent of the Euro coincides with the further development of electronic commerce, mail order, direct marketing, telemarketing and other forms of distance selling. EMU will make it easier to conduct cross-border business through such channels, for example providing price transparency in online purchase research.

The arrival of the Euro raises other issues in connection with pricing, advertising and promotion. For example, important questions arise as to the definition of price points and to the management of conversions. One of the most obvious impacts of the Euro will be the need to convert all prices into the new currency and familiar prices; for instance, 10 million lira will often convert into unfamiliar and unattractive totals (in this case €5,164.57). As a consequence firms must consider the possibility and implications of price rounding or, to achieve an acceptable price point, may have to ask suppliers to alter the way the product is manufactured. Any rounding will have implications for margins. In our example of a converted price of €5,164.57, a rounding-down to a simple and attractive price of 4,999 Euros equates to an effective price reduction of 3.19%. While a higher price of 5,199 would still look good, rounding up could cost the trust of customers and is certain to hit their pockets.

Marketeers and retailers must also consider various pressures relating to the need to establish price lists in Euros and to introduce systems of dual pricing for the transitional period. By 2002, all documentation indicating price references – catalogues, price lists, advertising material etc. – will have to be fully adjusted. Before this time, efforts may be made to undertake the dual display of prices in Euros and national denominations. In advertising, catalogues, shop-floor displays etc., businesses must consider how to incorporate Euro pricing and must decide the extent to which prices will be shown in dual form.

Planning and preparation

As we have seen, the introduction of the Euro will affect the markets, products, linkages, financing and information systems of business firms in many different ways. What a company needs to do will depend on the nature of its business, whether it is based inside or outside the Eurozone, and the extent to which the company trades with enterprises located in Eurozone markets.

If a company is based inside the Eurozone, it must:

- conduct a business impact analysis (identifying the areas which will be affected by the Euro);
- define how it will operate in the Euro environment (during and after the transition period);
- establish a conversion framework–timetable;
- consider budgetary and manpower provisions.

Impact analysis can be conducted with reference to the strategic and practical issues addressed in the previous section. Study may be facilitated by the formation of project groups or project teams encompassing managers from each of the organization's major functions. Meetings with external partners (e.g. suppliers, customers, financiers) could also prove useful in assessing the Euro's potential impacts and firm requirements. At some point a changeover plan–strategy must be defined. This should look to optimize the opportunities resulting from the Euro and to organize an efficient and cost-effective changeover. Encompassed here must be a decision as to when the switchover should be made and to which functions. Essentially, each enterprise has a choice between three approaches:

1. wholesale changeover at the start of the transitional period,

2. partial use of the Euro during the transitional period or

3. big-bang conversion at the end of the transitional period.

If a company chooses the first option, internal business systems are switched over to the Euro at the start of the transitional period. In effect, the business converts to an internal Euro environment while retaining the capability for dealing in national denominations with small suppliers and other economic agents who have not already made the change to the Euro (European Commission, 1997, p. 19). This approach has been witnessed in the case of many MNEs such as Siemens and Philips. In the Philips example, Euro price lists were available from 1 January 1999 and the company was receiving and issuing Euro invoices from this date. Since 1 January 1999, Eurozone intercompany transactions have also been conducted in Euros and financial reporting has been completed in the new currency. In essence, the Euro has been established as the business's functional currency for its Eurozone operations.

If a company choses the second option (partial changeover), some internal tools–activities are progressively switched (e.g. invoicing) but a complete changeover to the Euro is delayed until 1 January 2002. This approach is typical in many SMEs. For example, Gres Catalan (a small ceramics and bricks business in Barcelona, Spain) is looking to steadily increase Euro invoicing (even with countries outside the Euro zone). The company sees that such a move before the 2002 deadline will eliminate many of the costs of operating in and trading with different currencies. The business will not adjust all of its internal systems until the end of the transitional period. In the third approach (delayed changeover), an organization switches to the Euro in a 'big bang' at the very end of the transitional period. This approach is likely to apply where companies have little incentive to use the Euro and/or where commercial relations throughout the transitional period continue to be based on national denominations (European Commission, 1997, p. 19).

Companies may look to use the Euro from an early stage in order to:

- lower transaction costs by trading and invoicing in the Euro,
- access financial services in Euros,
- simplify internal accounting and reporting (by using a single denomination),
- avoid possible resource shortages in 2002 (e.g. in information technology), and
- gain first-mover advantages over rivals.

(see European Commission, 1997)

Companies may look to delay using the Euro until January 2002 owing to:

- a high frequency or volume of cash transactions,
- the cost of developing systems capable of working in two denominations,
- interest in standard changeover packages (which may slowly emerge), and
- rivals, customers or other interlocutors also organizing for a late changeover.

(see European Commission, 1997)

Of course many service companies (e.g. banks and software providers) have been able to position themselves as front-runners in the provision of Euro systems and services. Few companies have benefited as much as the fast-growing German software business, SAP. Its case is examined in Case Study 4.2 and highlights many of the issues raised in this section.

KPMG's detailed work with 307 European companies (KPMG Consulting, 1998) suggests that companies of various nationalities and types are still experiencing difficulties in calculating business impacts and in operationalizing strategies designed to ensure EMU readiness. Although 94% of firms in KPMG's 1998 sample said that they had a strategy for EMU, 40% of companies had still failed to estimated the costs of adaptation and fewer than half of respondents said that their companies had a budget. KPMG's 1998 survey also provides evidence that companies are focusing on the information technology, finance and treasury aspects of EMU to the neglect of external (and strategic issues). As of September 1998, only 12% of the 307 firms surveyed claimed that their EMU strategy covered pricing policy and only 8% said that it covered branding. The result according to KPMG is that the heralded structural effects of EMU, 'affecting everything from price points and packaging to supply chains and the location of workforces and plant' are being weakly addressed. Its 1998 report bemoans '...the impression that companies continue to give is that they are blind to these threats and opportunities' (KPMG Consulting, 1998, foreword). Unsurprisingly, the report highlights a greater level of preparation among EUR-11 firms than among those companies in Scandinavia (where only Finland is a present EMU participant) and in the UK. Company nationality is defined by the location of European headquarters.

Two-tier Europe: life on the outside

Although companies in other EU–EEA markets may experience few of the direct benefits of the Euro, nonetheless effects will be firmly felt on those firms conducting business or aspiring to conduct business with organizations in the Eurozone markets.

First, many firms in EUR-11 markets will be expecting UK exporters (like other 'outsiders') to produce a price list in Euros and, potentially to deal, invoice and take payments in Euros. As Floyd notes (1999, p. 4), firms will need to make the necess-

CASE STUDY 4.2   SAP and the Euro

Few companies have benefited as much from the Euro as SAP, the fast-growing German business software company.

A large part of its empire was built on helping businesses prepare for the changeover to the single currency next year.

'Scared or prepared', ran one of its advertising slogans, as it touted software to help businesses cope with the period between the start of monetary union in January 1999 and when Euro notes and coins are introduced in 2002.

This software allows customers to use the Euro as their main, or house, currency while preserving details of original transactions in whatever currencies they are carried out.

Companies using SAP's system can pay taxes in D-Marks while still working mainly in Euros. They can keep the Euro as their chief currency but still be able to accept 'late' payments in other currencies.

SAP was founded in the early 1970s at Walldorf, near Heidelberg, but is now a true mulitinational with offices around the world. It urges companies to think over the full business ramifactions of the Euro.

One of its selling points is that companies can gain a competitive edge by acting quickly, using its software, in key areas that would be affected by the Euro, including purchasing, administration, logistics, sales, controlling, accounting and finance.

SAP itself will begin reporting its financial accounts in Euros from January next year.

'The Euro is a selling point for our systems', says a spokesman. 'Therefore we have to be a front-runner in providing financial data in Euros as well.'

SAP believes the Euro will have some impact on the prices it charges for its systems across Europe.

'Price differences based on currency differentials will disappear', says the spokesman. 'In general we welcome this since it will make the overall market more transparent. In the long run this will help us to sell more of our products.'

It set up a working party early in 1996 to study the implications of the introduction of the Euro for its 10,000 installations and 400,000 users in Europe.

'We already had some experience of currency reform in Germany, and the currency devaluations of countries such as Poland', says Hans-Joachim Würth, who led the group. 'That required similar procedures.'

After gathering information from customers all over Europe, SAP developed a currency converter package which runs on top of its existing software installations without disturbing the original software.

Companies do not have to switch immediately to the Euro after next year but can continue to work with several currencies for a period.

Businesses can use the time this saves to concentrate on crucial strategic issues that have been thrown up by monetary union, says Mr Würth.

'Right now a lot of businesses are still confused when they talk about converting to the Euro', he says. 'Many are looking at a Big-Bang change-over.'

SAP has looked at the problem clients face in changing their own price lists to the new currency and even their pricing strategy.

'The Euro will change their business strategy and they need the business software to support that', says Mr Würth.

SAP began to run the first 'pilot' Euro conversions last year. 'We found our first willing customers', he adds. 'Our first training classes on how to do the conversion were in December 1997.'

So far SAP has spent around DM10 million on its own preparations for the single currency. In contrast, in developing systems and services to help customers deal with the Euro, Mr Würth estimates that it has spent around DM60 million to date.

SAP is convinced it is worth it.

Source: Financial Times, European Economy Quarterly Review, 30 October 1999

ary investment in computer technology and absorb the related costs. A Barclays bank survey, reported by IBEC, found that one in four British firms have already been asked by customers or suppliers to deal in the Euro from the beginning of 1999 and that 50% of 300 large businesses surveyed expected to be using the Euro by September 1999 (Irish Business Employers Confederation, 1999). Many large companies such as Siemens have invited their UK suppliers to invoice in Euros, and the UK's Northern Development Company has found that many UK suppliers in the North East are already expecting to be billing and invoicing in the currency. This reflects the fact that a large number of purchasers (including inward-investing MNEs) have already switched to the Euro for accounting purposes and for the links that UK companies form in international supply chains.

Second, businesses need to be very aware of the implications of the single currency for their ability to compete in European markets. UK exporters looking to compete for business in countries such as France, Spain and Italy have the disadvantage (relative to their Eurozone competitors) of exchange rate risk exposure, transaction costs and, in all likelihood, higher interest rates. For example, a French company will be able to sell its wares throughout Euroland without any risk of losing money because of the changing value of the franc. A British company, on the other hand, must run an exchange rate risk. If the pound falls in value against the Euro, its goods will become cheaper in France and elsewhere in the EUR-11, while French products will become more expensive here. If the pound is strong (as it has been in 1998 and 1999) UK goods will become more expensive in EUR-11 markets and rival goods from Europe will become cheaper to sterling buyers. Regardless of the direction of currency movements, it will only be the UK company that faces the exchange rate risk and associated costs.

Third, British firms in international supply chains could be supplanted by rivals within the EUR-11 market who share the same currency as their contractor. Although supply and sourcing decisions will continue to be influenced by a wide array of factors, the evidence of such risk is already there. For example, Nestlé Ireland is planning to switch its sourcing from the United Kingdom to the Eurozone because of the cost savings associated with common currency imports.

Equally, a number of factors configure to make EMU a major issue even for those firms uninvolved in cross-border trading in Europe or operating at its margins. First, the Euro will expose a great many to greater competition from market-hungry MNEs. In turn, this could apply severe pressure on local suppliers to reduce their margins. Companies of all shapes and forms should evaluate whether the introduction of the Euro will enhance competition in their home markets and, if so, how they will be affected (AMUE, 1998). Second, countless firms in the UK will be affected if both FDI and the UK financial services 'suffer' as a consequence of the UK's opt-out. As in Sweden, Denmark and Greece, the advent of the Euro adds to existing fears about national competitiveness. As discussed in the next section to this chapter, advocates of EMU have claimed that the Eurozone economies will become more attractive locations for investment, offering lower transaction costs, exchange rate stability and access to cheaper Euro-denominated capital markets.

The UK perspective

It would appear from the preceding analysis that businesses outside of the Eurozone may face a series of competitive disadvantages arising from relative exchange rate risk and higher costs of borrowing. Such concerns have fuelled the debate in Britain about the merits and timing of UK participation, although this debate configures around commercial, constitutional and political arguments. Address of the UK position allows for a clarification of policy options in the United Kingdom and for a presentation of some of the main criticisms of EMU.

The current position

The present position of the UK government is that the conditions need to be right before the UK joins the single currency but that the principle of future membership is established. This follows the UK's opt-out of first-wave entry. Although Labour insiders and senior Cabinet figures have talked up EMU membership, a majority of the UK cabinet have, to date, been persuaded that EMU represents a 'difficult sell' to a sceptical UK public. No single public opinion poll has shown majority support for EMU entry (or anything like it) and the public may even be growing more doubtful as to the merits of the Euro. A poll by Salomon Smith Barney Citibank and Mori in late 1999 showed that 58% of the British public remained opposed to EMU membership and that only 27% proclaimed support for Euro adoption (*Euro Quarterly Review*, *Financial Times*, 10 September 1999). While the Government has been encouraged to 'push' the Euro by many of the UK's leading firms, even the business community has evidenced divisions on the currency issue.

The Blair administration has now set up the prerequisite of measured economic convergence through an assessment of five economic tests. According to government officials, this represents clear support for EMU (and the principle of UK entry) but reflects a reality of underpreparation, divergent business cycles and untested EMU experience.

The five economic tests which have to be met before Britain enters are as follows:

1. business cycles and economic structures in the UK and Euroland would have to be demonstrably compatible;

2. EMU would have to be likely to promote growth and jobs in the UK;

3. there must be evidence of sufficient flexibility in the operation of the stability pact and in Euro-markets to respond to economic shocks;

4. EMU will have to create better conditions for companies to invest in the UK;

5. EMU will have to have a neutral or positive effect on the competitive position of the UK's financial services industry, particularly the City's wholesale markets.

These five tests extend the limited usefulness of the Maastricht convergence criteria and highlight a number of issues for interpretive analysis. The real task here rests with the demonstration of cyclical convergence and, within this, of the capacity of the UK economy to live with Euro interest rates on a permanent basis. For a sustained period, UK interest rates have been higher than long-term continental rates and the initial Euro rate of 3.0% (January 1999) was less than half of that applying in the UK economy at the point of the Euro's launch.

The Blair Government has also made a pledge to hold a referendum on any decision to take Britain into a single currency. Although the timing of any such referendum remains unclear, it is now unlikely to be held until after the next general election which will take place at some point prior to May 2002. Whatever the outcome of that ballot (should it occur), the context of any future referendum on the Euro will be one of deep political division. The official opposition (the UK Conservative Party) has hardened its policy of keeping Britain out of the single currency, in sharp contrast to that of the third force in British politics, the Liberal Democratic Party. The Liberal Democrats remain the most enthusiastic of the British parties for the single currency but have evidenced little unity with the Labour government on the currency question, accusing it of weak leadership. These tensions were exacerbated in early 2000, when Britain's self-exclusion from the Euro (and the high rate of sterling) were cited by senior BMW executives as foremost among their reasons for selling off the Rover car company, its ailing British subsidiary. Indeed, the fact that the pound has been pushed to ever higher levels against the Euro has brought new problems for the UK government. Not only has sterling's dramatic appreciation against the Euro made life difficult for British manufacturers and exporters, fears have been raised that a future fixed conversion rate for sterling against the Euro would be prohibitively high. Depreciation of the Euro against sterling – its value declined by 10% in 1999 from a starting rate of 70.4 pence – also does damage to the assumption that the Euro will be a strong and stable currency. While the Euro may well recover lost ground – in early 2000, it traded at a low-spot of just 60 pence – a falling currency is typically perceived as a weak one.

Of course the focus of Britain's debate has shifted from the academic question of whether a future Euro might replace the pound (like other EU currencies) to the question of whether the established Euro should replace the pound. On this question, British business people, like the public as a whole, are deeply divided. So what are the arguments articulated by the 'pros' and 'antis' and of the commentators and economists on whom they can draw?

The case for joining

The case for joining rests with the economic advantages of EMU and with the competitive and political disadvantages that Britain may face as a consequence of 'staying out'. According to its advocates, the Eurozone, or 'Euroland' as it is sometimes called, will be a zone of economic stability, within which effective business planning can take place and growth be enhanced. Internal price stability, a lower external (Euro) risk premium and lower real interest rates as well as sustained economic growth are all conducive to business efficiency and to efficient business planning. Fixed exchange rates also promise to put an end to the days of currency instability in Europe, eliminating exchange rate risk on cross-border transactions in the EMU core. Were Britain to shun the Euro then it would miss out on these advantages with the gain in competitiveness of the EMU group eroding our own ability to compete. For example, as Eurozone rivals benefit from lower interest rates, taking on larger loans and investing in future technology, borrowing costs for British firms will likely remain higher and their customers will be penalized by higher relative mortgage repayments. Of course, there is no certainty that Euro rates will be lower in the long term but, for the last twenty years, UK rates have averaged 3.5% more than those in Germany. This has put British firms which borrow in sterling at an immediate competitive disadvantage (see Simon, 1997, pp. 7–8). With doubts over Britain's long-term commitment to anti-inflationary disciplines outside of EMU and with the ECB's statutory commitment to low inflation and price stability, Britain could for some time suffer an interest rate premium over Eurozone rates.

Most of these points (greater stability for business planning, lower borrowing costs for businesses and reduced exchange rate risk exposure) have received prior treatment in this chapter and can be grouped with the following 'positive' aspects of Euro changeover raised in unit-level examination:

- reduced transaction costs
- better information on input costs and competitor prices (transparency)
- deeper financial markets and new capital options
- simplified book-keeping and treasury management
- speedier (cross-border) transactions
- scope for pan-Euro marketing, labelling and packaging

Elsewhere, a persuasive case for UK membership of EMU can be built on a number of broader arguments. For example, if Britain stayed outside the Eurozone, seeking to profit from competitive devaluation, its partners might retaliate with protection. If it stayed outside of the Eurozone burdened by an overvalued currency, its export performance would probably suffer. The second of these concerns seems the more relevant at the time of writing with a number of companies (including major foreign investors) warning that their position is being eroded by the pound's strength (see Case Study 4.3). Already, 'a number of large multinationals have pulled out of the (North-East) region including Siemens and Gilette; [and] Toyota has also threatened to pull out of the UK if the UK does not adopt the single currency' (Floyd, 1999, p. 3). Note of the BMW case – with its sell-off and break-up of the Rover car group – has already been made, although it is contestable that the exchange rate was a primary factor in the company's decision to axe Rover.

Another economic concern is that, outside of the Eurozone, the position of the City of London as Europe's premier financial capital might be undermined. Although this claim appears to be have been exaggerated (London has a booming Eurobond market and is performing well outside of the Eurozone), it is to be emphasized that international financial services in Britain employ around 150,000 people, generating approximately £15 billion in annual invisible exports. Any threat to this industry arising from self-exclusion would have to be taken seriously.

Some commentators have also warned that, if Britain shuns the Euro, it will become marginalized from economic policy decisions that will inevitably affect it.

CASE STUDY 4.3 | **Japanese investors give warning over exchange rate difficulties**

Membership of the Euro would reduce exchange rate uncertainty and make it easier for companies to make long-term investment decisions, according to a new report. The report by the National Institute for Economic and Social Research (NIESR), Britain's leading economic think-tank, follows the recent warning by Nissan, the Japanese carmaker, that the strong pound is threatening the future of its plant in Sunderland. It will add to cabinet tension over whether to make a more aggressive case for joining the Euro.

Sterling's strength against the single currency has created acute dilemmas for industry, highlighting the cost of staying out of monetary union. Nissan is not alone. Other big carmakers have said their position is being eroded by the pound's strength and the UK's Invest in Britain Bureau (IBB) has warned of problems ahead for Japanese investors, especially in the electronics sector with warnings of cutbacks at Aiwa and Hitachi in Wales and Toshiba in Plymouth.

Since early May 2000, when the pound hit its highest level in fourteen years on a trade-weighted basis, it has shed 10% of its value against the Euro. But, at DM3.10 (July 2000) the pound is still 40% above where it was four years ago. In part, falling interest rate expectations have driven the exchange rate lower. But the tumble also reflects the rehabilitation of the Euro, until recently the sick man of the foreign exchange markets.

The slide does not lessen Nissan's concerns. Its factory is only now feeling the lagged effects of the pound's recent strength. Also, more worrying than the outright level of sterling are its steep gyrations, which, if continued, will make it difficult to predict future profitability.

Paul Meggyesi, senior economist at Deutsche Bank in London, says the Euro's revival, coupled with the expected narrowing of interest rate differentials between the UK and the Euro-zone, will push sterling even lower. By the end of the year, the pound should have fallen back to below DM3.00, not far from levels considered by industrialists to be sustainable. But this will not mean an end to the problems for the Nissan plant in Sunderland. Exchange rate volatility is unlikely to go away, Mr Meggyesi says. Nissan recognizes this.

While the carmaker did not call directly for Euro membership, or action to weaken the pound, it demanded measures to ensure currency stability.

The NIESR report is definitive. It says that signing up for economic and monetary union is the answer. Joining the Euro, it says, would both reduce exchange rate uncertainty and increase price stability. The effect would be to help companies make long-term investment decisions, fulfilling one of Gordon Brown's economic tests for joining.

Unhappily for Nissan and other pro-Euro businesses, the exchange rate is also a stumbling block to membership. Were Britain to join at the pound's current level, the loss to competitiveness would be severe and lasting.

Moreover, greater stability against the Euro will require convergence between the UK and the Euro-zone economies. Analysts say there is little evidence that business cycles are moving closer together.

All this puts the chancellor in a quandary. Aside from public hostility to the Euro, which makes a campaign in favour of membership politically unpalatable, it is unclear when economic conditions will be right. Until then, complaints from business will grow.

Source: Financial Times, 1 July 2000

For example, when the ECB hikes its interest rates, a Britain outside EMU will find it very hard not to follow suit. This argument is predicated on the likely power and influence in the wider Europe of a common European monetary policy, the ECB taking over from the Bundesbank in this regard. If Britain adopts the Euro, so the logic runs, at least it will have a seat on the board of the European Central Bank and a vote in all its decisions (Palmer, 1997). The UK would also play its part in the Euro (x) Committee of the EU's ECOFIN Council. In similar vein, certain analysts have argued that, irrespective of the economics of the argument, Britain's hopes to play a lead role in the EU, to shape EU agendas and to influence the course of important negotiations may be undermined by the lack of commitment to the EMU project. Wolf makes the point that:

> The EU is not doomed to be an over-regulated, centralised behemoth, though it could turn into one. With its global perspective, stable democracy and liberal traditions, Britain can play a valuable part in preventing it from doing so. That in turn requires participation in EMU. (Wolf, 1997, p. 52)

Staying out: the case for self-exclusion

The basic political argument for retaining our own currency is that adopting the European single currency could prove a decisive step towards turning Britain into a region or province of a federal European order. By complementing the Single Market with a common monetary policy, the EU has taken a further and important step towards a United States of Europe. Most of Europe recognizes the political aim of monetary union and, while this final fate rests with further political decisions, if the UK adopts the single currency there will be further and significant surrender of economic and financial sovereignty. As encapsulated by Jeremy Nieboer (1998), Senior Partner at Gouldens City Solicitors:

> Under the combined effects of EMU and the Stability Pact, which regulates deficits, we will lose our currency, our £; we will lose our fluctuating exchange rate; we will lose control of our interest rates; we will lose the control of our money supply; we will lose our ability to deficit finance (except in very narrow limits); and we will lose our national bank and management control over our national reserves... No nation can be properly regarded as an independent political entity without these rights.

Monetary integration might of course (depending on your perspective) imply a pooling rather than a loss of sovereignty but it should be clear that Eurozone Finance Ministers have to operate within a regime in which a European Central Bank sets monetary policy and in which each member country (subject to tight fiscal constraints) submits its budgetary and other economic plans to a committee off-shoot of the main ECOFIN Council. Contrast this with the UK's present independence. The UK has the freedom to manipulate its own exchange rate as a safety valve in times of depression, to set interest rates in tune with its own domestic conditions and to operate fiscal policies free from external control. There must also be concern that membership of monetary union may put Britain on a path towards higher business taxes which, the IoD argues, constrain companies on the Continent. In the view of such institutions, any erosion of the advantage Britain enjoys through its lower aggregate tax burden constitutes a threat to British orders and jobs. Although such harmonization does not follow inevitably from EMU, cross-border flows of capital are more sensitive to differences in tax in the absence of exchange rate risks. Consequently, EMU may heighten internal EU concerns over tax competition and operate as a driver for future harmonization efforts (see the concluding section to this chapter).

There are of course a number of telling criticisms of the EMU project itself. A single monetary policy conducted for and behalf of a number of states has a fundamental weakness. A 'one size fits all' interest rate is unlikely to be appropriate for all parts of the Union at the same time. Just as a common rate fails to serve the particular needs of bouyant and sluggish regions within a single country, so at any given moment, different EU states would probably benefit from variable rates. For example, in 1999, several EUR-11 countries appeared to require a 2–3% interest rate to stimulate demand (if not an even lower rate) but others such as Ireland, Portugal and Finland appeared to require higher interest rates to slow growth and to stem inflationary booms. Elliott (1997, pp. 31–2) comments that 'even in the hypothetical scenario that the nirvana of fundamental economic convergence could be achieved, there would still be the risk of asymmetric shocks hitting one part of the EU more than others'. Those affected are no longer able to set interest rates or exchange rates in direct response. This would not be so problematic were there a mechanism for transferring resources on an adequate scale from rich to poor regions of the currency zone, but such a mechanism does not exist. The US has a federal tax base that amounts to 25% of GDP and makes extensive compensatory transfers; the EU has one of only 1.4% and cannot. Were it able to do so, this would imply a form of fiscal federalism and a further step towards political union.

Another fundamental challenge is that the characteristics of the Eurozone do not match those of an optimal currency area (OCA). Countries between which there is a high degree of factor mobility are viewed as better candidates for monetary integration since factor mobility provides a substitute for exchange rate flexibility in promoting external adjustment (Mundell, 1961, quoted in Baimbridge et al., 1998). Although factor movement has been greatly stimulated by the SEM, fundamental differences in language, culture, labour regulations etc., impede the sort of (human) factor movement characterizing OCAs and assisting them in responding to asymmetric shocks. Those brandishing OCA theory to highlight the perils of EMU membership issue a stark warning. Where economic divergence cannot be addressed by exchange rate flexibility, where divergence (or shocks) cannot be dealt with by labour mobility, and where there has been no adoption of a redistributive federal fiscal structure, the only remaining alternative is higher unemployment, which will rise as existing differences become exacerbated through cumulative causation. This may have serious consequences for political and social cohesion (quoted in Baimbridge et al., 1998).

Therefore, and looking ahead to possible UK membership, there must several genuine concerns. The first is that a uniform interest rate set in Frankfurt for the whole of Europe will fail to match the rate that would otherwise be set by the Bank of England to take particular account of economic conditions in the UK. Second, even if those conditions were harmonized and totally convergent, there would always be the danger of an asymmetric shock (for example a decline in world oil prices) hitting the UK harder than other Eurozone states. In those circumstances, the possibility of competitive devaluation and/or of unilateral interest rate changes would no longer exist although the UK would still retain flexibility over fiscal policy. Third, any system of fiscal transfers at EU level implies a degree of fiscal federalism and raises concerns over the proportionality of EU funding and the UK 'budgetary burden'.

A number of other arguments against British membership can also be made pointing to the essential differences between the UK and Eurozone economies. Recycling their earlier cautions, Baimbridge *et al.* (1998) characterize this line of thinking when remarking:

> Compared to most EU members, Britain possesses the following characteristics: a lower level of unfunded pensions; a greater volume of high technology exports; a business structure more orientated to services; an economy where income from overseas investment is greater than from manufacturing exports; a relatively small agricultural, and a relatively large gas and oil sector; a system of variable-rate finance that makes owner-occupiers uniquely sensitive to interest rate changes; a currency linked by foreign exchange markets more closely to the US dollar than to any EU currency; and a comparatively sizeable financial sector related to Wall Street and Tokyo rather than to Frankfurt or Paris. These differences are profound, indicating that EMU is unlikely to foster British prosperity.

Picking out some of the different concerns here, the UK is particularly sensitive to interest rate changes as a consequence of its high level of variable-rate mortgage debt. It is also the case that the UK trading cycle is closer to that of the United States and that the cycle of sterling is closer to that of the dollar. With reference to convergence between UK and European business cycles, the HM Treasury (1997, p. 17) reports:

> Our economic cycle is not in line with others. Although there should be some convergence, it is not yet safe to assume that it will be sufficient for some time . . . for the time being, the UK cycle remains closer to that of the United States.

Membership of EMU may also be problematic in the light of divergent approaches to pensions financing. Currently, continental European states pay the overwhelming proportion of pensions and, by and large, these are not provided for on a funded basis. Our pension provision is not state bound and future unfunded liabilities are only a fraction of those of our continental partners (generally in excess of 100% of GDP). There are concerns, therefore, that that EMU entry may open up the UK tax-payer to future financing of continental pension liabilities. This argument has a natural attraction to Eurosceptics although in truth the Maastricht Treaty stipulates the non-transferability of pensions liabilities.

Continuing this emphasis on divergence, it may also be argued that EMU is inappropriate for Britain's pattern of international trade. We are clearly less dependent on EU trade than any other country, with only half of our visible and invisible trade conducted with other EU economies. That is a lower figure than almost any other country. Consequently, the trumpeted savings arising from exchange rate fixity are not going to be so significant for us as for other EU countries and the pay-back on the massive conversion costs involved in making British firms 'Eurofunctional' will not be so great. The British Retail Consortium estimates that the retail sector, with its costs of labelling, its training, its tills and its software, will suffer a cost alone of up to £3.5 billion (Nieboer, 1998). There may also be a concern that the single currency area (characterized by very different labour conditions to those prevailing in the UK) could find itself blighted by high employment. In the absence of strong cyclical growth, the conditions for high employment within Euroland simply do not exist. First, some Euroland labour markets are characterized by inflexible labour systems, high social and wage costs (see Chapter 6). Second, the task of the ECB is to promote the control of inflation above all other objectives including growth and jobs. It may therefore fail to look beyond the issue of price stability and to consider the social and political effects of the tight monetary policy to which it is committed. All of these arguments should be given consideration in assessing the merits of UK entry.

Finally, here, a different kind of point might also attract our attention. The ECB is governed by bankers independent of national governments and the Community institutions. If Britain were to accept the Euro then it would have to embrace the idea of independent ECB governance. Although the Governor of the Bank of England would sit in the Governing Council of the European Central Bank, the UK government would have no direct hand in its monetary policy decisions. Furthermore, the ECB is hardly an open or transparent institution. Its Council meetings are held behind closed doors, and neither its minutes or voting records are published.

All of these arguments, therefore, raise serious doubts about the wisdom and purported benefits of UK EMU entry. UK campaign groups such as Business for Sterling, present these and other arguments as a part of their case for 'keeping the pound' and for rejecting the Euro.

EMU and EU tax harmonization

As is clear from the terms of 'the British Debate' one important question is the extent to which monetary union will lead to tax harmonization in the EU. As considered, any collectivization of fiscal policy, which is the balance of government revenue through taxation and government expenditure, implies a further strengthening of political union and the possibility of higher (standardized) tax rates. At present, the EU has little control over tax policies with national governments retaining broad control (subject to some harmonization) of sales taxes, excise duties, income and corporation taxes. Such freedoms contribute to varying average tax levels – from 36% of GDP in the UK to around 60% in Denmark and Sweden – and to a patchwork of tax measures and treatments.

With respect to taxation, it is possible to establish a solid argument that differentials in taxes (especially those applying to sales and profits) provide the basis for internal 'tax competition'. Tax competition means competing for a larger share of productivity, markets and investment by cutting tax rates. In a context of derestricted capital movements, inward investment may be lured by lower taxes on corporate profits and, in the absence of agreed minima, there may be a spiral down to ever-lower levels. Consequently, given that cross-border flows of capital are more sensitive to differences in tax in the absence of exchange rate risks, EMU may be predicted to accentuate tax competition in the Single Market. Already since 1996, the average corporate tax rate in the EU has been reduced by about 3% to 36% (KPMG International, 1999). An apparent stimulus to EU initiatives on tax harmonization is therefore unsurprising although it is probably erroneous to claim that the averaging out or banding of rates is an inevitable consequence of a single currency. As Hawksworth and Cussons (1999, p. 9) contend this is not the case either in theory or in practice:

> From a theoretical perspective, complete tax harmonisation across a group of countries would be inevitable only if companies were completely mobile and there were no other differentiating factors between these countries. In fact, it is costly to relocate existing companies and tax is only one of many factors influencing investment location decisions. This view is confirmed by practical experience in countries with federal structures such as the U.S., Canada, Switzerland and even Germany; this shows that there is still considerable scope for state and local governments to vary corporate tax rates within a single currency zone.

Although evidence is unclear at time of writing, EU initiatives on tax harmonization do appear fairly active. Currently being debated by EU finance ministers are measures to eliminate distortions in the taxation of capital income, measures to eliminate withholding taxes on cross-border interest and royalty payments, and measures to regulate the use of preferential tax regimes. It is worth stating here that the EU already operates a system of harmonized VAT rates (see Chaper 3) and has three significant directives with important tax implications: the Mutual Assistance Directive, the Parent/Subsidiary Directive and the Merger Directive (see Hawksworth and Cussons, 1999, p. 10).

A number of other recent developments are also noteworthy. First, it is clear that the Commission remains committed to setting up a definitive VAT system with standardized rates. The status of its VAT Committee was upgraded in early 1998. Second, the EU states signed a code of conduct pledging action on harmful tax competition in the ECOFIN Council in December 1997. This has led to the formation of a Code of Conduct Working Group on harmful tax competition along with a number of EU subcommittees focused on various tax issues. The Code of Conduct on Business Taxation requests member states to adopt certain principles and empowers them to 'discuss the tax measures of other member states and to evaluate whether they are harmful'. Member states can then be asked to amend taxes with a view to eliminating any harmful measures. The number of measures now being raised in the Code of Conduct Working Group appears to be growing rapidly.

Third, the Commission appears to be using indirect methods of enforcing harmonization, such as the application of articles of the Treaty on state aids, to bring about corporate tax convergence. This has already happened with Ireland's special 10% tax (applying to manufacturers locating in designated enterprise zones) judged in contravention of EU rules on state aids. Ireland has been forced to abandon this 10% rate (Ireland's top corporate tax rate is 36%) and to apply, by 2003, a 12.5% corporation tax rate on almost all trading activity. A limited number of projects specified on a list agreed with the Commission will be entitled to the 10% tax rate until the end of 2005 or 2010.

It is also clear that support of tax harmonization has been growing in certain member states. For example, the Austrians and Germans stamped their six-month presidencies of the European Union (1998–99) with calls for future EU tax harmonization. Although controversial German Finance Minister Oskar Lafontaine was ousted from his post in early 1999, others in German and EU politics have taken up the cause of wider tax harmonization and have championed the case of qualified majority voting on tax issues in the European Council.

The scope for fiscal harmonization in the EU is, however, limited by a number of factors.

First, businesses tend to like diversity, 'in that they can then pick the regimes that suit them' (see Cussons, 1999). Consequently, it is improbable that concerted pressure for harmonization of tax rates will extend from the business community despite the fact that businesses may benefit from the elimination of discriminatory tax measures.

Second, the EU involves the harmonization of developed countries with diverse and complicated tax and fiscal systems. This complexity is growing and wide disparities exist in the effective rates of taxation in the member states. These apply to both direct taxes such as corporation rates and to indirect taxes such as sales duties. For example, although standard VAT rates only range from 15% in Luxembourg to 25% in Sweden (see Table 4.1), sales tax rates for all goods actually vary from 1% to 38% when account is made of reduced and super-reduced rates applying to specific items. Corporate tax rates also show a significant range with the UK having a much lower headline rate than the likes of Germany and France (see Table 4.1).

Third, tax harmonization impacts on the very foundations of a government's control and management of its economy. The harmonization procedure upsets the status quo and is likely to face serious political obstacles. This can be demonstrated in the past rejection of Commission plans for VAT standardization and, more recently, in the tortured progress of the so-called 'Savings Directive'. This proposes a minimum 20% withholding tax on gains made by individuals in another EU member state and is being flatly opposed by the UK government.

Finally, and of huge significance here, tax harmonization measures continue to require the unanimous approval of all member states. As Cussons (1999) puts it, 'Under the Treaty of Rome and the Maastricht Treaty (and now Amsterdam), tax is one of the few remaining areas where one of the 15 member states can actually stop the whole show by just saying "no, I won't agree to that measure"'. If, as some have argued, tax issues were able to be decided under QMV then the prospect of far-reaching tax harmonization would be much greater.

Table 4.1 Tax rates in Euopean Union member states

Country	Standard sales tax rate (1 May 2000)	Corporate income tax rate (1 January 1999)	
Austria	20.0	34.0	
Belgium	21.0	40.17	
Denmark	25.0	32.00	
Finland	22.0	28.00	
France	19.6	40.00	
Germany	16.0	52.31 (retained profits)	43.60 (distributed profits)
Greece	18.0	35.00 (listed)	40.00 (limited liability)
Ireland	21.0	28.00	
Italy	20.0	41.25	
Luxembourg	15.0	37.45	
Netherlands	17.5	35.00	
Portugal	17.0	37.40	
Spain	16.0	35.00	
Sweden	25.0	28.00	
United Kingdom	17.5	31.00	

Note: Corporation taxes are calculated taking account of standard corporate income taxes and effective municipal taxes. A simple comparison of tax rates is of limited value given variations in the coverage of corporate taxation and in the nature of deductions and rate depreciations. The relative tax burdens imposed by different governments range from 1.4% of GDP in Germany to 4.0% in Italy. EU states apply reduced and super-reduced VAT rates on certain items.
Source: European Commission; KPMG

Conclusion

The logic and rationale of EMU is that common European monetary authority and a single currency will contribute to a healthy economic environment that inspires confidence, growth and wealth creation. According to its advocates, EMU should deliver greater price stability, lower interest rates and lead to the release of investment capital across the Union. Although the theoretical claims behind such claims are at least contestable, Europe places great store by these positive effects and expects a major impact on business and competition as a result. Business in Europe is making solid preparation (including many UK firms) and despite the complexities of a three-year transition, undertakings are beginning to see the benefit of conducting trade in a single currency. What is still uncertain, however, is the degree to which other areas of policy will be harmonized, particularly on the tax and fiscal side, and whether or not the Eurozone will perform under the fiscal constraints of EMU. Concerns also endure that EMU will prove unsustainable in the absence of further economic convergence and that the limitations of a 'one-size-fits-all' interest rate will be fatally exposed. The fate of the Euro against other major currencies is also unclear. Europe's new currency unit has been surprisingly weak in its first year-and-a-half with a dramatic 20% decline in value against the rival US dollar. Although its strength (and stability) should improve with the betterment of economic conditions in the more sluggish Eurozone markets there is much ground to recover. One way in which EMU might also gain strength and credibility is through the delayed entry of those countries (the UK, Sweden, Denmark and Greece) excluded or self-excluded from 'first-wave' entry. The Euro will represent a heavier monetary mass with these countries in, with its market extended by another 85 million consumers. However, the recent decision by the Danish people not to apply for the adoption of the Euro as their currency (September 2000) leaves only Greece as a confirmed future entrant.

For all of these variables, it is entirely clear that the introduction of the Euro represents a momentous change for Europe's business environment and a critical step towards economic union. In Chapters 8 and 9 further discussion will be made of this change with attention turned again to the strategic implications of the Euro and to marketing in a single currency area. This analysis should provide a useful complement to the form and nature of study provided in the present chapter.

Review questions for Chapter 4

1. What is the difference between a system of fixed exchange rates and the European monetary systems initiated in the 1970s?

2. What factors contributed to the crisis in the ERM in 1992–93? What has happened to the system since this time?

3. What are the key objectives of European Monetary Union?

4. In what sense do monetary unions involve the centralization of economic policy-making?

5. What is the difference between monetary and fiscal policy-making?

6. Do you consider that European Monetary Union involves a loss of sovereignty for member states?

7. The introduction of the Euro is associated with a three-year transition period. Can you explain the stages and timetables attaching to this period? Why do you think a staged transition has been chosen?

8. How might a single currency be of advantage to businesses in Europe?

9. What are some of the strategic and technical challenges presented to undertakings by the introduction of the Euro?

10. Identify five key arguments for and against the UK adopting the Euro.

11. What is the UK Government's current position on EMU?

12. What do you think are the advantages and disadvantages of a national referendum on the Euro?

13. What are some of the difficulties in achieving a greater harmonization of sales and business taxation in Europe?

14. Do you consider complete monetary and fiscal harmonization to be possible without political unification?

Web guide

See also Web guide for Chapter 2.

Institutions and authorities

EUROPA: Euro entry site @ http://europa.eu.int/euro/html/home5.html?lang=5

EUROPA: Euro Links (the institutions and member state authorities) @ http://europa.eu.int/euro/html/liens5.html?lang=5#group0

The European Central Bank (ECB) @ http://www.ecb.int/

The Bank of England on EMU @ http://www.bankofengland.co.uk/publica.htm#europe

Deutsche Bundesbank on EMU @ http://www.bundesbank.de/en/presse/wwu/eurokommt.htm

News and developments

FT Euro: European Economic and Monetary Union (registration required) @ http://www.ft.com/emu/

EU Business News: Economic and Monetary Union @ http://www.eubusiness.com/emu/index.htm

BBC News: the Euro @ http://news.bbc.co.uk/hi/english/events/the_launch_of_emu/euro_home/default.htm

Transition aspects

Association for the Monetary Union of Europe (AMUE) @ http://amue.lf.net/

Federation des Experts Comptables Européens (FEE) @ http://www.euro.fee.be/

References

AMUE (1998) Euro preparation guide for companies (online). (http://amue.lf.net/business/sme/english/smeindx.htm).

Baimbridge, M. Burkitt, B. and Whyman, P. (1998) Is Europe ready for EMU? Theory, evidence and consequences, *Bruges Group Occasional Papers*, no. 30.

Bishop, G. (1997) How EMU would strengthen the City of London, in *Britain and EMU: The Case for Joining*, Centre for European Reform (CER), London.

Connor, T. (1998) The single European currency – implications for business units, *European Business Review*, **98**(1), 45–50.

Currie, D. (1997) *The Pros and Cons of EMU*, Economist Intelligence Unit.

Cussons, P. (1999) PriceWaterhouseCoopers European economic outlook: harmonization questions (online) (http://www.pwcglobal.com/gx/eng/ins-sol/spec-int/eeo/eeo-harmonisation.html).

de Silguy, Y.T. (1998a) EMU and Business in the UK, Speech presented at the 5th EuroWirral Conference, 13 November 1998 (online) (http://europa.eu.int/euro/html/page-dossier5.html?dossier=215&lang=5&page=1&nav=5).

de Silguy, Y.T. (1998b) The Euro, vital complement to the Single Market, Speech presented at the French Chamber of Commerce in Great Britain, London, 26 November 1998 (online) (http://europa.eu.int/rapid/start/cgi/guesten.ksh?p_action.gettxt=gt&doc=SPEECH/98/265|0|AGED&lg=EN).

Elliott, L. (1997) The case for staying out, in, Kettle, M. *et al.*, *The Single Currency. Should Britain Join?*, Vintage/Guardian Press.

European Commission (1997) *EMU and the Euro: How Enterprises Could Approach the Changeover*, Office for Official Publications of the European Communities.

European Commission (1998) *Convergence Report 1998*, 25 March 1998, Brussels.

FEE (1998) *The Euro: Changing Your Information Systems*, Fédération des Experts Comptables Européens, Brussels.

Floyd, D. (1999) Life outside the Euro: is the UK really losing out?, *Journal of European Business Education*, **8**(2), 1–11.

Harrison, D.M. (1995) *The Organisation of Europe: Developing a Continental Market Order*, Routledge.

Hawksworth, J. and Cussons, P. (1999) Business tax harmonisation in the EU, *The Tax Journal*, **505**, 21 June 1999, 7–10.

HM Treasury (1997) *UK Membership of the Single Currency: An Assessment of the Five Economic Tests, October 1997*.

Irish Business Employers Confederation (1990) EMU: frequently asked questions (online) (http://www.ibec.ie/euro/faqs/index.htm#Q).

Johnson, C. (1996) *In with the Euro, Out with the Pound*, Penguin.

KPMG Consulting (1998) *Europe's Preparedness for EMU: Economic and Monetary Union Research Report 1998*, KPMG.

KPMG International (1999) *KPMG Corporate Tax Rate Survey – January 1999*, KPMG International Tax Office.

Marsh, P. (1999) Price is right for most companies despite the Euro: single currency has yet to make an impact and differences across the Continent remain, *Financial Times*, 4 August 1999.

Mundell, R.A. (1961) A theory of optimal currency areas, *American Economic Review*, **53**(1), 657–64.

Nieboer, J. (1998) A Speech to the Political Action Group for Europe, 23 May 1998, *Bruges Group Papers*.

Palmer, J. (1997) The case for joining, in Kettle, M. *et al.*, *The Single Currency: Should Britain Join?*, Vintage/Guardian Press.

Piggott, J. and Cook, M. (1999) *International Business Economics: A European Perspective*, Longman.

Simon, D. (1997) EMU, the route to a confident, competitive Britain, in *Britain and EMU: The Case for Joining*, Centre for European Reform.

Vowle, J. (1999) We've all got big blues over the Euro – IBM faces euro conversion issues, *Computer Weekly*, **50**, 1 July 1999.

Wolf, M. (1997) The danger of dithering, in *Britain and EMU: The Case for Joining*, Centre for European Reform.

5 Competition, aid and industry: EU policy action

Central themes

- Competition policy and the Single Market
- Concerted practices
- Abuse of dominance
- Concentrations and European merger control
- Regulating state aid at EU level
- Regional aid and structural assistance
- EU cohesion policy
- Common policies for European industry
- Backing research and technological development
- Fostering enterprise
- Competition and industrial policies: challenges and relationships
- Future action

Introduction

Chapters 3 and 4 examined the moves towards the creation of a Single Market in Europe and how the process of monetary unification is evolving as a means and method of strengthening the internal market regime. What should be clear, however, is that, to operate efficiently and smoothly, the Single Market requires effective national and transnational competition rules. Without such frameworks, the EU economies would be undermined by private and public barriers to trade and the role of competition in the Single Market would be much diminished.

The purpose of this chapter is to examine the defence and facilitation of the Single Market by EU competition rules and to explore the contribution made by EU legislation to the development and freedoms of industry and enterprise in the new European marketplace. Analysis extends to the significant interlinkages between the

EU's policies on competition, industrial and regional development. While these policies can be addressed separately, it is clear that state assistance to regions and to industry within EU states can distort or threaten to distort competition in the Single Market as a whole. Indeed, the competition articles of the Community Treaty prohibit many forms of state assistance while establishing conditions under which specific aids may be granted.

EU competition policy: defending and facilitating the Single Market

There is little benefit in removing tariff and non-tariff barriers to internal trade if firms are then faced with restrictive practices or with other anti-competitive activities permitted by the absence of effective anti-trust rules. Accordingly, the EU has looked to tackle private and public barriers to competition through regulation and the construction of a broad legal framework. It has established legally binding rules and obligations in order to:

- *Prevent firms from colluding by price-fixing, cartels and other collaborative strategies.* This is in order to stimulate competition and to prevent oligopolists from behaving in a quasi-monopolistic way.

- *Prevent firms from abusing positions of market dominance.* That is, to control such actions as monopoly pricing, discriminatory pricing and fidelity rebates, which can do damage to competition and to consumers.

- *Control the size to which firms grow through acquisition and merger.* This is aimed at ensuring that acquisitions do not seriously (and adversely) effect competition within defined markets and at preventing monopolies from reaping supernormal profits.

- *Restrict state aid to indigenous firms.* This is aimed at limiting the competitive advantages gained by 'supported' firms over unsupported counterparts and at ensuring that firms are not shielded from the real competitive pressures bearing on their markets.

In satisfying these aims, the EU (through its executive arm, the European Commission) can be said to have 'a double mandate'. On the one hand, it must work alongside national competition authorities in ensuring that restrictive and anti-competitive practices are forbidden and to prevent the formation of EU-wide or regional oligopolies that impede competition and penalize consumers. On the other hand, its actions must reflect the realities of global competition and the need for Europe to possess larger, cross-border undertakings in order to compete in global markets. This is just one of the challenges posed in framing EU competition policy and requires a policy of sufficient flexibility (see Story, 1996, p. 277).

In legal terms, the basis of this policy rests with Articles 81–89 of the Community Treaty and with the European Merger Control Regulation, no. 4064/89 (as modified by Regulation no. 1310/97). These instruments forbid a number of measures and practices that impair competition within the Common Market and which distort intra-Community trade. Anti-trust rules, associated primarily with Articles 81 and 82, have been in operation since 1962. These have provided Commission jurisdiction over national and international anti-trust concerns where there is a distortion in competition in the Common (or Internal) Market. As considered, tasks encompass the policing and regulation of concerted practices undertaken by commercial entities (Article 81) and the abuse of dominant trading positions (Article 82). The EU's Merger Control Regulation has been in place since 1990. This provides an important complement to Articles 81 and 82 and gives the Commission specific power to police mergers and the acquisition of more market share by undertakings where there is evidence of a Community dimension. An undertaking is defined as any entity engaged in commercial activity regardless of its legal form, ownership and the way in which it is financed. Articles 87–89 constrain the flow of public capital to domestic industries. The Treaty assumes in Article 87 that any aid granted by a state or through state resources in any form shall be incompatible with the Common Market if it distorts or threatens to distort cross-border competition. This does not preclude all categories of state assistance to indigenous firms – state aid granted for specific purposes may be compatible with the Common Market – but imposes clear controls on the support of domestic industry by public authorities in each of the member states.

Competition, free markets and efficiency

Although it is tempting to move directly to these legal instruments, an examination of the EU's anti-trust rules and performance is best oriented around an understanding of competition itself. Welfare economics suggests that competition is 'good' and, in the neo-classical view, competition is seen to promote an optimal distribution of resources in society. The existence of many buyers and sellers, efforts at profit maximization by independent firms and the absence of barriers to the movement of goods or factors of production, are all assumed to make positive contribution to the effective functioning of the market. The Austrian and Chicago Schools have taken a more tolerant view of monopoly power (arising when there are serious imperfections in the market) but competition has remained the prevailing ideal of Western society and economy. As Burke *et al.* put it (1991, p. 8): 'people in business usually subscribe, both intellectually and financially, to an ideology of competition'.

Market structures

In actuality, economic theory distinguishes between four main types of market structure, suggesting how firms behave differently under different competitive forces. These four market structures are:

- perfect competition
- monopolistic competition

- oligopoly

- monopoly

Perfect competition

Perfect competition, as an ideal market structure, provides a yardstick against which to judge the nature and efficiency of other market forms. Given that 'perfectly' competitive markets have (1) many buyers and sellers (who cannot fix prices), (2) no entry or exit barriers, (3) a homogenous product, (4) complete information, and (5) firms acting independently of one another (and seeking to profit maximize), the satisfaction of its full condition is nigh impossible. Only in a small number of markets, for example for commodity products such as eggs, rice or wheat, is there any approximation of these conditions. These products will sell on a market based on their comparative costs and are essentially undifferentiated. Prices are only distorted by variance in transport costs and by forms of government intervention (e.g. in the form of price supports).

Monopolistic competition

Monopolistic competition is the name given by economists to that form of imperfect competition that takes place between competitive companies supplying similar but differentiated (non-identical) products. Competition applies to price, product quality, labelling, advertising and promotion. Here then, the concept of branding emerges as a core feature of competition. Unlike perfect competition, each good is slightly different in composition and/or brand image. Markets of this type are expected to consist of a large number of firms entering and exiting the market with a good measure of freedom. A number of European markets for consumer and electrical goods are of this type.

Oligopoly

Under oligopoly a smaller number of larger firms enjoy a greater degree of market power and there is no longer complete freedom of entry into the industry. Under these conditions, firms may be inclined to collude (e.g. to fix prices or output) and may progress to do so, especially where public policy controls are weak or absent. Even in the absence of such collusion, the predominant concerns of firms are with the actual and potential actions of others, with the threat of new entrants, and with the risk of substitutes. Firms are interdependent in the sense that alterations to output or pricing by one in the industry will induce a response from the others. Therefore, although price leadership is possible, oligopolists tend to eschew aggressive price competition and rely heavily on product innovation, differentiation, branding and advertising. The European automobile industry (dominated by a small number of high-volume manufacturers) provides example of oligopolistic competition in Europe, as do the European aerospace, paper and pulp industries.

Monopoly

Monopoly provides the opposite extreme to perfect competition. Only one firm (or a group acting as one) is producing in the market, exercising substantial or total control over market supply. Entry barriers are high – causing other firms to remain outside of the industry – and supernormal profits may exist to be exploited from a protected position. Several monopolies have characterized the European business environment over the last twenty years, although their number has been greatly reduced by processes of market deregulation and privatization. Most, like Deutsche Telekom (prior to 1998), have encompassed governmental control of the business and protection by refusal to grant licences to other potential suppliers, capital requirements, patent rights etc. According to welfare economics, monopolies are 'bad' be they in the public or private sectors in that they result in a higher price charged and lower output produced than under perfect competition. Monopolies also tend to be less efficient. With state-owned examples in particular, X-inefficiency can be significant, a factor prompting several European nations to embark on wide-ranging privatization programmes in the 1980s and 1990s.

The theoretical comparison of a firm facing no competition (a monopolist) and a firm operating in a perfectly competitive market is shown in Figure 5.1. Perfect competition dictates that the price for the industry (and thus for the firm) is determined by the intersection of the supply curve (which is also the marginal cost curve) and demand (which equates with average revenue) and is shown as P_0 in Figure 5.1. If, however, the industry were to be taken over by a single firm (a monopolist) and costs and demand are initially unchanged, the marginal revenue curve for the industry must lie within the original average revenue (demand curve). Thus the price charged by the profit-maximizing monopolist is P_m, higher than under perfect competition, and the output Q_m lower than under competitive conditions. The monopolist therefore charges higher prices to the market and has no incentive to increase levels of output. Equally, there is no incentive to reduce costs and promote internal efficiency to raise price/cost margins as the firm is already earning super-

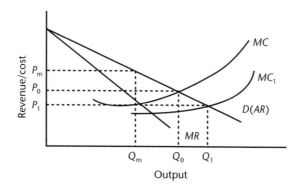

Figure 5.1 Perfect competition versus pure monopoly

normal profits. In reality, the price charged by the monopolist may or may not be higher than under perfectly competitive conditions. Much depends on whether or not the monopolist benefits from economies of scale. Where they do, the marginal cost curve moves to MC_1 and the price charged would be lower than under perfect competition.

Within the EU, the only firms that could feasibly be considered as perfect monopolies are the enduring nationalized industries. These firms, often regarded as political policy instruments, are renowned for their inefficiency. Diseconomies of scale, bureaucratic systems and poor management by civil servants rather than trained business people have all been cited as factors resulting in poor productivity, profits and overpriced goods and services. Such X-inefficiency (the gap between actual costs and those theoretically attainable) is often postulated as a problem specifically associated with large nationalized organizations. Overcoming these problems, however, is not merely a question of privatization. Turning public monopolies into privately owned monopolies is likely to be more detrimental than beneficial to the public good. Private monopolies unlike their public counterparts are not compelled to provide goods and services which are unprofitable and without some form of compulsion by regulation, may fail to do so.

Where the industry is characterized by a large number of small players, that is competition is imperfect (monopolistic), firms face a downward-sloping demand curve (see Figure 5.2) as products are differentiated from their competitors' and thus not complete substitutes. The small scale of firms also means limited scope for generating scale economies in production. The industry demand curve reflects total demand for industry output at all prices assuming all firms in the industry charge that price. An increase in the number of firms in the industry will shift the demand curve for each firm to the left as market share falls. Thus, in the EU, as new entrants are encouraged to enter markets and stimulate competition, demand for each individual firm will fall along with their corresponding level of market share.

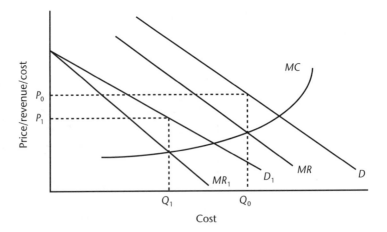

Figure 5.2 Imperfect competition versus new entry

In Figure 5.2, the firm's marginal revenue curve is shown as MR, its marginal cost curve MC and its demand curve D. As the firm is a profit maximizer it will set MC equal to MR and produce output Q_0 at price P_0. With new competitors entering the market (which is likely given the above-normal profits being earned by established companies), the firm's demand is reduced. The demand curve moves to D_1, marginal revenue curve to MR_1 and price falls to P_1 and output to Q_1. Profit-maximizing firms under these conditions are likely to reduce their costs and improve their internal technical efficiency as a way of preserving cost price margins and thus levels of profitability. Quite unequivocally, the theoretical model of intensified competition predicts increased efficiency.

Alternatively, in oligopolized markets decisions are made on the understanding that any change in strategy is likely to meet competitor reaction. This raises the likelihood of firms colluding – several European examples will be established in this text – completing explicit or implicit agreements with their competitors to actively avoid competition. Therefore, by co-operating on levels of shared output oligopolists may behave as monopolists aggregating marginal costs and equating them with marginal revenue for the whole industry. Collusion of this kind involves explicit agreement and a high degree of co-ordination, which, as the number of players increases, is hard to sustain. Any increase in output by one player will immediately depress prices and prevent the realization of optimized profits. More commonly, firms in oligopolized markets do not, as a matter of course, involve themselves in aggressive price competition which can potentially lead to price wars and be damaging for all players. Instead, oligopolized markets are characterized by competition based on differentiation rather than on prices. As collusion and cartels curb the extent to which firms engage in price competition and promote heightened technical efficiency the Commission has specifically targeted these practices as detrimental to competition and the achievement of a Single European Market. However, because oligopolized firms are not exempt from competition they do not ignore efficiency altogether.

The stimulation of differentiation and new product development are also critical elements in the promotion of efficiency through competition. Dynamic efficiency, which refers to the rapid development of new technologies and products, is essential for firms to keep one step ahead of their rivals in highly competitive markets. Improvements in organizational form, production techniques, management systems, products and services, and distribution systems, performed continuously, all contribute to enhancing the competitive potential of firms to compete both in the EU and in other international markets. Whilst technical efficiency involves establishing the most appropriate processes to facilitate best practices, dynamic efficiency concerns the ongoing evolutionary development of the organization. Both are fostered through competition which means that firms who do not continue to develop in line with other competitors will either be taken over or simply fail to survive.

EU competition law

It is to be recalled that the EU's rules on competition are in direct relation to:

- concerted (or restrictive) practices,
- abuse of dominant positions,
- concentrations (by merger or acquisition), and
- state aids.

In the terms of Wilks and McGowan (1995, p. 261), these operate as a form of 'economic constitution' guaranteeing the maintenance of liberal order and ensuring that competition in the internal market is not distorted. The articles concerned (and associated regulations) apply only in so far as the behaviour or practice at stake affects trade between member states. This is intended to distinguish the scope of Community law from that of national law.

Concerted practices (Article 81, ex Article 85)

Article 81 (ex Article 85) bans cartels, price-fixing and other forms of collusion, where such has the effect of restricting competition within the common market. It asserts that such practices are 'incompatible with the common market', forbidding all agreements between undertakings which have as their object (or effect) 'the prevention, restriction or distortion of competition'. Paragraph 1 of the Article explicitly prohibits those agreements and concerted practices which:

(a) directly or indirectly fix purchase or selling prices or any other trading conditions;

(b) limit or control production, markets, technical development or investment;

(c) share markets or sources of supply;

(d) apply dissimilar conditions to equivalent transactions with other trading parties;

(e) make the conclusion of contracts subject to acceptance by the other parties of supplementary obligations which, by their nature or according to commercial usage, have no connection with the subject of such contracts.

Paragraph 2 declares such agreements to be void unless exempt under the 'group' or 'block' exemptions set out in the Article's third paragraph. Delimiting the effective coverage of Community controls, these exemptions can be seen to cover:

(a) *Specialization agreements* – horizontal production agreements which involve the participating firms each specializing in the production of a particular product or product group. The justification for permitting this kind of activity is to allow small and medium-size firms the potential to rationalize production efforts, improve their efficiency and strengthen their competitive position *vis-à-vis* larger firms. Consequently the exemption only covers agreements between small and medium-sized firms based on market share and turnover. Twenty per cent market share on specialized products and combined turnover of €500 million are the current thresholds. Other stipulations dictate that agreements must be reciprocal and must only apply to the nature of products and not to the volume of production or prices.

(b) *Exclusive distribution agreements* – where stipulations are made by the manufacturer on the permissible sales territory and the sale of competitor products. These are sometimes considered beneficial as a result of their ability to promote efficiency in distribution as well as facilitate unification. The concept of parallel imports is critical here, as traders other than exclusive distributors who buy from third parties in other markets provide competition for the firm that has been granted exclusive rights. Any attempts to hinder parallel importing therefore render the group exemption inapplicable. Equally, no restrictions may be applied in respect of prices or customers, and agreements cannot be made between competing firms as this will lead to market sharing, except where one or both parties have an annual turnover of less than €100 million. There has been some infringement of these rules in the European motor vehicle industry, where a block exemption covering distribution and servicing agreements continues to apply.

(c) *Exclusive purchasing agreements*, such as those for beer and petrol (EEC/194/EEC), involve the reseller agreeing to buy exclusively from a specific manufacturer. These restrictions can make it difficult for competitors to penetrate the market and consequently there are limitations on the duration of such obligations (five years) and on the nature of products covered (applying only to those which are connected to each other).

(d) *Patent licensing agreements*, which may pose restrictions in terms of territorial rights and the exclusivity conferred on the licensee, do provide access to technologies for those firms without the potential to innovate, and market access for small innovating firms lacking the capacity to sell on a pan-European scale. Three main principles cover the group exemption in this case: a degree of protection afforded to both the licensor and licensee to ensure continued R&D effort by the innovator and ensure a favourable environment for technology transfer, assurance of effective competition and intra-EU trade for patented products and legal security of the contract partners. Territorial restrictions cannot be enforced, although licensees may only sell in other licensees' territories in response to unsolicited orders, they may not actively sell or manufacture. Regulations do not exempt obligations for licensees to buy materials and components from the licensor (often undertaken to protect the invention) to pay a minimum royalty, to observe technological secrecy and use the technology only in connection with production of the designated product.

(e) *Research and development agreements*, which have always been regarded favourably by the Commission, are permissible so long as competition in the final consumer market is preserved. This means that controls are applied to competing firms who jointly exploit technologies (limiting them to 20% joint market share for products which may be improved or replaced by the new technology), and all parties are afforded right of access to results and freedom of distribution.

(f) *Franchising agreements*, which have become more prevalent in the EU in recent years, usually involve licences covering industrial or intellectual property rights (trademarks, brandnames or know-how). They are regarded as having a generally positive effect on competition allowing franchisors to develop a wide and uniform distribution network without major investment. This has the potential to introduce new competition (particularly for small and medium-size firms), allows rapid expansion and extends interbrand competition. This clearly benefits consumers as it offers them wider choice and the advantages which result from standardized, efficient distribution. Franchise operations are seen as being very different from exclusive distribution and purchasing agreements as a result of the advantages offered, although the block exemption applies only to distribution and service franchises and not to those in the manufacturing sector.

(g) *Know-how licensing*, like patent licensing, benefits the economy by facilitating technology transfer and innovation although territorial restrictions can stifle competition. As a result of the irreversible nature of knowledge transfer (once attained it cannot be retracted), the Commission was keen to provide greater legal certainty for involved parties on how agreements fit into existing competition policy. The policies which apply to patent licensing also apply here with provision being made for restrictions which are not considered to be damaging to competition: obligations to maintain the secrecy of know-how by the licensee after termination of the agreement; obligations that the licensee divulge any experience gained in exploiting the know-how and the granting of non-exclusive licences to the licensor when improvements and new applications are revealed. By permitting such arrangements the potential to maintain a degree of monopoly over know-how is designed to facilitate its licensing (and implicitly its sharing).

Special exemptions may also be awarded where the harmful effects of restrictive agreements are more than compensated for by particular benefits. Article 81 identifies four conditions for the granting of such exemptions:

1. where improvements are made in production, distribution or economic progress such as cost reductions or capacity increases;

2. where a fair share of the benefits accrues to consumers (be they final consumers or trading companies) such as lower prices or the improved quality of goods and services;

3. only agreements which actively contribute to the additional benefits will be permitted;

4. a degree of competition must exist in a substantial part of the goods and services supplied.

As explained in the European Parliament's fact-sheet on EU competition rules:

> (in aggregate) these exemptions are designed to simplify the Commission's administrative task so it does not have to deal individually with too many concerted practice cases and make it easier for companies to fulfil their obligations by giving certain types of action a general prior exemption. (European Parliament, 1999a)

With similar aim, and given the desire to promote co-operation amongst and between smaller enterprises, Article 81 also excludes concerted practices (with a Community dimension) below agreed thresholds. Where the aggregate turnover of the involved parties is less than €200 million, and where the goods or services covered by an agreement represent less than 5% of the total market, Article 81 shall not apply and notification is unnecessary. This is the so-called '*de minimus*' principle further detailed in the Commission's 'Notice on Minor Agreements'. Also exempt are activities between parent companies and their subsidiaries or between the subsidiaries themselves. As these activities involve one economic unit, they fall outside of the scope of Article 81 except where the subsidiary is deemed to have freedom to determine its own course of action.

Dominant positions (Article 82, ex Article 86)

Article 82 addresses a rather different problem: the abuse of a dominant trading position. Dominance itself is not prohibited but abuse of it is, at least if it affects trade between member states. In the basket of EU competition rules, the place of Article 82 is important in that there will always be a fear that large firms (enjoying a dominant market position) may make it hard for smaller firms to compete. To guard against what might be termed 'abuse' of market advantage, the Article asserts:

> Any abuse by one or more undertakings of a dominant position within the common market or in a substantial part of it shall be prohibited as incompatible with the common market insofar as it may affect trade between Member States.

The Article gives examples of abusive practice, including:

- low pricing with the object of eliminating a competitor
- discriminatory pricing between or within member states
- retaining customers by granting fidelity rebates
- limiting production, markets or technical development to the prejudice of consumers
- unjustified refusal to supply
- imposing supplementary obligations which have no connection with the purpose of the contract

In recent practice, four principal criteria for establishing market dominance can be discerned from the decisions of the Commission and the ECJ:

1. an undertaking's relative market share (greater than 40% implies dominance)
2. an undertaking's independence from its competitors
3. the ability to eliminate competition
4. dominant relationships with customers and suppliers

These criteria provide the acid test in assessment of cases and some flexibility in assessing a firm's impact on its market.

Applying Articles 81 and 82: the role of the Commission

The Commission is responsible for application of the rules under Articles 81 and 82. It investigates cases on application by a third party (complainant) or on its own initiative. Despite notification procedures and the welter of exclusions considered previously, there are numerous instances where such investigation is necessitated and where formal decisions are reached. As regards complaints, the number received by the Commission in 1998 pursuant to Articles 81 and 82 was 192. Most of these were of manifest Community relevance with only a small number of notified cases referred back to member state authorities. As regards the number of cases instituted by the Commission on its own initiative, these numbered 101 in 1998, the same number as in the previous year (European Commission, 1999a). Figure 5.3 locates these figures as part of a six-year trend towards increased complaints, investigations and formal decisions.

A formal obligation to act is provided where a 'complaint' is made by a third party (say a company or trade association) normally through a national competition authority. Only where the complaint relates to behaviour falling within the scope of Community jurisdiction will the national authority pass the matter on to the European Commission. If the complainant has a legitimate interest in the termination of the behaviour under question and can show why and how the alleged infringement prevents fair competition, then the Commission is obliged to investi-

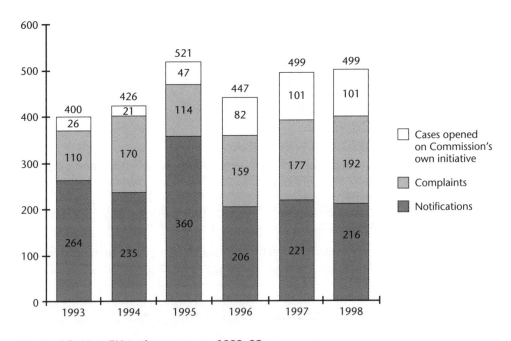

Figure 5.3 New EU anti-trust cases, 1993–98
Source: European Commission (1999a, p. 45)

gate the situation. Where investigations show that the complainant has a legitimate claim, the Commission must take the necessary steps to put an end to the infringement. Where no proof of infringement can be found, the Commission is obliged to inform the complainant of its decision and the reasoning behind it and give him or her the chance to provide further information.

The first stage of assessment normally involves the collection of information through either direct requests or formal investigations. This involves not only firms suspected of infringing rules but also third parties who are in a position to clarify certain information as a result of their proximity to the market. Investigation teams have complete freedom to enter company premises and to consult company documents, taking copies of any records they consider pertinent to the case. Although companies do not have to admit investigators, failure to do so will result in the Commission ordering the firm to comply by a formal decision and a daily penalty of between €50 and €1,000 can be imposed in addition to a lump sum fine. Visits are usually unannounced to prevent documents being destroyed in the interim. Where there is evidence of violation of Community rules, hearings will be held with the companies for the purpose of subsequent assessment and to establish the facts of the case before verdict.

In reaching its decisions (and in determining its penalties), the Commission must weigh up the deliberate nature, gravity and duration of any infringement where discovered. Guidelines authorise a 'starting point' for fines at €1 million but the Commission is at liberty to impose fines of up to €1,000 million or 10% of the annual turnover of the parties concerned, whichever is the larger. For very serious infringements, fines should start at no less than €20 million with the Commission taking into account the different roles and resources of the undertakings concerned. Fines should be paid within three months although they are subject to possible appeal. One case where Commission-imposed fines were successfully contested was in the case of the European chemicals cartel. In April 1999, the European Court of First Instance cut fines for Elf Atochem (France), ICI (UK) and Société Artesienne de Vinyle (France) from a combined total of €6.1 billion to €4.29 billion, reducing individual levies by between 33% and 66%. The original Commission fines, which followed exposure of a price-fixing cartel between twelve European chemicals companies, were rejected on the grounds of 'flawed calculation of company market shares' (*Financial Times*, 21 April 1999). However, while these firms enjoyed success in their appeals, dangers in such action exist. Interest is added to the value of the fine if any appeal is unsuccessful.

To encourage companies to co-operate more closely with the Commission when it is probing alleged breaches of EU rules, the institution has now introduced a 'leniency' system under which firms involved in anti-competitive practices may have their fines reduced by assisting with a Commission investigation (see Case Study 5.1). Such assistance – after an investigation has been started and where a company does not substantially contest the facts on which the Commission bases its allegations – should encompass co-operating with officials and supplying them with information relevant to their investigations (*European Voice*, 5 July 1999). Cartels, of course, are mostly secret agreements between companies, and without such co-operation it is difficult and time consuming for the investigating unit to unravel and to expose the full extent of secret dealings.

Collusion and market-fixing – the application of Article 81

In the Commission's view, cartels keep the least efficient companies in the market, keep prices high, weaken the production process and inflict considerable damage on the economy in general. Former EU Competition Commissioner, van Miert has described them as 'pernicious arrangements'. Those engaged in this sort of behaviour, he claims, 'damage not only their customers but also themselves by restricting efficiency and innovation'.

Although private cartels are by no means easy to uncover, offenders are often flagged by customers faced with continual price rises from all producers and by rival firms being squeezed by the actions of large groups of market players. Therefore, while the first responsibility of business managers with regard to competition policy is to ensure compliance, 'business managers must be also alert to competitors acting in contravention of the policies' (El-Kahal, 1998, p. 50). Tip-offs in the building industry, for example, have resulted in industry scrutiny and dawn raids on suspected firms, resulting in confiscation of documentation. Thermal insulation, stainless steel and ready-mixed concrete all provide example of market sectors which have come under scrutiny. Certain characteristics of the industry perhaps contribute to this tendency for collusion:

1. there is a relatively small number of suppliers in each national market, making it easier to negotiate co-operative market sharing and price fixing;

2. material costs are a relatively small proportion of total development costs which means that customers are more concerned about delivery schedules than price;

3. many of the materials are bulky, raising transportation costs, localizing competition and severely restricting cross-border trade;

4. customers are often able to hand on price rises to end-users and demand tends to be inelastic.

Evidence suggests that DG-IV (the Commission's Competition Directorate) has had increasing success in busting cartels tied to the building industry with, in many cases, fines resulting of up to 10% of company turnover. For example, on 30 November 1994, the European Commission imposed fines totalling ECU 248 million on thirty-three cement producers found to have participated in secret arrangements to rig markets over a period of more than ten years. The decision affected suppliers in the then twelve EU states as well as in Norway, Sweden and Switzerland. The largest fines were imposed on Italcementi (ECU 32.5 million), la Société de Ciments Française (ECU 24.7 million), Lafarge Coppee (ECU 22.8 million) and Blue Circle (ECU 15.8 million). Another price-fixing agreement involving sixteen steel makers (including British Steel) was also broken around this time, leading to total fines of £78 million. In this case, the parties were judged guilty of breaching competition rules over a ten-year period by fixing prices of beams supplied to the

---

| CASE STUDY 5.1 | Hot water for heating pipe partners |

In 1998, cartel partners – ABB, Løgstør, Henss/Isoplus, Sigma and six other firms – were found guilty of secret market-sharing, price-fixing and bid-rigging in the European market for insulated heating pipes. The firms were also found guilty with respect to attempting to eliminate a market competitor. It was a complaint in 1995 from this firm, Powerpipe of Sweden, that sparked the Commission's initial investigations.

Evidence was provided that these companies had colluded since 1990, progressing to cartelize a European market worth around ECU 400 million. Three interesting case features stand out. One is that the fine against cartel-giant, Asea Brown Boveri, at €70 million, was the third largest ever levied on an individual company under the EU's Article 81 (ex. 85). Two, the cartel continued for nearly a year after the investigation was launched. And three, Asea Brown Boveri 'won' a 30% reduction in its own fine after co-operating with Commission officials. This of course is tied to the 1996 leniency notice providing for a 10–50% reduction where companies provide substantial information. The scale of ABB's individual fine prior to this reduction reflected the fact that the company was the effective ringmaster, ABB's former Executive Vice-President effectively co-ordinating the cartel arrangement.

building industry and sharing out the market among them. More recently, the European Commission fined ten companies a total of ECU 92.21 million in 1998 for running an elaborate cartel in insulated heating pipes (see Case Study 5.1).

A wide variety of other industries have also faced the same kind of analysis – carton-boards, sugar and plastics to name but a few – leading to further success for a now formalized Commission cartel unit. In July 1994, the Commission announced fines totaling over £100 million on nineteen companies found to have fixed prices over several years in the market for cardboard packaging. In 1998, the Commission also prohibited an agreement between four sugar producers who had developed a collaborative strategy of higher pricing. Fines totalling ECU 50.2 million were imposed on the participating companies – British Sugar, Tate & Lyle, Napier Brown and James Budgett. Further cases were concluded in the areas of stainless steel and of ferry services in the Adriatic waters.

Abuse of a dominant position – the application of Article 82

Preceding analysis has made clear that while a dominant position is not, in itself, considered to be detrimental to the economic health of the EU, abuse of that position, hindering the maintenance of effective competition by acting independently of competitors and customers, runs contrary to EU objectives. Relating back to the basic ruling, it has to be proved that the firm is abusing its dominant position in the product market or a major proportion of it.

Much as the Commission has acted to invoke Article 81, so it has acted to apply Article 82. In fact, the number of formal cases pursuant to the Article has increased steadily over recent years. According to its XXVIIIth Report on Competition Policy, the Commission concluded six cases under the Article in 1998 and launched a

---

CASE STUDY 5.2 **Brussels probe into drinks giant**

European Commission inspectors have conducted dawn raids at Coca-Cola premises over the last two days in a probe into whether the world's largest soft drinks maker is abusing its dominant position in three European Union markets. The officials, investigating practices in Germany, Austria and Denmark, raided Coca-Cola offices in those countries and in the UK, where the company's main bottler for Austria has its headquarters. The raids are the prelude to an investigation into whether the world's biggest brand name abused its position in those markets by offering retailers incentives to increase sales volumes, carry the full range of Coca-Cola products or stop selling competitors' drinks.

News of the probe is another blow to Coca-Cola in Europe, where it is recovering from a health scare that originated in Belgium last month and saw its drinks swept from the shelves in four EU countries. In May it was forced to drop plans to acquire the Cadbury Schweppes soft drinks business in most of the EU after Van Miert, competition commissioner, sharply criticized it for failing to notify Brussels of its plans. The probe marks an increasing interest by the Commission in the relationship between large suppliers and their distributors. The Commission carried out similar dawn raids on Interbrew, the world's fifth largest brewer, last week as part of an investigation into whether the Stella Artois brewer was abusing its dominant position in Belgium. Coca-Cola confirmed that the raids – which it described as 'unannounced visits' – had taken place and said it was co-operating fully. Commission officials yesterday stressed that the Brussels executive was only at the beginning of its investigation to establish whether there was sufficient evidence to launch a full case. If it did, and found Coca-Cola guilty of abuses, it could mean fines of up to 10% of the turnover of the businesses involved.

In addition to the Coca-Cola premises, Commission officials entered offices belonging to three anchor bottlers – companies that bottle its products and in which it has stakes. These were Coca-Cola Beverages, the London-based bottler for central and eastern Europe, Coca-Cola Nordic Beverages, which is controlled by Carlsberg, the Danish brewer, and Coca-Cola Erfrischungsgetranke, the German bottler. The Commission has also written to retailers and distributors to seek their views.

Officials would not comment on whether the Commission's actions resulted from a complaint from a competitor, although they said this was often the case with such inquiries.

Source: Financial Times, 22 July 1999

number of fresh investigations. The upward trend in action has continued in 1999 with the Commission initiating a number of investigations focused on supplier–distributor relationships (see Case Study 5.2) and examining various concerns relating to telecommunication and Internet services. Internet infrastructure and related services are of particular interest in that the Commission confronts substantial challenges with respect to market definition. As in its management of AOL Europe's complaint against Deutsche Telekom – in early 1999 AOL accused the German giant of predatory pricing and discriminatory practice through its own Internet subsidiary company – the Commission must ask which aspects of Internet services constitute separate markets.

Of those recently concluded cases, two provide a quick illustration of the issues attaching to the application of Article 82. In the *Amministrazione Autonoma dei Monopoli dello Stato (AAMS)* case, Italian cigarette producer and distributor AAMS had a dominant position on the Italian market for the wholesale distribution of cigarettes. The Commission ruled that the company was imposing restrictive distribution contracts on a series of foreign producers. The effect was to protect AAMS's own sales and to limit the access of foreign cigarettes to the Italian market. In 1998, the Commission fined AAMS ECU 6 million and ordered it to put an end to the infringement. In the *British Airways* case, the UK carrier was fined €6.8 million in early 1999 when found to be creating an illegal barrier to airlines wishing to compete against it. BA was found to be in breach of Article 82 by offering extra commission to travel agents that promoted its tickets over those of the airline's rivals. These included complainant Virgin Atlantic. The Commission has warned that other airlines could face similar penalties where found to be operating anti-competitive loyalty schemes with travel agents.

The concept of the market

The concept of market to which the Commission refers when assessing an agreement or practice from the viewpoint of Articles 81 and 82 is of critical importance. In specifying criteria there is a heavy reliance on case law (see Case Study 5.3). Three important points require establishment:

1. Articles 81 and 82 apply to situations where anti-competitive practices may affect trade between member states. EU competition rules are only violated if a 'substantial part' of the SEM is affected. This could involve several countries or just one, depending on circumstances.

2. It is crucially important to define the nature and extent of the product markets covered by an agreement. In this respect, case law has established the principles that definition should rest with the identification of a homogenous and separable product area. Products need not be identical but at least substitutable and whether items are substitutable depends on how customers use them, their

---

CASE STUDY 5.3 **United Brands and the concept of 'relevant market'**

The United Brands case (United Brands v Commission, 1978) provides a classical illustration of the difficulty of defining the relevant market and the use of the substitutability rule. United Brands were accused of charging unfairly high prices for bananas in some member states while acting as a major supplier of bananas to the European market as a whole. The court therefore had to determine what constituted the product market for bananas and, thus, whether the firm could be charged with abusing a dominant position pursuant to Article 82 (then Article 86). Essentially, the Court had to suggest whether the banana market was a unique market or one in which consumers would readily switch their buying behaviour to other fruits if the price of bananas rose (whether there were interchangeable substitutes). Ultimately, the court determined that as bananas cater for different dietary requirements, their specific qualities influence customer preference and substitution to other fruits is unlikely. Thus the market for bananas was judged to be distinct. The abuse of market dominance concerned a geographic market defined as the Community market minus UK, France and Italy where national intervention in the banana market provided preferences to other producers at that time.

prices and characteristics. Debates at this level are not purely technical but are of fundamental importance. As Fitzpatrick poses (1995, p. 56):

> Clearly it is in the interests of a slipper producer accused of abusing a dominant position to argue that they operate in the (broader) footwear market as their market share is thus reduced.

3. Markets also have a geographic scope comprising an area where the conditions of competition are homogenous. This also requires definition in investigations as, quite clearly, restrictive practices and abuses of dominant positions relate to particular markets, whatever their extent and identity.

The role of the member states

Treaty articles in the anti-trust field apply only to an agreement or dominant position in so far as they impede trade between member states. Hence, where an agreement has no perceptible effects on trade flows between the member states then domestic competition law applies. Most member states have their own competition laws and authorities, and these are important to anti-trust regulation inside individual EU countries. Although EU law is binding on all member countries, national governments are free to operate their own national legislative frameworks and to determine the nature and scope of domestic anti-trust rules. Indeed, while some member states have re-modelled their domestic competition policies on the principles of EU law, significant differences in national rules on competition persist (see Turner, 1995). For example, while Finnish competition law now relies almost entirely on EU legislation, German competition rules (especially on market dominance) remain strongly influenced by preceding domestic codes.

Thus, while domestic legislation can be closely aligned with the principles of supranational law, and while there is close co-operation between national and supranational authorities, national competition bodies remain independent and important authorities in their own right, governing those many competition infringements that lack a Community dimension. To illustrate this point, the following examples of recent national action may be considered:

1. In 1997, the Finnish Competition Council imposed on Finland's major dairy products company Valio a competition infringement fine of FIM5 million. This was for its abuse of a dominant position in the national liquid dairy products markets.

2. In 1997, Germany's competition authority, the Bundeskartellamt, detected a cartel of power cable manufacturers in the German market. Case investigation concluded in 1998 with fines totaling DM280 million.

3. In the summer of 1999, Volvo Car UK admitted supporting secret agreements to fix its car prices in the UK. This admission followed an investigation by the United Kingdom's Office of Fair Trading (OFT) which uncovered evidence of an agreement by Volvo dealers not to offer discounts beyond set levels. Volvo has given assurances that it will not support price-fixing cartels operated by its dealers.

National courts and competition authorities also have a central role to play in support of the Commission's activities at EU level. The power to apply the provisions of Articles 81 and 82 are vested simultaneously in the Commission and the national courts (direct effect) and it is open for complainants to commence legal proceedings with reference to Community articles in their national courts. Meanwhile, competition authorities in the member states play a crucial rule in detecting breaches of Community competition rules within their own territory.

It is also clear that in the decentralization process envisaged by the Commission for the future execution of anti-trust cases, national competition authorities are to be central players. Where national authorities are approved by the Commission and where they can guarantee effective protection of individuals' Community competition rights, they may in future receive and execute decentralized anti-trust complaints pursuant to Article 81 (see Davison and Fitzpatrick, 1998). Although European competition authorities vary tremendously in terms of their experience, reputation and sophistication, the Commission is having to consider such a 'decentralization' of powers in an attempt to reduce and to focus its case burden.

Mergers and acquisitions (The European Merger Control Regulation, no. 4064/89)

Articles 81 and 82 make no specific provision for the control of European concentrations (acquisitions or mergers) which will often create or strengthen a dominant market position. In December 1989, a European Merger Control Regulation (MCR) no. 4063/89 was agreed in order to fill this void and to strengthen the Community's ability to regulate M&A activity. The rules under this regulation – as recently amended by Regulation 1310/97 – allow prior investigation and thus prevent mergers that would give rise to an abuse of a dominant position on the Community market before they happen. The Commission is empowered to declare a concentration with a Community dimension (CCD), pulling it under its sole jurisdiction, and to assess its compatibility with the common market. Incompatibility is established where that concentration creates or strengthens a dominant market position so as to impede effective competition. Where a concentration lacks a Community dimension it comes under national competition policy rather than EU regulation. Investigation applies to companies in all economic sectors when they are proposing a concentration by means of merger, acquisition or the creation of a joint company and where the concentration has a Community dimension. With effect from September 1990, this dimension has obtained where:

- the combined turnover of all parties is in excess of €5 billion;
- the aggregate EU-wide turnover (of each of at least two of the undertakings) is in excess of €250 million;
- each of the companies concerned generates no more than two-thirds of its aggregate Community-wide turnover in one member state.

With many cross-frontier concentrations remaining below these thresholds, efforts have been made to extend the scope of the MCR. Amendments made to

Regulation 4064/89 by Regulation 1310/97 now ensure that mergers will be considered as having a Community dimension, where they fall below the (original) 'global' thresholds but satisfy the following requirements:

- the merging parties must have a combined worldwide turnover of more than €2.5 billion;
- in each of at least three member states, the combined turnover of all the companies concerned must exceed €100 million;
- in each of these three countries, the total turnover of at least two of the companies concerned must exceed €25 million;
- the aggregate Community-wide turnover of each of at least two of the undertakings concerned must exceed €100 million.

The two-thirds rule also applies to this second category of Community mergers of which fourteen cases were notified to the Commission in 1998 (amounting to 6% of all cases).

In effect, the Commission now has the competence to examine cases of a smaller scale and where multiple referral – to the authorities of three or more member states – would otherwise take place. These cases will now benefit from the simplicity and legal security of Community-level control or 'a one stop shop' for merger approval. This change to EU merger controls emerged as an alternative to a reduction in the global and Community thresholds set out in Regulation 4064/89. The French, Spanish, German and British governments all rejected Commission proposals to lower the aggregate worldwide turnover threshold to €2 billion and the aggregate EU-wide threshold to €100 million.

Defining the market

Again, as in anti-trust investigations, the task force has to decide what constitutes the market. On the surface this appears to be an easy task whereas in practice it can be highly complex. As discussed with reference to Articles 81 and 82, the Commission has traditionally taken a narrow view of what constitutes a market, building on the concept of demand side substitutability. Indeed, the Commission's Notification of Acquisitions form provides the following definition:

> A relevant product market comprises all those products and/or services which are regarded as interchangeable or substitutable by the consumer by reason of the products' characteristics, their prices and their intended use.

Nevertheless, supply side factors have also been considered. The case of metal containers serves to highlight this point. In the takeover of the British company Metal Box Packaging by the French concern Carnaud, the market was, initially, taken to be metal containers. Conversely, in parallel mergers between USA metal packaging companies the product market has been defined to encompass metal containers, glass bottles and plastic containers. The Commission's argument for taking a narrower definition of the market centred on production switching difficulties in the context of glass, plastic and metal packaging. Calculations of market share, highly dependent on the definition of market boundaries, showed a wide disparity in the Metal Box case. Whereas the merged firm would have had a combined turnover of £2 billion in a packaging market worth £35 billion, in the more narrowly defined metal packaging market it would have had a dominant position and thus have been rejected under new legislation. Similar claims were made by the Commission in the merger of Metallgesellshaft and Safic Alcan (1991), where the differing production techniques of natural rubber and latex meant they were treated as separate products resulting in a narrow definition of the market. Debates about identifying the 'relevant market' when undertaking an appraisal were also central to the *de Havilland* case (1991) in which the Commission vetoed Aerospatiale's (France) and Alenia's (Italy) attempts to take over Canadian aircraft maker de Havilland. In assessing the competition effects of the proposed concentration, the Commission defined the product market ('regional turbo-prop commuter aircraft') and subdivided the market into segments in such a way that gave the highest market share possible to the concerned parties. Its decision to block the acquisition therefore rested, in large part, with its methodology of describing and analysing the market.

Questions of distinction also apply to services. In analysis of proposed concentrations in accountancy, insurance, financial and Internet access services, the Commission has established (and employed) evidence of the existence of separate and distinct markets, for example, statutory auditing (within accountancy services), credit insurance (within commercial insurance) and 'universal connectivity' (within the realm of Internet services). Here, and in more traditional sectors, if markets are defined too narrowly this can prevent mergers which do not distort competition and which may actually increase efficiency. Alternatively, if markets are defined too broadly then they will permit mergers to go ahead which act against the public interest by permitting a dominant market position to be attained.

Of course, along with product market definitions, there are also geographic boundaries to be considered as with cases pursuant to Articles 81 and 82. In seeking to assess the homogeneity of competition within a geographical area, the Commission's decisions have taken into account several factors. Among others, we can count the geographical distribution of market shares, transportation costs (which dictate the distance goods may be moved economically), market entry barriers, cultural preferences (which suggest whether or not goods stand a chance of penetrating foreign markets) and differing competitive conditions. Different cases have resulted in very different geographic market definitions. In a number of concentrations tied to the automotive components sector (see DENSO–Magneti Morelli and others) the relevant geographic market has been identified as that of the European Economic Area (EEA). Such a definition has been based on the reasoning that:

- transportation costs within the EEA are not significant
- there are no obstacles to intra-EEA trade
- prices are similar throughout Europe
- suppliers tend to serve the entire EEA from only a few plants located within it

- similar conditions of competition apply throughout the EEA

- suppliers tend to treat the EEA as a distinct product market in planning their production, sales and marketing activities.

In other cases and in certain sectors of activity marked by global competition, the Commission has carried out competition analyses on markets that it deems to be 'worldwide'. With respect to transatlantic airline services (e.g. the Boeing–McDonnell Douglas case), telecommunications alliances (e.g. Atlas–Global One) and other markets such as steel and platinum, the Commission has identified 'world markets' in a number of recent cases. As is made clear by EU officials (European Commission, 1999a, p. 44):

> As globalisation of markets progresses, the Commission is increasingly carrying out competition analysis on markets which are not confined to Europe ... [and] even where the market is identified as 'European', the Commission may take account of potential competition from other geographical areas when assessing a transaction.

Procedure and action

Companies involved in agreements or mergers or considering mergers which could affect competition within the EU, and which could fall under the MCR, should notify the European Commission in advance. The first imposition by the Commission of a financial penalty for a failure to do this was in 1998. The nature of the applications procedure has been very clearly outlined. Within a week of announcing the merger the firms involved must complete and return to the Commission a notification form which comprises detailed questions covering a wide range of aspects including prices charged in the EU and relative market shares. Although the detailed nature of the questions included on the form has caused a certain amount of dissent among firms, the Commission asserts that it is necessary if they are to make a stage I decision (within thirty days) once the prior notification requirement has been complied with. At this first stage, the Commission may decide:

(a) that the notified concentration falls outside of the scope of the Regulation,

(b) that the notified concentration falls within the scope of the Regulation but does not raise serious concerns, or

(c) that the notified concentration falls within the scope of the Regulation and requires detailed consideration on the grounds that there are serious doubts about the concentration's compatibility with the common market.

In the first example (a), supranational authorities are uninvolved in any subsequent appraisal. In the second example (b), clearance is provided at stage I (perhaps subject to minor remedies). In the final example (c), unless the notification is withdrawn, a detailed investigation is conducted in to whether or not the proposal creates or strengthens a dominant position on the relevant market. There is a four-month time limit to such an investigation (second stage proceedings) culminating in a formal Commission decision. The proposed merger cannot go ahead until the Commission's final decision has been taken. At this stage, the parties are provided with fresh opportunity to modify their concentration plans (so as to avoid their rejection) and many plans are actually withdrawn in order to avoid an adverse final decision. For example, phase II investigation was already under way in 1998 when merger plans were withdrawn between publishers Reed Elsevier and Wolters Kluwer. The Commission found grounds for concern about the merger's impact on competition in the global markets for academic journals and books, for professional books on law and taxation (in a number of EU member states) and for various kinds of dictionary and business publications. Amid growing concerns that it would either block the merger or demand large-scale divestments, the £17 billion merger plan was abandoned.

Although the Commission has formally vetoed only a handful of mergers under the MCR, it is clear then that many planned tie-ups have been scrapped or abandoned (following EU investigation) before a formal decision has been made necessary. It is also clear that several mergers (e.g. Nestlé–Perrier and Zeneca–Astra) have been authorized on strict conditions and subject to undertakings established at the point of stage I or stage II proceedings. These points should be borne in mind when considering the bottom-line figures in Table 5.1. These highlight only a small number of formal prohibitions – just ten up to and including September 1999 – including those made in the cases of Bertelsmann–Kirch–Premiere and Deutsche Telekom–BetaResearch. Both of these merger plans were linked to the German digital pay-TV market and were blocked by the Commission in 1998. Since the end of the reference period for Table 5.1 (September 1999), two further mergers have been formally blocked: an all-Swedish merger of truck, bus and coach builders Scania and Volvo and a proposed merger between UK tour operators Airtours and First Choice.

Table 5.1 Summary statistics pertaining to the European Merger Control Regulation, September 1990–May 1999 (inclusive)

Total number of notifications to the Commission	1,051
Total number of notifications to the Commission to a decision[a]	991
Total of final descisions taken at stage I	937
Number deemed compatible with the common market	*833*
Number deemed compatible with the common market with undertakings	*35*
Number deemed outside of the scope of MCR	*50*
Number leading to partial–full referral to member states	*19*
Total of final decisions taken at stage II	54
Number deemed compatible with the common market	*11*
Number deemed compatible with the common market with undertakings	*31*
Number prohibited	*10*
Number of other decisions	*02*

[a] Figures between total decisions and notifications do not summate due to withdrawn notifications.
Source: European Commission

The rules on state aid (Articles 87–89, ex Articles 92–94)

Although the EU has developed a role in the supporting of certain industries and regions by financial assistance, the Commission has a further responsibility to prohibit state aids if they affect the EU in any way. Under the terms of Articles 87–89, the Commission must ensure that national governments do not unfairly favour their own national businesses over those of other EU countries through the use of direct payments, grants, soft loans, tax concessions and other forms of aid (see Box 5.1). Such aid can frustrate free competition in the EU not only by preventing the most efficient allocation of resources but also by giving a substantial competitive advantage to domestic producers.

As a general rule, Article 87 determines that all state aid to business is illegal insofar as it affects trade between the member states of the EU. However, paragraphs 2 and 3 of Article 87 list various categories of aid which are permissible. This provides member states with some genuine scope for public intervention in support of regions and/or national industry and to support such wider Community goals as 'economic and social cohesion'.

Under Article 87(2) the following types of aid are permissible:

(a) aid having a social character, provided that such aid is granted without discrimination related to the origin of the products concerned;

(b) aid to make good the damage caused by natural disasters or exceptional occurrences;

(c) aid granted to the economy of certain areas of the Federal Republic of Germany affected by the division of Germany, insofar as such aid is required in order to compensate for the economic disadvantages caused by that division.

Under Article 87(3), the following may also be considered to be compatible with the common market:

(a) aid to promote the economic development of areas where the standard of living

---

BOX 5.1

Types of aid instrument

- Grants
- Interest subsidies received directly by the recipient
- Tax credits and other tax measures
- Tax allowances, exemptions and rate relief
- Reductions in social security contributions
- Sale or rental of public land or property at prices below market value
- Equity participation (including debt conversions)
- Soft loans from public or private sources
- Participatory loans from public or private sources

is abnormally low or where there is serious underemployment *(a platform for many national regional-aid schemes)*;

(b) aid to promote the execution of an important project of common European interest or to remedy a serious disruption in a national or regional economy;

(c) aid to facilitate the development of certain economic activities or of certain economic areas, where such aid does not adversely affect trading conditions to an extent contrary to the common interest;

(d) aid to promote culture and heritage conservation where such aid does not affect trading conditions and competition in the Community to an extent that is contrary to the common interest;

(e) such other categories of aid as may be specified by decision of the Council acting by a qualified majority on a proposal from the Commission.

Hence, a wide range of national- and Union-level investment subsidies are available under specific conditions and particular classes of aid (e.g. regional aid measures) are given clearance where in accordance with Treaty terms. It should be clear, therefore, that state aid control at EU level is not about prohibition of aid but about attenuating action that unduly distorts competition in the European Union. The central task rests with monitoring and regulating 'assistance' and with defining (and amending) the conditions under which states may provide specific forms of structural and/or regional assistance. Accordingly, the Commission has sole responsibility for checking that national aid schemes, which must be notified by member states under Article 88(3) of the Treaty, are compatible with the aims of the Treaty. In all circumstances, aid measures must conform to Treaty obligations and must be limited to the minimum necessary to achieve the desired purpose. For example, any and all sectoral aid must, to be acceptable, aim to restore long-term viability by resolving structural problems including, where necessary, the reduction of capacity. State aids are quite capable of falling foul of these rules and the Commission will ban assistance that is not compatible with the SEM or that is being misused. The most celebrated example here was the coming to blows of the Commission with the German federal government (and the regional German government of Lower Saxony) in 1995. At this time, the Commission blocked DM240 million of a proposed DM780 million in 'regional' subsidies for Volkswagen to build two plants in the East German state of Saxony. The Commission ruled that the aid was illegal because VW had first agreed to invest DM3.5 billion to assist East German development if it received clearance for this sum. When the carmaker scaled down its total investment, improperly, it received the same sum of aid. In this case, as in others, a Commission decision prompted an immediate legal challenge via the European Court of Justice.

Rescue and restructuring aid

Among the most commonly granted aids (and among the most controversial) are those given on an *'ad hoc'* basis. State aid that is granted *'ad hoc'*, i.e. outside established frameworks or schemes, is generally given for restructuring or rescuing companies. Member states must demonstrate that all finance is directed towards restructuring and be limited to the minimum necessary to enable restructuring to be undertaken. As concerns endure that such allocations may serve to preserve operators which would otherwise exit the market, a further principle (although one inconsistently applied) is that such aid be a one-off. Very simply, this 'one time, last time' rule means that rescue aid, say for restructuring an ailing state champion, should only be granted once. According to the Commission (European Commission, 1999b), slightly more than 50% of *ad hoc* aid supports the restructuring of companies in the steel and shipbuilding sectors, although *ad hoc* aid has been provided in a variety of manufacturing sectors, in financial services and in air transport (see Case Study 5.4). Grants make up more than half of all such aid, with soft loans, equity injections and the use of guarantees representing other aid forms.

CASE STUDY 5.4 **It's plane unfair. Rescue aid for airlines stirs up trouble**

Previously enjoying protection, the air transport sector has undergone a process of gradual liberalization – achieved since April 1997 – with many European airline companies scrambling to restructure their organizations in light of new market freedoms. Several member governments, keen to launch their champions into the private sector, have looked to *ad hoc* aid to smooth transitions and to springboard major restructuring programmes.

These efforts have brought many into negotiation with EU and industry authorities and have led to the European Commission backing, if amending, a number of controversial schemes. For example, in 1998, the Commission reconfirmed approval of French Government aid to Air France – its privatizing carrier – after its original decision (of 1994) had been overruled on the intervention of the European Court of First Instance. The Court upheld complaints by industry rivals that Air France had enjoyed unreasonable freedoms under the terms of the original deal which had held out the prospect of some FR20 billion ($3.3 billion) worth

of restructuring aid. The airline had moved to add seventeen new planes to its fleet as a part of its 'restructuring' and had enjoyed unfair terms of competition against rivals lacking equivalent support and long since transferred to the private sector. Under the terms of the amended deal, Air France must continue with debt reductions and its partial privatization, and will now face stiffer competition on a number of routes.

Rival carriers BA, SAS and KLM, still hopping at this decision, have also pleaded unfair competition as the Commission has approved government aid for Olympic Airways (Greece) and for Alitalia. In the latter of these two cases, the Commission has cleared (though downscaled) a substantial rescue package for the debt-ridden Italian carrier worth L2,750 billion. Strict conditions have been attached to the deal including manpower reductions, divestitures and a requirement that the Italian government open up Alitalia monopolies on non-EU routes.

Arguments surrounding subsidies

Economic theory has generally failed to advance a persuasive case in favour of state subsidies although there may be specific cases where state aid is justified as a result of market imperfections. The first is where the social benefit may be greater than the benefit derived by the individual firm, that is where there are externalities (spill-over effects). For example, it is argued that some research and development (R&D) initiatives result in greater social benefits than returns to the individual organization. Second, in high technology sectors, which are consumptive of up-front capital and R&D costs, there are high returns to scale which make it difficult for firms to compete with incumbents (the infant industry argument). Third, there are instances where, as a result of imperfections in information in the capital market, firms are more able to assess the risks of new projects and new investments than the credit institutions. This results in lenders charging high interest rates making socially desirable investments unprofitable for the private firm and providing a case for government-supported loans. Finally, there may be cases where (on social grounds) help is needed to create jobs and to overcome barriers to future competitiveness.

However (and irrespective of the security of these claims), the bulk of such subsidies in Europe go not to new industries with a future or to those generating positive externalities, but to ailing giants in industries such as ship-building, coal-mining and motor vehicles. As succinctly put by *The Economist* publication in a scathing attack on European subsidies (*The Economist*, 1997, p. 75):

> The benefits of competition between European airlines, car makers, energy firms, banks, chemical companies and the rest have all, at various times, been dissipated by governments that have merrily bailed out losers. Cost control and efficiency go out of the window when firms expect state support if things go wrong. Strained public budgets are stretched further by the cost of subsidies.

This statement highlights just some of the reasons why subsidies may not work even in the circumstances previously considered:

1. Governments tend to be less able to pick winners than the private sector because their decisions are often obscured by social pressures and a lack of expertise.

2. Government-supported R&D may simply replace private sector R&D and may not add to a net overall increase in activity.

3. Even if there appears to be an economic case for a subsidy, calculating the exact amount is difficult and can result in too much subsidy being paid which can worsen the distortion.

4. Export subsidies paid to firms in one country are likely to be matched by governments in others, leading to a subsidy war which acts as a drain on national resources.

5. The economic costs of subsidies can be high. As governments find money for subsidies, public budgets are stretched and/or tax policies impact adversely on incentives to work.

6. Aid is often a way for governments to delay or prevent the demise of failing industries and/or non-viable businesses with no long-term benefits as it simply puts off inevitable closures and redundancies.

Given such debate, and the financial and political investments associated with public aid decisions, it is relatively unsurprising that state aids are such a sensitive area of EU activity. Indeed, the EU's determination to rein in the granting of state aids (especially those given on an *ad hoc* basis) has come into sharp conflict with the determination of many member governments to use aid, in one form or another, in order to protect domestic industries (see Case Study 5.5). The scope for discretionary assistance under Article 87 and the matter of consistent (or inconsistent) application of EU rules adds to this combustible mix. At the heart of present argument, the Commission continues to warn that current aid levels are dangerously high. According to the findings of its seventh survey on state aid in the European Union (European Commission, 1999b), state aid volumes to industry (manufacturing) have been fairly consistent in recent years, at an average of €37.7 billion a year between 1995 and 1997 (see Table 5.2). The EU's former Competition Commissioner, van Miert, has described this as a substantial problem resulting in serious market distortions in many sectors. This position is well supported by the

---

CASE STUDY 5.5 **European industry still dependent on state aid**

European enthusiasm for state aid shows little sign of cooling off, according to new figures presented by the EU's competition commissioner, to the European Parliament yesterday. Subsidies given to manufacturing industry in the European Union between 1995 and 1997 amounted to an annual average of €37.7 billion. Excluding Sweden, Finland and Austria (which joined the EU in 1995), the figure was 36.4 billion compared with 42 billion for the same countries during 1993–1995 – a 13% drop. However, the fall was almost exclusively because of a sharp decrease in aid levels in Germany (where aid to the former communist Länder dropped by 30%) and to a lesser extent France and Italy. There is no downward trend in the overall figure once subsidies to Germany's eastern Länder are stripped out.

'The continuing high level of aid and the fact that the current decrease is due to an exceptional reduction in Germany provide strong reasons for the Commission to maintain its pressure on state aid in the Community', said the report on state aids. 'Aid measures should not be allowed to protect industries or non-viable businesses and thereby provide a means to export unemployment from one member state to another', it concluded.

The figures are likely to intensify pressure on member states to give stronger, possibly binding, commitments to reduce overall aid levels, viewed as a serious distortion to the single market. Although the Commission has waged a relentless battle against anti-competitive subsidies, its efforts have made little headway in countries such as Germany and France, which continue to support companies through direct grants, tax breaks and guarantees. Officials fear that aid levels could go even higher now that the single currency has been launched and state assistance becomes one of the few ways left for governments to protect companies from more intense competition.

The report shows sharp disparities between member states with aid levels in Greece six times higher than in the UK and Sweden, the lowest subsidisers. Although the EU's four biggest economies – Germany, Italy, France and the UK – still account for most of the aid to manufacturing industry, their share of total industry aid in the EU has decreased from 87% to 82%. Germany accounts for 37%, Italy for 28%, France for 12% and the UK for 5% of the total of aid granted to the pre-1995 EU-12.

Source: Financial Times, 30 March 1999

Table 5.2 State aid to industry in current prices, 1993–97 (million Euro)

	1993	1994	1995	1996	1997
Austria	0	0	489	495	616
Belgium	784	998	952	1,149	701
Denmark	561	558	648	727	797
Germany	19,675	20,167	15,798	12,920	11,794
Greece	646	355	656	582	723
Spain	1,127	1,062	2,568	2,745	1,966
Finland	0	0	401	327	426
France	5,306	4,110	3,243	3,773	5,750
Ireland	368	307	313	434	454
Italy	11,325	9,354	10,826	9,930	9,443
Luxembourg	41	42	47	46	45
Netherlands	509	531	661	687	670
Portugal	376	571	428	705	467
Sweden	0	0	366	405	369
United Kingdom	1,124	1,298	1,482	1,668	2,050
EUR-15			38,877	36,594	36,272
EUR-12	41,812	39,356	37,621	35,367	34,860

Source: European Commission (1999b)

Union of Industrial and Employers' Confederations of Europe (UNICE), which says that companies damaged by unfair state handouts to competitors should be compensated.

Controlling state aids: future issues

The Commission is now looking at reform of notification procedures and to concentrate its vetting work on cases involving large volumes of *ad hoc* aid. Some 60% of applications for state aid are approved after fairly brief investigation and the Commission intends to use the device of block exemptions to limit and to concentrate its case work. These should apply to small amounts of aid, to aid for SMEs, to the many aid forms designed to encourage R&D and to measures in support of environmental protection. Brussels is also talking in terms of a more open policy on state aid, looking to compile and to publish as much data as possible on aid volumes. DG-IV describes this as 'one primary means by which the Commission is able to demonstrate that it is constantly keeping a close watch on public interventions' (European Commission, 1999b, pp. 1–2). In addition, the EU is likely to take an increasingly tough view of failures to notify aids and of attempts to abuse the principle of rescue aid. Many of its previous 'rescue' clearances (e.g. of French aid to Air France and to Credit Lyonnaise) have provoked legal challenge on the grounds that subsidies were without proper account of restructuring proposals or of previous subsidies. The Commission can also be expected to continue its crackdown on preferential tax rates. As considered briefly in Chapter 4, the Commission ruled in July 1998 that Ireland's 10% corporate tax rate for investing manufacturing companies constituted a form of state aid. This suggests that predatory tax regimes are now a clear target.

Competition and regional policy

The concentration of regional aid in the most disadvantaged areas forms a common objective of both the EU's regional and competition policies. In effect, *if* an aid (or package of measures):

- is used sparingly,
- is a part of a coherent regional development strategy,
- is directed towards a region eligible for Community assistance according to defined EC rules, and
- is notified by the member state under Article 88 of the TEC (ex Article 93)

then it may be exempt from the Community's general restrictions on state assistance (see previous section).

Member states also have a margin of room to direct aid payments to regions not eligible for Community assistance (or for EU structural funding) but where a region- and state-aid scheme falls under one of the exemptions provided in Article 87(3)(a) or Article 87(3)(c). This establishes a complex relationship between regional policy and competition law and highlights a lack of complete consistency between the EU's policy on regional state-aid schemes and its regional policy. In this context, member states are themselves granting regional aid through national and subnational authorities to regions eligible under the Structural Funds and/or to regions eligible under Article 87(3). Alongside these efforts, but forming only a small part of the total regional-aid spending in the member states, the EU is dispersing development finance to designated areas in pursuit of agreed regional policy goals. These goals have evolved slowly since there was no original Treaty obligation on the member states to develop a co-ordinated regional policy. Since the early 1970s, successive Community declarations have recognized both the tensions brought about by regional disparities and by the centripetal effects of the Single Market regime. Today, the member states are committed to an area of social and economic cohesion with Article 158 of the TEC (ex Article 130a) declaring:

> ... the Community shall develop and pursue its actions leading to the strengthening of its economic and social cohesion. In particular, the Community shall aim at reducing disparities between the levels of development of the various regions and the backwardness of the least favoured regions or islands, including rural areas.

Regional state-aid schemes and national-level authorities

The task of ensuring that less prosperous regions are helped is primarily in the hands of the member state authorities. As has been suggested, assistance may be directed towards regions which are eligible for the Community's own assistance (under the so-called Structural Funds) or to regions eligible under Treaty Article 87(3). However, while all EU countries give capital grants for regional development and operate enterprise zones and related schemes, some do so with greater frequency and with greater generosity than others. In Spain, for example, up to 50% of total costs of new investments can be given in the form of direct cash subsidies, depending on the size of the investment and the number of jobs created. To qualify, investments must be made in areas designated as Zonas de Promoción Económica and projects must be valued at over Pta15 million. As explained elsewhere:

> ... grants can be used for the purchase of land, development of sites and property, purchase of capital equipment and research and development (Peck *et al.*, 1996, p. 57)

Similar types of support can also be found in Greece, Portugal and Italy. In Italy, the Contributo in Conio Capitale (CCC) has been particularly prominent in assisting corporate locations in the Mezzogornio and Calabria. Here, subsidies may provide for 50–75% of the set-up costs associated with new investments. This level of support has parallel elsewhere in the southern part of the European Union but contrasts sharply with an average equivalent allowance of 10–20% in most northern EU member states (see Griffiths, 1994, p. 48).

EU policy and financing

While there are some inconsistencies between the regions which are supported under national regional policies and those which are supported under Community instruments, the latter are designed to support and to bolster national efforts in their most disadvantaged regions. The Communication from the Commission to the member states on the links between regional and competition policy of the Treaty (98/C 90/03) stresses a broad if imperfect consistency in the number and identity of regions covered under national and Community measures.

Community efforts provide broad support for national development measures by part-financing schemes and projects designed and implemented at national and/or regional level. In fact, projects associated with the EU's policies (and funds) must be 'co-financed' and involve co-operation between actors and authorities at European, national and subnational level. Funding (which should complement not replace that provided by the member states) comes predominantly from three sources:

1. the European Investment Bank (which grants cheap loans for special projects),
2. the EU Cohesion Fund (supplying finance to environmental and infrastructure projects in Spain, Greece, Portugal and Ireland), and
3. the so-called Structural Funds (*the European Regional Development Fund; European Social Fund; & European Agricultural Guidance and Guarantee Fund*).

The three Structural Funds (ERDF, ESF and EAGGF) have financed a number of European regional and social aid projects drawn up by the member states and/or the Brussels-based Commission. In the programming period 1994–99, fund assistance focused largely on specific types of problem regions identified by numbered objectives:

Objective 1 status. Regions whose development had been lagging behind as determined on the basis of relative per capita incomes. Eligibility applies where average per capita income is below 75% of the EU average. In the period 1994–99, regions of this nature included the West of Ireland and the Italian Mezzogornio. During this period, financing of projects in objective 1 regions accounted for 67.6% of all spending under the Structural Funds.

Objective 2 status. Declining industrial areas, for example former coal and steel regions such as the Ruhr, Piedmont and South Wales. In the period 1994–99, 11.1% of Structural Fund spending was channelled into these regions.

Objective 5b status. Regions defined as vulnerable areas in low-income rural regions and not designated as objective 1 areas (no region may receive assistance under more than one objective). Accounting for 4.9% of the Structural Fund budget between 1994 and 1999.

Objective 6 status. Areas defined as thinly populated such as those of the new member states, Finland and Sweden. Accounted for 0.5% of the programming budget, 1994–99.

Taken together, the regions covered by objectives 1, 2, 5b and 6 accounted for just over 80% of the Community's total ECU 154.5 billion assistance under the Structural Funds between 1994 and 1999 (http://www.inforegio.cec.eu.int/dg16_en.htm). The remaining money was targeted on a number of cross-regional issues (in relation to a set of further numbered objectives) and on Community Initatives (CIs). The cross-regional issues tackled included:

- long-term unemployment and the socio-economic integration of excluded groups (objective 3),
- unemployment associated with industrial change (objective 4), and
- the structural adaptation of fisheries and agriculture (objective 5a).

It is worth noting here that, for each budget or funding period, member states designate their own areas or 'regions', with statistical justifications for all inclusions (by objective area). From this basis, regions have been eligible to put together project proposals and (where successful) to receive structural funding. Most of the money paid out to objective 1 regions actually comes through the ERDF, which focuses on infrastructure, human resources and productive investment. The ESF has had the principal aim of encouraging job creation in areas of high unemployment (objective 2 areas) and of providing assistance for the development of new and appropriate skills. Thus its main emphasis has been on supporting training and retraining schemes. The fund has also provided money to help to retrain employees unfamiliar with new technologies, migrant workers and women who are returning to full- or part-time employment. EAGGF money (Guidance Section) has been spent on intervention and export subsidies in the agricultural sector. Funding is designed to help rural communities to diversify away from traditional forms of production to new areas of agricultural activity such as forestry, while at the same time preserving the fabric of rural society.

Regional and social aid in 2000–06

For the period 2000–06, a new system of European regional and social aid has been introduced with expenditure targeted on a streamlined list of three objective areas (Regulation 1260/99). An average of €26.2 billion (at 1999 prices) is to be spent per annum, as against €24.1 billion over the period 1994–99. An aggregate total amount of €213 billion is to be complemented by €46.80 billion worth of regional spending in the Candidate Countries of Central and Eastern Europe. Currently, the Commission estimates that eighty-five of eighty-nine considered CEE regions would be eligible for objective 1 status. This provides a present interest in directing Community funds into Candidate Countries so as to encourage their development.

The specific budgets, as well as the list of objective 1 regions for this period, have now been determined. Eligibility will continue to apply where a NUTS II area (member region) has an average per capita income of below 75% of the EU average and where member states have included that region on their objective 1 maps. A total budget of €127.5 billion shall apply for the period with financial allocations for each member state now set. The regions covered in 2000–06 include those of eastern Germany (except the former East Berlin), those of Greece (the entire country), ten Spanish regions, France's overseas departments, the west of Ireland, the Italian Mezzogiorno (with the exception of Molise), and the Austrian Burgenland. The objective 1 list also takes in the different regions of Portugal (with the exception of Lisbon and the Tagus Valley), six thinly populated regions in Finland and Sweden, and four areas in the United Kingdom. The UK regions, South Yorkshire, West Wales, Cornwall and Merseyside, will receive annual average support of €2,234 million. This represents 8.5% of the EU total. Throughout the EU, special transitional support amounting to €8.4 billion has been provided for those regions (e.g. the Highlands and Islands, and Northern Ireland) that are currently covered by objective 1 but which will be excluded from 2000.

Areas may qualify for the new objective 2 under the industrial, the rural, the urban or the fisheries strand, where there is experience of major socio-economic change. In keeping with the priority that the European Union gives to tackling the problem, unemployment is now established as the main criterion for inclusion. At the time of writing, member governments were still working on their maps of objective 2 areas but two central facts were known. First, objective 2 regions combined should cover no more than 18% of the total EU population (this compares with 23% with respect to objective 1). Second, those areas that lose their status (and this will apply to many UK regions) will be assured of transitional funds. Governments are expected to put forward NUTS III areas (larger territorial units) but states may attempt to broaden effective coverage by pursuing designations based on alternative NUTS classifications such as NUTS IV (local authority districts and unitary authorities) and NUTS V (wards). It is expected that around €4 billion will be allocated to the United Kingdom for areas eligible for objective 2 of the Structural Funds between 2000 and 2006.

The new objective 3 will provide for ESF backing of anti-poverty action and for the promotion of education, training, employment and equal opportunities. It should also be noted that €8,760 million has been set aside for four broad Community Initiatives (CIs):

- INTERREG (developing cross-border and inter-regional co-operation);
- URBAN (revitalizing depressed urban areas);
- LEADER (focused on rural development);
- EQUAL (combating inequalities in the labour market).

The Community has historically operated CIs but is now looking to consolidate over a dozen previous initiatives operational in the programming period 1994–99.

EU industrial policy

Our focus on EU regional policy measures was launched by questioning the very legality of regional state assistance in the EU member states under the EU's competition rules. Moving us away from this field, but with no less importance to the shaping of competition in Europe, is the issue of industrial policy-making in Europe. The EU's approaches to industry and competition are hardly unified but competition and industrial policy are closely related. Competition policy aims to offset market failures arising from scale economies and market power. Industrial policy (at least in part) is designed to offset other sources of market failure which arise in the production process. Moreover, like competition policy itself, the European Commission regards industrial policy not as an end in itself but as a means of facilitating and defending the Single Market.

With respect to industrial policy, the EU's role is largely restricted to co-ordination and to setting an overall framework for industry to operate within. All member states of the EU have their own industrial policies and there has been little effort to substitute these or to erode sovereign authority in this field. The Treaty on European Union describes the task as ensuring that 'the conditions necessary for the competitiveness of European industry exist' and the detail of Treaty provision makes clear the need for co-operation between EU, national and subnational authorities. With respect to the EU's own tasks, the Treaty defines four central challenges:

- speeding up industry's adjustment to structural changes;
- encouraging an environment in which initiative can thrive and in which undertakings, particularly small and medium sized, can develop;
- encouraging an environment favourable to co-operation between undertakings;
- fostering a better exploitation of the results of innovation and of research and technological development which are of potential value to industry.

A brief history

EU industrial policy originated with the sectoral concentration of the Paris Treaty (1951) which initiated a series of interventions in the coal and steel industries. However, no mention was made of industrial policy in the Rome Treaty, and, although pressures for the development of a coherent European approach intensified during the 1970s, national authorities tended to look to domestic measures in support of their ailing industries (e.g. steel, textiles, coal and ship-building). The lack of a clear mandate at Community level provided little scope for co-ordinated efforts towards reform and restructuring at a time when protectionism and other forms of government paternalism were widely employed. Even as a tug-of-war developed between supporters of more (e.g. France and Italy) and less (e.g. the UK and the Netherlands) interventionist policies, support for greater Community competence failed to swell. For many member states, there were already important sectors, e.g. coal, steel and agriculture, where national governments had ceded powers and where promotional activities to the advantage of Community undertakings could be jointly pursued.

Despite this, in the build-up to the IMP, the Council of Ministers adopted a 'Transnational Plan' designed to improve the competitiveness of European industry through technological and industrial innovation and through enhanced co-operative arrangements. In the period after the completion of the single market, EU industrial policy gathered speed around such objectives and found clearer direction. The 1993 White Paper on Growth, Competitiveness and Employment (European Commission, 1993) identified a number of issues concerning European competitiveness including the need to capitalize on the Community's industrial strengths, to develop industrial co-operation and strategic alliances, and to target measures to ensure the competitive functioning of markets. Today, EU industrial policy appears to have consolidated around these established principles and the further objectives of promoting the access of European enterprises to the global market and of achieving success in the new information markets. Consequently, in seeking to address the challenges of global competition and in order to promote fair and liberal competition in the major industrial sectors, the member states have distanced themselves from many of the principles of the 1970s, therein rejecting insularity and blanket protectionism. While 'industrial planning' is far from a redundant concept, European authorities now largely subscribe to a mix of non-interventionist and (strategic) interventionist measures. In principle, these are to be taken within the context of an open and competitive Community market, and with the purpose of responding to inherent industrial weakness and to new forms of competition.

To complete this overview, the EU's industrial policy is now strategically designed to help European business and industry to compete in the global marketplace (not to shield it from global market pressures) and to maximize the potential benefits of the SEM. Although a framework for an integrated industrial policy is really yet to emerge (such a *project* still runs the serious risk of political defeat), revisions to the Treaties have established a reasonably clear and coherent mission for common efforts. The amended Article 157 TEC (ex Article 130) highlights the need for policies to:

- encourage an open and competitive industrial sector,
- smooth adjustments to structural change,
- promote small and medium-sized enterprises,
- encourage co-operation in R&D, and
- modernize the industrial role of public administrations.

Supplementation has followed in the form of successive communications by DG-III (the directorate responsible for EU industrial policy). In 1999, these have stressed the further need to:

- eliminate institutional and regulatory barriers to the development of venture capital, and
- to reinforce intangible investment in research, skills and training.

Backing research

Perhaps top of the agenda for improved competitiveness is the continued promotion of research and technological development (R&TD). Knowledge-based industries are now outstripping traditional sectors in growth, capitalization and exportability and, throughout industry, innovation is the key. In information technology, for example, 78% of revenue comes from products that did not exist two years ago (EUR-OP News, 1999).

Since the SEA, R&TD has enjoyed its own Treaty Title and EU policy has expressed the clear objective of 'strengthening the scientific and technological bases of Community industry' (Article 163 TEC, ex Article 130f). In present shape, policy aims to encourage industrial competitiveness by the promotion of R&TD activities and to co-ordinate Community-wide research efforts. EU action is designed to complement national policy (all EU governments provide clearance, tax rebates and other incentives to firms prepared to engage in collaborative R&D) and to give momentum to EU-based research. The EU directly undertakes its own research activities (through its Joint Research Centre) and promotes and finances shared-cost or contract research between private companies, research institutes and public bodies throughout the EU. Since the early 1980s the development, sponsorship, co-ordination and financing of such research – usually to about 50% of the total cost – has been pursued through a series of Framework Programmes dating back to 1983. Several research development projects have also been in place, such as RACE (telecommunications), BRITE (industrial technology) and ESPRIT (information technology).

The fourth framework programme (1994–98)

Under the fourth framework programme, ECU 13.1 billion was spent on research and technological development in information and communications, industrial technologies, biotechnology, the environment, transport and energy. Elsewhere, funding was attached to technological co-operation with non-EU countries (ECU 790 million); dissemination and application of results to small and medium-sized enterprises (ECU

600 million), and to the training and mobility of researchers (ECU 785 million). The overriding aim was to make the Community activities more selective so as to increase the economic spin-offs from Community research and to enable European industry (and subcontractors) to go back on the offensive in international competition. As noted in Chapter 3, there has been some evidence of success in this regard with an increased total of some 36,469 patent applications filed in EU countries in 1996. If not all of this improved performance can be attributed to the EU Framework Programmes, it is nonetheless noteworthy that, in 1998, 6,200 new projects were launched under the Community Framework, involving some 28,000 partners and creating more than 90,000 collaborative links (European Commission, 1999c). According to the Commission's research and technology directorate, these figures confirm 'the central position now occupied by [the EC] Framework Programmes in the landscape of European research' (European Commission, 1999d).

The fifth framework programme (1998–2002)

The fifth framework programme (FP5) sets out the present priorities for the European Union's research, technological development and demonstration (RTD) activities for the period 1998–2002. These priorities have been identified on the basis of a set of common criteria reflecting the major concerns of increasing industrial competitiveness and the quality of life for European citizens. Specifically, twenty-three key actions are to be resourced under a €14.96 billion budget. The funding for FP5 – up 4.5% in real terms on FP4 – is divided between what the Commission calls 'horizontal' and 'thematic' programmes, each indicated in Figure 5.4.

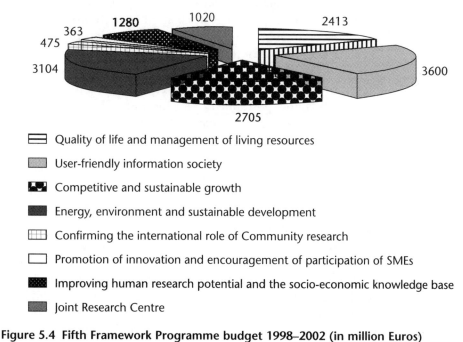

Quality of life and management of living resources

User-friendly information society

Competitive and sustainable growth

Energy, environment and sustainable development

Confirming the international role of Community research

Promotion of innovation and encouragement of participation of SMEs

Improving human research potential and the socio-economic knowledge base

Joint Research Centre

Figure 5.4 Fifth Framework Programme budget 1998–2002 (in million Euros)
Source: European Commission

The horizontal programmes attract a €3,138 million share of the FP5 budget. Focus is on:

- expanding Europe's socio-economic knowledge base (one key action);
- ensuring SME research promotion;
- confirming the international role of Community research; and
- developing the EU's own Joint Research Centre.

The thematic programmes attract a €11,822 million share of FP5 funding and encompass twenty-two of the twenty-three new 'key actions' and the areas of research that they cover. Focus is on:

- life science (six key actions);
- the information society (four key actions);
- sustainable industrial growth (four key actions); and
- energy and the environment (eight key actions).

Within this framework, individual action areas include the acquisition of critical technologies for aeronautics (aerodynamics, flight mechanics etc.) and the development of economical, efficient and clean technologies for road and rail vehicles. These and other projects are significant in their promotion of innovation and adaptation in European commercial sectors and directly involve a small community of innovative firms. In Starlab for example, fifty-six partners – thirteen of them industrial companies – are working on six biotechnology projects involving lactic acid bacteria (micro-organisms that develop in milk) and the improvement of food product qualities and safety. Participation in such projects may also sow the seeds for profitable collaborations and/or for independent corporate growth. For example, thanks to the support of the ESPRIT programme and of two German lens and glass companies, the Dutch company ASM Lithographics has become a global market force in the printing of the integrated circuits found in microprocessors. In another case, Pirelli is now positioned to exploit new commercial advantages from a steel cord–rubber adhesion technology developed with Rhône Poulenc Chimie and scientific partners in the BRITE–EURAM Euro-tyre project. Pirelli claims that tests have demonstrated the superiority of the new wire–rubber adhesion system and that it will be incorporated into its next generation of top-end car tyres.

Critics of the EU's technology policies have, however, made persuasive claim that, since the inception of Community R&D activities, there has been lots of research and little development. For some, the EC has concentrated unduly on pre-competitive research (lying between basic research and applied commercial development) and has been slow in moving R&D close enough to the market. Of course the failure of high-profile projects such as High Definition Television (HDTV) has added fuel to the critics' fire. Critics also point out that the EU's research budget continues to represent only about 5% of overall civil R&D spending in Europe. Despite this, there is renewed optimism that Community R&TD efforts are now more commercially driven and better targeted. The EU is encouraging European firms to take full advantage of collaborative research activities and, in many cases, is putting up the money. Its insistence on transnationality promotes cross-border activity (at least two partners from different EU countries must participate in a project) and proposals are evaluated on merit, not proportional to member state quotas.

Enterprise policy

The Commission has addressed many of its recent communications in the different policy fields towards the specific needs of small and medium-sized enterprises (SMEs). The broad aim has been to initiate further expansion and to create the optimal competitive environment for SME business success, growth and co-operation. The single clearest manifestation of this has been the establishment of a separate Directorate-General (and Commissioner post) for Enterprise, thereby creating a technical distinction between industrial policy and enterprise policy.

The first measure establishing Community enterprise policy was the organization in 1983, following a proposal from the European Parliament, of the European Year of Small and Medium-Sized Enterprises and Craft Industry. At its meeting in Luxembourg on 2 and 3 December 1985, the European Council decided to institute an assessment of the impact of Community proposals on SMEs and the preparation of measures to simplify their administrative, tax and regulatory environments. A new SME 'task force' was set up in June 1986 and a concerted programme was launched later that year with two overriding aims: creating a favourable environment for SME activities and providing services to support growth and to maintain their flexibility. On the first point, the Commission concerned itself with fostering entrepreneurship, improving the administrative, competitive and regulatory environments of smaller businesses, and with modifying company law. On the second, training and information initiatives figured large, particularly in relation to export procedures, company formation and growth, innovation and co-operative agreements. The 1986 initiative was followed up in 1989 with a new Council Decision on the improvement of the business environment and the promotion of enterprise, and the allocation of more resources to the policy. It was also at this stage that the new Directorate-General XXIII for Enterprise was established. Since these foundations were put in place, enterprise policy objectives have been pursued through three multi-annual programmes. The most recent of these was adopted on 14 November 1996 to cover the period 1997–2000. This now provides the legal and budgetary basis (€127 million) for the Community's SME policy actions with the following principal objectives (European Commission, 1996):

- to simplify and improve the administrative and regulatory business environment;
- to improve the financial environment for enterprises;
- to help SMEs to Europeanize and internationalize their strategies;
- to enhance SME competitiveness and improve access to research, innovation and training;
- to promote entrepreneurship and support special target groups.

The different elements, services and initiatives here are comprehensively profiled by DG XXIII at the following URL location address: http://europa.eu.int/en/comm/ dg23/guide_en/index2.htm. In the context of present analysis, and given earlier commentary on SMEs in Europe, two elements of enterprise policy are considered subsequently.

Communication and SME co-operation

In achieving many of its enterprise policy aims, the Commission has taken it upon itself to co-ordinate information provision to ensure that firms are fully aware of their rights and opportunities in the European marketplace and to put Europe's SMEs in easier contact with one another. This has resulted in organizational contact schemes such as 'Europarternariat' and the establishment of 275 European Business Information Centres (EICs) across the EU, often linked to existing organizations such as chambers of commerce. The European Commission, which is anxious to exploit the potential of EICs for the maximum benefit to SMEs, has appointed EICs as 'first-stop shops' providing a first port of call for expert service and advice. This implies that the EICs will refer businesses to other specialized networks or organiz- ations when very specific assistance is required. The Europarternariat scheme is designed to encourage small and medium-sized businesses from all over the Community (and third countries) to establish business relationships with their counterparts in less-favoured regions or those suffering from industrial decline. Under the programme, biannual events are organized where heads of SMEs from external regions which meet the specific criteria for participating in the scheme are brought into contact with those in the host region. On average, 30–40% of enter- prises in the host region conclude co-operation agreements as a result of a Europartenariat conference.

Co-operation initiatives have in fact been paid reasonable attention since the early days of EC enterprise policy with the formation of the BRE correspondents network in 1983 and the BC-NET network of business counsellors in 1988. These initiatives assist SMEs (of any kind) with defined free, part- and full-cost services in their search for financial, technical and commercial partners across Community borders. BC-NET handles both confidential and non-confidential requests and takes the inexperienced or building enterprise through a series of stages. Although varying from case to case, this typically encompasses the design of a co-operation profile and the registration and circulation of various details via the BC-NET data- base.

Research and Development: Integrating SMEs

In the light of the preceding analysis, it is also noteworthy that the Commission has actively encouraged the inclusion of SMEs in the Community R&TD programmes. Some theorists argue that research monies should be channelled into larger grants and concentrated on fewer advantaged players. However, there is no proof that larger institutions are better placed than smaller ones to develop or to profit from new technologies and this kind of thinking has been flatly rejected by the

Commission. Brussels Enterprise and Research staffs have published statistics claiming that Europe's SMEs are innovating twice as much (per employee) as large companies. Indeed, the Commission has placed great emphasis on the record of involvement of over 12,000 SMEs in the R&TD activities in the first four framework programmes. Technology stimulation measures for SMEs were actually introduced in twelve of the specific RTD programmes under FP4 and there is a specific SME unit within the Commission services responsible for RTD. Under FP5, horizontal programme number two, *'Promotion of innovation and encouragement of participation of SMEs'*, will also make better use of research results by smaller firms and create a single entry point for SMEs to EU programmes (EUR-OP News, 1999).

Conclusions

Without the EU policies on competition and industry, the benefits of the Single European Market would be simply undermined. National or regional competition authorities are ill-equipped to grapple with problems posed by commercial behaviour beyond their home markets and, in isolation, national measures in support of industry (research and enterprise) could neither confront common challenges nor avoid conflict. Equally, although hardly unified, the EU's approaches in these fields are interdependent in the extent of issue overlap and in many of their objectives. Many of the problems and limitations associated with the development and execution of policy are also shared. Although the EU has secured jurisdiction over certain competition cases, the enforcement of competition rules throughout the EU still rests heavily with national authorities and, as with industrial policies, the relationship between EU and national-level authority is complex. Ultimately, business firms must pay specific attention to the regulatory and financial frameworks attaching to these policies. These require a careful audit so as to ensure compliance with legal requirements and/or the maximization of commercial opportunities. The absence of effective monitoring, at least of those areas with possible effect on a given business firm, may lead to competitive disadvantage.

No single chapter could do justice to these different policy areas and the reader is carefully directed both to the references attaching to this chapter and to the web links provided. In particular, the issue of global competition rules is certain to figure prominently in the forthcoming debates of the WTO Millennium Round. Equally, with respect to the treatment of industrial policy issues in this chapter, analysis has been deliberately selective and has reflected some of the concentrations of earlier passages. It must be especially clear that, in the broader sense, the Community's industrial policy extends to the management of dynamic change, success and failure in specific industrial sectors. Among these, we can count Europe's 'Sunrise' industries – that is emerging high-tech industries such as advanced telecommunications – and those 'Sunset' industries such as coal and ship-building suffering from excess capacity and now in long-term decline.

Review questions for Chapter 5

1. The EU's competition rules are seen as a 'pillar' of the Single Market. Why is this?

2. What are the main areas covered by EU competition rules?

3. In the field of anti-trust, what are block exemptions and why are they considered necessary?

4. What is the relationship between EU level and national competition authorities?

5. What factors lay behind the introduction of a specific Merger Control Regulation?

6. What are some of the implications of widening the scope of the EC Merger Regulation?

7. Why is it important for companies to consider the implications of competition law? What can be the consequences if firms remain ignorant of them?

8. What forms of state aid does the EU try to prohibit and what are the grounds for such action?

9. What are some of the difficulties encountered in attempting to control state aids in Europe?

10. Certain forms of state assistance to industry are legal under Article 87. Why is this?

11. What forms of regional aid assistance can you identify? Can you explain the relationship between regional aid at state level and regional assistance at EU level?

12. Why has the EU concerned itself with the development of enterprise and the promotion of entrepreneurship?

13. What is the function of EU research and development policy? Have EU programmes contributed positively to R&TD efforts in Europe?

14. Identify other aspects of EU industrial policy.

Web guide

Competition Policy and issues

European Parliament: Policy Fact Sheet @
http://www.europarl.eu.int/dg4/factsheets/en/#3

EUROPA: Competition Policy Summary @ http://europa.eu.int/pol/comp/index_en.htm

EU Business News (Competition News) @
http://www.eubusiness.com/competit/index.htm

The European Commission: Competition Directorate-General @ http://europa.eu.int/comm/dgs/competition/index_en.htm

XXVIIIth Report on Competition Policy (Commission of the European Communities, 1999) @ http://europa.eu.int/comm/dg04/public/en/rap98.pdf

Seventh Survey on State Aid in the European Union in the Manufacturing and Certain Other Sectors (Commission of the European Communities, 1999) @http://europa.eu.int/comm/dg04/aid/en/rap7.pdf

Industry, research and enterprise

The European Commission: Enterprise Directorate-General @ http://europa.eu.int/en/comm/dgs/enterprise/index_en.htm

The Fifth Framework Programme of the European Community for Research, Technological Development and Demonstration Activities (1998 – 2002) @ http://europa.eu.int/comm/research/fp5.html

Regional aid–policy

INFOREGIO http://www.inforegio.cec.eu.int/

References

Armstrong, K. and Bulmer, S. (1998) *The Governance of the Single European Market*, Manchester University Press.

Burke, T., Genn-Bash, A. and Haines, R. (1991) *Competition In Theory and Practice*, Routledge.

Cecchini, P. (1988) *The European Challenge 1992: The Benefits of a Single Market*, Wildwood House.

Davison, L.M. and Fitzpatrick, E. (1998) An assessment of Community interest, Community dimension and decentralisation in EU competition policy, *European Business Review*, **98**(3), 160–7.

Economist (1997) The addicts in Europe: state aid, *The Economist* (US), **344**(8044), 22 November, 75.

El-Kahal, S. (1998) *Business in Europe*, McGraw-Hill.

EUR-OP News (1999) *Supplement on Research Policy*, no.1 1999, European Communities Publications Office.

European Commission (1993) *Growth, Competitiveness and Employment – The Challenges and Ways Forward in the 21st Century*, COM(93) 700 final.

European Commission (1996) *Third Multiannual Programme for SMEs in the European Union (1997–2000)*, COM (96) 98 final.

European Commission (1999a) European Community Competition Policy – XXVIIIth report on competition policy, 1998 (online) (http://europa.eu.int/comm/dg04/public/en/rap98.pdf).

European Commission (1999b) Seventh survey on state aid in the European Union in the manufacturing and certain other sectors (online) (http://europa.eu.int/comm/dg04/aid/en/rap7.pdf).

European Commission (1999c) *Research and Technological Development Activities of the European Union – 1999 Annual Report*, COM (99) 284.

European Commission (1999d) Community research: a continued dynamism closer to the needs of society, Press Release, 21 June 1999, Brussels (online) (http://europa.eu.int/comm/dg12/press/1999/pr2106en.html).

European Parliament (1999) Fact sheet: the Single Market – rules on competition (online) (http://www.europarl.eu.int/dg4/factsheets/en/3_3_.htm).

Fitzpatrick, E. (1995) Articles 85 and 86: control of restrictive practices and abuses of dominant positions, in Davison, L. and Fitzpatrick, E. (eds), *The European Competitive Environment: Texts and Cases*, Butterworth-Heinemann.

Griffiths, G. (1994) Hand-outs don't help out, *European Business*, February, 48–9.

Peck, F., Stone, I. and Coteban, M. (1996) Technology parks and regional development in the Southern European periphery: the Andalucia case, *European Urban and Regional Studies*, **3**(1), 53–65.

Story, J. (1996) EC competition policy: the merger and acquisition directive, in Cadot, O., Landis Gabel, H., Storey, J. and Webber, D. (eds), *European Casebook on Industrial and Trade Policy*, Prentice-Hall.

Turner, C. (1995) Competition policy in the member states: a Case of Convergence?, in Davison, L. and Fitzpatrick, E. (eds), *The European Competitive Environment: Texts and Cases*, Butterworth-Heinemann.

Wilks, S. and McGowan, L. (1995) Disarming the Commission: the debate over a European cartel office, *Journal of Common Market Studies*, **33**(2), 259–75.

6 The European workforce: change and regulation

Central themes

- EU social policy
- The Social Charter/Chapter
- UK policy and opt-outs
- Working time
- Worker consultation and information
- Equal opportunities
- EU labour markets
- Women and the European labour market
- Unionism and Eurocorporatism
- Employment policies
- Deregulation and employment reform
- The flexibility debate
- Transitions in work

Introduction

Like those policies previously examined, the EU's 'social' policy is of major consequence to business environments throughout Western Europe. Covering such areas as equal opportunities for men and women, working conditions, and health and safety at work, the policy contributes to both the rights and the experiences of the EU workforce and to the regulatory environments of their employers. Specifically, the supranational regulation of employment and social matters has created a situation in which working rights and employment conditions are being slowly harmonized around a set of basic or minimum standards. Thus, while the EU continues to offer a patchwork quilt of employment rules and practices, the reality has dawned of an open EU labour market in which workers are free to work wherever there is opportunity and where prevailing laws and protections often have their basis in Community-level agreement. It is these issues that dominate the present chapter, providing a conclusion to our early concentration on the business consequences of EU integration. It is clear, however, that any examination of social and employment policy-making in the European context must link with examination of structural change in European labour markets and with address of new practices in work and production. As we shall see, many changes are being experienced at this level, including the greater use of working time and contractual flexibility. In short, workers and employers throughout the EU are adapting to a labour environment in Europe that concerns not only new forms and centres of regulation but also new patterns of work and organization.

Analysis begins with the EU's record on social and employment questions. The EU's attempts to harmonize (and to improve) work and employment conditions across the member states are among its most controversial of interventions and highlight many of the structural and policy issues salient in this area. Each extension of Community authority has been associated with debate and argument over the balance of legislative power between the member states and EU institutions and over the challenges inherent in economic and organizational change in Europe. Indeed, since the Community's landmark 'Charter of Fundamental Social Rights of Workers' (1989), argument has raged over the direction and contribution of European policy measures and over the efficiency of European employment systems in a context of global competition. Although new Titles on employment and social matters have now been fully integrated into the Treaties, questions of work and employment still provoke discomfort between EU partners and a competition of policy prescriptions. Indeed, while the member states have declared their intent to work together and to co-ordinate their employment policies, questions still surround the direction of future action and the bridging of ideological divisions between the member states. These divisions have contributed to and have been compounded by repeated disagreement over the role and use of supranational legal instruments in the social and employment fields.

The social dimension and its impact on business

The early stages of social policy

The social dimension has always been considered as an integral part of the European integration process. Provisions of the Paris Treaty (1951) related to questions of health and safety (Article 56, ECSC Treaty) and the Treaty of Rome (1957) stated clearly that there should be an improvement in the working and living conditions of all Community citizens.

In the preamble and Articles 117–122 of the EEC Treaty (*Rome Treaty*), emphasis was placed on:

- harmonized living and working standards,

- equal pay for equal work by men and women,

- working conditions and worker safety, and

- vocational training.

The Treaty also established a European Social Fund (Article 123, EEC Treaty) in order to increase employment prospects and mobility throughout the Community, as well as the principle of free movement for Community workers (Articles 48–51, EEC Treaty).

Despite such provision, the scope for action on common social policy-making was initially quite weak, with a lack of effective policy instruments and inadequate enforcement of embodied Treaty principles. The only area of real activity was the co-ordination of social security systems for migrant workers, and it was not until the early 1970s that EC social policy was truly established. Following the Paris Summit of 1972 – at which a number of member states spoke of facilitating economic and social cohesion in the EEC – a (joint) Social Action Programme (SAP) was launched along with a review of the European Social Fund (ESF). This Social Action Programme led to landmark legislation in the social-employment field after what has been described as a period of 'benign neglect' (see Mosley, 1990). Between 1974 and 1979, directives were adopted on working conditions, training and promotion, health and safety, and equal opportunities. Noteworthy here were Directive 75/117 on the approximation of laws relating to the application of the principle of equal pay between the sexes, and Directive 76/207 on the implementation of the principle of equal treatment for men and women in most aspects of employment. A further directive on equal treatment in social security matters was also passed in the late 1970s (Directive 79/7) although proposals concerning parental leave and equal state retirement ages were not adopted at this time. Employees were also given protective rights in situations of collective redundancies (Directive 75/129) and the transfer of undertakings (Directive 77/187).

However, it was only with the accession of Jacques Delors to the Presidency of the European Commission (in 1985) and with the advent of the Internal Market Programme, that EC social policy really took off. Delors is widely credited as having played a lead role in developing the idea of a *'social dimension'* to Community integration and of channelling fears over internal market consequences into support for *'l'éspace sociale'*. A series of speeches and working papers in 1985 and 1986 ensured that social commitments and workers' rights were placed on the EC agenda and the Commission actively promoted the idea of expanded social programmes. Following the ratification of the Single European Act (1987), the Commission began to give greater substance to its ideas. Fears were now raised throughout the Community that Single Market freedoms might lead to the erosion of workers' rights and of health and safety standards throughout Europe. Although investors would continue to base investment and location decisions on a multitude of factors, investors would now be free (in an open Community market) to relocate from higher-cost and heavily regulated centres to those characterized by lower levels of business regulation, pay, and employee protection. Apart from the economic and social dislocations suggested by such a transfer of capital resources, one effect might be to encourage countries or regions to compete with each other for jobs and investment by reducing their own standards of workplace protection. Certainly, where national legislation imposed relatively higher social and employment costs, such regressive action might be necessary so as to prevent a haemorrhage of inward investment and employment – a process referred to as *social dumping*. Accompanying the problem of social dumping was the problem (and reverse tendency) of *social tourism*. In the new Single Market, workers, or more especially non-workers, might tend to migrate from disadvantaged regions with poor social protection to those with better opportunities, rights and protection (Alcock, 1996).

Community officials had long held that intervention towards a strengthened social dimension might help to improve European productivity and competitiveness. The Commission could now promote a baseline of minimum employment and social rights as an available (and potentially profitable) means of ensuring that the Single Market 'did not lead to a rush to the bottom in workplace conditions' (see Armstrong and Bulmer, 1998, p. 230). While there would be difficulties in achieving closer and upward harmonization of national measures, the Commission could now maintain that only enforceable Europe-wide planning and harmonized European standards could counteract the tendency of social dumping and prevent a depression (under market forces) of employment and social standards throughout the Community. Significantly, any regression from existing levels of provision might lead to a popular reaction against the IMP and to social and political discontent in specific Community regions.

The Social Charter

On 17 May 1989, the Commission produced a new document entitled *'Community Charter on the Fundamental Social Rights of Workers'*. This Charter set out a set of basic social rights (to be guaranteed under Community law) and committed the Community to the improvement of living and working conditions within the SEM. All of the Community governments except Britain proclaimed support for this Charter, with six governments (including those in Bonn and Paris) immediately calling for the preparation of detailed legislation. At the Strasbourg Council in December 1989, the UK was again isolated as the other EC governments adopted the draft Charter and agreed to the principle of a new Social Action Programme. In its detail, the approved Social Charter listed forty-seven actions to be taken at Community level – about half of them needing legislation. These were to cover such ground as freedom of movement, employment and remuneration, living and working conditions, equality of treatment, information and consultation (on management decision-making), and health and safety in the workplace. In all, the Charter specified twelve areas of entitlement (for workers and citizens) and encompassed a commitment to translate agreed and guiding principles into concrete and legal measures. These twelve areas, and attaching declarations, provided an echo of many of those essential principles enshrined in the European

Social Charter of the Council of Europe, which was signed at Turin on 18 October 1961.

An outline of the main themes (and principles) of the Social Charter is given below. It should be clear that it was a wish to continue along the path laid down by the Social Charter (which itself did not have legal force) that motivated eleven of the twelve member governments to attempt subsequently to import a *'Social Chapter'* into the Community Treaties. Although future analysis will be made of this attempt – and of the resulting compromise – the following presentation reflects the extension of Community Charter principles into the Social Chapter and the resulting *'Agreement on Social Policy'* (as annexed to the Maastricht Treaty). Given British obstructionism on social regulation ahead of and throughout the 1990–91 IGC, this agreement was concluded between the other eleven member states so as to allow for further progress towards a strengthened social policy. As of 1999 and the final ratification of the Amsterdam Treaty, this agreement has been fully incorporated into the main Community Treaty (new Articles 136–145, TEC) bringing final coherence to the various provisions on social policy affecting the fifteen member states.

Right of freedom of movement

According to the Social Charter, each citizen of the EC (now EU) should have the right to freedom of movement throughout the territory of the EU and to 'establishment' for the purposes of work or training. This freedom – established in the Rome Treaty itself – should only be subject to minor restriction, where justification might rest with concerns over public security or public health. At an operational level, the right to freedom of movement must enable any citizen to engage in any occupation or profession in the EU under the same terms as those applied to nationals of the host country subject to the provision of Community Law (see also Chapter 3). This right implies entitlement to equal treatment in all fields, including social and tax advantages, and the search for work. Furthermore, social protection must be extended to all citizens of the EU engaged in gainful employment in a country other than their country of origin on terms identical to those enjoyed by workers of the host country. Essentially, this means treating workers moving in the EU much as one would treat workers moving from one part of a member state to another. Discrimination in terms of low wage rates and a lack of social benefits, say against south Europeans working in northern European states, is implicitly barred.

Employment and remuneration

In general, a key principle of the Social Charter (and of the Agreement on Social Policy) is to establish fair remuneration for all employment in the EU. In effect, this means establishing an *equitable* wage defined as 'a wage sufficient to enable a worker to have a decent standard of living'. This contrasts with the idea of a *minimum* wage which is normally defined as a minimum level of remuneration guaranteed by law. As of 1999, legal national minimum wages were in place in eight member states (Belgium, Greece, France, Luxembourg, the Netherlands, Portugal, the UK and Spain). There has been no firm proposal for a uniform minimum wage across the EC/EU and the UK's national minimum wage was only introduced in 1999.

Improvement of living and working conditions

Living and working conditions are not discrete entities. We all spend a large part of our lives at work. The quality of the workplace, the work we do, the way we are treated and the extent of our own self-determination at work, all have an effect on our general quality of life and of the efforts we make at work. It has long been recognized by the best employers that it is not in their best interests to treat labour as a mere factor of production and that time spent on considering employee utility in the workplace is often rewarded by higher productivity and lower absenteeism.

A general aim of the single European labour market is to lead to an improvement in the living and working conditions of workers in the EU. The Social Charter provided significant prescription on the organization of work, with an emphasis on flexible working time arrangements and on establishing a maximum duration of working time per week. The later summary of legislative action demonstrates the significant attention of the Commission, social partners and member states to improving conditions in all forms of employment including: contracts of fixed and unfixed duration, full- and part-time work, and temporary work.

Right to social protection

Since the Social Charter agreement, the member states have been in agreement that social security arrangements should be harmonized in their structure but not in their value across the EU. The payment of unemployment benefits at the German level in Portugal, for example, would encourage people in Portugal never to work again. The principle established is that all workers, whatever their status, shall enjoy social security cover proportional to length of service, their pay and their financial contribution to the social protection system. Workers who are unemployed or otherwise excluded from the labour market shall receive appropriate benefit. Where this is not unemployment benefit and where such a person does not have adequate means of subsistence, they shall be able to receive a minimum income and appropriate social assistance.

Right to freedom of association

One of the basic statements of the Social Charter was that every employer and every worker in the EU shall have the right to belong freely to any professional or trade union organization of his/her choice. This right shall entail recognition of the right to belong to a trade union. Therefore some governments and some firms which did not allow trade union membership for certain occupations have been forced to reassess their restrictive practices as these principles have acquired legal status. This general right to trade union membership also extends to the freedom to negotiate and conclude collective agreements rather than to have conditions and pay awards imposed. It also relates to the right to renounce the aforementioned rights without any personal or occupational damage being suffered by the person concerned. In other words, it means that if workers refuse to join trade unions, then they have a right to do so. This implies that closed shops may not be implemented. The establishment and utilization of procedures of conciliation, mediation and arbitration for the settlement of industrial disputes are encouraged.

Right to vocational training

The intention in the Social Charter was that every European worker should have the opportunity to continue vocational training during his/her working life. Public authorities, companies and trades unions are thus encouraged to set up and operate continuing and permanent training systems, enabling every citizen to undergo training and retraining throughout his/her working life. Moreover, leave for training purposes and for periodical training, particularly as a result of technological developments, is to be encouraged. Every EU citizen shall have the right to enrol for occupational training courses, including those at university level, on the same terms as those enjoyed by nationals of the member states in the country in which the courses take place.

Right of men and women to equal treatment

As considered, equal opportunities for men and women have been a central platform of EC/EU social policy since its very inception. The Social Charter reiterated the basic principles of Article 119 of the Rome Treaty (now Article 141, TEC) and envisaged that action on remuneration, access to employment, social protection, education, vocational training and career development would be intensified. However, as has been seen in the UK, despite having had Equal Pay Acts for almost twenty years, the degree to which this is workable depends largely on the responses and behaviour of employers. Many still choose to discriminate against women. When it comes to discrimination (either active or passive) or through negligence, the scope for avoidance of legislation is enormous. This is a continuing feature of the female employment experience in Europe, as discussed later in this chapter.

Right to information, consultation and participation of workers

Among those principles rejected by the UK Government pre-1997, the Social Charter states that 'information, consultation and participation of workers must be developed along appropriate lines', taking account of the laws, contractual agreements and practices in force in the member states. Although the issue of worker consultation was not central to the Single Market programme, the Commission had long held the belief that a common market needed generalized rules on information and consultation of the workforce (see the Vredeling Proposal of 1980).

The Internal Market strengthened the case for relevant EC legislation and the Commission's favour for new provisions found support among several governments, especially those accustomed to works councils at national level. Existing

Community-wide provision was limited (and largely ineffective) with restriction to decade-old directives on consultation *vis-à-vis* collective redundancies and on the safeguarding of workers' rights in conjunction with the transfer of undertakings. With a view to the implementation of the Charter, the Commission's Second Action Programme provided for an instrument on the increase in worker representation and consultation (on a works council or parallel board) in 'European scale undertakings'. The succeeding account of legislative outcomes reveals the role of the European Works Councils Directive in satisfying this particular aim. Both the ETUC and ECOSOC had supported the specific targeting of European transnationals and, according to Hall (1992, p. 550), this was influential in ensuring that all provisions not specifically connected to transnational circumstances were excluded. Following agreement on European works councils, attention has shifted again to the establishment of procedures for information, consultation and participation in national scale undertakings.

Since a basic aim of the EU is to stimulate growth and employment, the Commission has been happy to promote the role and importance of participatory arrangements such as profit-sharing and share-ownership schemes. Such ideas are also expressed in the Social Charter. Experiences of worker participation in a number of forms, and from a number of sources, show that there are benefits associated with these arrangements (see Weitzman, 1984; Cable, 1988). Not only does it seem to be in the interest of workers to have a share in profits and/or a role in planning in their workplace, the evidence also shows that it is in the interests of businesses themselves. An involved workforce is likely to judge atmosphere at work in a better light and, as such, is likely to work harder, be absent less and be less likely to move to other firms, taking their skills with them. Surprisingly, perhaps, some trade unions have been wary of co-operative arrangements, profit-related pay and worker share-ownership schemes which, ostensibly at least, advance the principle of worker participation.

Protection of children and adolescents

According to the Social Charter, appropriate measures must be taken in the workplace with a view to providing basic protection for children and adolescents with a minimum employment age to be fixed at no less than fifteen years. One aim is to ensure that young people get a thorough preparation for employment via the provision of vocational training. Another is that they should receive equitable remuneration (in accordance with national practice) when in gainful employment.

Health protection and safety at the workplace

The Single European Act (1986) gave the EC new powers in the area of health and safety. The SEA states that there should be greater effort to improve workers' health and safety and a harmonization of conditions across the member states. These objectives were restated in the Social Charter, thereby encouraging the adoption of new minimum requirement directives as a development of existing health and safety provisions.

Rights of the elderly

According to the Social Charter, every EU citizen in retirement shall be entitled to receive a minimum income giving him/her a decent standard of living. This shall include citizens who, having reached retirement, are not entitled to a pension (because they have never been part of the labour market) and those who have no other adequate means of subsistence.

Rights of the disabled

The Charter also refers to the combating of social exclusion and to the fullest possible integration of the disabled into working life. Objectives on disability include greater access to employment and training opportunities, improved mobility for disabled persons, transport and housing.

From Charter to action

The attempt to transform the Social Charter into legislation began quickly (see Rhodes, 1991; Wise and Gibb, 1993). Before the end of 1989, a Second Action Programme had been submitted to the Council of Ministers and two General (or Framework) directives had been concluded. First, the Council concluded a General Directive requiring all member states to recognize as equivalent regulated professional qualifications obtained in any and all member states (Directive 89/48). Second, the Council concluded agreement on a new framework for the protection of health and safety in the workplace (Directive 89/391). Fourteen new directives would extend from this particular agreement with progress enabled by the ground-breaking provision for qualified majority voting (on health and safety issues) under the new Article 118a of the SEA. In the aftermath of the Strasbourg Council, the Council also proceeded with discussions on main contractual terms, protection of pregnant women's rights and benefits and maternity leave, signalling a breadth of focus consistent with the solemn declarations of the Social Charter. However, just as prior to the SEA, difficulties in converging national laws and in achieving unanimous political support for social measures, meant that many proposals made by the Commission were not enacted. Despite this and indeed because of the EC's lack of legal muscle in the field, the member states negotiated a new 'Social Chapter' for inclusion in the EC Treaty. By the point of the Maastricht Council in December 1991, it was envisaged that this Chapter would:

- bring amendments to Articles 117–122 of the 1957 Treaty,
- give a Treaty basis to the objectives of the Social Charter,
- extend EC/EU competence into new areas such as social security and the protection of employees (allowing for unanimous decisions in the Council),
- extend the scope of qualified majority voting (QMV) to several new areas, and
- provide for greater consultation with the 'social partners' in the development of employment and social policies.

However, despite these limited ambitions and a number of exclusions – pay, rights of association and the right to strike, were all left out – the UK government would refuse to endorse the draft Social Chapter. The UK's central argument was that the costs of the Social Charter/Chapter were prohibitive and would cause the costs of businesses to increase while suffocating them in over-regulation. Fears were also raised that the United Kingdom could be outvoted on a wide range of damaging legislation which could be adopted by qualified majority voting (see Box 6.1).

BOX 6.1

A social Europe – understanding the UK position

Until 1997, the UK's position remained largely unchanged from the influence of Thatcherism. Intervention in labour markets and in the relationship between employers and employees was seen as unnecessary regulation, which would ultimately impose increased costs on jobs leading both to uncompetitive industry and to higher unemployment. In this view, the social dimension represented a continental approach to labour market management based on regulation and statutory obligation that contrasted with a British approach based on low burdens on business, voluntarism and flexible working practices. Freedom from Social Chapter constraints would boost the competitiveness of United Kingdom firms in world markets and increase their capacity to create and to maintain jobs. Moreover, the 'social dimension' also threatened to revive and to extend the power of the unions (e.g. through strengthened works councils) and would leave Brussels in control of new and important powers.

For Mrs Thatcher and her supporters, the idea of a social Europe (and of harmonized social and employment measures) was entirely misguided and was symptomatic of the centralist and corporatist tendencies she associated with the Community. Her infamous Bruges Speech in late 1988 berated a socialist, centralist agenda threatening to reverse the direction of domestic market and trade union reforms and to steal further powers from the British Parliament. Even her successor John Major, determined to place Britain 'at the heart of Europe', could not endorse the Social Chapter, with senior ministers condemning the plan as a 'job-destroying machine'. Indeed, Major's erstwhile Trade Secretary, Ian Lang, once described the Chapter as a 'socialist virus' and accused its supporters of wishing to 'sign a blank cheque' (*DTI press release 96/725* of 30 September 1996). Before his government's eviction in the General Election of May 1997, Lang was to claim that the adoption of the parental leave directive in maternity or adoption cases would have cost British companies £200 million if the Maastricht opt-out had not protected them. The claim was also made that the imposed directive limiting working hours (the so-called Working Time Directive) would cost UK industry over £2 billion (*Daily Telegraph*, 1 October 1996). The strategy devised to apply this measure to the UK (identifying it as a health and safety measure and thereby bringing it under Article 118a of the modified Rome Treaty) was the source of an ill-fated legal challenge and of wide condemnation within Conservative and industry ranks.

The direction of British policy was changed dramatically with the election of a Labour Government in May 1997. While in opposition, the Labour Party had repeatedly attacked Conservative warnings as alarmist and had suggested that the Commission was only offering improved standards of worker protection and the prospect of German-style worker participation. The Labour party was also able to highlight that Article 2 of the Social Chapter provided assurances that legislation would avoid imposing administrative, financial and legal constraints in a way which held back the creation and development of SMEs. Immediately after their election victory, Britain opted in to the Social Chapter, committing itself to extend the rights and benefits of the Chapter to the British people. In so doing, it established a more pragmatic approach to the issue encapsulated in the words of a post-election press release by the Foreign and Commonwealth Office:

> We do not accept that the British People should be second class citizens with less rights than employees on the Continent. We want our people to enjoy the right to information about their company and parental leave to be with their family, as good as those who work on the Continent, often for the same companies ... partnership between innovative management and a committed workforce is the key to a competitive company. We will test all future proposals under the Social Chapter by whether they promote competitiveness and help us to meet our goal of a skilled, flexible workforce. (*FCO press release* of 4 May 1997)

The effect of this policy shift was to immediately extend a small number of measures (adopted under the Agreement on Social Policy) and to smooth the way for the incorporation of the Social Chapter into the main body of the Community Treaty. This process was completed at the Amsterdam European Council in June 1997. Measures now applying in the UK and previously avoided under the Social Chapter opt-out concern the consultation of workers in European-scale undertakings, the burden of proof in cases of sexual discrimination, the rights of part-time workers and the right to parental leave.

The result was a separate agreement, among the other member states, annexed to the main body of the Treaty on European Union in the form of a special protocol, and re-affirming the commitment of the eleven to develop the rights set out in the Social Charter. Significantly, this 'Agreement on Social Policy' established a second route to binding social legislation at EU level with provision for qualified majority voting on working conditions, the information and consultation of workers, equal treatment of men and women, and the integration of people excluded from the labour market. In essence, where unanimous agreement could not be secured on a social proposal or where decisions could not be reached by a qualified majority under the Treaties (as under Article 118a), discussions could now bypass the United Kingdom. At this stage, the 'social partners' – the European Trade Union Confederation (ETUC), the Union of Industrial and Employers' Confederations of Europe (UNICE) and the European Centre of Public Enterprises (CEEP) – would have to be consulted on all proposals under consideration, becoming co-actors within the social area. These groups would enjoy the power to conclude independent collective agreements, which might later be turned into EC law.

The first practical results of this evolving Euro-corporatism were the adoption of Framework Agreements on parental leave and on part-time work. In both these cases, a succeeding Council Directive gives legal validity to the terms of agreement without itself containing any further or substantive provisions in relation to individual rights. The full text of the Framework Agreement is attached as an annex to the final Directive.

Social Europe: the key legislation

The European Union has passed a number of laws (directives) in recent years, which aim to improve employment rights in all European countries and which reflect the objectives of the Social Charter. By popular identification, these include:

- the European Works Council Directive (94/45/EC),
- the Directive on Parental Leave (96/34/EC),
- the Part-time Workers' Directive (97/81/EC),
- the Directive on Burden of Proof in cases of Sexual Discrimination (97/80/EC),
- the Working Time Directive (93/104/EC), and
- the Pregnant Workers' Directive (92/85/EC).

Most organizations in the EU will be affected in some way by this new legislation, with potential impact in the areas of work organization, recruitment, training, promotion, benefit and retention. Organizations operating on a European scale, and expanding beyond national frontiers, will face additional challenges and requirements tied to worker consultation and participation. As considered, a number of these Directives have only applied to the UK since 1998. This is explained by their original conclusion under the provisions of the Social Protocol and by the dumping of the UK opt-out in the summer of 1997. Both the Working Time and Pregnant Workers' Directives have applied since the early–mid-1990s. This is due to their introduction under Article 118a of the Rome Treaty (as revised by the SEA) and their identification as measures designed to improve health and safety at the workplace.

The following sections provide a summary of the content of these six Directives, which add to that existing rump of social and health and safety legislation passed by the EU Council since 1975:

- the Directive on Collective Redundancies (75/129/EEC),
- the Equal Pay Directive (75/117/EEC),
- the Equal Treatment Directive (76/207/EEC),
- the Directive on Transfers of Undertakings (77/187/EEC),
- the Social Security Directive (79/7/EEC),
- the Directive on Insolvency of Employers (80/987/EEC),
- the Occupational Social Security Directive (86/378/EEC),
- the Directive on Equal Treatment for Self-employed Men and Women (86/613/EEC), and
- the Framework Directive on Safety and Health of Workers at Work (89/391/EEC).

Council Directive 94/45/EC 'on the establishment of a European Works Council or a procedure in Community-scale undertakings and Community-scale groups of undertakings for the purposes of informing and consulting employees'

Reviving early proposals from 1990 (OJ 91/C 39/10), the European Works Council Directive (EWCD) was the first piece of legislation to be passed under the Social Protocol and was adopted by qualified majority without the participation of the UK. The aim of the Directive is to improve the information and consultation of workers by requiring, in transnational companies over a certain size, regular meetings of management and labour to discuss company policies and employment practices. Those meetings must take place in a cross-frontier consultation structure composing of at least thirty members and detailed in a written agreement. The Directive applies to:

- companies with at least 1,000 employees within the member states;
- companies with at least 150 employees in each of at least two participating member states;
- EU-scale groupings of companies with at least 1,000 employees within the EU and at least two undertakings in separate EU states with at least 150 employees.

Regulations to implement the EWCD in the UK came into force on 15 December 1999. They will apply to all UK-based companies with at least 1,000 employees in the European Economic Area (EEA) and with at least 150 employees in two of the EEA's member states. While several British based companies have long been complying with the EWCD on a voluntary basis (e.g. United Biscuits and GKN), the new measure is expected to bring some 200 additional companies within the scope of the Directive, of which 110 will be UK based. Nearly 100 companies headquartered in other member states will now be embraced by the Directive as the inclusion of the UK workforce puts them above the Directive's thresholds (http://www.incomesdata.co.uk/brief).

The Commission has now adopted a proposal for a Council Directive on information and consultation of employees in national companies with at least fifty employees. As under the EWCD (applying to European scale undertakings) obligations are imposed on the covered undertakings to inform and to consult their employees about issues directly affecting work organization and their employment contracts. The aim in consultation shall be to seek to reach prior agreement on the decision concerned. The Commission wants to establish a framework that fully enshrines into law the fundamental right of workers to be informed of and consulted on changes likely to impact upon them. The Vilvoorde case in 1997, in which the Renault car group decided to close its Belgium production facility without any prior consultations with worker representatives, exposes the limitations of the EWCD and of the EU Collective Redundancy Directive. Similar proposals on information and consultation rights were submitted as a part of the stalled Fifth Directive on Company Law.

Council Directive 96/34/EC 'on the framework agreement on parental leave concluded by UNICE, the CEEP and the ETUC'

This Directive guarantees workers of either sex the right to a minimum period of unpaid parental leave following the birth or adoption of a child. The leave can be taken to a total of three months (in one single block or by the aggregate of shorter periods) at any time between birth/adoption and a child's eighth birthday. Unless covered by voluntary allowances, this leave is unpaid. In all circumstances, it is in addition to and separate from paid maternity and paternity leave. About half of the EU member states give fathers the statutory right to a short period of paid leave at the time that their children are born. 'Paid' maternity leave, although provided in many different forms, is a universal principle throughout the EU.

Many EU states exceed a three-month guarantee of unpaid parental leave through their existing national legislation and will have to make few if any changes to existing law and practice. Nonetheless, the Directive is important in providing basic minimum standards across the EU and in establishing improved or original statutory terms in a small band of countries, including Greece, the United Kingdom and Ireland. Moreover, the Directive establishes some basic guarantees that have not always applied in the EU states. For example, the Directive makes it clear that an employee who takes parental leave is entitled to return to the same or equivalent job at the end of the period of leave and is protected from dismissal on the grounds of application for or absence on parental leave. These European-derived rules on parental leave are now contained in the United Kingdom's Employment Relations Act 1999 and have started to come into effect. The UK's new Employment Relations Act also takes into account a stream of case law on maternity issues extending from the European Court of Justice.

Council Directive 97/81/EC 'on the framework agreement on part-time work concluded by UNICE, the CEEP and the ETUC'

This Directive follows on from the discussions of the social partners on atypical and temporary work. The Directive provides equal contractual terms and conditions (pro rata) for 'part-time' workers with regard to pay, holiday entitlements and occupational sick leave. Unless different treatment can be justified on 'objective grounds', employers must treat their part- and full-time workers with equivalence. Thus, the Directive also makes it unlawful to discriminate unfairly against part-time workers with regard to bonus, shift and other additional payments made to comparable full-time staff, access to vocational training and promotion at work.

The term 'part-time worker' refers to an employee whose normal hours of work, calculated on a weekly basis or on average over a period of employment of up to one year, are less than the normal hours of a comparable full-time worker. Companies are also expected to provide 'timely information' on the availability of part-time and full-time positions in the establishment and to take measures to facilitate access to part-time work at all levels of the enterprise, including skilled and managerial positions. As far as possible, employers should give consideration to requests by workers to transfer from full-time to part-time and vice versa should the opportunity arise. A worker's refusal to transfer from full-time to part-time work or vice versa should not in itself constitute a valid reason for termination of employment.

The European Commission has also now adopted a proposal for a future Council Directive transposing the recent framework agreement (between the social partners) on 'fixed-term' work into EU law. This measure, which will have been enacted prior to the publication of this title, is set to curb the abuse of successive fixed-term contracts and to remove discrimination against temporary employees relative to permanent staff.

The new emphasis at EU level on atypical workers' rights must be seen in the context of structural change in European labour markets and with reference to the changing constitution of European workforces. Today, just over 15% of the 155 million workers in the EU work on a 'part-time' basis. As far as the proportion of part-timers in the total workforce is concerned there are effectively three camps of economies in the EU. First, there is a northern rump of economies where the number of part-time workers as a proportion of total employment is above the EU average of 16.6% and where flexible working arrangements have become well established. This is a group led by the Dutch. Second is a cluster of economies just below the EU average mark (e.g. France, Germany and Sweden) with between 10% and 16% of all workers working part time. A third group of member states consists of those who have had traditional restrictions on the use of part-time contracts and where the number of part-timers is under 10%. Some detail on national rates is provided in Table 6.1.

Table 6.1 Part-time employment as percentage of total employment

Country	Both sexes (1997)	Women (1997)	Men (1997)
Austria	10.8	22.0	02.1
Belgium	17.4	34.3	05.0
Denmark	17.9	24.7	11.9
Finland	08.5	11.7	05.3
France	15.5	25.6	06.3
Germany	15.0	29.8	03.3
Greece	08.7	14.2	05.3
Ireland	16.7	27.1	08.0
Italy	12.4	24.0	05.1
Luxembourg	10.7	25.3	02.1
Netherlands	29.1	54.6	10.6
Portugal	07.9	14.1	02.7
Spain	07.9	16.6	02.8
Sweden	15.7	24.5	06.7
United Kingdom	23.1	40.1	07.6
EU-15	16.6	30.6	05.5
OECD Total	14.2	23.4	06.7

Defined by a common standard based on thirty hours worked or less per week
Source: Labour Force Statistics 1977–1997, 1998 edition © OECD 1999

Council Directive 97/80 'on the burden of proof in cases of discrimination based on sex'

Building upon the directives on equal pay and equal treatment adopted before 1980, Directive 97/80 aims to ensure that the measures taken by member states to interpret the principle of equal treatment are made more effective by:

(a) including a definition of indirect discrimination, and

(b) by redefining the nature of burden of proof in cases of discrimination based on sex.

Specifically, the burden of proof in sex discrimination cases is effectively reversed with the respondent now responsible for establishing that there has been no breach of the principle of equal treatment. Member states are required to bring into force the laws necessary to comply with the directive by 1 January 2001. In the UK, employers facing sex discrimination cases already need to demonstrate that they did not discriminate so as to avoid an inference of discrimination being drawn against them. In this sense, the Directive will have less dramatic effect in the UK than in other member states.

Council Directive 93/104 'on the organization of working time'

Unlike the previous Directives considered here, the Council Directive on the organization of working time (hereafter the 'Working Time Directive' or WTD) was adopted under Treaty provision on the basis of Article 118a of the Treaty of Rome. As considered, this article sets the goal of promoting improvements in the standards of health and safety of workers in the EU, allowing for measures to be passed by qualified majority vote. The aim of the WTD is to ensure that workers are protected against adverse effects on their health and safety caused by working excessively long hours, inadequate rest, or disrupted work patterns. Consequently, the working time directive provides for:

- a forty-eight-hour limit to the working week (workers may exceed these hours if they elect to do so),
- a minimum daily rest period of eleven consecutive hours a day,
- a rest break where the working day is longer than six hours,
- a minimum rest period of one day a week,
- a statutory right to annual paid holiday (totalling four weeks), and
- a maximum of eight hours night work in any twenty-four-hour period.

The directive is implemented in UK domestic law by the Working Time Regulations 1998 (Statutory Instrument 1998/1833) which entered into force on 30 September 1998. According to the Office for National Statistics, the Directive is set to have a major social and economic impact in the UK given that over a quarter of all working fathers in Britain work in excess of a fifty-hour week (*source*: UK Office for National Statistics, 1997). At the time of writing, the UK Government was involved with other member states in considering Commission proposals covering working time arrangements for a number of excluded sectors including transport and health. This is likely to result in a future modification of the WTD and to the inclusion of some of the 5.6 million people working in the excluded sectors. It is now clear, however, that there will be no immediate extension of the Directive to health workers such as doctors and nurses (see Case Study 6.1). The ETUC has led the calls for an end to these exclusions, highlighting the plight of health and transport workers throughout the European Union. Workers in these sectors regularly experience sixty- to seventy-hour working weeks (http:/www.etuc.org). The exclusions themselves are a direct result of the watering-down of original working time proposals. Modifications were brought at the insistence of the UK government with a number of specific exclusions supported by other member states.

The entire issue of working time continues to attract attention (and headlines) throughout the EU. By the end of 1999, France will have fully enacted two laws cutting the number of working hours per employee to thirty-five (without any

---

CASE STUDY 6.1 **No working time prescription for EU doctors**

The maximum working week for junior hospital doctors in the European Union should not be reduced to the normal statutory forty-eight-hour limit for thirteen years, EU ministers agreed yesterday.

The deal delighted British ministers, who had pressed for a delay, but infuriated the European Commission, the EU's executive, and the medical profession. It could be overturned as a result of pressure from the European parliament.

The commission had suggested that the forty-eight-hour maximum, already applied to most other EU workers, should be implemented within seven years.

Padraig Flynn, acting social affairs commissioner, who has championed working hours limits, said yesterday's deal was morally unacceptable. Patients would continue to be treated by doctors who were exhausted and have their health endangered, he said.

The drive for a thirteen-year implementation period was led by the UK, although countries including Ireland, France and Italy had argued for longer than the commission's seven years.

Frank Dobson, health secretary, insisted the agreement by Europe's social affairs ministers would enable 'us to bring junior doctors inside the forty-eight-hour working time directive within a realistic time scale'.

He argued for extra time to train 6,000 new doctors needed to cope with the hours limits. But the British Medical Association, the doctors' trade union, said there were 35,000 junior doctors in training and it took only seven years for them to become consultants.

British junior doctors are limited to a fifty-six-hour week by a voluntary agreement but surveys have shown one in six works longer than this.

The BMA said it was 'extremely disappointed' at the EU agreement. 'We are going to write to every candidate in the European parliamentary elections and ask them to overturn this ludicrous proposal', said Andrew Hobart, chairman of the junior doctors committee.

Under EU law, working hours regulations must be agreed by member countries and the European Parliament jointly. Parliament has already said it wants a forty-eight-hour week for doctors to be implemented within four years.

Ann Widdecombe, shadow health secretary, said the agreement would 'plunge doctors' morale even lower' and could risk patients' lives.

Source: Financial Times, 26 May 1999

regression in terms of pay) and laying down the principles of a new working time regime including rules on the calculation and payment of overtime. According to this legislation, a statutory working time 'limit' will be set by January 2000 at an average of thirty-five hours per week (over twelve months). This will apply to all companies employing more than twenty people. On 1 January 2002 this statutory limit will be extended to all companies with twenty employees or fewer. Companies that reduce the working week to thirty-five hours will be granted a reduction in the social security contributions they have to pay on low-waged jobs. Already, the average French employee works just 1,599 hours a year, among the lowest totals in the OECD group (see Table 6.2) and below 40 hours a week (see Table 6.3).

Legislative action in France follows several years of attempts by the state to encourage companies to reduce working hours for their existing employees by col-

Table 6.2 Average number of hours worked annually per person, 1998 (selected OECD countries)

Japan	1,864 hours	United States	1,833 hours
France	1,599 hours	Germany	1,580 hours
Ireland	1,797 hours	Norway	1,401 hours
Sweden	1,551 hours	UK	1,587 hours
Greece	1,930 hours	Spain	1,821 hours

Source: Adapted from *Economic Growth in the OECD area: recent trends at the aggregate and sectoral level*, OECD Working Paper (ECO/WKP (2000)21) © OECD, 2000

Table 6.3 Average working weeks in the EU member states, 1998

Country	Full-time female (in industry)	Full-time male (in industry)
Austria	39.8	40.2
Belgium	37.5	39.1
Denmark	37.7	39.3
Finland	38.2	40.1
France	38.7	40.3
Germany	39.3	40.4
Greece	39.3	41.7
Ireland	41.5	41.5
Italy	36.3	39.7
Luxembourg	37.4	40.3
Netherland	38.5	39.2
Portugal	39.6	42.1
Spain	39.6	41.2
Sweden	40.0	40.2
UK	40.7	45.7
EU average	39.0	41.3

Note: Data for the Irish Republic 1997. EU average calculated using 1997 data for the Irish Republic
Source: Social Trends, 1998, National Statistics © Crown Copyright 2000

lective agreement as a way of creating more employment opportunities. Collective agreements on working time (at industrial and company level) are the preferred option of most EU states and in many continental countries have contributed to some progress toward reduction of the working week. The French approach is a controversial policy response to a national employment crisis and it remains to be seen what concrete effects the legislation will have both on national competitiveness and employment. While a fuller debate on working-time is taking shape in Europe, working time arrangements enshrined in legislation have been accused of hindering labour market flexibility and of impeding job creation (OECD, 1994). Certainly there are fears at Community level that the limits being introduced in France will put up employers' costs as staff opt to do more overtime.

Council Directive 92/85 'on the introduction of measures to encourage improvements in the health and safety at work of pregnant workers'

The Directive, which member states were obliged to enforce by the end of 1994, requires employers to take all appropriate steps to ensure that neither a pregnant worker nor her unborn child is exposed to a health risk in the workplace. The Directive also sets out certain employment rights for pregnant women:

- they cannot be dismissed for pregnancy-related reasons;
- they cannot be forced to work nights if this will damage their health;
- they have the right to at least fourteen weeks maternity leave, during which time they must either be paid or receive an adequate allowance;
- they must take two weeks compulsory maternity leave before or after confinement.

While the directive has been broadly welcomed, it is also clear that the commitments with respect to maternity leave and pay are really rather minimal, imposing only a series of minimum requirements. In this sense, the directive does little to eliminate the marked variations across the EU in, *inter alia*, the length of 'paid' maternity leave (which ranges from fourteen to twenty-eight weeks), the percentage of it that is compulsory and the level at which it is paid. These variations are highlighted in Figure 6.1. The Directive also includes a non-regression clause establishing that provision must not have the effect of reducing the level of existing national protection.

In their detailed study of the Pregnant Workers' Directive, Armstrong and Bulmer (1998, pp. 239–40) recall that the UK again disputed the EC's competence to regulate maternity provision on the basis of Article 118a and contributed to a watering down of proposals. With its specific fears about the upgrading of UK legislation (and associated costs), the UK was foremost in diluting the terms of agreement *vis-à-vis* the level and duration of maternity benefit. In the Council voting, much as with the WTD, the British government abstained while contesting the legal base of the Directive.

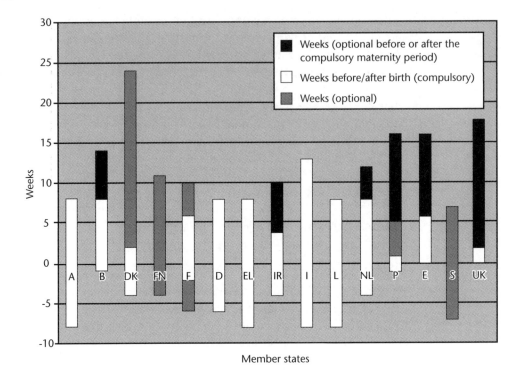

Figure 6.1 Maternity leave provision in the EU member states (minimum eligible period)
Note: Zero equals week of birth
Source: European Commission (1999)

CASE STUDY 6.2 | **EU social measures: little protest among UK's biggest companies**

Most large UK-owned companies believe the European Union social chapter, with its consequent legal regulation, is important in safeguarding employees' rights.

More than half favour the harmonization of employment regulation across the EU. Only 17% said they wanted the UK to opt out of the social chapter.

These are the conclusions of the first large independent study of the impact of the new EU-inspired employment law on the UK on the bigger companies. The survey was carried out by City Research Associates, the poll organization, for Lovell White Durrant, the international law firm. It is based on interviews with human resource directors employed by one in ten of the 750 largest companies in the UK.

But 80% of the directors voiced concern that the

social chapter would increase bureaucracy and business costs. The main criticism concerned the implementation of the working time regulations from last October. Nearly two-thirds of corporate respondents supported their introduction. This involves a maximum forty-eight-hour working week limitation by agreement for most employees, paid holiday entitlement and protections for shift work. But 83% said the regulations had created unnecessary red-tape.

More than two-thirds of directors said their companies had varied or opted out of the working time regulations and most said some of their employees continued to work longer than forty-eight hours a week. But only just over 10% believed that the regulations had adversely affected profitability.

The survey also found wide support for the

European Works Council directive requiring large companies with employees in more than two EU states to establish advisory and information councils. Some 70% believed that companies should be required to inform and consult employees on most or all business planning matters that substantially affected them.

Opinion was more divided over the statutory right to unpaid parental leave. More than half those surveyed said that they already allowed their employees to take parental leave in addition to annual holiday entitlement and statutory maternity leave. But a quarter of the sample were firmly opposed to the introduction of unpaid parental leave by regulation.

There was overwhelming support for the part-time directive that provides part-time workers with the same fundamental employment rights as those who are employed full-time, with 95% backing this.

Source: Financial Times, 16 August 1999

EU labour markets

Much of the debate over the Social Charter/Chapter in the UK has concerned the extent to which supranational regulation on social and employment matters threatens the traditional features and 'flexibility' of Britain's Anglo-Saxon market model. This very suggestion raises the existence of competing labour market models in Europe, over which there has been much recent debate.

Anglo-Saxon and 'Continental' models

References to the Continental social market model are in truth something of a simplification. Europe's mainland is really home to a number of distinct socio-economic models, Nordic, Latin, French, Italian and Germanic, with several authors identifying a plurality of capitalisms in Europe (see Crouch and Streeck, 1996). Despite this and as forwarded by Albert (1991), a group of neighbouring countries – Germany, the Netherlands, Switzerland and Austria – share a form of capitalism – 'Rhenish capitalism' – in which the emphasis is on collective, long-term efforts and on the reconciliation of economic efficiency with the principle of social justice. A special feature of this Rhenish model is the principle of co-determination, which describes the involvement of works councils in the management of companies and which provides a framework for social partnership at industry and enterprise level. Rhenish capitalism is also characterized by high relative wage payments (gross employee earnings) and strict statutory requirements attaching to recruitment, training, remuneration and the termination of employment. Employee rights in such areas as sick pay, paternity and holiday provision are also well developed. Consequently, in employee remuneration, in the social security expenses employers must pay and in their vocational training expenditure etc., employers in the Rhenish economies have a relatively high cost burden. This can be seen quite clearly from the data presented in Table 6.4. In Germany especially, punitive labour costs are contributing to a cycle of job destruction (and investment flight) despite the compensatory effects of superior productivity rates. Although Germany continues to attract a high percentage of

Table 6.4 Eurostat estimates of hourly labour costs in industry (current exchange rates), 1996

	Hourly labour costs in ECU	... of which direct costs (%)	... of which direct remuneration (%)	... of which indirect costs (%)
EU15	20.2	73.7	n/a	26.3
Euro-zone	21.6	71.2	63.4	28.8
Belgium	25.8	67.4	55.5	32.6
Denmark	23.0	92.0	n/a	8.1
Germany	26.5	74.4	62.7	25.6
Greece	9.6	76.0	69.9	24.0
Spain	14.9	73.6	73.5	26.4
France	22.5	66.9	57.2	33.1
Ireland	13.8	83.5	73.2	16.5
Italy	17.2	66.0	65.5	34.0
Luxembourg	19.3	84.0	71.8	16.0
Netherlands	22.6	74.9	64.7	25.1
Austria	24.6	70.4	61.3	29.6
Portugal	6.1	75.3	69.1	24.8
Finland	19.7	75.1	63.8	24.9
Sweden	23.9	67.7	60.7	32.3
UK	n/a	n/a	n/a	n/a

Note: The term 'labour costs' means the expenditure borne by employers in order to employ workers. These costs can be subdivided into two main categories: direct costs and indirect costs. **Direct costs** are mainly direct remuneration (i.e. gross amounts, before deduction of taxes and social security contributions payable by employees) irregular bonuses and gratuities, payments to employees saving schemes, payments for days not worked and benefits in kind. **Indirect costs** include the social security expenses the employer must pay, vocational training expenditure, taxes, etc. If the employer receives any subsidies, these may be deducted from the costs.
Source: Eurostat, 1999

investment in high-technology industries, blue-collar jobs in traditional manufacturing sectors are being lost in large number. As Bloch (1998, p. 3) puts it:

> German magazines and newspapers are replete with photographs of and articles about German firms such as Puma manufacturing in the Czech Republic or Nivea in China. ... [and] Germans are investing increasingly overseas, with a special emphasis on Asia.

The Anglo-Saxon model, as evidenced in the United Kingdom and the US, provides clear contrast with the Rhenish model (Albert, 1991). Labour and employment systems in these countries are based chiefly on individualisation in pay, reward and recruitment. Systems are also characterized by more voluntarist principles. Labour is easier to hire and to dismiss, and payroll taxes and redundancy payments are typically smaller and less burdensome. Neo-liberal principles dominate economic planning and companies are generally more-oriented towards profit and share-holder value than to notions of social partnership. These differences are well illustrated in Doughty and Woodhead's (1999) comparative portrait of the German and British employment cultures. They note:

1. Average hourly wage costs in Germany total the equivalent of £17.10. This compares with just £10.22 in the UK.

2. In the UK, approximately 70% of total labour costs are attributable to gross employee earnings. In Germany, just 55% of total labour costs are tied to employee payments.

3. Employees in Germany are entitled to fifteen days off a year for public holidays. In England, workers get eight days off a year for public holidays.

4. German public sector workers receive a month's extra pay every year as an automatic annual bonus.

5. Working women in Germany get a total of fourteen weeks maternity leave (eighteen for multiple births) at 100% of earnings. UK women receive 90% of earnings for six weeks of maternity leave and a low flat-rate payment of about £60 a week for a further 12 weeks.

6. German workers receive generous terms of sick pay and the state retirement pension pays 75% of full salary. These entitlements significantly exceed their equivalent in the UK.

7. German workers also have the right of 'mitbestimmung', or 'co-determination', which means that they can choose members of a company's supervisory board. No such culture exists in the UK.

Labour market flexibility and the flexibility debate

The contrast between these labour market models and between national employment systems is often associated with the debate over labour market flexibility. In particular, inflexibility in Continental labour markets is often cited as the main factor contributing to the EU's relatively poor record of private sector job creation and to its present unemployment record. Indeed, the comprehensive OECD Jobs Study of 1994 (OECD, 1994) identified the need for greater flexibility in European labour markets and greater competition in product markets as the key to bringing down European unemployment levels (see Table 6.5). But what is labour market flexibility and what does it involve?

The concept of labour market flexibility is much disputed. Neither the notion nor the term itself has agreed meaning. In one view, labour market flexibility equates with minimalist regulation of employer behaviour and with the operation of economic agents in a largely unregulated labour market. In another, it equates more accurately with the evidence of forms of (working) time and contractual flexibility, and the ability of firms to enagage and dispense with labour. Put together, these different views of labour market flexibility hint at four different dimensions of flexibility (see Rhodes, 1994, p. 136):

> *external (numerical) flexibility*: the ability to recruit and to dismiss manpower in accordance with changing market conditions;
>
> *internal qualitative flexibility*: the ability to (re)deploy workers within the firm;
>
> *internal quantitative flexibility*: the ability to vary the hours and duration of workers through the use of a combination of part-time, full-time and fixed-duration contracts;

Table 6.5 National unemployment rates, percentage (August 1999)

Country	Rate of unemployment (%)
Spain	15.7
Italy [1]	12.0
France	11.0
Greece [2]	9.9
Finland	9.9
EU-15	9.3
Germany	9.2
Belgium	9.1
Sweden	7.0
Ireland	6.6
United Kingdom [3]	6.5
Portugal	4.7
Austria	4.3
Netherlands	3.2
Luxembourg	2.8
Others	
United States	4.2
Japan	4.7

Note: Cited unemployment rates are Commission estimates based on the standardised ILO definition of unemployment. According to the International Labour Organization (ILO), unemployed persons are those aged fifteen and over who are without work, who are available to start work within the next two weeks and who have actively sought employment at some time during the previous four weeks.
[1]As at January 1998, [2]as at January 1998, [3]as at April 1998.
Source: Eurostat, 1999.

pay flexibility: the ability to alter pay rates in line with changes in demand, performance and/or operational conditions.

On this basis, the UK, with its limited government, decentralized pay bargaining and flexible working arrangements, would appear to be the most flexible of all of the EU economies. Ireland and the Netherlands also provide example of flexible labour markets. In Holland, where an emphasis has been placed on work-sharing arrangements, the proportional rate of part-time employment is now higher than anywhere in the EU. Without jettisoning the principle and institutions of 'social partnership', a flexible labour market has been delivered providing for the greater participation of women and of the long-term unemployed (see Hartog, 1999). Like Holland, Denmark also scores well on quantitative and external flexibility. Part-time and temporary labour rates are now relatively high and legislation on dismissals and redundancy pay is quite liberal. Notably, both of these systems continue to combine a high level of 'flexibility' with active labour market policies and extensive individual and social protections. In the Danish case:

> This is accomplished not by putting strict legal demands on behaviour of the individual employers, but by setting up institutions that facilitate both negotiated solutions

involving the social partners and flexibility at the individual level in moving between firms and jobs. (See Madsen, 1999)

In combining features of negotiated flexibility and individual protection, these 'intermediate' models arise as a possible template for reform elsewhere in Europe. In all of these cases, some market deregulation has been undertaken in order to foster greater flexibility but a dialogue between companies, employees and the state has remained central to 'activist' employment strategy (see Case Study 6.3). Equally, the evidence of increased labour market flexibility in Italy, Germany and Spain, owes much to the interventionist policies of public authorities in these societies (see Morgan, 1996). France too, is modernising its employment system and achieving a higher level of market flexibility within the framework of active public policy initiatives. This makes it clear that an equation between labour market flexibility and labour market deregulation is a gross simplification.

CASE STUDY 6.3 Small states, big ideas

Small is beautiful used to be a fashionable slogan nearly thirty years ago. It was then applied to small companies. Now apparently it can also be used to cover the employment performance of small nation states with open market economies.

A study of today's jobs revival in western Europe focuses on four small countries with remarkable improvements in their labour market performances – Austria, Denmark, Ireland and the Netherlands. Could they provide the motor to pull the European Union out of high unemployment?

The Netherlands and Austria are enjoying 'full' employment with only about 3% of the labour force without work. In Denmark, male unemployment has fallen to less than 4%. Even more impressive has been the improvement in the employment rate of the adult labour force, generally regarded as a more accurate measure of employment creation. Between 1985 and 1997 in the Netherlands there was a 9% growth in the employment rate from 57.7% to 66.7%, while in Ireland the improvement was 6.4% – extending the employment rate from 51.4% to 57.8%. But the most significant gains were in the female employment rate – up by 15.4% in the Netherlands during the period, by 13.2% in the Netherlands and 7.4% in Austria.

There are interesting differences between the employment trends of the countries studied. But the ILO study argues that all four have been successful on at least three grounds.

They reduced unemployment levels significantly during the 1990s. They have achieved relatively high employment rates and ensured significant growth. Perhaps more importantly, they are already among 'the highest ranking countries in the world in terms of efficiency, equity and labour market performance'.

The ILO report sums up several studies carried out after the UN's 1995 Copenhagen social summit. It ought to be required reading for policy-makers who still believe the main way to improve employment opportunities is by deregulation, privatization and labor market flexibility.

As Peter Auer, the report's author, argues 'It is not the countries that have reduced social spending most, have curbed government intervention drastically or minimized social partnership that are the leading successes today. It is rather those which have retained while adapting their institutions.'

'These institutions were not in fact too rigid to survive ... The special European way of dealing with change, filtering it through established labour market institutions, leads to positive results', the author concludes.

The report accepts that 'there is no unique European model'. Each EU member state has labour market institutions which are the product of specific cultures, traditions and alliances. Although there are common factors at work – such as social partnership, an extensive net of social protection and the maintenance of social dialogues between employers, trade unions and governments – considerable variations are evident.

The relative success of their employment record

appears to owe next to nothing to neo-liberal policies of deregulation, privatization and labour flexibility beloved of the US and UK governments.

All four countries have some common factors. First, the ILO report argues, is the relevance of corporate governance and macroeconomic policy co-ordination. 'A climate of confidence' has apparently been created between the state, employers and trade unions. Social partnership has ensured agreement on social security and labour market reforms.

Second, the countries surveyed have practised price, interest and exchange rate stability and provided selective fiscal stimulation.

Third, activist labour market strategies emphasizing training and modernization to improve job search have been crucial. This has involved a 'new implicit contract between benefit recipients and the different benefit administrations with a new stress on rights and duties'.

Here are at least two lessons for the larger European economies wrestling with mass unemployment. The ILO believes 'democratic corporatism' – a dialogue between companies, employees and the state – is vital. Second, it argues that 'economic openness pays off and there seems to be no longer-term negative effects of globalization on the labour markets of the developed countries'.

But there is a more fundamental conclusion. The concept of full employment needs to reflect in fresh way the 'new heterogeneity of working life'.

Mr Auer explains, 'participation in full-time permanent work must be an option for everyone at certain points in an individual's career'. But 'while the regular public or private labour market (including dependent employed and self-employed) should remain the main destination, many of the transitional labour market statuses such as education and work, work and retirement, socially useful work, active labour market measures ... should be included in a new notion of full employment'.

Source: Financial Times, 27 January 2000

EU employment strategy

A discussion of national reform efforts highlights the extent to which national policies are now co-ordinated under an active EU employment strategy. While member states maintain their exclusive competence in confronting unemployment and job creation, each EU government must now treat their employment policies–practices as a matter of *'common concern'*. This follows agreement under the Amsterdam Treaty and at the Luxembourg Special European Council of 20–21 November 1997. The Luxembourg Summit marked a turning point in the Community's address of employment questions – as a dedicated 'Employment Summit' – and was critical in accelerating the introduction of a new employment strategy ahead of formal ratification of the new Community Treaty. As a consequence of these agreements, joint employment guidelines are to be published on an annual basis and each member state now submits a national action plan (NAP) for employment. Since 1998, express aims have included:

1. improving employability and promoting re-employment,

2. the development of entrepreneurship,

3. encouraging adaptability and flexibility in businesses,

4. strengthening policies for equal opportunities,

5. reducing and simplifying tax and regulatory burdens on employers, and

6. achieving reductions in unit labour costs.

Interestingly, the Employment Guidelines 2000 (adopted at the Helsinki Summit in December 1999) and the Joint (Commission and Council) Employment Report 1999 refer specifically to modernizing work organization and forms of work, with the aim of improving competitiveness, productivity and organizational flexibility. It is worth recording here that the seeds of an EU Employment Strategy are found in the Commission White Paper, *'Growth, Competitiveness and Employment'*, published in 1993 (Commission of the European Communities, 1993). This paper led to agreement on a joint European employment strategy at the Essen European Council in December 1994, elements of which are manifest in the new EU employment guidelines.

Policies for equality: tackling gender gaps

Concerted action towards the promotion of equal opportunities (between the sexes) appears as a central theme in the (EU) Employment Guidelines adopted since the signing of the Treaty of Amsterdam. Member states have agreed to translate their desire to promote equality of opportunity into increased employment rates for women and into equal treatment for a gender, which has continued to confront discriminatory treatment (in various forms) and under-representation in many sectors and occupations. What then are the gender gaps characterizing European markets and what are the obstacles and disadvantages confronting female workers in the EU?

Participation

The role of women on the labour market of the European Union has become more and more important over the past twenty years. Their proportion of the labour force and total employment are steadily rising and greater numbers of female workers have been competing for full-time and part-time employment. Despite this, rates of female participation in the EU countries still compare poorly with male participation rates.

The average rate of female participation (58.3%) masks considerable differences between the member states (see Table 6.6). In Denmark, for example, 75.1% of women of working age are 'economically active' but in Spain, Greece and Italy the female activity rate is below 50%. As a result, women are over-represented in unemployment figures in many EU countries and are under-represented in most economic sectors. Changes in the industrial structure of employment in favour of services have tended to encourage higher rates of participation – along with many other factors – but, to bring more women into the workforce, women must be better positioned to compete for jobs (especially for stable and highly qualified employment) and for promotion. Amongst measures which might assist here, we include stricter enforcement of anti-discrimination laws, the co-ordination of working

Table 6.6 Female labour market participation rates, 1987 and 1997

Country	1997	1987
Austria	61.9	53.0
Belgium (a)	56.5	50.6
Denmark	75.1	76.8
Finland	71.3	72.9
France	59.8	56.5
Germany (b)	61.8	54.5
Greece (a)	47.5	41.5
Ireland	50.4	38.5
Italy	44.1	43.4
Luxembourg	60.9	45.8
Netherlands	62.2	48.8
Portugal	65.1	56.9
Spain	47.1	37.7
Sweden	74.5	79.5
United Kingdom	66.8	62.4
EU-15	58.3	52.5
OECD Total	59.6	n/a

Note: (a) Figures for these countries are for 1996; (b) 1987 figures are for West Germany only
Source: Labour Force Statistics: 1977–1997, 1998 edition © OECD, 1999

hours with the school timetable, and the promotion of work-sharing arrangements (as undertaken in Holland). Improved childcare facilities, the greater availability of training and retraining schemes for women (and the unemployed), and systems of special leave for both parents are also necessary targets. Of course neo-classical theories of labour supply suggest that women are unlikely to match male participation and reward structures while they are primarily responsible for housework and childcare. These responsibilities cause many women to gain less work experience than men or to abstain and/or withdraw from the labour force in greater (relative) numbers.

Occupational segregation

Occupational segregation by sex is a continuing problem. It is a major source of gender inequality, of labour market rigidity and of economic inefficiency (see Anker, 1997). Evidence suggests that occupations are often stereotyped as 'male' or 'female' and that women either gravitate or are directed towards 'female jobs' which are concentrated in lower-paid, lower-status sectors. This is sometimes referred to as '*horizontal segregation*' and is supported by empirical evidence of a numerical concentration of women in lower-paid service occupations and in sectors such as textiles, agriculture, cleaning and retail services. Again, these sectors are relatively poorly paid and are associated with a large number of part-time and temporary positions.

The gendering of work is fairly similar in all member states, except among the self-employed. In the UK, 'the general position is slightly more favourable to women' (Townsend, 1997, p. 120) but gendering remains clear. *'Vertical segregation'* refers to the imbalance between sexes in terms of representation in managerial and executive positions (within the same occupations) and to the problems faced by women in climbing occupational ladders (see Helms and Guffey, 1997). Throughout the EU, fewer than 4% of company directors are women and there is no significant evidence to suggest that any real changes are occurring in the degree of vertical segregation in the EU. In the UK, a survey by the Labour Research Department (1997) shows that women account for only 1.7% of executives and just 4.2% of all directors among the top 100 companies listed on the stock exchange. Further down the management chain, women have enjoyed greater success but still constitute a minority. In organizations signed up to the pro-equality Opportunity 2000 programme (e.g. British Telecom, Marks & Spencer and Tesco), women account for only 17% of senior managers, 31% of middle managers and 41% of junior managers (Johnston, 1997). Even in public life in Europe, women are poorly represented in decision-making structures. In one of his final speeches, former EU Social Affairs Commissioner, Padraig Flynn (15 April 1999) bemoaned that, overall in the EU, only 17% of the members of national parliaments are women and that women account for only 21% of ministers of national governments (http://www.ecu-notes.org/News).

Pay and remuneration

Another feature of gender inequality in Europe rests with the question of pay and remuneration. Although there is a general tendency for women's earnings to converge with those of men, average female earnings still run well behind male earnings. The latest available data suggests that, on average, women earn at least a quarter less than men (see Table 6.7). Calculations are based on full-time employees in all economic activities except agriculture, education, health, personal services and administration. In the UK, despite a narrowing of the pay gap by 9% between 1975 and 1995, there is still an average earnings gap of 26.3% across all regions and sectors of industry.

Table 6.7 Female gross hourly earnings as a percentage of men's (full-time earnings, bonuses excluded)

Belgium	83.2	Italy	76.5
Denmark	88.1	Luxembourg	83.9
Germany[a]	76.9	Netherlands	70.6
Germany[b]	89.9	Austria	73.6
Greece[c]	68.0	Portugal	71.7
Spain	74.0	Finland	81.6
France	76.6	Sweden	87.0
Ireland	73.4	UK	73.7

[a] Old Lander; [b] New Lander, including East Berlin; [c] Industry only.
Source: Eurostat 1999

Fundamentally, these averages reflect those structural differences in the characteristics of female employment previously considered. Fewer women than men occupy management positions and the imbalance in the representation of women or men in certain economic sectors is another key factor. It is also true to say that, on average, working women are younger: 44% are under thirty compared with 32% of men (Eurostat, 1999). This is because less of the older generation of women work and many women stop work to raise children. The consequence is that women tend to have less seniority and fewer opportunities to be in management positions, which in turn has an impact on salaries. Gunderson (1994), as cited in Anker (1997), manages to identify five specific sources of male–female pay differentials highlighting these and other factors. These include:

1. differences in human capital endowments (such as education, age and experience),

2. intra-occupational differentials (differences in pay within the same occupation),

3. differences in pay for stereotypical 'male' and 'female' skills (with 'male' skills more highly rewarded),

4. differences in jobs desired (with many women actively seeking part-time hours), and

5. differences in the jobs available (with men dominating higher paid positions and occupations).

The existence of intra-occupational differentials in particular is clearly inconsistent with EU policy and a wide variety of explanations may exist including covert discrimination. In terms of job applications, salary agreements and increments, a lot of factors may be used to decide between two candidates which can obfuscate whether or not any sexual discrimination was involved in the final decision. In this context, despite a clearer definition of indirect discrimination in recent legislation (e.g. Council Directive 97/80/EC) the potential for covert discrimination will always exist.

Opinion towards women and towards labour market equality

Important in understanding the differences between (female) working experiences in Europe are male and social attitudes to women at home and at work. While this issue is given some treatment in Chapter 10, it is to be noted here that progress towards greater labour market equality will be closely tied to behavioural and attitudinal factors in the EU societies themselves and their impact on corporate and public policies. In improving equality in the workforce, countries are starting from very different points and perspectives both in terms of their policies and practices and in terms of overriding attitudes towards women. For example, a traditional view of women as housewives and 'nest-builders' is still quite strong in the southern member states (with their deeply Catholic traditions) and in Germany. A number of these countries are being forced to redress their attitudes not simply because of the new legislation on equal opportunities but as a result of the changing age structures of their populations and of populations throughout Western Europe. Between 1995 and 2015, for example, the numbers in the twenty to twenty-nine-year-old age group are forecast to drop by as much as 20%. This will ensure a more feminized workforce as well as requiring a fundamental change in attitudes to the recruitment and retention of older workers. Women, like older male workers, will be required to make up shortfalls of professional workers in many sectors, requiring reassessment of education and training requirements and a corresponding change in social attitudes.

The UK displays one of the highest proportions of women in the workforce among the EU states. Equally, and despite its appalling provision of childcare for working women, the UK is regarded (by some observers at least) to have fostered a more positive working environment for women than that found in many other member countries. The country has recognized the economic necessity of introducing women into a wide spectrum of functions and, in theory at least, this has resulted in greater opportunities for female workers. Certain sectors, however, such as engineering, remain bastions of male dominance and boast few women in top management positions. Moreover, the UK has a long way to go in order to match the superior childcare facilities and (female) education and training records boasted by the Scandinavian markets. Attitudes towards female participation in the labour market are especially progressive in countries such as Denmark and Sweden where there is evidence of an infrastructure to support high rates of (female) economic activity. In these societies women fit easily into institutions, which encourage good living standards and are encouraged to pursue their careers in parallel with their family lives. Childcare facilities in organizations are common and career paths take into account career breaks for maternity and childcare.

The European Union and industrial relations

Analysis has already attested to the emergence and perceived desirability of workers' participation and consultation in national and transnational companies in the EU. Attention has been paid to the nature and intention of the European Works Council Directive and to the possibility of new workers' consultation provisions for national-scale undertakings. However, how are the European economies tied or differentiated by their wider systems of industrial relations and what are some of the characterizing features of trade unionism in Europe?

Highly corporatist countries in the EU include Austria, Belgium, Germany and the Nordic countries. In these societies, trade union movements have been powerful political actors for many years and industrial relations systems have relied heavily on collective bargaining as the dominant means of representing employees' interests. Participation by workers in company decision-making is generally evident and is structured around a variety of institutional forms such as works councils, leading to varying degrees of co-determination (see Case Study 6.4). In the Nordic countries especially, the proportion of the employed working population who are trade union members has remained comparatively high and the principle of social

CASE STUDY 6.4 Co-determination and German industrial relations law

Co-determination is founded in German industrial relations law. In companies of more than 2,000 employees, there must be supervisory boards where 50% of the representation comes from employees other than management. In addition, works councils, which can be, and are, established in companies of more than five people, have consultation duties and rights of veto. The works council is elected by the whole workforce but, not surprisingly, tends to be dominated by trade unionists. In larger companies these representatives may work full time on council duties. The rights of veto exist over work practices, overtime arrangements, holiday arrangements and some aspects of employment procedure. However, the council has no direct power enabling it to prevent dismissal although it tends to have influence especially with regard to redundancy arrangements.

In the larger companies the co-determination arrangements on the supervisory board mean that workers can influence the business strategy and plans of the company. At their quarterly meetings all decisions of the management board must go through the supervisory board for approval. However, strict 50% voting rights are generally tightly enforced and a casting vote is always in the hands of a chairperson – a shareholder representative. Even though this right exists, practice of the supervisory boards tends to be to attempt to reach a consensus.

German employers do have some doubts about giving workers so much influence and one specific concern is that worker representatives have to be given access to full information about company strategies and plans. However, employers are well aware of and do promote the positive aspects of the co-determination schemes. These include positive productivity and motivation effects based on an enhanced atmosphere at work, a reduced feeling of 'them and us' and a knowledge of the firms' longer term plans which reduces the tendency to hypothesize for the worse. However, to some extent, in some companies, the supervisory boards may be little more than rubber stamping devices. In effect, decisions may have been taken by management a long time before they go before the supervisory board. Management is able to present large amounts of seemingly convincing evidence to the board and then press for a decision to be taken quickly in the name of efficiency and progress. A more indirect benefit of co-determination is that it tends to protect firms and, therefore, senior management from hostile takeover bids and, to an extent, senior managers have been able to hide behind their supervisory boards at times of possible merger activity. On the other hand, where mergers are being discussed they can be done so without worker representatives on the supervisory boards knowing about them.

consensus has been central in socio-economic policy-making. Elsewhere, while union membership has declined dramatically (see Table 6.8) and a movement to firm-level bargaining processes has been observed, institutionalized consultation between government and organized interests remains a recognizable feature. For example, in Ireland, Italy, Spain, Portugal, Greece and the Netherlands, unions have played a significant role in setting the framework for responsible wage policies and in many recent labour market changes. These countries offer varying models for employer–employee dialogue at enterprise level but place an emphasis on such interaction and attaching notions of 'social partnership'.

Consequently, although labour unions in Western Europe lost over 4.5 million members in the 1990s and offer a mixed picture, their role remains significant. Levels of unionization remain higher than elsewhere (e.g. the United States) and one in three employed persons in Western Europe is still a member of a trade

Table 6.8 Trade union density in EU member states, 1950–95

Country	1950	1955	1965	1970	1975	1980	1985	1990	1995
Austria	61	64	63	62	56	58	58	46	43
Belgium	37	n/a	n/a	46	53	57	54	51	53
Germany[a]	36	38	38	38	37	41	39	33	30
Denmark	53	59	63	64	67	80	73	71	82
Spain	n/a	n/a	n/a	n/a	30	14	14	17	15
France	33	21	19	21	23	17	15	10	9
UK	44	45	43	49	52	55	49	39	32
Greece	n/a	n/a	n/a	36	n/a	37	37	34	n/a
Italy	45	43	29	38	43	54	51	39	39
Ireland	37	n/a	n/a	53	55	57	56	50	38
Netherlands	43	41	40	40	38	35	29	25	26
Portugal	n/a	n/a	n/a	59	52	59	52	32	32
Sweden	67	71	68	73	75	88	92	82	83
Finland	34	33	42	51	67	70	69	72	81

[a] Figures for Germany relate to West Germany except for 1995 figures

Figures show the progression of trade union density (percentage of employed working population who are trade union members) over time

Source: European Trade Union Information Bulletin 1/98, page 12

union (see Visser, 1997). Equally, although collective bargaining has declined in extent and influence across the EU, it remains legitimized and embedded in the institutions of most West European countries (see Towers, 1997). Once again, however, the UK presents something of an exception. There is a virtual absence of institutionalized consultation between government and organized interests in the UK, and worker consultation and participation is largely limited to multinational companies (with EU-wide interests). A decentralized, private sector collective bargaining system has become predominant and union membership remains in steep decline. In the first half of the 1990s alone, the number of employed union members fell by 1,581,000. Despite the closer harmonization of UK and Continental European labour law, it is unlikely that unionism in Britain will either return to its past glories or take on the form exhibited in its more corporatist neighbours.

Although trade union influence can be excluded from systems of workers' representation (e.g. works councils), local and national unions will continue to play an important role in managing and regulating the large-scale transformations taking place in working environments throughout Europe. A number of factors including changing management and productive techniques, and the internationalization of firms and markets, provide challenges for workforces in Europe and for those representing employee interests. In this context, the preservation and recognition of unions as important national and local actors is of fundamental importance given the need for protection against the exercise of arbitrary power by employers and the employee's right to information and consultation. Moreover, given the present interdependence of European markets and (social) legislation, concerted efforts are required of national employee groups so as to maximize and to unite the worker's voice at the European level. In this regard, the role of the European Trade Union Confederation, which has worked as quite an effective vehicle for worker representation at the EU-level, is of considerable importance. At this stage, relationships between the ETUC and the Union of Industrial and Employers' Confederations of Europe (UNICE) are generally positive and have produced a series of Framework Agreements leading to Council action. Paradoxically, declining trade union memberships across Europe in the 1980s and early 1990s may have helped to foster the development of a form of Euro-corporatism, with national-level unions forced to consider both transnational organization and concerted (coalitional) bargaining efforts. On this note too, there is some evidence of emerging cross-national links between unions from different countries. As Visser (1997) highlights, while there is 'a national embeddedness' to the European union movement, cross-border co-operation has increased between industrial unions (e.g. in chemicals and printing) in Germany, Austria, Switzerland and the Netherlands, as well as between union federations in Belgium and the Netherlands.

Transitions in work

According to many commentators, we are now living in a post-Fordist era of industrial production (see Piore and Sabel 1984; Wood, 1989). Problems arising from large-scale production methods based on Taylorist and Fordist principles have encouraged many firms to move away from traditional mass production techniques and to introduce more flexible production and management processes. These changes have had a major impact on the workplace, on attitudes towards work and on working experiences. Not only have we seen new emphases on smaller-scale units, on teamwork, and on quality, but 'flexible firms' have looked to forms of working time flexibility (i.e. part time and shift working) and to contractual flexibility (short-term contracts and subcontracting) as a contribution to their own flexibility. Equally, new technologies and working practices have raised profound questions over the skills and training of workforces. The present section pursues some of these issues and considers the concept of modern (post-modern) work and industrial division.

Flexible specialization and the growth of subcontracting

Among the recent trends in industrial organization in developed market economies has been that of *flexible specialization*. As a result of the recession of the early 1980s there was a drive by many firms in developed markets to reduce their costs and to improve their responsiveness to changing market conditions. One way of meeting this goal was to move to a flexible firm structure involving a vertical disintegration of the production chain through outsourcing and 'contracting

236

out'. Central here was a division of organizational activities into core and peripheral activities. The core activities which were central to the work of the firm would be kept 'in house' and carried out by full-time permanent workers. The peripheral activities would be carried out by temporary workers (under atypical contracts) and/or would be subcontracted. The firm has then reduced its overheads and can react to peaks in demand by increasing the amount of temporary labour it uses and/or increasing the amount of subcontracting. Internally, efforts would also be made to use smaller-scale, 'flexible' production teams and to introduce flexible technology and continuous innovation of products and processes. Attached here is an understanding that smaller scale units (utilizing technological modes of operation) enable production to be specialized and encourage the unit to be more flexible and responsive to changing demands. In this context, workforces throughout Europe have been increasingly required to cope with new production techniques and technologies and with non-traditional working arrangements including variable working hours and new patterns of work organization. These requirements can be more fully illustrated by advancing a model of five 'interactive' elements central to flexible management and to flexible production systems throughout Europe (see Figure 6.2).

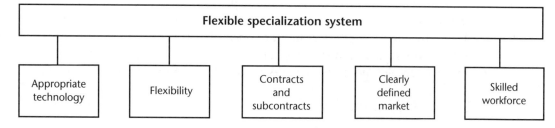

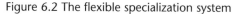

Figure 6.2 The flexible specialization system

Appropriate technology

The flexible specialization concept is associated with the employment and integration of flexible technology and the use of skilled operatives. Technologies associated with production, information and communications and, in particular, computer-aided design (CAD) and computer-aided manufacture (CAM), are seen to provide many opportunities for reorganizing production. In association with reorganization on the factory floor and new opportunities for franchising and subcontracting, many of these developments have made smaller-scale, specialized, batch production possible. As the machinery dedicated to fixed assembly operations becomes obsolete, it is often being replaced with multi-purpose capital equipment. The traditional arguments that there are benefits of economies of scale underlying mass production are looking less convincing. In their place is an argument which suggests that economies of scale are being replaced in importance by economies of scope, that is economies associated with flexible, multi-product production using flexible technology.

Flexibility

We observe trends towards multi-product production, increased customization, new demands for quality and environmental attributes, caused by more sophisticated consumer needs and wants. These sorts of trends can only be serviced through more flexible modes of production and working arrangements.

Subcontracting and contractual flexibility

At the limit, flexibility and the need to be responsive mean that workers may be needed at one point in time but not at another. The implication of this is that a 'flexible firm' will distinguish between core and peripheral workers, only employing on a permanent basis those workers (core-workers) who are core to the operations of the business. This thesis/model suggests that peripheral workers will be added and incorporated through part-time working arrangements, casual employment and temporary contracts, as and when required by the firm. These workers will generally receive fewer rewards than the core-workers, and will have short-term and/or interrupted contractual associations with the firm (see Atkinson, 1985).

The flexible firm is also likely to make use of subcontracting. In many instances, it will be cheaper and more efficient to use external firms; themselves specialized, to carry out particular tasks. Such firms are likely to be relatively small. Large firms are increasingly operating in this way, recognizing that internalizing all their tasks is not always the most cost-effective mode of operation. The use of small firms undertaking contract work enables the large firm itself to maintain a degree of flexibility and prevent over-employment. In some cases extensive production networks are formed.

Clearly defined market

In the past, large mass production techniques have relied on mass demand for the product being produced. This meant that production was highly sensitive to changes in aggregate demand and, in particular, to recession. Now, smaller quantities of much more specialized products can be produced profitably because the technology is available to do it and because markets are growing internationally, such that even the most specialized products are likely to have sufficiently stable markets in terms of demand. A Single European Market accelerates this sort of trend and small enterprises which may not be able to find a significant market in their own member state may find a viable one in the wider European market. This also means that new smaller firms, based on the twin characteristics of flexibility and specialization, are able to survive alongside their much larger conglomerate counterparts, relying on niche markets, meeting specialized demands and offering a more responsive and personal service.

Skilled workforce

The dominant ideology behind the post-Fordist scenario is that new flexible processes work most efficiently where workers themselves take on responsibility for the planning, programming and functioning of their work. This often means that fewer, more skilled workers are employed and that they are expected to carry out a wider variety of tasks. Emphasis therefore is on flexibility and versatility and on the ability of the worker to offer and to acquire expertise in different areas as their work demands. It might be argued that this movement towards functional flexibility and multi-skilling mirrors best practice within Japanese industry. With workers increasingly controlling their own work patterns, worker motivation can increase and quality can be improved.

Flexible working and production – the evidence?

The trend towards flexible production is now well established in Europe and has contributed significantly to new patterns of flexible working in Europe. Table 6.9 shows, for example, that a significant number of jobs are now 'non-permanent'. This label encompasses 'temporary' and 'fixed duration' contracts. Earlier analysis has also attested to the growth of part-time employment in Europe, which continues to play a greater role in the overall European labour market than temporary work. There has also been a considerable increase in self-employment in the EU countries and in the number of small businesses in Europe, as considered in the very introduction to this title. Many of these small firms have been artisan in nature, co-operative in organization, and flexible in production. Several commentators have also evidenced an increase in subcontracting and outsourcing arrangements involving European firms. For example, a recent study by Simmons and Kalantaridis (1996) provides discussion of small business growth in peripheral Greek regions as a result of the decentralization of production by large-scale German textiles firms. Brewster *et al.* (1997) provide clear evidence that in all major

Table 6.9 Percentage of full-time and part-time employees with temporary, fixed-term contracts

Country	1983	1996
Austria	n/a	8.0
Belgium	5.4	5.9
Denmark	n/a	11.2
Finland	n/a	17.3
France	3.3	12.5
Germany	n/a	11.0
Greece	n/a	11.0
Ireland	6.1	9.2
Italy	6.6	7.5
Luxembourg	3.2	2.6
Netherlands	5.8	12.0
Portugal	n/a	10.4
Spain	n/a	33.6
Sweden	n/a	11.6
United Kingdom	5.5	6.9

Source: Eurostat, 1997

West European countries there has been a significant increase in subcontracting. In Germany and the Netherlands, half of all organizations surveyed in their research indicated that their use of subcontracting had increased. In Spain, Switzerland, France, Finland, Ireland and the UK, one-third or more of all organizations surveyed had increased their use of subcontracting. The authors note that there appears to be generally less uptake of subcontracting in Ireland and the Nordic countries (Denmark, Finland, and Norway) but that subcontracting is still used by a substantial number of firms.

Comparative studies evidence a plethora of flexible production systems throughout Europe, from production by small firms in regional networks to the organization of labour into smaller integrated units within the larger enterprise. In fact, the diverse ways in which post-Fordist flexibility has contributed to a new industrial order in Europe are well highlighted by the two competing cases of Italy and Germany.

Italy

'Third Italy' in the centre and north-east of the country, encompasses some of the most dynamic and innovative industrial entities in modern Europe involved in the production of household goods, textiles and industrial parts. A growing number of SMEs, representing the peak of Italian manufacturing quality, have formed production and export networks and/or have been absorbed (as suppliers) into the production networks of larger companies such as Benetton. In broad terms, the success of these companies (and their networks) has been based on the integration of craftsmanship with new productive technologies and techniques. Such strategies as outsourcing (to Eastern Europe and North Africa) and the shortening of production cycles have also ensured that many firms have been able to produce a much larger range of goods (reacting more quickly to changes in demand) and to reduce their total manufacturing costs. Another aspect of the 'flexibility' of Third Italy has been that firms have been able to enter and to exit niche markets at greater speed (e.g. in the fashion markets) exploiting their smaller scale and more flexible working practices. While these firms and networks have confronted stiffer competition in recent years, their flexibility and innovation have continued to contribute to the fortune of several districts and to the strength of Italian manufacturing as a whole. Although local firms are increasingly 'integrated' into international networks and markets, the longstanding traditions of familialism and artisanship in the Italian regions remain, and public policy actions continue to support small and family business development. One of the parallel aims of this sort of investment has been to prevent migration to the cities and the deindustrialization and depopulation of rural areas.

Germany

In Germany, flexibility has been attained within many companies through the use of general purpose, high-tech equipment and machinery. Additionally, many west German firms have decentralized production, contracting out to lower-cost regions.

Many firms have also reconceptualized the relationship between the manufacturing process and the role of workers therein. For example, in automotives, movement has been observed to smaller-scale production groups which revolve around common technology, the control of several machine tasks from one computer, and the responsibility for quality control devolved to the associated team of workers. In traditional Fordist plants such as the monster VW plant in Wolfsburg, this has been a slow and difficult process. At a governmental level, succeeding federal and regional-level authorities have offered state aid for technological innovation based on quality circles which has aided shop-floor technological advances and movement towards post-Fordist production techniques.

An evaluation

While it is tempting to suggest that post-Fordist production is humanizing where the assembly line is dehumanizing, a calmer view is necessary here. A general increase in worker satisfaction resulting from the movement away from repetitive working is a welcome result but, in a world of production flexibility, labour may be faced with a new problem: that of uncertain employment. Fixed-term, part-time and temporary contracts, subject to competitive bidding, may become the reality of the future and analysis here has attested to a numerical increase in part-time and temporary positions throughout European industry. Moreover, the trend of labour-intensive mass production continues in Europe's developing markets (and in the wider developing world) where wages are low and environmental concerns are easily overlooked. The 'new international division of labour' has seen many low-skilled, repetitive, production line tasks simply exported from the EU to these developing markets under the control of transnational corporations.

Quality management systems and new work practices

Aside from the adoption of new technologies and more flexible production methods, competitive advantage may increasingly rest with the type of management system adopted in a company and with the quality considerations of the firm. In this context, it is to be noted that the introduction of quality management systems at enterprise level in Europe is also having a major impact on many employees in Europe, in particular on those working in larger-scale manufacturing companies. Central elements of total quality management (TQM) include teamwork, worker–management dialogue and quality circles, features which reflect a view that quality is all-pervasive and that the responsibility for quality belongs to everybody in the organization.

Teamwork and quality circles

Teamwork especially is central to many parts of the TQM system where workers have to feel that they are part of an organization. Teams of workers will often be brought together into problem-solving groups, quality circles and quality improvement teams, so involving individuals in making decisions and in responsibility for

CASE STUDY 6.5 Teamwork drives performance improvement at Denso Manufacturing UK Ltd

Denso introduced their first quality circles in 1993. Their quality circles are made up by members from the same line or department who meet to address problems which affect their normal working activities. These teams meet to investigate problems selected by the team themselves. They are self-directed and concerned with problems that affect their ability to work effectively. Problems are tackled one at a time and once one problem has been resolved the team does not disband but moves on to tackle the next problem. Apart from the role of quality circles in problem-solving, Denso considers that the fundamental objectives of the teams are to promote team working, to provide an opportunity for the personal development of participants and to improve the working environment for associates. In other words, while the fact that the teams resolve problems on the line is important, it is not the sole driving force behind them. The company has a total of thirty-three quality circles which involve 270 associates – some 36% of the workforce. This represents a substantial commitment to the development of their people and to involving associates in the continuous improvement of processes for which they are responsible. Indeed, the programme has grown to such an extent that it has now become part of the annual planning cycle with:

- a timetable for the formation and registration of quality circles and the presentation of results,

- a time plan for quality circle activities during the year,

- a performance monitoring programme for quality circle activities,

- quality training for circle leaders,

- an annual Director's award for the Denso UK quality circle which demonstrates the best effort and

- on-site and European competitions to identify quality circles which have achieved the most significant improvements in performance.

Quality circles form at the start of each year and meet over a six- or twelve-month period, after which they make a presentation to the Managing Director. Participation is voluntary and teams usually meet for an hour every second week, either during the normal working week or in overtime if necessary. A quality circle committee meets once or twice each year to review circle activities over the previous period and to make plans for the next.

Alongside these quality circles, the company has two further team types – 'project teams' and cross-functional 'TIE working groups'. Project teams are management led and directed. Cross-functional teams are set up to address defined problems involving more than one function. Project teams are responsible for resolving individual problems and hold regular meetings with local managers to review progress and remove obstacles. In addition to resolving the problem, the teams are responsible for communicating with all employees affected, to stimulate their involvement in the problem-solving process and to gain their support. To demonstrate support and commitment, Denso's Managing Director attends these meetings at three-monthly intervals. Once the problem has been resolved, the team tasked with its investigation is disbanded. TIE working groups are cross-functional groups set up to improve the efficiency of production lines by eliminating waste and inefficiencies. These teams are inter-departmental and management led and their role is to focus primarily on productivity improvement. They have a typical duration of four to six months and, unlike quality circles, are disbanded once the project aim has been achieved.

Denso considers that the fundamental objectives of its production and management teams are to promote teamworking, provide an opportunity for the personal development of participants and to improve the working environment for its employees.

Source: Adapted and revised from the Denso case note by Malcolm Munro-Faure @ http://www.mcb.co.uk/nsqt/denso.htm

their work and for the work of others. Teamwork, communication and commitment across the organization are used as means of improving productive and organizational efficiency in relation to such elements as inventory or stock control, planning, control and monitoring (see also Chapter 10).

The greater role of teamworking and of quality circles in Europe-based factories merits some extended comment. A quality circle is usually defined as a group of workers, doing similar work, who meet together regularly under the leadership of their supervisor in order to identify and solve work-related problems and to recommend solutions to management. Teams implement those solutions once they are agreed. Central to any discussion in the quality circle is the key issue of quality of work done. A key feature of quality circles is that people must be invited to join them, not forced to do so. There are no formal rules governing the size of quality circles, but very large groups are difficult to manage and become unproductive. The impact of quality circles is to make workers feel needed, as well as acting as a monitor on quality and a forum in which new working arrangements can be discussed. Many firms offer bonuses to individuals or groups who can come up with new systems or new practices in their work area which will ultimately save the company money. Although quality circles can be linked with production line technology, often their use has been associated with a move away from the production line towards team-based production, where several tasks in the production of a good rather than one task are done by a group of people.

One example of a company committed to such working methods is Denso Manufacturing UK Limited which was set up as a joint venture between DENSO of Japan and MAGNETI-MARELLI of Italy in 1990. With a turnover of £92 million, the business is growing at the rate of £20 million per year – supplying evaporators, condensers, heaters and air-conditioning units for customers including Toyota, Audi, Jaguar, Land Rover and Volvo. The company involves 900 employees (called 'associates') in three main types of team set up to improve performance and to address different problems. A summary of its case is presented in Case Study 6.5.

Conclusions

The adoption of new production and management systems and of flexible working practices is of course taking place in an increasingly 'intelligent' EU economy. In fact, just as the organization of production is being transformed by new productive technologies and by new managerial techniques, so the information technology (IT) revolution is impacting on the very composition of employment and on the nature of working relations in Europe. The dynamics of technological change are already allowing firms to reconsider many of their policies and organizational practices, some of which may have been in place since the industrial revolution. Bloch (1998), for example, provides discussion of the role of networked computerization in simultaneously engaging German and American car designers on recent Ford motor vehicle projects and in allowing a number of German banks (e.g. Deutsche

Bank) to curtail their labour-intensive branch networks. Indeed, the very notion of the physical and fixed workplace is likely to be challenged by the growth and consolidation of virtual (on-line) organizations and by the transfer of many jobs into 'cyberspace'. New forms of employment unexamined in this chapter (e.g. tele-working) are also becoming more prevalent as new forms of communication technology create new options for organizations and their employees.

Some commentators argue that a second industrial divide is now under way, based on new technologies, flexibility, changing management practices and participatory arrangements. If this is the case, then the outcome is likely to be a very different workplace to the divisive, mass production factory, common in post-war Europe, and will involve forms and modes of work as yet little experienced. In this context, those people who do work will increasingly need specialist and transferrable skills and will become accustomed to more frequent career moves and breaks. Many low-skilled jobs will be eliminated and much duplicated work eradicated. This presents a changing set of challenges to employers, employees and public policy-makers throughout the EU, including the need for life-long learning (and skills acquisition), the resolution of tensions between short-term needs and long-term training, and the regulation of variegated employment practices and environments. The role of the EU in managing these challenges is likely to become ever more important.

Review questions for Chapter 6

1. To what extent do you think that an effective 'social dimension' is essential to a Single European Market?

2. If workplace legislation becomes more and more harmonized, are there any reasons to think that some countries may find themselves losing some of their competitive advantage?

3. Explain the distinction between the Social Charter, the Social Chapter, and the (Maastricht) Agreement on Social Policy.

4. What factors contributed to the distinctive UK position on social issues between 1985 and 1997?

5. How might we legitimize the UK's recent decision to end our opt-out from the Social Chapter?

6. Identify arguments against and in favour of statutory limits on working time.

7. How has EU legislation contributed to patterns of worker consultation and information in European companies? What national practices exist to promote employer–employee dialogue and to involve workers in management decision-making?

8. What advantages and problems might result from systems of worker representation?

9. Do the structural problems of Continental labour markets make the case for an

American-style labour market and for wholesale deregulation of 'social market' models?

10. What evidence do we have of new employment strategies in Western Europe? Are there any common threads to present reform paths?

11. What do we mean by occupational segregation by sex? How far is such segregation evident in the UK and in other EU markets?

12. What sort of pressures are impacting on trade unions in the European Union? What is the likely result of these pressures in terms of trade union organization in the future?

13. Explain the concept of flexible specialization and its HR effects. What are the main elements in a flexible specialization system?

14. Explain the relationship between new work practices in Europe and the introduction of quality management systems.

Web guide

National policies and EU legislation

European Commission: Employment and Social Affairs Directorate @ http://europa.eu.int/comm/dgs/employment_social/index_en.htm

European Employment Observatory (EEO) @ http://www.ias-berlin.de/

International Labour Organization (ILO) @ http://www.ilo.org/

EU Business News (Employment News) @ http://www.eubusiness.com/employ/index.htm

OECD @ http://www.oecd.org/

Industrial relations

The European Trades Union Congress (ETUC) @ http://www.etuc.org/

The UK Trades Union Congress (TUC) @ http://www.tuc.org.uk/

EIROn-Line (European Industrial Relations Observatory) @ http://www.eiro.eurofound.ie/

EMIRE (Employment and Industrial Relations Glossaries) @ http://www.eurofound.ie/information/emire.html

ELCID (European Living Conditions Information Directory) @ http://www.eurofound.ie/information/elcid.html

References

Albert, M. (1991) *Capitalism Against Capitalism*, Whurr Publishers.

Alcock, P. (1996) *Social Policy in Britain: Themes and Issues*, Macmillan.

Anker, R. (1997) Theories of occupational segregation by sex: an overview, *International Labour Review*, **136**(3), 315–39.

Armstrong, K. and Bulmer, S. (1998) *The Governance of the Single European Market*, Manchester University Press.

Atkinson, J. (1984) *Flexibility, Uncertainty and Manpower Management*, no.89, Institute of Manpower Studies.

Atkinson, J. (1985) Manpower strategies for flexible organisations, *Personnel Management* **28**(1).

Bloch, B. (1998) Globalisation's assault on the labour market: a German perspective, *European Business Review*, **98**(1).

Braverman, H. (1974) *Labor and Monopoly Capital: The Degradation of Work in the Twentieth Century*, Monthly Review Press.

Brewster, C., Mayne, L. and Tregaskis, O. (1997) Flexible working in Europe: a review of the evidence, *Management International Review*, **37**, 85–103.

Cable, J. R. (1988) Is profit-sharing participation? Evidence on alternative firm types from West Germany, *International Journal of Industrial Organization*, **6**, 121–37.

Commission of the European Communities (1993) *Growth, Competitiveness, Employment*.

Crouch, C. and Streeck, W. (eds) (1996) *Les Capitalismes en Europe*, Edition Française, La Decouverte.

Doughty, S. and Woodhead, M. (1999) German giant may move here (Germany's expensive workforce), *Daily Mail*, 26 February 1999.

Gunderson, M. (1994) *Comparable worth and gender discrimination: an international perspective*, International Labour Organization, Geneva.

Hall, M. (1992) Behind the European Works Council Directive: the European Commission's legislative strategy, *British Journal of Industrial Relations*, **4**, 547–65.

Hartog, J. (1999) The Netherlands: so what's so special about the Dutch model?, *ILO Employment and Training Papers*, Employment and Training Department, International Labour Office, Geneva.

Helms, M. and Guffey, C. (1997) The role of women in Europe, *European Business Review*, **2**, 80–4.

Johnston, P. (1997) A woman's place is not in the boardroom, *Daily Telegraph*, 4 January 1997.

Madsen, P.K. (1999) Denmark: flexibility, security and labour market success, *ILO Employment and Training Papers*, Employment and Training Department, International Labour Office Geneva.

Morgan, J. (1996) Structural change in European labour markets, *National Institute Economic Review*, **155**, 81–9.

Mosley, H. (1990) The social dimension of European integration, *International Labour Review*, **129**(2), 147–64.

OECD (1994) *The OECD Jobs Study: Facts, Analysis, Strategies*, OECD.

Piore, M. J. and Sabel, C. (1984) *The Second Industrial Divide: Possibilities for Prosperity*, Basic Books.

Rhodes, M. (1991) The social dimension of the Single European Market, *European Journal of Political Research*, **19**(1), 245–80.

Rhodes, M. (1994) Labour markets and industrial relations, in Nugent, N. and O'Donnell, R. (eds), *The European Business Environment*, Macmillan.

Simmons, C. and Kalantaridis, C. (1996) Entrepeneurial strategies in Southern Europe: rural workers in the garment industry of Greece, *Journal of Economic Issues*, **30**(1), 121–42.

Teague, P. (1989) *The European Community: The Social Dimension. Labour Market Policies for 1992*, Kogan Page.

Towers, B. (1997) Collective bargaining, democracy and efficiency in the British and US workplace. *Industrial Relations Journal*, **28**(4), 299–308.

Townsend, A.R. (1997) *Making a Living in Europe*, Routledge.

Visser, J. (1997) European trade unions in the mid-1990s, *Industrial Relations Journal*, **28**(1), 113–18.

Weitzman, M. (1984) *The Share Economy*, Harvard University Press.

Wise, N. and Gibb, R. (1993) *Single Market to Social Europe: The European Community in the 1990s*, Longman.

Wood, S. (ed.) (1989) *The Transformation of Work: Skill, Flexibility and the Labour Process*, Unwin Hyman.

7 The transition economies: Central and Eastern Europe

Central themes

- The Communist legacy
- Post-Communist transition
- Privatization
- Enterprise restructuring
- Banking reform
- EU–CEE trade
- EU enlargement
- Pre-accession strategies
- Foreign direct investment
- Entering CEE markets

Transition and change

As an important part of Europe, we cannot fail to give some consideration to the huge changes which continue to occur in Central and Eastern Europe and their impact on European businesses. These changes are now a decade old and the region's transition to the market mechanism, although resulting in huge social costs, has opened up a vast economic region marked by rapid enterprise creation and by fledgling free markets. A number of countries in the region are now experiencing sustained economic growth but purchasing power continues to be low and living standards remain poor when compared with Western levels. Given future economic growth and continuing attractions for resource-seeking businesses, few international businesses in Europe (or worldwide) will disregard these countries in the years ahead. Increased political stability and the prospect of EU accession should also add to the attractiveness of countries selling state-owned businesses to private investors (privatization) and deregulating their economies to promote greater competition.

Despite this, ten years after the fall of the Berlin Wall, Central and Eastern Europe continues to present a varied picture, with nations moving forwards (and westwards) at different speeds. In the Balkans, for example, reforms have lacked continuity and incomes and output have declined dramatically to below 50% of 1989 levels. In the former Soviet Union (FSU), most economies are still grappling with negative growth. Russia – which has experienced negative growth in all but two years in the last decade – has lost half of its pre-reform output. Here, transition strategies have served to enrich the former Communist nomenklatura and transition has become synonymous with decline. Societies have lurched towards a form of rough justice capitalism in which crime, corruption and inequality are the dominating features.

The purpose of this chapter is to examine these trends and to account for the state and transformation of regional business environments. Emphasis falls not only on the considerable potential for commercial development in the region but also on the continuing impediments to economic and political progress outside of Central Europe. Attention is paid to the features of transition, to the degree to which individual economies have accepted the need for change, and to the varying paths of reform and liberalization. Some reasons for investing in the Central and Eastern European region are offered together with an assessment of the forms and consequences of inward foreign direct investment (FDI). Much of the chapter is also concerned with the changing nature of relations between the European Union and the Central and Eastern European countries (CEECs). While early chapters have covered several issues in connection with the EU, more needs to be said about the challenges and processes of EU enlargement and about the membership objective shared by many Central and Eastern European governments. Selected cases and statistics are presented from a number of different sources, updating the statistical profiles of the preceding edition of this work. Again, as with earlier discussion of the EU theatre, further observations on the strategic challenges confronting CEE firms and of operational issues in the region's markets feature in the second half of the book.

The Central and East Europeans

Despite historical reference to the 'Eastern bloc', Central and Eastern Europe is not a homogenous area. The countries of the region differ widely with regard to ethnic compositions, languages, historical identities, industrial structures and economies. The approach taken here is to distinguish between three main groups of countries. Firstly, there are the countries of 'Central Europe', consisting of Poland, Hungary, the Czech Republic, Slovakia and the former Yugoslav republics of Slovenia and Croatia. While separate reference is sometimes made to the Baltic states (Lithuania, Estonia and Latvia) these are generally included with this group. European Communities' reports and statistics on the Central European Candidate Countries (CECCs) also aggregate Romania and Bulgaria with this group. This reflects their strong orientation towards economic integration with the West (and with Central Europe) and their fellow status as prospective EU members. In other respects, however, Romania and Bulgaria are more logically included with a range of countries in South-Eastern Europe, typified by lower income levels, delayed structural reforms and relative instability. This group of countries also includes Albania, Macedonia and the remaining Yugoslav republics, and is frequently refered to as *'the Balkans'*, given the dominant geographic feature of the region. This practice is emulated in the present study. A third group consisting of Russia, the Ukraine, Belarus and Moldova is referred to here as the *'European NIS'* (newly independent states). While the reader should be clear that the former Soviet Union encompassed fifteen republics (including some in Central Asia), these four states constitute the remaining 'European' part of the old USSR.

As can be seen from Table 7.1 the smaller countries of the region have populations similar to the size of Belgium and the Netherlands (the smaller EU states). Despite this, population figures highlight the size and importance of the Central and Eastern European countries when taken as a group. For example, the ten countries that are 'candidate' EU members (hereafter the CECCs) have a combined population of some 105 million. Of this total some 97 million persons are already linked through the Central European Free Trade Area (CEFTA) providing for a degree of intra-regional trade and economic integration. Outside of this group, and

Table 7.1 Population of Central and Eastern Europe, 1997 (mid-year)

Country	Million
EU Candidate Countries	
Bulgaria	8.3
Czech Republic	10.3
Estonia	1.4
Hungary	10.2
Latvia	2.5
Lithuania	3.7
Poland	38.6
Romania	22.6
Slovakia	5.4
Slovenia	2.0
Sub-total	*105.0*
Others	
Albania	3.3
Belarus	10.2
Bosnia & Herzegovina	3.7
Croatia	4.6
Macedonia (FYR)	2.0
Moldova	4.3
Russia	147.1
Ukraine	50.5
Yugoslavia	10.6
Sub-total	*236.3*

Source: UN/ECE *Statistical Yearbook 1999*

taking into account the majority of former Yugoslav and Soviet republics, another 236 million persons may be counted. It is also clear that a small number of regional markets, notably Poland, Russia and the Ukraine, have substantial domestic populations. Over time, as markets develop and as living standards increase, populations of this scale will emerge as a serious variable in the investment equations of many international businesses. Indeed, many firms such as Fiat, BAT and McDonalds are already making investments in Poland and in Russia conscious of the potential revenues to be gained from their large and incipient domestic markets.

Incomes and living standards

A number of the CEECs have started a catching-up process with Western Europe in terms of income per capita and living standards. On the whole, however, living standards in Central and Eastern Europe are generally low and consumer markets remain underdeveloped by Western standards. Despite several years of consistent growth, only 25–30% of the population in Central Europe has enjoyed any real increase in incomes since 1989 and around 20% has seen a significant fall (Meth-Cohn, 1999, p. 14). Moving into the Balkans and the European NIS, most people have seen a significant drop in their incomes with millions squeezed out of the

Table 7.2 GDP per capita in PPS (% of EU-15 average), 1998

Country	Average
EU Candidate Countries	
Slovenia	68
Czech Republic	60
Hungary	49
Slovak Republic	46
Poland	39
Estonia	36
Lithuania	31
Romania	27
Latvia	27
Bulgaria	23
EU-15	100
EU-15 (Selected countries)	
Luxembourg	169
Denmark	119
Germany	108
United Kingdom	100
Spain	79
Greece	68

Note: PPS is an artifical unit based on real purchasing power standards.
Source: Eurostat, 1999

labour market and/or impoverished by the declining value of their wages and savings.

For the region's ten EU candidate countries, GDP per capita (in PPS) falls below 50% of the EU level when averaged out across countries. In 1998, the range applying to these income levels was from 23% of the EU average in Bulgaria to 68% in Slovenia (see Table 7.2). As the data reveals, not one of this group has a per capita income at a national level above the EU-15 average. Most Central European 'regions' are also less than half as wealthy as the average EU region. The Czech region of Praha (surrounding Prague) is, in fact, the only Central European region to have real income levels above average EU (regional) levels.

Differences in average incomes are even more pronounced when comparison is struck with the rest of Eastern Europe (see Table 7.3). For example, Russia (at $5,042) has an average income per capita figure (in PPP) which is 4.1 times lower than the average EU figure (at $20,400). In turn, Russia's average income levels compare favourably with those in other former Soviet Republics and to many of those in South-Eastern Europe. Consequently a significant gap in real incomes between Western and former Communist Europe is matched by chasms in income and welfare throughout Central and Eastern Europe itself. Most obvious here are the growing differentials between the fast-reforming, west-oriented countries of Central Europe and the ailing economies of the Balkans and former Soviet Union.

As discussed later in this chapter, several factors have combined to preserve and to accentuate these differences. For a start, CEECs have embarked on the road of reform from different starting points. As noted by Stern (1998, p. 3), variations in initial conditions concerned the length of period of central planning, past experiences of market economics, existing levels of economic reform and private enterprise, levels of debt, economic structures, human and natural resource

Table 7.3 GDP per capita 1998 in PPP (US$) – selected transition economies

Country	Per capita income
Slovenia	14,880
Czech Republic	12,900
Hungary	10,680
Slovakia	10,050
Poland	8,430
Croatia	7,020
Estonia	5,456
Russia	5,042
Bulgaria	5,010
Romania	4,990
Lithuania	4,425
Latvia	4,136
Ukraine	3,330

Source: Business Central Europe Magazine Statistical Database (01.01.2000)

endowments, and the state of macroeconomies. In this context, countries like the Czech Republic (with past experience of capitalism) and Hungary (with its early engagement with market-style reforms) have generally had a huge advantage over the Balkan economies and the European NIS. It is also fair to say that differences in the success and progress of reform efforts have been influenced by a country's geo-graphical proximity to Western markets with evidence of a broad distance decay effect on both trade and investment flows between Western and CEE markets. Hungary especially has benefited from its shared border with Austria (and by impli-cation with the entire EU) and Poland and the Czech Republic from their proxim-ity to Germany and the core EU markets. Also relevant is the extent of social, political and national fragmentation arising from the collapse of Communist auth-ority. As Wolf (1999, p. 2) insists:

> the dislocation involved in the fragmentation of the Soviet Union was greater than any-thing that happened in Central and Eastern Europe, except in the former Yugoslavia. This is why the Baltic countries suffered deep initial ouput losses, despite vigorous reforms.

Differences in reform efforts, and in the focus of transition policies, have also widened the gap between Central and Eastern Europeans. In general, those tran-sition economies that have pursued reform most vigorously have recovered from the transformational recessions that characterized the region after 1989. Indeed, various indices of reform progress evidence a strong correlation between faster growth in transition economies and the pursuit of determined liberalization and structural reform. The importance of this factor – and on the strength of political support for reforms – is demonstrated in the varying cases of Poland, the Czech Republic, Bulgaria and Russia. As noted by Ellman (1997), similar economic pack-ages were proposed and introduced at some stage between 1989 and 1992 in all of these countries. Where conditions and determination allowed for full implemen-tation (as in Poland and the Czech Republic) economic recovery and the growth of private sectors have been impressive. In others (as in Bulgaria and Russia) failures in implementation have contributed, along with other factors, to ongoing economic and financial crises.

The gap between the aspirations to Western living standards and the reality of what is being achieved (and is likely to be achieved in the near future) is a source of popular discontent in CEE societies. For people throughout the region, a decline in real incomes, higher prices and unemployment have been the most obvious manifestations of the 'new Capitalism', outweighing the supposed gains of political and economic freedom. Since most states began to liberalize their economies in the early 1990s, millions of jobs have been lost and inflation has eroded savings and purchasing power, forcing millions into impoverishment. Today, according to the World Bank, over 40% of the region's population live below the poverty line (Meth-Cohn, 1999, p. 14). This represents a ten-fold increase since 1989 and hints at the emergence of massive inequalities of income in societies from Prague to Kiev. Throughout the region, a gulf has opened up between entrepreneurs, property-owners and select private sector workers (on the one hand) and a number of other social groups that have seen little benefit from the transition to capitalist democracy. Although social experiences have varied from country to country, Ellman (1997) observes that:

> the losers have tended to include older (former) employees, those working in agriculture, manufacturing, coal mining, and the state sector, the newly unemployed, ethnic minorities (e.g. Romanis or Russians living outside Russia), children, large families, and the less educated.

Despite these tensions and disappointments, governments realize that they must continue with the reform process and see it through to some sort of conclusion. In the Central European states, persistence with reform has been key to a revitalization of output (and growth) following the transformational recessions of the early 1990s. These recessions were marked by an extraordinary decline in industrial production, with falls across the region amounting to average per annum declines of more than 10%. Indeed, despite adverse external developments in 1998–99 – most notably the financial crisis in Russia and the conflict in Kosovo – most of the Central European states have sustained their economic growth throughout the final years of the 1990s. Although the crisis of the Czech Koruna in May 1997 has slowed down the Czech economy (see Table 7.4), short-term difficulties extending from poor bank management and insufficient industrial restructuring should not mask the Czech Republic's strong macroeconomic performance since 1993.

For these countries, therefore, it is possible to talk of two 'developmental phases' in the post-Communist era. What this highlights is an initial period of economic contraction (transformational recession) and a subsequent period of reform-driven

Table 7.4 Real GDP change (% change against previous year)

Country	1990	1991	1992	1993	1994	1995	1996	1997	1998	1999
EU Candidate Countries										
Bulgaria	−9.1	−11.7	−7.3	−1.5	+1.8	+2.9	−10.1	−7.0	+3.5	+2.0 [2]
Czech Republic	−1.2	−11.5	−3.3	+0.6	+3.2	+6.4	+3.9	+1.0	−2.7	−0.9 [2]
Estonia	−8.1	−13.6	−14.2	−9.0	−1.8	+4.2	+4.0	+11.4	+4.2	−3.9 [1]
Hungary	−3.5	−11.9	−3.1	−0.6	+2.9	+1.5	+1.3	+4.4	+4.9	+4.1 [3]
Latvia	−3.5	−10.4	−34.9	−14.9	+0.6	−0.8	+3.3	+8.6	+3.6	−1.3 [2]
Lithuania	−6.9	−5.7	−21.3	−16.2	−9.8	+3.3	+4.7	+6.1	+4.5	−4.8 [1]
Poland	−11.6	−7.0	+2.6	+3.8	+5.2	+7.0	+6.0	+6.8	+4.8	+2.3 [1]
Romania	−5.6	−12.9	−8.8	+1.5	+4.0	+7.2	+3.9	−6.9	−7.3	−3.9 [1]
Slovakia	−2.5	−14.6	−6.5	−3.7	+4.9	+6.9	+6.6	+6.5	+4.4	+1.8 [2]
Slovenia	−4.7	−8.9	−5.5	+2.8	+5.3	+4.1	+3.5	+4.6	+3.9	+4.5 [1]
Others										
Croatia	−7.1	−21.1	−11.7	−8.0	+5.9	+6.8	+6.0	+6.5	+2.7	−1.1 [1]
Russia	−3.0	−5.0	−14.5	−8.7	−12.7	−4.1	−3.5	+0.8	−4.6	+1.8 [2]
Ukraine	−3.5	−8.7	−9.9	−14.2	−22.9	−12.2	−10.0	−3.2	−1.7	−2.0 [1]

Note: [1] – as of June, 1999; [2] as of September 1999; [3] preliminary
Source: Business Central Europe Magazine Statistical Database (01.01.2000)

growth which has generally slowed towards the end of the decade. For most Central European countries, the second of these phases appears to have started at some point between 1993 and 1994, although Poland's recovery – encouraged by a 'big bang' reform effort – can be traced back to as early as 1992 (Carlin and Landesmann, 1997, p. 78).

In contrast to these Central European states, whose output levels have been restored to between 75% and 120% of 1989 marks, Russia, the Ukraine and the Balkan states remain mired in recession. These countries have been dependent on Western largesse in preventing acute economic and financial crises and (with the exception of Romania) have failed to register any sustained positive economic growth since 1990 (see Table 7.4). Output levels remain depressed at between 45% and 50% of 1989 levels.

The Eastern bloc prior to transition

There were several important features to the Communist model that existed in the Soviet Union and Eastern Europe prior to 1989–90. In political terms, the Communist Party infiltrated and dominated all institutions of government such that there was no effective separation between the Party and the machinery of the state. Even at local levels of government and public administration, the Communist Party ensured the selection of personnel from within its own ranks by maintaining lists of jobs and of Party members to fill them (the nomenklatura). Mass organizations, education, the press and television were all tightly controlled, and police-state methods were employed to ensure compliance with state (communist) authority (see Kearns, 1994). If these controls were ever to prove insufficient as in Hungary 1956 and Czechoslovakia in 1968, Soviet military power was deployed to quell opposition groups and protests.

In economic terms, the features of state control, state ownership and central planning were defining. As explained by Lavigne (1995, p. 3):

> First, in such a system, economic life was under the control of a single party, whether or not the party was called communist. Second, the economic institutions were based upon collective, or state ownership of the basic means of production [the concept of 'social' ownership was advanced in post-war Yuogoslavia]. Third, compulsory central planning was the main co-ordinating mechanism, with an increasing but still subsidiary role devoted to market instruments.

In fact, in the socialist economic system of the post-war era, assets were owned and controlled by the state to the extent that that where people might work and what enterprises might produce were strictly determined by the state ministries. Decisions on resource allocation, production, distribution and pricing were made by state committees working to five-year and annual plans. Each sector of the economy and each enterprise was required to meet specific production targets set by central government and measured primarily by quantity rather than quality of output. Consequently, and with little heed to actual consumer demand, organs of the state were substituting for the role and functions of the market in deciding how to allocate resources and what to produce.

This system was first manifest in the Soviet Union in the 1920s following the Bolshevik or Communist revolution of 1917. It was broadly replicated across Eastern Europe between 1948 and 1953, by which time the Stalinization of the Communist model was fully complete. While some of this communization was spontaneous (notably in Albania and Yugoslavia), much was achieved under direct Soviet influence and intervention. The terms of post-war settlement had created a sphere of Soviet influence east of Berlin, and Stalin was set on creating a buffer zone of satellite states between the Soviet Union and the West. This zone would be marked by Communist political and economic development and by the occupation of the Red Army. Therefore, while states such as East Germany, Czechoslovakia, Hungary, Poland, Romania and Bulgaria maintained their 'independence', these became mirror images of the USSR, with local leaders accepting both the disciplines of the command economy and the structures of Communist (single-party) authority. Soviet leadership was imposed both through military controls (via the Warsaw Pact Agreement and dispersal of Red Army forces) and through the Council for Mutual Economic Assistance (CMEA or Comecon). This was the Soviet bloc trading order in which, according to command principles, particular countries and centres specialized in particular categories of products.

The failures of the Communist system

Although it is tempting to date the transition to market democracy in Central and Eastern Europe back to the fall of the Berlin Wall on 9 November 1989, in reality Polish elections had already established a non-Communist majority in June 1989. However, ailing Communist authorities throughout the Eastern bloc had effectively commenced the process of economic transition before this event. In Hungary major steps on the way to the market were made as early as 1988 with the introduction of new company laws which allowed state enterprises to convert themselves into joint stock companies and (from 1 January 1989) for 100% foreign ownership. Even in the Soviet Union itself, the ill-fated restructuring or 'perestroika' of the late 1980s introduced new enterprise rights and co-operative freedoms while retaining central command of the economy. These early reform efforts reflected a realization that the socialist economic system was collapsing under its own inherent flaws and, in the Polish and Hungarian cases at least, exposed the weakening grasp of national Communist parties. Although the centrally planned economies had worked relatively well for for a number of years (industrialization had ensured substantial economic growth), there had been a major slowdown in economic growth in the 1970s and 1980s. During this time, the classic inputs of land, energy and raw materials all became less plentiful, and production costs began to rise (Kennedy, 1993). In the Soviet Union, oil extraction costs had escalated, with easily exploited reserves depleted and new oilfields developed at high cost. These problems were exacerbated by the massive inefficiencies of the state-owned enterprises (SOEs) which – protected from the forces of competition – were typified by managerial inefficiency and worker carelessness. While state officials might penalize inefficient enterprise managers, businesses themselves were not subject to the disciplines of the market and would always find the state willing to subsidize their activities. These institutions soaked up huge government subsidies and were simply unable to develop quality production to the market in appropriate volumes. The system under which they operated neither encouraged quality nor could accurately predict the level of demand for all products, including those parts and materials central to productive processes. Although prices would be set and subsidized at artificially low rates, bottlenecks in production and failures to accurately match demand and supply were a persistent problem. These difficulties were matched by a limited range of available consumer products such as motor vehicles (generally of lower quality), with industrialization heavily concentrated on armaments and heavy industry. Workers were often drawn into these new industries from the countryside (itself collectivized) and subjected to heavy production methods. To compound these problems, a lack of investment in transport infrastructure contributed to grave distribution problems that further exacerbated the problems of production bottlenecks and, in the worst of cases, resulted in food queues and rationing.

By Western standards, spending on new manufacturing sectors was also minuscule and economies were unable to rectify massive quality and technology gaps with the West. International trade (outside of the CMEA), a major engine of economic development, was stymied by administrative restrictions on foreign trade and by the fact that Central and Eastern currencies were not convertible. Foreign borrowing helped at various times but contributed to massive levels of foreign debt (sovereign debt). Efforts to meet financial obligations by printing money (which became widespread) created repressed inflation which, when coupled with the shortages, led to black markets in many goods.

As recalled by Kearns (1994, p. 381), 'the development of such an economic situation was fatal to the legitimacy of the Communist regime'. Given the absence of free elections in their coming to power and other political freedoms, '...such legitimacy as existed rested on the Communists' claim to both economic superiority and a more equal society'. In similar vein, although speaking specifically about the Soviet system, Kennedy observes 'had the economy been working properly there would have been far less criticism of the leadership' (1993, p. 235). As it was, the daily evidence of shoddy consumer goods, of terrible housing and of targeted privileges (for senior party members and apparatchiks) stood in contrast to the regime's claims that its system was both superior and egalitarian (see Kearns, 1994, pp. 381–2; Kennedy, 1993, pp. 235–6). Claims of this nature were also undermined by the spread of satellite and television images of Western lifestyles that Communist authorities could do little to control. Indeed, while the uprisings against Communist authorities (between 1989 and 1990) were generally peaceful, this did not mask the deep disenchantment of many Central and Eastern Europeans with their Communist leaders or the hunger for a new democratic order. Throughout the region, Communist governments were forced to resign (or into power-sharing agreements with non-Communist parties), their demise accelerated by the removal of assurances from an ailing Moscow that it would intervene to sustain Communist authority outside of its own borders. Although some Eastern European Communist parties clung on to a presence within new multiparty governments, most were defeated in the free elections that characterized 1990 and 1991. In Hungary, a centre–right coalition government was formed in March 1990 casting the former communists into a form of political opposition that few in Central Europe had ever thought possible. Indeed, it was not until October 1992 that any free elections in Eastern Europe were to return former communists to power (in Lithuania). By this time both the politics of Communism and the very map of Eastern Europe itself had become almost unrecognizable. In particular, after a failed crackdown in the Baltic Republics and an attempted coup against President Mikhail Gorbachev (by Communist hardliners), the Soviet Union slipped towards its end on 31 December 1991.

The nature of transition

The concept of 'transition', therefore, as applying to Central and Eastern Europe, refers to the movement away from a command to a market economy and to the creation of a new system for the generation and allocation of resources. This process involves a range of policy reforms and institutional actions including market deregulation, price liberalization, privatization, enterprise restructuring, and banking and financial sector reforms. The introduction of new market-based systems also entails concerted policy action directed towards macroeconomic stabilization and a massive reorientation of foreign trade and external economic relations towards Western markets and institutions. In the following sections some of these features of transition are examined with address of the form and progress of reform in a range of Central and Eastern European states. The fundamental nature of these changes (coupled with the need for political reforms) makes the problem of transformation in Central and Eastern Europe quite different from the development problem of raising per capita incomes in poor market economies. Even in the more economically advanced countries of Central Europe, such as Poland, Slovenia, Slovakia, Hungary and the Czech Republic, there is unfamiliarity with the mechanics and institutions of market-based capitalism and a nest of challenges surrounding financial, legal and intitutional reform. Socio-cultural and political tensions, such as those arising from ideological, ethnic and national divisions, can also weaken the cohesion of central governments and complicate the process of economic reform (witness the case of Yugoslavia).

Market deregulation

Market deregulation (or liberalization) involves removing legal restrictions to the free play of markets and to the establishment of private enterprises. It is a process common to all transitional economies although one that has been managed variably and at different speeeds. It should be recalled that before the collapse of

Communism in 1989–90, governments in Eastern European countries exercised tight controls over prices and outputs (setting both through state planning) and, with only minor exception in Poland, Hungary and Yugoslavia, precluded private sector firms from operating in all sectors of the economy. Foreign economic activity was also limited to the exchanges of Comecon (at least in substantial part) and foreign ownership of enterprises was strictly prohibited. Consequently, structural measures aimed at creating private market economies have included privatization, the introduction of competition policy (and the dismantling of state monopolies), foreign trade liberalization (permitting enterprises to engage in foreign trade), reform of the banking and financial sectors, and price liberalization (the release of previously fixed and unrealistic prices). These measures are central to the establishment of market conditions and to the facilitation of enterprise restructuring.

Macroeconomic stabilization

Measures aimed at structural transformation have generally had to be launched within the context of (national) macroeconomic stabilization programmes. Although varied in their forms, macroeconomic stabilization programmes have usually consisted of measures designed to curb inflation and to balance government expenditure. For example, in the early years of economic reform in Hungary, Poland and Czechoslovakia, efforts were directed at controlling hyperinflation and at improving current account and fiscal balances. These included increases in taxes, the introduction of convertible currencies (and their consequent devaluations), the reduction of subsidies, and other cuts in government expenditure. In Poland, where huge inflationary pressures were unleashed by quick moves to the market, restrictive monetary policies extended to the creation of positive real interest rates and to the direct regulation of bank lending. Rigid incomes policies were also introduced during the early stages of reform. While the implementation of many structural reforms (especially enterprise privatization) can be realized over a number of years, stabilization measures have generally been required from the onset of market-oriented reforms. This reflects both the initial impact of the movement away from central planning – e.g. the inflationary consequences of price liberalization – and the contingency of much Western lending on tight fiscal policies. It must also be recognized that stabilization measures were required regardless of the course and patronage of reforms. For nearly all of the CEECs, the legacy of the Communist era included over-employment (and high prospective welfare costs), repressed inflation, large budget and balance of payments deficits, and (in certain cases) high levels of sovereign debt.

Most of the governments and central banks in Central and Eastern Europe began the implementation of stabilization measures from the onset of market-based reforms. In Poland and Czechoslovakia, where a rapid 'shock therapy' model of transition was selected, stabilization measures were quickly introduced as new enterprise laws, subsidy cuts, currency conversions, price and trade liberalization led to rising levels of inflation and to an initial deterioration in current accounts and fiscal balances. In Hungary too, which had for many years been taking gentle steps towards a market economy, wide-ranging stabilization measures followed demonopolization laws and a (Privatization) Transformation Law in July 1989. The Baltic and Balkan countries largely followed suit in 1992–93, tightening fiscal and monetary policies and embarking on piecemeal structural reform. In Russia, structural reform and tentative stabilization policies were finally pursued from 1992 onwards although the dramatic measures prescribed by the IMF were never fully implemented.

Price liberalization (and the curse of inflation)

During these early years of reform, inflationary pressures were immense. Large budgetary deficits (due to enterprise financing and the lax nature of monetary and fiscal policies) provide one explanation, with many governments often increasing the money supply to finance their expenditure. Inflationary pressures in CEECs also resulted from monetary overhangs and from the ending of soft loans and subsidies to many state-owned enterprises (SOEs). As Harris explains (1999, p. 131), the ending of state loans to businesses at negative rates of interest and of direct subsidies and payments forced many businesses in CEE markets to quickly raise their prices in order to cover true production costs. There was also an initial trade-off between instant currency convertibility and inflation (see Ellman, 1997). Instant convertibility required deeply undervalued exchanges rates, 'which contributed to inflationary explosions at the beginning of many [national] stabilization programmes' (Ellman, 1997). A root cause of inflationary pressures, however, has been the removal of price controls. It is clear that, at the onset of market liberalization,

Table 7.5 Inflation (change in % against previous year)

Country	1997	1998	1999	Annual peak since 1989 (and year)
EU Candidate Countries				
Bulgaria	1,082.3	22.3	6.2 [2]	1,082.3 (1997)
Czech Republic	8.5	10.7	2.5 [2]	56.7 (1991)
Estonia	11.1	8.2	3.3 [3]	1,076.0 (1992)
Hungary	18.3	14.3	10.6 [1]	35.0 (1991)
Latvia	8.4	4.7	2.4 [3]	951.0 (1992)
Lithuania	8.9	5.1	0.3 [3]	1,021.0 (1992)
Poland	14.9	11.8	7.3 [3]	585.8 (1990)
Romania	154.8	59.1	54.8 [2]	256.2 (1993)
Slovakia	6.1	6.7	14.2 [2]	61.2 (1991)
Slovenia	8.4	7.9	7.8 [1]	554.6 (1990)
Others				
Croatia	3.6	5.7	4.3 [1]	1,517.1 (1993)
Russia	14.8	27.6	50.5 [1]	1,528.7 (1992)
Ukraine	15.9	10.6	n/a	5,371.0 (1993)

Note: [1] – As of November 1999; [2] as of December 1999; [3] preliminary
Source: *Business Central Europe* Magazine Statistical Database (01.01.2000)

prices for food, goods and services were artificially low when compared with world prices. This established a margin for increase in consumer prices that contributed to early experiences of hyper-inflation. 'The more complete the initial price liberaliz-ation, the bigger the initial price explosion' (Ellman, 1997). Peaks of annual infla-tion are highlighted in the final column of Table 7.5. These underscore the severity of inflationary pressures experienced in the CEECs following the abandonment of Communism, with peak (annual) rates reaching over 1,000% in specific cases.

The data in Table 7.5 provide some evidence of the improved control of inflation in recent years, although rates throughout the region remain high by Western European standards. A continuing disinflation process is being supported by the operation of tighter monetary policies (partly through pressure from international bodies such as the IMF) and by the continued decline of input prices. In the CECCs, continuing inflationary pressures relate primarily to the rapid growth of real wages. Inflationary pressures also continue to emanate from further adjustments in admin-istered prices and from indirect tax measures, such as the introduction of VAT in Slovenia.

Privatization

Among the structural measures necessary to establish market economy, we have already identified the privatization of enterprises or the transfer of businesses from the state to the private sector. Privatization has been seen to play an important role in improving state budgets (through sale proceeds and/or reduced subsidies), in ownership change, and in the breaking-up of state monopolies. It has also been seen as central to the restructuring of enterprises, in providing for efficient man-agement of firms at the expense of former SOE stakeholders, and to bringing in Western investment capital, expertise and technology. Privatization has also been viewed among CEE governments as a means of reducing the state's administrative burden and of creating a broad basis of support for market reforms through mass participation. Thus, the popular image of privatizations in Western societies – essen-tially as a source of financial gain and competitive efficiency – has been promoted in the CEECs alongside a number of wider benefits. In fact, it is only really in a number of states (in Hungary and Estonia for example) that governments have con-centrated on the outright sale of state assets to strategic (Western) investors. Other countries have pursued populist 'give-away' voucher-type programmes and/or 'insider privatization' to privatize swathes of industry, combining these methods with conventional capital-based privatization. While such methods have some-times facilitated speedy privatization, they have not always brought great budget-ary benefits or deep-level enterprise restructuring.

The evidence on privatization in the CEECs is that this is an aspect of structural reform that few countries have found easy, that few have managed to complete and that has been marked by numerous and varied methods. Indeed, the different routes to privatization in CEE states can be seen to include:

1. the restitution of enterprises to their former owners;

2. the transfer of small state assets such as shops and restaurants by sale or lease (generally with favour to current employees);

3. the privatization of firms through employee or management buy-outs;

4. mass privatization by which 'free' vouchers transferrable for shares in privatized firms or in investment funds are distributed to all adult citizens;

5. capital privatization (sale at full or significant price to strategic investors – including foreign investors);

6. insider privatization (selling firms or firm assets to enterprise insiders, often at reduced prices).

The privatization processes underway in Central and Eastern European economies, have evidenced a mix of these methods. Indeed, when we examine the scale of operations and the spectrum of privatization schemes across the region, it is clear that privatization has taken (and continues to take) a variety of forms both within and between countries.

The Czech Republic

In the Czech Republic, restitutions to former owners and the auction of small-scale enterprises took place quickly as a precursor to the privatization of large-scale enterprises. Following these auctions, centred largely on small hotels, outlets and factories, a first wave of large-scale transfers (involving nearly 1,000 Czech enterprises) was then completed in 1992 through a mass privatization programme. This programme was based on the issue of voucher point books at a symbolic nominal price. Adult citizens (who were eligible to receive 1,000 voucher point books) were thus able to become individual investors in single enterprises or in investment funds (IFs). These funds quickly attracted a large share of all voucher points and then bid for the shares on offer in the privatization programme. Individual investors (and IFs) received confirmation of their share ownerships in the middle of 1993 (see Potts, 1999). Foreign strategic investors were also able to buy large blocks of shares in enterprises from the newly created National Property Fund (NPF). This fund retained significant stakes in nearly all major companies. After some delay, resulting largely from the turbulence during the partition of Czechoslovakia, a second wave of large-scale transfers was commenced in late 1993 involving nearly 700 companies. This privatization round proceeded on a similar basis. More recently, the Czech government has embarked on the direct sale of stakes in strategic companies in the telecommunications, banking and petrochemicals sectors and has developed plans to accelerate industrial privatization.

Several criticisms have applied both to the nature and scope of privatization efforts in the Czech Republic. First, little restructuring of enterprises was undertaken before mass privatization. Second, it is only fairly recently that the state has turned its attention to the privatization of banking and utilities. Third, although there are plans to sell around a dozen large state companies over the next few years (from a variety of sectors), many more will stay in state hands including firms such as Budvar (beer) and CEZ, the country's big power producer (see Kapoor, 1999).

Fourth, although the voucher system has succeeded in enabling mass privatization in Czech Republic, the nature of the approach has meant that there have been no major revenues for the state (and for enterprise restructuring) as a consequence of the voucher privatization of nearly 2,000 enterprises. Finally, because IFs are partly owned by leading state banks, this creates a situation in which banks are often lending money to companies which they also 'own'. Significantly, the current shake-up of the Czech banking system is already seeing the return of many unreconstructed companies to state control adding to the volume of Czech 'corporate dross' that nobody wants to buy (see Kapoor, 1999).

Hungary

By contrast, the focus of Hungarian (large-scale) privatization has consistently been the attraction of significant foreign investment through auctions and direct sale. Privatization revenues have accounted for almost one-third of FDI and have promoted considerable organizational restructuring in privatized Magyar enterprises. As early as January 1990, the Hungarian government sold the state lighting company, Tungsram Light, to General Electric (of the US) and subsequent rounds of privatization have seen foreign investors establish majority or large minority stakes in key enterprises in the electricity, gas and telecommunication sectors. In Hungary, privatization has reached an advanced stage with movement into transport, banking and financial sectors. Indeed, although the state retains 'golden shares' in strategic firms such as MOL (the main oil and gas importer–producer), privatization is virtually complete. Compared with the Czech Republic, there are relatively few (inefficient) enterprises left in state hands and a large section of control of important industries is now under foreign management.

Poland

In Poland, although small-scale privatization has been completed swiftly and successfully (Ziljstra, 1998; Potts, 1999), large-scale privatization has proceeded slowly. The overall rate of privatization, while encouraging, has been slower than that of Hungary and the Czech Republic where almost 90% of state-owned enterprises have been privatized (Schoenberg, 1998). In fact, there are still nearly 3,000 enterprises which are either state owned or in which the Treasury is the sole or majority owner. Most of these companies have remained in poor financial shape (Ziljstra, 1998). The country's 'mass' privatization programme – the National Investment Fund (NIF) Programme – has accelerated the pace of privatization but, to date, this has had only limited coverage. In this scheme, over 500 state enterprises have been allocated to NIFs with each receiving a lead shareholding in a small number of enterprises and a minority holding in an additional number managed by other NIFs. Privatization units (vouchers) have been made available to all Poles at just over £10.00, with these units converted into shares in the fifteen different NIFs. Each NIF is listed on the Warsaw stock exchange and each is characterized by powerful outsider shareholders (see Potts, 1999). A total of 25 million Poles have involved themselves in this process. The government now plans to sell stakes and to undertake partial flotations in key companies drawn from many sectors including oil and energy, insurance and banking, chemicals, pharmaceuticals, transport and ship-building. In late 1999, the Polish government seemed to be acting on this promise with, among several moves, a (partial) flotation of leading refinery and petroleum company Polski Koncern Naftowy. This stock market flotation was reported to have raised $515 million. During the final weeks of 1999, SwissAir also became a strategic investor in Poland's national airline Lot, buying a 10% stake for $180 million with plans to increase that to 38%. The government is now also proceeding with the sale of a strategic stake in Tele-komunikacja Polska (TPSA) to France Telecom, a deal expected to close early in 2000.

Russia

In Russia, privatization has also worked with a voucher scheme component (see Potts, 1999). In a first wave of privatization (1992–93), approximately 6,000 medium to large-scale enterprises auctioned a proportion of their shares for vouch-ers distributed to all adult citizens. A number of shares in these enterprises were retained by the state or allocated to incumbent managers. As in other cases exam-ined (e.g. the Czech Republic), vouchers could be used to buy shares at auction in individual enterprises or could be entrusted to investment funds. Alternatively, they could be sold to speculators set on investing in specific enterprises or in investment funds (Potts, 1999). The Russian scheme gave particular preference to incumbent managers and employees. These 'stakeholders' would be able to buy up controlling shares in their own enterprises (at reduced price) before public auction of the remaining shares. This meant that a form of 'insider control' was created in newly privatized firms in Russia, with managers often consolidating their control by pro-gressing to buy shares from their employees. The approach also created limited scope for restructuring of enterprises as it brought in little foreign investment (or expertise) and exposed few companies to increased (external) performance pressures.

A second wave of privatization (which began in 1995) has included a controver-sial shares-for-loans scheme. Under this scheme, a small but powerful group of bankers have secured lucrative shares in selected natural resource companies at 'knock-down' prices (see Bush, 1999). These shares have been secured through the conversion of special bonds issued by state authorities in exchange for much-needed loans and financing. The Russian government now appears to be turning its attention to the auction-based sale of partial shares in high-profile companies such as Svyazinvest (the state-holding company in the telecommunications sector) and in various energy-sector-related concerns. What is clear, however, is that the privat-ization process has been bedevilled by the financial, political and economic insta-bility of post-Soviet Russia and that there is much domestic opposition to forms of privatization that surrender to the control of insiders.

Reflections

These histories demonstrate that the need to privatize huge numbers of firms in quite difficult conditions has led to a variety (and creativity) in privatization methods. The major methods of privatization in the Czech Republic, Hungary, Poland and Russia have been discussed and have highlighted such variation as the weight of sales to strategic investors (outsiders) in Hungary and the dominance of insider privatization to employees and managers in Russia. While it is not possible here to consider other states at length, it should be registered that such heterodoxy also characterizes privatization processes in and between other countries in the region. In tiny Moldova, for example, privatization has taken place through mass privatization, national patrimonial bonds, small-scale cash privatization and sale by tender. Lithuania's privatization efforts have combined spontaneous privatizations of small-scale enterprises with the sale of company shares for vouchers and the sale of (larger) assets for cash. In most cases, mass voucher-based programmes have had a natural attraction and, while the analyst is struck by the variety of different methods in use, the dominance of voucher privatization can be easily demonstrated. Direct sales through open auctions and public listings have the virtue of bringing in much needed resources (capital, expertise etc.) but for large-scale privatization to be achieved through such methods there has to be an attractive basis for sale and substantial capital resources. The problem, as noted by Potts (1999), has been that '[l]imited western interest and domestic savings, combined with problems of valuation and the need to create an effective stock market, reduce the possible speed, effectiveness and scope of [such] privatization at full price'. Privatization by such methods has only been possible for a limited number of SOEs and, after a wave of foreign buy-outs of potentially profitable firms, western interest has been limited.

Looking at the progress with privatization (both small scale and large scale), it is clear that some CEECs have fared better than others. Privatization efforts in Hungary (especially), the Czech Republic, Poland and Estonia are really quite advanced. Croatia, Latvia, Lithuania, Slovakia and Slovenia have also transferred a large number of enterprises to private ownership. Outside of these countries, progress has really been quite unimpressive. Having already discussed the limited achievements of successive Russian governments, it is also the case that privatization programmes in Romania and Bulgaria have been extremely limited and that privatization processes have barely begun in the Ukraine, Belarus and the wider CIS.

Enterprise restructuring

Successful enterprise restructuring depends not only on privatization but also on competition in the product market and the imposition of financial constraints. This point is made emphatically by Carlin and Landesmann, who write:

> The role played by a credibly hard budget constraint, of bank reform, of the promotion of the private sector, of privatization prospects, and of competition in the product market to the separation of good from bad managers and to eliciting restructuring effort from good managers is clear...privatization per se is not a substitute for the other elements of the policy package. (Carlin and Landesmann, 1997, p. 23)

In Central Europe at least, the introduction of privatization laws has been accompanied by the introduction of anti-monopoly laws and by the promotion of the private sector. Support for liberal trade regimes has also been quite high and increased competitive pressure from foreign (as well as from domestic firms) has been central to the encouragement of enterprise restructuring (see Heinrich, 1995; Carlin and Landesmann, 1997). Repeatedly, international bodies such as the IMF and the EBRD have associated enhanced market competition with the stimulation of enterprise reform. With respect to financial constraints (as imposed on enterprises), the elimination of subsidies and reductions in 'soft finance' play an important part in bringing about changes in the structure of enterprises. Where cuts have been made in such financial support, enterprise restructuring is accelerated. In Poland, for example, hard budget constraints on companies have forced many to sell off assets and/or to engage in considerable labour-shedding. Changes in the law since 1992 have also induced banks to renegotiate non-performing loans and to change their lending behaviour so as to weaken support of unprofitable enterprises. Where strict bankruptcy laws have also applied (e.g. in Hungary) such pressures have led to multiple closures or to operational restructuring. According to the EBRD, as a result of the introduction of bankruptcy legislation in 1991, 9% of Hungarian industrial enterprises representing 24% of industrial output and 35% of total exports had been registered as being in bankruptcy or liquidation within twelve months. A shake-out of inefficient and bankrupt enterprises has continued since this time despite some relaxation of the law. Effective bankruptcy regimes are an important component of transition and play a key role in identifying firms with no future in a market environment and in increasing financial discipline. Arguably this is one of the key failings of the Czech transition model where large-scale closures (at least in early transition) were prevented by delayed introduction of a bankruptcy code and through the writing-off of much enterprise debt. The Czech case, however, bears no comparison with Russia, where a largely unreconstituted enterprise sector has faced rather soft-budgetary constraints. In Russia, only a small number of large and very large enterprises are as yet subsidy-free (see Alfandari *et al.*, 1996, cited in Carlin and Landesmann, 1997).

Small business development

The privatization of the large industrial units and their restructuring may be less significant in the long run than the development of small and medium-sized businesses. A significant small business sector not only carries an immense potential for making an economy prosperous but also distributes that prosperity to a larger segment of a country's population. Moreover, small business tends to be less environmentally damaging. The lack of significant social benefits in Central and Eastern European countries is already driving people into enterprising ways of generating incomes and an abundance of new small businesses is to be found in any large town. In Poland, where transition has taken place at a rapid pace, the growth of the private sector has been fuelled by the vast number of start-up companies and the economy now virtually relies on its small companies. These firms – two-thirds of which are one-man or one-woman businesses – contribute significantly to an estimated total of 4 million small and medium-sized private sector enterprises in the CECCs. Eurostat estimates that 3.3 million such enterprises were already registered in the CECCs by the end of 1995. While this rate of growth is not yet matched in the NIS, large numbers of small private firms are emerging despite many obstacles to market entry.

Much can be learned from the development of small businesses in Europe and particularly from the work of local authority development agencies in countries such as the UK and Italy. Again there is an apparent contradiction between the creation of a market economy and the need for government (particularly local government) support and planning. In the EU local governments have been successful in creating and supporting business parks, managed workspaces, small business advisers, co-operative support networks, grants and low-interest loans. In many cases projects have built on local resources and skills and where appropriate have been linked to such things as local tourism or the particular ethnic mix of a region. These types of developments are being considered by governments in Central and Eastern Europe and, in some regions, are in their early stages of development. However, there is limited availability of finance and venture capital for SMEs throughout Central and Eastern Europe and most enterprise creation takes place with equity provided from savings, friends and relatives. According to Pissarides (1998) this can be attributed to underdeveloped capital markets in the CEE region in which access to credit is still easier for state and other large enterprises and in which SMEs continue to face higher levels of nominal interest rates. While banks in all societies generally consider the credit risks to SMEs to be higher than those applying to larger enterprises, the average 2–5% that SMEs pay above what larger enterprises pay for loan finance in the OECD economies is tiny compared with that extra premium paid by SMEs in the CEECs. Therefore, for a significant development of new business to take place, local banking sectors must be strengthened (and further commercialized) and incentives must be created for banks to lend to SMEs. Equity and bond markets must also be developed so that the financing needs of SMEs can be served more efficiently (see Pissarides, 1998, pp. 4–5).

CASE STUDY 7.1 Entrepreneurs find ways to profit

For Dinu Patriciu, one of the wealthiest men in Romania, doing business in the 1990s has been about getting in first.

After the fall of Nicolae Ceausescu, the Romanian dictator, Mr Patriciu was the first person to register a private company in the country – called Alpha, it was given the registration number 00000001. An architect by profession, Mr Patriciu was also among the first to grasp the value of property. Just before Bucharest land prices took off amid the high inflation of the early 1990s, he sold a car and a video recorder and put the money into property. Simultaneously, he received a string of architectural contracts from others wanting to develop sites.

The boom later fizzled out and some of Mr Patriciu's projects were never built. But the fees were paid, and Mr Patriciu was on his way to financial success. Today, aged forty-nine, he runs a business group that includes property development, asset management and Rompetrol, one of Romania's largest oil companies with its own refinery.

He has his problems, notably with a loss-making

267

shipping company he founded. However, the group as whole, which employs about 2,000 people, makes profits of 5–10% of turnover which Mr Patriciu says will this year reach $120–130 million and $200 million next year.

Mr Patriciu says that determination and chance played an equal part in his success. 'I was stubborn and I was lucky', he says. He was also fortunate. As one of Romania's top architects he taught at Bucharest University, which had extensive national and international contacts. In the 1980s, he won an international scholarship which led to work overseas and, as he says, 'contact with the market economy'.

Mr Patriciu's story highlights one of the most important economic and social trends of post-Communist eastern Europe – the rise of the entrepreneur. Once the chains of totalitarianism were broken, business people grasped opportunities to make money – as free market theorists said they would – even in the toughest macro-economic conditions such as those in Romania.

The scale and importance of newly created private business vary greatly between countries. The biggest number of active entrepreneurs is probably in Poland, where business has been stimulated by traditional independence of mind, by frequent contact with relatives and others in the West and by favourable macroeconomic policies.

Hungary, too, has generated many businesses, notably in high technology, where some companies have been so successful that they have moved lock, stock and barrel to the US. Czech companies, stifled by red tape and economic stagnation, have done less well. In the former Soviet Union, the most successful have been those who have won control of oil, gas and other natural resources businesses, quickly turning themselves into some of Europe's wealthiest people.

Entrepreneurs also often differ in their origins. Some, like Mr Patriciu, made use of their existing skills and contacts. Others had businesses before 1989, especially in Poland and Hungary, where small-scale private enterprise was tolerated.

For example, Wojciech Kruk, president of Kruk, Poland's best-known jeweller, runs a business started by his family in 1840. It never closed, operating in basement workshops during the height of Stalinist oppression. Today, Mr Kruk has a turnover of $10 million a year, employs 300 and is considering a stock market flotation.

Many business people are former members of the communist political elite. Directors of state-run factories often, through privatization, won personal control of all or part of their old operations. This element is strongest in Russia and Ukraine, where a new phrase has been invented to describe the process – 'nomenklatura capitalism'.

Rem Vyakhirev, chief executive of Gazprom, the gas group, is one of the more successful of thousands of former officials. Anti-communist politicians often condemn nomenklatura capitalism as unfair, but, at least within the former Soviet Union, the Communist party had such a grip on talent that there are few alternative sources of well-educated people with business experience.

Outside the former Soviet Union, ties to the old regime are less important. In terms of numbers, the most important school of entrepreneurship is small-scale trade.

Taking goods from one place to another, often across borders, allowed tens of thousands to accumulate a little capital in the 1980s and early 1990s and later to establish a shop, a bar, a workshop or a software company. Among them is one of Poland's richest business people, Zbigniew Niemczycki, who began in the 1980s by trading goods including fruit juice and now employs about 1,000 people at his group called Curtis International.

For a younger generation, such possibilities still exist but offer a long hard road to success. Some try to short circuit the process by working as employees for a while to accumulate cash and experience.

For example, in Hungary, thirty-one-year-old Erno Duda – who first made a name for himself managing Copy General, a US-owned chain of copy shops – left the company to set up a student restaurant in Szeged, his home town. He impressed some local lawyers who asked him to join them in establishing LP Invest, a venture capital group.

Recently, he was so struck by one high-technology company which approached LP Invest that he decided to help finance it and work for it full time. The company, Solvo, makes sophisticated blood-testing kits for use in chemotherapy. 'Business is creative', says Mr Duda. 'I love a challenge'.

He also likes the freedom to make his own decisions and the perks of being in charge. LP Invest's office, from where he runs Solvo, has its own swimming pool. 'Where else could I have that?' he asks.

Source: Financial Times, 10 November 1999

Financial sector reform and development

The development of an infrastructure for the market economy also necessitates a transformation of financial institutions (and legislation) and the development of new capital markets. This is suggested in the preceding observations on privatization, enterprise restructuring and small business development. Indeed, just as new legal systems have had to be introduced to transform patterns of ownership and to create new property rights, so new financial and banking systems (and capital markets) have had to be introduced so as to underpin and to operationalize the new market systems. In this context, CEE banks and other financial institutions have to be modelled on Western equivalents (specifically EU forms) and must execute the role of these institutions. In short, market-driven institutions need to be established to attract savings, to provide links between savers and investors, to lend to creditworthy customers and to provide an efficient clearing and settlement system. With respect to their practices, and as discussed with regard to the restructuring of enterprises, banks must also enforce repayments and impose hard budget constraints on enterprises (*EBRD Transitions Report*, 1998, p. 15).

Banking and financing systems are still under development in the CEECs and the structural impediments to banking sector reform and development are immense. Despite the privatization of some commercial banks, several large commercial banks remain in state hands. Many of these banks are also debt ridden and are plagued by non-performing loan problems. Combined with poor credit practices and inadequacies in banking supervision, these factors have already led to severe sectoral crises in Latvia, Lithuania and Russia. Even fast-reforming countries (notably the Czech Republic) have seen 'substantial disturbances in the form of failures of medium-sized or large local banks' (see *EBRD Transitions Report*, 1998, p. 20). In addition, most countries evidence a deep resistance to majority foreign control of domestic banking sectors and to downscaling of banking sectors. Such weakness and the underdevelopment of financial sectors throughout the region are a genuine brake on growth in the CEECs. Banks continue to play only a modest role as providers of investment finance and capital markets continue to lack maturity. Even where commercialization and privatization have proceeded at greatest pace, banks continue to lack experience in private sector lending and other skills and methods of work are as yet poorly developed. The struggle for sectoral reform is profiled further in Case Study 7.2.

CASE STUDY 7.2 **Bank reform struggles for pace**

Few countries in central and east Europe have been spared banking crises, as the region has made its painful transition to a market economy.

Governments have often been wary about surrendering control of state-owned banks and have been reluctant to give up the powers of patronage and influence conferred on them by their seats on the bank boards.

Political leaders have had to learn the hard way, however, that financial reforms and healthy financial institutions lie at the heart of the transition process and are the foundation stones of a strong economy.

In fast-track reform countries such as Hungary, Estonia and Poland lessons were taken on board early. It has been no coincidence that a fast pace of sustainable growth has been accompanied in most cases by determined efforts to restructure the banking sector and to privatize state-owned banks, in particular through the sale of large stakes to foreign strategic investors.

However, the current spate of bank privatization deals across central and east Europe from Croatia to Bulgaria and from Romania to the Czech Republic shows that a decade after the start of transition even the worst laggards are seeking to catch up with the pace set by the front-runners.

The most recent convert is Slovakia, where the reform-minded government elected a year ago recently announced plans to spend Sk87 billion ($2.13 billion) on restructuring the country's fragile banking sector with the aim of privatising the three leading state-owned banks by the end of next year.

'We want to be in the first wave of entrants to the European Union (from central and east Europe)', says Brigita Schmognerova, Slovak finance minister. Development of the financial sector including bank privatization, as well as plans for corporate restructuring and reform of bankruptcy legislation, are key moves aimed at improving the competitiveness of the Slovak economy, she says.

The Slovak government admitted in its restructuring plan that 'the growing problems of corporate sector indebtedness and banks' non-performing loan portfolios are adversely affecting the Slovak economy and neither can be resolved without the other'.

Governments in most countries remain convinced that only foreign groups have the capital and know-how to modernise their banks.

In the neighbouring Czech Republic, the minority Social Democratic government is in the midst of the privatization process and the struggle to catch up with the fast-track countries of the region that have stolen a lead in the race to complete negotiations on EU membership.

Prague is having to confront the tough realities of what can be afforded in cleaning up the problem banks before privatization and what price can be expected from interested investors.

The state-owned banks offer interesting acquisition targets for Western banks seeking to expand in the region because they often control significant market shares, but at the same time investors are wary of taking on risky loan portfolios heavily burdened by bad debts.

Erste Bank, Austria's second largest bank, has recently bid to acquire a 52% stake in Ceska Sporitelna, the largest Czech savings bank. The Austrian group is seeking to become the leading regional retail bank in central Europe, and it regards the takeover of the troubled Czech bank as the keystone for pursuing this strategy.

Andreas Treichl, Erste Bank chief executive, said the bank's offer was based on the group gaining substantial protection against the Czech bank's existing portfolio of non-performing loans, however. It was not prepared to bid 'if we must worry about the credit risk in the loan portfolio. We can only do this if we limit ourselves to the management and operational risk'.

The gains for the successful bidder could also be substantial, however, and it is the prospects for strong growth that have fuelled Western banks' interest both in privatizations and acquisitions in the region as well as in start-up operations.

Big privatization deals completed this year include Poland's sale of a controlling stake in Pekao Bank, the biggest privatised bank, to UniCredito of Italy for $1.1 billion and the Czech Republic's sale of a dominant stake in CSOB, the fourth-biggest bank, also for $1.1 billion, to KBC of Belgium.

Foreign banks' share of the banking market in central and eastern Europe jumped last year from 20% to 32% and is set to rise further according to Bank Austria. It estimates that while the region's total banking assets grew last year by 11 per cent to Sch3,155 billion, foreign banks' assets leapt 82% to Sch1,020 billion.

It says that the region's banks have plenty of scope for rapid growth given the low level of penetration of banking into the economy. Total bank assets in the region reach only 66% of gross domestic product, compared with 266% in Austria and 173% in Germany.

Source: Financial Times, 10 November 1999

Trade re-orientation and entry into the international economic community

Central and Eastern European governments have also turned their attention to integrating themselves more fully into the global financial and commercial systems. Aside from the construction of new relations with the European Union (EU) and with other European institutions, this has encompassed membership of the World Trade Organization (WTO) and significant efforts to gain access to international capital from such institutions as the EBRD, the World Bank and the International Monetary Fund. Another feature of transition in Central and Eastern Europe has been the establishment of new trading links with Western nations and the re-orientation of foreign trade. The collapse of institutional trading relationships between the former members of the CMEA (a primary cause of the collapse of industrial output in CEECs following 1989–90) has necessitated a substantial re-orientation of trade towards Western Europe and the re-integration of the CEECs into the international trading order. This in turn has contributed to the pressures for trade liberalization and to significant changes to the commodity structure of exports with major changes required to the nature and type of products being sold.

Prior to 1988 EC trade flows with Central and Eastern Europe were relatively insignificant. Although bilateral trading links between individual countries did exist, there was neither mutual recognition nor contractual relations between the European Community and the Council for Mutual Economic Assistance. Individual EU members were not supposed to enter into agreements without prior consultation with the European Commission and state traders such as the Soviet Union, East Germany and Czechoslovakia, enjoyed no group trading preferences with the European Community. Of the major CMEA economies, only Romania received special trading concessions because it was categorized as a developing country. Eastern bloc exports to the EC markets were also frustrated by quality problems. The quality and design of many products made in Central and Eastern Europe were so inferior that these products were virtually unsaleable on Western markets. Other serious obstacles included the inconvertibility of Eastern bloc currencies, the state monopoly of foreign trade, red-tape and political–bureaucratic interference (see Lavigne, 1995, p. 84).

Geographic restructuring and the 'new' commercial relations

In Central Europe, there was a significant switch in trade patterns towards the EU and EFTA markets during the early stages of transition. Indeed, between 1989 and 1993, regional exports to Western Europe increased by an annual average of 12% (Faini and Portes, 1995). Earnings arising from these exports helped to generate hard currency inflows at a difficult time in the reform process, providing means for the importation of Western energy and technology and for the servicing of sovereign debts. This geographical restructuring of trade has continued in subsequent years despite the revitalization of intra-regional trade by the formation of CEFTA.

Table 7.6 CEC trade by key partners (in billion ECU)

| | Imports | | | Exports | | |
Partners	1993	1997	% share 1997	1993	1997	% share 1997
World	61.50	122.72	100.0	50.86	93.98	100.00
EU	32.19	71.81	58.5	26.52	55.52	59.1
Germany	13.28	28.54	23.3	12.53	27.11	28.8
Italy	4.24	10.46	8.5	3.17	6.66	7.1
NIS	11.43	14.18	11.6	6.38	10.09	10.7
Russia	8.73	11.70	9.5	3.88	6.00	6.4
CECs (intra)	7.14	12.57	10.2	8.10	13.16	14.0
USA	2.34	4.71	3.8	1.29	2.26	2.4
Switzerland	1.23	1.89	1.5	0.63	0.83	0.9

Source: Eurostat, 1999

Indeed, while 14.0% of CEC exports go to other countries in the region, 59.1% of all CEC exports are now destined for the EU market (see Table 7.6). For those countries dominating this trade – Hungary, Poland and the Czech Republic – the EU is an even more significant trading partner accounting for nearly 70% of total export trade. Trade flows are dominated on the EU side by Germany and Italy, which together represent almost 70% of EU trade with the group.

Contributing to the strengthening of trade links post-1989 (and to this broad re-orientation of foreign trade) has been the progress of the Central European countries up the EU's hierarchy of trading preferences (see Chapter 12). Following the conclusion of 'first-generation' trade and co-operation agreements between 1988 and 1990, access to EU markets has been regulated by the trade provisions of multi-issue association agreements with the EU. For Poland, Hungary, Slovakia and the Czech Republic, the commercial provisions of these agreements – known as Europe Agreements (EAs) – have been in place since March 1992. As at the Copenghagen Summit in June 1993, these agreements have been occasionally revised so as to improve terms of trade and in order to address Central European concerns over trade impediments and liberalization timetables. The basis of EAs, now also covering Romania, Bulgaria, Latvia, Lithuania, Estonia and Slovenia, is the principle of reciprocal free trade in non-agricultural products by the year 2004. Based around the principle of asymmetric liberalization, these agreements also involve the guarantee of free EU market access for industrial exports by 1999. In this regard, while the EU has stuck to its basic commitment, the member states have made full use of special conditions applying to steel, coal, textiles, chemicals and other sensitive sectors so as to restrain import flows to 'acceptable levels' prior to this date. These conditions, as established in a series of special annexes and protocols to each of the Europe Agreements, have ensured tariff and/or quota restrictions in some of these sectors as late as 1998. Although these restrictions have now been lifted, they have previously stymied exports in exactly those sectors where the transition economies have enjoyed a comparative advantage (see Dyker, 1993; Faini and Portes, 1995). The fear is now that the EU may compensate for their absence by subjecting its associates to anti-dumping actions and other contingent forms of protectionism. Since 1992, Brussels has taken a number of such actions against its associates, shielding sensitive industries from competition and creating negative spillover effects for other CEC exporters. Imports of ammonium nitrate from Lithuania and Bulgaria, of haematite pig iron from Poland and of steel tube fittings from Slovakia have all, for example, been the focus of controversial definitive anti-dumping duties.

Despite this, and short of final EU membership, the asymmetric liberalization of the Europe Agreements establishes that the EU's trade concessions to Central Europe are now largely in place. In fact, the terms of the EAs now commit the candidate countries themselves to demanding liberalization timetables and to opening up their own markets to EU goods and services by 2004. This will establish new competitive pressures for indigenous firms in Central Europe and create further export and investment opportunities for Western businesses. Already, the balance of trade has tilted decidedly in the EU's favour with heavy demand for Western products in transition markets. Reference to Figure 7.1 highlights a trade deficit with the EU (in 1997) of some €21.61 billion with the EU enjoying a significant surplus in machinery and transport equipment, road vehicles, electrical machines and appliances. The main EU trade deficits with the region are apparent in products that are not very capital intensive including clothing and textiles where EU imports marginally outstrip exports to candidate countries. Indeed, the use of trade data to reveal comparative advantage suggests that the Central European Candidate Countries are relatively efficient in the production of natural-resource-based and labour-intensive products (see Brenton and Gros, 1997). The relative efficiency of a number of other sectors is forecast to improve in the years ahead. These include paper, chemicals, metal products and mechanical engineering.

The Balkan economies and European NIS have also experienced a strong re-orientation of trade towards Western markets. However, discounting its more favourable treatment of candidate countries Bulgaria and Romania, the EU has stopped short of establishing preferential trading terms with these countries and has yet to advance the idea of association. This has meant that East European states have been relatively disadvantaged in commercial terms (at least compared with the Central European countries) and have had less success in overcoming many of the trade barriers encountered when attempting to enter EU markets. Agreements range from basic trade and economic co-operation agreements (as existing with Albania) to so-called Partnership and Co-operation Agreements (PCAs) as concluded with the European NIS (Russia, the Ukraine, Belarus and Moldova). Although more will be said later about the broader content of these agreements, the trade provisions of PCAs merit present commentary. As introduced by interim agreements in the first half of 1996, these cover trade in goods, payments, competition, standards co-operation, conformity assessment and customs. Although the

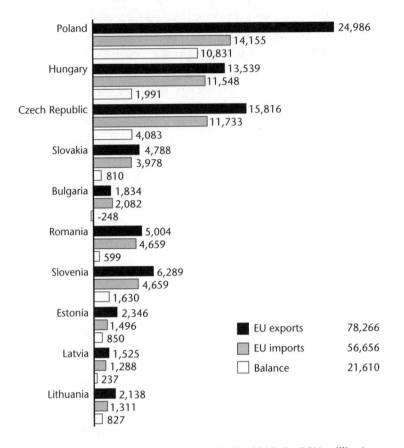

Figure 7.1 EU trade with the candidate countries in 1997 (in ECU million)
Source: European Commission, 1998

PCAs raise the possibility of an FTA between a signatory country and the EU (through future negotiation), they do not establish a timetable for full liberalization or commit the EU to that result. Instead, agreements consist of the limited extension of tariff concessions (most favoured nation treatment on goods), the elimination of several quantitative restrictions (these were in place on over 300 commodities exported by Russia as of October 1995), and an improvement in export opportunities in areas such as textiles and steel still to be regulated by quota. The agreements also reduce substantially the scope of certain EU commercial instruments such as anti-dumping procedures and safeguard actions, though these means of contingent protection are provided for (e.g. Articles 17 and 18 of the EU–Russia PCA). Anti-dumping rules now apply in accordance with GATT provisions and a consultation clause is granted. It is also to be noted that the PCAs extend MFN terms for the cross border supply of a limited range of services (an innovation here) and provide conditions for freedom of establishment of companies and of capital movements, although Russia can still apply restrictions on capital outflows.

While these terms have granted NIS products better treatment and access to the European market, they clearly fall well short of those agreements concluded with the Central European countries and are essentially 'non-preferential'. Indeed, with respect to trade and commercial relations, the PCAs do little more than confirm that the European NIS will be treated by the EU as if they were members of the WTO (a possible future objective for these states). Significant trade concessions depend on further negotiation and the number of sensitive sectors identified by the EU (and therefore subject to significant import restrictions). Inclusions such as nuclear products and space launches suggest the EU's continuing ability to control Russian imports in strategic areas. Nonetheless, these agreements are an important part of the process of commercial re-orientation in the former Soviet states and in encouraging increased trade flows between these countries and EU markets. Figures for the full set of newly independent states (but dominated by Russia and Ukraine) show that the European Union is now the NIS' most important Western trading partner, taking more than €26 billion worth of imports from the NIS in 1996 (or more than 33% of the NIS' total exports). Trade between the European Union, Russia and the other NIS has been growing strongly since 1989 and the NIS as a group are now running a big trade surplus with the European Union. The major part of Russian–NIS exports to the EU is fuel, energy and raw materials. Exports of timber, chemicals and metals are on the rise and Russia (in the face of continuing restrictions) is beginning to actively seek new export possibilities in relation to military aerospace production and nuclear materials.

Transition: progress and challenges

The preceding analysis has highlighted a number of key points. First, while there has been no universal agreement as to the best strategy for transition towards market capitalism in the CEE region, a number of essential elements can be recognized as being central to the transition process. These include market deregulation, price liberalization, privatization and enterprise restructuring, banking and financial sector reforms, macroeconomic stabilization, and progressive integration into international financial and commercial sytems. Second, while a number of CEECs have opted for rapid transformation (or for 'shock therapy'), most have taken a slower path to reform. By and large, those economies that have adopted more rapid programmes of change have seen an improvement in their economic fortunes and have succeeded in attracting the larger slice of international capital investment (a point to be given more serious examination in the later stages of this chapter). In fact, it is now possible to distinguish between those economies well down the road to successful market economies (e.g. Poland, Hungary, the Czech Republic, Slovenia and Estonia) and those whose reform efforts have progressed at a slower pace. Among this second set we find a varied mix of regional economies oscillating between progressive and revanchist measures. Here, divisions are now evident between the likes of Bulgaria (see Case Study 7.3), intensifying reform efforts after years of crisis, and economies such as that of the Ukraine marked by a continued paralysis in economic decision-making. Third, throughout the CEECs there are outstanding tasks. As seen

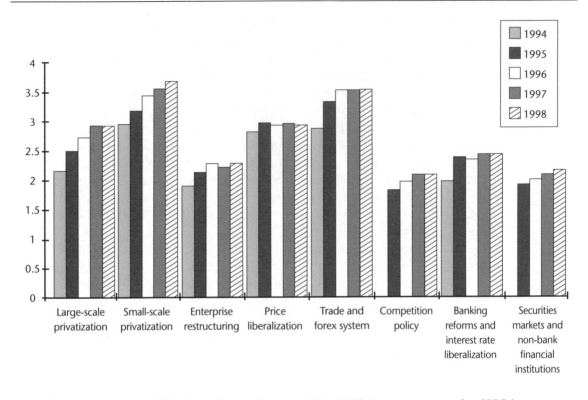

Figure 7.2 Movements in EBRD Transition Indicators, 1994–1998 (average across the CEECs)
Source: EBRD *Transition Report* 1998

in Figure 7.2, the EBRD's transition indicators (averaged out across countries) high-light restructuring requirements in eight major categories. With a score of 1 repre-senting little change from old regimes, it is clear that much progress is to be made in areas such as enterprise restructuring and banking reform before scores are reached that signal Western standards (e.g. scores of 4 or 4+). Of course such ratings mask the variations in national performance, but even in the better-performing states, much remains to be done *vis-à-vis* financial sector reforms, corporate gover-nance issues and deep-level enterprise restructuring. In addition, efforts still have to be made in all societies to create a secure basis for long-term competitiveness and to reduce state aids. These challenges sit alongside those tied to the control of inflation and government spending, and to the tackling of unemployment and environmen-tal despoilment. It is to these two subjects (i) unemployment and labour market conditions; and (ii) environmental conditions and improvements, that analysis now turns.

Unemployment and CEEC labour markets

Under the centrally planned system, the right to work was guaranteed and every worker had some rights to choose his/her job. The latter part of this was subject to

CASE STUDY 7.3 Bulgaria – progress at last?

For the past two years, Bulgaria has provided the economic success story the International Monetary Fund has so lacked in other parts of the world, as emerging markets have lurched from one crisis to another.

When government ministers are asked about their commitment to the reform process, the reply is invariably that the targets have to be met because they are stated in the agreement with the IMF, the programme is open and transparent, and it is publicly available on the government Internet site, in both Bulgarian and English.

Certainly, the economic policies of the past two years have represented a clear break from Bulgaria's recent chaotic past, which was marked by severe banking and foreign exchange crises, financial indiscipline, mounting budget deficits, towering losses in state-owned enterprises, stalled privatization and, finally, hyperinflation.

The progress has been remarkable. Helped crucially by the introduction of a currency board in the summer of 1997 (which fixed the exchange rate of the Bulgarian lev to the D-Mark at 1,000 leva to 1DM and provides full foreign currency backing for domestic money in circulation), the centre–right government, led by Prime Minister Ivan Kostov, has brought much-needed stability to the Bulgarian economy. (From 1 July in a further reform, the lev will be redenominated to one new lev for 1,000 old leva).

Inflation as shown in the consumer price index had dropped to only 1% in December year-on-year from 578.5% a year earlier.

'The currency board system has brought stability to economic decision-making', says Martin Zaimov, deputy governor of the Bulgarian National Bank. 'We can forecast far more. During the worst times you could plan for a couple of weeks only. Now people can plan years ahead.'

Foreign exchange reserves have been rebuilt with international support from a low of $400 million in January 1997 to more than $2.5 billion. The private sector now accounts for about 67 per cent of gross domestic product (GDP), up from 42% two years ago.

Backed by the restrictive terms of the IMF agreement the government budget achieved a surplus equivalent to 0.9% of GDP last year. The target is to achieve a broadly balanced budget in the medium term. The government is forecasting a budget deficit of 2.8% of GDP for 1999 taking account of various steps to cushion the blow of the tough structural reform measures that should be implemented this year.

Unemployment fell to about 11% by the end of last year from 14% a year earlier.

After the ravages of recent years, the economy began to show some modest growth last year. The progress is real but still fragile. The finance ministry currently estimates that GDP grew by 4.5% last year, albeit from a shrunken base. Gross domestic product declined by 6.9% in 1997 and by 10.1% in 1996 in the final year of the previous socialist government.

According to figures from the European Bank for Reconstruction and Development, GDP in Bulgaria last year was still only 66% of the 1989 level, ten years after the start of the transition from a command to a market economy.

Despite the stabilization successes of the past two years, the daunting challenge still facing the government is to put Bulgaria on a path of sustainable growth at a time when the economy still faces tight external limitations.

Under the three-year, $864 million IMF programme agreed last September, the government is targeting growth of 4–5% a year, but Dimitar Radev, deputy minister of finance, accepts that that is unlikely to be achieved in 1999. Against the background of the slowdown in the world economy, the finance ministry is currently forcasting growth of 3.7%.

The economy slowed sharply in the second half of last year. Industrial sales fell by 9.4% in 1998 owing to the fall in world prices for key exports, such as metals and chemicals. Exports fell by 12% in value last year.

Activity is seriously constrained by the lack of capital. The banks, burned by their experiences in the recent years, remain very cautious lenders. They hold much of their assets as low-yielding deposits in German banks and in government securities, and new lending has been negligible.

Privatization revenues should help to finance

the current account deficit during the next two years, with the government seeking strategic foreign investors for assets such as the telecoms utility, the leading state-owned banks, Bulgartabak (the tobacco industry), the Neftochim oil refinery and Petrol (the state-owned service stations).

Green-field site foreign investment will be urgently needed as the receipts from privatization diminish, however, and it is crucial that the government makes progress on infrastructure projects in areas such as power generation and distribution, and municipal services, where foreign capital is also supposed to play a big role.

A key test of foreign investors' appetite for Bulgarian risk should come later this year with both the Republic of Bulgaria and the capital city of Sofia planning to make their debut on the international bond market. Acceptance of the bonds by international investors would provide a crucial vote of confidence in the current government's economic policies.

Stuart Eizenstat, US assistant secretary of state, warned on a recent visit to Sofia that the government still had to take many 'courageous and painful economic decisions'. Privatization had been slow, bureaucratic and had lacked transparency. Efforts to reform the state apparatus and to root out corruption and red tape had to be intensified.

'Sustained, energetic reform' was critical, he said, but if it took place, 'in a few years we may be describing Bulgaria as the Balkan Tiger'.

Source: Financial Times, 8 March 1999

considerable control, however, because of particular shortage areas and a degree of regional planning. Nevertheless, this policy resulted in 'full employment' and a well-trained workforce in the East, with 85% of all workers in former East Germany, Poland and Hungary having completed some form of vocational training. That is not to suggest that central planning cured unemployment. A characteristic of that system was massive underemployment; in other words, most people had jobs but many were not employed fully or efficiently in them. Equally, while there is little doubt that the level of technical competence was high among many workers, large numbers were demotivated or passive and did not consider that extra effort was required to carry out tasks speedily or to the highest standards. There were also very few differentials in wage levels between jobs and no meritocracy in terms of promotion and career advancement. Among other things this meant that many capable individuals were held back at a lower level in company structures and that managers and directors were often in place owing to their party loyalty rather than to their ability to do the job.

Unemployment has become an inevitable consequence as markets are liberalized and as workforces are rationalized and plants closed. The average Labour Force Survey (LFS) unemployment rate for the whole region – excluding Albania, Macedonia and Yugoslavia – already averages 12.7% (1998) and, with further structural reforms ahead, regional unemployment levels might climb to between 20% and 25% of the workforce. In the long term, lower unemployment levels are expected in the 'fast-track' countries but, in many cases, unemployment levels are rising rather than falling (see Table 7.7).

It was foreign nationals in the East who were the first to be hit by the wave of dismissals and redundancies in the early 1990s. Linked to this was a growing wave of xenophobia and nationalism. The most prevalent nationalities working in East

Table 7.7 Unemployment rates in the CEECs, 1990–98

Unemployment (%)	1990	1991	1992	1993	1994	1995	1996	1997	1998
Bulgaria	1.7	11.1	15.3	16.4	12.8	11.1	12.5	13.7	12.2
Croatia	11.4	13.2	13.2	14.8	14.8	15.1	15.9	17.6	18.6
Czech Republic	0.8	4.1	2.6	3.5	3.2	2.9	3.5	5.2	7.5
Estonia	na	na	na	6.5	7.6	9.7	10.0	10.5	na
Hungary	1.9	7.4	12.3	12.1	10.4	10.4	11.4	11.0	9.6
Latvia	na	na	2.3	5.8	6.5	6.6	7.2	7.0	9.2
Lithuania	na	0.3	1.3	4.4	3.8	6.1	7.1	5.9	6.4
Poland	6.3	11.8	13.6	16.4	16.0	14.9	13.2	10.3	10.4
Romania	0.4	3.0	8.2	10.4	10.9	9.5	6.6	8.9	10.3
Russia	na	0.0	4.8	5.3	7.1	8.3	9.9	11.2	12.4
Slovakia	0.8	0.0	4.8	12.2	14.8	13.1	12.8	12.5	15.6
Slovenia	4.7	8.2	11.5	14.4	14.2	14.5	14.4	14.8	14.6

Source: Business Central Europe Magazine Statistical Database (01.01.2000)

European countries had been Vietnamese, Cubans and Angolans. In countries such as former East Germany it was common to find Poles and, in Hungary, Bulgarians had often found jobs. In other words, there was a migration from the poorer East European countries to the more wealthy. These people too have often been sent back to their countries of origin. Subsequently it was women who were made redundant. In countries such as former East Germany 75% of women's jobs were traditionally reserved for them. On reform, such rights to work were lost and female participation rates fell dramatically. Increasingly, as financial constraints have been tightened on enterprises and as businesses have been liquidated, large numbers of male jobs in both industry and agriculture have also been lost and totals for long-term male and youth unemployment have escalated. The decline in male industrial employment especially reflects the scale of industrial restructuring in the region and the high over-employment before transition. Eurostat estimates that, between 1990 and 1997, employment in industrial sectors fell by more than 6 million people or by almost a third. Employment fall-out in industrial sectors is further expected as slow-track reformers advance processes of privatization and industrial restructuring.

Structurally, the private sector share of employment in the CEECs has been expanding rapidly. From a level of less than 10% of total employment in 1990, the private sector's share reached almost 70% in Poland, Latvia and Lithuania in 1998. Throughout the region, private sector shares of employment are now in excess of 50%. Equally, while agriculture continues to account for a substantial portion of total employment in all countries except the Czech Republic, the transition years have been characterized by the growth of service sector employment. Services now account for the largest share (and for growing shares) of total employment in most Central European countries.

Average wages continue to lag well behind Western levels but, in most countries, are showing a steady increase (see Table 7.8). While increased wage levels are helping to improve the welfare of many workers and their families, one point of concern here (and one factor militating against larger declines in regional inflation) is the evidence that the growth of real wages is continuing to outstrip increases in labour productivity. The consequent increases in unit labour costs are a potential threat to CEEC competitiveness, especially in those labour-intensive industries currently dominating exports.

Table 7.8 Average monthly wage ($) in the CEECs, 1990–98

Average monthly wage ($)	1990	1991	1992	1993	1994	1995	1996	1997	1998
Bulgaria	157.5	55.0	87.7	116.9	91.5	113.1	79.4	76.3	106.5
Croatia	435.1	402.3	111.0	147.1	359.2	552.0	597.2	595.5	649.5
Czech Republic	182.6	128.5	164.3	199.6	239.5	307.8	356.4	337.3	362.1
Estonia	na	na	na	na	130.7	186.2	234.3	256.9	293.1
Hungary	212.8	239.8	282.2	295.2	316.8	309.5	307.0	306.7	316.0
Latvia	na	na	na	na	119.0	161.0	183.5	211.8	225.9
Lithuania	na	na	na	na	91.0	163.3	193.5	202.3	288.1
Poland	na	na	213.0	215.7	231.3	285.5	323.8	324.9	355.2
Romania	138.6	97.6	82.6	103.1	109.8	138.3	138.4	121.8	153.0
Russia	18.9	26.2	23.8	62.1	107.3	115.5	157.2	181.9	114.2
Slovakia	178.7	127.7	160.6	175.3	196.4	241.9	266.0	274.4	283.9
Slovenia	900.2	609.9	627.9	666.1	734.6	945.0	953.9	901.2	943.7

Source: Business Central Europe Magazine Statistical Database (01.01.2000)

The environment

Around the period of the first edition of this work, it was characteristic of many discussions surrounding Central and Eastern Europe to pay particular attention to environmental issues. This was not only because of the general increase in environmental awareness in these countries but because of growing evidence of the horrendous environmental legacy of Communism, including widespread air, water and soil pollution. Throughout the 1990s these concerns have been underscored by the exposure of ecologically destructive practices in CEEC industry, by the evidence of heavily polluted hotspots (see below) and by high levels of imported pollution. In particular, Europe's Scandinavian and Alpine states, have complained bitterly about substantial levels of imported pollution from east of their borders. Indeed, while Western agencies have expressed concern about the environmental threat to human health and to the natural environment in the old Eastern bloc, much of the concern has rested with the ramifications of their situation for Western nations (and their environments). In this regard, substantial air pollution in the 'Black Triangle' has been a particular worry. The Triangle itself, which stretches from Lower Silesia (Poland) to Southern Saxony (Germany) and Northern Bohemia (the Czech Republic), is marked by the highest concentration of air pollution in the whole of Europe. High annual emissions and concentrations of air pollution (primarily by sulphur dioxide) are directly linked to the domination of brown coal mining, heavy and chemical industry in the regional economies. Despite recent reductions, the depositions of sulphur and other acidifying substances are at their European maximum over this blighted area (European Environment Agency, 1999, p. 143).

Returning to the broader picture, the main causes of the environmental situation in the CEECs are these:

1. many years of maintaining an energy and structural policy characterized by large-scale use of brown coal;

2. heavy industry involving intensive use of energy and raw materials, high energy consumption and outdated production processes;

3. high levels of untreated effluent from key industries, the discharge of organic waste products from agriculture and the uncontrolled disposal of domestic waste;

4. long-term neglect of environmental management and low funding for environmental protection measures;

5. the underdevelopment and underproduction of environmental protection technology.

On a human level, in the worst affected of countries such as former East Germany, Poland and the Czech Republic, emissions of sulphur dioxide affect over 30% of the population directly and the number of respiratory diseases among children has more than doubled in the last fifteen years. The number of children suffering from endogenous eczemas has also risen sharply to about 30%. Such high levels are also taking a toll on the natural environment with many forests severely damaged. According to Hlobil and Holub (1997), only 26% of the Bohemian Forest, 45% of the Saxonian Forest and 22% of the Silesian Forest remains undamaged (cited in European Environment Agency, 1999, p. 143). The situation with water sewage treatment is also grave. While water management standards have improved significantly over the last five years, only a minority of CEE populations enjoy proper sewage treatment facilities (see Table 7.9). Even in the Czech Republic, where 59% of the population enjoy such facilities, the state of water quality 'remains serious' with high levels of toxic substances in aquatic ecosystems (OECD, 1999).

Table 7.9 Environmental indicators for Poland, Hungary and the Czech Republic

	Sulphur dioxides kg per capita	Public waste water treatment plants % of population connected
Czech Republic	68	59
Hungary	67	32
Poland	61	47
EU–15	27	73

Source: OECD Environmental Data Compendium, 1999 edition © OECD, 1999

The current situation

Developments in recent years have been positive as a consequence both of improvements in environmental legislation and of the restructuring of industry and industrial practice. There is some evidence to suggest that harmful factory emissions have dropped throughout the region and that wide-ranging clean-up programmes have begun to have a positive effect. According to the European Environment Agency, between 1989 and 1996, the air emissions from the largest Black Triangle sources, were 'reduced significantly'. Sulphur dioxide emissions were reduced by 50% in Poland and the Czech Republic, and by 30% in the eastern part of Germany. Nitrogen oxide emissions also dropped by an average of 50% (European Environment Agency, 1999, p. 143). These falls can be largely attributed to a shift away from use of brown coal (and towards gas and other fuel types) and to retrofitting of many large power plants with desulphurization equipment. Despite this, the problems and challenges extending from the environmental situation in the CEECs are still enormous. Factory emission levels in Central Europe alone are still two-and-a-half times higher than in the West and, in the Czech Republic, sulphur dioxide emissions (per capita) remain the highest in OECD–Europe (OECD, 1999). Furthermore, all countries continue to fall well short of EU standards on urban waste water, drinking water, waste disposal and the release of dangerous substances into rivers and oceans. In this context, it is clear that environmental standards need to be further defined and that the application and public enforcement of environmental legislation need to be strengthened. At industry level, substantial investments need to be made in new environmentally acceptable technologies and multiple problems in relation to energy production and usage need to be confronted. There is still a huge waste of energy in CEE industry (even among viable firms) and the promotion of fuel efficiency and renewable energy sources is difficult as traditional energy costs remain low. Indeed, hundreds of conventional power plants need to be weaned off coal (and on to cleaner-fuel alternatives) and nuclear power stations need to be brought up to international safety standards or even decommissioned.

In the long run, the implementation of environmental reforms will result in modern and more efficient industries, cleaner energy production, and improved and cost-effective urban environmental infrastructure services. However, and in spite of clear economic benefits from these investments, quick implementation will be difficult owing to scarce financial and other resources. In its Agenda 2000 report, the Commission concluded that to achieve full compliance with the environmental *acquis* (the full body of EU environment law), total investment costs for Central Europe were likely to be around €100–120 billion. The bulk of the investments will be needed for air pollution abatement, water and waste water management, and for control and disposal of municipal and hazardous waste (http://www.ends.co.uk). Total clean-up costs for Central and Eastern Europe (including the former Soviet Union) have been estimated at around €300 billion. As the financial assistance from the EU and other international agencies will only cover a minor part of all the resources required, effective prioritized management of the process is crucial.

Success will be dependent upon careful strategic planning and cost-effective programmes in the candidate countries. Fundamentally, the massive costs involved will only be met by economic growth in the CEECs and by steady investment both by national governments and by private sector investors. However, in the short term at least, improving the environment and implementing EU standards will mean closing the worst-polluting coalmines, power plants and factories, retrofitting viable facilities left in the state sector, and forcing private sector firms to invest in more expensive environmentally friendly capital equipment. This means difficult decisions at different levels of government and an additional burden on firms at a time when many are struggling to compete or even to survive. In the absence of such restrictions, or given weak enforcement, when a decision has to be made as whether to prioritize environmental spending or other forms of expenditure, the decision may be all too predictable. While this dilemma is not unique to firms operating in the transition economies (see Chapter 11) it is arguably more acute for those operating in the difficult financial conditions of transition environments.

Having to live in poor environmental surroundings is also a major disincentive to Western businesses wishing to move into Central and Eastern Europe. At the very least, companies are dissuaded from locating assets and personnel in polluted areas and countries competing for investors will be 'judged partly on the clarity of their laws on liability for past pollution and on how soil and ground water contamination is measured today' (Simpson *et al.*, 1996, p. 37). The need to improve environmental conditions on grounds of health and efficiency thus fuses with the role of environmental action in attracting inward investment and in satisfying some of the essential requirements for future EU membership. It is to this issue that we now turn.

CEE development and integration with the European Union

As is clear from the preceding analysis, much of the transformation in CEE environments is marked by attempts to adopt or to emulate West European practices and principles. If the issues are examined in greater detail, it becomes clear that there are wide-ranging efforts directed at aligning domestic legislation with EU legislation in a variety of fields. While the environment is an important area, harmonization with EU laws and standards is also being pursued in such areas as competition law, financial services regulation and consumer protection. These efforts reflect the determination of many CEE governments to enter their countries into the EU and the EU's requirements for entry. A number of CEECs have made applications to join the EU – Hungary and Poland (in 1994), Romania, Slovakia, Latvia, Estonia and Bulgaria (in 1995), and the Czech Republic and Slovenia (in 1996). In March 1998, the EU opened formal entry talks with the Czech Republic, Estonia, Hungary, Poland and Slovenia (along with another candidate country, Cyprus). For nearly two years, this placed the remaining candidates into a second stream characterized by the absence of formal entry negotiations and a more distant promise of future EU membership. At the Helsinki Summit in December 1999, the EU member states finally agreed to open formal negotiations with these remaining countries – Bulgaria, Latvia, Lithuania, Romania and Slovakia – also adding Malta and Turkey to their list. Thus ten CEECs (among a total of thirteen candidate countries) are now engaged in EU entry talks and are continuing to make far-reaching economic, political, social and legal adjustments with the target of future EU membership. The existing member states have remained vague about when the negotiations with the most advanced countries might conclude but the European Commission has signalled that accession is unlikely before 2004 given both the expected length of future negotiations (covering 80,000 pages of EU legislation) and the timetables attaching to ratification procedures. Moreover, the EU has indicated that it will only open new 'chapters' or tracks of negotiations with an individual candidate (there are thirty-one in total) where it is convinced that progress can be made. Few involved in the process expect a first wave of entries before this date and it is clear that the finishing line, optimistically set at 2000 by former German Chancellor Helmut Kohl, keeps moving backwards.

While the prospect of future EU membership for Central and Eastern European countries was raised by the very fall of Communism, it has only been since the Copenhagen Summit of 1993 that the EU has been formally committed to eastward enlargement. At this summit, the EU took the important step of confirming that present and future signatories to agreements of association ('Europe Agreements') were eligible for EU membership. The EU also established an 'entry test' at Copenhagen, since referred to as the Copenhagen Criteria. These include the essential requirements of a stable democracy and a fully functioning market economy. Aspirant members must also demonstrate a good record on human rights (including the protection of minorities and respect for the rule of law), the capacity to cope with competitive pressure and market forces within the Union, and the ability to take on the obligations of membership (the *acquis communautaire*). In each of these areas the applicant countries are subject to progress reports issued by the European Commission. When progress reports were presented in October 1999, these showed that all the candidates still face a heavy workload in preparing for accession. However, differences between the applicant states as regards compliance with the eligibility criteria are such that it is possible to identify those moving at greatest speed towards the full satisfaction of EU entry requirements. Hungary and Poland appear to have made greatest progress to date and are thus likely to be among the first wave of CEE entrants. Slovenia has also made progress since 1997 but must speed up its privatization efforts and further facilitate the restructuring of enterprises. All three of these front-line applicants attract some criticism for the state of their administrative, political and judicial systems. Areas such as state aid, environmental law and farm reform are also subject to some criticism.

The EU's pre-accession strategy

Discussion of the debate surrounding EU enlargement raises the various strands of

EU assistance for Central and Eastern Europe already established. The EU has operated a coherent pre-accession strategy since 1994, which now integrates:

1. formal association (or 'Europe') agreements,

2. bilateral accession partnerships, and

3. a multidimensional programme of financial aid and technical assistance.

The association agreements ('Europe Agreements')

In October 1991, Jacques Delors called on the EU to prepare for an EU of twenty-four, or even thirty, members. His answer to the collapse of the economic system in Eastern Europe and the growing demand from EFTA countries for EU membership was to devise a system of so-called concentric circles. This would see the present EU membership at the centre, the EFTA countries in a second ring, and Central and Eastern Europe in an outer ring. Circles were to be linked by their own internal agreements and would be built around the EU through the device of external agreements. These ranged from agreement on the EEA between the EU and the EFTA countries (see Chapter 3) to a bundle of fairly uniform association agreements with applicant countries from Central and Eastern Europe.

Association agreements were initially negotiated between the EU and Poland, the former Czechoslovakia and Hungary in 1991. These agreements built on bilateral trade and economic co-operation agreements struck in the later 1980s. Succeeding agreements were later extended to Bulgaria and Romania (in 1993) and to Estonia, Latvia, Lithuania and Slovenia (in 1995). Replacement agreements for the Czech Republic and Slovakia were also concluded in 1993 following the partition of Czechoslovakia. In all cases, these agreements conferred the status of 'associate members' on the CEE signatories, set national paths for progressive legislative convergence with the EU, and provided for far-reaching economic, political and financial co-operation. The EU's decision at Copenhagen (June 1993) to confirm the status of CEE associates as future EU members brought an even higher status to these agreements and corrected what was for some, a glaring omission in the original deals. Looking at the content of these agreements, apart from providing for free trade in industrial goods and for the preferential treatment for exports of agricultural products (see previously), the EAs also committed the new associates to introducing similar legislation to that of the Union in the areas of competition rules, state aids, and intellectual, commercial and industrial property. The agreements also provided for national treatment for establishment and operation of enterprises and for improved rights of movement for workers, although not for free mobility between EU and CEE states. In the political sphere, a key feature of the association agreements was the formalization of bilateral political dialogues between the EU institutions and the applicant governments. These dialogues have been conducted primarily through so-called Association Councils and have involved regular and systematic meetings at ministerial levels on most areas of Union policy. The EAs also raised the possibility of the early participation of associate countries in various Community programmes on cultural, technological and environmental questions.

The accession partnerships (APs)

Bilateral accession partnerships have been in place since early 1998 and are central to what the European Commission now calls its enhanced pre-accession strategy. These partnerships (established with all ten applicant countries) are aimed at guiding the applicants towards European Union membership by supporting their preparations for membership. This builds on the EU's launch of the Agenda 2000 programme in 1997 which established a profile of all the internal and external measures needed to achieve eastward enlargement. Under the APs, support is provided for the applicants' membership efforts by setting out both the priority areas for further work and the financial assistance from the EU available to help tackle these problems. Thus, unlike the earlier Europe Agreements, APs focus specifically on preparing the applicant CEECs to meet specific membership criteria set by the Copenhagen European Council.

EU assistance to Central and Eastern Europe

Since the reforms in the Eastern bloc took place, the EU and its member states have increased the amount of aid going to Central and Eastern Europe. In particular, specific EU programmes such as PHARE and TACIS (which provides grant finance for the NIS) have been established to help with the transition process and to channel large amounts of capital into specific development projects throughout the region. Public money from the EU member states along with that from other OECD group economies has also been channelled into Central and Eastern Europe through the European Bank for Reconstruction and Development. The EBRD is not actually part of the EU but is jointly owned by fifty-eight governments, the European Union and European Investment Bank. It is based in a member capital (London) and derives a majority of its capital from the EU and EIB. From 1991 to 1997, the EBRD had made available nearly €14 billion worth of financing. The bulk of approved EBRD projects have been in the Czech Republic, Hungary, Poland and Russia. In capital terms, the largest recipient of EBRD loans and investment since the launch of the bank in 1991 has been Russia. Financial institutions account for the largest slice of the EBRD's disbursements (over 35%) but emphasis has fallen increasingly on transport and energy projects and on manufacturing and environmental clean-up operations (see Box 7.1).

The EU's dedicated aid programme for the CEECs, PHARE, was set up in 1989. For ten years, it has functioned as the world's largest grant assistance effort for Central and Eastern Europe, committing some €11.1 billion to programmes promoting private sector development, transport and telecommunications infrastructures, nuclear safety and environmental improvements. Between 1999 and 2006, the EU's pre-accession aid package (worth €24 billion) will be administered under a re-

BOX 7.1

The EBRD

Since its creation in 1991, the EBRD has provided direct financing for private sector activities, restructuring and privatization in transition economies and has provided funding for the infrastructure that supports these activities. While its present reputation is good, this has not always been the case. In 1993 it emerged that the EBRD had spent twice as much on its running costs and offices as on loans and investments to the east. Its then President Jacques Attali was forced to resign. Since 1993, the EBRD has reestablished its reputation by emerging as an effective 'pump primer' for economic and enterprise development in Central and Eastern Europe. The main forms of its financing have been loans, equity investments (shares) and credit guarantees tied to sizeable projects. It is only really through providing guarantees to other lenders, such as commercial banks, that the EBRD involves itself in providing finance to smaller-scale projects and entrepreneurial schemes. In this respect the EBRD–EU regional finance facility for the ten EU accession countries is an important step, providing term loans and equity finance to financial intermediaries so as to facilitate the expansion of lending to small and medium-sized enterprises (SMEs). By and large, the EBRD has exercised a conservative lending strategy and has stuck largely to safe ventures with governments, blue-chip firms, banks and public agencies. For example, the EBRD's ECU 102 million contribution to Volkswagen's ECU 3,490 million investment in Czech car company, Skoda, was hardly risky or innovative and could easily have been served by a traditional commercial bank. However, as private banking has developed in Central Europe and as privatization programmes have edged towards completion, the EBRD has taken greater risk with larger investments in countries such as the Ukraine, Bulgaria and Russia. Although concentration has continued to rest with larger (often complex) projects, levels of risk have increased and substantial losses are being incurred as a consequence of the economic instability in Russia. Despite this the Bank remains committed to Russia and the NIS. Many of its projects such as the innovative Kamchatka energy project in Russia (for which it has provided a $100 million loan) are long-term projects at early stages of development and are set to have a substantial transition impact.

launched PHARE programme – dubbed PHARE2 – and two parallel instruments, ISPA and SAPARD. ISPA will finance projects in transport and the environment and SAPARD will finance agricultural sector improvements. The future job of PHARE, which means 'beacon' in French, is to focus solely on preparing the ten candidate countries for EU membership. Thus, between 1999 and 2006, around 30% of PHARE assistance will be channelled towards institution building, which includes the strengthening of democratic institutions and public administrations. This is to ensure that public services are ready to apply the *acquis*. The remaining 70% of PHARE financing will go towards more traditional investment support, although with reduced emphasis on transport, agriculture and the environment (now covered by ISPA and SAPARD).

The EU has resolved to only fund projects that tackle priorities set out in the Accession Partnership and to ensure that more money is spent on development rather than on supervision and/or consultancy services. It has also made clear that candidates are expected to show that proposals are cost-effective and that the necessary technical and institutional arrangements are ready to deliver those projects. These insistences are welcome, along with the broad re-organization of EU aid efforts, given some of the significant problems with EU aid programmes prior to 1999. While these programmes have helped beneficiary countries bring about economic, legislative and social progress, several problems have been noted. First, as highlighted by Echikson (1997), nearly two-thirds of the aid money previously spent has gone to 'highly-paid Western consultants, including wealthy multi-national consulting and accounting groups'. Second, money approved by the EU's political leaders under PHARE has often never been spent. The same problem has applied to the TACIS programme where, in one notorious case, the EU Court of Auditors noted that only a third of $180 million allocated to improve Ukrainian nuclear safety had been disbursed. Third, months have often been needed to get EU programmes up and running and many projects have been outdated before tenders have been made and accepted. Fourth, failing projects have been rarely terminated even where performance has been poor or where interim objectives have been barely satisfied. Fifth, project proposals have often been poorly conceived or have simply not been ready for implementation. Concerns have also been raised over the lack of transparency in programme administration and the misappropriation of funds. The present re-orientation of PHARE should go some way to dealing with some of these past difficulties but the EU must strengthen its oversight of pre-accession aid spending and concentrate on fewer, strategically important projects.

EU enlargement – costs and benefits

Of course the existence of a pre-accession strategy reflects the prospect of future EU enlargement to Central and Eastern Europe, and some comment has already been made on the progress and scheduling of entry talks. The admission of Central and Eastern European countries to the EU has a good number of supporters. These supporters are able to point to both political and economic benefits. Politically, the re-integration of the Central and Eastern European countries (or at least a number of CEECs) with the rest of Europe will promote democracy and stability throughout the continent, cementing processes of democratization and marketization east of Berlin. A wider EU might also be assumed to carry greater weight and influence in international fora, maximizing and harmonizing the 'European voice' in world affairs. Economically, (eastward) enlargement should see the EU population rise by up to 30% with the possible integration of 100 million more consumers into the Single Market. Enlargement should also provide a further stimulus to pan-European trade and investment and accelerate the economic development of transition states. Deeper market integration holds a clear potential for welfare gains on the part of all parties, arising in the form of traditional efficiency gains, increased exploitation of economies of scale and a medium–long-run growth bonus. With specific regard to investment effects, there would be manifold benefits for foreign investors extending from the further strengthening of the institutional, commercial and legal linkages between the CEECs and the EU. Investors not only would have greater confidence in the long-term security of the CEE region, but might also benefit from the ending of residual restrictions on the transfer of employees, goods, services and capital.

However, the idea of extending EU membership into Central and Eastern Europe runs up against a number of obstacles and cautions. For the applicant states, concerns surround the full exposure of indigenous industry to Single Market freedoms (and competition). Fears are raised that SEM integration will lead to a 'wipe out' of home-country firms in vulnerable sectors such as heavy engineering, steel and agriculture. Equally, although applicant countries have maintained their bids for membership, the introduction of EU standards in various areas has demanded much adptation of national law (and much expenditure). Harmonization with EU laws and standards in such areas as social and environmental protection may also pose a threat to the present competitive advantage extending from present national standards. From the perspective of incumbent EU states, a number of concerns are evident:

1. Fears that eastward enlargement of the EU could make the EU too cumbersome to function efficiently and lead to an increase in conflict management difficulties.

2. Fears that eastward enlargement could lead to a weaker, multispeed EU marked by greater internal disparities (between members) and the wider use of opt-outs.

3. Difficulties in 'funding' enlargement given the relative economic underdevelopment of applicant states and the financial underpinnings of EU policies on agriculture and the regions (see below).

4. The belief that the EU should concentrate on deepening its integration rather than on admitting new members (widening).

5. Worries about a flood of cheap imports as a direct consequence of eastward enlargement. With Eastern Europe strong in labour-intensive industries, enlargement is feared as likely to aggravate the slump in labour-intensive industries in current member states.

6. Fears over a flood of economic migrants as the citizens of CEEC states secure the right to move freely across the EU territories. This right is a notable omission from those provided under the Europe Agreements.

These fears have not prevented the establishment of a pre-accession strategy nor have they dissuaded the Council of the European Union from backing the goal of eastward enlargement. What is clear, however, is that the concerns listed above have contributed to the EU's internal arguments over enlargement and to the fragmentation of pre-accession efforts. The condition of entry talks (which in most cases are little advanced) and the continued absence of target entry dates also reflect the worries of incumbent EU members. Many of these concerns are now being used to support calls for transitional arrangements at point of entry (e.g. initial restrictions on the movement of CEE workers throughout the EU) and for full compliance with the Copenhagen criteria.

While a full evaluation of these arguments is beyond the scope of the present study, it is beneficial to provide some further explanation of the specific concerns relating to the financial consequences of enlargement. These concerns are central to the debate about the timing and format of EU extension and to the EU's internal review of its own fiscal, policy and institutional arrangements. The reader is reminded that many of the issues surrounding institutional reform have been previously considered in Chapter 2.

The financial consequences of enlargement

On the EU's side, it is clear that enlargement will inevitably have consequences for certain common policies and for the Community expenditure associated with them. This has also been the case with past enlargements but, given the economic characteristics of the present applicants (relative underdevelopment and large agricultural sectors), unparalleled concerns are raised over the future funding and operation of the EU's agricultural and regional policies. Available estimates of combined fiscal costs range from 0.1% to 0.2% of EU-15 GNP. Thus, as remarked on by Keuschnigg and Kohler (1999), 'given that the Union's own resources amount to no more than 1.27% of national GNPs, approximately 10% of the Union budget is at stake'. At the policy level, allowing for progressive cuts in farm spending and subsidies in the years ahead, conservative estimate suggests that the costs to the CAP of CEEC membership may be around €10 billion. As eastern farm products switch from the external protection regime of the CAP to its internal price and income support structures, CAP expenditure will be inflated and tariff revenues will be lost. On the structural policies, eastward enlargement could cost a similar sum at around €13 billion (Baldwin et al., 1997). While some calculations have virtually doubled this cost, it should be recalled that, under current rules, EU structural funding has to be matched by equal funding from state government (see Chapter 5). In this context, the European Commission has estimated that new members would be unable to absorb more than 4% of their own GDP with absorption capacities varying from case to case.

Whatever the precise costs, the budgetary consequences of eastward enlargement are clearly huge and member states have been locked in repeated internal debate over their meaning and management. Specific states such as Spain and Portugal, which receive significant monetary transfers under the EU's structural policies, have been determined to secure assurances over future financial allocations and have argued for the EU to strengthen its overall funding. Others, such as Holland and Finland, have been determined to hold EU spending to acceptable levels and to look to policy reform so as to make enlargement achievable. The scope for such tensions is considerable. Were the EU to stick to its present plan to hold spending to 1.27% of EU GNP, the financial allocations received by some existing member states would inevitably be reduced as a consequence of EU expansion.

The reform issues surrounding these policies are complex but the EU's challenge is to preserve the coherence and effectiveness of these policies (if not to improve them) while introducing new member states. On agriculture, therefore, the Commission has proposed to continue the broad direction of reforms initiated under the MacSharry Plan of 1992 (see Box 7.2). These involve progressive reductions in interventionist price supports for commodities such as cereals, oilseeds and beef, as well as duty and export subsidy reductions agreed with WTO partners under the Uruguay Round. Meanwhile, CEE farm sectors will have to undergo dramatic restructuring before membership can even be considered. While some are modest in scale and do not raise particular financial concerns (e.g. the Czech agricultural sector), others are large and encompass hundreds of thousands of relatively inefficient smallholdings. According to Schoenberg (1998), for example, the average farm size in Poland is approximately 8 hectares. In the UK, holdings under 10 hectares represent only a quarter of all farms. Under current CAP rules, this pattern to agri-sector activity in Poland (which alone has 4 million farmers) would equate with the eligibility of thousands of Polish farmers for a range of CAP subsidies, compensatory payments and income supports.

On regional policy, the challenge is to find a structure that allows any new members to receive manageable levels of aid and without creating uproar among the EU's present poorer members. Eighty-five of the eighty-nine CECC regions (at NUTS II level) are at present eligible for objective 1 funding as their per capita incomes are less than 75% of the EU average. The regional policy reforms discussed in Chapter 5 have gone some way to starting this process.

BOX 7.2

The Common Agricultural Policy

For forty years, the Community's Common Agricultural Policy (CAP) has sought to increase agricultural productivity in Europe and to stabilize agricultural markets and farming incomes. As a consequence of its operation, the EU experiences the free movement of agricultural products across and between the member economies on the basis of common prices, common rules on competition and central administration by the EU. The principle of Community Preference gives priority to the sale of EU produce via extensive regulation of imports, levies and customs duties, price subsidization and other forms of domestic market support. Since internal EU prices are higher than those on world markets, the CAP must protect domestic producers and the internal market against cheap imports and fluctuations by the use of such means. Within this there is considerable variation. Although common prices, external barriers and market interventions are used to control agricultural production and to stabilize markets in general terms, external protection and intervention cover about two-thirds of agricultural production in the EU and external protection without intervention covers about one-third. In the former cases, protection through levies and customs duties is combined with the formal maintenance of EU prices above certain minimum levels. Specific agencies exist for key Community products such as cereals, milk powder, beef and veal, which buy up supplies when at their highest so as to stabilize market prices.

This policy framework has undergone a number of significant changes in recent years inspired by internal financial constraints, persistent agricultural surpluses and external demands for EU agri-market liberalization. CAP reform in the 1990s – extending from the 1992 MacSharry Plan and the 1994 WTO Agreement on Agriculture – has helped to reduce internal budgetary and supply pressures and to expose EU producers to greater competition. Specifically, the EU has been looking to adopt:

◀

- A pricing policy geared more to the market. Interventionist price supports for commodities such as cereals, oilseeds and beef are being drastically cut.
- Full and on-going compensation for that reduction through compensatory payments (made on a hectarage or headage basis).
- Progressive implementation of measures to limit the use of factors of production such as the set-aside of arable land.
- Reduced duties and export subsidies, the WTO Agreement demanding a tariffication of variable levies and charges, and providing for duty and export subsidy reductions.

The priorities for the European Commission were to ensure that European agriculture would become more competitive (on both the EU and global markets) and to facilitate satisfaction of international and tightening environmental requirements. This had to be achieved without prejudice to CAP principles and with sensitivity to the need to protect farmers' livelihoods. These priorities have been fully upheld in the latest package of measures forming a part of the Commission's Agenda 2000 proposals.

Several actions have now been made the basis of Council agreement, including further reductions in price supports, increases in (compensatory) direct payments, and a considerable simplification of policy rules. This policy is again designed to improve the competitiveness of EU agriculture and to avoid future surpluses. The Commission argues that lower prices will benefit consumers and leave more room for price differentiation in favour of quality products. Greater market orientation will importantly prepare the way for the integration of new member states. Additionally there will be increased emphasis in the new CAP on food safety and on environmental concerns.

Foreign investment in Central and Eastern Europe

Up until the First World War, foreign investment was a very important feature of the economies of the countries in Central and Eastern Europe. Foreign owner assets were an extensive part of the manufacturing sector and over half of mining production. During the First and Second World Wars, the liberal regime that had allowed this to happen was tightened and much foreign-owned property was placed under state control. Prior to and during the Second World War, the majority of firms still under foreign control were expropriated and assigned to German companies. Eventually, during the nationalization programme between 1944 and 1950, control was placed in the hands of the Communist governments. In the 1960s the state control of production remained binding but some Communist governments began to see that there might be certain advantages in foreign investment and it began to be accepted that limited investment could help with some of the problems of relative underdevelopment. Most of the inward investment centred around co-production activities, where control was still held by the state. Towards the end of the 1970s it became clear that these types of arrangements had not brought with them the hoped for technology transfer and associated benefits, and regulations were loosened still further. Even this move did not bring with it significant new investment, because Western companies were still reluctant to invest in countries which they perceived to be politically unstable.

There can be little doubt now that all countries in Central and Eastern Europe are in favour of attracting foreign direct investment. This occurs when a firm invests overseas to produce and/or to market a product in a foreign country, establishing both ownership and control over a company (or other foreign assets). Thus FDI may take the form of an acquisition of an existing company in the local market, some form of equity investment with local partners (involving part ownership and control of overseas facilities), or the establishment of new overseas facilities. Thus an important distinction is raised between FDI and FPI (foreign portfolio investment) which concerns passive investment in foreign firms (or investment funds) and which requires no management effort by the investor. FPI does not generally involve an investor taking a significant equity stake in a single foreign business entity.

The attractions of FDI

Foreign direct investment into Central and Eastern Europe is likely to speed up the process of industrial development and modernization. This belief is based on the the expectation that inward capital inflows will augment low domestic capital supplies and bring with them new technology and management methods. The experience to date is that, in virtually all cases, the better organization introduced in factories belonging to foreign firms has led to rapid increases in labour productivity. The technology transferred (although not always the most up to date) has been more modern than those hitherto employed. The countries of Central and Eastern Europe are also banking on foreign investment in helping them to access new markets (to strengthen their export potential) and to improve their balance of payments problems. It is central, therefore, that foreign investment brings with it the capability for export growth and import substitution. A further bonus of foreign investment is that it can help to create greater market competition and to break down old state monopolies. This is especially the case where investment is tied to privatization processes. Against this is the possibility that, in some instances, foreign investment can actually reduce competition. This can happen when transnationals close off entry to markets, where they secure exclusive supply rights, and suck up or kill off local companies to acquire local monopolies. Indeed, the benefits brought by foreign investment should not obscure the fact that there are often less welcome facets to this sort of activity. For instance, cross-border acquisitions can sometimes hamper trade. A study by the UN's Economic Commission for Europe (ECE) found that big multinationals such as foreign automakers often lobby for, and get, trade concessions from Central European governments such as quotas and tariffs on competitors' imports. These concessions are often an effective precondition for investment (Papp, 1995, p. 9). In other cases, investors have been able to secure tax concessions and favourable terms for profit repatriation. The governments of all countries confront a key dilemma: if legislation is too restrictive and/or if investors' demands are not treated sympathetically, foreign capital will go elsewhere; if legislation is too liberal and/or too many concessions are made, revenue streams will be reduced and large slices of profit removed abroad. This reality gives foreign firms some very strong bargaining power with which to play off different countries looking for new investment.

We also see that foreign investment is concentrated in specific locations. To date, the overwhelming proportion of inward FDI into Central and Eastern Europe has been located in Poland, Hungary, Russia and the Czech Republic. Within these countries, foreign investors have also tended to target big urban areas with good infrastructure and easy access to office space and production facilities (e.g. Praha in the Czech Republic and the Mazowieckie, Śląskie and Wielkopolskie Voivodships in Poland). In this sense, the preference of foreign firms to pay somewhat higher rents and wages in order to operate in the most developed and favourably situated locations is, in itself, contributing to Central and Eastern Europe's own core and periphery problem. The benefits of a border with the EU have been very clear. For example, Hungary has benefited significantly from its border with Austria (see Case Study 7.4) and Poland and the Czech Republic from their borders with Germany. On the other hand, Bulgaria, located on the wrong side of the former Yugoslavia and at distance from the core EU market, has found it relatively difficult to attract investors.

CASE STUDY 7.4 **Curtain fall rings changes for Austrian managers**

At the moment, the Austrian economy is humming along successfully. The good figures for growth and unemployment can largely be attributed to two factors from outside the country: entry into the European Union in 1995 and the opening up of the east European markets to Austrian exports and investments. EU membership has led to considerable growth in exports to western countries such as France and Spain. But it was taking the opportunities that rose from eastern Europe's return to capitalism and democracy that really got Austria's economy moving.

A few figures might demonstrate this regional boom. Austria's exports to the newcomer on western industrial markets, Hungary, equal those to Switzerland with which it has had a strong trading relationship for many decades. Sales to tiny Slovenia almost come up to those to Japan and China combined.

And what is true for the whole economy is also reflected by intra-company exports: the supplies of Opel Vienna to its sister plant in Hungary's Szentgotthard of engine parts such as cylinder heads, equal Austria's total exports to countries such as Israel or Ireland.

Similar ties exist within the networks of other multinational companies which span the region: Philips Austria sends crucial parts of its VCR machines to an assembly facility in Szekesfehervar, also in Hungary.

Henkel produces detergents in several chemical plants for sale in the region. Audi's engines from Gyor, Hungary, find their way into the cars of various Volkswagen models, among them the Skodas of Mlada Boleslav in the Czech Republic.

Austria's largest contribution to the Audi plant – situated only fifty kilometres from its border – was physically small but nonetheless high in added value. With development facilities in Germany running at full capacity, the engineering company, Magna Steyr Daimler Puch, in Graz received the order to develop the sports car Audi TT on the basis of the VW Golf's platform. Steyr also supplied additional engineering work up to the very production start of the car in Hungary.

Many Austrian managers had been taken by surprise soon after the Iron Curtain came down. 'We kept calculating again and again', says Herbert Reimitz, a former production director of Philips Austria. 'But by combining production facilities in Austria and in Hungary we were actually competitive with Asian suppliers.'

Similar to Philips many other local companies, even smaller ones, went international. Berndorf, a non-ferrous-metal group, runs a cutlery factory in Slovakia. Wienerberger, a producer of building materials, acquired dozens of brick and pipe plants across the region.

Fronius, a welding gear specialist, set up shop in the Czech Republic. Meanwhile, thousands of Austrian joint-ventures popped up all over the region, many of them founded by Mittelstand companies which had never before thought about going abroad.

This picture is mirrored on the very top by international groups running their regional networks from Vienna. While ABA, the Austrian Business Agency, was less able to attract international investment in the production sector, it proudly points to a number of new headquarters in Vienna of companies ranging from pharmaceuticals to chemicals and from international consultants to IT providers. Of the 400 US companies in the country, about eighty run their regional business from this location.

Still, not everyone in Austria wants to see these dynamics. A recent poll among small business managers in Burgenland, Austria's easternmost province bordering Hungary and Slovakia, said that more than half of them are pessimistic about EU enlargement. Only a quarter of them has developed an offensive strategy and hoped to gain additional markets in the east.

Shortly before Austria went to the polls on whether or not to join the European Union, a large part of the population was undecided or even opposed to the entry. The Freedom party – and the Greens – mobilized for a 'No'.

Then the government and Austria's still important social partners – industrialists and unions – started a strong campaign that was not limited to posters and TV advertisements but went down to the shopfloors where workers and managers knew exactly how important the European market was for them. The result was a solid 65% majority in favour of the Union.

A similar effort might be necessary focusing on EU enlargement. Austrian workers cannot be assured that they will keep exactly the jobs they hold today. But they ought to know that many of their future jobs will be closely tied to those of their colleagues in the East.

Source: Financial Times, 26 November 1999

Location of investments

Hungary was the first country to receive significant FDI flows in 1991, mostly in the form of acquisitions under the national privatization programme. Poland and the Czech Republic began to attract significant sums from 1992 onwards, with massive FDI flows surging into these countries in the early–mid-1990s. By 1996, Hungary, Poland and the Czech Republic claimed approximately two-thirds of total inward regional investment between them. The bigger investments in these markets such as in the automobile industry (e.g. Fiat SpA in Poland, General Motors in Hungary, and Volkswagen AG in the Czech Republic) or in the electrical sector (e.g. Electrolux and General Electric in Hungary) involved substantial capital imports and demonstrated the long-term plans of Western firms in Central Europe (see Agarwal, 1996). Over the last few years, Poland has led the way, emerging as the biggest single destination for FDI in the whole of Central and Eastern Europe. According to PAIZ (the Polish National Agency for Foreign Investment) cumulative FDI in the country stands at in excess of $35.5 billion (as of June 1999) with $7.5 billion worth of foreign capital investments attracted in 1998 alone. Most of this capital has come from large foreign companies, with over 500 separate firms investing a minimum of

$1 million. Businesses from the US and Germany have topped the list of foreign investors, followed by those from Italy, the Netherlands, France, the UK, Russia and Korea. Each of these countries has been the source of inward investment worth in excess of $1 billion. In the case of Germany and the US, the cumulative value of investments has reached $6 billion and $5 billion respectively.

Alongside the big three (Poland, Hungary and the Czech Republic), Russia has also emerged as a significant destination for inward investors into Eastern Europe. Foreign participation in its telecoms and oil sectors has strongly increased since 1996. As evidenced in Table 7.10, a number of smaller countries such as Estonia, Lithuania and Slovenia have also shown a growing attraction despite their relatively smaller scale. In terms of FDI per head, in 1998 Estonia outperformed all the CEECs including Hungary whose inflows have fallen with privatization deals drawing to a close (*Business Central Europe Magazine*, November 1999). Compared with the rest of the world, however, these countries have only performed modestly in attracting international capital investment. Relative investment levels remain low when compared with other developing markets. Sinn and Weichenreider (1997) highlight an accumulated stock of FDI in the region by 1996 ($43 billion) lower than that accumulated by just Argentina and Mexico. It is important to remember here the history of these young market economies and the contribution of their Communist heritages to shortages of managerial know-how and to underdeveloped infrastructures. Bureaucracy and corruption within administrative sectors have also worked to make operational environments quite difficult while many investors have been led elsewhere by the evidence of political and economic instability in many of the region's markets. More will be said about such issues subsequently.

Table 7.10 Foreign direct investment flows, 1990–98

Foreign direct investment flow ($m)	1990	1991	1992	1993	1994	1995	1996	1997	1998
Bulgaria	13.0	56.0	42.0	40.0	105.0	82.0	100.0	497.0	270.0
Croatia	na	na	13.0	77.0	95.0	83.0	509.0	196.0	350.0
Czech Republic	72.0	523.0	978.0	580.0	1,038.0	2,732.0	1,138.0	1,300.0	1,400.0
Estonia	na	na	na	157.0	215.0	199.0	111.0	128.0	565.0
Hungary	300.0	1,651.0	1,487.0	2,294.0	1,684.0	4,945.0	2,828.0	1,436.0	1,971.0
Latvia	na	na	43.0	51.0	155.0	244.0	376.0	515.0	200.0
Lithuania	na	na	25.0	30.0	31.0	72.0	152.0	328.0	950.0
Poland	89.0	100.0	300.0	600.0	500.0	1,100.0	2,800.0	3,000.0	7,500.0
Romania	18.0	37.0	73.0	97.0	341.0	417.0	263.0	1,224.0	884.0
Russia	na	na	700.0	400.0	500.0	1,700.0	1,700.0	3,800.0	1,100.0
Slovakia	18.0	82.0	130.0	200.0	309.0	304.0	295.0	197.0	330.0
Slovenia	4.0	41.0	113.0	111.0	374.0	429.0	221.0	213.0	306.0
Ukraine	na	na	200.0	200.0	100.0	400.0	500.0	600.0	700.0

Source: Business Central Europe Magazine Statistical Database (01.01.2000)

Determinants and motivations

What then lies behind these patterns and the particular attraction of a number of Central European economies? Well, first of all, there is strong evidence that 'the level, location and motive of FDI in the region are all powerfully associated with progress in transition' (Lankes and Stern, 1998, p. 8). In short, firms typically prefer to operate in the most developed CEEC markets where they can expect a good degree of macroeconomic stability and where they can benefit from improvements in structural and institutional fundamentals. Poland, Hungary, the Czech Republic, Estonia and Slovenia, for example, all exhibit good levels of economic growth and (relatively) stable legal frameworks. Each has low levels of country risk (at least by East European standards). Investment has also been attracted owing to progress with privatization and the liberalization of investment laws, both important aspects of transition. While extensive privatization has ensured the availability of many low-priced assets, FDI has been encouraged by favourable investment laws and the removal of many restrictions on foreign business participation. In Poland for example, as noted by Schoenberg (1998), 'profits and dividends can be easily repatriated, as can proceeds of share sales and liquidations'. Inward investment incentives are also available for capital inflows exceeding €2 million, with further investment reliefs available in a number of designated special economic zones (Stemplowski, 1996, as cited in Schoenberg, 1998).

By contrast, the low rates of investment in most Balkan and NIS economies reflect less favourable conditions for investment extending from a plethora of economic, legal and political difficulties in these countries (see Case Study 7.5). Problems often cited include complex and changing investment regulations, poor enforcement of ownership and property rights, widespread corruption, political instability, currency instability and slow-moving privatization programmes. Many of these countries also face an uphill task owing to the small size of their domestic markets, poor-quality infrastructures and low income levels. In brief, 'unfavourable investment conditions ... shortcomings in the implementation of reforms, and in particular in the way the business of government is conducted, remain a deterrent for private investor activity' (Lankes and Stern, 1998, p. 8). If individual economies prove the exception to the rule, then this is explained by their unique attractions. In Russia's case, higher levels of investment over the last decade reflect the country's positioning both as an important oil and gas economy and as Eastern Europe's largest single market (see Case Study 7.5).

Geographical proximity to Western markets and EU candidacy also separate the CECCs from a number of less-advanced economies in the wider Eastern Europe. These factors are particularly relevant for cost-motivated investments as opposed to those primarily seeking new markets. This distinction – between cost-motivated resource-seeking firms on the one hand and market-seeking firms on the other – is of particular significance. While the two are in no sense exclusive, they have often been contrasted in attempts to further unravel the motives for FDI in developing markets.

For companies looking to *acquire foreign resources* through direct investment (raw materials, assets, production efficiency etc.), cheap assets have been widely available

CASE STUDY 7.5 Investors still cautious about Russia

Vladimir Putin's victory in Russia's presidential election has prompted many long-term investors to re-examine a delicate calculation: the potential attractions of the vast Russian market set against its huge existing pitfalls.

'We are seeing the first wave of fresh interest in Russia since 1998', says Scott Blacklin, president of the American Chamber of Commerce in Moscow. 'It was easy for companies to cross Russia off their list over the last two years, but now the lawyers and accountants here are saying that lots of companies are putting their toes in the water again and doing due diligence.'

Portfolio investors certainly have reasons to cheer. Since the beginning of the year, the economy has been picking up steadily, commercial Soviet-era debt has been restructured, the credit rating agencies have begun to prepare upgrades and Eurobond and share prices have increased sharply.

But the enthusiasm of those who look for short-term speculative gains stands in sharp contrast to the more cautious approach of foreign direct investors. Their expertise and capital may be vital in developing the fledgling Russian economy, but many have had bitter experiences in the past, and are reluctant to commit substantial sums over a long period.

Russia's size, its 147 million population, the strength of its education system and the poorly developed market system ought to offer enormous potential for foreign investors.

While most of them remain coy about figures, some have been able to turn a profit. McDonald's, which has opened fifty-two fast food outlets since 1990, claims to have been in the black since the mid-1990s.

Undeterred by Russia's latest crises, Philip Morris, the US tobacco company, and Caterpillar, the US engineering group, have both opened factories on the outskirts of St Petersburg in the last few weeks. Fiat of Italy has signed a joint venture in Nizhny Novogorod with Gaz, producer of the Volga car.

Yet all these projects are the result of very long-running and often frustrating negotiations. The Swedish furniture manufacturer Ikea, for example, began talks with the Soviet authorities in 1988. It has only recently opened its first branch.

According to official figures, direct foreign investment across the country was just $4.2 billion in 1999, up from $3.3 billion in 1998 and down from a peak of $5.3 billion in 1997. 'That is still tiny, even compared with other parts of eastern Europe', says Sergei Prudnik, an analyst with the brokerage Troika Dialog in Moscow.

As Eivind Djupedal, regional head of Cargill, the international agricultural production and trading group puts it: 'I think Russia has to rank among the most difficult operating environments in which we work anywhere in the world'.

A case in point was the contract killing of a senior executive at Baltika, a highly successful Scandinavian-controlled brewery in St Petersburg, at the start of the year.

But there are many other, mostly prosaic, obstacles, such as the long and contradictory tax code and the ubiquitous bureaucracy. As a result of strong cultural differences and disagreements with local partners, many companies prefer to undertake 'green-field' investments, or to have, at the very least, majority control in any joint venture. But that can still leave them vulnerable to a market in which foreigners are viewed with suspicion – as tempting targets for criminal groups and politicians alike.

Joel Hellman, an economist with the European Bank for Reconstruction and Development, argues that it is the lack of respect for property and contract rights, and for the role of minority shareholders, that remain the principal barriers for potential investors. 'So far, the positive signs are few and far between', he says.

For companies that are already present in Russia, however, there have been some indications of change over the past few months.

Last December, BP-Amoco, the petroleum giant, and other shareholders won back control over their investments in Sidanco, a Russian oil company, after alleged abuses to the bankruptcy process.

Earlier this month, the US–Russia Investment Fund won a court ruling that appeared to bring to an end challenges brought by former 'red directors' and the federal state property ministry, questioning the legality of the controlling stake it acquired last year in Lomonosov, the historic St Petersburg porcelain factory.

And Karl Johansson, managing partner of Ernst & Young for Russia, points to a meeting last month of the Foreign Investors Advisory Council (FIAC), which represents many large investors in Russia and which he co-ordinates. Mr Putin himself attended, and impressed delegates by his attentiveness and 'hands-on' approach, as well as pledges to create enhanced tax deductions.

The problem is that Mr Putin has so far issued no economic programme, and the statements he has made on the campaign trail have proved contradictory. He has called for a 'dictatorship of law', a fight against corruption, and indicated support for the free market and foreign investors.

But he has also endorsed protectionism and state intervention, and is seen as still being too closely linked to a number of disproportionately influential business 'oligarchs', against whom he has so far shown no sign of action.

Mark Bond, president of the Anglo-Russian Finance & Investment Corporation, says: 'Most investors will wait for another two to three months. We still don't know who Putin is, or what he will do. The initial impression is good, but has he got enough support people around him?'

His own experience is salutory. After long delays and attempts at intimidation against him, he achieved a court judgment last year compensating him for $7 million in shares his company had purchased in the privatisation of Baikal Airlines – which had been expropriated by the local administration. But officials have refused to implement the judgment.

Without changes to the current system, he argues 'The only direct investors that can operate in Russia are huge companies with enough political power to lobby and big resources to throw at the problem. As soon as you rear your head here, you can get shut down immediately'.

Source: *Financial Times*, 4 April 2000

in Eastern and Central Europe since the beginning of reforms. Production facilities and company assets have been available (cheaply) as a consequence of privatization processes and cheap raw materials have raised the prospect of low-cost inputs for cost-oriented firms and/or vertical integration opportunities. Critically, low wage rates (at least by Western standards) have represented a golden opportunity to undertake manufacturing tasks at relatively low cost, often in the context of less restrictive environmental regulation. The low cost of labour in the CEECs has been a major factor in the location decisions of many companies. Automakers Fiat, VW, General Motors and Ford, have all cited low labour costs as one of a number of motives for locating new investments in the region (see Case Study 7.6). The former head of Asea Brown Boveri's European operations, Eberhard von Korber, was even drawn to describe the region's labour cost advantages as 'a gift of history' (*Business Central Europe Magazine*, April 1996). This conclusion could be quickly drawn from comparing wage rates in the company's Czech and Polish subsidiaries with those in Germany and Switzerland. In the company's new Central European subsidiaries, wage levels were running at barely a tenth of those prevailing in Germany. Other companies involved in labour-intensive production in areas such as textiles, clothing and consumer electronics, have also looked to Central and Eastern European markets as a low-cost production–export base. However, if cheap labour costs have represented an inevitable attraction to many cost-oriented firms, it is one likely to be eroded over time and in the course of convergence of CEE economies towards EU income levels and environmental standards. Indeed, while cost advantages have influenced many previous foreign direct investments, foreign investors in CEE countries have been mostly motivated by domestic market potential and/or the possibility of servicing regional markets from a Central–Eastern European location. In the Communist era, the region was typified by shortages of both consumer and industrial goods and high levels of demand are expected over time. Demand levels for industrial goods such as glass, cables, chemicals, power supply and engineering products have already proved attractive to firms looking to expand their markets. Consumer markets for items such as tobacco, televisions, cars and household goods are growing rapidly. Potential market growth is also an attraction to service sector operatives with many sectors such as banking, retailing, telecommunications, tourism and hospitality management, short on Western experience and offering excellent potential (Paliwoda, 1997). Many foreign firms want to be in the market-place ready to supply this demand and/or, in some cases, to use regional platforms for wider access to European markets (e.g. a Polish base for easier access to the Russian market). Daewoo, for example, has made shipments of cars to target CEFTA and EU markets from its main venture in Poland. The EU exempts duties on cars from the ex-Communist state (even if produced by Asian companies) if they have a local content of at least 60% of their manufactured value. This provides a significant attraction given the 10% duty on direct motor vehicle imports into the EU from Korea itself.

Economic sector of investment

The analysis of data from CEEC investment agencies confirms the fact of concentration of capital at industry level. In Poland, for example, statistics issued by PAIZ highlight the major attractions of the manufacturing sectors with food processing, transport equipment manufacturing, chemicals, pulp and paper and other non-metal goods all prominent. Significant capital has also been invested in financial intermediation, trade and repairs, and the construction sector. Italian auto-maker Fiat heads the list of individual foreign investors with $1.4 billion worth of investments, followed by Korea's industrial giant, Daewoo ($1.38 billion). United Pan-Europe Communications ranks third on the list with investments reaching $1.15 billion. Fourth place is taken by the Russian Gazprom ($1.11 billion). A number of positions in the top ten list (see Table 7.11) belong to investors from the financial sector including UniCredito Italiano ($1.04 billion), Bayerische Hypo und Vereinsbank AG ($1 billion), and Allied Irish Bank Plc ($746.7 million).

In the Czech Republic, important industries with high levels of foreign capital allocation include: energy, construction and property development, chemicals, pharmaceuticals, metals, finance and management consultancy. In finance, Citibank Praha (with American capital), Banka Haná (with Belgian capital), and Volksbank (with Austrian capital), have all seen inward investment in equity. In the energy field, well-known energy producers and distributors from Germany, the Netherlands, France, Sweden and Great Britain have all taken part in share purchases of Czech energy companies. This includes the entry of the British company National Power into Elektrárny Opatovice. Marked foreign investor participation has also been felt in the consumer goods and food industries. According to the Czech National Bank, '[i]nterest in these Czech industries is connected to the still comparatively lower labour costs, the possibility of increasing domestic sales and expanding capacity applicable also for exports to third countries' (http://www.cnb.cz/en/ archiv/bp97/finan.htm).

Table 7.11 Major foreign investors in Poland (as of 30 June 1999).

NO.	INVESTOR	INVESTED TOTAL (US$ mn)	PLANS (US$ mn)	ORIGIN	ACTIVITIES
1	Fiat	1,405.2	na	Italy	Automotive, banking, insurance
2	Daewoo	1,385.8	457.8	Korea	Automotive, electrical machinery and apparatus, construction, insurance
3	United Pan-Europe Communications	1,150.0	na	Netherlands	Media and entertainment
4	RAO Gazprom	1,109.6	625.8	Russia	Construction and energy
5	UniCredito Italiano	1,045.3	250.0	Italy	Banking
6	Bayerische Hypo- und Vereinsbank AG	1,000.0	500.0	Germany	Banking
7	Allied Irish Bank Plc	746.7	na	Ireland	Banking
8	EBRD	703.4	na	International	Banking, capital investment
9	Metro AG	598.0	650.0	Germany	Wholesale and retail trade
10	Polish-American Enterprise Fund	505.0	na	USA	Capital investment
11	Adam Opel AG	500.0	200.0	Germany	Automotive
12	ING Group NV	470.0	na	Netherlands	Banking, insurance
13	IPC	465.0	30.0	USA	Pulp and paper
14	Reemtsma Cigarettenfabriken GmbH	417.1	150.0	Germany	Tobacco processing
15	Commerzbank AG	413.1	na	Germany	Banking
16	Philip Morris	372.0	80.0	USA	Tobacco processing
17	Coca-Cola Beverages Plc	360.0	na	Great Britain	Food processing and beverages
18	ABB Ltd	341.6	182.8	International	Machinery and equipment, electrical machinery and apparatus
19	Harbin BV	325.9	na	Netherlands	Food processing
20	Saint-Gobain	317.0	120.0	France	Glass

Source: The Polish Investment Agency (PAIZ)

CASE STUDY 7.6 Carmakers pile into Central Europe

Mr Peter Bognar, a twenty-eight-year-old maintenance engineer, earns the equivalent of DM700 (£250) a month at Audi's engine plant in Gyor, western Hungary. In the Czech Republic to the north, Mrs Vaclava Buriankova, a forty-eight-year-old body-shop worker, takes home the equivalent of about DM650 at Skoda's car plant in Mlada Boleslav.

Both could make around eight times as much in Germany. Such huge disparities are one of the reasons why some of the world's leading car companies have invested in central and eastern Europe since the collapse of Communism in the early 1990s. 'For west European carmakers, faced with near permanent overcapacity and low trend growth, the prospects in the east are too tempting to pass up', says Mr Simon Miller, automotive analyst at UBS Securities in London.

More than $8.9 billion (£5.3 billion) has been committed to new plants in the region in the past six years by the four biggest investors: Germany's Volkswagen; Adam Opel, the General Motors German subsidiary; Fiat of Italy; South Korea's Daewoo. Spending by the less ambitious Suzuki of Japan and Ford of the US takes the total to more than $9 billion.

Low pay is not the main reason why they have headed for central and eastern Europe. While investment grants and tax incentives have played a part, soaring demand on the back of generally buoyant economic growth has been the main draw when sales in traditional markets such as the US, western Europe and Japan have been sluggish.

The explosion in sales in the former East Germany shows the potential. Registrations exceeded 777,000 units in 1992 – the peak year of a post-reunification boom – compared with a fraction of that in the former German Democratic Republic. Although sales have fallen since, they have stabilized at about 600,000 units.

And although demand in Poland, Hungary, the Czech Republic and Slovakia has also been volatile, the trend has been decisively upwards. Poland – the biggest and most populous country in the region – was Europe's fastest growing car market last year. Sales jumped 41% to 373,542 units, making it Europe's eighth biggest new car market, according to Samar, a local consultancy. Registrations should hit 450,000 by 2000, it reckons.

Sales in the Czech Republic reached 128,701 units in 1995 from 104,142 the previous year. In Hungary, sales have yet to exceed their peak of 90,000 units in 1994. But after collapsing to 68,800 following a government austerity package in 1995, registrations climbed last year and should reach 76,000 units in 1997.

Volkswagen, Europe's biggest carmaker, has led the investors into this new market. This has been partly the result of political pressure after reunification – the group is 20% owned by the west German state government of Lower Saxony. It will have spent DM3.2 billion on new car and engine plants in the former East Germany by 2000.

VW has also invested elsewhere in the region. It has allocated DM3.7 billion to acquire and modernise Skoda, the Czech Republic's leading carmaker, by 2000. In Hungary, VW's Audi subsidiary expects to have spent DM1 billion over the same period. More modestly, the group has also invested in Slovakia and Poland.

Opel has been almost as ambitious. It has ploughed DM500 million into a showcase new 'lean production' car factory at Eisenach in the former East Germany. The lessons learnt at Eisenach will be incorporated at the DM500 million plant under construction in Poland, to supersede a DM30 million assembly unit in Warsaw. A further DM700 million has been invested to assemble cars and engines in Hungary.

Fiat and Daewoo have concentrated on Poland. The Italian company has spent $1 billion on acquiring 80% of FSM – now Poland's biggest carmaker. Another $800 million is going into two new models by 2002.

Daewoo's ambitions are so big it has bought two Polish vehicle-makers since 1995. The largest, FSO, is being groomed to build a new generation of Daewoos now taking to the roads in Korea.

The boldness of these four carmakers contrasts with the caution of the other car companies. Although others concede that demand will eventually rise significantly, they are much more pessimistic about the immediate potential for sales growth.

Such arguments often disguise self-interest: many of the financially strapped European carmakers face overcapacity in their home countries. Many would prefer to export vehicles from their domestic plants rather than to build new factories in central and eastern Europe. They argue that it will be easier to export to the region once countries such as Poland and Hungary join the European Union and have to cut high tariffs on imports.

They also point out that the advantages of investing in low-wage economies are limited: pay accounts for no more than 10% of the costs in a capital-intensive car plant; and wage levels are rising fast in these countries.

The big investors acknowledge salaries are climbing. But they say it will be years before they reach Spanish or UK levels, let alone those in western Germany. Even after re-unification, pay in the former Communist East is still 15–25% below that in the West – and that ignores the more generous fringe benefits in the latter.

The big investors emphasize the importance of gaining an early foothold in these growing markets by establishing local plants. 'A local presence is essential to building goodwill', says Mr Albert Lidauer, managing director of Opel Hungary.

However, Opel and VW expect their investments to serve a wider region than just the countries in which they are located. General Motors last month said its Hungarian operation would lead its push into the Balkans. Both companies also have their eyes on a bigger prize – the vast but still untapped markets of the former Soviet Union.

Meanwhile, Daewoo sees a double benefit in Poland: local production will provide a back-door to sales in western Europe if exports from Korea were ever threatened, as well as a bridgehead to the east.

And the evidence suggests the spoils will indeed go to local manufacturers. Opel has led Hungary's car market for the past five years, with more than 20% of sales in 1996. Suzuki, another local manufacturer, came second with 19%.

In Poland, Fiat took 42% of sales last year. Together with Daewoo (26%) and GM, the three biggest brands accounted for more than 75% of sales in 1996.

Such data may explain why Toyota, Japan's biggest carmaker, which has so far steered clear of building cars in the region, is having second thoughts. Mr Akira Yokoi, its head of international operations, says it is now looking closely at local production.

But there is a special reason why German carmakers have been in the vanguard. Their green-field factories in eastern and central Europe are convenient test-beds for more flexible production methods, which would be resisted by their unionized workers in Germany.

'When you start from scratch, you can be very efficient', says Mr Lorenz Kostner, head of VW's East German engine plant.

Moreover, the threat of shifting investment to the East has given management a lever to negotiate productivity concessions from their traditionally pampered domestic workforce.

The Chemnitz plant, which has been VW's most productive engine unit for the past two years, contracts out dozens of tasks which would be done by VW workers in the west, to cheaper third parties. Similarly, Audi chose to assemble its new sports cars in Hungary because its highly flexible contracts suit a model for which demand will be very seasonal says Mr Karl Huebser, managing director of Audi Hungaria Motor.

VW and Opel know they must tread carefully to avoid being accused of 'exporting' jobs to the east or of 'blackmailing' their West German workers into giving up hard-won privileges on pay and conditions.

Such concerns can provoke some extraordinary corporate doublespeak. Last year, Mr Adreas Schleef, Audi's head of personnel, justified the decision to shift work to Gyor because it corresponded to the company's strategy of 'enhancing our competitiveness, corporate growth and safeguarding employment, each of which influences the others in a kind of magic triangle'.

But there is no alchemy behind the companies' ultimate intentions. They believe much of what is being learnt at the new plants in the east will eventually be applied at home. 'Whether for VW or Opel, the aim is to transfer the experience back to western Germany', says one executive who has worked for both companies.

Mr David Herman, Opel's chairman and a tough-talking former lawyer, is characteristically succinct.

'We have expressed, through our decisions, the element that time is pressing. Having a new plant on your doorstep is different from having it in Indonesia.'

  High-cost manufacturers such as VW and Opel believe they have no other way to fight the threat of rising imports from lower-cost Asian rivals in western Europe. For them, the factories in the east are vital lifelines to developing new markets for tomorrow and to protecting those of today.

Source: Financial Times, 12 February 1997

Modes of entry

Although later chapters in this book provide for further address of strategic responses to change in European markets, it is useful to comment here on market entry strategies for Western firms considering direct investment in Central and Eastern Europe. Through such analysis, we can learn a good deal more about the new business environments of Central and Eastern Europe and of some of the motivational factors now applying to foreign investment in the region. This section provides a brief review of some of the entry methods which are appropriate to the situation to be found there and which involve direct investment. These include three broad options, all involving substantial commitments in terms of capital, organization and management input:

(a) independent ventures (constructing new facilities or premises as an independent company or entrant),

(b) local company acquisitions, and

(c) joint ventures with local organizations.

Although these methods are used outside Central and Eastern Europe they are particularly appealing to both governments and firms looking to invest in Central and Eastern European markets. As investment entry modes they are not to be confused with licensing or franchising agreements (which are contractual in nature) or with methods of entry where the company's products are produced outside of the overseas market and exported in (see Chapter 8).

Independent ventures (new developments)

A number of foreign investors have selected new developments (or green-field projects) as a method of entry into CEEC markets. Toray for example – a Japanese textile firm – heads a list of several Japanese companies including Matsushita (televisions), Nissho Iwai (metals) and Denon (electronics) establishing new (green-field) production facilities in the Czech Republic. Western multinationals such as IBM and Philips have also featured green-field site investments as a part of their investment plans for Central Europe. Although acquisitions offer advantages, companies may choose to build if no desired company is available for acquisition, if acquisition is harder to finance, and/or if engagements with existing companies might present substantial problems for the investor. Compared with participation in or with existing businesses, start-ups may also allow firms to more easily implement their intentions and to avoid many of the problems associated with potential partners. These may include obsolete factory facilities and technologies, inefficient methods, poor management and sub-optimal locations. However, there are inevitably both advantages and disadvantages in a green-field site strategy. Although capital and land costs are generally much lower than in the EU, building a new factory, plant or distribution facility suggests substantial set-up costs. It is only really appropriate if the investor's strategy is one of long-run market penetration. In the Toray case investment costs were estimated by CzechInvest at $150 million (*Business Central Europe*, May 1997). Market entry may also be delayed by the time taken to complete the investment, building, equipment and training requirements etc.

Company acquisition

Acquisition refers to the process of buying (or buying into) an existing organization. Distinction should be drawn between total or full acquisitions (resulting in 100% ownership) and 'partial acquisitions' which give the investor part ownership of a local firm and a role in the management of that enterprise. There are many reasons for seeking acquisitions in Central and Eastern Europe. Buying an existing company gives the buyer not only labour, local management and market know-how, but also a whole organizational structure. Through acquisitions, a company may also gain established brand identity, an existing company base and, potentially, an established distribution network. Equally, the costs and difficulties associated with building new facilities are generally much higher than upgrading existing premises, capital equipment etc. (although such costs should not be underestimated). However, a very careful examination of potential acquisitions is needed and the strategy of buying into existing enterprises faces a number of potential drawbacks. As captured by Harris (1999, p. 315), 'Premises may not be particularly suitable for new production processes [and] capital equipment is likely to be outdated'. There may also be resistance from existing management and/or employees and hidden liabilities from such things as pension funds and previous environmental damage. Thus, '[a]lthough an existing CEEC business may seem attractive at first, the costs of bringing it up to EU standards may be significant' (Harris, 1999, p. 315).

Analysis has already referred to several notable acquisitions including VW's acquisition of the Czech car company Skoda and General Electric's acquisition of Hungarian lighting company Tungsram. Other noteworthy examples include the sale of Hungarian firms Chinion to Sanofi of France (pharmaceuticals), Lehel to Electrolux of Sweden (electrical goods), and the 60% holding in Matav (the Hungarian telecoms operator) secured by Deutsche Telekom and Ameritech. In Poland, British purchases have included Pilkington's 83% stake in International Glass Poland (IGP), United Biscuits' 99.7% acquisition of ZPC San SA, and GEC

Alsthom's acquisition of 60% of Konstalu, the Polish tram producer (see Schoenberg, 1998, for further analysis).

Joint venture agreements

This mode of entry involves some form of equity investment leading to the sharing of ownership (and control) of overseas facilities with one or more local partners. In most cases, the investing and local firm(s) join to create a new business entity and maintain their legal independence. Features of JVs include shared inputs (e.g. capital and technology), shared outputs (profits, losses and R&D results), a degree of joint control over decision-making, and a common commercial policy (adapted from Davies *et al.*, 1996, p. 25).

With respect to the market entry strategies of Western firms looking to do business in Central and Eastern Europe, a joint venture can help a firm to enter untapped markets quickly and generally at lower cost than either a green-field start-up or a full local acquisition. Joint ventures can also allow an investor 'to assess from the inside the valuation of assets (of a potential target) and to proceed to full acquisition with full and proper knowledge of the productive capabilities and market values of the enterprise' (Paliwoda, 1997). For these and other reasons (e.g. restrictions on foreign ownership shares), Western firms appear to be using joint ventures as a preferred method of market entry for Central and Eastern Europe (see Brouthers and Bamossy, 1997; Paliwoda, 1997; Davies *et al.*, 1996). Examples include Thomson Polkolor, a joint venture set up in Poland between local television set and tubes producer Polkolor and the French electronics giant Thomson. Telecommunications equipment makers Alcatel and Ericsson have also undertaken joint ventures with RomTelecom, the privatizing Romanian telecommunications giant.

Governments in the region have been actively encouraging joint venture activity as a means of gaining inward investment and technology transfer and in order to sell part stakes of conglomerate firms, aiding the privatization process. Typically, the Western partners' contribution has been in the form of cash, manufacturing know-how, machinery and components, management expertise and links to Western markets. Motivation has rested with the existence of clear market opportunities, access to valued resources and/or interest in backdoor acquisitions. Eastern partners have generally contributed land, (cheap) labour, buildings and equipment and, in many cases, local market knowledge and distribution networks. In the Shell and Rompetrol JVA for example, Shell's goal was in obtaining exclusive rights to Romanian oil reserves. It sought access to natural resources and was willing to contribute technology, management and financial resources. As the state oil and gas monopoly in Romania, Rompetrol was interested in improving the exploitation of its domestic reserves and was looking for Western technical skill, management expertise and financial resources. In addition to its monopoly market, it offered local skills, beneficial wage rates, government contacts and local market knowledge (quoted in Brouthers and Bamossy, 1997).

The most important consideration in a joint venture is the selection of a partner.

Sharing activities and resources is difficult, so careful consideration has to be given to finding a partner that has complementary skills or resources. Another key consideration is that of control given that factors resulting in JV failure include conflicts over decision-making, perceptions of unequal costs and benefits, strategy and goal variance between partner firms. In most joint ventures in the CEECs, western partners have been the dominant parties, assuming primary strategic control for the venture. However, a number of studies have suggested that the conditions necessary to encourage positive employee performance and learning in joint ventures include the sharing of responsibility between local and foreign managers (see Cyr, 1997; Cyr and Schneider, 1996).

It should be noted that there are other business structures (involving equity investment) that are sometimes described as joint ventures by their participants. An example here would be the form of quasi-acquisition suggested when a company secures the particular assets of a target company combining these with certain of its own operating assets (Davies *et al.*, 1996, p. 25). Confusingly, other co-operative agreements (although not involving equity investment) can also be described as 'joint ventures'. In this case, the concern is with what may be more accurately described as non-equity joint ventures or non-equity associations.

Conclusions

The prospects for foreign direct investment in the CEECs depend crucially on internal developments in recipient countries, on the region's future relationship with the EU, and on the relevance of CEECs to the international business strategies of Western firms. If in the future the situation in Central and Eastern Europe continues to evolve in a way which is favourable to foreign investors, then this will encourage an increasing flow of new investment into the region and foreign capital investment will continue to function as an important driver for the modernization process. In this context, Western governments and institutions should remain supportive of such investments. If, however, the attractions of low asset sales, low wages, and dynamic markets are lost, then international investors will likely look elsewhere. Some may even be encouraged to do so if little is done to tackle the current scale and unpredictability of corporate and other taxes and/or if changes in unit-production costs and business regulation erode or challenge existing operational advantages. In this sense, future membership of the EU may be something of a dual-edged sword.

There is no doubting the commitment of CECC governments to this aim or the progress of many transition economies towards satisfying the EU's eligibility criteria. Throughout this chapter, we have seen that, in the more advanced countries, rapid liberalization has contributed to economic progress in these societies and that these same countries have made strenuous efforts to satisfy the demands of the EU (adopting large slices of its *acquis*). In a genuine sense, these economies – Poland, the Czech Republic, Slovenia and Hungary in particular – have created new business environments that are favourable to foreign investment and to continued private sector development. Much remains to be done – especially in terms of enterprise restructuring, fiscal control and the facilitation of new enterprise – but hopes for the second decade of transition are high. However, it is the variation in reforms and macroeconomic performance across countries that is perhaps the clearest feature of the first ten years of transition. As we have seen, liberalization and privatization have been slow-moving in much of Eastern Europe, and governments in South-Eastern Europe and the European NIS have done relatively little to reduce the obstacles to foreign investment and to the growth of new enterprise. In the years ahead, these business environments will be marked by more dramatic upheavals as governments intensify their efforts to complete liberalization and to lay the basis for macreconomic stability. The failure to do so will lead inevitably to acute financial and economic crises and, potentially, to political disorder and civil conflict.

Review questions for Chapter 7

1. How and why did the command economies of Central and Eastern Europe collapse?

2. Outline the basic requirements for the transition of centrally planned economies into market-based economic systems.

3. What were some of the early effects of transition?

4. Which countries have advanced furthest towards market-based systems and what factors have contributed to their progress?

5. Why has transition failed to bring prosperity in so many countries and to a number of social groups?

6. Why has privatization proved so difficult in the CEECs? Can you identify the strengths and weaknesses of different routes to privatization?

7. Why is the development of a small business sector important in Central and Eastern Europe?

8. Discuss the importance of financial sector reform in establishing business environments conducive to investment and private enterprise.

9. Outline what you would expect to be the pattern of unemployment in Central and Eastern European countries over the next few years.

10. Is there a straightforward trade-off between environmental protection and economic development in the East?

11. What efforts have been made to integrate the economies of the EU and Central and Eastern Europe? How far would you agree that the EU has promised a great deal and delivered relatively little to Central and Eastern Europe?

12. Why do so many CEECs target membership of the EU? What are some of the costs and benefits of EU membership for both existing and prospective members?

13. Western businesses are getting involved in business arrangements in Central and Eastern Europe. How would you explain the differences in the concentration and forms of these investments?

14. What are some of the major motives for Western investment in Central and Eastern Europe? Can you highlight some of the difficulties encountered by investors and the possible deterrents to inward investment?

Web guide

Organizations and institutions

European Commission (Enlargement, covering the CECCs) @ http://europa.eu.int/comm/enlargement/index.htm

European Commission (External Relations, covering the NIS and South-Eastern Europe) @ http://europa.eu.int/comm/external_relations/index.htm

The European Bank for Reconstruction and Development (EBRD) @ http://www.ebrd.com

Country reports and data

The CIA World Factbook (country profiles) @ http://www.odci.gov/cia/publications/factbook

The Library of Congress Country Studies @ http://lcweb2.loc.gov/frd/cs/cshome.html

UN/ECE Statistical Yearbook Europe (basic country–market information) @ http://www.unece.org/stats/trend/trend_h.htm

US Department of State Background Notes: Europe and the New Independent States @ http://www.state.gov/www/background_notes/eurbgnhp.html

News services and intelligence

BBC News (Europe) @ http://news.bbc.co.uk/hi/english/world/europe/

BBC News (EU enlargement special) @ http://news.bbc.co.uk/hi/english/special_report/1998/eu_enlargement/

EUBusinessNews (Eastern Europe) @ http://www.eubusiness.com/easteuro/index.htm

Business Central Europe Magazine @ http://www.bcemag.com/

Radio Free Europe – Radio Liberty @ http://www.rferl.org

Central European Business Daily @ http://www.nsl.co.uk/cebd/

Central Europe Online @ http://www.centraleurope.com

Central Europe Business @ http://www.ceebiz.com

Central Europe Review @ http://www.ce-review.org

OLIN Intelligence Project (Eastern Europe and Russia) @ http://khan.interaccess.com/intelweb/eeurope.html

References

Agarwal, J.P. (1996) Impact of Europe agreements on FDI in developing countries, *International Journal of Social Economics*, **23**(10/11), 150–63.

Alfandari, G., Fan, Q. and Freinkman, I. (1996) Government financial transfers to industrial enterprises and restructuring, in Commander, S. and Schaffer, M.E. (eds), *Enterprise Restructuring and Economic Policy in Russia*, World Bank.

Baldwin, R. *et al.* (1997) The costs and benefits of eastern enlargement: the impact on the EU and Central Europe, *Economic Policy*, April, 127–76.

Brenton, P. and Gros, D. (1997) Trade reorientation and recovery in transition economies, *Oxford Review of Economic Policy*, **13**(2), 65–76.

Brouthers, K.D. and Bamossy, G.J. (1997) The role of key stakeholders in international joint venture negotiations: case studies from Eastern Europe, *Journal of International Business Studies*, **28**(2), 285–308.

Bush, J. (1999) Crash course, *Business Central Europe*, November, 41–2.

Carlin, W. and Landesmann, M. (1997) From theory into practice: restructuring and dynamism in transition economies, *Oxford Review of Economic Policy*, **13**(2), 77–105.

Cyr, D. (1997) Culture and control: the tale of East–West joint ventures, *Management International Review*, **37**(SPEISS), 127–44.

Cyr, D. and Schneider, S.C. (1996) Implications for learning: human resources management in East–West joint ventures, *Organization Studies*, **17**(2), 207–26.

Davies, E.M.M., Kenny, B. and Trick, R. (1996) UK joint venture activity in the Czech Republic: motives and uses, *European Business Review*, **96**(6), 22–9.

Dyker, D.A. (1993) Free trade and fair trade with Eastern Europe, *RFE/RL Research Report*, **2**(26), 39–42.

Echikson, W. (1997) *The East: The EU Rethinks its Funding to the East*, RFE/RL.

Ellman, M. (1997) The political economy of transformation, *Oxford Review of Economic Policy*, **13**(2), 23–32.

European Environment Agency (1999) *Environment in the European Union at the Turn of the Century*, EEA.

Faini, R. and Portes, R. (1995) *European Union Trade with Eastern Europe: Adjustment and Opportunity*, Centre for European Policy Research.

Harris, N. (1999) *European Business*, 2nd edition, Macmillan Business.

Heinrich, R.P. (1995) *Enterprise restructuring and privatization in the transition? Evidence from Hungary and the Czech Republic*, 40th Atlantic Economic Conference, Williamsburg, 6–11 October 1995.

Kapoor, M. (1999) The big shift, *Business Central Europe*, November, 43–4.

Kearns, I. (1994) Eastern and Central Europe in the world political economy, in Stubbs, R. and Underhill, G. (eds), *Political Economy and the Changing Global Order*, Macmillan.

Kennedy, P. (1993) *Preparing for the Twenty-First Century*, Harper Collins.

Keuschnigg, C. and Kohler, W. (1999) Eastern enlargement of the EU: how much is it worth for Austria?, *University of Saarland Economic Series*, no.9904, November.

Killing, P. J. (1982) How to make a global joint venture work, *Harvard Business Review*, 120–7.

Lankes, H.-P. and Stern, N. (1998) Capital flows to eastern Europe and the former Soviet Union, *EBRD Working Paper*, no.27.

Lavigne, M. (1995) *The Economics of Transition: from Socialist Economy to Market Economy*, Macmillan.

Meth-Cohn, D. (1999) Was it worth it?, *Business Central Europe*, November, 14–19.

OECD (1999) *Czech Republic*, OECD Environmental Performance Reviews.

Paliwoda, S.J. (1997) Capitalising on the emergent markets of Central and Eastern Europe, *European Business Journal*, 9(1), 27–36.

Papp, B. (1995) Equal footing, *Business Central Europe*, September, 9–11.

Piggott, J. and Cook, M. (1999) *International Business Economics – A European Perspective*, Longman.

Pissarides, F. (1998) Is lack of funds the main obstacle to growth? The EBRD's experience with SMEs, *EBRD Working Paper*, no.33.

Potts, N. (1999) Privatization: a false hope, *The International Journal of Public Sector Management*, 12(5).

Schoenberg, R. (1998) Acquisitions in Central Europe: myths and realities, *European Business Journal*, 10(1), 34–8.

Simpson, P., Daniels, W., Kravagna, S., Leslie, J. and Stravnik, A. (1996) Clean growth?, *Business Central Europe*, June.

Sinn, H.W. and Weichenreider, A. (1997) Foreign direct investment: political resentment and the privatization process in Eastern Europe, *Economic Policy*, **24**.

Stemplowski, R. (1996) Poland: on the road to the European Union. *European Business Journal*, **8**(3), 38–43.

Stern, N. (1998) The future of the economic transition, *EBRD Working Paper*, no.30.

Wolf, M. (1999) Central and Eastern Europe: transition proves long and hard, *Financial Times*, 10 November.

Ziljstra, K. (1998) Privatization in Hungary, Poland and the Czech Republic, NATO Parliamentary Assembly Economic Committee Reports (online) (http://www.naa.be/publications).

The strategy and structure of European business

8 Strategy and the Single European Market

Central themes

■ Determining opportunities and threats

■ Defensive and offensive strategies

■ Foreign market screening

■ Market entry

■ Export strategies

■ Licensing and franchising

■ Joint ventures and alliances

■ Acquisitions

■ Managing cross-border operations

■ Structuring European organizations

Introduction

The movement towards the completion of the Single Market and the wider developments examined in the first half of this text have been discussed as critical elements in a changing European business environment. In the following chapters, attention shifts to how business organizations are responding to these changes and to the challenges of the Single Market environment. Changing conditions and market structures in this 'theatre' are demanding that many firms devise new organizational structures and strategies as they search for competitive positioning in their home markets and/or to take advantage of emergent market opportunities. For a firm to succeed, its strategy must be consistent with the environment in which it operates and a 'fit' must be achieved between its strategy and organizational structure.

In this chapter, analysis begins with the various ways in which companies may respond to the needs of the Single European Market. We explore the many issues and challenges involved in developing a business strategy for Europe and in establishing–consolidating cross-border (European) operations. Having established a model of the strategic management process, efforts are made to examine the various methods by which companies may diversify into new markets. As we shall see, firms can do business in other EEA nations via exporting, licensing, franchising, joint ventures and the many forms of direct investment. As they expand across borders and grow their businesses, firms will confront new pressures tied to the co-ordination and control of their activities. These pressures are also examined here.

Elsewhere, of course, whole books have been dedicated to the subject of European strategic management and to the structure of cross-border operations. Restricting assessment to a single chapter is impossible and, by necessity, the present chapter is supported by a series of dedicated concentrations. In Chapter 9, focus shifts to marketing strategies and challenges in the new Europe. In Chapter 10, the cultural challenges inherent in cross-border activity and management are addressed. In Chapter 11, attention is turned to the formulation and implementation of ecologically competitive strategies and to the philosophy of total quality environmental management. At this stage, an argument will be made that, through the pursuit of key operational objectives, businesses in Europe can look to improve business performance and to gain competitive advantage. Across these chapters, the intention is to demonstrate a wide array of differing strategic problems and solutions relevant to the European theatre, albeit with concentration on the markets of the European Economic Area and the Internal Market regime. It should be clear that earlier chapters (e.g. Chapter 4 on monetary union and Chapter 7 on CEE transition) have already provided some discussion of the strategic implications of key developments in European marketplaces. The concentrations that follow advance and strengthen this early analysis and allow for a necessary synthesis of principal themes. Finally, Chapter 12 offers something of a change in the direction of study, providing a final evaluation of the role of European business in the global economy. Here, concentration falls on the globalization of markets and the inherent challenges for European firms in becoming global players. This chapter provides a final opportunity for discussion of the involvement of European firms in international markets and competition.

Analytical framework

While there is no blueprint for a successful competitive strategy and there are a variety of routes to market growth in Europe, models that can provide guidance to European business managers in (a) formulating competitive strategic plans and (b) operationalizing those plans, make a useful contribution. Whether they are embraced, modified or rejected, such designs can work as a springboard for successful business development and as a means of conceptualizing the strategic management process. This chapter looks to advance one such framework, the principles and stages of which provide the model for subsequent study. While this framework does not suggest a standardized approach or one unique for business in Europe, it does at least integrate many of the essential tasks and questions associated with the two interrelated aspects of business strategy: *formulation* and *implementation*. In the

Critical questions   Strategic issues

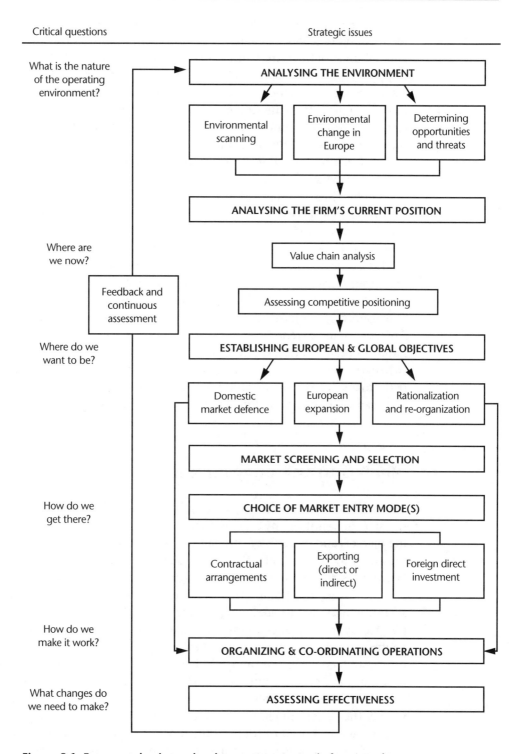

Figure 8.1 European business development: a strategic framework

present view, the central challenge in the formulation of business strategies is to identify and to reconcile changing environmental conditions and the competences and resources of the firm. Thus, while turns and directions in strategy are a response to opportunities or needs created by changes in the external environment, those responses are also shaped and modified by the possession of firm-specific resources and capabilites. After the strategy is formulated, implementation is essentially concerned with how resources are mobilized to accomplish the strategy. Attention is turned to the establishment of appropriate organizational structures and to systems of co-ordination and control. Again, this interpretation of strategy guides the succeeding analysis which is organized around the framework and principles of Figure 8.1. Implicit here is a suggestion that 'strategy' is a multi-staged process which seeks an answer to a succession of questions concerning the situation, resources, organization and commitments of a firm in an ever-changing environment.

As seen in Figure 8.1, the first steps in the formulation of a competitive single market strategy concern the determination of the strategic situation which an organization faces. It is here that our analysis really begins as such an understanding provides the background against which future strategic choices may be made and against which ideas can be shaped or influenced (Johnson and Scholes, 1993). Analysis should extend both to features of the operating environment (what is the nature of the operating environment?) and to analysis of the firm's current position (where are we now?). The challenge is to make sense of the variables affecting the performance of the organization as well as to understand the organization's strategic capability given the forces at play inside and outside of the organization.

Analysing the environment

The process of information gathering on external forces and conditions provides the starting point of any strategic audit. This not only concerns the state of existing markets and patterns of competition (the competitive or task environment) but must also involve a study of the contextual or remote environment. At this level, attention is directed to the socio-demographic, cultural, political and technological features of organizational environments, to modelling current influences under such headings, and to predicting future changes. The external environment is complicated by the tendency towards change and changes in both the operational and contextual realms of organizational environments will (a) underscore the nature of future strategic decisions, and (b) challenge assumptions on which past strategic decisions have been formulated. While different environmental forces will be more or less important to different organizations, all organizations will need to take a view of their environments (scanning those environments for change and development). Each will need to consider the most useful ways of understanding and dealing with the information available. Given that environmental influences can emanate not only from local and national sources but also from international developments, the boundaries of such exercise can often be broad. Indeed, the environments in which European business is conducted consist generally of important elements attaching to different spatial levels – e.g. the local, (subnational) regional, national, international and global. From this basis, companies can begin to determine the nature of their strategic situations and to develop strategic plans both with 'knowledge' of the competitive forces that shape their industries and of the broader influences in the environment.

Environmental scanning (competitive environments)

Environmental scanning or auditing frequently begins with an investigation of those external factors and influences which are more or less immediate and which directly influence the capability of an organization to position itself against its rivals. The aim is to provide a clear overview of the task environment for current strategic development and to synthesize the various information sources providing insight or data on key dimensions. It is not just the nature and scope of the information which is critical to environmental analysis, but the way in which this is prepared and interpreted.

One means of modelling information and of examining competitive environments is to make use of the five-forces model developed by Harvard Professor Michael Porter (1980). This model (see Figure 8.2), which has broad applicability to a variety of situations and industries, manages to capture the powerful forces of industry dynamics in a simple format and has become an academic and industry standard. In essence, it shows a range of factors in the competitive environment

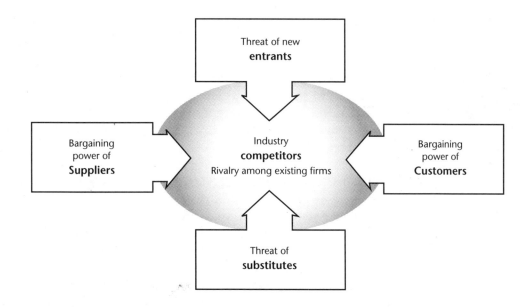

Figure 8.2 Porter's five-forces model
Source: Based on Porter (1980, page 4)

that are significant to a company. The strength and importance of each of these factors (forces) will vary from market to market, but all are relevant to the competitive dynamics confronting any firm in any given industry. Specifically, the firm is seen to be pressured by:

1. the bargaining power of its buyers,
2. the bargaining power of its suppliers,
3. products or services that may be a substitute for what the firm offers,
4. potential new entrants to the market, and
5. its existing competitors.

According to Porter, what a firm can charge for its products, the costs it incurs and the investments it needs to make in order to create or to sustain market entry barriers, are shaped by these competitive dynamics (five forces).

As a method of modelling the firm's current position, the five-forces model is of value to most organizations. Because of the range of factors examined (and their simple organization), industry competitive analysis can be undertaken relatively simply and the balance of power within industries closely examined. Structural analysis can be conducted at local, national or international level, given the circumstances of the firm and the purpose of the study. In all cases, and at all levels of analysis, the five-forces framework can be employed simply for descriptive purposes (to describe what is going on in an industry at any given time) or, more usefully, as a means to identify and recognize both the relative position of a firm within its industry and the main issues that need its attention (Johnson and Scholes, 1993).

As we shall see, strategists can also utilize the Porter framework to analyse the specific competitive dynamics a firm might encounter if it was to enter a new geographic market. By using the five-forces analysis, the strategist can model the competitive forces associated with the country–product market and identify each of those factors which might threaten a foray into that theatre. One central issue will be the barriers to entry the firm might have to overcome in establishing a market presence (e.g. the cost of access to distribution channels in the target market). The role of such analysis in foreign market screening is given consideration at a later stage in this chapter/framework.

Environmental scanning (contextual environments)

In completing a stategic audit, what is more difficult to ascertain (and to conceptualize) is information on the more remote influences on business activity and competition. We are reminded that in examining the business environment a useful distinction can be made between between influences of this kind – such as cultural, demographic, political, legal and technological developments – and those factors which tend to have a more immediate effect on the day-to-day operations of a firm and which are centralized in competitive industry analysis. In fact, Figure 8.3 suggests that, at the highest level, diverse political, economic, social, legal, ecological

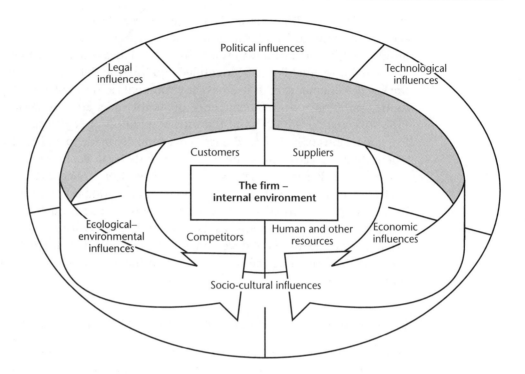

Figure 8.3 The business environment: a modelling

and technological forces provide the overarching framework within which any organization or industry operates.

While Porter's five-forces framework provides us with an obvious starting point for analysis of the immediate or operational environment of firms, in de-layering this higher level of environment – the general or contextual environment – it has only limited attraction. For example, technological developments (offering product substitutes) may emanate from outside the task environment and political decisions (e.g. on market liberalization or taxation) are often critical in the shaping and reshaping of industry competition. In short, managers need also to work at a different level of analysis (the macro-level), auditing those environmental influences important to organizations but emanating from outside of their task environments. Movement to consider environmental influences at this level can enhance the general understanding gained by a structural analysis directed towards the key forces at work in the immediate or competitive environment.

How then do we study the contextual environment and what role might such focus play in strategic analysis? Although this question was given some treatment in Chapter 1 (where we characterized key features of European business environments) it is useful to restate here both the ways in which organizations can conceptualize their wider environments and the nature of key forecasting/modelling techniques. A classical method – and one popularized for its simplicity and broad applicability – is PEST analysis. PEST analysis establishes examination of four categories of influence – political, economic, social and technological – which affect business activity in a variety of ways. The central idea is that a number of aspects of these environments should be identified and listed so that the company is aware of the key developments in its business environments and can plan strategically for its future. Variations on this theme encompass the integration of legal factors into a PEST-style analysis (SLEPT) and the further addition of ecological factors to those five dimensions (PESTLE). Reference is occasionally made to a PLESCET framework, where the PEST acronym is amended to include legal, ecological and cultural factors/pressures. Businesses may use such frameworks to conceptualize their business environment at all spatial levels, to model their national environments, those of host or target countries, or 'transnational' environments such as the European single market. However, there is a danger that by simply listing pressures, the relative importance of different developments may be overlooked. This problem can be overcome by amending the basic analysis to incorporate some sort of ranking or coding system.

Environmental analysis and the European domain

Analysis conducted at the European level (or in any sense in 'international' terms) is a challenging task. For effective modelling/forecasting, a broader range of knowledge will have to be aggregated and assimilated, and the firm will confront a high degree of environmental complexity.

The transnational firm

Let us take the example of a European financial services company looking to profile or to assess the political forces/influences central to its numerous market operations in Europe. Many European financial service providers fall into this category including HSBC and Axa, the renowned French insurance group. At once, it is clear that firms of this nature (given their presence in many national markets) must pay careful attention to the policies, outlooks, and legislative actions of different 'national' administrations and regulatory authorities. But it is also incumbent on such firms to analyse and to monitor changes in EU competition law, and to survey developments in the EU financial services legislation. The regulatory framework of the industry is being profoundly shaped by the processes of decision-making played out in the EU institutions, and by developments in Community law. Sticking with the most obvious area of concern (financial services legislation), the European Commission's right to initiate policy proposals in the financial services sector already covers mortgage services, insurance and assurance, consumer credit, bank branch accounts, capital adequacy, electronic payments, and the licensing and supervision of financial services in general. Recent efforts to create a single financial services market (see Chapter 3) have profoundly affected the freedoms of such companies and have encouraged processes of industry concentration and consolidation. Developments at the global level, such as the recent WTO Agreement on Financial Services, must also be assessed and evaluated for their likely impact on European (and wider international) financial services frameworks.

Emerging players

Where a firm may be little developed as an international player but looks to identify cross-border threats and opportunities, then the challenges of European environmental analysis are also clear. While most companies would be aware of key trends and factors in their home markets, their knowledge is likely to be more chequered with respect to markets abroad and/or to the European theatre as a whole. Equally, changes in the political, economic, social and legal superstructures of other nations may be harder to predict and to anticipate (see Bennett, 1997, p. 209). As companies begin to target specific overseas options/opportunities, the demand for knowledge and the breadth of knowledge requirements are likely to grow. In such circumstances, management will need to focus on exercises directed towards detailed market screening (see later sections), assessing both the general characteristics of the country or countries in which it senses opportunity and the specific nature of the product market including its size, rate of growth, and long-run profit potential.

The nature of such exercise will depend largely on the precise objectives set by the firm but it is clear that, where a company seeks to diversify into new geographic–product market(s), it may initially need to undertake or pay for detailed country–market profiles. Surveys of this kind can provide a base of information from which to investigate future market opportunities and are often a precursor to more tailored market research and project evaluations. It is also clear that the company will confront differences and variations in national conditions/ environments that may impinge on its strategic planning. In an area such as culture, the analyst is almost certain to be confronted with a different set of cultural attitudes, customer tastes and values. While progress can be made to identify cultural subgroups which cross traditional geographic boundaries, cultural norms and values will not simply echo those in the home market. Differences need to be understood so that they can be brought into future marketing and management strategies (see Chapters 9 and 10).

Although companies may focus attention on a narrow range of markets or one region within the Single Market, the volume and scope of information for a manager researching a large number of countries is likely to be considerable. The challenge of assessing its impact on company development is highly complex. Again, complexity is added by the existence of Community-wide regimes and regulations (with direct effect across Community markets) and by the frequent transposition of EU-level decisions into national laws in such areas as employment and social legislation, environmental and consumer protection. Consequently, a process of EU legislative auditing can prove productive and a source of competitive advantage. As discussed in Chapter 2, many players are ceding competitive advantage to rivals who are (a) better prepared to implement legislation set at the supranational level

Source	Publisher or Manager	Nature of information (and related URL)
EUR-lex	Managed by the European Communities Publications Office	The EU's main legislative database. Provides access to consolidated legislation in force and links to the 'C' and 'L' series of the Official Journal of the European Communities (*see below*). (http://europa.eu.int/eur-lex/en/index.html)
Pre-lex	Commission of the European Communities	Information on all European Commission legislative proposals and communications. Provides links to COM documents, Official Journal, Bulletin of the European Union, documents of the European Parliament and more. (http://europa.eu.int/prelex/apcnet.cfm?CL=en)
Official Journal of the European Communities	Commission of the European Communities	Contains the texts of all secondary legislation, draft legislation and official announcements and information about the activities of Community institutions. Divided into three sections: Legislation (L series); Notices (C series) and Supplements (S series).
General Report on the Activities of the European Union	Commission of the European Communities, Secretariat-General	An overview of policy development in all areas during the previous year. (http://europa.eu.int/abc/doc/off/rg/en/1999/index.htm)
Bulletin of the European Union	Commission of the European Communities, Secretariat-General	Reports on the activities of the Commission and the other Community institutions. Ten issues a year. (http://europa.eu.int/abc/doc/off/bull/en/welcome.htm)
Eurostat	Commission of the European Communities, Statistical Agency	Various reports and publications covering economic indicators, social and demographic trends, industry performance and so on. (http://europa.eu.int/eurostat.html)
SCADPLUS/ SCADPLUS Bulletin	Commission of the European Communities	Detail on Community policies, legislation and institutions plus a weekly analytical bulletin containing bibliographical references of the main Community acts, publications of the European Institutions and of articles from periodicals. (http://europa.eu.int/scadplus/sitemap_en.htm)
The Legislative Observatory	European Parliament	The Parliament's new and updated legislative database. (http://www.europarl.eu.int/r/dors/oeil/en/observ.htm)
EU Information Handbook	EU Committee of the American Chamber of Commerce, Belgium	Valuable handbook (annual updates) specifically designed for business professionals. (http://www.eucommittee.be/)
European Access	Chadwyck-Healey	EU current awareness bulletin covering policies and activities of the European Union. Extensive bibliographic references and specialist commentary. (http://www.europeanaccess.co.uk/home/home.htm)

Figure 8.4 Sources of information in EU legislation and business regulation

and (b) better positioned to monitor, track and influence proposals and political dialogues at their early stages of development. In obtaining information on EU-level developments and legislative initiatives, firms may consider exploiting one or several of the information systems listed and summarized in Figure 8.4.

Determining opportunities and threats

Although strategic planning may not always begin with the approaches outlined, the formulation of competitive strategies is best enabled by a systematic approach to environmental scanning. Formal reviews have the potential to identify the key opportunities open to the business and to highlight possible threats such as new competition, future regulatory controls, and so on. Further, by establishing a profile of the impact of environmental factors on the organization (either actual or predicted), managers can decide whether or not the immediate concern should be defence or attack.

The identification of potential opportunities and threats facing a business is often pursued through a SWOT analysis–matrix. SWOT is a simple tool which encourages a basic environmental audit and links that audit to an evaluation of a firm's own strengths and weaknesses. By identifying a firm's strengths (S), weaknesses (W), opportunities (O) and threats (T), strategic planning can be reinforced by a clearer picture of organizational resources/performance and by a simple modelling of environmental influences. A model of the kind developed by Ansoff (1984) can also allow for the integration of various environmental influences into a framework designed to identify the major threats and opportunities characterizing a firm's environment (see Figure 8.5). The ability to adjust the events/issues according to the findings of an environmental survey and to weight factors according to their impact gives this type of approach great flexibility. By working through the model, a firm can 'calculate' the degree to which each event or issue is thought to enhance or to inhibit the success of its strategies and can 'identify' the degree to which different strategies pose a threat or opportunity to the firm given its predicted environment.

It is clear of course that many opportunities and threats for businesses in Europe are arising out of the creation of the Single European Market and out of progress towards a common currency area. Given their role as important agents of change, finding out what threats or opportunities arise from these processes is a basic step in strategic analysis of the new European business environment. Although the elements highlighted in Figure 8.6 relate only to the general opportunities and threats posed by these developments, it should be clear that such threats or opportunities could be given clearer meaning to the individual business through a dedicated audit.

The opportunities of the Single European Market have been well documented and are outlined in Chapter 3 of the present work. In short, the removal of barriers between the member states offers up the potential for organizations to treat the whole of the SEM as their domestic market and thus the scope to increase output and to engender greater scale economies and a more efficient operating position. In reality,

Environment sector	Opportunity/ Threat	Weighting [1]	Importance [2]	Impact on firm's strategies [3]			Σ–	Σ+
				S1	S2	S3		
Technology	1							
	2							
Political								
Economic								
Social								
Etc.								

Σ–

Σ+

Note

1 Indicates the degree to which the event is judged to be a threat or opportunity.
   On an ordinal scale from 1–5, 1 represents a weak T/O, and 5 a strong T/O.

2 Indicates the degree to which the weighted event has, or will have, an impact on the firm's strategies.
   On an ordinal scale from 1–5, 1 represents little impact, 5 a great impact.

3 The impact each event has on each of the firm's strategies is calculated by multiplying the weighted score
   by the importance score. A large positive (negative) score represents a strong opportunity (threat).

   The row sums indicate the degree to which each event/issue is thought to enhance (+) or inhibit (–) the
   success of the firm's strategies. The column sums indicate the degree to which each strategy is itself thought
   to pose a threat or opportunity to the firm given its predicted environment.

Figure 8.5 The firm's environment threat and opportunity profile (ETOP)

however, these opportunities are blighted by the threats facing organizations currently operating in the EU (and wider EEA), including increased competitive activity in their traditional markets. More will be said about this later in this chapter in relation to the establishment of overall objectives. In similar vein, the complement to the Single Market of a single European currency (and of European monetary union) translates into a series of broad threats and opportunities for commercial undertakings operating in or across European markets. Today and for some time into the future, analysis of the European business environment should encompass the acquisition and ordering of clear and up-to-date information on what is happening with monetary union, as well as forms of business and market impact analysis. Complexity is added to these tasks by the creation of a two-tier Europe, in which the adoption of a single currency is particular to a subgroup of EU member states (currently eleven in number) and by current uncertainties over the effects and benefits of monetary union.

The consequences of European Monetary Union have been much debated and have been given some examination in Chapter 4 of the present work. In short, the introduction of a single currency (the Euro) and the elimination of exchange rate risk in Eurozone markets offer up the potential for organizations to operate across internal borders without the burden of foreign exchange transaction costs and free

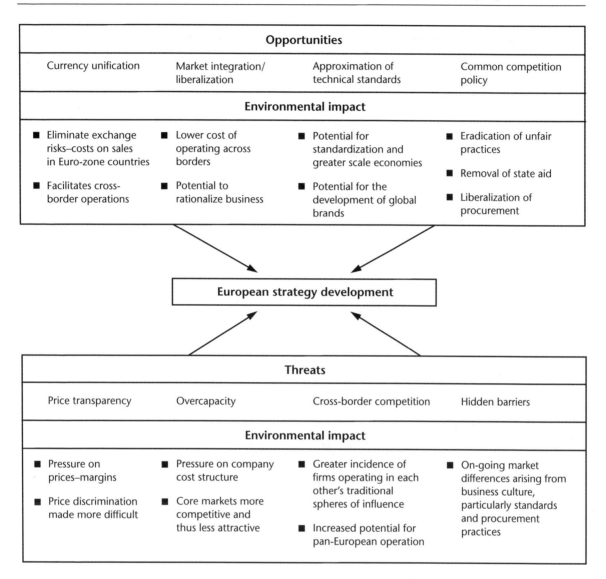

Figure 8.6 Opportunities and threats within the European environment

from exposure to the risks associated with fluctuating foreign exchange rates. Businesses may also benefit from improved access to overseas buyers and suppliers, easier capital movements and greater price stability. Lower average interest rates should also result in lower capital borrowing costs. In practice, however, these opportunities are likely to be blighted by the costs and threats facing organizations in a single currency area. Possible threats to those currently operating in the EU include increased competitive activity in home markets and the threats posed to discriminatory pricing practices (and future profitability) by the greater comparability of prices across national borders. Again, more will be said about this later in this chapter in relation to the establishment of overall objectives.

CASE STUDY 8.1 Environmental change and the European television industry

For more than forty years, most European countries sported two or three television channels provided by state-owned broadcasters and paid for through taxes and licence fees. Some countries, such as the UK and Italy, ventured into the field of commercial television, although their forays were relatively limited and offered only limited additional choice for customers. In some countries, restriction on advertising was severe. In Germany, for example, the two state channels were permitted to take advertising, in five minute blocks, for twenty minutes a day except for Sundays and holidays. The extent of regulation severely curtailed competition both within each country and between countries. Massive deregulation in the 1980s changed the market dramatically. Technology and political pressures served as the catalysts of change, with advances in satellite and cable communications technologies diluting the argument that state control of scarce airwaves was in the public interest. Between 1980 and 1994 the number of TV channels in what was then twelve EU states rose from forty to 150, with over one-third being delivered by satellite ('Feeling for the future: a survey of television', *The Economist*, 12 February 1994). While most channels continued to service their domestic audiences, a small number such as Eurosport and MTV-Europe were now targeting pan-European television audiences for the very first time. In turn, this growth in broadcasting space and platforms led to an explosion in advertising expenditure and to new challenges for television companies in filling the vastly expanded airtime.

Such change rocked the television industry Europe wide with a massive increase in broadcasting space and in competition among broadcasters. State broadcasting monopolies such as the RAI in Italy lost huge chunks of their market share to private networks. But this is not the end of the story. In recent years, a new wave of technological developments has swept through the television industry bringing new competition and challenges to the market and a host of new entrants from the IT and telecommunications fields. The central aspect of this recent technological change has been digitization with rapid progression through different platforms (e.g. terrestrial, satellite and cable) towards digitized, interactive television services. In the UK, viewers now have something like eighty-five channels available to

them and, through digital service providers such as Sky and ONdigital, are gaining first experience of two-way communication via the television set.

Commercial implications

Deregulation, the explosion of satellite and cable television, and the digital revolution, have raised many issues for industry operatives throughout Europe. While the consumer can expect more choice and control as a consequence of these developments, incumbent firms now face new competitive pressures as a result. Challenges are tied to the development and operationalization of new interactive technologies, to funding, service design and differentiation.

Rewards for future success are likely to be substantial. Larger projected audiences will allow commercial broadcasters to collect increasing advertising revenues, with increasing scope for 'narrowcasting' (concentrating advertising messages on specific 'niche' audiences). Even for publicly funded broadcasters such as the BBC, the digital revolution offers opportunity to combine a traditional 'licence-fee' based policy with subscription services and revenues. Five pay-TV channels have already been launched by the Corporation as a part of a joint venture with the cable and satellite company, Flextech. The blurring of industry boundaries – with television broadcasters, telecommunications and computer companies all becoming part of a wider 'media entertainment' – also presents scope for synergistic gains between firms with complementary skills and competencies.

Many companies remain uncertain about the sort of investments and collaborations required in order to survive in the television industry of the twenty-first century and are nervous about the risks from heavy investments and exposure in uncertain markets and technologies. Despite this, companies such as Fininvest and Canal+ have begun to prepare for the future by forging alliances across industry and national lines and by thinking in terms of pan-European production and distribution. Fininvest of Italy, for example, has invested heavily in other European markets, expanding into French, German and Spanish broadcasting systems as a partner in La Cinq in France, Telefünf in Germany and Telecinco in Spain. The company has also moved into Belgian cable systems with La Cinque (see http://www.stanford.edu/~cjacoby/eurotv.html).

Conclusions

This case example typifies the movement and progression in European business environments over time and outlines the various environmental inputs and influences affecting industries and their operatives at different spatial levels. Analysis has shown that dramatic changes taking place in the industry over recent years have been linked to culture (e.g. the changing demands, habits and expectations of television viewers), politics (deregulation and the liberalization of state monopolies) and technology. Not all industry environments are as volatile, but the case of the European television industry highlights the complexity of external business environments and their tendency towards change.

Analysing the firm's current position

The previous section has highlighted the role of environmental scanning in the process of strategic analysis. Given that strategic change can be regarded as a reaction to environmental change, such exercise is clearly central to the process of defining and formulating superior competitive strategies. Ultimately however, 'any organization must pursue strategies which it is capable of sustaining...[and] this requires a good understanding of the strategic capability of the organization' (Johnson and Scholes, 1993, p. 115). In essence, when a firm asks 'what strategic factors do we need to focus on in order to be competitive in the future?', an understanding of operating environments must co-join with an understanding of the resources available to an organization in supporting its strategies and of the firm's existing strategic capability. Indeed, a resource-based view of strategy suggests that internal organizational factors, resources and capabilities structure the organization's response to its external stimuli.

At this stage in our analysis, we look at how firms can more fully assess their positions and at the notion of competitive advantage across a series of strategic dimensions. While we have determined that a key step in understanding the position of an organization is to build a picture of the environment in which the organization functions, the ability of a company to penetrate European markets, or even simply to protect its position within an 'open' European market depends to a great extent on the nature and quality of its various resources. For example, sound technological management, more efficient production processes, efficient procurement of quality raw materials or more responsive decision-making can all enhance a firm's performance *vis-à-vis* rivals in the industry.

Value chain analysis

A useful framework for identifying the resources 'available' to an organization and how they are the sources of the firm's competitive advantage has again been provided by Michael Porter (see Porter, 1985). Porter's *value chain analysis* separates the internal components of a firm into five *primary* and four *support* value-creation activities (see Figure 8.7). Thus, we may identify efficiency in one value-creation activity (e.g. production) as a key source of value and as a source of competitive advantage. Of course, the primary activities of a firm – production, inbound logistics, outbound

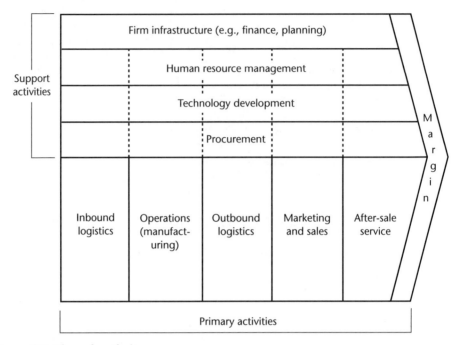

Figure 8.7 The value chain
Source: Based on Porter (1985, page 46)

logistics, marketing and sales, and after-sales service – draw on the variety of support activities in their on-going management. Put very simply, support activities provide the inputs that allow the primary activities of production and marketing etc. to occur. An effective human resource function, for example, ensures that the firm has the right people in place to undertake primary tasks efficiently, as and when necessary. It is the value that each of these activities adds to the product or service, both independently and in integration with other value-creation activities, that must finally be assessed in order to truly understand the sources of the firm's competitive advantage. Value must be assessed from the viewpoint of the end-user with the value of a product or service seen as a function of how much customers are willing to pay for it and of how many customers are willing to purchase the product or service.

More will be said about the integration and configuration of different value-creation activities in the later stages of this chapter as attention turns to how organizations might establish some type of 'multinational' structure and to the implementation of cross-border strategies. At this stage what is important to understand is how organizations can analyse their current position along the various dimensions of the value chain, identifying how the major activities performed create buyer value and examining their integration and synthesis. Ultimately, it is the configuration and co-ordination of resources which provide strategic capability.

Competitor analysis

A value chain analysis can provide a useful starting point for assessing the elements or competences which constitute a company's strengths and weaknesses. The chal-

Issues	Dimensions	Rating				
		1	2	3	4	5
Inbound logistics	Cost–price					
	Relationships					
	Quality					
	Flexibility					
	Reliability					
Production	Cost–efficiency					
	Local responsiveness–adaptation					
	Technology					
	Flexibility					
	Relationships					
Organization	Flexibility					
	Efficiency					
	Mechanism for integration					
	Responsiveness–local autonomy					
	Centralization of critical issues					
	Relationships					
Technology	Flexibility in development					
	Responsiveness to local needs					
	Efficiency in R&D					
Finance	Mechanisms for managing risk					
	Efficiency					
	Effectiveness of systems					

5 = a very strong competitive position, 4 = strong, 3 = average, 2 = weak and 1 = very weak

Figure 8.8 Competitor assessment matrix

lenge now is assessing how the firm compares in relation to its major competitors and with assessing the company's competitive position. This process can be advanced by constructing a simple matrix such as that highlighted in Figure 8.8. This can then be used to assess the company's own strengths and to rate/assess rival firms. While such an approach has many limitations (e.g. the ratings of organizations are obviously subjective), it permits a highly transparent means of assessment along the various dimensions of the value chain and a visual representation of areas in which the organization boasts clear strengths and weaknesses relative to its main competitors.

This position has then to be assessed according to the importance of the various dimensions in the current–future operating environment. Thus, with cost pressures now facing most organizations as a result of competitive intensity across the EU, cost factors must be weighted highly. In addition, as organizational flexibility and the need to adapt quickly to changes in the market and consumer demands become prerequisites for competitiveness, flexibility will also derive a high weighting. Alternatively, an issue such as manufacturing technology may be weighted lower if the firm is operating in a sector where production technologies are mostly standardized.

By multiplying the derived ranking by the calculated weighting, a weighted score of the organization's strengths along each dimension can be worked out. Table 8.1 provides an example of this process. In such way, an organization can establish areas of weakness and highlight the resources, processes and skills that give it competitive advantage. However, the business environment is highly dynamic and organizations must also consider future competitor reactions and developments before they can establish optimal directions for strategy development. To do this, they must also pay attention to:

- firms' core competencies – areas of business in which competitors display clear comparative advantages which are sustainable in the long term;

- firms' likelihood to react – the changes in strategy they may introduce in response to changes in both competitive activity and industry change;

- resources – the extent of competitors' resources and thus their ability to react–develop new strategies;

- culture – traditional behaviour of competitors and their overall management culture (e.g. centralized versus decentralized, or their propensity to enter into alliances versus a tendency to internalize core technologies and skills).

Information on these types of issues is likely to be limited and analysis along these lines necessarily speculative. However, by monitoring firms along these dimensions there is greater scope for considering lines of future action and the creation of contingency plans to cope with eventual outcomes.

Table 8.1 Calculating weighted scores for competitor assessment (production)

Factor	Weight	Rating	Weighted score
Cost/Efficiency	0.8	4	3.2
Local responsiveness	0.3	2	0.6
Technology	0.2	3	0.6
Flexibility	0.7	4	2.8
Relationships	0.6	3	1.8
			9

Establishing European and global objectives

Once firms have undertaken a full review of their operating environments and of the sources of their competitive advantage, they will then be in a position to decide on or to reassess their objectives. As we shall see, firms may well look to concentrate on defending and/or strengthening existing markets. Alternatively, firms may look towards overseas expansion as a means of achieving business growth. Foreign market expansion may be achieved through penetrating markets with existing products or by developing new products for new markets. These options are not mutually exclusive and many firms are likely to pursue a mix of defensive and offensive strategies.

Domestic market defence

Despite the new competitive freedoms of the Single European Market, for reasons of resources or other constraints, some companies may not aspire to developing cross-border activities or to overseas expansion. Their major challenge (and immediate concern) will be that of '*domestic market defence*'. This suggests a series of efforts and actions designed to make it expensive and difficult for new competitors to establish themselves in the firm's domestic (home) market. It should be clear that many organizations will derive the major part (if not all) of their sales from their domestic marketplace and, consequently, that defence of their home territory is likely to be the critical short-term objective for a large number of firms. In most cases, defence of existing business operations at home is likely to be considered a 'safer' option than overseas expansion.

Where customers exhibit high levels of loyalty and where returns on investment are good, it may also be desirable to focus attention on keeping existing customers (and keeping them satisfied) rather than attempting to generate loyalty among a new customer group (see Lynch, 1994). In such circumstances, maintaining and improving the position domestically may be more advantageous than expanding into new geographic markets which may be more competitive and/or which may be difficult to access. Given this defensive orientation, firms should find a strong position behind which to defend the market (these will be based on a firm's comparative advantages), then calculate carefully how they can force up a competitor's costs of entry, deny them the segments and customers on which their market entry strategy will depend for success, and attack their weaknesses (Dudley and Martens, 1993). On all accounts, efforts should be made to strengthen the domestic competitive position by such steps and to avoid 'do-nothing' strategies. If the competitive threat is high, firms may even strike up kinds of co-operative agreements with potential rivals as a means of protecting their own market position. Examples include:

1. licensing-in – agreeing to produce a product for another company (in return for an up-front fee and royalty payments) instead of facing up to competition from the product in the market;
2. cross-licensing – bilateral arrangements through which firms swap licenses between themselves so as to make and market each other's products and to avoid duplicating each other's activities;
3. distribution agreements – providing the distribution network for the competing firm wishing to enter the market rather than facing competition from a new product line;
4. bilateral marketing agreements – which can vary from simple bilateral deals wherein each party sells the products of its partner in its own domestic market, to more complex agreements involving cross-shareholdings and/or the formation of jointly owned marketing subsidiaries.

However, it would be wrong to assume that all firms can strike up co-operative agreements with potential entrants as a means of protecting themselves from new entry.

Marketing and licensing deals, whether operating in one direction or on a bilateral basis, are more likely to occur where there is complementarity between products (and thus the potential for extending the product range) rather than direct competition where the products of the new entrant might potentially cannibalize the products of the incumbent. All of these co-operative routes provide one further strategic advantage: they allow firms to internationalize their outlook without necessarily internationalizing their business. In other words, even in the simplest case of licensing in technology from a foreign player, organizations are able to learn more about operations outside of their traditional sphere of influence and, in so doing, develop a broader understanding of the nature and scope of the European marketplace. This may give them an edge in their own domestic environment.

Whatever the elements and scope of a defensive strategy, dependence on a single domestic market brings with it the inability to offset home-market risks through business operations in other markets, some of which may throw up better profit potential. It is also clear that defence strategies do not come cheap and that it can prove expensive to sustain businesses under prolonged assault. Price and advertising–promotion wars, for example, while potentially protecting the firm from encroachment in the short term, cannot be sustained in the long term without concomitant cost reductions. The downward pressure on prices resulting from the opening up of markets and increased price transparency in the EU economies (see Chapter 4) will make defence of markets on prices alone a very dangerous route to contemplate. Companies need to ask themselves whether they wish (or can afford) to enter into a series of aggressive moves and countermoves, particularly if the new entrant (or potential entrant) has deeper pockets and a wider resource base on which to draw. Again, however, doing nothing is equally dangerous. Sitting back and wondering what will happen if and when a competitor takes an aggressive stance and moves into existing territory runs the risk of being undermined in competition for existing customers.

Pre-emptive defence thus emerges as the preferable objective or option and companies should look not simply to hold the line against competitors but to aim their defensive strategies at increasing their own competitive advantage. In this context, strategic options may also be seen to include mergers and acquisitions, joint ventures and alliances. While much of the analysis of these arrangements concerns their role as powerful mechanisms for market expansion (see the succeeding sections), buying up or coupling with the competition rather than facing it head on, can often contribute to the defence of existing markets. Such partnerships can lead to a sharing of risks and a pooling of resources and skills, enabling 'partners' to bring enhanced competitiveness to the marketplace. Manufacturing abroad can also help in finding cheaper and more efficient sources of production to compete with competitors in existing markets (Dudley and Martens, 1993, p. 167).

Defending strategic position: rationalization and reorganization

International firms will also have to pay close attention to competitive threats in their home (domestic) markets. Most will remain closely wedded to their home economies and will calculate that defence of backyard territory is essential to their long-term success at home and abroad. For example, the £6.8 billion merger between British insurance companies Commercial Union and General Accident was designed to give them greater strength and security in their home market, as well as power to wield in the wider European market (*The Economist*, 2 January 1999, p. 5). This said, in cases where firms derive a profit from a number of individual markets in Europe, the concept of 'defence' takes on broader meaning. Here, we are effectively concerned with the support or consolidation of an existing strategic position across a number of geographic markets and, in many cases, across a number of different product markets. Among many possible objectives, such a business must ensure the highest overall efficiency in its business functions and structures, must look to improve its responsiveness to customer needs and wants, and to contain and (where possible) to reduce its costs. The firm may even consider expanding linkages with other organizations as a means of defending strategic position. Closer relations with suppliers and distributors may also be sought as a means of extending power throughout the value chain. With the completion of the SEM, transnational businesses are also likely to look towards restructuring and rationalizing their activities as a means of enhancing their overall efficiency. In this sense, they may consider a number of options such as divesting peripheral activities (and re-focusing the business on core activities) and/or closing down less-efficient business units and rationalizing distribution and production.

Since the onset of the Internal Market Programme, many companies have looked to reorganize production facilities for a single regional market, rather than duplicate facilities for each separate national market. Unilever, for example, has rationalized its European detergents business, moving to manufacture standardized products in a small number of cost-efficient plants, and to introduce standard packaging and advertising. Prior to SEM completion, the company had different detergent operations in most EC markets, leading to much duplication in assets and marketing and to occasional tensions between central and subsidiary managers. At the same time, many companies have discovered that diversification can mean diluting effort in areas of core competence. From Alcatel to Monsanto, multinational corporations have been busy slicing off some of their businesses and have been looking to concentrate on fewer core activities in Europe and elsewhere. Such actions are likely to support or to enhance the efforts of international firms to defend strategic position in Europe and to reduce capital demands on their businesses.

In this context, the reader is directed towards Case Study 8.2 on Pilkington, the international glass company. In the period of the early 1990s, Pilkington redefined its strategy and structure in the face of serious competitive pressures in Europe. Signficantly, the company refocused its work on a narrower range of products for a wider European market and rationalized its production. Pilkington also made a number of strategic moves so as to strengthen its position in its home territory. The reader may also consider the case of Philips, the European electronics giant. As a result of mounting competitive pressures in Europe and worldwide, Philips has re-aligned its business in recent years through a mixture of rationalization, divestments and organizational restructuring. The company's latest results show a return to profitability after a difficult period (Case Study 8.3).

335

CASE STUDY 8.2 Pilkington Glass

Pilkington Glass is a UK manufacturing organization with its main production centre located in St Helens in Lancashire. Originally a family-owned domestic producer, the company expanded internationally earlier than many other organizations as a result of the success of its float glass production process which it licensed to a number of leading international manufacturers and exploited through foreign direct investment.

The European glass industry has been beset with difficulties in recent years. The emergence of non-EU competition (with Guardian of the USA establishing a green-field plant in Luxembourg and Asahi Glass of Japan taking over the German concern, Glaverbel) has put pressure on Pilkington and St Gobain of France, the industry leaders. A downturn in both the car and construction industries has exposed over-capacity in glass production and forced prices down, a situation not likely to improve as the forecast for growth is slow.

This situation has forced Pilkington to rethink its strategy for Europe. It has refocused its production plants on making a narrower range of products for a wider European market. Enabled by greater border freedoms, this approach is expected to enable greater scale-economies of plant, eradication of the duplication of effort and more efficient utilization of equipment by eradicating production process downtime. To achieve these benefits the firm has been forced to close one of its float glass production lines at its plant in St Helens. Annual cost savings are expected to be substantial, as much as £10 million over two years, permitting the firm to compete more effectively with low-cost producers such as Guardian.

But while all this points to greater efficiency in the firm's centralized production location, what of the company's ability to effectively meet demand within the narrower user groups suggested? A change to the company's marketing efforts has also been required – a Europe-wide user-specific approach where location will mirror the developments of its major customers (particularly the car producers) which have already moved to Europe-wide production and procurement systems.

The company was also forced to reassess its distribution strategy in the UK. St Gobain, Pilkington's leading competitor in Europe, broke with tradition in 1990 and waived the unwritten agreement not to aggressively compete in Pilkington's home territory by purchasing *Solaglass*, the UK's second largest glass distributor. Pilkington, who had until then resisted the idea of increasing its involvement in domestic distribution, partly due to its protected status, but also because it was committed to the idea of being a cost leader, took three years to realize that defence of their domestic market was essential to long-term success. In 1993, they acquired the UK's largest glass distribution company.

Implications for European strategy

Pilkington, like many other organizations servicing the needs of major customers across Europe, is finding that the only way to survive as market pressures hot up is to stay close to their customers in their sales and marketing provision. However, Pilkington cannot contemplate the establishment of small-scale manufacturing units to service the needs of customers in different centres due to the enormous plant economies required to operate in the glass industry. The next best approach is therefore to establish proximate sales and marketing operations which can deal with customer needs and requirements, while maintaining centralized production as a means of preserving economies and profit margins.

Re-organization alone is not, however, seen as sufficient to tackle the challenges. The company has been forced to rationalize its operations and re-focus its activities on a smaller range of products and services in order to maintain levels of efficiency and ensure that it can generate and sustain comparative advantage in all areas of the business. It has also been forced, by an aggressive challenge from its leading competitor, to concentrate attention on defending its home market territory.

CASE STUDY 8.3   Philips thinks again

Philips is the largest consumer electronics company in Europe. Throughout the 1990s, the company had been beset by serious difficulties and had lost further market share to Japanese rivals such as Sony Corporation, Sharp Electronics and Matsushita. The company's problems have been numerous. The organization has been forced to cope with an unwieldy international corporate structure, to overcome an unfortunate gap between its ability to innovate and to successfully market its products, and a high local cost base (in Holland and West European markets). Throughout much of the 1990s, the Group reported heavy annual losses.

Back to basics

One of the central threads of the Group's restructuring efforts has been to concentrate on fewer core activities and to divest many of the firm's peripheral businesses. In 1988, Philips sold its telecommunications business to Alcatel of France, in 1989 it announced the sale of its defence businesses in the Netherlands, Belgium and France to Thomson CSF and, in 1990, it announced the sale of its domestic appliance business to Whirlpool of the USA. In the mid to late 1990s, a new wave of restructuring under new president Cornelius Boonstra saw the company sell or close several more businesses. By 1999, the company had sold its stakes in Grundig (electronics) and Polygram (films and music) and had jettisoned further businesses in such areas as car systems, passive (electronic) components and cable television. The company is now focusing greater attention on its remaining, more focused portfolio, encompassing business and consumer electronics, lighting, personal care products, semiconductors and imaging equipment. In these core areas of company activity, greater competitive demands, increasing costs of R&D and greater pressures to speed up the process of new product development require the closest focus.

Rationalization

Prior to the Single Market, the company had light and television factories in nearly every EC country producing to varying national standards and positioning itself close to end-consumers in a series of partition markets. Like many other European firms, the organization operated a fragmented multidomestic regional strategy and quickly found itself with too many plants of insufficient size to fully exploit the economies of scale presented by an integrated European market. Through a series of plant closures and mergers, Philips has attempted to enhance its overall efficiency and to better exploit scale and location economies. Today, value-creation activities are concentrated on fewer sites and management centres and the company has significantly reduced its operational costs. The company continues to try to reshape its European–global production network and to find the right organizational structure for its various geographic and product divisions.

European expansion

While growth strategies can be based on expansion in the domestic market, firms may well look to international strategies as a way of extending their business. Figure 8.9 provides a simple matrix of the various growth strategies available to organizations and highlights the possibility of overseas expansion with new and/or existing products.

For the individual firm, four questions are critical to the definition of a proactive strategy directed towards overseas expansion and European business development:

1. the nature of market opportunities abroad;
2. the basis on which the organization might seek to achieve a competitive position in a foreign market or group of foreign markets (competitive strategies);

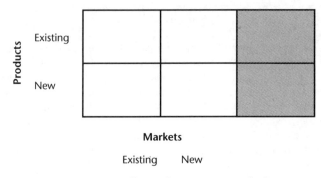

Figure 8.9 Matrix of potential growth strategies

Table 8.2 The transferability of comparative advantage

Source of advantage	Scope for transferability
Product technology (patent protected)	High but may be copied or improved upon as technologies change/improve.
Process technology	High, but again are time dependent. Limited scope for exploitation through exports owing to plant capacity and establishing new plant abroad is highly resource intensive.
Quality and systems control in manufacturing	Can lead to cost advantages although additional transportation costs through exporting may erode the advantage. Just-in-time systems with local suppliers have to be developed abroad in the event of foreign investment which can take time and be difficult to achieve if relations already exist between suppliers and customers.
Productivity	May be linked to production location and therefore only transferable via exports wherein the advantage may be eroded via high transportation costs. Also, may be difficult to sustain in the long-term as competitors have the potential to improve their efficiency by operating in a wider European market.
Marketing expertise	Often the most difficult advantage to transfer as branding, positioning, distribution and promotion often have to be adapted to local market conditions.
Service	Service and customer relations cannot be transferred and require dedicated resources to establish in overseas markets.

3. the direction which an organization might choose to take (for example expanding into new geographic markets with existing products or diversifying into new markets with new products);

4. the methods through which market expansion might take place.

The answers to these questions rest with internally and externally directed research. Although many firms will have a broad sense of foreign market opportunities (and threats), expansion into specific markets as a part of an active strategy should be underpinned by careful market screening and by exacting assessment of the transferability of organizational competences. Of course, advantages developed in one country may not be transferable to another. It is important, therefore, to analyse the extent to which different advantages can actually be transferred, before any decision on expansion can be made. Table 8.2 gives some indication of the nature and scope of different types of competitive advantage and the ease with which they may be transferred between different member states of the EU. What is clear is that the nature of core competences will often dictate the means by which companies choose to compete in a foreign market (their competitive strategies) and their methods of market entry (entry strategies). More will be said of this in the succeeding sections.

Market screening–selection

In deciding whether and where to expand, it will be necessary for any company to identify potential market(s). While this process can often be unstructured, market identification is best managed through a systematic review of foreign environments, which can be formalized around an examination of country- and market-specific factors. In addition to looking at information on market size, future growth, product match, consumer segments etc., a company looking to expand into new markets will also have to model the competitive forces at play in those environments, evaluating levels of competition, barriers to entry etc. 'The relative sophistication of the market(s) in terms of branding, product range and product flexibility will also be relevant in making the judgment on competitive forces and opportunities' (Watters 1995). Such analysis is clearly necessary in order to identify possible opportunities and to answer such basic questions as 'is there a market opportunity?', 'what is the size of that opportunity in market x, y, z?', 'what are the possible barriers to market entry?' Product–market factors may even be incorporated into a market selection grid along with a series of contextual factors hinting at degrees of political and economic risk and the nature of legal, regulatory and cultural environments. Values or scores for each country or region could be assigned to each of the chosen factors and (in a comparative exercise) countries ranked in terms of their market attractiveness and long-run profit potential.

Basic country data is available at the embassies of the countries in question, from trade ministries (e.g at the DTI) and from commercial bureaux–attaches in the target market. Chambers of commerce and business intelligence services also provide basic country information, albeit generally as a (fee-based) commercial service.

Newspapers, news magazines, on-line bureaux and news centres, can also prove the source of valuable inputs. Institutions such as the UN, World Bank, IMF, OECD and WTO publish periodic studies–reports on most European countries.

Industry–market data may be found in various institutional publications such as the European Commission's 'Panorama of EU Industry' or via company reports, trade journals and statistics. Chambers of commerce, embassies, national commercial representations in target markets, trade ministries, banks, distributors, newspapers, customers and suppliers may also be the source of useful information. A mixture of qualitative and quantitative data is likely to apply and analysts must deal with the nature, contradictions and biases of secondary evidence.

The issue of market selection–identification is taken further in Chapter 9 where attention is paid to the analytical and creative processes of defining product markets in Europe and of identifying customer groups (market segments). It is clear, however, that, in profiling and comparing options and in ranking countries in terms of contextual and market-related factors, such examinations play a central part in the rational development of international strategies (Ellis and Williams, 1995, pp. 230–5). Through a rational, systematic analysis of country- and market-related features, contribution is made to the identification of potential opportunities and to the choices surrounding 'competitive' and 'market entry' strategies (see below).

Competitive strategies

Competitive strategies are means by which companies gain marketplace advantages over their rivals. In this sense, a firm will look to compete in foreign markets (and to secure competive advantage) on the basis of one of three 'generic' strategies: the least-cost strategy, the differentiation strategy and the niche strategy (Porter, 1980). Its choice of strategy will be influenced by the structure and dynamics of the target market, by the source(s) of its comparative advantage, and by the time horizons applying to its foreign market interests.

The least-cost strategy involves competing as the lowest-cost operator in the industry. The strategy works best where there is a large demand for standard products and where a company can exploit economies of scale in production and distribution. Sustainable cost leadership means having the lowest cost compared with competitors over time.

The differentiation strategy involves producing a range of well-differentiated products that meet the specific needs of customer segments. These products have unique characteristics and are hard to imitate. By offering uniqueness (product uniqueness, service or delivery uniqueness), manufacturers can charge higher prices.

The niche strategy focuses on a narrowly defined segment of the market in which the aim is to fulfil the needs of special customers in that niche. Within the niche, the firm can look to become a cost leader *(cost focus)* or to exploit differential advantages *(differentiation focus)*. Niche firms possess specialized knowledge which gives them long-term competitive advantage (Porter, 1980).

Table 8.3 attempts to highlight cost-, differentiation- and focus-related assets in relation to different 'strategic drivers'. These drivers are based on an assessment of

Table 8.3 Matching assets to competitive drivers

Assets	Competitive drivers in the EU
Cost related	**Cost leadership drivers**
Access to inputs	Relationships with suppliers. Larger scale production units permitting economies in purchasing.
Appropriate production capacity	Greater potential for scale economies through production in larger units
Location	Operation of fewer large scale operating units in centres offering cost advantages.
Market coverage	Learning curve effects – the more products sold and the wider the coverage the more likely the company will develop cheaper means of production/distribution.
R&D capability	Shared costs of R&D through linkages with other competitors.
Time to market	Greater flexibility in reaction (either technological or market investment) can lead to first mover advantages.
Brand development	Establishment of Euro-brands can reduce duplication in advertising and raise entry barriers.
Differentiation related	**Differentiation drivers**
Technological know-how	Continuous product development required to stay one step ahead of the competition in aggressively competitive markets.
Firm/product reputation	Creates barriers to foreign entry and raises loyalty among existing customer franchise.
Distribution channel	Can protect against entry. Innovation in distribution can change the rules of the game and customer purchasing habits. Joint ventures give access to closed distribution channels.
Market knowledge	Customer awareness essential for targeting differential effort particularly for servicing small specialized markets with specific needs now possible/desirable in the new Europe.
Service network	Differentiation through service becoming more important as products standardize (particularly in industrial sectors).
Marketing personnel	Personnel with wide experiences of European market able to generate better awareness of areas for standardization and adaptation.
Integration	Either with internal units or partners can lead to better responsiveness, improved knowledge and greater flexibility to add value through different parts of the value chain.
Focus related	**Focus drivers**
Geographic spread	'Cherry picking' of markets which offer greatest potential gives rise to better resource allocation.
Portfolio focus	Focus on core strengths means excellence in one area rather than fair performance in several which generally results in easier defence.
Managerial skills	Current management skills may not always transfer to new businesses outside of geographic and product sphere.
General	**General cost drivers**
Information technology	IT as a means of integrating business organizations and improving efficiency.
Financial capacity	Shapes amount of money available for new investments.
Culture	Centralization potential enhanced through the opening up of borders – may not fit with company culture.
Government/union relationships	Government and union goodwill can facilitate expansion/contraction objectives.

Source: Verdin and Williamson (1994, page 12)

those factors now at play in the EU which are having an impact on the strategic choices of firms. Thus, while the nature of assets will have a significant influence on the choice of competitive strategy, it is the exploitation of assets which fit with overall market and industry drivers which will lead to a position of sustainable competitive advantage.

Market entry strategies

Where a business does decide to serve product markets other than in its indigenous local or national market, then it must also choose between a number of different entry modes. In doing so it must establish some method (or combination of methods) drawn from three generic groups: *export entry modes, contractual entry modes and investment entry modes* (see Root, 1987). For different businesses, these different methods will have varying attraction. For example, where a firm's competitive advantage (its core competence) is based on control over technological know-how, this competence may be easily threatened by contractual arrangements (i.e. licensing and joint venture partnerships) which can sometimes lead to technology leakage. In all cases, entry mode decisions are complex and are likely to be influenced by a number of considerations, some of which are captured under the headings of Table 8.4. To examine these issues properly, the following section is dedicated to entry mode decisions and to the strategic options enjoyed by firms looking to expand in Europe. For the reader concerned specifically with the CEE markets, a reminder is provided as to the content of Chapter 7 where examination is made of some of the principal investment options available to Western firms. Once more here, the analysis suggests that the selected entry mode must conform to the particular country, industry, firm and product-related factors faced by the entering firm. This is the essence of the contingency theory of market entry strategies. Each of the available options – exporting, contractual relationships and foreign direct investment (establishing forms of ownership control) – has clear implications for the selecting firm in terms of the level of its resource commitment, the form of its market servicing and the degree of direct control it will enjoy over its European market activities.

Choice of market entry mode(s)

As hinted above, the foreign market entry decision is complicated by many factors and by the wide array of operational strategies available to firms. Each of these operational strategies boasts its own strengths and weaknesses and managers will need to consider these carefully when deciding which to use.

Exporting

Exporting means the sale abroad of an item produced, stored or processed in the supplying firm's home country. In practice, the term covers a variety of alternative

Table 8.4 Factors impacting on the choice of foreign market entry mode and market servicing

Costs	Physical location	Product characteristics	Company resources and objectives	Government intervention
Exporting	**Exporting**	**Exporting**	**Exporting**	**Exporting**
■ Potentially high distribution costs from peripheral location.	■ Known structures and systems in domestic market.	■ Large and bulky products preclusively expensive to export.	■ Exporting is generally considered to be the most cost-effective form of market servicing as it involves limited financial outlay.	■ Domestic governments likely to be supportive of exporting as it raises balance of trade and thus likely to provide support packages.
■ Adding capacity to existing domestic operations leads to scale economies.	■ Physical distance from market can raise questions in consumer's mind regarding ability to deliver.	■ High-technology products may require technical selling capabilities and after-sales service which may be better achieved by the firm itself rather than relying on third parties.	■ Effective management of intermediaries via co-operative links and the development of good working relationships can substantially raise the costs of exporting.	■ Within Europe, free access to markets means government ability to restrict imports severely limited to safety and consumer welfare issues.
■ Domestic production costs rise if products for foreign markets need to be adapted for cultural differences due to down-time and re-tooling.	■ Distance from the market in terms of information and market monitoring (although might be able to overcome difficulties by using the services of market based intermediaries) and thus may not automatically see directions for adaptation and differentiation.	■ Highly differentiated products which can command high prices in the marketplace can withstand the costs of transportation although the differential benefits may be best communicated by company employed sales staff rather than those of an intermediary.	■ Firms often continue to export even when economic factors dictate greater involvement due to habit and familiarity. Indirect exporting is generally used by those firms 'dabbling' in foreign markets and selling excess capacity.	■ Exporting still not likely to be favoured where access to public procurement contracts desirable due to continued local preference.
■ Domestic production costs may be higher or lower than those pertaining in foreign markets owing to differences in the local price of resources.				

343

Table 8.4 *continued*

Costs	Physical location	Product characteristics	Company resources and objectives	Government intervention
Foreign investment ■ Set-up costs may be high. ■ Duplication of effort in business functions (e.g. finance, marketing personnel). ■ Local manufacturing costs may be lower. ■ Shorter transportation distances.	**Foreign investment** ■ Close to the market and customer needs and wants more obvious. ■ Operating environment alien in early stages of investment which may lead to cultural misunderstanding.	**Foreign investment** ■ Offers greater potential for monitoring changing needs and demands and differentiating products accordingly. ■ Shorter distribution channels for bulky products. ■ Locally placed for providing technical support. ■ Closer to foreign customers and thus easier monitoring of competitor technology and differentiation.	**Foreign direct investment** ■ Foreign direct investment involves maximum commitment to foreign markets and can be highly resource intensive where the investment takes the form of a manufacturing facility. ■ Only firms seeking to expand international activities in a proactive manner are likely to contemplate foreign investment. ■ Firms seeking a fast return on investment may opt for a takeover rather than a green-field operation due to the existing operation's ability to generate rapid profits.	**Foreign direct investment** ■ Freedom of capital movements in Europe means freedom of investment without government intervention. ■ Regional support for investment in economically deprived areas.
Contractual arrangements ■ Share risks with another player. ■ High management costs for establishing and maintaining the relationship. ■ Lower distribution costs because close to the market.	**Contractual arrangements** ■ Local partner helps overcome cultural and physical distance. ■ Reliance on local partner may stifle learning and make increased commitment hard to achieve later on.	**Contractual arrangements** ■ Where product technology is the essence of a company's competitive advantage, contractual arrangements may be less popular as they can lead to technology leakage. ■ Quality may be difficult to maintain where production is carried out by third parties.	**Contractual arrangements** ■ Resource commitment can be lowered through contractual arrangements and be spread between more than one firm. ■ Relies on the ability of organizations to work co-operatively, and choice of partner critical.	**Contractual arrangements** ■ Favourable attitude towards contractual arrangements shown by EC Commission owing to technology sharing potential.

options including those involving independent intermediaries and those where the firm takes control of all operations. In turn, these distinctions throw up three important issues:

1. there are various modes of exporting for which cost structures and risk vary enormously;

2. different modes of exporting offer the organization disparate degrees of control;

3. various types of market intermediaries exist to support the export activities of firms.

Indirect exporting

With *indirect exporting*, an exporting business uses home-based middlemen or market intermediaries to sell its goods in foreign markets. This means that the firm does not have to deal directly with foreign firms or customers and can invest relatively little in establishing a (foreign) market presence. Intermediaries may or may not take title to the goods and may or may not work exclusively for the exporting firm. Such depends on the terms of agreement with the manufacturer and on the type of intermediary. For example, export houses and trading companies will tend to buy from the firm and sell products abroad for profit. Products will be represented along with those of various non-competitive manufacturers. By contrast, confirming houses sell on behalf of the manufacturer on a commission basis providing various export services.

Indirect exporting can be an attractive option for firms exporting for the first time with (a) little export experience and/or (b) little or no knowledge of the chosen market(s). However, by operating through intermediaries, companies depend on the ability of third parties to actively sell and promote their products abroad and will suffer from a lack of contact with the (foreign) customer. Although (foreign) sales can be achieved through these forms of exporting, it can also be shown that indirect methods of exporting yield the lowest levels of foreign market penetration.

Direct exporting

Through direct exporting, a business looks to sell directly to customers in foreign markets. One option is to set up an export department and to service the needs of the customer directly from the home market. Another option includes the use of middlemen based in the overseas market. Such middlemen may include 'local' sales agents (appointed by the manufacturer) or foreign distributors. This is sometimes described as direct agent–distributor exporting. Agents will generally take orders on a commission basis and will assume no risk or responsibility for the product. Foreign distributors will normally take ownership of the goods and sell them on for profit. Territory exclusivity is normally required by these (overseas) intermediaries. Companies may also use (establish) their own sales organizations in overseas markets. In this case, sales branches (offices) and subsidiaries can be separated out as two distinct options, not so much because they offer distinct services, but because their legal status differs.

Whereas a branch is regarded in law as a direct extension of the parent firm into a foreign country, sales subsidiaries are individual companies in their own right. Rather than sell the company's products on commission they, like distributors, buy stock from group manufacturing units and sell it on for profit. Importantly, therefore, sales and marketing subsidiaries provide a channel for internal company transfer pricing.

In whatever form, local sales establishments can 'recruit local staff who are experts in the nuances of the local market, [who are] fluent in the language of the host country, and who possess wide-ranging contacts with local businesses and institutions' (Bennett, 1997, p. 220). They can also offer a route to the better co-ordination of marketing and after-sales service and can help to overcome some of the many difficulties in finding, managing and controlling local commission agents and independent distributors (Bennett, 1997, p. 220).

Exporting firms

In attempting to identify and exploit foreign market opportunities by export, firms may be judged to be either proactive or reactive. Proactive firms engage in a deliberate search for export opportunities, establishing proper systems for the export function and for procuring foreign sales. Reactive firms have a more passive attitude in seeking exporting opportunities and are typically characterized by opportunistic or accidental export involvement. It is clear that these two types reflect different outlooks and patterns of export behaviour, with the former actively canvassing for export business and the latter 'picking up' sporadic export orders. In this context, it is interesting to note that almost all models of export development (e.g. Crick, 1995) view the firm's involvement in export operations as an evolutionary and sequential process (see the discussion in Leonidou and Katsikeas, 1996). Pulling various models together, we might differentiate between exporting firms in the 'pre-engagement phase' (where firms are selling their goods solely in the domestic market but may be considering export activity), the 'initial phase' (where export activity is passive and sporadic) and the 'mature phase' (where firms are active pro-curers of regular export business).

For most organizations, especially those lacking previous experience and organization in foreign markets, export-based strategies have clear attraction. They do not require a great deal of investment or carry a great deal of risk. It is clear, however, that organic development of a business from scratch, through the export of products, management skills and investments, can be a slow and difficult task and that other development paths based on either contractal entry modes or some form of equity investment abroad may provide for quicker progress (see Blackwell, 1980). It is also clear that many firms that initially expand their product sales out of the company's domestic market progress to more committed forms of international business.

Contractual arrangements

Firms may enter new markets by forming (non-equity) contractual associations with local entities. Such associations may include technical agreements and service contracts, which are touched on elsewhere in this book. As a category, contractual entry modes also encompass licensing and franchise agreements, contract manufacturing agreements and (non-equity) joint ventures. These entry modes are explored below.

Licensing

Licensing agreements involve a company (or licensor) granting rights under contract to intangible property such as patents, copyrights, trademarks or procedures. Agreements specify the terms of use and the payment for use. In the case of an international licensing agreement, the owner of the property (the licensor) grants rights to an overseas firm (the licensee). Such agreements can offer the licensor a number of advantages, including regular income (from the licensing of its property) and inexpensive development of foreign market interests. Licensing can also be used where impediments exist to more direct forms of investment. For example, where government restrictions militate against the firm choosing any other option, where it is not technically feasible to establish a direct market presence and/or where the limited resources of the firm prevent other forms of market servicing being followed, licensing can be an attractive option. Licensing may also be regarded as a transitory mode offering the licensor the opportunity to test demand and product acceptance (with a view to subsequent direct investment) and/or to gain a foothold in a competitive sector.

Notwithstanding these benefits and the fact that licensees carry much of the risk of failure, numerous uncertainties remain. Because licensing involves a market sale of embodied knowledge (e.g. technology) to a host country producer, there is a risk that the agreement will create a competitor. For example, a licensee may use acquired knowledge in ways which have not been paid for to create new products in competition with the licensor. The danger is loss of technological advantage which is the lifeblood for firms in many sectors. Problems may also exist in terms of licensee quality standards, the basis and continuity of royalty payments, and the circumstances under which the agreement may be terminated. Consequently, many licensing agreements look to detail criteria for quality, payments and terminations in exacting license contracts.

Franchising

Franchising is a form of licensing prevalent in the services and retail. Rather than a company simply granting the rights to its commercial–industrial–intellectual property to another business, franchising involves selling a total business concept or format. In return for an up-front payment and succeeding royalty payments, the franchisor provides the franschisee with some combination of its name, trademark, methods, equipment and/or display materials. As well as providing these ingredients to run the business (and various forms of training and management support), the franchisor may also impose a set of rules as to how the franchisee should run the business. In most cases, franchisees must follow standardized business techniques and are subject to some control by the franchisor. In illustration (although its case has many unique features), the Italian clothing retailer Benetton has a complex system of controls over its 'franchised' retail outlets. All Benetton outlets ('franchise' holders) are required to sell the company's products on an exclusive basis, to follow the company's basic merchandising concepts, and to choose from a set menu of shop layouts and fixture selections. Traditionally, these formats have been seen to promote open and colourful displays. 'Franchisees' have also had to work under a centrally determined pricing policy and to adhere to standard opening hours. By such mechanisms, the company has looked to retain quite tight control over its merchandising and its identity in the 'global' high street (Jarillo and Martinez, 1988, p. 75).

Whereas many licensing agreements are set up on an *ad hoc* basis, often initiated by the licensee, franchising represents a dedicated approach to earning management fees on an international scale and a committed approach to expanding geographically. In this way, American companies such as McDonald's and Kentucky Fried Chicken (fast food), Chem-Dry (dry-cleaning) and AlphaGraphics (see Case Study 8.4) have all secured an extensive international franchise network throughout Europe. Indeed, a large number of North American firms have viewed franchising as 'a valuable channel for transatlantic penetration of the European market' (Chapman, 1997). Many European firms, including Benetton (clothing), The Body Shop (cosmetics) and OBI (the German-based DIY superstore), have also acquired an international reputation and presence through the franchising option.

Burlage (1997) highlights that, apart from the viability of the franchise concept, the success of a franchise hinges on the calibre and commitment of the franchisees. He notes that international franchisors, in particular, have often failed to pay close enough attention to the experience, commitment and funding of franchisees in new markets, 'selling, or rather mis-selling, their franchise rights to the first willing investors'. This problem hints at some of the basic disadvantages of international franchising. The commitment and quality standards of franchisees cannot be guaranteed and the geographical distance of the firm from its foreign franchisees can make control over quality and marketing quite difficult. A franchisor may also have to penetrate a foreign market by setting up a master franchisee and giving that 'local' entity the rights for that country or region. Much of the success of the franchise strategy will then come to rest with the ability of this organization to develop an efficient network of subfranchisees. For lesser-known businesses brands, it can also be difficult to attract investors. Even where investment can be attracted to the venture, adjustments or adaptations to the product–service may be required given variations in local tastes and preferences. Despite these problems, there are many examples of successful international franchises and international franchising is now widespread in the EU where franchising itself accounts for 1.3 million jobs and an annual turnover approximating €75 billion. Traditional areas for international franchises such as fast food, retail, cleaning and maintenance services are now being joined by such fast-growth areas as consultancy, computer and internet services (Chapman, 1997). Such growth reflects the many advantages of international franchising. As with other forms of licensing, the costs and risks associated with foreign market access are minimized (with franchisees assuming much of the capital risk) and international presence can be achieved relatively quickly.

CASE STUDY 8.4 AlphaGraphics expands in Europe via franchising

From a foundation of 250 print shops in the United States, AlphaGraphics, the Arizona-based company, has established an important European bridgehead, and it has used franchising as the key to its strategy.

It has twenty-five of its fifty overseas outlets in Europe, and has plans for expansion in countries such as Germany and Russia.

'Printing lends itself to franchising because, with our production scheduling system, there is nothing we don't know about how much turn-around time is needed for each job', says MaryPat Sloan, managing director of AlphaGraphics' Moscow operation.

'Employee issues, accounting, how much a machine costs to get into a building; these will all vary from country to country. But once that machine is in, you are in the AlphaGraphics system.'

The print shops are interlinked on the group's world digital communications and document transmission network. 'It's a nightmare to trail off for a sales trip to Japan and cart a mass of business cards and manuals', comments Andrew Pindar, chief executive of GA Pindar, master franchisee for Britain and Ireland. 'We transfer information electronically, print it locally and have it waiting for the sales director in Tokyo on arrival.'

This helps maintain confidentiality, something which the physical movement of documents cannot guarantee. In advance of a Russian sovereign bond issue on the London market, for example, 'London will transmit to us the proofing documentation', says Sloan. 'We can ensure the wrong people don't see it and that it is delivered to the right people.'

In countries such as Germany, sophisticated technology does not ensure such advantages. 'There are quality print and copyshops on every street corner', says George Pasveer, a Dutch national who is managing director of AlphaGraphics in Germany for Drescher, the German master franchisee. But Drescher, one of Europe's largest commercial printers, looks to AlphaGraphics to introduce US levels of service.

'Customer service is an under-used concept in Germany', said Pasveer. 'Fast turnaround time, catering to smaller customers rather than taking large-scale orders, a onestop shop from design to delivery, these are all areas where standards from the US can do well.'

'We print manuals for Motorola, and even doublesided business cards for Xerox – with one side in Cyrillic script', says Sloan of some typical Moscow orders. 'But teenagers come in for calendars made up with photographs of their girlfriends, or you get the local policeman wanting his car documents laminated. We deal with a cross-section.'

The Russian franchise has a five-year plan to invest $34 million in new print shops throughout the country. In Germany, AlphaGraphics which is based in Rutesheim, near Stuttgart, has a contract to set up sixty outlets in the next ten years.

AlphaGraphics has global annual turnover of $270 million, and last year advertised for master franchisees with capital of about $1 million in various European countries.

'I expect to be signing agreements in Greece and Switzerland within two months, and in Italy and France by the end of the summer', says William Edwards, senior vice-president at the company's headquarters in Tucson.

New franchisees spend a month training in the US. Thereafter there is 'a lot of hand-holding for the first half-year of business', says Pindar, 'answering questions like "what is a laminator?" and so on'. A note of caution is sounded by Pasveer, however, on franchisee training and the US approach to Europe. 'Americans should be coming to Europe for training, not Europeans going to the US', he says. 'Business is different here: languages, methods, markets. There has to be a concentrated approach to development.'

A balance of styles may be hastened by necessity. 'The US needs Europe', says Pasveer. 'The market is here. In five years it will be vital for businesses to be sending their computer files for graphics, not carrying everything around. There is a beautiful future.'

Source: The European, 24 April 1997

Contractual joint ventures

The various types of licensing arrangement share one common element: they all depend on the establishment of contracts with independent operators. Control is achieved via contractual arrangements rather than ownership, placing great emphasis on the choice of organization and the establishment of good, legal and workable contracts. In this sense, the types of licensing agreement previously examined can be associated with 'non-equity' or 'co-operative' joint ventures (JVs). These agreements (normally based on contract) involve the promotion of co-operation between independent entities but not (co-)investment in a separate commercial entity. Where co-operation extends into the creation of a separate commercial entity and involves equity arrangements, we are confronted with a different and more traditional category of joint venture examined later in this chapter (the equity-based JV).

Like strategic alliances (see below), contractual JVs can be thought of as finite co-operative ventures involving two or more organizations. Such ventures will often take on an international character and may represent a means of developing new links in new (geographic) markets through contractual (non-equity) association.

Strategic alliances–partnerships

While many contractual JVs are described as strategic alliances, the alliance concept incorporates a variety of co-operative arrangements between potential or actual competitors (see Vyas *et al.*, 1995). While alliances may often be based on some form of equity investment, the term may be directly applied to circumstances where two or more competitors (without equity association) work towards a specific strategic goal. Very often, this goal is associated with the development of a new product or process, but intellectual–technology sharing, cross-licensing and distribution arrangements can all be encompassed by the term.

Like the other approaches examined, alliances make it possible to enter new markets using the distribution networks and the specific knowledge of local partners. As Garrette and Dussauge observe:

> Thanks to the contributions of these partners, less effort and time has to be put into learning how to succeed in very different local environments, thus allowing for simultaneous and fast entry into multiple countries (cited in UNCTAD, 1999)

It is clear, however, that alliances/partnerships are usually entered into for reasons other than market access. According to Doz *et al.* (1986), more typically, the driving forces behind such coalitions are:

- the desire to share costs and risks in developing new products or processes,
- the modification of competitive terms between actual or potential rivals,
- the rationalization of production and sales operations,
- the desire to take advantage of complementary skills and capabilities, and/or
- the desire to benefit from increased economies of scale.

Strategic alliances have emerged as an important part of the industrial landscape in Europe, for example in the pharmaceuticals sector, in the various computer and communications technologies and in the international airline business. Firms such as Rhône-Poulenc, Ericsson, Deutsche Telekom, Cap Gemini and Lufthansa have all turned to intra-European and inter-continental alliances as a means of strengthening their competitive positions in regional and global markets. The multinational consortium, Airbus Industrie (AI) also provides demonstration of a successful multi-party alliance in the civil aerospace industry. The four Airbus partners – British Aerospace (BAe), Deutsche Aerospace (Dasa), Aerospatiale of France and Spain's Casa – have used their partnering to match their merged US rival, Boeing-McDonnell Douglas in the global market for civil aircraft. Firms such as Thomson, Bull, Philips and Siemens have also been involved in multiple research-based partnerships, encountering each other in many of the core technology projects of the EU-backed ESPRIT programme. For these and other companies, strategic partnering has provided a means of entering new markets, spreading costs and risks, combining skills for new product development and building critical mass.

While many alliances will continue to be aimed at capturing scale economies for 'defensive' strategies, European firms, keen to expand their international coverage, are likely to continue to see advantages in entering into such coalitions with other industry players in an attempt to pursue more dynamic strategies. Whether firms are engaged in defensive or offensive efforts, alliances are likely to be central to long-term strategic success. As put by one set of commentators:

> [I]n a changeable world of rapidly globalising markets and industries – a world of converging consumer tastes, rapidly spreading technology, escalating fixed costs and growing protectionism – globalisation mandates alliances, makes them absolutely essential to strategy. . . . In the fluid global market place, it is no longer possible or desirable for single organizations to be entirely self-sufficient. Collaboration is the value of the future. Alliances are the structure for the future. (Bleeke and Ernst, 1993)

Contract manufacturing agreements

This method involves the product being produced or assembled by an independent manufacturer in the foreign market under contract with the firm. Production may be marketed locally or returned to the principal for distribution in its home and/or third-country markets. The difficulty of this method lies primarily in finding a local manufacturer with the capabilities to produce sufficient quantities of the product and to the standard required. Even where such manufacturers can be found, direct supervisory control is unlikely. The main advantage, however, is that the company can avoid the huge costs associated with establishing their own manufacturing facility and yet exploit cheaper production costs. It may be particularly attractive for firms when the host market is not considered large enough to justify substantial (direct) investment and where there may be advantages in marketing a product as being locally produced.

Investment entry modes

Entry modes under this heading involve ownership of production units (or other facilities) in the overseas market, based on some form of equity investment (see Root, 1987). Many expanding businesses opt for ownership in some or all of their international ventures. This can be achieved via: acquisitions, (equity-based) joint ventures, green-field site developments and/or the establishment of wholly owned overseas subsidiaries. In many ways, the decision to establish ownership of facilities in the overseas market can be seen as a deeper-level commitment to a foreign market environment and as an investment in higher-level control of foreign operations.

Joint ventures (equity based)

Joint ventures (or at least equity-based joint ventures) involve the creation of a separate business entity under the joint control and ownership of two or more partners (see Chapter 7). Although many joint ventures (JVs) involve equal shareholdings, this need not be the case with many examples 'led' by one dominant party. Equally, some joint ventures involve 'passive' partners who invest money in the operation without taking an active role in its management.

As with licensing, joint ventures involve firms pooling their resources and combining critical assets, in particular technology from the entrant and local knowledge from the market-based partner. This can be greatly advantageous with many possible resources adding to the synergy of business linkages: e.g. complementary product portfolios (offering scope economy advantages), service networks, entrenched distribution networks (lowering distribution costs) and local business contacts. International joint ventures also permit firms to reduce their capital outlay in achieving international expansion and to spread risks with other players. This has been especially significant in the internationalization of many SMEs for whom joint venture agreements have been a popular option. In a joint venture, a firm's resource commitment is minimized relative to a wholly owned entry mode because of the shared resource commitment between firms. Joint ventures also provide an opportunity for the firm to learn about foreign market environments before independent investment–involvement. Increasing costs of R&D are also a significant factor behind the popularity of 'research joint ventures', defined as 'organizations[s], jointly controlled by two or more parent institutions whose purpose is to engage in research and development activities' (Vonortas, 1997, p. 577). The costs of technological development are ever-increasing, making it difficult for individual firms to withstand the costs of developing new technologies on their own. Equally, as firms rationalize and limit their own areas of technological strength, joint ventures allow them to co-operate with organizations in more diverse technological areas for the formulation of new basic technologies. As noted by Ohmae (1989):

> Today's products rely on so many different critical technologies that most companies can no longer maintain cutting-edge sophistication in all of them ... no one player can master all of them.

Several of the case notes that follow in this chapter highlight the usefulness of JVs in achieving various business goals, including expansion into new geographic markets, knowledge-sharing and product-market diversification. The European Commission also recognizes the value of joint ventures in promoting cross-border trade and investment, technology transfer, and (international) small business development. For example, the discussion of EU enterprise policy in Chapter 5, highlighted EU-backed SME information services such as (BC-NET) dedicated to creating international business links and venture co-operation.

Joint ventures are not, however, without their risks. Failures are common. Conflicting objectives between partners, conflicting business cultures and hidden agendas can all lead to the early demise of the venture, emphasizing the importance of careful screening and selection procedures (see Table 8.5). Similarly, continuance of a competitive rather than co-operative ethos in the management of the joint venture may mean that compromises cannot be reached and common objectives not found. For such reasons, many companies will develop joint ventures only after previous experience with 'partners', for example through a preceding distributorship or licensing agreement.

Despite these potential problems and pitfalls, joint ventures are now seen as one of the most popular answers to short-term growth and to overseas market expansion throughout the EEA and wider European market. European firms, keen to expand their international coverage and their technological strengths, have seen broad advantages in entering into such agreements in an attempt to maximize synergies in their strategy development and in order to quickly diversify into new markets. Joint ventures have been especially prevalent in the capital and knowledge intensive industries. For example, both Hoechst and Rhône-Poulenc (the merging pharmaceuticals and industrial chemicals businesses) have formed significant joint venture partnerships with each other and with other major participants involved in the life-sciences and industrial chemicals businesses. Hoechst's ventures have included its agrochemical business AgrEvo (with Schering) and Dade Behring (its diagnostics business with Dade International). The German giant has also formed a joint venture in the textiles dye sector with Bayer (DyStar) and Targor (a joint venture in the polypropylene sector with BASF). These ventures stand at the heart of a complex web of strategic partnerships and technology alliances. Since its privatization in 1993, Rhône-Poulenc has also formed many joint ventures in order to strengthen its many businesses. The Paris headquartered business has a 50% interest in Merial (genetics) and Pasteur Merieux-MSD (vaccines), two joint venture businesses formed with Merck. The company's 50% interest in Centeon, its blood plasma venture business with Hoechst, is now to be absorbed into the new business entity Aventis, the result of a progressive business combination between the two companies.

France Telecom provides example of another European firm which has made use of joint ventures (and strategic acquisitions) in order to grow its business in Europe. The context of telecommunications market liberalization has provided the firm with new opportunities to expand from its French market base and into a wider range of communications markets (Case Study 8.5). France Telecom joins many

Table 8.5 Joint venture design and management: some recommendations

Stage	Recommendations
Determining the need for co-operative alliances	Concentrate on strategic gaps (e.g. technology, distribution, quality of inputs, co-operative alliances, local market knowledge). Ensure venture is being entered into for positive strategic reasons and not just because the firm feels obliged to jump on the bandwagon. Ensure joint venture fits with firms' overall objectives (defence, expansion and rationalization). Look beyond economic and technical acquisition to learning, knowledge and skill acquisition. Consider risks and resource pooling.
Partner selection	Cast the net widely. Don't just enter into ventures with known organizations (e.g. existing suppliers) because they are there. Review various alternatives to find best match. Look for synergies and complementarities. If firms are too closely aligned, there is the risk of on-going secrecy and a lack of transparency. Assess company culture as well as economic factors. Look at traditional lines of action and historical developments.
Selection and negotiation	Bring everything to the table, as a way of building trust. If you are honest and open, then partner more likely to follow suit. Determine the importance of the JV to the partner. If it is peripheral for them, but significant for you, different commitment balances may lead to problems later. Look beyond obvious objectives and try and determine if the partner has a hidden agenda (e.g. pre-emptive strategy leading to full takeover). If you suspect hidden motives say so. Set realistic objectives. The early stages of the venture are likely to require a lot of adaptation and re-negotiation so don't expect a quick fix.
Management	Involve people in both organizations across a wide array of functions. The more people involved and committed the stronger the relationship. Be prepared to re-negotiate and adapt. As partners learn about each other the balance of power and decision-making may have to change and overall objectives be re-formulated. Don't hold hostages unless you can do this on a mutual basis. If you hold back technology or knowledge without the partner having a hostage in return, the venture will fail. Invest good people. If the skills and knowledge of the managers is marginal, so will be profits.

other telecoms and media giants such as Deutsche Telekom in making use of co-operative ventures in order to capitalize on Europe's growing telephony and Internet markets. Case Study 8.6 on Davidson-Marley BV, should also be read at this stage. This case highlights many of the triggers for partnership-based ventures and illustrates several of the inherent challenges in establishing and managing co-operative business development.

CASE STUDY 8.5 France Telecom's European growth strategy

France Telecom is one of the world's leading telecommunications carriers, with 1998 consolidated operating revenues of FRF161.7 billion (€24.6 billion), 33.7 million telephone lines in service and operations in more than fifty countries. In addition to local and long-distance telephony, France Telecom provides businesses and consumers with data, wireless, online, Internet, cable-TV, broadcast and value-added services. The 62% state-owned company held an initial public offering in October 1997. The company is now listed on the Paris and New York stock exchanges. At the start of the year 2000, its market value was estimated at £103 billion, putting it ahead of rivals British Telecom (£68.4 billion); Telefonica of Spain (£59 billion) and Telecom Italia (£57.2 billion). Only two 'European' telecoms companies could claim to be bigger – Deutsche Telekom, with a market capitalization value of £161 billion, and Vodafone Airtouch, with a market value of £157.4 billion (Source: Datastream Primark).

To benefit fully from the liberalization of the European telecommunications market, France Telecom is pursuing a European growth strategy based on fixed, mobile and Internet services developed with local partners (in collaborative ventures) in national markets throughout Europe. To this aim, it has made several key acquisitions and has set up a welter of joint venture and co-operative agreements throughout the European Economic Area. Since 1996, start-up companies have been launched, with national and international partners, in Belgium (Mobistar), Denmark (Mobilix), Switzerland (Multilink), Italy (Wind), the Netherlands (Dutchtone) and Spain (Uni2). These companies are on their way to becoming full service alternate carriers, offering converging fixed, mobile and Internet services. For example, Mobilix in Denmark (owned 54% by France Telecom) is making inroads into national residential and business sectors by offering competitive products and services in key service markets. The company has also recently concluded a partnership agreement with Sonae of Portugal so as to develop global telecommunications operations in Portugal. This agreement will enable the development of activities that will position the telecom provider as a key

player in January 2000, when the Portuguese telecommunications market is fully liberalized.

France Telecom has also consolidated its European market position through joint ventures with cable operators. Ventures have been launched with Casema (Holland) and NTL of the UK, in which France Telecom has taken a small equity stake. Given its aim to create full-service fixed-mobile-Internet carriers in Europe, the company has also moved to acquire a number of Internet access providers. For example, in November 1998, France Telecom acquired the Internet service provider EuroNet BV in Belgium, which is developing operations in Benelux. Through this subsidiary, France Telecom launched its Wanadoo Internet gateway service in Belgium, taking the subscriber base (in four European countries) to above 1 million users. Strategically, one of the company's present targets is to build a new high-speed Internet network with the assistance of its affiliated national operators, providing end-to-end connectivity between forty cities in sixteen European countries by the year 2000.

Another aspect of France Telecom's international strategy is to offer transnational services to multinationals. The business maintains a one-third ownership stake in the nascent Global One joint venture with Deutsche Telekom and US firm Sprint Corp. This venture provides a full range of international voice and data services to multinational companies. Wider relations with Deutsche Telekom are, however, under review. This follows DT's failed takeover bid for Telecom Italia in 1999, a move which angered France Telecom and some of DT's other European partners. According to the French, the move for Telecom Italia (headed off by Olivetti) broke the terms of an established bilateral co-operation agreement between the French and German heavyweights. It is unclear as to whether both parties will continue together in the Global One venture, although the company is successfully expanding its customer base. Prior to this fall-out, the France Telecom–Deutsche Telekom alliance was one of the world's leading sectoral alliances and was characterized by significant cross-shareholdings and co-investment in emerging markets.

CASE STUDY 8.6 Davidson-Marley BV

Background to the two parties

Marley Plc is one of the leading manufacturers of building materials in the UK with several international manufacturing subsidiaries. While the main areas of its business are in the construction industry, the company also boasts a well-established operation supplying quality components to the UK car industry.

The car industry has changed significantly in recent years. Many companies are now looking to sole sourcing of many of their supply needs as a means of simplifying buying processes and tying in organizations to meet their specific needs. Time frames for delivery and product development are also shortening, and there is a growing trend towards closer integration of supply and assembly and the pursuit of common goals and adding-value objectives. Manufacturers are also devolving design responsibilities to their suppliers for sub-assemblies, in return for single supplier status.

Davidson Instrument Panel is only one of thirty-three divisions of the US Textron conglomerate. With its two sister companies, Interior Trim and Exterior Trim, it makes up Davidson-Textron. Davidson-Textron is the largest supplier of instrument panels to the US market.

For some years Marley operated as a licensee of Davidson, using its technology to produce instrument panel skins and foam injections.

Ford approaches Marley

Marley had been producing instrument panels for Ford Sierras in the UK for some time. With the development of its plant in Genk, in the Netherlands, it approached Marley about the possibility of supplying instrument panels for their new world car. However, Ford's policy was clearly outlined as one of global sourcing and, although Marley was keen to develop its automotive business (and thus reduce its dependence on cylicial demand patterns in the construction industry), it was aware that it did not have the capacity, alone, to provide a global sourcing solution for Ford.

Marley were also concerned about the risks associated with the venture. There was no guarantee that the Ford venture would be successful.

The initiation of the joint venture

Against this backdrop, the possibility of a joint venture seemed attractive to Marley. It would allow them to reduce their risk, and it would extend global sourcing potential for Ford. For Davidson, there were equally sound reasons for contemplating an alliance. They were keen to expand their business beyond the USA, particularly in Europe where they had little presence.

The venture also offered Marley a number of associated benefits, not least the potential to learn about new manufacturing and business techniques from Davidson which had a proven track record of flexible manufacturing, workforce flexibility, teamwork and total quality management.

Location of the plant

Plant location was carefully considered. The first objective was to locate near to Ford so that just-in-time delivery could be successfully implemented. However, the companies were also aware of the importance of establishing in a position proximate to other car manufacturers which would potentially open up its market to new opportunities. The Born site, forty-five minutes from Ford, is also close to Volkswagen, Audi, Mercedes and NedCar and although these companies currently source much of their instrumentation internally, the joint venture is well placed to take advantage of any change in their policies. Marley have, therefore, also established a small marketing company responsible for assessing new business opportunities.

Getting the management right

It was decided by both parties to employ a local manager with considerable experience in manufacturing. As it was deemed important for the organization to 'fit into' the local culture, it was believed important for a local to drive the company's development. The recruited human resource manager and facility manager were also Dutch, the former boasting experience in a Japanese subsidiary in the Netherlands. These three individuals were charged with the responsibility of recruiting the 150–200 strong workforce, although strategies for recruitment, training and responsibility had been decided on earlier by representatives from the two parents. This led to some conflict in the early stages between the local managers and the parents, the former finding it difficult to operate freely within the strict guidelines established by the owner organizations.

Both parents committed skilled workers to the venture for a period of time to facilitate the smooth transfer of technology and know-how. It was strongly felt that this process should be rapid so as to allow local managers to quickly take on a feeling of ownership.

With local managers responsible for the long-term development of Davidson-Marley BV, there is a belief that they will carve their own career paths within the 'child' organization, separate from concerns about the future development of the two parent groups. This is believed to severely reduce the likelihood of conflict between the two parents.

Organizational structures

Davidson-Marley BV is a flexible organization, with flat structures (no more than four hierarchical layers) organized on the basis of teamwork and shared responsibility. Much training takes place 'on the job' by associates which were sent to Davidson's Canadian plant for an initial period to learn about the systems and structures to be employed. Workers are involved in all aspects of the business with training courses being run on the company's relationships with its parents, customers and the country.

The company, through its flexible manufacturing technologies and sequential delivery procedures, is focused on lean manufacturing and distribution. In order to enable a fuller understanding of the demands of their prime customer, employees are also sent to the Ford plant to understand the nature of Ford's production processes and thus their customer's demands. This is helping to strengthen links between Davidson-Marley and Ford.

Joint venture survival

Both of the parents of the joint venture are aware of what it takes to make a joint venture work:

1. shared objectives (a joint mission);
2. co-operation as equals (based on parity, no domination or paternalism);
3. openness, mutual trust and respect of others as persons and their values, capabilities and objective understanding of their intentions;
4. building on each other's strengths;
5. reducing each other's limitations;
6. each has something the other needs (resources, access etc.);
7. pooled capabilities and resources permit taking on tasks neither could alone;
8. two-way flow of communication (breakthrough of communication blocks);
9. mutually perceived benefits;
10. commitment of leadership and middle management to find some shared values, without ignoring the fact that they are not identical;
11. co-learning flexibility;
12. a win-win orientation.

Implications for European strategy development

The above review of the Davidson-Marley BV joint venture raises a number of important points:

1. Many firms in the modern environment are reluctant to go into new ventures alone. In such a highly competitive environment, sharing risks can bring great rewards and mean individual companies are not unduly exposed to problems associated with business failure.

2. Managing joint ventures is far more than simply identifying joint opportunities. It is about committing resources and effort to attain mutually beneficial outcomes. This requires time, effort and good people. A failure to dedicate sufficient resources will ultimately result in failure.

3. A critical aspect of a successful joint venture is its people. Not only does the venture require good management, but in a European context, managers who can successfully operate in the local environment. By recruiting local managers into the venture, Davidson and Marley were demonstrating a willingness to be adaptive to local cultural nuances. Neither firm is Dutch, and therefore some degree of personnel sensitivity at an operating level is essential.

4. Equity joint ventures of this kind involve the creation of a separate entity which needs to develop a personality and business culture of its own. It is interesting to note that one of the only areas of conflict which has arisen is that between the par-

ents and local management. By attempting to enforce tight rules on the local operation the parents have frustrated the process of the company developing its own way of doing things. Nevertheless, the parents have shown a degree of sensitivity here recognizing that once managers from the parent firm have transferred their knowledge and know-how, they should leave the business up to the managers on the ground.

5. The final checklist in the case suggests that European managers proposing a joint venture must keep in mind the purpose and intent of the

venture as the business develops. It is only in this way that they can preserve the longevity of co-operation without seeking ways of sub-optimising and using the venture for their own ends.

Based on two case studies:

Schuler, R. and Van Slujis, E. (1992) Davidson-Marley BV: establishing and operating an international joint venture, *European Management Journal*, **10**(4) December, 428–36.

Schuler, R., Dowling, P. and De Cieri, H. (1992) The formation of an international joint venture, *European Management Journal*, **10**(3) September, 304–9.

(Mergers and) acquisitions

Acquisition refers to the process by which a firm controlling one business (or set of businesses) acquires control of another by gaining a majority of its voting shares. This may involve the first firm bidding for and buying the shares of a second for cash or swapping them for shares in the acquiring company (an exchange offer). This is sometimes described as a 'takeover' and may be 'hostile' or 'friendly' in nature. Larger transactions may be structured as 'business combinations', leading to newly merged entities managed by executives from both parent firms. This is possible where firms are of equal stature and where there is mutual interest in creating a new business and management structure. To a degree, this confuses the distinction between acquisitions and *mergers*, which are the result of the mutual agreement of two firms to come together. Indeed, merger and acquisition (M&A) activities are generally bracketed together.

Through mergers and acquisitions, firms can move into entirely different industries–markets (unrelated diversification). Where business strategy focuses on expanding the scope of the organization within its existing industry (related diversification), firms have two basic options. First, they may acquire others at the same stage in the production process, something refered to as *horizontal integration*. Second, firms may 'acquire' other firms in the same industry but at different stages in the production of a good, something referred to as *vertical integration*. In cases of forward *vertical integration*, the acquired business will be further down the production line towards the consumer (i.e. a vehicle manufacturer acquiring a dealership). In cases of backward vertical integration, the acquired business will be further up the production line towards the raw-material stage (i.e. a publishing company acquiring a pulp and paper producer).

The 'acquisition' (or takeover) of former SOEs in Central–Eastern Europe by Western businesses was considered at some length in Chapter 7 (CEE transition). In the present context, it is clear that such investment offers clear possibilities for indigineous and 'outsider' businesses to develop market presence in EEA economies and to diversify into new markets. European giants such as Danone, British Airways, Allianz and Alcatel (see Case Study 8.7) have all achieved significant business growth through acquisitions, integrating many smaller companies into their grow-

---

CASE STUDY 8.7 Alcatel grows through acquisitions

Alcatel NV, the French-based but Dutch-registered telecommunications equipment giant, provides a successful example of a transnational European firm using acquisition as a means to expand both inside the EEA and in the wider global market (see Charles, 1996). Since its merger (as CIT Alcatel) with ITT in 1986, Alcatel NV has developed a leadership position in several telecoms equipment markets via a series of strategic acquisitions. The company continues to make acquisitions of both small and large firms in building its strategic position in the switching equipment market, in the cables sector, in the transmission equipment sector and in the subscriber equipment market. These acquisitions have contributed to a worldwide sales performance of €23 billion (on 1999 figures) and the company's presence in more than 130 countries.

In the cables sector, European acquisitions have included Cableries de Dour of Belgium, Irish Cable, Holet in the Netherlands, STC Submarine Cables in the UK and Italco in Italy. In Germany, several businesses have been acquired including Vacha Kabel and the former cable business of Daimler Benz/AEG.

With the consolidation of the switching market and with the movement to digital switching, transmission equipment businesses have also been a target. To date, the key acquisition has been of Telettra from Fiat in Italy. Acquisition activity also features centrally in the company's efforts to expand outside of Europe and into the lucrative Asian and American markets. Alcatel's growth in North America has been facilitated by four recent acquisitions, DSC, Packet Engines, Assured Access Technology and Xylan. The DSC acquisition is of particular strategic importance. The company is a well established among regional operators and complements Alcatel's strengths, particularly in high-speed transmission, intelligent networks and rapid access systems. These strategic acquisitions have helped the company to consolidate its position in key sectors outside of Europe and to plug holes in its product lines. In Europe and worldwide, Alcatel is committed to getting into new businesses that will help it deliver next-generation networking equipment to carriers and corporations.

---

ing businesses. Retailers such as Carrefour (France), Metro (Germany), Tesco (UK) and B&Q Plc (UK) are also looking across borders for targets and making acquisitions in other EU territories. B&Q's $4.1 billion takeover of Castorama Dubois (France) in 1998 was one of the largest deals between European retailers in recent years. In pharmaceuticals and industrial chemicals, there have also been several significant cross-border acquisitions and exchange offers forging consolidation within the European industry. These have included Roche's (Switzerland) acquisition of Boehringer Mannheim (Germany) in 1997, and the Hoechst–Rhône-Poulenc 'business combination'. This sector has been marked by intensive domestic and cross-border M&A activity in Europe including the formation of Astra-Zeneca (between Astra of Sweden and British firm Zeneca) and Novartis (through the merger of Swiss firms Sandoz and Ciba-Geigy). Nestlé too, in the food and drinks sector, has made consolidation and growth through acquisition central to its international business strategy. The Swiss giant (studied further in Case Study 8.8) acquired the Italian mineral water concern San Pellegrino in 1997 and Spillers Petfoods of the UK in 1998. Through these strategic acquisitions, the company has strengthened its positions in the European–global bottled drinks and pet food markets. All of these firms have recognized that acquisitions are a means of: rapid international expansion, reinforcing strategic product areas, securing new technical and market knowledge, and building critical mass.

American firms too have been very active in the European acquisitions market. In the mid-1990s about one-quarter of all acquisitions in the EU were made by US firms. While the motivations for takeover have varied from case to case, US firms have often viewed acquisitions as a means of achieving rapid market penetration (with fast return on capital and learning opportunities), of getting around market barriers (e.g. local content rules, tariffs and rules of origin requirements) and of securing undervalued assets. These perceived 'advantages' can be aggregated with a number of other points in assessing the possible attractions of acquisitions and takeovers in achieving international business expansion. For example, with an acquisition:

1. cultural, management and legal difficulties in the early set-up period in a foreign market can be avoided or more easily assimilated;

2. the purchase 'package' may include critical assets – technology, skilled indigenous managers, brand names and distribution networks;

3. companies may find it easier to gain access to local capital;

4. no further capacity is added in the market, reducing the risk of competitive reaction.

Nevertheless, several problems may be inherent in the takeover mode. First, integrating the foreign operation into the firm, not only in terms of physical systems but also as regards its management culture, can be difficult. This includes the problem of generating good communications systems between the two organizations, which is fundamental to integration and co-operation. Second, the purchaser has to evaluate the worth of the assets, which is not always obvious as a result of potential synergies between the assets of the firm and the target acquisition. Third, the costs of searching for a potential target can be high, adding to the overall cost burden of this strategy. Finally, governments/regulators may prevent acquisitions because they fear lessening competition or market dominance by foreign enterprises. In Chapter 5 we discussed how the EU regulates cross-border merger and acquisition activity (above set thresholds), primarily under the terms of its European Merger Control Regulation, EC 4063/89. The acquisition strategies of many firms have been affected by this regulation. More recently, the German national company has raised several concerns over the 'hostile' attempt of telecommunications company Vodafone Group PLC to acquire German media group Bertelsmann.

Green-field site developments/wholly owned subsidiaries

Acquisitions and joint ventures involve firms acquiring or investing in existing businesses or establishing equity stakes (with other firms) in new commercial entities. Through such options firms can gain new market access for existing products or diversify into new geographic and product markets. Alternatively, firms may choose not to invest in or with other businesses but to pursue an independent (investment-based) venture as a means of achieving new market access and of maximizing the benefits of foreign market presence. Such ventures may range from the creation of a wholly owned sales–marketing subsidiary in a host market through to the construction of a fully operational 'green-field' manufacturing facility. Foreign sales–marketing subsidiaries and assembly units are usually designed to maximize the benefits of having a presence in a given market. Through a foreign market location firms are able to raise confidence about their ability to deliver and to service products as they minimize the geographic distance between the source of supply and the customer. They are also better positioned for the purpose of gathering market information, increasing sales, developing local links and reacting more quickly to market changes. Green-field options also give freer choice of location, investment in the most up-to-date technologies and management practices, as well as financial commitment which matches existing market potential (see also Chapter 7). New ventures may also benefit from government incentives. Many governments offer packages to investing firms to foster inward investment in economically depressed regions as a means of promoting economic welfare (see Chapter 5).

Reviewing lines of action

The strategic alternatives available to firms have been clearly categorized for the sake of analysis. In practice, there is a high degree of overlap both within and between generic groups. For example, while joint ventures are grouped together here with other forms of direct investment, we have seen how many JVs are better described as non-equity contractual associations. This demonstrates that the boundaries between our generic modes (as well as specific operational strategies) are less than clear cut. It is also common for firms to employ more than one strategy at the same time in the same geographic market, possibly because different products in the portfolio demand a different approach or because different options complement each other in achieving a strong market position. For example, a joint venture may involve a licensing agreement with the partner designed to protect a patented technology or brand name. These points are reinforced by some of the case study material already presented. Finally, we should not lose sight of the fact that many of these strategic alternatives can play a role in achieving objectives other than market expansion. On this note, the reader is directed to Figure 8.10

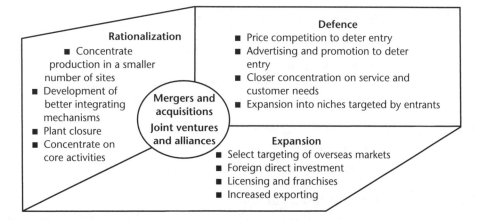

Figure 8.10 Strategies for reaching European objectives

which suggests how different strategic alternatives can help in achieving different types of European objectives – e.g. defence, rationalization and expansion. As highlighted earlier in the chapter, these lines of action are not mutually exclusive and certain strategies (e.g. joint ventures, acquisitions and alliances) may permit the achievement of objectives along a variety of dimensions.

Organizing and co-ordinating operations

Strategic research demonstrates that most problems relating to strategy emerge not in the formulation stage but in how firms organize themselves to implement their strategic plans. What follows is an overview of the kind of organizational/operational issues facing European-scale undertakings post-SEM. Concentration rests with:

(a) the location and *configuration* of value chain activities (e.g. production, procurement and R&D) and

(b) organizational design and *co-ordination*.

Value chain configuration

According to Porter (1986), the international business must achieve a suitable form of configuration. That is, it must decide on where to locate value creation activities and between dispersed configuration and concentrated configuration. Dispersed (or decentralized) configuration means having value creation activities in many countries; while concentrated (or centralized) configuration means having value creation activities in one central location (i.e. in the firm's home market). An array of possibilities exist along this continuum. Further decisions regarding the configuration of activities on a European/international scale are concerned with the question of what a firm should do itself or what it should outsource. In the literature on international strategic management this is often presented as the choice between internalization and de-internalization.

The organization of production

A concentration on production strategies (and the organization of production in European-scale undertakings) highlights the nature of some of these choices and associated issues. Firms are essentially faced with three key decisions when organizing and managing their production for Europe:

1. Where do we produce?
2. Who produces?
3. How to source the materials and inputs necessary for production?

Where to produce?

At one level, this involves an assessment of the trade-off between centralized and decentralized production organization benefits. Centralization assumes that advantages (e.g. maximum benefits from the economies of scale) accrue from large-scale single-point production. Decentralization, on the other hand, assumes that greater advantages arise from carrying out production nearer to the end-consumer, maximizing the firm's responsiveness to local needs, tastes and requirements. A decentralized strategy may appear to make greatest sense when there are high pressures for local responsiveness, whereas a centralized strategy is attractive where demands for local responsiveness are minimal and where firms are able to produce–market a standardized product.

As competition in Europe intensifies, firms are looking to find flexible solutions to the production challenge which combine advantages of both centralization and decentralization. Figure 8.11 summarizes these strategies and demonstrates that certain approaches to manufacturing permit the achievement of both efficiency and effectiveness in production. One such strategy is that of 'flexible specialization' (alluded to in Chapter 6). Flexible specialization permits highly efficient production in multiple small-scale manufacturing units. Production units of this kind, usually relying on computer-aided design (CAD) and computer-aided manufacturing (CAM), permit greater flexibility to respond to customer demands and service specialized needs profitably. Small batches can be produced cost effectively and thus efficiency does not rely on mass production and the pursuit of scale economies.

Cases such as Benetton (see Chapter 9) and Lucas Girling (the UK engineering firm) point to how an organization can be both efficient (low cost) and effective (market responsive) using decentralized manufacturing based on flexible production techniques. Through the adoption of 'flexible specialization', CAD and CAM, these companies have been able to establish a decentralized network of small plants capable of batch size, profitable production. Thus, even with decentralization, they are able to achieve both adaptability and efficiency. Alternatively, some organizations, particularly those with existing operations in a number of member states, are capitalizing on the greater opportunities for plant specialization wherein plant economies can be achieved by individual manufacturing units concentrating on single products, or a narrow range of the company's portfolio. This allows the

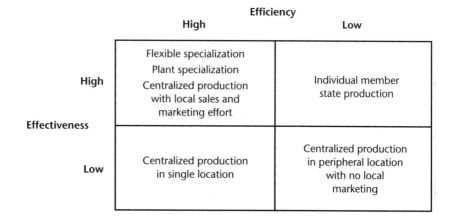

Figure 8.11 Assessing the benefits of production location

removal of effort duplication and thus greater plant efficiency. Within the EU, the removal of barriers between member states and thus the greater freedoms to export, mean that this approach to production can yield higher benefits than was the case in the past.

Perhaps the most popular route to combining the benefits from centralization and decentralization is that which involves centralizing production but decentralizing distribution. In this approach, organizations can combine the benefits of scale economies in production ('efficiency') with local responsiveness in sales and marketing ('effectiveness'). More will be said about this in Chapter 9 on European marketing strategies, but it is clear that many organizations are aware that one of the easiest ways to combine efficiency and local market responsiveness in an integrated European economy is to treat the manufacturing and marketing functions as discrete entities. These can be locationally divided so as to produce better customer focus in conjunction with rationalization and efficiency.

Using the framework outlined in Figure 8.11, organizations can assess both their and their competitors' manufacturing strengths and weaknesses along the two dimensions of efficiency and effectiveness and discover how well the organization of their manufacturing compares. Poor performance on either dimension may well force the company to reconsider its manufacturing in line with the approaches outlined which are becoming more popular across Europe as markets open up and competition intensifies.

Who produces?

Organizations may either choose to produce themselves or enter into some kind of contractual relationship with another organization to produce on their behalf (such as a licensing or franchising agreement, management contract or subcontracting arrangement). Critical to the management consideration in this respect are the cost implications associated with these choices and the concept of control. Internalization of activities (the firm producing itself) implies high control which is often believed to be a source of advantage. Full or high control over production gives managers free choice over strategies and operational decision-making which can be hard to achieve when working with a third party. Nevertheless, firms have to trade off the additional costs incurred in gaining control and in day-to-day management of operations, against the benefits of ownership. De-internalization of activities (through contract) means that organizations may avoid some of these costs but, in many cases at least, see their control over assets and/or operations seriously weakened. Certainly, a number of issues need to be written into licensing, franchise and management contracts in order to preserve a good degree of control:

- situations under which the contract may be terminated (failure to fulfil obligations),
- geographical–market boundaries for exploiting the asset,
- obligations for information sharing in the event of technology–process improvements,

- obligations for marketing and promotion, and
- systems for quality testing.

Assessment of the company's position with regard to who undertakes production therefore needs to involve the cost implications associated with particular options as well as the issue of control. The associated comparative matrix is shown in Figure 8.12.

Figure 8.12 suggests that 'best practice' with regard to the internalization versus externalization decision is subcontracting. This approach can afford cost and control maximization. A trend towards subcontracting in European industry was alluded to in Chapter 6 and it is evident that competitive success can be derived by firms hiving off parts of the production process and focusing on core strengths. For example, the contracting out of major parts of production by the leading Japanese car manufacturers has given them many advantages over their rivals. By subcontracting parts of the production process (e.g. components manufacture, plating, subassembly work etc.), these organizations have been able to dedicate more time and resource to increasingly important value chain activities such as technology development, product commercialization and marketing. Many European automanufacturers have followed suit, 'contracting out' a wide range of tasks/activities so as to improve their efficiency (lowering fixed costs) and to raise flexibility. It must be registered, however, that the matrix is heavily simplified. As previously considered, the development of water-tight licensing franchising management contracts can afford high levels of control, particularly for organizations experienced in these operational modes. Coca-Cola's bottle licensing agreements, McDonald's multinational franchising agreements and Holiday Inn's management contracts for example, all pay testament to the fact that well-constructed contracts can result in good levels of control. It should also be clear that the possibility of subcontracting may not exist where firms must protect their technological and brand advantages (such as in the pharmaceutical industry), where quality control is criti-

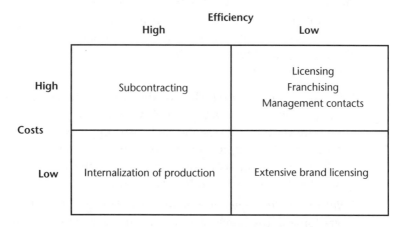

Figure 8.12 Assessing the benefits of internal versus external production

cal to competitive success or where component inputs and subassemblies do not feature.

How to source production?

In developing their production strategies, firms must determine whether or not there is advantage in adopting a pan-European or global sourcing policy and on the nature of their relationships with their suppliers. Firms which rely on their domestic market only for the supply of inputs are faced with less flexibility than organizations which adopt a pan-European (or global) sourcing policy. Although domestic sourcing means firms can avoid problems of cultural uncertainty, long distances in distribution channels, exchange rate fluctuations, and political and economic risks, it also means that firms have less choice over the quality and type of inputs available to them. Indeed, pan-European sourcing (or global sourcing) can provide:

- access to lower cost raw materials and components,
- access to raw materials and components not available domestically,
- access to higher quality inputs (which may include better technologies), and
- less reliance on a small number of possible suppliers (which reduces risks).

In the current European market, liberalization and the removal of barriers have raised the potential for firms to source across a wider market and realize some of these advantages. Take-up of such opportunities has, however, been slow, as cultural uncertainty and exchange rate fluctuations have tended to dog the ease with which firms can operate across borders. The move towards a single European currency will undoubtedly facilitate the process although cultural differences and geographic distances will remain.

In deciding whether a European or national sourcing policy is preferable, firms will need to assess not just what is available but what will best serve the common operational objectives of cost, quality, delivery and flexibility. They must also analyse their supply practices in conjunction with other methods employed in their industry sector and test them against key changes in the European operating environment and developments within their own industry.

In all cases, a key issue will be that of how to structure relationships with suppliers. Essentially, firms have three options available to them when sourcing raw materials and components:

1. *Buy on the open market.* Here quality and efficiency depend on the buyer power of the organization (and its ability to dictate prices and quality) and the purchasing relationships established with suppliers. There are obvious risks associated with this approach: the possibility of suppliers going out of business; reliance on quality control methods and delivery schedules; the possibility of a supplier being purchased by a competitor.

2. *Internalize the supply of raw material.* This can be achieved via backward integration and the purchase of upstream organizations or the establishment of raw material processing plants or component manufacturers. Efficiency depends on

the ability of the organization to successfully integrate operations into the over-all organization. The main risk associated with this approach is the inflexibility to choose between alternative sources of supply, which is particularly critical when technology change is rapid and new, more efficient, suppliers emerge in the marketplace.

3. *Quasi-integration.* While quasi-integration is akin to purchasing on the open market, it differs in one key respect. Rather than establishing an arms-length buyer–seller relationship, the buyer and supplier co-operate closely and exten-sively share information. Popularized by the Japanese, such arrangements are now typical in the global car industry and are increasingly being used as a means of cost management in a wide array of industrial sectors from computing to clothing manufacture. Co-operation may take a variety of forms: technological co-operation (wherein the companies work together to establish new supply inputs tailor made to the manufacturer's requirements), investment co-operation (involving the manufacturer assisting the supplier in improving production capacity or quality to ensure high standards of inputs), and supply co-operation, wherein the companies work together to establish just-in-time (JIT) supply and production scheduling (see Box 8.1). Relationships may be based on medium-term or longer-term contracts, and may sometimes be exclusive. It is clear, how-ever, that some organizations depend on a multiplicity of suppliers in sourcing raw materials and components and thus the cost of managing supplier relationships in this style can be preclusively high. Equally, where supplies are of a commodity nature, the motivation to establish linkages may be less as there is no scope for technology co-operation. Ultimately, the decision is one of balance between careful cost manage-ment and quality and co-operative commitment in adding value.

BOX 8.1 | **Just-in-time systems**

Just-in-time systems are credited to the Japanese who developed and began to use them in the 1950s. Slowly, such management techniques have been adopted but many European firms have been relatively slow to recognize the benefits of such systems. Just-in-time is a programme directed towards ensuring that the correct quantities of materials are purchased or produced at the right time and that there is no waste. Materials and/or services are purchased or generated in exact quantities and just at the time they are needed. The primary objective is therefore to improve quality through the elimination of waste and in turn the system demands that stocks or inventories of raw materials, semifinished and finished products are kept to a minimum. This results in cost savings for the following reasons:

- less capital has to be invested in inventories
- inventory items do not become obsolescent or deteriorate
- less space is required to keep inventories
- stock control costs are minimized.

JIT is not purely about inventory reduction, however. It is essentially good management with ▶

problem-solving, planning and decision-making taken further down the ladder of authority. The whole system is often linked with worker incentives, staged promotion systems, performance-related payments, regular retraining and often, in Japan, guaranteed lifetime employment.

The benefits of JIT management systems and techniques are evident in many Japanese firms and increasingly in US and European ones as well. For example, Nissan's automobile assembly plant in Murayama, Japan, schedules its supplies by computer link and updates the schedule every fifteen to twenty minutes. Suppliers deliver between four and sixteen times a day, with an on-time delivery performance of 99.9%. This allows Nissan to keep only one day's stock throughout its whole system. An important outcome of the JIT technique is a programme for improving overall productivity and reducing waste. This leads to cost effective production or operation, and delivery of goods or services, in the correct quantity, at the right time and which exactly meet the requirements of the customer. This is achieved with a minimum amount of equipment, materials, people and warehousing. Once again, a key operational concept is that of flexibility.

In Europe, JIT systems are becoming more popular. Companies such as Massey-Ferguson, GKN, IBM, 3M and Lucas have introduced and consolidated JIT systems, while there are many Japanese firms operating JIT systems in their plants in Europe (including Nissan). Just-in-time is now widely recognized as being able to provide another competitive edge and for this reason we are likely to see its implementation become even more widespread in Europe over time.

The organization and configuration of R&D activities

The centralization–decentralization trade-off can also be seen in relation to the choices surrounding the organization and configuration of research and development. Until recently, many multinational firms took the decision to centralize their global R&D activities. Centralization might be pursued for a variety of reasons:

1. the need to control the development of new technologies on which the company's future competitiveness may rest;

2. economies of scale in R&D where very large amounts of resource can be concentrated into single centres with no duplication of effort;

3. the fear that foreign research departments may be a source of leakage of ideas and knowledge.

Lately, the decentralization of R&D functions has begun to feature in the strategies of multinational firms as they seek to derive maximum advantage from regional and/or global organization. Bartlett and Ghoshal (1990), outline a number of competing approaches:

Centre for global. This is the approach traditionally followed by multinationals. While there are advantages in terms of control and scale economies, this approach runs the risk of being insensitive to local market demands in the leading markets of the world.

Local for local. This approach suggests conducting research in all target markets in order that the technologies which are developed match with local market demands. While beneficial in terms of local adaptation, the approach implicitly involves duplication of effort and a tendency for subsidiaries to 're-invent the wheel' in an attempt to maintain the local autonomy.

Locally leveraged. Under this arrangement management can take the most creative and innovative developments from its various subsidiaries and share them with other subsidiaries worldwide. The main disadvantage here is that there are frequently impediments to transferring products from one market to another – particularly cultural differences and local market demand condition.

Globally linked. The final approach (promoted by Bartlett and Ghoshal as the optimum solution to the technology development challenge) involves the establishment of flexible linkages between research teams from various global–regional centres. Structures of this kind allow companies to exploit synergies in technology development at the same time as exploiting local leverage advantages. The major drawback to this approach is the cost of co-ordination and the complexities of managing the linkages on an ongoing basis.

None of the approaches, therefore, emerges as adeptly suited to the changing global or European environment. Each has its advantages and disadvantages. This points to managers developing flexible systems which allow them to maximize a variety of advantages from the different approaches, while at the same time minimizing the costs and managerial complexities. This may mean having major centres for R&D in a number of key locations, with a series of local R&D support offices acting more as idea-generating centres than capital-intensive research laboratories. Co-operation between these units may be viewed as an important means of ensuring that local markets are catered for. Ideas emanating from developments in one department can be communicated to the group and tested against conditions in other markets where they may potentially prove as successful. This kind of thinking reaffirms the importance of the marketing department's information exchange role in the research and development process (see Chapter 9). By combining forces, different marketing subsidiaries around Europe can compare their knowledge and experience of different customer segments in the various member states and demonstrate areas of similarity and difference. These can either be communicated to centralized development centres or decentralized units in different countries, which may then work co-operatively rather than independently.

Organizational design: control and co-ordination issues

It is not just the configuration of the value chain that is the key to international competitiveness, but also the way in which the firm structures itself and achieves internal control and co-ordination of its various parts (see Porter, 1986). Effective organizational design and co-ordination on a European (or global) scale is complex and challenging. It requires difficult choices as to the location of authority for strategic and operational decisions and the integration of international activities within the operating structure of the firm (e.g. within or alongside functional and product divisions). Again, the trade-off between centralization and decentralization is central to the strategic challenge as decisions are reached as to the extent to which directives are made at the top of the organization and passed down, or are delegated to and carried out at lower levels (e.g. subsidiary level). Historically, most organizations operating across Europe have developed decentralized multidomestic business structures with loose co-ordination and a great deal of autonomy being afforded to national operating subsidiaries. This contrasts sharply with the centralized hub model characterizing many Japanese companies, in which top management at headquarters impose a direct and central control over their international affiliates and subsidiaries. The rationale for decentralized structures (low co-ordination) is that managers at local level have a better understanding of the conditions in which they operate than managers at central headquarters. In the European case, where cultural diversity and market fragmentation have raised demands for the local adaptation of many products (and of strategies to support those products), this approach has had much attraction. Subsidiary managers have often been afforded a high level of decision-making autonomy to make necessary strategic adjustments and to enhance the flexibility and (local) market responsiveness of the firm.

While this approach has enabled many European MNEs to make decisions in accordance with local conditions, it has also tended to lead to duplications of effort (e.g. in marketing, research and development) and to tensions between the senior managers of subsidiaries and corporate parents. Some of the central benefits of more centralized systems include the elimination of unnecessary duplication of functions (leading to greater cost effectiveness) and clearer lines of authority and strategic reponsibility. With Single Market completion (and with the greater harmonization of business standards and operating conditions across Europe), many firms have looked to move away from these 'federal' arrangements, looking again at the balance between centralization and decentralization. Figure 8.13, based on the work of

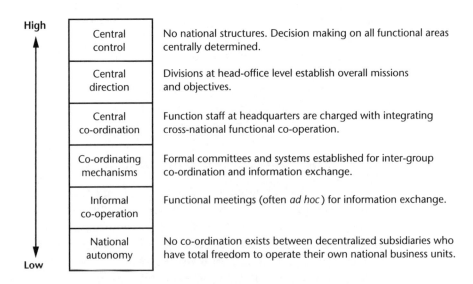

Figure 8.13 Continuum of business integration

Blackwell *et al.* (1993), suggests the different levels of integration possible across a continuum in which centralized control lies at one extreme and decentralized control at the other. The organizational structures which fall within the middle tier of this continuum appear to afford some of the advantages of both high and low co-ordination.

New organizational models

Recent research on the organizational structures of MNEs points to a movement away from traditional hierarchies and towards heterarchies and matrix structures. In such cases, attempts are made to represent teams, units and managers at multiple levels in the process of strategic decision-making and to blend the various divisions of the organization: functional, product and geographic.

A *'heterarchical'* firm is one characterized by multiple centres of control and by managerial decision-making processes that straddle national boundaries (see Hedlund and Rolander, 1990). A heterarchicial firm in Europe may therefore have its financial centre in London (close to the London stock market), its R&D centre in Germany (in a centre of technological excellence where good researchers are abundant), its European headquarters in Paris (responsible for co-ordinating EU-wide strategy development), production units or subsidiaries in the UK, Italy and the Netherlands (the last of these responsible for distribution co-ordination) and *ad hoc* teams for global brand development. Some centres will have responsibility for just one function (or part responsibility throughout the network), others responsibility for several functions and/or cross-functional management processes. Within this format, foreign units are not just 'outposts' of the organization responsible for implementing strategies at a regional/market level, they are part of a complex network of authority and learning, where experiences and knowledge acquired locally are communicated to the centre(s) as a way of shaping future direction for the corporation as a whole. The guiding direction is solving common problems, and this is achieved through the sharing of information, knowledge and resources throughout what has become a multicentre network. Hedlund and Rolander (1990) describe organizations such as this as holographic with information being stored and acted on at all levels and not monopolized by strategic thinkers at the centre. They note that sophisticated information exchange systems and normative mechanisms (such as a strong corporate culture) provide facilitating mechanisms for the establishment of highly integrated business structures. A further feature of the heterarchy is the flexibility to establish coalitions with other parties as a means of building synergies in the global or European environment. On this basis, European firms such as Cap Gemini (the Paris-based management consulting and information technology group) and companies such as Alfa Laval, Atlas Copco and Sandvik (from Scandinavia) begin to fit the description. These organizations have a fairly large number of influential overseas centres and are organized as multicentre networks with less than traditional hierarchies (see Forsgren, 1990; Nilsson *et al.*, 1996).

In many ways, heterarchical firms are similar to those 'transnational' firms that have assumed matrix-type organizational structures. These firms are sometimes described as multipoint networks in which the old centre relinquishes much of its strategic domination of overseas centres and in which relatively high degrees of centralization for some operating decisions mix with relatively high degrees of decentralization for others (see Bartlett and Ghoshal, 1989). Complex matrix structures are adopted to establish reporting relationships and in order to integrate and to co-ordinate a multiplicity of strategic actors. For example, the matrix structure might consist of product divisions intersecting with functional departments and/or geographical divisions. Because of the interaction between product, geographic and functional groups, matrix structures can facilitate the flow of information throughout the organization and can bring different perspectives to bear on important decisions. ABB (Asea Brown Boveri Ltd), the world's leading power engineering company, is one of the most discussed corporate cases in this regard. Under former CEO Percy Barnevik, the company adopted a complex matrix structure with the organization headed by an executive committee and divided by business areas, company and profit centres, and country organizations. In the mid-1990s, fewer than 100 headquarters staff were running 1,200 companies worldwide with what Parnevik's successor Goren Lindahl called 'effective decentralisation under central conditions'. Since Barnevik's departure as CEO in 1997, ABB's approach has evolved but managers from different countries, divisions and centres continue to work together under a matrix design. Matrix structures can be complex organizational arrangements and will not always work well. In particular, the use of dual or multi-dimensional command with intersections between functional, product and geographic divisions, can result in confusion as to what everybody is responsible for and over who reports to whom.

This section began with identification of the joint challenges of co-ordination and configuration in the context of international business structures. Several factors make these tasks more difficult for international businesses, which must establish, integrate and control relations between their domestic and foreign facilities, and which must establish a workable balance between centralized and decentralized authority. Bringing these themes together, Case Study 8.8 on Nestlé – the Swiss-based international food and beverages company – offers practical insight into the way one organization has attempted to solve the problem of achieving balance and efficiency in its organizational structure.

Building for flexibility

Successful implementation of strategies in Europe throughout the next decade will dictate firms designing structures for flexible and creative strategy development and implementation. Change in the EU is rapid, partly because of the new agenda for Europe-wide business, and partly because of increasing competitive threats in the global environment which mean shorter technology–product life-cycles and thus more rapid changes in the European competitive environment. Long gone are the days when firms could develop a technology, protect it with a series of patents, launch it internationally and live off the benefits until the patent was close to expiry. Reverse engineering, resulting not only in the 'copying' of technologies, but

CASE STUDY 8.8 Organizational design and management at Nestlé

Nestlé SA is Switzerland's largest industrial company, and the largest food company in the whole of Europe. The company is a true multinational enterprise. In 1999, the company boasted 230,929 employees in some 509 factories scattered across some seventy countries. By the end of 1998, worldwide sales were totalling 72 billion Swiss Francs (approximately $50 billion).

With such a spread of activities one of Nestlé's major corporate concerns is establishing the roles and responsibilities of both head office and subsidiary managers and the organizational structures capable of facilitating effective management of its extensive operations.

The head office retains control over the company's strategic direction. Essentially it has responsibility for:

- geographic expansion and concentration
- acquisition decisions
- research on world commodities and mandates
- divestment of poorly performing products and non-desirable assets acquired through acquisition
- monitoring of performance reports
- control of money (including in which denomination it is to be held)
- product research (to ensure duplication kept to a minimum)

With this responsibility, the head office operation is able to keep a careful watch on overall business activities and shape the overall direction of the company. A good example of this has arisen recently in terms of the firm's plans for geographic expansion. Greater attention to LDCs (particularly China) as the potential areas for future growth can be directed from the centre. In relation to acquisition decisions, central control enables the organization to maintain its policy as an independent manufacturer–wholesaler–marketer, avoiding vertical expansion into supply chains (plantations) or distribution networks (retailers).

The importance of controlling acquisitions centrally cannot be overstated. Based on a policy of expansion through acquisition rather than greenfield development, on the grounds that purchasing existing companies with recognized brands and customer franchises is more cost effective than attempting to establish new businesses worldwide, the company is often faced with problems of integrating new businesses into the existing corporate network. This is further hampered by the fact that often acquired businesses do not wholly fit with the company's overall corporate direction and thus require careful post-acquisition management, often involving divestment and rationalization. For example, following the acquisition of the Buitoni-Perugina operation, the organization were forced to divest the printing and packaging business which did not fit the organization's future development strategy. Equally, following the takeover of Rowntree in the UK, the organization was forced to rationalize production activities in the UK, a contentious issue which could not be charged to local management.

Although this appears to suggest the company is highly centralized, there exist various layers of responsibility and organizational co-ordination below this top corporate level. At subsidiary level, area managers have great discretion with regard to pricing, distribution, marketing and staffing. Local managers have discretion over take-up of new products, being able to refuse their addition into the portfolio if they are considered unacceptable to local market needs. In addition, they are given freedom to adapt products to suit local market conditions as long as the adaptations are not considered harmful to the company's overall objectives. Nestlé's flagship coffee – Nescafé instant – is consequently blended and coloured slightly differently in a wide array of world markets.

The company has continued to devolve power to the local regions and to simplify head office procedures in an attempt to make the whole organization more responsive to the highly dynamic global marketplace. Flatter organizational structures at corporate level and simplified reporting procedures have speeded up decision-making. At the corporate level, general managers have been employed who are responsible for different regional groups, rather than different product groups. At the same time, in an effort to ensure that such devolvement of power does not result in less overall control and integration, the company has established policies to bring corporate and subsidiary management closer together:

- Moving individuals between jobs at subsidiary level and jobs at head office level. This encourages permeation of company culture.

- Meetings and training programmes which bring managers from various subsidiaries together. This facilitates the cross-fertilization of information and knowledge.

- Encouragement of language development so that head office staff can converse with managers in their subsidiaries in at least French and English, and preferably Spanish and German.

European management implications

This brief overview of some of the policies and practices of Nestlé highlights a number of important issues for organizational design and management:

- Many companies now operating in Europe are not only concerned with developing effective systems for Europe but are looking at their overall global activities. The establishment of

regional group managers at corporate level demonstrates Nestlé's awareness of the growing trend towards organizing their business according to global regional development.

- Organizations need to find mechanisms for both centralization and decentralization. Nestlé's decision to centralize up-stream and support activities (R&D, finance, acquisitions etc.) but decentralize downstream activities (particularly sales and marketing effort) is not unique. Work by Ohmae (1985) based on Porter's value chain theory highlighted this tendency. Although it is possible to argue that Europe may provide scope for increased centralization, continued cultural differences and tastes (particularly for products such as foodstuffs) mean this trend may be slow.

- Integrating mechanisms are a powerful tool to ensure closer co-operation between devolved parts of complex organizations. Regular meetings and briefings and the circulation of staff emerged here as methods by which this may be achieved. Other alternatives might include established systems for information exchange through IT, intra-group newsletters, combined technology forums etc.

often improvements on it, means that reliance on patents to secure long-term sustainable advantage is risky to say the least. More important, in the modern world, is the design of systems and structures which permit continuous technological improvement as a way of staying one step ahead of, or at least level with, the other players in the game. Similarly, as production techniques are changing, and mass production is no longer the only means of efficient manufacturing, scale advantages are being eroded by flexible specialization in production. When this factor is coupled with a resurgence in the marketing field of satisfying the demand of specific groups of consumers, rather than attempting to generate markets which afford scale opportunities, flexibility in customer servicing, possibly through adaptation, is re-emerging as a prerequisite of competitive success (see chapter 9).

Strategic managers must review the way in which they view their asset base. It is no longer a case of summing up the scale and dominance of fixed assets, it is a case of developing flexible assets, many of which may be intangible:

1. Buyer power relating to the scale of purchasing may be superseded by co-operative links with suppliers prepared to offer similarly attractive deals to smaller companies with whom they strike up long-term relationships.

2. Economies of scale in manufacturing may be superseded by flexible specialization where productivity rates can be matched and advantages enhanced through closer proximity to customers and shorter distribution channels.

3. Reliance on patents and trademarks may be undermined by co-operative R&D developments which give firms access to a wider knowledge pool and new technologies.

4. Relationships with a number of distributors or bilateral marketing arrangements may offer firms wider distribution coverage than those who have sunk resources in establishing their own distribution networks. It also permits the flexibility to swap partners or distributors as market conditions and customer buying behaviour changes.

Managing for flexibility is therefore about determining the most effective balance between fixed and flexible assets, which may mean divesting parts of the business in favour of developing looser affiliations with third parties and partners. Implementing strategies flexibly is therefore about 'stage managing' the organization of the value chain but not necessarily owning its constituent functions.

Assessing effectiveness

Finally, and returning to the framework presented in Figure 8.1, strategic planning is an iterative process requiring continuous adaptation and reformulation. This has never been more the case than in today's business environment wherein the pace of change, both environmental and technological, is far more rapid than has ever been the case before. Firms which rest on their laurels of past strategic success are unlikely to be the winners of the future. Evaluation is critical and feedback loops need to be established to ensure that unprofitable strategic outcomes are re-evaluated rapidly so that the firm does not expose itself to undue risks. Criteria for assessment can be divided into two categories:

1. *quantitative measures* such as export market share, return on investment, sales growth, and profitability;

2. *qualitative measures* such as improved quality perceptions by customers, better relationship management, and improved goodwill.

Quantitative measures, while requiring a considerable amount of effort in compilation and analysis, are obviously easier to amass and assimilate than qualitative measures which dictate targeted research effort, both within and without the organization. Nevertheless, a failure to accurately measure outcomes will invariably result in misguided perceptions of the success or otherwise of strategic moves and make the re-development of new strategies difficult.

Also at issue is the time frame for evaluation. Poor performance of UK firms in recent years has often been attributed to short-termism which hampers the effectiveness of their strategic planning worldwide. Concerned about share performance and the reactions of the City there is a tendency to set strict time frames for profit realization in new ventures and pull out of ventures before they have realized their true potential. Competing with the likes of the Japanese, who measure effectiveness via market-based measures rather than pure profit related measures, UK firms are restricted in their ability to plan organically and for the long term.

Conclusion

Change in the European (and global) operating environment is causing organizations to carefully re-think their strategies. Many 'domestic' firms are now looking towards internationalization and to offensive strategies, where they face a series of complex choices concerning the selection of markets, methods of entry and operational strategies. For European-scale undertakings or MNEs, the intensity of competition is being heightened and traditional success factors such as scale economies are now being challenged. Today, success appears to rest with the development of systems and structures for enhanced flexibility and with deriving balance in strategic objectives: between defence and expansion strategies, centralized decision-making and decentralized autonomy, standardization and adaptation, and internalization and de-internalization. While there is clearly no blueprint for achieving these complex balances, it is evident that firms must pursue strategies that 'fit' with their changing external environments and with their internal strengths. Equally, ignoring the opportunities offered by relationship development across the value chain is also likely to lead to inferior performance.

In the remaining chapters (Chapters 9–12), we build our analysis, looking at the issues and challenges now confronting European firms in the different dimensions of their business. Chapter 9 focuses on the challenges of marketing in the new European environment and on marketing management. Although marketing is an integral part of firms' strategy development, change in the discipline, along with new challenges posed by integration and technological development, mean that the topic is worthy of further and separate comment. Equally, while the point has been emphasized, it is not possible for firms to plan and implement their strategies independently of the cultural context of European business. Failure to take account of the cultural nuances between markets may result in expensive mistakes and, while standardization may be possible in a variety of business functions, firms need to look closely at the markets of Europe to identify both the commonalities and the differences. These issues are discussed in Chapter 10 along with some prescriptions for effective cross-cultural management. Chapter 11 examines the formulation and implementation of (ecologically) sustainable and quality-based strategies. Environmental management and quality management are increasingly becoming a part of firm's strategic focus and deserve specific attention. Subsequent to these concentrations, Chapter 12 examines European business in a global context, exploring the interlinkages between European and extra-European economies and some of the activities of European firms in the global business arena.

Review questions for Chapter 8

1. How important is strategic analysis in the development of competitive strategies? What are some of the key components of such analysis?

2. What are some of the challenges in studying and conceptualizing external organizational environments? Why is environmental analysis central to the process of strategy formulation?

3. What factors may contribute to a decision to grow a business via overseas (European) expansion?

4. How might countries screen foreign environments so as to identify and to compare market opportunities?

5. How does the need for control over foreign operations vary with the nature of a firm's core competencies? What are the implications for the choice of entry mode?

6. What other factors may influence the choice of foreign market entry mode?

7. What are some of the advantages and drawbacks of export-based strategies? Discuss the issues involved in working with export intermediaries.

8. Discuss the advantages and disadvantages associated with the licensing of proprietary technology to foreign businesses.

9. Explain the popularity and growth of international franchises.

10. What kind of companies may benefit from entering into strategic alliances and joint ventures?

11. What lessons for successful joint venture management can be derived from the case material presented in this chapter?

12. Why do so many MNEs look to grow their businesses via acquisitions?

13. Why must firms achieve a 'fit' between their strategy and structure? What sort of trade-offs are at issue when multinational firms determine their organizational structures?

14. How has Nestlé maintained its multidomestic philosophy while centralizing a number of key functions (e.g. R&D)?

Web guide

Market data (general characteristics)

The CIA World Factbook (country profiles) @
http://www.odci.gov/cia/publications/factbook

UN/ECE Statistical Yearbook Europe (basic country/market information) @ http://www.unece.org/stats/trend/trend_h.htm

US Department of State Background Notes: Europe and the New Independent States @ http://www.state.gov/www/background_notes/eurbgnhp.html

The Library of Congress Country Studies @ http://lcweb2.loc.gov/frd/cs/cshome.html

Business regulations (national characteristics)

UNCTAD/WTO @ http://www.intracen.org/

Companies: profiles and performance

Biz/ed company facts @ http://www.bized.ac.uk/compfact/comphome.htm

Hoover's online: company and industry information @ http://www.hoovers.com/

Financial Times: European performance league @ http://www.ft.com/euroleague/

References

Ansoff, H. I. (1984) *Implanting Strategic Management*, Prentice-Hall International.

Bartlett, C.A. and Ghoshal, S. (1989) *Managing Across Borders*, Hutchinson.

Bartlett, C. A. and Ghoshal, S. (1990) Managing innovation in the transnational corporation, in Bartlett, C. A., Doz, Y. and Hedlund, G. (eds), *Managing the Global Firm*, Routledge.

Bennett, R. (1997) *European Business*, Pitman Publishing.

Blackwell, N. (1990) Way around Europe: the adoption of the right approach to a European development strategy is critical, *Management Today*, August, 86–7.

Blackwell, N., Bizet, J. P., Child, P. and Hensley, D. (1993) Shaping a pan-European organization, *McKinsey Quarterly*, **2**, 94–111.

Bleeke, J. and Ernst, D. (1993) *Collaborating to Compete*, Wiley.

Burlage, F. (1997) Don't jump in feet first – do your homework, *The European*, 24 April, 26.

Chapman, P. (1997) Life-saver in a perilous sea of job losses, *The European*, 9 October, 39.

Charles, D. (1996) Alcatel: a European champion for a globalising market, in Nilsson, J.-E., Dicken, P. and Peck, J. (eds) *The Internationalisation Process: European Firms in Global Competition*, Paul Chapman Publishing.

Crick, D. (1995) An investigation into the targeting of U.K. export assistance, *European Journal of Marketing*, **29**(8), 76–94.

Doz, Y., Hamel, G. and Prahalad, C.K. (1986) Controlled variety: a challenge for human resource management in the MNC, *Human Resource Management*, **25**(1).

Dudley, J.W. and Martens, H. (1993) *1993 and Beyond: New Strategies for the Enlarged Single Market*, Kogan-Page.

Economist (1994) *Feeling for the future: a survey of television*, 12 February 1994.

Economist (1999) *The urge to merge*, 2 January 1999.

Ellis, J. and Williams, D. (1995) *International Business Strategy*, Pitman Publishing.

Forsgren, M. (1990) Managing the international multi-centre firm: case studies from Sweden, *European Management Journal*, **8**, 261–7.

Hedlund, G. and Rolander, D. (1990) Action in heterarchies: new approaches to managing the MNC, in Bartlett, C. A., Doz, Y. and Hedlund, G. (eds), *Managing the Global Firm*, Routledge.

Jarillo, J.-C. and Martinez, J.I. (1988) Benetton SpA (A), in Hendry, J. and Eccles, T. (eds), *European Cases in Strategic Management*, Chapman and Hall.

Johnson, G. and Scholes, K. (1993) *Exploring Corporate Strategy: Texts and Cases*, 3rd edition, Prentice-Hall.

Leonidou, L.C. and Katsikeas, C.S. (1996) The export development process: an integrative review of empirical models, *Journal of International Business Studies*, **27**(3), 517–51.

Lynch, R. (1994) *European Business Strategies: The European and Global Strategies of Europe's Top Companies*, Kogan Page.

Mahon, J.F. and McGowan, R.A. (1998) Modeling industry political dynamics, *Business and Society*, **37**(4), 391–2.

Nilsson, J.-E. Dicken, P. and Peck, J. (eds) (1996) *The Internationalisation Process: European Firms in Global Competition*, Paul Chapman Publishing.

Ohmae, K. (1985) *Triad Power: the Coming Shape of Global Competition*, Free Press.

Ohmae, K. (1989) Managing in a borderless world, *Harvard Business Review*, May–June, 152–61.

Peng, M.W. and Ilinitch, A.Y (1998) Export intermediary firms: a note on export development research, *Journal of International Business Studies*, **29**(3), 609–20.

Porter, M. E. (1980) *Competitive Strategy*, The Free Press.

Porter, M. E. (1985) *Competitive Advantage*, The Free Press.

Porter, M.E. (1986) *Competition in Global Industries*, Harvard Business School Press.

Porter, M. E. (1990) *Competitive Advantage of Nations*, Macmillan.

Root, F.R. (1987) *Entry Strategies for International Markets*, Lexington Books.

UNCTAD (1999) *World Investment Report 1999, FDI and the Challenge of Development*, UNCTAD, Geneva.

Verdin, P. and Williamson, P. (1994) Successful strategy: stargazing or self-examination?, *European Management Journal*, **12**(1), 10–19.

Vonortas, N.S. (1997) *Co-operation in Research and Development*, Kluwer Academic Publishers.

Vyas, N.M., Shelburn, W.L. and Rogers, D.C. (1995) An analysis of strategic alliances: forms, functions and framework, *Journal of Business and Industrial Marketing*, **10**(3), 47–60.

Watters, R.D. (1995) International business development – what are the considerations?, *Journal of Business and Industrial Marketing*, **10**(3), 61–73.

9 Marketing in the 'new' Europe

Central themes

■ The changing marketing environment

■ The marketing mix

■ New marketing theories

■ Segmenting European markets

■ Pan-European strategies

■ Standardization versus adaptation

■ Branding and pricing

■ Communications and logistics

■ International direct marketing

■ Internet marketing

Introduction

This chapter follows on directly from the last chapter on strategies for Europe. It was highlighted there that marketing and sales are an important part of the value chain of business activity and as such are subject to re-adjustment in the new European business environment. Given the important place of marketing in the strategic planning of firms, it is appropriate to give this one element separate treatment. As with the chapter on strategy, it is difficult to do justice to European Marketing within a single chapter. So much has been written about the subject that it is hard to fully reflect all the issues within the obvious constraints here. Nevertheless, the present chapter should extend student knowledge of an evolving discipline and provide fresh appraisal of changing marketing practices in the dynamic European region. Analysis also adds to that existing coverage of EU legislation (as relevant to commercial undertakings), providing brief assessment of some of the restraints arising from EU legislation on the implementation of European-marketing strategy.

While the question of marketing was raised in Chapter 8, it should be clarified that marketing directs the R&D function, sets prices, specifies the place where the product will be sold (aims the products) and concerns the product's promotion and sale. Even this functional interpretation may be too limiting as for many theorists, '[i]t is the whole business seen from the point of view of its final result, that is from the customer's point of view' (Drucker, 1955). It should also be clear that when discussion is made of marketing goods and services that a number of subdivisions are being crossed (see Campbell, 1997). For example, we may make a distinction between industrial products (or marketing) and consumer products (or marketing). The former category consists of those goods and services purchased by businesses rather than by final consumers. Normally, these industrial products undergo some form of further processing (e.g. rubber in vehicular-tyre production) or, in their final form, enable service providers to carry out their work. The latter category, consumer products, consists of goods and services purchased by end-users (final consumers). In turn, consumer products can be subdivided into durable items, that is those with medium–long-term utility such as motor cars, and fast-moving items that tend to have a short–medium-term utility and that are bought little and often (e.g. food products).

Changing environments

Throughout the early chapters of this work, the business environment of the new Europe has been extensively addressed. The policies and structures of the EU, industry, work and culture in Europe have all been examined and thus provide some backdrop to our present discussions. As a consequence, it should be entirely clear that, for nearly 19 million enterprises in Western Europe, barriers to trade and communication in Europe are coming down fast. The EU alone provides a single market of some 376 million consumers in which transnational communities are emergent and in which businesses are increasingly subject to common rules and standards. The introduction of a single currency brings greater transparency to this market (providing for easier price comparisons) and confronts its marketers with new levels of competition. Any understanding of marketing in Europe must rest with account of these developments and with appreciation of their operational and psychological effects. The marketing environment consists of all those external actors and forces that affect a company's ability to develop and to manage transactions and relationships in the market, and these European developments play a central part.

There are, however, a number of other inputs as yet unaddressed that represent important influence in the way that business firms are thinking about their marketing efforts and are carrying them out. At this early stage in this chapter some of these 'lead' influences require introduction.

First, insofar as marketing theory represents the intellectual environment of European marketers, new ideas and principles are beginning to impact on and/or to reflect marketing practice in Europe. New orientations and interpretations are challenging traditional assumptions about the marketing mix and are shifting the strategic emphasis in marketing strategies towards longer-term and strategic partner relationships.

Second, and with respect to the changing technological environment of

European businesses, new communications technologies, in particular Internet-based technologies (such as electronic mail and the World Wide Web), have, in a short space of time, revolutionized the practice of marketing communications. As considered later in this chapter, wired and on-line systems are providing cost-effective vehicles for rapid (and interactive) customer communication, for advertising and promotions, and for the management of commercial transactions. The conjunction of new and old media forms is also a key issue in the development and diversification of international direct marketing activities which have emerged as a central feature of the marketing landscape.

Third, concentration must also fall on the changing face of European sales and media legislation. Along with that on production standards, packaging and distribution (at both national and supranational levels), legislation in this field adds another dimension to the legal and regulatory environment of European marketing. Although national rules on advertising rules predominate, the standardization of regulations across the European Union is on the agenda and fields of product and sales legislation have already been subject to some integration. While the issues are complex, it should be clear that the future and further harmonization of communications legislation would make it easier, cheaper and more efficient for firms to 'tap' international market segments and to reach them through pan-European advertising campaigns. The entire process is affecting the rights and freedoms of all agents active in the marketing relationship.

Fourth, and although some attention has already been paid to culture and society in Europe, any address of European marketing must closely assess the meaning and implications of convergent consumer clusters in Europe. Consumers throughout Europe are increasingly viewing the same media and are giving greater meaning and cohesion to the concept of Euro-consumerism. Their needs, tastes and behaviours are increasingly similar and companies are speaking and thinking in terms of transnational markets and segments. As we will see, this entails a series of difficult but strategically important choices concerning the design, marketing and delivery of products or services and an emphasis on pan-European solutions.

This chapter addresses each of these trends, the combination of which is leading to more interactive marketing and to more uniform demand, product and service solutions.

Changing marketing practices

It is these trends, and the development of global competition, that are shaping marketing in Europe. For example, the erosion of commercial barriers in Europe and the birth of the Euro-consumer have encouraged several companies to standardize their products and to sell them in much the same way across the Continent. Consumer products adopting such a strategy include Delacre biscuits, Chanel perfumes and Cartier watches. Under parallel influence, and through such avenues as catalogue sales, direct mail and telephone selling, international direct marketing activities are also on the increase. Direct selling techniques are now being used to sell a wide variety of products and services to specified consumer segments within and across national borders, with European firms now more experienced in international direct marketing (IDM) than their American counterparts (see Iyer and Hill, 1996). Relatedly, there is also a trend towards database marketing (DBM) which is providing a more interactive approach to customer contact management and a platform for relationship-type strategies. The database is used to provide computer-aided sales support and to maintain accurate customer, competitor, market and company information. Also advancing is the phenomenon of electronic commerce (e-commerce). The world wide web (WWW) and Internet-based technologies are providing marketers in Europe with new reach, speed and efficiency in all aspects of their work. A common theme of current marketing scholars is that dynamic marketers (and their firms) will be those that embrace these new technologies and combine with these established instruments of marketing communication to provide an integrated communications approach. There is no suggestion that this is easy but a warning that organizations failing to respond to the new avenues of communication are likely to get left behind.

Again, the present chapter examines all of these trends along with key themes receiving traditional emphasis in chapters on European and cross-border marketing. These include the growth, form and efficiency of pan-European marketing strategies, the relative value of network and hierarchical marketing structures, and the growth and attractions of Euro-brands. An address of these themes takes us to the heart of the *standardization versus adaptation* debate that has attracted singlemost attention in traditional narratives on European marketing. This debate is given an initial outline here and is then pursued at various stages within what is by necessity a much broader framework of analysis.

The standardization–adaptation debate: an introduction

At the outset of the Single Market initiative, many theorists alluded to greater opportunities for pan-European standardization of products (brands), services, distribution and promotion. The conditions for such efforts are now fertile with further momentum provided by purported cultural homogenization and the arrival of a single European currency. Despite this, standardized strategies in Europe continue to face difficulties in a context of cultural, linguistic and regulatory differences between European countries. Consequently, businesses in Europe must continue to ask how far, if at all, it is appropriate to:

(a) design and deliver 'standardized' products and services (across national market boundaries)

and

(b) promote those offerings through uniform pan-European campaigns.

The product/market-specific nature of these choices must be stressed. For example, where cross-national segments display more uniform needs and buying behaviour, and where cultural differences do not necessitate adaptation, markets may be served efficiently by standardized products and services. Supplying a single unmodified product (which itself affords economies of scale in research and production) can also lead to the standardization of marketing and distribution methods. In cases of product modification, extra promotional costs have to be incurred, while standardized products raise the possibility of uniform (pan-European) promotions. Conversely, where varying subgroups display different needs and tastes, where there are local requirements in relation to such matters as packaging and technical standards, and where cultural differences require significant adaptations, it is to be believed that market-by-market adaptation will be preferable. Rather than creating universal products and looking for common Europe-wide solutions, product modification may be more appropriate (along with other changes in placing, pricing and promotions) leading to the execution of differentiated international marketing strategies. The decision of which approach is preferable is, therefore, product–market determined and no one single prescription is possible. Both approaches are likely to exist together in the new European environment.

More about this debate will be said later but, as many commentators have identified, the argument is a variant on the debate about global cultural homogenization and the emergence of global markets. As with its regional microcosms, the debate at this level centres around the desirability of standardizing products or services for broadly defined international market segments. It was Levitt (1983) who triggered this debate by stating that consumers' needs and interests are becoming increasingly homogenous worldwide and that substantial economies of scale in production and marketing can be achieved by supplying global markets through standardized solutions. Since Levitt unfolded this controversial argument, much discussion has taken place over the opportunities for, and barriers to, standardization. Rival hypotheses have emerged, with a 'glocalization' hypothesis encouraging firms to develop global orientation but to adapt their marketing efforts to local or regional conditions ('think global, act local'). Again, more will be said about such choices at later stages in this chapter where we make close reference to the strategic decisions of European firms and marketers.

The theory of marketing: new ideas, new thinking

Although it might seem unusual to commence with reference to theory, it might be recalled that theory can be used as a guide for action and as a means of translating our experiences into an ordered collection of thoughts and interpretations. In theory, of course, the underlying ethos of marketing has never changed: that is, the concept concerns finding out what customers want and delivering it. Despite this, there is no universal agreement as to how marketing should be defined or conceptualized or which methods of marketing communication are the most effective. Marketing theory is a relatively new invention (at least in ordered form) and the breadth and complexity of the function sustains a lively discourse.

The traditional view

For many years, the 'marketing mix' approach has provided an ascendant theory of marketing, offering a factor-based classification of the key marketing variables. The idea of 'a mix' developed originally from a notion of the marketer as a blender of ingredients, with the marketer combining different means of competition (see Culliton, 1948). The concept was formalized by Borden in the 1950s and then adapted and simplified by McCarthy. McCarthy (1960) developed the view that marketing, as a specific function of business management, could be split into four functional areas representing a 'mix' of key activities. These activities (or elements of marketing) are represented in Figure 9.1 and concern (a mix of) price, product, place and promotion policies. In this view, marketing:

■ specifies the design and features of the *product*,

■ determines the *price* that will be charged for the product,

■ specifies the *place* where the product will be sold, and

■ concerns the *promotion* of the product to the target market (place).

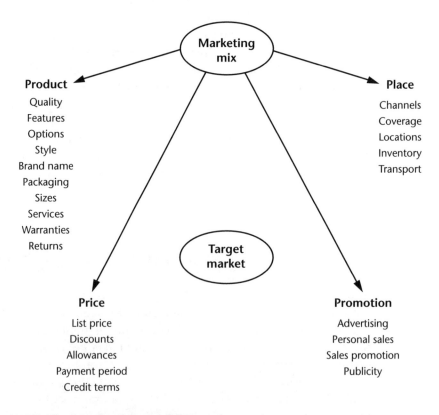

Figure 9.1 The four Ps of the marketing mix
Source: Based on Kotler and Armstrong (1993, page 41)

A fifth P ('people') has been promoted by a number of writers and, in recent years, reference has been made to the six Ps, with Kotler (1986) adding 'politics' and 'public relations' in his innovative work on megamarketing. Most marketing text-books forward the various Ps (conventionally four) as the basis of the 'marketing mix' and argue that a firm's marketing mix will normally (but not necessarily) have to be adapted for international (as opposed to purely domestic) marketing. This is as a consequence of the many differences that exist across geographic markets in relation to development, legal frameworks, cultural tastes, competitive situations etc. The idea that marketing is about managing discrete business functions has also given legitimacy to the functional structuration of the firm and to the concept of the 'specialist' marketing department. In turn, by suggesting that marketing is solely concerned with managing elements of the marketing mix in specific situations, marketing has often been promoted as a function best managed at a local level. Therefore, international marketing efforts across international organizations have often been decentralized with individual subsidiaries sometimes pulling in different directions.

New ideas and concepts

The traditional view of marketing is giving ground. Although it may be too early to signal a paradigm shift, there are clearly new threads and dimensions to recent marketing scholarship that both question the sufficiency (and utility) of the marketing mix concept and consider marketing as something more than a collection of ordered functions. Much of this new thinking is associated with the growth of interest in industrial and services marketing.

A number of theorists have contended that market-driven management in modern business environments (such as those in Europe) requires a concept of marketing that goes beyond the idea of 'mix management'. The modern concept of marketing, they argue, should rest with the notion of anticipating and responding to customer needs and with defining and delivering customer value in a market-oriented business strategy (customer orientation). This strategy should be geared towards profitable transactions and relationships with target customers. For example, Frederick Webster, a leading American theorist, makes it clear that what is really at issue is not a series of tactical choices as to how to place, position and to promote a product, but:

> ... a strategic process of defining what constitutes superior value, developing it and delivering it to customers [at a profit].

For Webster (1998, p. 239):

> ... value is defined in the marketplace by customers in terms of how well the product or service meets their expectations.

This echoes the earlier thoughts of Philip Kotler, one of the pioneers of contemporary marketing theory. According to Kotler (1984):

> [Progressive] outside-in companies take their clues from the marketplace. They spot

unmet needs and translate them into business opportunities. They define target groups and develop a value-delivery system that is superior to competitors who are serving the same market.

For the theorists of the Nordic School, the traditional view of marketing has also created an unhealthy separation between marketing and other business activities such as design, technical and customer service. Such a separation militates against the development of customer or market orientation in all functions of the firm. In particular, in services marketing, where the customer interface is broad and where a firm seeks to cultivate strategic relationships with its buyers, then:

> [t]he internal interface between marketing, operations, personnel and other functions is of strategic importance to success. (see Gronroos, 1997)

Although more will be said of this later, the basic prescription is that of (re-)integrating the marketing function with other organizational activities. It is only this form of integration (interfunctional co-ordination) that can provide all departments with the market-related input necessary to make the organization truly market oriented. In such a view, not only efficient individual efforts but efficient collective efforts across the organization are necessary. The idea is of marketing and sales specialists ('full-time marketers') supporting and collaborating with 'part-time marketers' in other parts of the firm in order to ensure total perceived quality on the part of the customer (see Gummesson 1987, 1991, 1996).

Such ideas are closely associated with the work on 'relationship marketing' (RM) emerging out of the industrial and services marketing fields. Very simply, the RM concept begins with a view that marketing should be seen less in terms of a combination of policy elements (pricing, promotion etc.) and more in terms of relationships, networks and interactions. Relationships are contacts between two or more people, but they also exist between people, objects and organizations. Networks are sets of relationships, and interactions concern activities performed within specific relationships and networks. Within this conception, a stress is placed on customer connectivity and on meeting and exceeding customer expectations in a rolling series of transactions and exchanges ('relationship-type strategies'). As Gronroos puts it (1990, p. 16), in different situations, the function of marketing is:

> ... to establish, maintain and enhance (long-term) relationships with customers and other partners, at a profit, so that the objectives of the parties involved are met by a mutual exchange and fulfillment of promises.

These ideas (see also Blomqvist *et al.*, 1993; and Lehtinen *et al.*, 1994) are slowly influencing our perception of marketing fundamentals and the way in which we define marketing. Marketing is no longer seen as a 'function' which can be performed by a separate business unit, but in terms of tasks, processes and relationships which (a) link the many components of the firm and (b) link the firm to the marketplace. Accordingly, many successful companies are changing from being production driven (jettisoning a 'make and sell' mentality) to being market driven, wherein adoption is made of what Webster describes as a 'sense and respond' mentality.

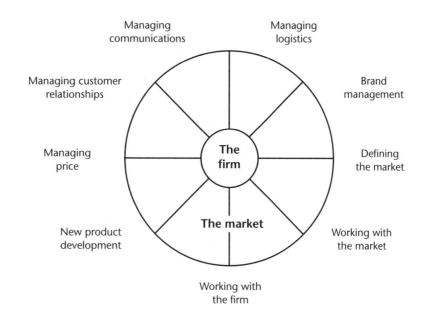

Figure 9.2 The dimensions of marketing: an alternative framework

Figure 9.2 reflects this thinking. The dimensions listed suggest an understanding of marketing as something that is interactive and reflect the co-requisites of market and customer orientation. While the essential simplicity of the four Ps modality has its own attraction, it is this alternative framework that is employed here in order to enable extended analysis of current and future marketing trends and choices in Europe. In parts this analysis is descriptive, providing overview and account of present trends; in parts it is prescriptive, based on propositions of change. The rationale for taking such an approach is the fact that theorists and business practitioners alike are generally agreed that change to a pan-European way of thinking is the only effective way of managing their marketing efforts (and strategic development) in the Europe of the future.

Defining the market

Based on earlier discussions about the European theatre, it is clear that the EU is not a single market in the sense of there being opportunities for adopting a unified mix of marketing policies which are appropriate across all markets. While Europe is moving closer together in so many ways, and while consumer tastes and behaviours are slowly converging, it is simply unrealistic to expect millions of 'Euro-clones' with the exact same tastes and purchasing styles. Equally, were such clones to exist, it is clear that legal, regulatory and cultural barriers continue to divide the European nations.

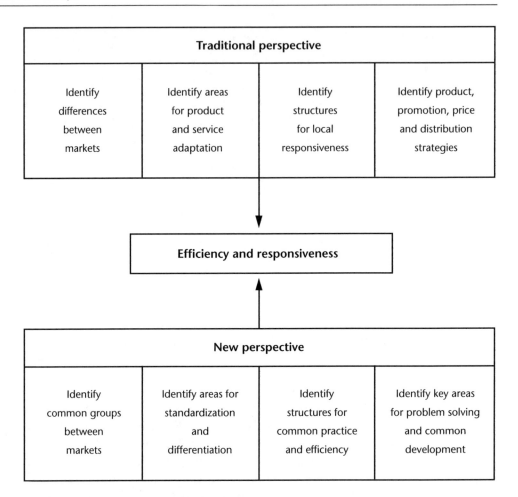

Figure 9.3 European marketing: changing perspectives

Segmenting European markets

Despite this, the analytical and creative processes of defining markets in Europe, of identifying the customer groups at which product(s) can be aimed, should be directed towards the targeting of transnational customer groupings. In the modern Europe, where the significance of national borders is much diminished (at least in commercial terms), marketing strategies should be devised on a pan-European basis and executed with sensitivity to local tastes and conditions. What this implies is that firms in the EU taking a traditional approach to European marketing (one involving a process of national geographic segmentation) should change the focus of their market research along a number of dimensions as depicted in Figure 9.3. Centrally, processes and structures that have made it difficult for firms to adopt a pan-European vision should be substituted by those that allow for transnational market segmentation and that facilitate the identification of common tastes, needs and requirements across national boundaries. From the basis of 'European market segmentation', firms will be better positioned to discover the types of person most likely to purchase their products (across different markets in Europe) and to identify areas for standardization and differentiation. Again, either a standardized promotional campaign can be devised or a customized approach adopted. This will depend on the salient features of the product and market in question.

Identifying customers

In this context, the adoption of distinctive demographic and geodemographic modalities of market research provides one route to the identification of cross-border segments. By examining some of these approaches we can look in greater depth at the whole issue of European market segmentation and extend consideration into some of the problems and difficulties of contemporary international market research.

Euro-clusters: geodemographics and the Euro-consumer

According to research associated with VanderMerwe and L'Huillier, companies in Europe can compete effectively in Europe by accurately targeting customers close to one another, but not necessarily living in the same country. These transnational clusters will have similar economic, demographic and/or lifestyle characteristics, despite the existence of national boundaries between them. Consequently, the idea is advanced that consumers living in different countries can be closer in profile to one another than to other consumers in their own country. In turn, managers working in those markets will need a fresh marketing approach:

> Rather than tackling each country or market separately, they will be able to tap large cross-cultural Euro-Consumer clusters. This will necessitate an adjustment in their marketing and operating strategies, from market segmentation and product planning to distribution and logistic network decisions. . . . Rather than look for one mass market or for consumers who fit old purchasing molds, they (managers) need to identify clusters of Euro-Consumers and adjust their strategies and operations to cater to these new transnational groups. (VanderMerwe and L'Huillier, 1989)

The six clusters identified by VanderMerwe and L'Huillier are:

- the UK and Ireland (cluster 1),

- Central and Northern France, Southern Belgium, Central Germany and Luxembourg (cluster 2),

- Spain and Portugal (cluster 3),

- Southern Germany, Northern Italy, Southeastern France and Austria (cluster 4),

- South Italy and Greece (cluster 5), and

Figure 9.4 VanderMerwe's European clusters

■ Northern Germany, the Netherlands, Northern Belgium, Iceland, Norway, Finland and Denmark (cluster 6).

These clusters are presented in Figure 9.4. VanderMerwe (1993) went on to suggest that Europe will continue to be a complex set of independent operating areas, each dominated by certain similarities. These include:

1. mass clusters with common consumer needs;

2. niche clusters (wherein consumers have similar but non-identical needs);

3. local and specialized clusters.

In this context, market integration in Europe should facilitate access to cross-national segments, eliminating many entry barriers and heightening the potential for standardized products and promotions.

Social group and life-style modelling

As El-Kahal (1998, p. 132) suggests, another basis for a general pan-European focus is to take advantage of demographic variables and distinguish between different social groups or segments across the Community. Again, the reasonable assumption underlying this approach is that different types of people, across Europe, will have similar demands for products and that they can be broadly grouped according to their interests, tastes and attitudes. The most frequently used segmentation bases are gender, age, occupation and income. Other variables include a person's stage in the family life-cycle and their type and place of residence. Precise frameworks vary, mixing and prioritizing different variables from this list. Many marketing specialists band people together into associated groups according to the occupation of the principal wage earner in a household. In this case, we are left with familiar letter–numerical descriptions such as C1s and C2s to describe different socio-economic groups such as 'lower middle class' (C1), 'skilled working class' (C2) and 'subsistence or under-class' (E). While these classifications are far from universal, a number of EU countries do follow the UK in using the above classifications and statistical authorities throughout Europe use comparable methodologies.

Broader efforts at social segmentation, and ones relying on a synthesis of age, income and other variables, can be seen elsewhere. For example, in the research of Guido (1992), evidence is presented of converging cross-national segments among young people, trendsetters and business people. A fourth category of more senior consumers (the so-called 'grey market') could easily be added to reflect the growing importance of Europe's expanding population of retirees and senior citizens. These and other social-group approaches are closely related to life-style-based analyses which identify in (European) consumers activity preferences and/or shared attitudes.

While precise divisions are somewhat arbitrary, it is entirely clear that marketers are targeting different socio-economic and life-style groups across European boundaries. For example, multinational companies have been heavily investing in researching European youth consumption patterns in order to better exploit the multiple markets in areas such as music, drinks, food, fashion, sports and tobacco (see Sumner-Smith, 1998). Companies have also been focusing entire marketing strategies on particular consumer groups. For example, Ikea, the Swedish furniture company, has long been focusing its marketing in Europe on relatively young consumers, with a common strategy of reasonably priced, self-assembly products. In recent years, the diversification of the apparel group Benetton into athletic and sports equipment (and clothing) has followed the growth of the 'active' market. This market is characterized by a growing number of adventurous young people with a taste for high-octane activities such as rollerblading, ski-ing, snowboarding and abseiling.

Residence and neighbourhood analysis

Residential analysis provides an alternative (if not dissimilar) means of conceptualizing and researching customer groups. Again, although individual approaches evidence some variability, assessment is based broadly on analysing similar socio-residential groups on the assumption that purchasing power and usage behaviour may be fairly uniform in similar neighbourhoods. The ACORN classification provides one such approach, separating one type of neighbourhood from another and providing marketers with a framework for targeting products and product promotion.

Providing a different picture of socio-economic groups, residential analysis may, therefore, allow businesses to segment transnationally and to tailor their marketing efforts to different groups within and across national boundaries. This may involve a focus on similar metropolitan areas in Europe (these are showing more similarities than urban and rural areas within national boundaries) and, within this, on comparable neighbourhoods.

European market research: some common problems

Despite the attractions of targeting Euro-consumer segments, researching customers and markets on a multinational basis is rarely straightforward. Marketers and market researchers must confront the following problems and issues:

1. *Language barriers*. Language differences pose real problems for identifying commonality of behaviour between different nationals. This refers not just to difficulties in translation but also comparability in meaning, which is linked to not just the words used but to semantic differences in understanding between different nations.

2. *Sensitivity of questioning*. The different peoples of Europe will demonstrate a different willingness to impart information. The Greeks, for example, may not be concerned about giving information on their income, whereas the British are very sensitive about the money they earn and the implications this has for their being stratified into different social groups.

3. *Different research techniques*. Many modern-day market research techniques are the product of American marketing activity and centre on individuals' ability to talk about feelings and emotions. Some country nationals, however, find this difficult to do and prefer more functional research questions.

4. *Cultural differences*. With cultural differences between the member states being so significant, and culture permeating the way in which groups and individuals behave and think, questionnaire responses from different nationalities need to be considered within their own cultural context. A failure to do this may well lead to misinterpretation of the real meaning of research findings.

5. *Suspicion*. In some countries, there is growing suspicion about the usage of information gathered through marketing research, which is leading to a growing reluctance to participate in research exercises.

6. *Statistical comparisons*. Serious complications attach to cross-country comparison of statistics, many of which are gathered locally using different conventions and reporting practices. For example, differences in demographic data, educational qualifications, family groups, social trends, advertising and promotional spending exist between member states. This makes meaningful comparison difficult.

7. *Fragmentation*. Because many multinational companies have decentralized structures (where each local centre has its own autonomy), 'own account' research, across different countries and markets, can often be fragmented, methodologically inconsistent, and diluted in effect.

For all of these reasons, and as many organizations continue to lack the necessary funds and expertise to conduct efficient multinational research, the popularity of major international market research companies such as TNSofres and ISPOS is increasing. The total European market for market research is now estimated at a staggering €4.7 billion (a little over 40% of the total world market) with Europe's ten biggest market research (MR) firms taking over half the industry's total revenue (http://www.esomar.nl/index.htm). Using standardized methodologies, these organizations have the capacity to assimilate and to integrate market research data from across Europe and to disseminate targeted findings on a customized basis.

Nonetheless, facilities for researching European markets are better and more extensive than ever before and firms continue to enjoy a number of options (Bennett, 1997, p. 242). Apart from the expert (and expensive) services of leading MR firms, businesses can commission market research from smaller agencies in their home countries and/or from local research firms in target (foreign) markets. Many national market and marketing research associations are also geared up to provide clients with Europe-wide market data and have formed networks through such structures as ESOMAR (the European Society for Opinion and Marketing Research). National statistical services are also now much better developed and Eurostat (the EU's statistical service) provides a number of relevant publications (e.g. *Panorama of EU Industries*) and databases such as CRONOS and REGIO. Between these publications–databases, the EU is providing the sort of basic macroeconomic and demographic data increasingly valued by market researchers (see also Bennett, 1997, pp. 241–3).

Working with the market

Whatever the parameters of a firm's market, for any company to succeed it must become truly market oriented. According to Frederick Webster (1998) market-driven companies segment the market efficiently and strategically, identify which customers they want, focus on customer benefits and service (sensing and responding to customer needs) and build strong long-term relationships. These are not the only components of market-driven action but are essential if a firm is to work successfully 'with', rather than simply 'in' its different markets.

Customer focus and orientation

In this theory, and implicit in the framework advanced in this chapter, everything starts with customers, their changing definitions of value, and the challenge of offering solutions to customer problems. As noted in earlier commentary, there is a growing belief in the area of marketing that customers want solutions not products. As consumerism has developed in Western economies customers have become more discerning and demanding of suppliers and are continually looking for products which add more value (whether this be aesthetic, technological or performance and quality). Furthermore, 'because customers continually acquire more experience and new information, especially from competing marketers, their definition of value keeps changing' (see Webster, 1998, p. 238).

In short, it is no longer strategic for firms to simply 'produce and sell'; alternatively they must 'enquire and provide' in an increasingly dynamic context. This means re-thinking the way in which they interact with their market and developing structures which permit market-driven decision-making. A key part of this process is changing the mind-set of the organization to think in terms of customer focus and problem solution ('customer orientation'). This requires solid information about customers, their needs, requirements and buying patterns. Defining the business as a service business offering solutions to customer problems becomes the key to defining opportunities for growth and greater profitability. A bank, for example, does not want to purchase a computer system. What it wants is a tool which facilitates financial planning and permits the establishment of a sophisticated customer database. The bank customer, on the other hand, wants a solution which spans his/her day-to-day financial transactions including deposits and withdrawals, the payment of bills, ease of access to his/her money at any time, services for foreign travel and holidays, credit and loans, etc.

Therefore, producing standardized goods for mass consumer markets appears to hold less sway than developing solutions for the individual and being sensitive to individual requirements ('pervasive customer focus'). As Webster concludes (1998, p. 240):

> A market-driven company focuses on what the customer is buying – that is, on customer benefits – not on what it is making in the factory and selling. ... The successful global marketer aims to achieve 'mass customization', the tailoring of product offerings and communications to individual customers and small market niches.

Managing relationships with intermediaries

It is not only the final consumer firms need to concern themselves with; they also have to consider the role of intermediate purchasers or re-sellers such as wholesalers, distributors and retailers. These have a potentially important role to play both in the success of the product in the market and in the experience of the customer. It is therefore critical that firms attempt to develop strategic relationships not only with final customers but also with intermediaries.

Intermediaries can provide a number of important services for the manufacturer:

1. providing warehouse facilities – building and breaking bulk;

2. distribution – utilizing existing channels to reach (foreign) customers;

3. providing market intelligence – gathering and passing on information to the manufacturer on which future strategies may be based;

4. providing a visible market presence – increasing awareness and confidence by having a physical market-based representation (foreign intermediaries can provide firms with a surrogate presence in overseas markets);

5. managing relationships – between manufacturer and customers;

6. administrating – responding to inquiries, taking and processing orders;

7. providing customer service – technical advice and repairs along with advice on product usage (for end-users), product storage and display (for retailers);

8. minimizing cultural distance – serving as a learning post for the company to understand the foreign market and, when staffed by local managers, a means of reducing the foreign image of the firm and overcoming local language barriers.

By working together, manufacturers and intermediaries have the potential to add value. However, it is entirely clear that there is much scope for conflict between manufacturers and their intermediaries. Conflict may arise for a number of reasons:

1. Intermediaries and manufacturers may disagree on price. Intermediaries may cut prices in order to move stock, lowering the returns for the manufacturer.

2. Conflicts arise in the way the product is marketed. Intermediaries, based on their closeness to the market and understanding of customers, sometimes perceive products as uncompetitive, which gives them less incentive to promote them. Equally, helpful advice made by the intermediary to the manufacturer is frequently ignored as it fails to fit with the manufacturer's understanding of the product and competition based on experience from other countries.

3. Intermediaries fear over-performance. By promoting a product and achieving a certain level of business, the intermediary can encourage firms to establish their own distribution functions, removing their business from the intermediary.

4. The intermediary is often faced with divided loyalties. Dealing with a number of competing products means that the intermediary is not solely dedicated to the manufacturers' product, which dilutes the amount of selling effort provided by the salesforce. Generally, they sell those products which earn them the highest commission or for which there is a strong demand generated by high promotional expenditure, a high degree of attractiveness (be it brand name or technological sophistication) or greater reliability.

Conflict can be overcome through one of two methods, control or co-operation. Control involves a series of rewards and sanctions based on targets set by the manufacturer. Although they can prove successful in raising performance, they do little to nurture good relations between the two parties as they continue to support a buyer–seller-type relationship. In so doing, the individual parties continue to suboptimize. While the intermediary may be inclined to improve sales performance, there will be little incentive for him or her to improve additional complementary functions such as information gathering and dissemination, which can be critical to future strategic planning for the manufacturer. Co-operation emerges as the most favourable approach, wherein the manufacturer works closely with the intermediary, setting price levels which are acceptable to both parties, giving, receiving and acting on information, and providing adequate support and incentives.

While many firms assume that operating via an intermediary involves handing over the product at the docks or market border, nothing could be further from the truth. The challenge facing firms in the Single Market, particularly small firms for whom utilizing the services of the intermediary is their only available option, is to establish and preserve good relations. In the longer term this may involve technical staff placements in the foreign firm although, in turn, the acceptability of this approach depends on the development of good relations.

Concluding here, the Industrial Marketing and Purchasing Group alluded to the notion of tripartite relations in international marketing, the manufacturer, the distributor and the customer all becoming involved in the marketing process. This concept is consistent with much of the new thinking on market-driven action stressing the formation of strategic partnerships at all levels, e.g. with suppliers of raw materials and components, with re-sellers and chosen customers. Without this kind of relationship, it is impossible to ensure that product and service solutions are truly customer oriented. The complexities of tripartite customer management are highlighted in Figure 9.5.

While the above research centres on relationship management in industrial markets, there is no reason why these concepts cannot be equally transferred to

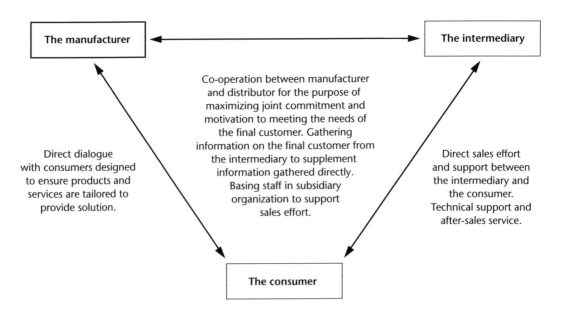

Figure 9.5 Developing tripartite customer relations

consumer markets. Companies need to ensure that they work closely with customers (by researching their needs and wants and understanding their purchasing behaviour) and develop good relations with retailers. If marketing managers are going to actively pursue the advantages which accrue from working with their customers to provide more tailor-made solutions and added value, intermediaries need to be incorporated in the value chain of the firm, whether they be internal or external to the organization. At one level, this would appear to suggest greater vertical integration within the value chain (gaining greater control over the firm–customer interface through ownership of distribution and marketing functions), although, as was stressed in Chapter 8 and above, control can be equally achieved through co-operation and relationship management.

Managing customer relationships

If we are to accept that modern marketing is relationship marketing, then managing these relationships is a critical function of the current day marketing department. A failure to deliver on time, an inability to cope with after-sales servicing and a failure to understand why customers come back (or fail to do so), mean that the organization does not have a foundation on which to build consumer loyalty or to establish long-term meaningful relationships with their market. In this context, managing ongoing relationships centres on three objectives:

1. managing quality;
2. providing service;
3. understanding customer needs and behaviour.

Managing quality

An important problem immediately arises when considering quality management: what is it and how can it be measured? There are no simple answers to this, and in many ways the only reliable means of measuring quality is through consumer research on past purchases. This gives manufacturers some indication of how well a product is performing relative to customer expectations. Post-purchase questionnaires are becoming a popular tool for monitoring opinions about quality issues. Satisfaction with product features and performance, and indication of faults and complaints can all be assessed using this technique.

Providing customer service

Providing service poses a completely different set of problems. For intermediaries, service quality is often measured in terms of a company's ability to deliver on time. Alternatively, from a consumer's point of view, service is more about providing adequate information and effective after-sales support.

The importance of delivery can be regarded in relation to future demand. Where a manufacturer fails to deliver on time, whether because of the firm's inability to secure adequate stock or respond rapidly enough to orders, or where there are unexpected problems such as poor weather conditions, the likelihood of the customer trading with them again is remote. This introduces the notion of the cost of lost sales into the management equation. In order to prevent this happening, firms have a number of options available to them:

1. they can establish a more centralized distribution facility which is better placed to respond quickly to orders;
2. they can employ more flexible manufacturing and distribution techniques;
3. they can rely on the services of locally based intermediaries to hold stock on their behalf (although problems of delivering to intermediaries will remain).

These issues are visited at greater length at a later stage in this chapter ('Managing logistics'). Regarding the provision of after-sales service, again manufacturers have a number of options:

1. Establish their own after-sales service provision in the local market (usually through local sales and marketing offices).
2. Employ a team of Europe-wide trouble-shooters prepared to go to any location within the EU at short notice (only really feasible where the number of customers is small).
3. Rely on the services of market-based intermediaries.
4. Allow customers to contact the organization quickly and easily through dedicated customer information and service centre(s). The reasons for contact may include bill query, warranty claim, product/service information or technical problems.

Understanding the customer

Firms need to continually enquire of their efforts, why do customers buy from us? In short, understanding relationships with customers is not just about identifying needs but also about understanding how and why these needs arise and in what way the firm equates with the solution or satisfaction of those needs (or not as the case may be). In this context, the emergence of the customer database must be considered as central to the efforts to understand customer purchasing and to establishing long-term customer relationships. Although more sophisticated methods of customer profiling exist, such as regression modelling, CHAID and neural networks, these remain to be fully exploited.

Customer databases

Throughout European sectors, databases of all shapes and sizes are being used to store useful information on actual and potential customers, to track customer purchasing patterns and to associate buying patterns with identifiable lifestyle characteristics. This provides organizations with a new level of customer knowledge and allows them to take a long-term perspective of their customer relationships. In particular, by continually updating information, the identification of key trends is easier to see and thus creative business solutions are easier to develop on a customized or tailored basis. For example, with the maturation of customer databases, it becomes easier for catalogue companies to distinguish between different buying groups to the extent that it can target the needs of smaller subsegments through smaller specialized catalogues. The only problem with databases (and database marketing) is customer suspicion and resistance. The concept smacks of a 'Big Brother' mentality, with the individual's behaviour mined and monitored by agencies over which he or she has little control. Therefore, the use of information gathered needs to be treated with great sensitivity and considered in the light of cultural norms and acceptance.

Working with the firm

Organizational structures

In achieving pervasive customer focus and in building relationships with strategic customers, the firm must also look inwards. As Peters makes clear (1990), if the philosophy of getting closer to the customer is not supported by intra-organizational dynamics (interfunctional collaboration and co-ordination) then structures will act as impediments not facilitators to this new way of thinking. This point takes us back to one of our earlier themes raised in relation to the emergence of new marketing theories. As considered then, marketing departments in recent years have been accused of working independently of other functions within the organization, of becoming islands without linkages to other departments. Often, this has meant that marketing departments, which may be adept at identifying the needs of customers and targeting products, have been frustrated by the failure of internal systems to permit group-wide value adding. With R&D departments and production operations ploughing their own furrow, it is inevitable that knowledge of markets will not be translated into improved product offerings. The various functions within the organization therefore require review (and closer integration) if European firms are to respond to the new environmental challenge.

So how can firms react? The first issue to stress is that all departments should be working in the same direction – to satisfy the needs of targeted consumers. This means the marketing function transcending other business operations and not merely being an adjunct to them. Indeed, some proponents of customer-oriented marketing have gone as far as to suggest that everyone in the organization needs to adopt a marketing role, thinking how their particular function relates to the needs of customers, both internally and externally (we can refer back to the Nordic School theorists here). If guided by a marketing department which is freed from the ties of its island status and permitted to operate across functions, various departments may be able to more clearly align their activities with the pursuit of customer value-adding.

This notion of pervasive customer focus, both internal and external, is reminiscent of the total quality management (TQM) principles alluded to in Chapter 6 (see also Chapter 11). Some theorists have argued that TQM is, in essence, a management tool for developing systems for internal and external marketing improvement. While it is way beyond the scope of this chapter to outline the varying arguments in this debate, it is useful to understand the parallels. Quality is driven from the top, through mechanisms to integrate and reinforce the notion of the customer as king, to remove inefficiencies and draw the organization together to meet a common purpose. New marketing challenges demand the same: an all-embracing ethos of customer orientation designed to find solutions to problems and not products to sell. This can only be driven by the top and through re-organization of the company into more cross-disciplinary groups charged with the responsibility of managing across functions and not perpetuating functional inefficiency.

Making the necessary adjustments is, however, far from straightforward. Whereas the marketing function is a relatively soft discipline in which change and new ways of thinking can be adopted quickly, company organization and production are hard disciplines which are far less flexible and require major investment before change can be achieved. The marketing department cannot, therefore, work alone in achieving the objectives of pan-European marketing and improved customization. Directives must come from the top with senior managers finding ways of altering organizational structures and functional competence to support new developments.

New product development

It was stated above that marketing departments need to work more closely with R&D departments to ensure that the products which are developed are those which cater for the changing needs of target customers and the different needs of customer segments. The marketer's role in new product development is, therefore, about providing a link between the market and the design department, with customers and R&D technicians both involved in the process. It also requires involving senior management, as changes in customer demand and purchasing patterns may have serious implications for future business objectives and directions. Figure 9.6 attempts to highlight the varying degrees of involvement of different players in different stages of the design process and thus the role of marketing departments in the new product development function. Although the processes described in the figure are highly simplified, it is easy to see the rationale for presenting the marketing department as the linchpin in the new product development process. They are the conduit of information between the market and the firm and between the

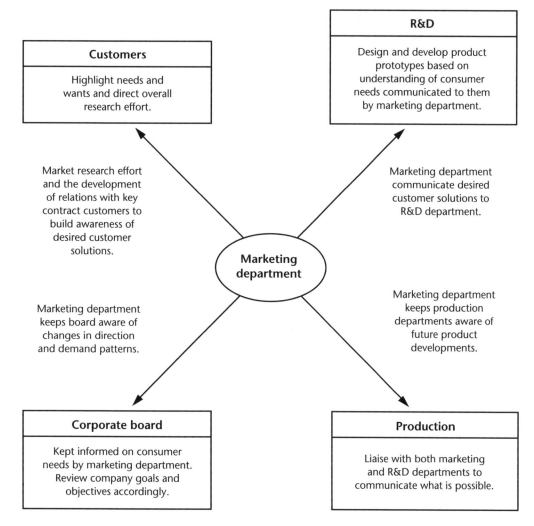

Figure 9.6 Marketing's role in product development

various departments involved in the product development process. Taking on a pivotal role means broader involvement of various stakeholders which can be further facilitated by project teams which bring members of all groups together at the same time to discuss and to solve mutual problems. As Saunders remarks (1994, p. 107):

> Such approaches, which encourage a pooling of expertise and the solving of problems jointly, represent a significant change to traditional practices, which were carried out on a sequential basis, with little co-operation and a low level of communication between the functions.

Whatever the precise view of the marketer's role, the significance of new product and process development has been given increased recognition in recent years and the value of close integration between design, manufacturing and marketing activi-

---

CASE STUDY 9.1 **Benetton: a story in product and process development**

Benetton began as a small family manufacturing business in Treviso in north-east Italy in 1965. Since this time, the organization has become a multinational giant with operations in over 120 countries and over 7,000 clothing stores worldwide. In 1997, global revenue topped $2 billion. Ambitious as a group, Benetton has been making several acquisitions (from supermarkets to tennis racquet manufacturers) and has recently been extending its clothing range from knitwear and sweaters (its core clothing product) to sports and leisurewear.

With respect to product and process development, the company has always focused on innovation. In many ways, it is the company's hallmark. In 1972, the company changed one of its central processes. Rather than dyeing the yarn, it turned its attention to dyeing garments, a process that could be completed in two hours for each batch. This has helped the company to respond quickly to differences in retail demand, heightening its market responsiveness. The company can introduce a great number of changes in articles, colours etc. in a very short space of time with machines adjusted to produce large numbers of articles in relatively small

batches. In addition, a wool softening technique (first identified in a firm in Scotland) has supported Benetton's ability to differentiate itself from its leading competitors. Today, production is quick and efficient because of a flexible production network, which encompasses over a hundred external contractors and two state-of-the-art company factories near Treviso. These manufacturing units, with extensive CAD and CAM facilities, give the company the ability to design and to produce up to 2,000 different garments a year and to cut 15,000 garments every eight hours. While knitting and assembling are performed throughout the network, production planning, design and development, cutting (by computer) and dyeing processes all remain centralized. External contractors are provided with much of the technical ability needed to run them, the exact quantities of raw materials necessary for production work, technical support and financial aid. Production strategy is based on producing to order for franchised shops, which are independently owned (see Chapter 7). This means less stockpiling of garments, reduced wastage and improved efficiency.

---

ties is now widely perceived. In this context, a firm that has a slower rate of new product introductions and the phasing in of product modifications is likely to be eclipsed by more innovative rivals and will waste opportunities for other improvements in performance. Conversely, and as explained by Wheelwright and Clark (1992), excelling at product and process development can provide a sustainable competitive advantage (see Case Study 9.1).

Creative thinking and development

If new product development is a matter of finding out what customers want (and then delivering it), the question begs, do customers always know what they want? Given that the certain answer to this question is 'no' and, that in many situations customers cannot identify or articulate their requirement with any real certainty, some theorists are now talking about the concept of market-sensing. Robertson (1994) suggests that market-sensing is about:

> Designing a product that consumers did not explicitly request. The challenge of course is to get out in front of consumers; to extrapolate and infer future customer needs. Yet

traditional forms of marketing research seldom seem to provide the insight necessary to engage in creative marketing.

Thus new product development is also about having visions. This does not merely mean innovative researchers doing their own thing, but marketing managers exploring trends in customer purchasing and demand so that emerging needs become explicit to the supplier organization before they have become apparent to the consumer. This is a far from easy task but organizations that master the art have the potential to create markets.

Product legislation and Euro-marketing

Practice has shown that legal aspects are still a significant obstacle to the development of a European product strategy, imposing various restraints. This question has already been addressed in discussion of Single Market arrangements (see Chapter 3) but a number of issues are worth re-stating here allowing for a deferred focus on labelling and packaging issues. For example, firms may still be required to adapt their products before they can be sold on the markets of partner countries whose product regulations differ from those applied in the country of origin. Although products legally marketed in one member state should be admitted in other member states (that is, in accordance with the mutual recognition principle), this is not always guaranteed. In the absence of conformity with a mutually recognized European or international standard, or if no standards are applicable, compliance with local regulations may need to be certified by a so-called 'competent body'. Another way may be to achieve a type-examination certificate through a so-called 'notified body'. In either case, certification may be dependent on product modification. Where the issue is a voluntary national standard rather than a statutory regulation, the producer still faces a situation wherein the voluntary standard is likely to hold a quasi-legal status (see Hildebrand, 1994). Moreover, if there is no clear legal compulsion to adapt the product and to have it certified in accordance with local rules, there may very well be a market-driven pressure. The absence of association with a publicly recognized standard may seriously hinder distribution and sales in the market in question.

Common specifications such as those created by European standards bodies are now widely applied in those product areas where Community directives have specified 'essential requirements' as regards safety, health, the environment and consumer protection. Significantly, although producers do not have to adopt existing European standards (a product *can* be legitimately marketed if it meets legislative requirements by any method), failure to do so creates disadvantage. Critically, producers who can show that their products are produced according to mutual standards will save time and money in gaining the required CE marking. In areas of industrial production subject to technical harmonization directives, the Conformité Européenne (CE) mark is a compulsory affixation to goods circulated within the EU market. As explained by Hildebrand (1994):

CE marking is a Community sign of a regulatory type. ... It signifies that industrial products are presumed to comply with all of the requirements in the directives that is to say the essential requirements of safety and all the other requirements which are collectively mentioned in the directive and which are the subject of an evaluation of conformity on the basis of appropriate procedures. Directives have been issued for toy safety, construction products, machine safety, telecommunication products, gas appliances, pressure vessels, electromagnetic compatibility, non-automatic weighing instruments, medical aid goods, and [elsewhere] ... The requirements also apply to goods coming from outside the European Union.

Given this backdrop and the requirement on companies to stay informed about the legal requirements applicable to their products, the stages of product design, testing and packaging must be journeyed with mind to legal and quasi-legal conditions in all target markets. Strategically, if those requirements are integrated in an early stage of the product development cycle, unnecessarily high adaptation costs may be avoided (Hildebrand, 1994). Firms should also be conscious that the European Product Liability Directive makes both manufacturers and importers liable for injuries caused by defective products, and that the EU's 'General Product Safety' Directive requires manufacturers to provide customers with full information on the potential risks from their products.

Managing pricing

Price is an important aspect of product positioning. Prices are decided not just as a means of deriving profit but as a means of giving signals to customers about the quality and nature of the product being offered. There are no universal rules as to what constitutes a good pricing policy but it is widely considered that pricing strategies will be determined by a combination of factors. These may include production costs, product maturity, the price of competitive products, the utility the customer attaches to the product, and the elasticity of demand of the product (i.e. how responsive the quantity demanded is to changes in the product's price).

Pricing in Europe

Although the IMP and EMU have both increased competition and have put downward pressures on prices in some markets, the European economies are characterized by wide price differentials over basic samples of goods (see Figure 9.7). To understand this, it is important to consider the main factors that keep national markets and prices apart:

1. As each member state market is characterized by a different competitive structure (with different local firms coming into play), local operating units need to have a degree of freedom to decide on the most appropriate pricing level for local conditions.

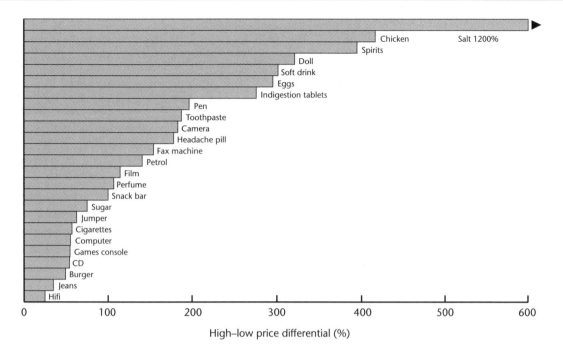

Figure 9.7 Price differentials by product, EU-15
Source: KPMG Consulting (1999, p. 3). Reproduced by permission of the publishers.

2. Different channel structures and degrees of retailer power between member states impact on the amount of mark-up required by distributors and retailers in each consumer market.

3. Differences between nations in terms of tastes and wants lead to different perceptions of product value. For example Italian branded goods may be perceived as chic in one market but unreliable in another (KPMG Consulting, 1999, p. 8).

4. Products sold in different EU markets may be at different stages in their life-cycles, allowing different prices to exist in different markets.

5. Many manufacturers have little certainty as to the level and range of their prices across Europe, meaning that prices can remain differentiated as a consequence of weak control over channel structures and by simple chance.

6. Price differences can also be associated with differential VAT and excise rates. Although the impact of these differences can often be exaggerated, standard VAT rates do vary within a relatively significant range (15–25%) and various categories of goods are associated with reduced and super-reduced sales taxes which further widen sales tax differentials.

Pricing for Europe

In this context, the potential (and attraction) of pan-European pricing in Europe

407

has remained extremely limited. The feasibility of more uniform pricing has been questioned in a context of very high spreads, and price harmonization has been viewed widely as a threat to profitability. Companies not only have continued to maximize their opportunities for price discrimination but have tended to obscure it and to deter parallel trade by making national adjustments to packaging, product size, service attachments etc. However, as price differences across the Eurozone become more transparent, and as buyers turn more and more to pan-European sourcing, there is the threat that firms will lose the potential to offer products at significantly different prices in different locations. The growth and encouragement of parallel imports exacerbates these dangers (see Box 9.1). Where firms resist establishing a standard price for all Europe-wide activities, they will almost certainly need to adjust their European pricing policies to fit much narrower price corridors. This will be most pressing where price dispersion between member states is due not to structural causes such as differences in consumer tastes and indirect taxation, but to deliberate market segmentation strategies.

Whatever European pricing solutions are adopted, for many firms, basic aspects of pricing now take on a European (if not global) character. Consequently, a broader level of price intelligence is required in order to understand European pricing (and price dynamics) and firms need to construct both a map of price levels throughout the value chain (by country) and of competitor prices across Europe. In strategic terms, firms must ask whether or not they want to aim for a large and/or increased market share across Europe or in individual European markets. In this case the

---

BOX 9.1

Parallel trading

In an attempt to encourage the erosion of price differentials (and to benefit consumers Europe wide), the Commission is actively encouraging parallel trading. Article 81 of the Treaty of Rome permits the institution to take action against any firm that tries to prevent intermediaries from parallel importing.

Parallel trade involves market intermediaries buying up goods in one market (where prices are low) and selling them in another (where prices are higher) at below the going market rate. This deters manufacturers from charging different prices in different markets and exploiting those markets where price elasticity is lower and where consumers are prepared to pay the higher price. To prevent grey or parallel markets from emerging, businesses are forced to harmonize prices to a certain degree to reduce the incentives for parallel traders. Apart from this threat to operations (and to profits), when grey products are seen as a legitimate source of supply, the manufacturer is threatened with a loss of control over where and to whom its products are sold. In turn, traditional market intermediaries lose confidence in manufacturers as they see their services being side-stepped.

In an increasing number of EU markets (e.g. motor vehicles), parallel or grey markets are emerging at some speed. With the arrival of the Euro, parallel traders will enjoy greater market security because exchange rate uncertainties are removed. This will allow parallel traders to guarantee making a profit on cross-border activities for an extended period of time (assuming that prices are not adjusted).

firms might consider a (market) penetrative pricing strategy. This would mean setting a low price (and correspondingly lower profit margin on each unit) as a means of expanding market presence, but selling a higher volume. This depends considerably on whether the product is elastic in demand. Alternatively, and in potential response to cross-national audiences, they may want to function as an international niche market producer. In niche markets, businesses may be able to set a high price (with a higher profit margin on each unit sold) because of limited supply and scarcity value. This is known as market skimming. These different strategies will have major implications for sales revenue and profits and firms should develop competing Europe-wide pricing scenarios.

Brand management

Branding issues have changed significantly in recent years and, increasingly, companies in Europe have looked to unite behind key brands and towards loyalty brand building. Such efforts are seen as a key to pan-European positioning and promotions and as a method of broadening product or service recognition across regional and global markets. Significantly, uniting behind key brands can lead to material savings on printing, packaging, distribution and advertising. This applies where brands use the same identity and the same name across borders. A brand is in fact best described as a name, term or symbol (or combination of them) which is intended to identify goods and services of one seller (or group of sellers) and to differentiate them from competitors. A brand name is a major investment (it may take several years to establish a clear and positive brand identity) but a good brand can be the company's strongest asset in the marketplace. Having once been satisfied by a branded product, customers then recognize the name or logo and may return to it. Registration of brand names and their attendant properties (e.g. logos) is absolutely vital. As Dudley and Martens explain (1993, p. 284), '[w]ithout legal protection against unauthorised use by other companies the brand name is worthless'.

That there is potential for pan-European brand development is undeniable. The tentative conclusion drawn earlier was that, while marked differences remain between markets, there is the potential to identify common customer groups between member states. The existence of these groups, combined with the ability to position and to place products across Europe (with only few commercial barriers), suggests that the dilution of resources among multiple brands is at best conservative. It is also clear that a 'Euromedia' of increasingly international advertising, satellite and Internet-based information flows provides new opportunities for transnational executions based on the existence of a transnational brand. This issue is addressed in the later section on communications strategies.

Euro-brands

If the firm sells several products in one country or across different countries, it must choose whether to allocate (or to preserve) separate brand names to individual products or to establish a generic brand identity (trade name and/or logo) across all products. The idea of a Euro-brand is tied to the goal of one brand name and logo working across all of Europe in much the same way as a truly 'global brand' can work across the world. This does not mean that everything is necessarily standardized – Danone, for example, markets BioYoghurt in France, England and Germany under the same name but with different packaging – but various aspects of consistency are to be assumed. Most usually, although not universally, this includes the name and the design of the product. Although the existence of Euro-brands creates scope for common positioning and brand communication, this may differ from market to market.

According to research on Euro-branding by Landor Associates (1998), moves towards a homogenous Eurobrand can be initiated from one of a number of scenarios, including totally fragmented brands, one of partial endorsement, or one where a common brand name or common visual identity is already shared. It is the first of these scenarios which is proving increasingly common in the EU. For example, in the case of Mars, several different brands such as Treets and Bonitos have been harmonised under the M&Ms umbrella. In the case of Campbells Biscuits Europe, five local brands have been consolidated into the unified Delacre brand that now enjoys pan-European or 'umbrella' packaging. There are also present moves to standardize the United Biscuits (UB) portfolio under a pan-European McVities umbrella as a part of a wider restructuring programme at UB. In the further cases of Barilla, Bonduelle, Bols and Philips, efforts have been made to harmonize names, looks and logos across the European region. In general terms, the exercise has been to maximize marketing efficiency and to promote international product identity (see http://www.landor.com/strategy/eurobranding).

Developing brand portfolios for Europe

In developing brand portfolios for Europe, many firms are acquiring brands that are often filling identified 'gaps' in global–regional brand portfolios. A good example here would be the recent acquisition of traditional English shoemaker Church by Italian fashion house Prada: Church's shoes are worn by various British icons, including such fictional characters as James Bond. Strategically, the brand will fill a small gap in the prestigious Prada portfolio. Buying an existing brand is comparatively cheaper than attempting to establish new brands as this requires considerable advertising backing to establish awareness and acceptance. It is also possible that, by acquiring different brands, firms can gain from new economies of scale and from additional leverage with retailers. On the first point, different ranges of products can be distributed together, the salesforce can handle larger volumes, and promotional efforts can be cross-subsidized. Of course, savings on printing, packaging and promotions etc. are only fully realized when the range of products use the same identity and the same name. On the second point, by offering more lines, there is a greater potential to command shelf-space. In turn, it may be in the retailers' interest to deal co-operatively with organizations servicing their needs across a variety of diverse product ranges. Acquiring brands also means acquiring production facilities – in the case above, a small manufacturing operation in Northamptonshire, England. Although acquired facilities may not be viable over the longer term, in the short term at least, organizations do not have to face the problems of manufacturing down-time or inflexibility in production.

Of course international portfolio development can also provide a platform for geographic market expansion. As Kapferer highlights (1998, p. 28), to launch Laboratoires Garnier in Germany, L'Oreal bought out a leading German brand Dralle, which had a popular local product, 'Beauty'. In 1995 this range was relaunched as Ultra-Beauty of Dralle with the signature of Laboratoires Garnier. Subsequently, L'Oreal placed a series of its own products into the market under hybrid labels before finally abandoning the Dralle name entirely. It is clear, however, that local brand recognition can be an extremely valuable resource and that many local brands are often held in great affection. Consequently, businesses must tread carefully towards the standardization of brands and the simplification of their portfolios. In the case of Nestlé, two brands are now used on the one product. While Nestlé has tended to preserve local product brands, all of the product brands in a given range are now federated under the roof of strategic brand identities such as Nestlé or Nescafé. The attempt here has been described as an effort to find equilibrium between consumer familiarity and marketing efficiency (Brabeck, 1998).

Options such as acquisition are rarely open to smaller firms, for whom concentration on a single brand or narrow portfolio is preferable. Therefore, international brand development (by acquisition or by other means) is likely to remain a preserve of multinational enterprises and not smaller European organizations. Nevertheless, the challenges for brand development in Europe, whether by multinationals or small specialist firms, are the same:

1. To establish a product which has a distinct image and offers consumers clearly defined differential advantages.

2. To maintain levels of quality and service.

3. To establish brand names and supporting advertising which have general appeal.

4. To use price as a means of positioning the brand effectively.

5. To clearly communicate brand objectives to third parties and partners.

A failure to focus on the above list of factors diminishes the effectiveness of brand development and may lead to misconstrued signals and market failure. Branding is therefore about establishing a clear picture in the minds of target customers and intermediaries of what the brand represents and why it is a preferable purchase solution to other products or services available in the market.

Managing communications

Once the product has been designed, priced, branded etc., marketing turns its attention to promoting the product to its target markets. In a traditional four-factor classification of marketing, this is described as 'placing' the product in its market. The practice of communicating product benefits and identity is widely referred to as 'marketing communications' which can be viewed on a continuum from non-personal forms of communication to personal forms of communication. The management of this activity is described by a number of titles including 'promotions management', 'communications management' and 'customer contact management' (Hartley and Pickton, 1998).

There are many different techniques or vehicles for marketing communications, for example personal or direct selling, public relations, promotions and advertisements. An exploration of some of these vehicles will allow us to confront the notion of a marketing communications continuum stretching from personal to non-personal models of communication and to look at the different dimensions of media-based promotions. Although there are forms of marketing communications which do not use the media (e.g. personal or direct selling), firms communicate with their customers through various media including traditional mass media forms (e.g. television, radio and newspaper) and 'new' media forms such as online services and interactive TV. The use of traditional media forms has tended to follow a passive (non-personal) one-to-many communication model whereby a firm reaches many current and potential customers through marketing efforts that allow only limited forms of feedback on the part of the customer. These may or may not be segmented. Relative to traditional media, new media, as a group, 'tend to afford greater consumer control and access to more differentiated content' with communications models based on varying forms of dialogue and interactivity (Hoffman, 1995).

Personal or (personal) 'direct' selling

Personal or (personal) 'direct' selling as traditionally conceived involves person-to-person communication and is therefore at one extreme of the marketing communications continuum. Very simply, it is a method of marketing and retailing goods and services direct to the consumer rather than by using retail outlets. Consequently, it is a closely targeted marketing promotion. Independent sales people call on customers and customer organizations in their homes and businesses, to present their products and services and to conclude sales. Goods are then supplied directly. Personal selling is suited to high-quality household, personal and industrial products where benefit might be derived from detailed explanation or demonstration of the product and/or from a more personal approach. Significantly, it provides an independent distribution channel for manufacturers in a context of growing retailer power.

Personal selling has an enduring appeal and, according to the Direct Selling Association, overall industry sales exceed £900 million per year in the UK alone. However, personal direct selling costs are constantly increasing. A study conducted by McGraw-Hill in 1990 highlighted the average costs of sales visits in EU markets.

These ranged from a high in Denmark of $1,439.62 to a low in Ireland of $128.18 per visit. Based on their evaluation that it takes six visits to secure a sale, the cost of single sale in the UK worked out at $1,822.99. With this in mind, it is unsurprising that there has been increased focus on new direct marketing (DM) techniques such as catalogue sales, direct mail, direct response marketing (DRM) and telephone selling. Direct sellers are finding increasing attraction in such methods which, while failing to afford the same kind of interface with the customer, do at least require the consumer to become 'active' in order to receive more information and/or to place orders (see Box 9.2).

BOX 9.2

Direct marketing in Europe

Direct marketing (DM) and direct response marketing involve the use of the database for targeted campaigns using addressable communications such as direct mail, mail order, teletext, direct response TV and telephone selling. There has been increased focus on such techniques throughout Europe as a consequence of several factors. At one level, operators have been faced with higher (personal) direct selling costs, growing retailer power and escalating (conventional) advertising costs. At a second level, multiple customer databases are leading to the production of good-quality lists of prospective customers, and advances in technology and mail delivery services have reduced distribution costs. Indeed, DM has been growing rapidly in most European states (including a number of 'high-response' Central European markets) and has taken on a genuinely transnational character. Leading players such as La Redoute are now taking over 100,000 European orders daily via various media (Iyer and Hill, 1996).

Cross-border marketing has been encouraged by the geographic proximity of European states, by the broad assault on commercial barriers in Europe and by the advance and efficiency of European postal, telephone and television services. At present, the European Commission estimates that direct marketing accounts for about a quarter of all commercial communication expenditure in and across the EU-15. The British market is prominent here. Recent estimates suggest that top UK brand companies spend over 40% of marketing spend on direct marketing. Within five years, this figure will rise to nearly 50% with the Internet playing an increasingly important role as a DM/IDM media (http:www.aig.org/).

DM and IDM activities do however face a number of difficulties. Various concerns continue to apply to cross-border payment collection (not least to security of payments) and different VAT rates bring added complexity. Some cross-border potential is also limited by varying data protection laws and by divergent legislation on advertising in Europe. Although the EU is looking towards greater harmonization in all of these areas, there is perhaps little it can do about consumer acceptance. For example, some people may be reluctant to order a product that they cannot see or touch. Having to return the good if it is not acceptable and having to wait up to twenty-eight days for delivery may also deter consumers from embracing methods of this kind. Equally, in the case of direct mail, the growing amount of 'junk mail' received by people may reduce the impact as the degree of overload means that none of it is read or digested. In Eastern Europe and Russia too, direct marketing is being held back by problems with distribution networks, by the continuation of bureaucratic constraints on business activities and by major infrastructure and other operational constraints (see McDonald, 1999).

Public relations

Public relations is marketing communication geared towards the promotion of a company and its image rather than to the promotion of a product (advertising tends to be discreet and indirect). PR or community involvement may take the form of sponsorship, press statements and conferences, open days, charitable contributions and associations. For example, BMW has sponsored numerous sporting events (including European professional golf tournaments) and a variety of art forms and companies throughout Europe. Major factors contributing to the growth of PR (and PR services) include the escalating costs of above-the-line advertising (see the next section), the relative absence of restrictive legislation on PR activities and the internationalization of markets. As firms increase their presence in overseas markets many look towards planned efforts at company and/or brand promotion. In this respect, PR consultancies have emerged in large numbers to offer specialist services. While smaller and medium-sized companies tend to manage PR 'in house' (PR does not come cheap), running large-scale and international PR drives is complex and expensive. Consequently, the cross-border PR of major multinationals in Europe often involves networks of agencies, including transnational firms (with multi-market expertise and infrastructure) and smaller operators who can bring more detailed local knowledge to the network. Indeed, while single agencies have managed pan-European PR, the average campaign consists of both country-specific work (by local network partners) and pan-European elements defined and co-ordinated by multinational agencies. The European PR structures of Motorola and IBM both conform to this 'mix-and-match' model which balances global (or regional) orientation with local needs and customization. IBM's twenty-eight-strong European PR agency network is led and co-ordinated by Ogilvy Public Relations. In each case, local agencies play an important part in executing an international strategy with local sensitivity and adaptations (see Goddard, 1999).

Advertising

Although product sales may be promoted through vouchers, coupons, point-of-sale displays etc. (below-the-line promotions), most of the energies and expenditures associated with product promotions concern 'above-the-line' advertising in which promotional messages are designed to convey a product's existence and benefits to target segments. Using various types of media, advertisements look to create demand for products (demand-pull advertising) and/or inquiries and leads for direct selling activities (demand-push advertising). Consequently, advertising – which can also be used for sales support and for company image building – concerns the communication of basic marketing messages and plays a critical role in product and market development.

Modes and media

Advertising budgets typically represent a sizeable proportion of combined marketing funds and marketers work on the assumption that these funds must be spent carefully and efficiently. In this context, the different media forms – *television, radio, magazines and newspapers, billboards and poster-boards, leaflets and handouts, and the Internet* – offer varying advantages and disadvantages. Each will have a greater or lesser utility depending on the nature of the product, target segment, marketing budget etc. (see Campbell, 1997, p. 168). For example, television may provide extensive coverage but its ability to convey complex messages (combining images and speech) translates into higher costs. Traditional media such as posters and newspaper adverts are cheaper but only allow for simpler messages (see also Campbell, 1997). On-line, advertisers are able to cut costs (net advertising is relatively cheap), to provide deep communications and to obtain immediate feedback through such channels as e-mail. However, the emerging types of on-line advertising such as interjacent adverts – those that feature between pages on third-party web sites – and thumbnail graphic hotlinks (to advertiser sites) are only in their infancy. Few advertisers have added an on-line component to their marketing plans and, as yet, there is little concrete data to suggest which, if any, of the on-line advertising techniques is proving successful.

Advertising expenditure

Across all media, the advertising expenditure of European businesses continues to grow. BMW spent a staggering $706.3 million on advertising in 1997 but even this figure is dwarfed by the extraordinary 'adspend' of Anglo-Dutch giant Unilever whose multiple brands include Birds Eye, Boursin and Persil. Unilever, which is the world's second largest consumer goods business behind Phillip Morris, has had an advertising budget of over $3 billion since the mid-1990s. In 1997 alone, it spent $5.939 billion on advertising worldwide. Since 1980, the overall value of EU advertising expenditure has increased by 73% in real terms with television spending up by 200% and newspaper advertising by 50% (Advertising Association, 1998). These two media account for 70% of all 'adspend' in Europe with aggregate advertising expenditure in the EU reaching a total of $74 billion in 1996. Annual rates of growth are expected at between 2% and 5% in the near term with growth in television advertising to be further stimulated by the continuing deregulation of European broadcasting. A number of national TV admarkets, including all of the Scandinavian markets, are growing from a relatively small base.

Creative policies for Europe: standardization versus customization

A key issue in international advertising is whether the firm should standardize its advertising campaigns or adapt them to meet the requirements of particular foreign markets (Anholt, 1993). Standardizing campaigns that cross borders can provide cost efficiencies in producing commercials, press advertisements etc. (e.g. less creative time to devise separate advertisements) and can contribute to a universal quality standard in creative presentation, message and copy. These advantages may be especially significant where brand values are fairly universal and where a universal product meets similar needs and occupies similar segments in different markets. In this context, uniform campaigns can help to steer brand positioning the same way in all markets together (Dudley and Martens, 1993). Equally, common executions across borders may have an attraction where a corporate culture and/or generic product set is being promoted (see Case Study 9.2) and where a product or brand is being launched. For example, Ford found it possible (and profitable) to launch its new Puma model through a uniform pan-European execution inspired by the Steve McQueen movie classic 'Bullitt'. Similarly, the Swatch Micro Compact car was launched across eight European countries in 1998 (but not in the UK) with the same creative artwork and strapline, 'reduce to the max' (see Gray, 1997, p. 14).

Despite the improved conditions for cross-border campaigns (e.g. more pan-European media, closer EU integration etc.), uniform pan-European executions are not always the answer. It remains extremely difficult to produce standardized ads and campaigns that will bridge national and cultural divides in Europe. Companies may find it impossible to get the same message across effectively in different markets and languages, and a lack of fine-tuning to cultural sensibilities may lead to weak local demand and/or difficulties in defending a product against competition. A genuine concern is that uniform pan-European campaigns may involve lowest common denominator messaging, appealing to everyone but capturing no-one. Language is a particularly complex issue in that ad messages must be relevant to each individual market. Apart from the costs involved with local language adaptation, names and phrases mean different things in different markets. For example, when Vauxhall launched its Nova car, the company realised that in Spanish the name meant 'doesn't go'. A similar confusion occurred with Wrigley's Spearmint gum, which in some East European states reads as 'shark's sperm' (see Barrett, 1997).

CASE STUDY 9.2 The 'mono-advertising' of Benetton

One business making use of standardized advertising campaigns is the apparel group Benetton. Benetton do not advertise their individual products, they advertise their corporate culture, the thing that embraces the organization and draws it together. It would be impossible to reflect the ranges of clothes sold in Benetton outlets in an advertising campaign, which would therefore do little for establishing company image across cultures. The solution was mono-advertising campaigns executed and delivered across European and global borders and symbolizing a radical and global corporate philosophy ('The United Colours of Benetton'). Striking and controversial campaigns that look to raise awareness of social and global issues, for example ads featuring Down's syndrome kids modelling Benetton clothing, and dramatic images of war, death and childbirth. The purpose is to provoke and to shock, to make people sit up and to think about political and social issues, to make them identify with a company which is prepared to stand out of line and to say 'I am different'. According to Luciano Benetton, the Chairman of the Benetton Group, such campaigns, which are free from tailoring to specific countries or markets, play well in free-thinking Europe and represent a legitimate means of tackling social and global issues. Critics say the company is exploiting sensationalism and the impressionistic qualities of young people in order to sell its jumpers.

For these reasons – and as a further consequence of different media structures and laws governing advertising in Europe – many pan-European campaigns are customized or 'adapted'. This means that alterations are made to a general concept so as to tailor the central message to each market efficiently and effectively. It is still possible to talk of a European communications strategy but, unlike standardized approaches where minimal adaptations are made in order to meet basic legal and language requirements, here, significant (local) modifications are made in one or more areas. For example, alterations may be made to the choice and balance of media channels, creative presentation (e.g. changes to straplines, use of actors or symbols), positioning (changes to the selling proposition and product presentation) and even to brand identity. These may be lesser or greater depending on the cultural differences between countries and/or market segments, the availability or non-availability of matching media, and the use and perception of the product in the countries at issue. As Dudley and Martens put it (1993, p. 328), the exercise is about 'sharpen[ing] the marketing attack' on a country-by-country basis within the context of an overarching European strategy. Thus, it should be clear that adaptive campaigns are removed from purely local approaches (where there is no international identity for the product) and from standardized communications, where identity, presentation and positioning are uniform across markets.

Legal barriers to cross-border advertising

This analysis raises the issue of advertising and promotions legislation in Europe and its effects on aspects of marketing. Differences in the interpretation of relevant Community directives and in national rules tied to the legal control of national media (and media structures) make cross-border advertising a continuous challenge. The same applies to national differences on the advertisement of certain products (see Case Study 9.3), to limits on the number of hours available for television advertising, to limits set on the amount firms can spend on advertising, and to rules regarding misleading advertising and sales discounting. Fragmentation presents businesses and advertisers with a series of different headaches, frustrating the execution of pan-European communications strategies and inflating the costs of cross-border service provision. Given these differences, it is easy to envisage (repeat) situations in which a brand is kept from being advertised throughout Europe with a uniform campaign because of country-specific advertising restrictions. Equally, it is easy to imagine a situation in which a magazine may not be sold in one country because it contains prohibited advertising. Indeed, two laws in one country alone (France) – the general ban on tobacco advertising and the prohibition of TV-based advertising for alcohol products over 1% ABV – inherently carry the risk of import restrictions placed on foreign media carrying such advertising.

Despite this, the EU's Expert Committee on Commercial Communications has reported little enthusiasm for the further harmonization of European communications legislation, with most member governments questioning the need for further action. In fact, member states are refusing to give up most of their own sales and advertising laws and are quite prepared to defend them where necessary. A dramatic

---

CASE STUDY 9.3 **Advertising restrictions in Europe: a picture of diversity**

Differences in toy and alcohol advertising regulation provide a clear picture of the differences in communications legislation throughout Europe.

1. *Children's toys*. European toy-makers and distributors confront a patchwork quilt of national laws on how they may advertise their products. In Greece, Sweden and Norway (for the under-twelves), toy advertising aimed at children is outlawed, and, in Belgium, it is prohibited from children's programming slots. Several complaints have been levelled against these bans, especially the blanket Greek law, which has sometimes been accused of being a crude protectionist measure. Interestingly, the Swedish Government has pledged to ban all TV advertising to children under twelve throughout Europe on what it calls 'moral and ethical' grounds. The country takes on the six-month presidency of the EU in 2001 and will hope to make progress both against those who want to preserve national sovereignty on such matters and those who want all such restrictions lifted.

2. *Alcoholic drinks*. There are a variety of national restrictions and controls in EU countries on the advertising of alcoholic beverages. In France the block on TV advertising for products over 1.0% ABV is similar but slightly different to that pertaining in Denmark where TV and radio advertisements are prohibited for alcohol over 2.25% ABV. However, in Germany, Britain and Luxembourg, there are no specific restrictions by media or alcohol content. Advertisers should not encourage excessive drinking or exploit the young but are subject only to voluntary codes (Britain having lifted an earlier ban on dark spirits advertising by television). Elsewhere in Europe, the picture becomes particularly complex. For example, a legal ban on spirits advertising on TV and radio applies in Ireland, and all alcohol advertisements are prohibited before sports programmes. On other media, a voluntary code is in operation. In Portugal, no alcohol advertising is permitted on TV before 22:00 hours and advertisements must not show alcohol being consumed (http://www.ias.org.uk/factsheets/advertising.htm).

---

case in point here is the response of the German government to the EU's recent effort to ban all advertising of tobacco and tobacco products within the EU by 2006. The German government has indicated that it will make legal challenge to this measure which it claims is a matter of public health and, therefore, for independent national authorities alone.

Overall, the body of EU communications legislation remains limited and concentrated on the establishment of 'minimum basic requirements'. For example, the Misleading Advertising Directive (84/450/EEC) establishes only minimum standards of protection against misleading claims addressed to consumers within Community member states. As discussed by Hildebrand (1994), the Directive 'expressly provides that Member States may introduce or maintain more stringent rules against misleading advertising. This means that the substantive rules for misleading advertising (in Europe) are still regulated by national provisions'. It has long been proposed that a directive on comparative advertising should coexist with this legal instrument so as to harmonize currently diverse laws and regulations on comparative claims. Among other things, this would allow advertisers (subject to common rules) to make direct comparisons between their own and competitor's goods or services. Elsewhere, the 'Television Without Frontiers' Directive

(89/552/EEC as amended by 97/36/EC) imposes a limit for advertising and promotions of 20% of any given clock-hour of broadcasting time and establishes some basic guidelines for teleshopping. The directive also contains two Articles (15 and 16) which regulate television advertising for alcoholic beverages, in particular the exposure of minors to such advertising.

Current evidence is of an *ad hoc* approach to regulating advertising and of a failure within both the Commission and the Council of the European Union to tackle the major differences that exist between member states' treatment of the same communication activities. In this context, a multiplicity of rules and provisions on both the national and regional planes, will have to be checked when a European advertising campaign is being developed. Marketers must also be attentive to the rulings of the ECJ which contribute to a growing body of relevant case law. For example, in the case *GB-INNO-BM* v. *Confederation do Commerce Luxembourgeois* (C-362/88), the Court ruled that 'under Articles 30 and 36 of the EEC Treaty an advertising campaign lawfully conducted in another Member State cannot be made subject to national legislation prohibiting the inclusion, in advertisements relating to a special purchase offer, of a statement showing the duration of the offer or the previous price'.

Internet marketing

In the present context it is incumbent on us to say a little more about the recent growth of Internet marketing in Europe. It is worth considering that the preceding version of this title (published in 1996) provided no examination of this new marketing channel, the rapid growth of which has proved one of the hallmarks of the mid–late 1990s. For the sake of clarification, it should be recounted that the World Wide Web consists of locations (URLs) or 'sites' which providers erect on servers and which users visit. With respect to business on the net, consumers (visitors) are able to search for information and/or advertising about products, to browse content (possibly advertiser supported), and/or to place an order for a product on-line. Therefore, like direct mail and catalogue sales, the Internet represents both a medium for firms to promote their products and a channel for distribution.

Internet penetration in Europe is increasing and recent growth has been faster than for the rest of the world. Europe already accounts for over a quarter of all global connections with an estimated 13 million Internet users amongst a 35 million on-line population. Strong future growth in Internet usage is expected from Italy, Spain and the Central European markets. Growth is also expected in France and in Germany where on-line populations have grown substantially since 1997. In relative terms, 'wired' populations are most significant in Scandinavia, the Benelux countries, Britain and Ireland (see Table 9.1). In fact, Scandinavia (especially Finland) has a higher density of wired population than the US.

Although the further penetration of the Internet will provide a boost to the region's e-commerce activities, there is little unity of agreement as to just how large on-line sales will become. Despite the emergence and growth of thousands of

Table 9.1 Computers (hosts) connected to the Internet per 1,000 inhabitants, select countries

	1992	1993	1994	1995	1996	1997	1998
Austria	1	2	3	7	11	14	19
Belgium	0	1	2	3	7	11	18
Denmark	1	2	4	10	21	33	55
Finland	3	7	14	41	56	63	89
France	0	1	1	3	4	6	8
Germany	1	1	2	6	9	14	17
Greece	0	0	0	1	2	3	4
Ireland	0	1	2	4	8	11	14
Italy	0	0	1	1	3	3	6
Luxembourg	0	1	1	5	9	12	17
Netherlands	2	3	6	11	18	26	38
Portugal	0	0	1	1	2	4	5
Spain	0	0	1	1	3	5	7
Sweden	3	5	9	17	27	29	46
Great Britain	1	2	4	8	12	18	24
Norway	4	7	11	20	35	68	72
Switzerland	3	5	7	12	19	27	33
USA	n/a	n/a	4	17	29	35	n/a
Canada	n/a	n/a	n/a	n/a	n/a	29	n/a
Japan	n/a	n/a	1	2	6	6	n/a
Bulgaria	0	0	0	0	0	1	1
Croatia	0	0	0	1	1	2	2
Cyprus	n/a	n/a	n/a	n/a	n/a	n/a	7
Czech Republic	n/a	0	1	2	4	6	7
Estonia	0	0	1	2	5	10	14
Hungary	0	0	1	2	3	7	9

Source: Ripe DNS Hostcount; Computer Industry Almanac; European Telework On-line

specialist Internet retailers such as lastminute.com in the UK (travel and leisure) and Sweden's Boxman.com (home entertainment), Internet retailers remain small in number and on-line sales remain modest. Total Internet commerce in Western Europe accounted for a mere 0.1% of total domestic expenditure in 1998 and only 1.5% of the European population have bought anything on-line (Schenker, 1999). In certain countries (e.g. France) teletext shopping is still more popular than on-line shopping. The French spent over $2 billion via their Minitel in 1997 but e-commerce spending totalled only $218 million (Dunlap, 1998). Thus, while consumers and firms are conducting on-line business in much greater numbers, volumes bear little comparison to those attaching to traditional media forms.

As Europe tackles the regulatory confusion surrounding e-commerce, more businesses will move on line to capture expanding audiences. It is also clear that cheaper Internet services, along with higher computer sales and increased customer confidence, should lead to more on-line consumer spending (see Case Study 9.4). However, for all the likely improvements in volume and access, basic questions of strategy remain to be answered. As Reynolds remarks (1998, p. 231), while e-commerce and marketing is in its period of infancy, 'it is unclear to what extent conventional marketing models and ideas can be transferred wholesale to an electronic channel'.

CASE STUDY 9.4 UK wired to shop on line

UK shoppers spent €2billion on the Internet in the past twelve months, a tenfold increase, according to research published in October 1999.

The surge in buying has been underpinned by several factors, including cheaper Internet service provision, higher computer sales, more web sites and growing consumer confidence in using the Internet to make purchases.

In the past four months, the number of people willing to use their credit cards for online shopping rose from 35% to 48%, according to the report by BRMB Internet Monitor. The number of people using the Internet for shopping increased by almost a third, to 2.5 million, in the past six months, representing a quarter of all Internet users in the UK.

Average annual expenditure rose 50% in the same period to €690 per person. The biggest spenders are those aged forty-five to fifty-five with Internet access at work. Their average annual on-line bills top €1,000.

Books, computer software and compact discs continue to be the most popular items purchased. However, holidays, electrical goods and cars made strong showings.

Internet banking was another favourite destination. The report said that 10% of UK Internet users now access their accounts online.

Meanwhile, a new web site that offers shoppers the chance to band together and negotiate discounts on goods and services opens in the UK this week.

Letsbuyit.com, which began trading in Sweden three months ago, has already attracted around 50,000 registered users. Web sites have also been established in Sweden, Denmark, Norway and Finland. Germany, Switzerland and Austria will follow shortly.

Users wishing to purchase a product file their request to the web site, together with the length of time they are willing to wait. When enough people have requested the same item, Letsbuyit.com goes to the manufacturer, or agent, and negotiates a discount.

Dubbed co-shopping in Sweden, users are able to monitor each co-shop event on the site to see how many people have signed up for a particular item.

John Palmer, who founded the company last November, said the business strategy was about giving power back to consumers.

Source: Financial Times, 2 October 1999

Managing logistics

Like marketing communications and the other tasks highlighted in this chapter, logistics management is an integral part of the combined marketing effort. Logistics strategies involve the identification, construction and control of supply chain structures or distribution channels. Establishing the right systems and structures for managing the distribution of physical products and information between the firm and the marketplace is of critical importance. Firms need to put in place systems which allow them to service the diverse needs of their customers speedily and efficiently. Costs should be minimised taking into account various strategic, customer service, legal and environmental constraints. While some aspects of logistics management in the new Europe have already been implicitly raised in the chapter a deal more needs to be said.

Channel structures

Supply chain or channel structures can take several different forms involving different configurations of wholesalers and distributors, sales intermediaries and retailers. Although the simplest structure is direct delivery from the manufacturer to the user or purchaser (no intermediaries or intermediate stocking points are involved), several distribution patterns exist. The length and complexity of these channels varies from case to case:

- manufacturer → consumer
- manufacturer → retailer → consumer
- manufacturer → intermediary (agent) → consumer
- manufacturer → wholesaler → consumer
- manufacturer → wholesaler → retailer → consumer
- manufacturer → intermediary (agent) → retailer → consumer
- manufacturer → intermediary (agent) → wholesaler → retailer → consumer

A firm that sells directly to user–purchasers (say by direct mail or via its own retail outlets) retains full responsibility for the storage, transport and sale of items, and for all credit risk. Where items are moved from producer to retailer (before reaching the final customer), the retailer bears the costs of storing goods awaiting sale and for merchandising the product. Where external stockists, distributors and sales agents are involved, the distribution channel takes on added complexity and the manufacturer's degree of control is loosened. Depending on the structure in question, the manufacturer may benefit from the transfer of the risk of product failure (producer to intermediary).

In selecting a distribution system, the producer should consider the following questions in respect to each alternative structure (quoted in Bennett, 1997, p. 273):

- cost of the channel,
- extent of control,
- whether the channel improves or worsens the image of the goods/brand etc.,
- geographic coverage of the channel,
- reliability of actors and agents,
- consequences for total order–delivery cycles, and
- probabilities of the non-availability of the product in certain markets.

The European dimension

Of course, assessment of these issues is being transformed by the expansion and development of the European Union and by the growth and strengthening of the Single European Market. These changes mean that manufacturers, wholesalers and distributors can design and execute their logistics strategies on a European scale. In this context, a nexus of factors is encouraging pan-European networks:

- The free movement of goods across internal EU borders and the removal of physical barriers (e.g. customs posts). This has reduced transit times (and company costs) associated with cross-border activity.

- As borders have opened up, firms have become better positioned to identify and to serve (dispersed) transnational market segments.

- Customers are becoming more demanding in relation to delivery times and want to buy goods at any time that is convenient for them. In turn, firms have needed to find systems which allow them to reach their customers speedily and efficiently and which satisfy their changing requirements for delivery of goods.

- Developments in rail and road networks across Europe, and across the Channel, are resulting in the faster movement of goods.

- A harmonization of transport regulations across Europe is opening up the potential for more Europe-wide solutions to logistics problems.

- Europe is witnessing the growth and emergence of third-party distribution companies.

With reference back to our earlier typology of channel structures, a number of options arise with regard to pan-European logistics. Saunders (1994, p. 187) identifies six likely strategies:

1. A firm may supply goods directly from a single point of origin to locations in any of the other countries – direct export – using its own transport or buying in a distribution service.

2. A firm may supply from a single point of origin to its own stockholding points in various locations in Europe. With faster delivery times and the declining influence of national borders, fewer points (or even a single centralized point) may now be needed to serve the Single Market.

3. A firm may supply through independent wholesalers and retailers.

4. A firm may be able to locate manufacturing plants in different parts of Europe and set up a supply network between them.

5. Where products have a European appeal, a retailer may expand into other countries and expand its distribution arrangements to accommodate common sources of supply.

6. European sourcing policies for a firm become more feasible either to serve a single location or a group of locations spread around the region.

The first option here rests with the idea of a centralized (European) distribution centre. While a firm may use its own warehousing, transport etc., there is an increasing propensity for firms to 'contract out' or to make use of the services of large European logistics organizations capable of handling distribution requirements on a Europe-wide basis. As well as transport firms supplying specific services (such as freight services), other companies have developed a range of services such as warehousing, logistics information, collection and delivery services that can be provided to customers on a third-party basis (see Saunders, 1994, p. 187). These services may even be 'dedicated', that is they are made exclusive to the client. For example, Hewlett Packard has a dedicated 15,000 square metre logistics centre in Amersfoort, Holland that helps it to ensure optimum supply of laser printers and toners to the European market. The company providing this service, Intexo, offers warehouse management, international road and airfreight forwarding services to a range of European and global clients (see Case Study 9.5). In fact, many firms in Europe have looked to centralize their distribution through the sorts of services offered by Intexo. The general aim is to reduce costs and to facilitate efficient pan-European delivery and servicing. In all cases, centralized distribution centres for Europe (EDCs) are made attractive by the logistical complexities and costs associated with large volumes of business across geographically dispersed markets.

CASE STUDY 9.5 | **Smith & Nephew move to new European distribution centre**

Smith & Nephew, one of the world's leading health care providers, has moved to a central warehouse (Intexo Veghel BV) for the European distribution of its woundcare and rehabilitation products. All of its rehabilitation and wound management products for Europe (except for France) now go through this Dutch distribution centre which entails 4,600 square metres of forwarding space. Intexo is a provider of European logistics services to the high-technology, healthcare and office products industries and includes Océ and Hewlett Packard among its many clients. Veghel is just one of its twelve European distribution centres. Smith & Nephew, which sells its products from Scandinavia to Southern Europe, has managed to boost sales, reduce inventory and improve on delivery times since moving its stock to Veghel. Except for the south of Italy and the very north of Europe it is now managing to get the products at their destination within two working days after receipt of order (adapted from http://www.logistics.com/news/).

While EDCs have grown in number and popularity, other firms have shown that the complexities and costs associated with customer dispersion can be effectively handled through alternative logistics management tools such as just-in-time (JIT) delivery systems. For example, the JIT stock response systems of Berghaus (backed by flexible production techniques) have allowed the UK company to restructure its relationship with European retailers. Retailer reluctance to stock large quantities of its specialty performance outdoor clothing, particularly those which only sell in specific weather conditions, meant that it was difficult to maximize the potential from market integration when large shipments were viewed as the only cost-effective means of servicing the market. New systems mean that the company has been able to shorten delivery times and relax minimum order quantities to a single garment. This shifts stockholding risk away from retailers which makes Berghaus a far more attractive supplier.

Distribution channels and EU rules

Throughout this chapter analysis has attested to the many possible restraints from EU legislation on the implementation of a Euro-marketing strategy. Sure enough, there are problems encountered in establishing a Europe-wide logistics and service network in the shape of EU rules.

First, and in general principle, agreements between undertakings that prevent, restrict or distort competition are blocked under TEC Article 81. Vertical agreements between manufacturers and distributors can fall under this rule of prohibition. Second, although certain types of vertical agreement are permitted under the so-called 'block exemptions' attaching to the Community articles on restrictive practices (see Chapter 5), these too can fall foul of Community rules. Critically, if any party or combination of undertakings associated with the distribution agreement makes use of black-listed measures, the benefit of the block exemption may be automatically withdrawn. For example, in the terms of the block exemption for motor vehicle distribution (Council Regulation 83/83 as amended by 1475/95), any direct or indirect hindrance of parallel trade is strictly prohibited. Equally, no dealer may refuse to supply a consumer simply because he/she is a resident of another member state or hinder the activities of intermediaries authorised by consumers. By its decision to fine Volkswagen/Audi for forcing its authorized dealers in Italy to refuse to sell VW and Audi cars to foreign buyers, the Commission has signalled that such practices will be heavily penalized and may even jeopardize the benefits of block exemption. This threat is raised in Case Study 9.6, which takes a broad overview of the many marketing challenges confronting auto-manufacturers at the start of the new millennium and highlights many of the themes and issues raised throughout this chapter.

It is clear then that, for a Euro-marketer, information about EC competition rules is essential to avoid a Euro-distribution strategy which is in conflict with the legal principles enshrined in the Community treaties. In particular, and as raised by Hildebrand (1994):

> When becoming a party to a distribution agreement, companies should check whether it is compatible with the conditions of Article [81] or, for an item which falls under a block exemption, the relevant EC regulation. In particular, clauses prohibiting parallel imports, granting absolute territorial protection or arranging market-sharing, export bans and resale maintenance schemes are forbidden.

CASE STUDY 9.6 Car-makers to rethink marketing strategies

The summer of 1999 has been hot and sunny for the world automotive industry. But on the horizon dark clouds are gathering that could force a fundamental rethink in the way vehicles are designed, manufactured, distributed and sold. Most car and truck manufacturers have already begun to prepare for a change of climate, suspecting that market conditions could soon turn chilly. Global relationships with suppliers are under review, and car-makers are reconsidering their control of assembly operations. At the same time, leading manufacturers have put their research and engineering teams to work on new fuel and power train technologies. Further downstream, companies such as Ford and General Motors of the US, Germany's Volkswagen and Toyota of Japan have begun to re-examine their dealer relationships and pricing strategies. They have all embraced a new customer focus, hoping to increase their exposure to areas such as insurance, finance, servicing and even recycling.

Several large vehicle groups have already embarked on bold consolidation moves to achieve critical mass, extend their global presence and drive out purchasing and technology costs. In the past year, Daimler Benz has merged with Chrysler of the US, Ford has acquired Sweden's Volvo Car Corporation and Renault of France has acquired an influential stake in debt-laden Nissan. In trucks, the rump Volvo group has finally secured control of Swedish arch-rival Scania. Meanwhile, General Motors has increased its stake in Suzuki and installed new management at Adam Opel, its main European subsidiary. Such deals and restructuring certainly create an opportunity to cut costs, but it remains to be seen whether they will create significant new opportunities for growth.

Nick Scheele, the president of Ford of Europe, believes future growth depends on a simple formula: customer satisfaction. 'There is relatively little difference [between car-makers] in technology and product quality. So what will cause a consumer to check out a Ford – we think it will be the sales and service experience.' To that end Ford has begun moving downstream from its core manufacturing expertise. The company has started to consolidate dealerships on both sides of the Atlantic. In Europe it has acquired Kwik-Fit, the fast-repair chain, along with its first car recycling plant in the US. Ford Credit, one of the world's largest financing businesses, has been strengthened – as has its insurance arm.

General Motors has pursued similar moves, overhauling its dealership functions in Europe and launching web-based sales platforms. It has also extended its bi-fuel range – cars powered by both regular gasoline and liquid petroleum gas – in a bid to capture more of the growing environmental market among fleet operators. All this activity signals an attempt by manufacturers to develop innovative products and to strengthen their brand values, according to John Lawson, head of automotive research at Salomon Smith Barney in London. 'The only way to make money is to offer brand differentiation that customers are willing to pay for', he says. 'That drives consolidation in terms of economics, pricing and product variety.'

That may be so, but there is a real question mark as to how much the manufacturers are in control of this process. For all their statements about customer service and increased marketing efficiency, their strategic shift is being driven largely by outside forces. In Europe, pricing strategies and distribution systems are being reviewed partly because the European Commission is expected to alter or abandon the fourteen-year-old system governing new car sales. The 'block exemption' has allowed manufacturers to sell and market new cars only through captive dealers, enabling them to control prices in different territories. Consumer groups have effectively complained (loudly) that the system discriminates against customers in large markets such as the UK and Germany. They claim prices for identical models vary by up to 40% in different parts of the EU, leading to allegations of price-fixing. The European Commission appears to agree. Earlier this year it fined Volkswagen a record £69 million for preventing German customers buying vehicles from Italian dealers. Similar investigations are pending against Renault, DaimlerChrysler and Opel. Manufacturers are therefore preparing for a possible dilution or end of the block exemption, pitching them in to competition with price-conscious independent dealers. Car prices, moreover, may come under further pressure when EU quotas on Japanese

CASE STUDY 9.6

imports are lifted next year, exposing European manufacturers to more competition from lean rivals including Honda and Toyota.

In North America, the overhaul of sales and marketing is being driven by the arrival of new Internet competitors such as Autobytel and car supermarkets, both threatening the existing franchise system [this process is coming Europe's way]. Elsewhere, hefty investment in new fuel technology – most notably zero-emission fuel cells – has been forced on the manufacturers by the threat of tougher environmental legislation. Proposals by some city authorities to ban polluting vehicles has also prompted the development of cleaner diesel engines and electric vehicles for urban areas. Of all the pressures facing carmakers, perhaps the most worrying is in recycling. A new European Commission directive, yet to be ratified, will force manufacturers to take responsibility for recycling all cars on the road from 2006. At best this will lead to significant cost-cutting and restructuring. At worst it could bankrupt those companies that fail to adapt to the requirements (see Chapter 11).

The financial burden imposed by such legislation – coupled to wholesale changes in retailing and distribution – represents a significant threat to the traditional shape of the automotive industry. In order to meet the costs involved, manufacturers will have to achieve more savings in areas such as distribution, research and development, and purchasing. In turn, that could lead to further consolidation. Looking to the horizon, most industry executives fear a period of extreme turbulence, and they have begun to make preparations.

Source: Financial Times, FT Auto/Retail Survey, 16 September 1999

Conclusion

In many ways, consumers throughout Europe are giving greater meaning and cohesion to the concept of 'Euro-consumerism'. Their needs, tastes and behaviours are increasingly similar and marketers are thinking and working in terms of transnational segments and customer groups. In this context, many businesses are opting for pan-European (or global) product strategies, in which a highly standardized product is offered across and between countries in much the same way. Brands are frequently standardized and advertising and promotions strategies 'unified' so as to reduce costs and to maximize the economies of scale. It is clear, however, that pan-European marketing should be devised and executed with sensitivity to local tastes and conditions. Where varying subgroups display different needs and tastes and where there are local requirements in relation to such matters as packaging and technical standards, it is to be believed that market-by-market adaptation will be preferable. Rather than creating universal products and looking for common Europe-wide solutions, an emphasis falls on product modification and on other changes in placing, pricing and promotions. The decision of which approach is preferable is, therefore, product–market determined and no one single prescription is possible. Both approaches are likely to exist together in an environment in which marketers must look to build strategic relationships with their customers and intermediaries and pay close attention to a complex web of legal conditions and constraints.

Review questions for Chapter 9

1. Define marketing. What is the marketing mix?

2. Explain why concentrating on differences between the member states is detrimental to taking a European view of marketing.

3. Explain the concept of market segmentation. How might marketers go about segmenting European markets?

4. How might firms undertake international market research? What are some of the major problems associated with the process?

5. What prescriptions would you offer for developing structures to facilitate marketing effort in the new European environment?

6. Explain the choices between undifferentiated or standardized strategies on the one hand and differentiated or adapted marketing strategies on the other.

7. In what circumstances might it be appropriate to standardize cross-border marketing communications?

8. What barriers exist to uniform pan-European advertising campaigns?

9. Discuss the possible role of Euro-brands in international marketing strategy.

10. What advantages do you think accrue from marketers working more closely with their customers?

11. Why would you suggest that interfunctional project groups and interdisciplinary teams are important in the modern marketing organization?

12. What is a distribution channel?

13. Outline some of the major issues attaching to the development of pan-European logistics and distribution networks.

14. In what sense is the development of a Euro-marketing strategy complicated by legislative provision? How significant has EU legislation become to marketers in Europe?

15. How are international marketing strategies being pursued through the Internet and through direct marketing techniques?

Web guide

See also Chapter 8.

Consumer and marketing research

Euromonitor @ http://www.euromonitor.com

ESOMAR (European Society for Opinion and Marketing Research) @ http://www.esomar.nl/

Mintel @ http://sinatra2.mintel.com/mintel/main/guidefr.htm (note that your library or organization may subscribe to a varying range of services)

Other links

Global On-line Marketing Centre (articles on e-commerce and Internet marketing) @ http://www.glreach.com/eng/ed.php3

Tilburg University: Marketing and Marketing Research @ http://marketing.kub.nl/magazine.htm

MELNET – Marketing Electronic Learning Network @ http://www.brad.ac.uk/acad/mancen/melnet/index0.html

References

Advertising Association (1998) Survey of European advertising expenditure 1980–1996, *International Journal of Advertising*, **17**(1), 115.

Anholt, S. (1993) Adapting advertising copy across frontiers, *Admap*, **28**(10).

Barrett, P. (1997) Abroad minded, *Marketing*, 24 April 1997, 20–1.

Bartlett, C.A. and Ghoshal, S. (1990) Managing innovation in the transnational corporation, in Bartlett, C.A., Hedlund, G. and Doz, Y.L. (Eds), *Managing The Global Firm*, Routledge.

Bennett, R. (1997) *European Business*, Pitman Publishing.

Blomqvist, R., Dahl, J. and Haeger, T. (1993) *Relationship Marketing: Strategy and Methods for Service Competition*, IHM Forlag.

Brabeck, P. (1998) Striking a Balance Between Familiarity and Efficiency, *Mastering Global Business*, Financial Times/Pitman Publishing, p. 235.

Campbell, D.J. (1997) *Organisations and the Business Environment*, Butterworth-Heinemann.

Culliton, J.W. (1948) *The Management of Marketing Costs*, Harvard University Press.

Drucker, P. (1955) *The Practice of Management*, Pan Books.

Dudley, J.W. and Martens, H. (1993) *1993 and Beyond: New Strategies for the Enlarged Single Market*, Kogan-Page.

Dunlap, B. (1998) The current state of European electronic commerce (on-line) (http://www.glreach.com/eng/ed/art/rep.eur12.html).

El-Kahal, S. (1998) *Business in Europe*, McGraw-Hill.

Goddard, L. (1999) Building PR teams to conquer Europe, *Marketing*, 24 June 1999, **34**.

Gray, R. (1997) Car clients back campaigns that cross borders, *Campaign*, 3 October 1997, **14**.

Gronroos, C. (1990) *Service Management and Marketing*, Free Press/Lexington Books.

Gronroos, C. (1997) From marketing mix to relationship marketing – towards a paradigm shift, *Management Decision*, **35**(3–4), 322–39.

Guido, G. (1992) What US marketers should consider in planning a pan-European approach, *Journal of Consumer Marketing*, **9**(2), 29–33.

Gummesson, E. (1987) *Marketing – A Long-Term Interactive Relationship*, Marketing Technique Centre, Stockholm.

Gummesson, E. (1991) Marketing revisited: the crucial role of the part-time marketers, *European Journal of Marketing*, **25**(2), 60–7.

Gummesson, E. (1996) Relationship marketing and imaginary organizations: a synthesis, *European Journal of Marketing*, **30**(2), 31–44.

Hartley, R. and Pickton, D. (1998) Telebusiness, sales and marketing in the 21st century, in Kanterelis, D. (ed.), *Business and Economics in the 21st Century*, Vol. II, B&ESI Anthology, pp. 53–64.

Heilbrunn, H. (1998) Interactive marketing in Europe, *Direct Marketing*, **60**(11), 56–9.

Hildebrand, D. (1994) Lawyers and marketeers – a European partnership?, *European Business Journal*, **6**(2), 45–54.

Hoffman, D.L. (1995) Marketing in hypermedia computer-mediated environments: conceptual foundations, *Working Paper no. 1*, Project 2000, Owen Graduate School of Management, Vanderbilt University, Nashville.

Iyer, R.T. and Hill, J.S. (1996) International direct marketing strategies: a US–European comparison, *European Journal of Marketing*, **30**(3), 65–84.

Kapferer, J.-N. (1998) Making brands work around the world, *Mastering Global Business*, Financial Times/Pitman Publishing, pp. 23–8.

Kotler, P. (1984) Reconceptualising marketing: an interview with Philip Kotler, *European Management Journal*, **12**(4), December, 353–61.

Kotler, P. (1986) Megamarketing, *Harvard Business Review*, **64**, March–April, 117–124.

Kotler, P. and Armstrong, G. (1993) *Marketing: An Introduction*, Third Edition, Prentice Hall.

KPMG Consulting (1999) *Pricing Policy White Paper*, KPMG EMU Unit.

Landor Associates (1998) EuroBranding (on-line) (http://www.landor.com/strategy/eurobranding/).

Lehtinen, U. *et al.* (1994) On measuring the intensity of relationship marketing, in Sheth, J.N. and Parvatiyar, A. (eds), *Relationship Marketing: Theory, Methods and Applications*, Centre for Relationship Marketing.

Levitt, T. (1983) The globalization of markets, *Harvard Business Review*, **61**, May–June, 92–102.

McCarthy, E.J. (1960) *Basic Marketing*, Irwin.

McDonald, W.J. (1999) International direct marketing in a rapidly changing world, *Direct Marketing*, **61**(11), 44–7.

Murray, J.A. and Fahy, J. (1994) The marketing environment, in Nugent, N. and O'Donnell, R. (eds), *The European Business Environment*, Macmillan.

Peters, I. (1990) *Liberation Management: Necessary Disorganization for the Nanosecond Nineties*, Alfred Knopf.

Reynolds, J. (1998) Reaching the virtual customer, in *Mastering Global Business*, Financial Times/Pitman Publishing, pp. 230–5.

Robertson, T. (1994) New developments in marketing: a European perspective, *European Management Journal*, **12**(4), 362–5.

Saunders, M. (1994) *Strategic Purchasing and Supply Chain Management*, Pitman Publishing.

Schenker, J.L. (1999) Barriers to trade, *Time Magazine*, **153**(25).

Sumner-Smith, D. (1998) Europe's youth is our future, *Marketing*, 22 January 1998, 29–31.

VanderMerwe, S. (1993) A framework for constructing European networks, *European Management Journal*, **12**(1).

VanderMerwe, S. and L'Huillier, M.-A. (1989) Euro-consumers in 1992, *Business Horizons*, **32**(1), 34–40.

Webster, F.E. (1998) Is your company really market-driven?, *Mastering Global Business*, Financial Times/Pitman Publishing, pp. 238–41.

Wheelwright, S.C. and Clark, K.B. (1992) Competing through development capability in a manufacturing-based organisation, *Business Horizons*, July/August.

10 Managing cultural diversity

Central themes

- What is culture?

- Analysing cultural differences

- Cultural diversity in Europe

- Culture, work and organization

- Challenges of cross-cultural management

- Intercultural effectiveness

- Corporate and national culture

- The cultural grounding of business practices

- European business culture and Japanese work practices

Introduction

Cultural difference is a term which is frequently bandied about by academic theorists and most people familiar with the European societies would agree that such differences exist. Nonetheless, culture is an issue which tends to receive scant attention. Although most people understand the generic implications of different cultures, whether or not they understand the specific features is more questionable. From a business viewpoint, considerable research indicates that some aspects of culture differ significantly across Europe and have a substantial impact on the conduct of business in different settings. In this sense, awareness and understanding of cultural differences can provide businesses and their managers with a basis for behavioural and strategic modifications (in different cultural settings) and can contribute to a better understanding of social-market dynamics. Sensitivity to cultural difficulties can also help managers to achieve a higher level of intercultural effectiveness and to avoid some of the pitfalls of cultural blindness. The history of international business ventures is littered with failures owing much of their demise to a poor understanding of how cultures differ. In the context of the EU, cultural similarities and disimilarities may also be the pivotal issue in determining areas for standardization or adaptation of products and services.

It is not possible within the confines of a single chapter to describe culture in Europe. Indeed, it is arguable whether any theoretical text could come close to explaining what constitutes the difference between the fifteen member states. Understanding culture is dependent on first-hand observation and experience. This chapter is not, therefore, designed to provide readers with everything they need to know about culture in Europe. Rather it is concerned with providing pointers to those elements of culture (primarily national and corporate culture) which need to be considered by managers developing their European business. With this in mind, our chapter, which develops on from discussions in Chapters 8 and 9 on European strategic issues, seeks to answer four basic issues:

1. What is culture and how will it impact on the strategies of European firms?
2. How can firms analyse cultural differences?
3. What are the main challenges of managing across cultures in the EU?
4. What systems and strategies can firms put in place to help overcome the uncertainties of European cultural difference?

Concepts of culture

Culture is essentially about people and the way in which they behave as a result of their background and group affiliation. It is not about individual behaviour (there are variations in individual behaviour within cultural groupings) but about shared systems of meaning within and across ascribed and acquired social groups. *Ascribed* social groups are those based on gender, family, age, ethnic, racial or national origin (affiliations determined by birth). *Acquired* group memberships, such as membership of political, religious or commercial bodies, are not determined by birth but are accumulated (and sometimes abandoned) during the life-cycle. Thus, van Maanen and Schein (1979) are led to define culture as 'values, beliefs and expectations that members of specific social groups come to share', and Hofstede (1991) is able to refer to 'the collective programming of the mind which distinguishes one group or category of people from another'. In more complex terms, Kroeber and Kluckhohn (1952) – who identify 164 separate definitions of culture – suggest that culture 'consists of patterns, explicit and implicit, of and for behaviour acquired and transmitted by symbols, constituting the distinctive achievement of human groups'. They add, 'culture systems may, on the one hand, be considered as products of action, on the other as conditioning elements of further action'.

These respectable definitions highlight a number of points which are generally shared in concepts of culture:

1. *Culture is a system of values and social norms (rules and guidelines directing behaviour), shared among a society or group of people.*

2. *Culture is not innate, but learned.* In other words, people are not born with an understanding of culture. It is rather something they acquire through the socialization process.

3. *It is shared, communicated and transmitted by members of a social set* and defines the boundaries between different groups. This point interacts with the previous point in that it is through reinforcement within the social group that culture is learned.

4. *There are various facets of culture,* many of which are interrelated, for example, traits of social organization may well be reflected in business organization in a particular culture.

These elements have important ramifications for the European and international manager. First, managers can, and indeed must, learn about the culture(s) in each foreign market in which they operate. Cultural differences across and within nations can affect the way in which business is practised and cross-cultural competence is vital for managers dealing in an international context. Second, as culture is determined by group behaviour, an awareness of group dynamics can be an important part of understanding cultural norms, particularly organizational structures employed in different member states. Third, the fact that different elements of culture are interrelated highlights the importance of identifying the individual facets and the way in which they interface with each other. Finally, analysing culture is not just about assessing how different cultural groups (and norms) differ from one's own but about reception, engagement and learning. A problem here, however, is that as individuals we are so steeped in our own cultures and ways of thinking that it is often difficult for us to fully understand other cultures or to embrace new ideas. For managers dealing in an international context, there is a natural tendency to judge situations, beliefs and actions in different cultures according to their own cultural norms. Eliminating this lack of cultural sensitivity, or what Lee (1966) called 'self reference criterion' (SRC), is difficult but can be assisted by four basic steps:

1. determining the problem or goal in terms of home country culture, habits and norms;

2. determining the same problem or goal in terms of host country culture, habits and norms;

3. isolating the SRC influence on the problem and how it complicates the issue;

4. redefining the problem without the SRC influence and solving it according to the specific foreign market situation.

This suggests looking carefully at those cultural factors which shape behaviour at home (understanding your own culture) and in the host market (understanding the foreign culture). What managers therefore need is a framework for assessing and analysing culture.

Frameworks for cultural analysis

The previous, albeit highly limited, review of cultural concepts provides some insight into the cultural issues to be addressed by European managers. It fails, however, to provide a clear framework for analysing culture, specifically for analysing the values and norms predominant within specific nation-states (national cultures).

One possible approach is to breakdown the socio-cultural environment into its detailed elements. Murdock (1945) developed an elaborate list of seventy culture universals which are present in all societies and which arguably make up the whole socio-cultural environment (see Table 10.1). The list has been reproduced here as it serves as a useful checklist of features for any cultural analysis. While to assess all these various facets of culture would be a highly complex task, individual elements can be isolated as key variables in certain situations. For example, if a company were to consider selling housing finance in a foreign market it may wish to consider the following elements: family, inheritance rules, kingroups, law, marriage, property rights and residence issues. In so doing it would become aware of specific elements of the foreign culture associated with family groups, their homes and the laws surrounding ownership and residency.

Table 10.1 Cultural universals

Age grading	Food taboos	Music
Athletic sports	Funeral rites	Mythology
Bodily adornment	Games	Numerals
Calendar	Gestures	Obstetrics
Cleanliness training	Gift giving	Penal sanctions
Community organization	Government	Personal names
Cooking	Greetings	Population policy
Co-operative labour	Hairstyles	Postnatal care
Cosmology	Hospitality	Pregnancy usages
Courtship	Housing hygiene	Property rights
Dancing	Incest taboos	Propitiation of
Decorative art	Inheritance rules	supernatural beings
Divination	Joking	Puberty customs
Division of labour	Kingroups	Religious rituals
Dream interpretation	Kinship nomenclature	Residence rules
Education	Language	Sexual restrictions
Eschatology	Law	Soul concepts
(after-life)	Luck superstitions	Status differentiation
Ethics	Magic	Surgery
Ethnobotany	Marriage	Tool making
Etiquette	Mealtimes	Trade
Faith healing	Medicine	Visiting
Family	Modesty concerning	Weaning
Feasting	natural functions	Weather control
Fire making	Mourning	
Folklore		

Source: Based on Murdock (1945, page 123).

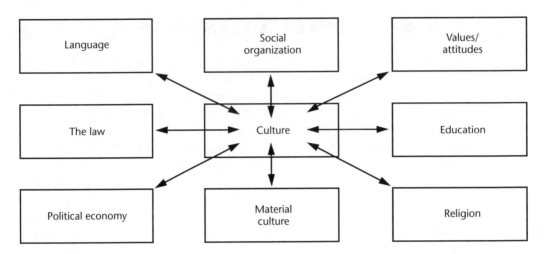

Figure 10.1 Generic aspects of the cultural environment

Arguably, however, these factors are too specific, and a more generalized understanding of people and their environments may provide a more realistic management tool. Many academics have preferred to opt for a more generic framework which provides for closer assessment of the main elements of culture that can have an impact on business in different societies. These include such features as language, education, religion, politics, economics, the law, social organization, attitudes and moral values. A typical framework is provided in Figure 10.1 and our initial analysis proceeds under such broad headings.

Language

Language is one of the defining characteristics of a nation and is a key element in the cultural mix. Both the spoken and unspoken means of communication provide a medium through which people can relate to one another and through which social norms can be transmitted and perpetuated. In a business sense, language forms the hub of communication between people and provides a means of firm-to-firm and company-to-customer communication.

The spoken language

Within the EU there are many spoken languages with eleven 'national' languages recognized and used by the European Union itself. Europe as a whole is home to over fifty different 'languages' (see Table 10.2) including a number of dialect forms. In specific EU countries such as Belgium, several languages exist at the same time – in this case, Flemish, French and German. Outside of the EU, in countries such as Switzerland and the Russian Federation, the existence of many languages is a characterizing feature of state society. While it does not necessarily follow that language differences create differences in culture or group orientation, the notion of a national culture can be a very fragile one where there is a multiplicity of languages,

Table 10.2 Languages, tongues and dialects in the European nations

ALBANIA
Albanian (Tosc dialect), Albanian (Gheg dialect), Greek

ANDORRA
Catalan, Castilian Spanish, French

AUSTRIA
German

BELARUS (BYELORUSSIA)
Byelorussian, Russian, others

BELGIUM
Flemish, French, and German

BOSNIA-HERZEGOVINA
Serbo-Croatian (Bosnian)

BULGARIA
Bulgarian, some Turkic languages

CROATIA
Serbo-Croatian

CZECH REPUBLIC
Czech and Slovak

DENMARK
Danish, Faroese, Greenlandic (Inuit dialect) (also German)

ESTONIA
Estonian, Lettish (Latvian), Lithuanian, Russian, others

FINLAND
Finnish, Swedish, Lapp, Russian

FRANCE
French, Provençal, Alsatian, Corsican, Catalan, Basque, Breton, Flemish

GERMANY
German, small number Sorbian and Frisian

GREECE
Greek, Turkish, Macedonian, Albanian, and French and English

HUNGARY
Hungarian

ICELAND
Icelandic

IRELAND
Irish (Gaelic), English

ITALY
Italian, and dozens of regional dialects, German, French, Slovene, Rhaeto-Romanic

LATVIA
Lettish (Latvian), Lithuanian, Russian, Byelorussian, others

LIECHTENSTEIN
German, Alemannic dialect

LITHUANIA
Lithuanian, Polish, Russian

MOLDOVA
Moldovian, Russian, Gagauz (Turkic dialect)

MONACO
French, Monégasque, Italian, English

THE NETHERLANDS
Dutch, Frisian

NORWAY
Norwegian, Lapp, Finnish

POLAND
Polish

PORTUGAL
Portuguese

ROMANIA
Romanian, Hungarian, German

RUSSIA
Russian, Tatar, Mongolian, Caucasian, Chechen and many others

SERBIA
Serbo-Croatian, Albanian

SLOVAKIA
Slovak, Hungarian

SLOVENIA
Slovenian, Serbo-Croatian, others

SPAIN
Castilian Spanish, Catalan, Basque, Galician

SWEDEN
Swedish, Lapp, Finnish

SWITZERLAND
German, French, Italian, and Romansch

UKRAINE
Ukranian, Russian, Romanian, Polish, Hungarian, others

UNITED KINGDOM
English, Welsh, Scots Gaelic

Source: adapted and derived from http://www.webofculture.com

and tensions between different groups may exist. A good case in point here would be the tensions that exist between the Basque-speaking minority and Spanish-speaking majority in Spain. While not all Basques support the separatist cause, at the very least Basque-speakers have a clear sense of their own cultural identity.

The failure to learn other languages may put individuals operating outside their own national market at a disadvantage. Communicating in the language of the host may be seen as a symbol of co-operation, faith and trust, and the effort in itself may be regarded as a way of communicating with foreign partners or customers. Equally, some people argue that it is impossible to understand other elements of culture without comprehending the medium through which that culture is perpetuated. In this respect, musicality, intonation and phraseology all serve as secondary communication signals which are lost on those with no grasp of the language. However, most people feel more confident communicating in their first language and are less than happy about conducting business in another language. Some may feel that this puts them at a disadvantage. This point can be connected to the fact that many people (and managers) in Europe have no second European language (see Table 10.3).

Those whose natural tongue is English may find security in the fact that English is rapidly acquiring the status of *the* language of international business. In a strictly European context, nearly 50% of EU-based adults can take part in an English-language conversation and four out of five secondary school students in the EU are actively learning the language. But while English is becoming the language of international business, knowledge of a local language can provide an improved basis for the understanding of local culture. British managers will therefore be handicapped unless they can improve on the low levels of language skills that exist at present.

The issue of language also surfaces with respect to translation. International businesses must look to ensure that the translation of a word or phrase into the local language has the desired meaning and does not communicate something unintended. As was raised in the previous chapter, literal translations and/or weak grasps of local language, have led to many marketing blunders. This was certainly the case in General Motors' advertising campaign 'Body by Fischer' (corpse by Fischer) and with the 'Nova' brand name. When spoken in Spanish, this sounded like 'no va', which means 'it doesn't go'. Budweiser has also been marketed in Spain as the 'queen of beers'. This clearly communicates the wrong message about the product (Ricks, 1997).

Silent language

Language refers not only to the spoken word but also to the various aspects of 'silent language' (see Hall, 1973). Aspects or dimensions of silent language are central to the communication process which consists of verbal and non-verbal elements. *The language of space* concerns personal surroundings and the distance between people during conversations. People's sense of appropriate distance is learned and differs among societies. Research suggests that closer conversational distance may be the norm in Latin European countries. On a different level, the French are more likely

Table 10.3 Percentage of people who can follow a conversation in another language

Country	Number of languages			
	0	1	2	3+
Belgium	50	22	18	9
Denmark	40	30	25	6
Germany	60	33	6	1
Greece	66	27	5	2
France	67	26	6	1
Ireland	80	17	3	–
Italy	76	19	5	1
Luxembourg	1	10	47	42
Netherlands	28	29	32	12
Portugal	76	14	8	2
Spain	68	26	5	1
United Kingdom	74	20	5	1

Source: Eurobarometer.

to lay out space in the workplace so that it facilitates interaction rather than to promote separation. *The language of time* includes response times for a written communication, punctuality at business meetings, the time it takes to make a decision, formal schedules and deadlines. All communicate different messages in different societies. While it is too easy to think in stereotypes, in Germany people are generally expected to be on time and any degree of lateness is often considered unacceptable. Conversely, in Mediterranean cultures a greater degree of flexibility exists regarding punctuality and there is a higher tolerance level for lateness.

Social organization and social stratification

Within cultural groups there are a number of smaller *social organizations* which have an important bearing on how people think and behave. For example, the family provides the central hub of most individuals' social sphere and it is here that many cultural values and norms are instilled. Equally, differences in attitude and behaviour within the workplace, for example meetings, decision-making processes, work delegation, leadership roles, communication and promotion issues, can all be tied to cultural factors and group norms pertaining in different societies. Although these factors appear small and relatively trivial, an understanding of the structure and dynamics of social groups can provide business managers (or cultural analysts) with a better insight into people's behaviour and cultural attitudes in different societies.

Societies also differ in their degree of *social stratification*. The weakening British class structure provides one demonstration of such stratification. In highly stratified societies, class groups often manifest themselves in the various institutions of society: in education, industry, politics and administration. For example, the Grandes Ecoles in France and the Oxbridge universities in the UK (Oxford and

Cambridge) draw large numbers from the privileged classes. These institutions are seen as bastions of tradition and tend to support the idea of social and/or managerial elites. Indeed as noted by Crawshaw and Spieser (1996), 'it is extremely hard to accede to a top management position in France without a Diplome de Grande Ecole'. Job status may serve as a surrogate for social class and as a form of social stratification. In Germany, engineers and those with a technical background are among the most highly thought of within society. This is part and parcel of their industrial background in which, traditionally, service sector professionals have been regarded as less important than those working in industry. The converse case is true in the UK where the dominance of the service sector has raised the profile of professional jobs, particularly in such disciplines as accountancy, finance and law. By class or surrogate, the social stratification of people within society has an important impact on various facets of culture such as buying behaviour, social aspirations, work and career objectives. The recruitment practices of firms in highly and weakly stratified societies are also likely to vary. Firms operating in less stratified societies are freer to seek out the most qualified employees, regardless of background. In highly stratified societies, however, recruitment procedures will need to take into account class differences among administrators and workers, and the absence of those with the 'right background' in management positions may lead to problems with networking, negotiation etc. with other local elites.

Education and training

Education is the medium through which individuals learn many of the skills and cultural norms necessary for their role within society and the workforce. From a European or international perspective on business, education is especially important in determining the attitudes, skills and aptitudes of individuals in a particular society.

Different educational systems across Europe show a polarization of opinion regarding the benefits of vocational versus pure academic programming. In the UK, for example, education has traditionally been operated independent from business with an emphasis on academic skills. This contrasts with the vocational emphases found in many schools, polytechnics and universities in countries such as France and Germany. Both systems offer advantages: the vocational system prepares students within the school environment for their job role in society while the academic approach provides the building blocks of learning on which employers may build. Thus, business managers operating in foreign markets will tend to find a close association between national systems of education and features of a country's economic environment.

The same applies to training, where attitudes have much to do with the historical development of different member states' educational systems and with contrasts in basic economic philosophy. For example, the UK, which arguably has one of the poorest records for education and training for a developed Western economy, has traditionally taken a laissez-faire approach to training, with employers responsible for the majority of training. It has often been argued that British employers see training as a cost, not an investment, and are therefore only concerned with 'doing the minimum' – training individuals for specific tasks rather than broadening their knowledge base and skills. In this sense, the UK case contrasts sharply with those of France and Germany. Successive governments in France have demonstrated a clear commitment to training and have given the right to training to all working people. A statutory minimum requirement has been established for training provision. In companies with ten or more employees, 0.15% of the wage bill must be dedicated to training (of which 0.3% must be channelled into training young workers and 0.2% into external training centres for employees on training leave). Many companies spend more than the minimum. In Germany, the fact that only around three-quarters of post-sixteen students remain in secondary education is not a reflection of poor educational attainment – at this age, many individuals enter into vocational training programmes. These are run jointly by the state and over 500,000 approved registered training companies. Even though the cost to firms is large, the benefits of training the workforce in appropriate skills is apparently justifiable. The ethos of training in Germany is also extended to management development programmes in which managers are encouraged to continually improve their skills by attending courses covering various disciplines from product and function specific courses to those more concerned with objective management techniques. With this historical background, it is arguable that Germany is well placed to deliver the kinds of people needed to work in the new Europe.

In repeated communications, the European Commission has suggested that without increased commitment to education and training, the advantages of the Single Market will accrue to the most highly educated and dynamic who will be persuaded to move to areas where the best jobs and conditions are available. In order to avoid a 'brain-drain' from the periphery to the centre, countries need to look carefully at their education and training provision over the next few decades. There is also a growing awareness that Europe must prepare individuals for new work practices and improve their skills within the workplace if EU firms are to survive in the increasingly competitive world marketplace.

The law

The diverse nature of the legal rules and frameworks pertaining to the fifteen member states of the EU has, for a long time, served to reinforce the differences between nations. Different laws and regulations continue to apply on an individual national basis, with customary rules and social norms (developed over many years) incorporated into common law. Thus the laws of a nation and its penalties for non-compliance are a reflection of those particular forms of behaviour which have come to be accepted as 'social norms'. Despite the many external sources of law (e.g. the EU), laws relating both to individuals and to organizations have their root in national customs, values and experiences. Moreover, while important test cases emerge that challenge existing legal guidelines and serve as a catalyst for change, few new laws are introduced without changes in the needs and/or values of society.

Political economy

Politics and economics have an important role to play in shaping national character. Many of the distingushing features of national economic and political systems were highlighted in earlier chapters and will not be reiterated here. Nonetheless, more needs to be said at this stage about the way in which a culture is affected by the political economy of a country (and vice versa).

Political systems, institutitions and processes vary by country and some appreciation of their basic elements is vital for students of business and for managers alike (see Chapter 1). It is clear, however, that the politics or political culture of a country is much wider than the formal structure of government and state politics. It encompasses the role, activities and communications of social institutions such as trade unions, business and professional associations, pressure groups and churches. It also encompasses the plurality of beliefs and political philosophies that mix and combine in a society (e.g. nationalism, liberalism, anarchism and socialism) and which, at different times, embed themselves in social and political institutions. In turn, these differences may reflect divisions of class, wealth, religion and race. Political cultures may also be more or less open. This reflects such qualities as the level of politicization across domestic constituencies, the openness and frequency of political debate, and the comfort associated with freedom of expression, political association etc. Nearly all of the EU states have liberal and open political cultures (at least by international standards) but this should not mask the significant differences that exist between these states, their political systems and cultures.

An 'economic culture' encompasses the dominant economic beliefs and perceptions in a society which, to some extent at least, legitimate the methods and goals involved in the ordering of economic life. At the highest level (that of state action):

> [t]he culture designates what will be perceived in the surrounding environment, how it will be interpreted, and which reactions will be considered appropriate ... [it] provides the litmus test that any economic policy must pass to be considered legitimate. (Rohrlich, 1987, p. 70)

Little here is controversial. Thurrow (1992) like many other analysts, has managed to show how the distinctive macroeconomic features and industrial policies of different Western states can be located in varying economic philosophies. He highlights a communitarian philosophy in France and Germany (contributing to a stronger record of state intervention and industrial planning) and an individualist or liberal philosophy in the UK (contributing to a more laissez-faire economic culture). In similar vein, although in specific comment on the cultural and economic context of modern France, Crawshaw and Spieser (1996, p. 1) are drawn to remark:

> Many features of the country's economic structure and development (such as the strong role of the state) can only be explained with reference to France's historical past and to the French nation's image of itself.

Firms and managers involved in international activities will quickly confront these differences as they move between countries and, in many cases, deal with governments and public authorities. This is not to say, however, that misperceptions or miscalculations are easily avoided. For example, it is possible, as argued in the *Financial Times* (28 March 2000), that a degree of cultural ignorance led BMW to believe that the UK government would intervene to assist the Rover Car Company (its ailing UK subsidiary) and other domestic manufacturers at a time of exchange rate difficulties in 1999–2000. In highlight of profound differences in German and British economic culture, the paper noted:

> In Bavaria, BMW is used to the extremely supportive regime of the CSU (sister party to the Christian Democrats), which has been in power since the first postwar German election. At federal level, Gerhard Schroder, the German chancellor, intervened to save Phillip Holzmann, the construction company, from bankruptcy. Economic policy still plays an important role. The UK's Department of Trade and Industry, on the other hand, has no industrial policy of this kind and makes few such interventions.

The influence of economic culture (philosophy) at the macro- or policy levels is only part of the story. Business organization in particular societies and other features of a microeconomic nature are also profoundly shaped by basic values and beliefs. These cultural attributes combine with the forces of modern technology and international competition to shape and to mould the ways in which firms do business, manage, and relate to their employees, customers etc. For example, the emphases among German businesses on reconciling the interests of clients, employees and shareholders, on vocational training and on quality workmanship are all culturally grounded. So too is the collective, liberal and consensual form of management seen in German industry (see Albert, 1991). The Rhenish model–philosophy which underpins this economic system is institutional and collective and is based on the principle of consensus. Its underpinning values encompass those of social justice, reward for hard work and social partnership (see also Chapter 6).

Material culture

Material culture relates to the way in which people regard material possessions and wealth and often serves to communicate important messages about different societies. Furnishings and trappings also make important statements about individuals in certain materialistic cultures such as the UK and Germany. This is often manifested in one-upmanship between friends and colleagues where individuals compete through their acquisitions of new technologies and gadgets to assert their social standing. In other cultural groups, particularly those of southern Europe, the family, relationships and friendships are typically considered more important than material 'things'. There are of course significant differences in material culture between cultural subgroups in individual countries and associations across national boundaries. For example, the international success of products and services such as Levi jeans, Swatch watches, McDonald's and Nike sportswear is often attributed to the notion that there is a global youth subculture – a pop culture – which exists irrespective of differences in language and social acclimatization in the local state. Again, this point was touched on in the chapter on European marketing strategies.

Material culture also dictates the way people regard pay and remuneration for work. In most Western European cultures people generally accept that the harder they work the greater will be the remuneration. Those people who desire more economic wealth are therefore likely to work longer and harder. Equally, employers who require extra effort from their employees, greater commitment or more loyalty, can often achieve their goals through providing the right economic incentives. This might take the form of favourable overtime conditions, pay rises, a better company car, or additional peripheral benefits such as pensions and private medical insurance.

Values and attitudes

Values and attitudes refer to commonly held beliefs about a variety of issues, which in turn determine common behavioural patterns. More specifically, values are the standards by which things may be judged and serve to shape people's beliefs and consequently their attitudes. This is probably the most elusive area of culture as values and attitudes only become apparent through interpersonal communication and interaction. There are no formal rules and guidelines, but the unwritten frameworks may be just as powerful in determining behaviour. 'The best thing about the British is their sense of humour!' This is a belief the British hold about themselves, but how do others view them? Mole (1992) suggests the Germans think they are idle, the Spanish regard them as arrogant, and the French as chauvinistic. In return, the English tend to think that the Germans are arrogant and pushy, that the French are rude, and Spanish idle. A major stumbling block to achieving a Single Market, and managing across cultures, may therefore turn out to be unqualified attitudes and stereotypical beliefs by each member state about its neighbours. Many of these feelings lie deep within the core of each society and are often based on past historical events, feuds, wars and misunderstandings. While firms operating on a pan-European scale will, over time, overcome some of these preconceived notions through their dealings with institutions from other member states, it is more the attitudinal block to viewing Europe as a Single Market which is likely to hamper true integration.

At this point, we may pause to consider the concepts of ethnocentrism and polycentrism. *Ethnocentrism* refers to the belief or attitude that one's own group is superior to others. Daniels and Radebaugh (1995) suggest there are three types of ethnocentric behaviour:

1. Differences abroad are ignored as managers are so steeped in their own cultural norms that they cannot see beyond their own social group. This kind of ethnocentrism demands careful review of foreign cultures and an opening up of attitudes before successful foreign operations can be achieved.

2. Managers are aware of environmental and cultural differences but do not translate these into strategy. This may result in under-performance in overseas markets.

3. Management is aware of differences but believes they can re-educate foreigners to adopt something new. While this kind of ethnocentrism can produce positive results through the introduction of innovative products or business practices which may give the firm an edge over indigenous companies, it may be dangerous. Foreigners may show high resistance to change, particularly if it means diverging from their own norms, ethics and morality.

Quite clearly, ethnocentrism can hamper progress in overseas markets, with managers failing to identify (or choosing to ignore) the different cultural norms and practices in different societies. Conversely, the *polycentric* business assumes that cultures are so different that, to a large extent, decision-making should be decentralized and left to managers in individual markets. These managers are then free to adapt products and practices according to local customs and norms, and the business will maximize its local responsiveness. The most extreme case, however, ignores the potential for standardization and harmonization and may ultimately result in inefficiencies and a loss of overriding control. Equally, if the practices adopted become so localized, there is little scope for the firm to innovate or behave as a change agent.

This returns us to the ongoing debate in Europe on the benefits and disbenefits of centralization versus decentralization. Whereas this was previously analysed from a strategic point of view, the cultural focus here points to the fact that managers in Europe must not just look for differences. It is imperative they look for similarities between different cultural groups and common business behaviours, which may cut across national boundaries. These may serve as the starting point for establishing transnational European objectives, messages and solutions.

Religion

Religion provides a foundation for attitudes, beliefs and values in a society, shaping individual and group behaviour. It helps to shape attitudes toward work and entrepreneurship, and influences material values within society. Religion also affects male–female roles and the structure of family groups. Understanding the dominant religion of a particular country, therefore, can provide business managers with a better insight into people's behaviour and cultural attitudes. In all cases, businesses should show sensitivity to the differences between principal and other religious groups.

Christianity is predominant in the EU states, with other religions such as Islam and Judaism underpinning the value systems of large minority populations. The major branches of Christianity in Western Europe are Catholicism and Protestantism. There is little agreement as to the economic implications of either Protestantism or Catholicism, but some have been drawn to highlight how Protestant ethics (which dominate in northern Europe) give particular emphasis to the importance of hard work and wealth creation. The research of Geert Hofstede (1980) and Fons Trompenaars (1993), which will shortly be considered, also suggests that Protestant societies are marked by a relatively high degree of individualism. This can be linked to the emphasis in Protestantism on an individual relationship with God and on personal responsibility. The orientations and economic implications of Catholicism are more ambiguous, but the same researchers have found that Catholics tend to score high on group choices and are lower on individualism. According to other analysts, including the famous German sociologist Max Weber, the Catholic emphasis on salvation in the after-life also fails to foster the same kind of work ethic found in the Protestant West.

Classifying national cultures and cross-cultural analysis

As has been commented, the values and norms ascendant in a foreign country are an historical product and are shaped by (and reflected in) a number of factors such as language, education, religion and social organization. By analysing the different European societies along these dimensions, we can gain some, albeit limited, insight into their different cultures. Unfortunately, by using such a model, there is a clear tendency towards cultural separation and the accentuation of broad value differences between societies. A different approach to cultural analysis rests with the classification (and clustering) of national cultures in terms of broad social values, management and organizational practices. Far from an academic exercise, it is clear that if we can identify cultural associations or distinctions between different countries, then international businesses may be directed towards (or away) from a standardization of their practices and management styles. For example, if the cultures of Spain and the United Kingdom result in different work-related values, an international business with operations in both countries should vary its management process and practices to take these differences into account. Conversely, if the cultures of Sweden and the Netherlands result in similar work-related values, a business with operations in both countries may standardize many of its processes and practices so as to maximize efficiency.

Classifying national cultures in terms of the importance attached to different values has been the preoccupation of many analysts. For example, in the seminal work of two Dutchmen, Geert Hofstede and Fons Trompenaars, we see the use of bipolar dimensions to describe the differences between national cultures in general terms, when managing, and when being managed. As explained by Hofstede, the position of a country on these dimensions allows us to make some predictions on the way their society operates, including their management processes.

The work of Geert Hofstede

Hofstede's original research – conducted between 1967 and 1973 – included a sample of 116,000 personnel (employees and managers) working in sixty-four national subsidiaries of the IBM Corporation (see Hofstede, 1980, 1983). In analysing the data, and in comparing national cultures, Hofstede created an index score for each of four dimensions. The scores for each country on each dimension were seen to describe its unique position against others, with 0 representing the lowest possible score. Hofstede's four dimensions are:

Power distance. This dimension indicates the extent to which a society expects and accepts inequalities between its people, and an unequal distribution of power and responsibility within its institutions and organizations. Countries with a high score (large power distance) are those which feature broad differences between individuals in terms of power, status and wealth, whose institutions are characterized by formal hierarchies, and whose populations consider a high degree of inequality as normal. In such societies, authority is largely centralized and subordinates are cautious about challenging or questioning the decisions and authority of their superiors.

Uncertainty avoidance. This index relates to the extent to which countries and their institutions establish formal rules and fixed patterns of operation as a means of enhancing security and of avoiding ambiguity and doubt. High uncertainty avoidance societies are marked by a strong preference for structured over unstructured situations.

Individualism–collectivism. This dimension relates to the degree to which people in a country prefer to act as individuals rather than as members of groups. At the high end of the scale are those (individualist) societies where ties between individuals are very loose and where individuals have a high sense of independence and self-responsibility. In organizational settings, individualists value freedom to make their own decisions and/or to adopt their own approach to the job. In addition, members of individualistic societies place an emphasis on personal liberties and on having sufficient time for personal or family life.

Masculinity–femininity. The more 'masculine' a society the more it values assertiveness and materialism. Masculine society also promotes competition, meritocracy, decisiveness and strong leadership. There is no particular concern for social or gender equality, with gender roles often defined quite rigidly. Feminine societies promote harmonious relations in the workplace (between men and women, managers and their employees) and place a strong emphasis on social partnership and gender equality.

Identifying cultural clusters

By plotting pairs of dimensions on the basis of Hofstede's original ratings, it is possible to identify groupings of member states in terms of their broad social and work-related values. Figure 10.2 (which plots uncertainty avoidance against power distance) and Figure 10.3 (which plots masculinity–femininity against individualism–collectivism) demonstrate this across two of the several matrices which can be developed using Hofstede's framework/data.

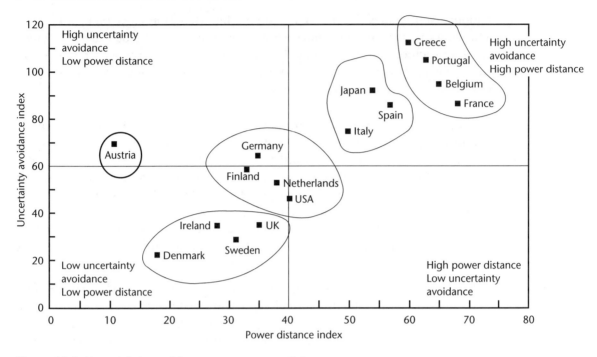

Figure 10.2 Uncertainty avoidance versus power distance

The uncertainty avoidance versus power distance matrix (Figure 10.2) shows five (albeit arbitrary) groupings of countries for the fifteen member states, with Japan and the USA included as comparators. While it is possible to identify broad regional groupings (that is some loose associations between clusters of north and south European states respectively) the boundaries are far from clear. Austria appears as an outlier, with a very low power distance index, and Belgium and France find themselves positioned with more distant Greece and Portugal. Above all else, the matrix highlights the contrasts between the EU states when taken as a whole.

In terms of masculinity–femininity versus individualism–collectivism (Figure 10.3), regional groupings can be more readily established. There is some association between the ratings of Greece, Portugal and Spain (all Southern EU states), between a Scandinavian grouping (and the Netherlands), and between a number of north–central Europeans marked by high masculinity and (reasonably) high individualism. Although the UK is separated out here (owing to its close association with the United States), the UK could easily be grouped with this latter cluster. A rogue case is provided by Italy, which along these dimensions shows more affinity with the north European states than with its fellow southern Europeans. It is worth recording here that the Scandinavian countries, along with the Netherlands, appear as the most feminine societies (low masculinity). These countries are characterized by a progressive attitude towards equality between men and women in work and society. Individualism is at its very highest in the Anglo-Saxon countries (the UK and US). It is much lower in Southern EU states such as Spain, Greece and Portugal. Japan provides an interesting example along these two dimensions, standing alone

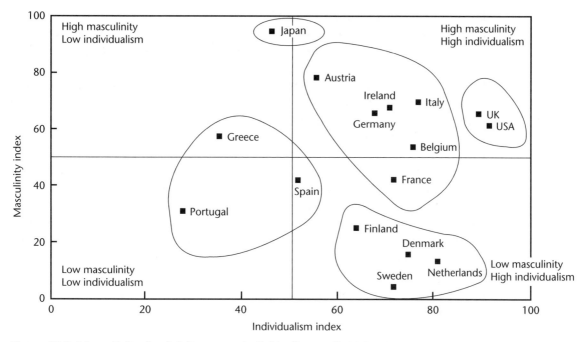

Figure 10.3 Masculinity–femininity versus individualism–collectivism

in terms of the masculinity index and characterized by an individualism score which is well below that of its principal economic rivals. This suggests great delineation between men and women in Japanese society and suggests a stronger commitment to the priorities and rules of specific social groups (e.g. the firm).

More recently, and following collaboration with Michael Bond, Hofstede (1986, 1991, 1995) has included a further dimension into his pioneering work on culture: *long-term versus short-term orientation*. Long term relates to such values as thrift and perseverance, while short-term values include respect for personal tradition, social obligations and 'saving face'. European (like American) cultures figure quite low in the rankings (the UK exhibiting an index of 25, Germany 29, the Netherlands 44 and Sweden 33). It is the East Asian cultures which show the most long-term orientation, including Japan with an index of 80.

The work of Fons Trompenaars

Similar research has been conducted and published by Fons Trompenaars who, in the 1980s, administered research questionnaires to over 15,000 managers and administrative staff in a number of companies across twenty-eight countries (Trompenaars, 1993). Trompenaars points out that a culture is distinguishable by the kinds of solutions it creates for certain problems, grouped under three headings:

1. those involving relationships with other people
2. those involving the natural environment
3. those involving the passage of time

Like Hofstede, he forwards a series of bipolar dimensions along which cultures can be assessed (see also Trompenaars and Hampden-Turner, 1997). One dimension – *sequentialism versus synchronism* – relates to the issue of time, its structuring and management. In synchronistic cultures, time is conceived as cyclical and repetitive, 'compressing past, present and future by what these have in common'. Ideas about the future and 'memories of the past' are both seen to 'shape present action'. In sequential cultures, 'time is seen to move forward, second by second, minute by minute, hour by hour in a straight line'. People conceive of time 'as a dotted line with regular spacing'. Such cultures are predominantly present oriented and will not attach much value to common past experiences nor to future prospects. 'Day-by-day experiences tend to direct people's life' (see Trompenaars and Hampden-Turner, 1997, pp. 120–40). A second dimension – *internalism versus externalism* – relates to relations with the natural environment. Trompenaars asserts that inter-nalistic people have a mechanistic view of nature, seeing nature as something which can be controlled and manipulated. By contrast, externalistic people have 'a more organic view of nature', believing that natural forces cannot be simply con-trolled as if nature were somehow mechanical. In externalistic cultures, an empha-sis falls on environmental harmony and on the concept of sustainable development.

Trompenaars' five remaining dimensions relate to the question of inter-personal relationships and work-related values. These dimensions are:

- universalism versus particularism (rules versus relationships?);
- Communitarianism versus individualism (the group versus the individual);
- Neutral versus affective cultures (controlled and subdued emotion versus high emotion and free expression);
- Specific versus diffuse relationships (engaging with others in specific areas of life (e.g. work) or diffusely in multiple areas of life);
- Achievement versus ascription (according status to people on the basis of their achievements or by virtue of class and seniority).

Only one of these directly echoes a Hofstede dimension: communitarianism versus individualism. To some extent, however, there are clear associations between a second Trompenaars dimension (achievement–ascription) and a second Hofstede dimension (power distance). Table 10.4 identifies the different business areas affected by these cultural dimensions. Interestingly, where associations can be made with the Hofstede dimensions, there is little consistency between the 'positioning' or classification of different countries. For example, Trompenaars identifies France, along with Germany and Italy, as among the more collectivist societies in Europe. Looking at the individualism (IDV) scores in Hofstede's study, these three countries score relatively well. These differences can be explained by several factors including the different questions used to measure individualism in the two studies, the contrasts between the two databases, and the different time-frames of the studies.

Table 10.4 Business areas affected by Trompenaars' cultural dimensions

Affective	Neutral
Show immediate reactions either verbally or non-verbally	Opaque emotional state
Expressive face and body signals	Do not readily express what they think or feel
At ease with physical contact	Embarrassed or awkward at public displays of emotion
	Discomfort with physical contact outside 'private' circle
Raise voice readily	Subtle in verbal and non-verbal expressions

Individualism	Collectivism
More frequent use of 'I' and 'me'	More frequent use of 'we'
In negotiations, decisions typically made on the spot by a representative	Decisions typically referred back by delegate to the organization
People ideally achieve alone and assume personal responsibility	People ideally achieve in groups which assume joint responsibility
Holidays taken in pairs, or even alone	Holidays taken in organized groups or with extended family

Specific	Diffuse
More 'open' public space, more 'closed' private space	More 'closed' public space, but, once in, more 'open' private space
Appears direct, open and extrovert	Appears indirect, closed and introvert
'To the point' and often appears abrasive	Often evades issues and 'beats about the bush'
Highly mobile	Low mobility
Separates work and private life	Work and private life are closely linked
Varies approach to fit circumstances, especially with use of titles (for example, Herr Doktor Müller at work is Hans in social environments or in certain business meetings)	Consistent in approach, especially with use of titles (for example, Herr Doktor Müller is Herr Doktor Müller in any setting)

Universalism	Particularism
Focus is more on rules than on relationships	Focus is more on relationships than on rules
Legal contracts are readily drawn up	Legal contracts are readily modified
A trustworthy person is the one who honours their 'word' or contract	A trustworthy person is the one who honours changing circumstances
There is only one truth or reality, that which has been agreed to	There are several perspectives on reality relative to each participant
A deal is a deal	Relationships evolve

Source: Based on Hoeklin (1995, pages 41–5).

Evaluating the models

While these studies are of some considerable value in highlighting national cultural differences and their impact within organizations, the conclusions and ratings associated with each should be approached carefully.

451

First, scope exists for cultural change across and within societies. As Hill remarks (2000, p. 100):

> Cultures do not stand still; they evolve over time, albeit slowly. What was a reasonable characteriisation in the 1960s and 1970s may not be so today.

Second, such analysis does not fully account for the diversity of subcultures within nations. Hofstede and Trompenaars are not blind to this fact but, judged simply, their results do not capture the distinction between culture and the nation-state. As stressed by Lane *et al.* (1997, page 31):

> Culture is not monolithic or uniformly manifested in a country. Not all people will react the same way, but rather certain reactions will be found statistically more often in a particular society. Because of the existence of subcultures, cultural homogeneity within any country cannot be assumed. Within larger cultures, there are pockets of smaller cultures that can be identified as holding different dominant values.

Worldwide clusters?

By compiling the findings of a number of cross-cultural studies, Ronen and Shenkar (1985) have been able to derive eight worldwide clusters based on 'shared' societal attitudes and work-related values. These clusters are shown in Figure 10.4, along with four independent states/cultures. Five of these clusters encompass European states:

- Anglo (with the UK and Ireland exhibiting more similarities to the USA than to other EU members),

- Nordic (the Scandinavian countries – Denmark, Sweden, Finland and Norway),

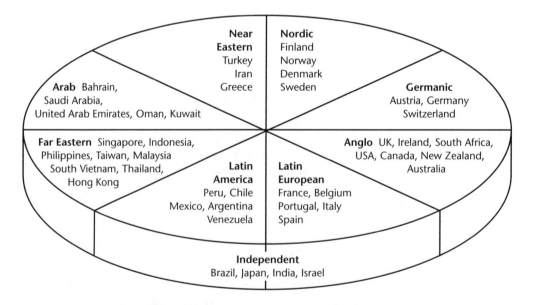

Figure 10.4 A synthesis of country clusters

- Germanic (including Austria, Germany and Switzerland),

- Latin European (Portugal, Spain, Italy, France and Belgium) and

- the Near East (distinguishing Greece and EU candidate Turkey from the rest of Europe).

There exists a degree of uniformity between these findings and the country clusters which emerge from Hofstede's research. Nevertheless, such relationships must be treated with caution. As noted by Daniels and Radebaugh (1995, p. 69): 'They deal only with overall similarities and differences among countries, and managers may easily be misled when considering specific business practices to use abroad'. Despite this, 'a company should expect fewer differences when moving within a cluster than when moving from from one cluster to another'.

High and low context

In different vein, and according to Edward T. Hall (1976), the cultures of the world (and of Europe) can be compared on a scale from high to low 'context' (Figure 10.5). In high-context (HC) societies (such as Japan, China and the Arab nations), a higher value is placed on interpersonal relations in assessing business proposals. People and businessmen tend to build strong and long-term links with others and to seal those links through close personal relationships. Because of these close interactions–relationships, there is little need for a stream of detailed (written) background information and lawyers and formal contracts *may* be used with less frequency. A high-context culture is also one in which the context in which a conversation occurs is just as important as the words that are actually spoken. Cultural clues are important in understanding what is being communicated implicitly. By contrast, in low-context cultures (the USA, Germany, the UK and northern Europe more broadly) people tend to compartmentalize their personal relationships, their work and many aspects of day-to-day life. Words used by speakers explicitly convey the speaker's message to the listener and the mass of information attaching to com-

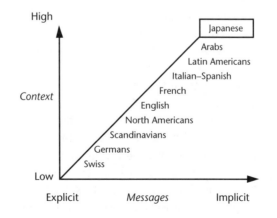

Figure 10.5 Hall's 'contextual' continuum of national clusters
Source: Based on Hall (1976)

453

munications is found in the explicit transmission. Managers look for a body of detailed, explicitly coded information when they make decisions or evaluate a new enterprise. In short, and in direct opposition to managers in high-context cultures, they feel the need for 'contexting' or for the filling in of background information. From a managerial point of view, this tends to mean that in low context cultures much emphasis is placed on formal documentation, legal agreement, fact-oriented and explicit communication.

According to Hall, the Latin European countries (especially the Mediterranean peoples) and Greece are a little higher on the context scale than the Germanic and Nordic nations. If this theory is accepted, there are many possible implications for management and strategy. Not least, efficiency in communication (in different cultural settings), would appear to hinge on an understanding of the degree of 'contexting' both preferred and expected. As Hall and Reed Hall (1995) put it:

> The key to being an effective communicator is in knowing the degree of information (contexting) that must be supplied. If you're communicating with a German, remember he or she is low-context and will need (prefer) lots of information and all the details, in depth. If you're communicating with someone from France, he or she is high-context and won't require (desire) as much information.

While not everybody accepts this theory, and while there are differences in the need for contexting in different circumstances in the same societies, Hall and Reed Hall (1995) are able to cite many examples from their executive interviews in order to support their general argument. They refer, for example, to one German manager working for a French firm who was astonished to find himself fired after a short spell in office. His complaint was that nobody told him what to do. They note:

> The opposite problem was encountered by a Frenchman who resigned from a German firm because he was constantly being told what he already knew by his German superior. Both his intelligence and his pride were threatened.

Cultural change

Much of the above analysis suggests assessing various cultures at a point in time. What is of equal importance is understanding how cultures change over time. As stressed previously, culture may change slowly as a result of evolution, or may change quite rapidly in response to internal strife or exogenous factors. Either way, 'it is important to note the time period associated with any information (or data) one uses to analyse culture' (see Lane *et al.*, 1997, p. 32).

Culture contains an inherent contradiction (Robock and Simmonds, 1989): on the one hand, individuals are keen to protect and preserve their own culture which suggests a degree of constancy. *Ethnocentrism*, the natural belief that one's own culture is superior to that of others, tends to perpetuate the existence of cultural barriers. Concerns that the Single Market will dilute individual country sovereignty (and the power of national state rule) also extend to worries that centralized decision making will not account for individual country nuances. Some observers argue that these fears will manifest themselves in growing nationalistic tendencies as individuals attempt to preserve their domestic cultural norms within the new Europe. This, in itself, asserts a change in attitudes and behaviour which serves to highlight the converse case: dynamism of the environments in which culture exists means that individuals will react to the challenges imposed by grouping together large masses of people with different social norms. Cultural change is therefore inevitable.

Each culture will yield a different propensity to change. Some cultures will readily accept new ideas, innovations and products, while others will put up a great deal of resistance. Much depends, then, on the proportion of the population likely to accept change. Rogers (1962) proposed five categories of people within each society, ranked according to their willingness to adopt new innovations (see Figure 10.6). Where societies are made up of a large number of innovators they are likely to be highly progressive and dynamic as change is accepted readily. They are also more likely to yield higher levels of innovation as individuals not only accept new developments but demand them as a matter of course. Alternatively, some societies yield a lot of resisters curbing the potential for change. The diffusion theory suggests that innovators and early adopters – the risk-takers in any cultural group – secure the fate of new developments. If consumers in these adoption groups regard the product as acceptable their attitude is likely to be mirrored by individuals in the other adoption groups. Acceptance slowly works through society until, ultimately, even the most resistant individuals find that common opinion has swayed their thinking.

The case of the hole in the ozone layer may serve to highlight how this process works. Originally, when it became clear that chlorofluorocarbons (CFCs) were creating a hole in the ozone layer, a number of individuals immediately reacted to this news by boycotting sales of aerosols which had this damaging effect. These people, many of whom formed pressure groups, were able to convince others that changing their buying behaviour of aerosols was necessary if everyone was to work together to save the planet. In turn, the manufacturers of aerosols were also persuaded by the behaviour of the innovators and early adopters (and government pressure) that attitudes were changing and thus developed more environmentally friendly aerosols in readiness for (and adding to) the acceptance of the early majority. This case is particularly interesting as it incorporates not only the changing attitude of customers for a particular generic product but also the changing

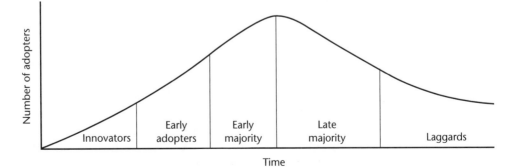

Figure 10.6 Product adopter categories

behaviour of manufacturers prepared to adapt in the face of dynamic market conditions. In this instance, the manufacturers who originally refused to change their behaviour, or who were slow to react, lost market share in favour of those who had made a more rapid adjustment to the exogenous pressure. The degree of nationalism displayed by a culture may also have an important bearing on the willingness to change. Those societies characterized by high degrees of nationalism tend to resist any new developments introduced from outside their immediate environs. Furthermore, this may be directed specifically against a particular nation or culture which is seen to challenge the status quo. Highly nationalistic attitudes tend to sustain barriers between individual nations and cultures.

Culture, management and organization

Before progressing here, it is useful to look in somewhat greater depth at the cultural differences between the fifteen member states and at the impact of culture on business and management in these societies. To do this, we return to Hofstede's dimensions: power distance, uncertainty avoidance, masculinity versus femininity, individualism versus collectivism and short-term versus long-term orientation. Case Study 10.1 at the end of this section provides a specific focus on the cultural differences and similarities between the UK and Germany.

Power distance

Figure 10.7 plots the power distance indices for the fifteen member states and includes those pertaining to the USA and Japan as a means of comparison. A high power distance culture is one where people accept and expect that power will be distributed unevenly and where people accept being told what to do by parents, teachers, managers etc. Relatedly, a high power distance organizational setting is one marked by rigid hierarchies and by centralized authority and decision-making. Employees will tend to accept that their boss has more power and expect (accept) command and instruction. Austria exhibits the lowest power distance score of the group, followed by Denmark, Ireland and Sweden. Austria, Denmark and Sweden, which feature legally mandated co-determination procedures for business, tend to have flat organizational structures, with decisions being more made by consensus than imposed by top-level management. Managers like to see themselves as practical and accessible. Relatively low scores are also attributed to Germany and the UK. Germany too, has adopted co-determination policies for management (as outlined in the case study in Chapter 6). Thus, while many decisions are centralized at top-management level, they are often made in consultation with worker representatives. Equally, as decisions are shaped in German firms by clearly defined rules, the exercise of personal command is unnecessary. In the UK, suggests Hofstede, organizations are akin to 'villages' with decisions based on negotiation rather than command and with many operational decisions decentralized to middle-level managers.

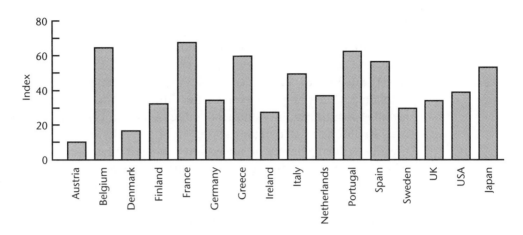

Figure 10.7 Power distance index for the EU member states, US and Japan

Therefore, although UK firms display steeper organizational pyramids (and are rarely characterized by formal structures for co-determination and employee involvement), managers at different levels of the organization are often given freedom to make decisions and will make decisions after consulting with subordinates. It is apparent therefore, that different business structures can lead to similar power distance scores. It is not just the scores themselves which managers need to concern themselves with, but what it is about the way companies in that country do business which leads to the score.

For the EU countries scoring high on the power distance index – Portugal, Spain, France, Greece and Belgium – other factors come into play in determining their autocratic business methods. In the southern European states – Spain, Italy, Greece and Portugal – the dominance of the family as the central focus of the individual (and resultant paternalistic business practices), means that lines of authority established in the home are often perpetuated in the workplace. Although decision-making may be shared in the firm (as in the family), there is an acceptance of senior authority which is bound by trust and loyalty and not formal contracts. France, on the other hand, which exhibits the highest power distance score, shows a marked tendency for centralization of decision-making and, while there is a degree of informal networking, management is often considered to be dictatorial and highly formalized. This is linked to the country's political regime of centralized authority reflected in business organizations through strict pyramidal hierarchies held together by strong unity of command and formal rules.

It is worth noting at this stage the value for power distance in Japan. It is a commonly misheld conception that Japanese management practices, which promote team-work and bottom-up management, implicitly mean flat organizational structures and consensus decision-making. This is not necessarily the case: although workers are encouraged to identify and help solve work-related problems, and management is receptive to their ideas and suggestions, decisions are made by senior managers who are highly respected and looked up to by the workforce.

Uncertainty avoidance

Figure 10.8 plots the uncertainty avoidance indices for the fifteen member states, Japan and the USA. High scores of uncertainty avoidance reflect the extent to which society attempts to shape rules and laws to provide safety, security and to deal with ambiguity. Conversely low scores reflect the extent to which individuals are comfortable with uncertainty and risk-taking. Again, uncertainty avoidance manifests itself in different social organizations. At home, rules, routines and efforts directed towards reducing levels of uncertainty, suggest high uncertainty avoidance. At school, acceptance of broad tasks and unstructured learning (low uncertainty avoidance) may contrast with highly structured formalistic learning with clear timetables and curricula. At work, a desire for formalized rules and little risk taking may contrast with great flexibility and high risk-taking.

Greece and Portugal, and to a lesser extent Belgium, France and Spain, exhibit high scores for uncertainty avoidance. As was highlighted earlier, the Romanic influence on certain of these nations, with centralized nationwide laws being established for common governance, means that cultures have been shaped wherein individuals and institutions expect to be guided by the rules and stipulations of the state or the organizations in which they work. Therefore, individuals not only welcome direction and orders, they depend on them. Conversely, Denmark, Ireland, Sweden and the UK exhibit low levels of uncertainty avoidance. Hofstede (1995) suggests that the Germanic part of Europe (including the UK) 'never succeeded in establishing an enduring common central authority'. Hofstede also argues that uncertainty avoidance is linked with Roman Catholicism, with nations dominated by the Catholic ethos showing higher scores owing to their strict adherence to religious codes of conduct.

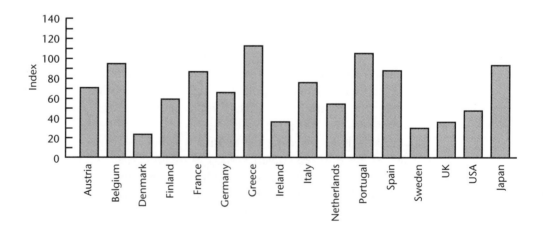

Figure 10.8 Uncertainty avoidance index for the EU member states, US and Japan

Masculinity–femininity

Figure 10.9 shows the indices for masculinity–femininity for the EU member states, Japan and the USA. Again, the graph shows broad differences across the member states. As noted earlier, in the home, the school and the workplace, masculine societies promote competition, performance outcomes, reward-based systems, assertiveness and decisiveness. Feminine societies on the other hand promote relationships, co-operation and compromise and a focus on life qualities rather than outcomes.

Austria, Germany, Ireland, Italy, Greece and the UK exhibit the highest scores along this dimension. Career aspirations and profit orientation drive individuals and companies. Performance is highly rewarded and class structures often promote an ethos of upward mobility – although this can be difficult to achieve as class systems tend to be self-perpetuating. Conversely, in Scandinavian countries such as Sweden, Denmark and Finland, much more emphasis is placed on the quality of work life and the well-being of workers rather than the maximization of profit. This is not to suggest, however, that goals are not important: instead, they are achieved through encouragement rather than driven by necessity. Also important in understanding differences between masculine and feminine societies is countries' attitudes to women at home and at work. As alluded to in Chapter 6, some Germanic and Latin European societies tend to have a more traditional view of the female role in society and lower rates of active female participation in the labour market. Nevertheless, most of these societies now have well-developed equal opportunities legislation, protections for women taking maternity career breaks, and good state-funded childcare facilities. In many cases, these provisions owe much to the course and impact of EU social and employment policies.

Conversely, the Netherlands and Scandinavian countries (which register the lowest scores on Hofstede's maculinity–femininity index) have recognized the economic and social value of introducing women into a wider spectrum of professions

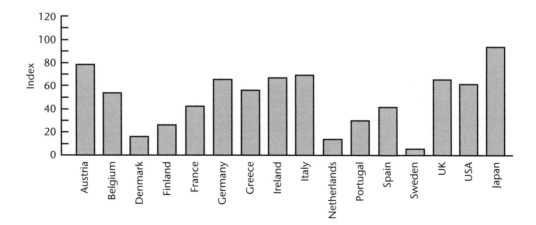

Figure 10.9 Masculinity versus femininity index for the EU member states, US and Japan

and functions and exhibit a more progressive view towards equality in work between men and women. The Scandinavian countries, given their high 'femininity' bias, are unsurprisingly supportive of women in their businesses. Women fit easily into institutions which encourage good living standards and are encouraged to pursue their careers in parallel with their family lives. Childcare facilities in organizations are common and career paths take into account career breaks for maternity and childcare.

Individualism–collectivism

Figure 10.10 outlines the indices along the individualism–collectivism dimension for the member states of the EU, Japan and the USA. In the home, this will mean differences between self-interest versus group harmony, self-actualization versus respect, the expression of personal opinions versus acceptance of group norms. These are translated in the education process to distinguish between learning how to learn versus learning how to do, and in the firm in the form of competing management values and worker practices (see below). As considered at an earlier stage in this chapter, the UK exhibits the highest score along this dimension. The UK, which in this respect is possibly more akin to the USA than other member states, encourages an individualistic ethos. Great store is placed on such management values as entrepreneurship and individual effort. People are often encouraged to operate alone and, frequently, can only get on at work by usurping others and competing for jobs and recognition. Various other member states exhibit slightly lower, but still significant, scores showing a tendency towards individualism rather than collectivism. The two clearest exceptions are Greece and Portugal, where collectivism is assumed to dominate. Hofstede (1995) argues that individualism is positively correlated with economic performance and national wealth, which possibly suggests the low scores for these two member states. The logic is less compelling, however, when applied to other cases.

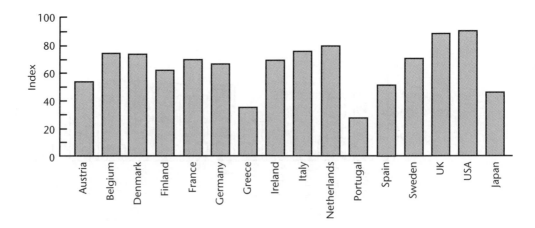

Figure 10.10 Individualism index for the EU member states, US and Japan

Japanese management practices (of which more later) are generally accepted to differ markedly from those pertaining in the West along this dimension. Teamwork and group effort have often been ascribed as one of the driving forces behind their success and Western firms, adopting elements of Japanese 'best practice', have attempted to introduce teamwork concepts into their organizations with varying degrees of success. To what extent this will change the behaviour of people in Western European society is debatable, but it does raise the issue (discussed later in this chapter) of the continuing practice for firms to adopt new management practices outside of their traditional spheres of cultural practice.

Short-term versus long-term orientation

The issue of short-termism was raised in Chapter 8. The UK has, for several years, been accused of taking a short-term view of planning and development which tends to lead to fire-fighting and strategies which can make a quick return rather than those which will ultimately result in long-term competitive success. Japan on the other hand has traditionally been thought of as taking a long-term perspective on decision making, looking to attain a long-term sustainable business position rather than short-term profit. It is not surprising, therefore, that the index for the UK is 25 and that for Japan is 80. Similarly, the figures for Germany, the Netherlands and Sweden are 31, 44 and 33 respectively. Much here relates to the way in which business interacts with the financial community. Japanese industrial groups – keiretsus – include at their core banks and other financial intermediaries. This means that Japanese firms tend to benefit from favourable terms for borrowing which allows them to take a longer view of investments and projects. Nevertheless, this alone does not give society its long-term cultural affinity. Stability at work and individual commitment to the organization (rather than self-development) also aid the continuity of management decisions and an ability to promote long-term goals which individual managers can see through from inception to ultimate conclusion. In Western nations, where individual worth is measured by outcomes, there is a tendency to try to make a fast impression and look for short-term profitable solutions which do not necessarily bring long-term success.

CASE STUDY 10.1 **Germany and the United Kingdom, a cultural perspective**

In many respects, Germany and the United Kingdom share much of their heritage. Both countries, like so many others in Europe, are a product of an amalgam of different economic and political forces emanating from different nations throughout both countries' histories. It is not surprising therefore that there is a degree of commonality between these two nations. But what is the extent of this commonality and how might it affect the way in which companies from each country do business in each other's national markets?

Germany and the United Kingdom – the Hofstede perspective

Figure 10.11 compares Germany and the UK along the four dimensions of Hofstede's research. It is clear that the two countries are very similar along the power distance and masculinity indices but show considerable differences along the uncertainty avoidance and individualism dimensions. But why? It is possible to argue that the UK's business culture is now more based on an American

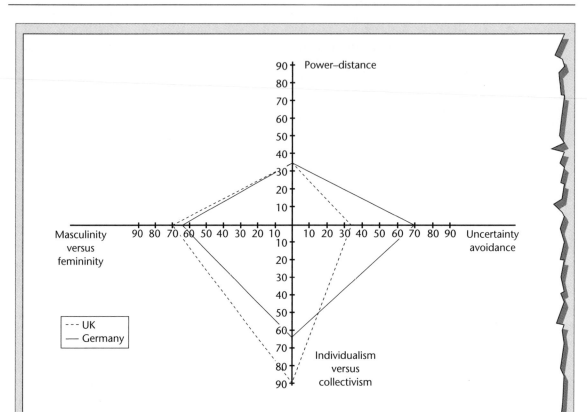

Figure 10.11 A comparison of Germany and the United Kingdom along Hofstede's four dimensions

rather than European model. Sharing the same (or at least very similar) language and displaying similar political and economic systems based on the exploitation of capitalist principles, the UK has forged a cultural path which has moved it away from its European neighbours. Germanic culture, on the other hand, the product of Bavarian influence, has shaped a markedly different set of principles in relation to individualism and uncertainty avoidance. But how does this manifest itself in business behaviour?

Personal relationships

Personal relations count for a lot in Germany. Business is frequently based on trust and 'seeing eye to eye' and this tends to form the cornerstone of negotiation. The British on the other hand place great store on affability and, generally, they only like to work with people they like. The difference between these two perspectives is this. The Germans are more prepared to work at relationships than the British who tend to recoil from dealing with people they do not get along with. This has important ramifications for the way people behave and interact at work. The Germans will persevere with colleagues and will attempt to build bridges and long-term relationships. This leads to stability in organizations and less movement of staff between business functions (unless for the purpose of gaining broader experience). This assists in continuity of management and the building of teams as well as close working relationships with partners and customers. This does not mean, however, that the Germans are closed to outsiders. Germans tend to be better at building

new relationships than the British, who, once they have established working partnerships (either inside or outside of the firm), are reluctant to change. Once they have developed a network of contacts, they are keen to preserve it and not extend it. This is why so many foreign firms are frustrated by their failure to gain contracts with UK clients. It is not because their products are inferior, or can offer no added value, but because they are happy to preserve the status quo. Conversely, the Germans will shop around for new products, new customers, new suppliers, new relationships. Because of the highly individualistic culture, with UK managers (or salespeople) you can deal with the individual. They have the authority to make decisions and secure deals. By contrast, as much German decision-making is centrally determined, it is harder to negotiate with German managers who refuse to bend rules and operate within tight limitations.

Communication

The British tend not to get to the point quickly. They find launching into business negotiations without first establishing some kind of rapport very difficult to do. They may talk about the weather, the state of the economy or crack a few jokes, as a means of breaking the ice before getting down to the matter in hand. The German mentality is the total opposite. They believe that business relationships can only be developed by talking business, and therefore get to the point very quickly. Differences also exist in how directly managers from different countries express themselves once they have got to the point. The British have a great tendency to couch difficult issues in terms and phrases which dilute the impact – soften the blow. This may mean the British saying 'yes' when they actually mean no. The Germans, on the other hand are very direct, even to the point of being brusque. It is this difference which has often led to British managers thinking the Germans they are dealing with as rude. They expect to hear a softer, more cushioned response; instead they may just hear an outright 'no'.

Rules and regulations

The German management system is steeped in rules and regulations. Everything is boiled down to specifications, contracts, documentation and the minutiae of small print. This can slow down the process of negotiation, and is frustrating for those intent on building relationships and mutual co-operation. Take, for example, a UK company which tried to enter into an inward licensing deal with a German chemical manufacturer. The UK company were keen to develop a relationship which would allow them to add value for customers. Their focus on people, rather than systems, meant that they wanted to talk to a variety of people in the German organization and get to know them on a personal level – particularly marketing and sales people who would be charged with the responsibility of getting the product into the market and thus developing the new product's potential. The German company, on the other hand, were eager to finalize the specifications and technical details and continued to send financial and legal representatives to the meetings. They believed there was little point in their potential partner talking to the sales staff until they had finalized the legal transfer of the technology and the financial targets. They also couldn't see the point of introducing more people into the meetings until the existing team had achieved its purpose. The result was a lack of trust, a failure to fully communicate and, ultimately, the failure of the venture. Communications is thus clearly more than just talking to people, it is about understanding different information and exchange requirements, which in this case did not happen.

Conclusion

What is apparent from this cursory overview of some of the differences between Germany and the UK is that the two countries show very different behaviour patterns in the way they conduct business which have the potential of complicating the way in which people from outside of the nations deal with them. Cultural sensitivity is critical to ensuring that such differences do not pose problems and result in a failure to consolidate contracts and relationships. What is also apparent is that there are a number of contradictions between different facets of each country's culture. This partly stems from the fact that cultural analysis, which always tries to reduce things to their simplest level, is not wholly sufficient in providing a framework for assessment, but also relates to the fact that culture is so complex and deep-seated in a society that it manifests itself in very subtle and not always apparent ways.

Corporate culture

What is corporate culture?

Corporate culture differs from national culture as it refers to the way in which attitudes are expressed within a *specific* organization. Corporate culture is sometimes labelled 'organizational culture'. It is the product of the firm's own history and development which may, for multinational organizations, be an amalgam of experiences in a number of national marketplaces. It is, therefore, unique to the individual organization and carves out a path for behaviour and practices which may be distinct from other firms operating within the same national culture. Of course national cultures can help to determine corporate cultures and in different national cultures, one or more 'types' of corporate culture tend to dominate *(see later)*.

According to Trompenaars & Hampden-Turner (1997, p. 158), three aspects of organizational structure are important in determining corporate culture:

1. the general relationship between employees and their organization;
2. the system of authority defining superiors and subordinates (including structures and styles of management);
3. the general view of employees about the organization itself.

Within the literature on organizational cultures, there are essentially two schools of thought:

1. organizational cultures are becoming free from the particularities of specific national cultures and are converging (the cultural convergence perspective);
2. organizational cultures are directly linked to the cultures of societies in which organizations operate, with different national cultures having real consequences for the corporate cultures observed.

Those supporting the first viewpoint believe that management practices and business cultures across the globe are converging as globalization results in technological similarities, new interdependencies and a homogenization of tastes and values. Those supporting this viewpoint believe that such forces have a more pervasive effect on management styles and processes today than national cultural dimensions. Those taking the alternative view bow to the notion that there are increasing similarities in technology, production techniques and communication, leading to some similarities in corporate cultures across countries. However, those challenging the convergence hypothesis assert that management practices and organizational authority structures continue to be shaped significantly by national cultural norms.

Corporate culture and national culture

Theoretically, it is possible to associate national cultural characteristics with different corporate and management cultures. A number of corporate cultures and management styles are presented in Table 10.5 and are related to Hofstede's notions of power distance, uncertainty avoidance etc. Accepting the simplistic nature of these associations, it is possible to project different corporate and business cultures onto Hofstede's dimensions of national culture and to affirm national patterns of corporate culture. Compare France, Italy and Sweden. Each of these countries exhibits different scores along the four original dimensions proposed by Hofstede. By plotting these scores for the four countries, and assuming that they have an impact on company culture for firms with their main operating base in each of these member states, it is possible to compare corporate cultures pertaining in firms from each nation. This is demonstrated in Figure 10.12. Swedish firms, therefore, are expected to demonstrate decentralized and democratic decision-making with high levels of worker consultation, common communication and understanding. Managers are also given freedom to make decisions outside of formal rules and are encouraged to think innovatively. French firms, on the other hand, are expected to show high formality in their rules and structures, authoritarian and coercive management practices. While innovation is encouraged, this can only take place within the strict regulatory rules. Consultation is encouraged, although not necessarily as the basis of ultimate decisions. Finally, Italian firms are likely to show similar characteristics to their French counterparts, with rather less emphasis on authority and coercion and more emphasis on results and profit.

Even those with only a cursory knowledge of the workings of European firms will be aware that there is some validity in these distinctions, with firms from the various countries highlighted exhibiting characteristics in line with these distinctions. However, suggesting that all firms within each country display all these characteristics to the same degree would be entirely misleading. Firms of a different size and background can vary enormously and those which have been exposed to different cultures as part of their normal day-to-day business practices (through working with intermediaries, selling to final customers, acquisition of foreign organizations, joint ventures or alliances) are likely to have adopted a corporate culture and managerial ethos quite distinct from that of companies with little or no exposure to foreign environments/cultures. It may even be possible to suggest that multinational organizations are likely to be more akin to each other than they are to other organizations within the nation in which they are headquartered. This relates back to an earlier

Table 10.5 Corporate culture and management styles

National cultural characteristics	Business structure	Corporate culture	Management style
High power distance	Hierarchical structures with power determined by level in the pyramid	Centralized decision-making and control	Authoritarian and coercive
Low power distance	Flat organizational structures – heterarchies possible	Decentralized decision-making and consultation of lower managers and the workforce	Democratic and open to ideas
High uncertainty avoidance	Formalized structure (possibly hierarchical) functional structures with much centralization	Job specialization and clear delineation of individual job roles and functions	Dependence on documentation and written rules
Low uncertainty avoidance	Loose organizational structures – task oriented and teamwork with high decentralization	Job mobility and little attention paid to titles and roles; generalism encouraged	Freedom afforded to individuals to take responsibility and make decisions
Individualistic	Line functions support individual effort; often hierarchical with clear lines of career development	Encourages entrepreneurship and competition between employees; low loyalty and high inter-company mobility	Freedom to express opinion; encouragement of innovative thinking
Groupist	Flat organization structures and focus on interdisciplinary teams and functions	Encourages co-operation and common purpose – usually established at the top but communicated through management levels	Process oriented, focus on encouragement and involvement at lower levels (although not always decision-making power)
Masculine	Functional departments made accountable	Reward systems based on profit; low loyalty	Aggressive – results oriented
Feminine	Process orientation	Focus on worker welfare leads to consultation and communication; high loyalty	Decisions made on the basis of common communication and understanding

Source: Based on Lachman, Nedd and Hinings (1995)

argument and suggests that levels of development and common experience can shape companies as much as domestic national characteristics. The cumulative point here must be that it is difficult to characterize organizations without 'getting inside' and learning first hand what systems and practices they have adopted as a

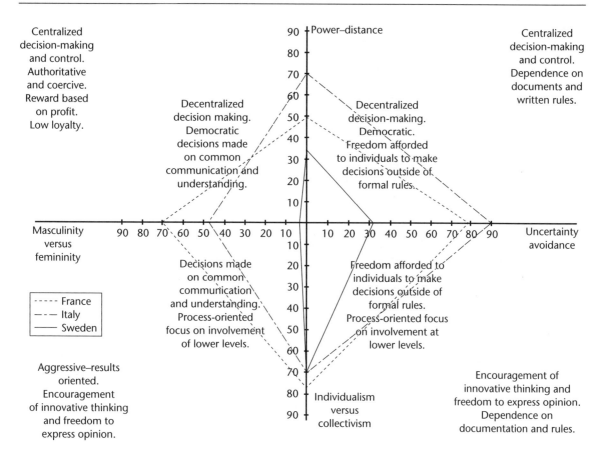

Figure 10.12 Corporate cultures and management styles for France, Italy and Sweden

result of their experiences and historical development. While corporate culture may be influenced by dimensions of national culture, there is no simple 'cause-and-effect' relationship between national culture and corporate culture.

Nevertheless, it is possible to characterize 'types' of organization (organizational culture) and to suggest which countries exhibit which cultures in greatest number. This is a further aspect of the work of Fons Trompenaars with Chistopher Hampden-Turner (see Trompenaars and Hampden-Turner, 1997). Trompenaars defines four types of corporate culture and comments on the degree to which these structures are manifest in specific countries. These cultures are identfied as:

1. the family (France and Spain score highest for this type of corporate culture),

2. the Eiffel Tower (Germany scores highly for this type of corporate culture),

3. the guided missile (the UK scores highly for this type of corporate culture) and

4. the incubator (Sweden scores highly for this type of corporate culture).

The characteristics of these four corporate cultures are presented in Table 10.6 with Trompenaars' national patterns of corporate culture presented more completely in

Table 10.6 Characteristics of Trompenaars' four corporate cultures

	Family	Eiffel Tower	Guided missile	Incubator
Relationships between employees	Diffuse relationships to organic whole to which one is bonded	Specific role in mechanical system of required interactions	Specific tasks in cybernetic system targeted on shared objectives	Diffuse, spontaneous relationships growing out of shared creative process
Attitude to authority	Status is ascribed to parent figures who are close and powerful	Status is ascribed to superior roles who are distant yet powerful	Status is achieved by project group members who contribute to targeted goal	Status is achieved by individuals exemplifying creativity and growth
Ways of thinking and learning	Intuitive, holistic, lateral and error-correcting	Logical, analytical, vertical and rationally efficient	Problem-centred, professional, practical, cross-disciplinary	Process-oriented, creative, ad hoc, inspirational
Attitudes to people	Family members	Human resources	Specialists and experts	Co-creators
Ways of changing	'Father' changes course	Change rules and procedures	Shift aim as target moves	Improvise and attune
Ways of motivating and rewarding	Intrinsic satisfaction in being loved and respected. Management by subjectives	Promotion to greater position, larger role. Management by job description	Pay or credit for performance and problems solved. Management by objectives	Participating in the process of creating new realities. Management by enthusiasm
Criticism and conflict resolution	Turn other cheek, save others' faces, do not lose power game	Criticism is accusation of irrationalism unless there are procedures to arbitrate conflicts	Constructive task-related only, then admit error and correct fast	Must improve creative idea, not negate it

Source: from *Riding the Waves of Culture*, Fons Trompenaars and Charles Hampden-Turner, Nicholas Brealey Publishing, London

Figure 10.13. Importantly, Trompenaars makes a number of warnings to those interpreting these findings: first that the corporate types he suggests are 'ideal types' which seldom exist; second, that while national patterns of corporate culture may be detected, these patterns are in no sense universal, with different countries exhibiting a mix of preferences and forms; third, that there is a close relationship between organizational size and organizational culture irrespective of national setting. As he writes:

> Smaller companies wherever located are more likely to take the family and incubator forms. Large companies needing structure to cohere are likely to choose Eiffel Tower or guided missile forms. ... In France, for example, smaller companies tend to be family and larger companies Eiffel Tower. (Trompenaars and Hampden-Turner, 1997, p. 179)

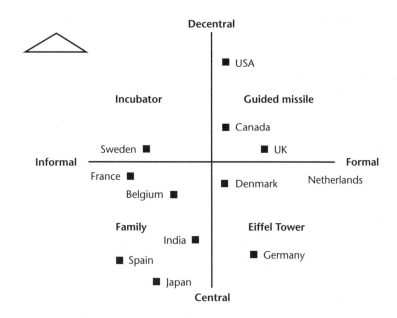

Figure 10.13 Trompenaars' national patterns of corporate culture
Source: from *Riding the Waves of Culture*, Fons Trompenaars and Charles Hampden-Turner, Nicholas Brealey Publishing, London

Other commentators have used different dimensions to establish types of corporate culture and organizational structure.

Process versus results

Peters and Waterman (1982) have argued that strong cultures are more *results oriented* than weak ones which are more process oriented. By a strong culture, they were referring to the degree of homogeneity in perceptions about practices and ways of conducting business according to the norms of the firm. There are various advantages and disadvantages associated with strong cultures which are highlighted in Table 10.7.

Pragmatic versus normative

A different distinction can be made between *pragmatic* and *normative* cultures. This essentially measures the degree of customer orientation displayed by the organization. Pragmatic organizations tend to drive from the centre, whereas normative organizations tend to be driven by functions lower down the value chain (sales and marketing in particular). This is obviously a fundamental issue in modern-day Europe wherein firms are grappling with the problem of balancing centralization and decentralization (efficiency and market responsiveness). To an extent it is possible to argue that all European firms are demonstrating a trend towards more pragmatic management styles as they endeavour to find ways of improving their

Table 10.7 Advantages and disadvantages of strong corporate cultures

Advantages	Disadvantages
Goals are easier to achieve as the culture drives all employees not just towards the same ends, but to the same ends via the same means.	Although goal alignment may be easy to achieve, the goals may not be the right ones. They may be unethical or uneconomical.
With everyone pulling together, organizations tend to be more efficient with less time wasted in conflict and disagreement.	Strong cultures do not always give rise to motivation. UK public sector organizations, for example, have very strong cultures but are notoriously bad at motivating
Leads to high levels of employee motivation. There is 'comfort' in working for an organization with clearly defined ways of doing things even if these are idiosyncratic.	staff. It is possible to argue that strong cultures can generate a variety of different attitudes towards the organization not all of which are conducive to motivation.
Organizations with strong cultures often incorporate practices which make working for them rewarding such as participation in decision-making, again determining good motivation.	Organizations can become too introspective and wrapped up in their history and fail to focus on the present and future development.
Strong cultures tend to learn lessons from past experiences and learn the best ways of doing things.	Changes in the operating environment can mean that old rules no long apply. There remains the question of causality. Does a strong culture result in good performance, or does a good performance help to strengthen company culture?

Source: Based on Hannagan (1995, pp. 250–1).

marketing effort in the EU market which is increasingly competitive and challenging. Without an outward looking focus on customers it is impossible for them to survive. With this thinking in mind, it is clear that this cuts across all of the national managerial determinants discussed above and suggests that there is the possibility of 'Euro-firms' developing which display common cultural characteristics and business norms. This tends to support the argument that ultimately corporate culture can converge across the EU.

Job versus employee

Some organizations consider their workforce purely as an economic asset, expendable at any time. Others are more concerned about the welfare of their employees and consider not only their job role but their personal well-being. Differences of this kind obviously have a bearing on the way in which managers liaise and co-operate with staff lower down the organization, training and individual development. Implicitly, differences of this kind impact on motivation and loyalty. Within the context of the EU, it is again possible to argue that things are changing. A spate of recent EU social measures (see Chapter 6) have set out a number of minimum standards which require many organizations to shift their thinking about employees and to offer improved working terms and conditions. While a good number of organizations in different EU states will find little challenge here, the demands of this new legislation dictate major cultural change among many UK organizations.

Management across cultures – managing diversity

There is no doubting from the previous analysis that Europe is, and will remain, a marketplace in which different cultural norms prevail in different (national) markets. While we observe a greater harmonization of corporate culture, business practices and approaches, at a deeper level, differences in national identity and in societal attitudes and values throughout Europe endure (see van Dijck, 1995). Strategic management for Europe then is about matching organizations not just to one homogeneous environment but to several, culturally distinct environments, and *managing diversity*. Even allowing for the greater harmonization of business practices and approaches (for which there is some genuine scope), it is unlikely there will ever be a truly single homogeneous European culture. While this has led some to argue that the proposed benefits of the Single Market – e.g. greater opportunities for achieving scale economies – can never truly be realized, they are perhaps missing the point. The cultural diversity of Europe need not be considered as a barrier to achieving Europe-wide objectives but a facilitator of achieving improved competitive advantage. In the following sections, we try to give some depth to this point and to further explore the question of intercultural effectiveness.

Intercultural effectiveness

A part of any Euro-manager's reality is the intercultural nature of his or her interactions. Consequently, managers in international businesses require a thorough understanding of the environments in which they operate ('cross-cultural literacy') and the ability to communicate cross-culturally. This is sometimes referred to as 'intercultural effectiveness'. In this context, Wills and Barham (1994) suggest that successful international managers share a number of important traits:

1. Cultural empathy – an ability to 'get into the heads' of the people they deal with from other cultures. This requires putting aside one's own assumptions when dealing with foreign managers or customers and opening up to alternative perspectives and ways of behaving.

2. The power of active listening – cultural empathy depends on an ability to listen and to absorb what is being heard. This means not thinking of a response before the other person has finished talking. In this way, it is possible to learn how others look at things from a different perspective. It also requires managers to look for 'hidden meanings' and covert thinking.

3. A sense of humility – an acceptance that you can learn from others and your own mistakes.

4. Self-awareness – demonstrating emotions improves the openness of interactions and helps to build trust between parties.

5. Emotional resilience – a failure to express emotions is not the same thing as emotional resilience. The failure often stems from an individual suppressing their emotions. Emotional resilience refers to the ability to express emotions

and deal with difficult situations without the emotion hampering the effectiveness with which a situation is handled.

6. Risk acceptance – emotionally resilient managers tend to view the concept of risk differently from other managers. They accept that cross-cultural dealings expose them to risk and thus they develop mechanisms for understanding levels of discomfort, survival techniques, ways of learning from the outcomes (whether they are positive or negative).

7. Emotional support of the family – the family providing a 'comfort zone' and a place for alleviating stress and supporting the challenge of risk and complexity.

8. Curiosity to learn – an active interest in seeking out the new and unfamiliar; learning by doing and continually adding new layers of knowledge to old.

9. Orientation to time – 'living in the here and now'. Making the most of existing opportunities and not pondering on what has passed or what is to come except to learn from past experiences and plan for the future. Essentially, they are controllers of their time and not servants to it.

10. Personal morality – taking responsibility for decisions and, through a respect for people, encouraging empowerment of others.

With such an extensive list of personal qualities required for managing across cultures it is not surprising that there are major issues to be addressed by international businesses and their human resource (HR) managers. Thought must be given to how those with cross-cultural skills can be attracted and 'bought in' (the recruitment challenge) and to how both new and existing managers can be developed into good international managers (the training challenge). It is not just about developing managers in job functions but about developing them as people to cope with the complex environments in which they operate and to manage cross-cultural interactions.

So how do firms encourage the development of such managers and skills as a means of managing cultural diversity and of attaining competitive advantage? Advantages can accrue from incorporating new personnel initiatives in the overall strategic plan for Europe. Creating career paths which include operating in various member states, developing reward schemes which reflect cross-cultural learning and emphasizing language learning by providing in-house programmes (as well as recruiting good language graduates), all have the potential to foster the development of effective Euro-managers.

Tijmstra and Casler (1992) suggest that an international or pan-European manager needs to go through four distinct aspects of learning: awareness, knowledge, skills and attitudes. Knowledge, they argue, is a hard element which can be delivered through training courses on such issues as:

- the European business environment (socio-political, economic, business sector and technological)

- European management dynamics (the diversity of business cultures and variations in management values)

- the Europeanization process (transnational structures, transnational processes, European identity and cross-cultural communication).

Conversely, awareness, knowledge, skills and attitudes can only be shaped through on-the-job experience and exposure to other cultures. Training of managers is therefore imperative at both a pre-occupation and post-occupation level. In this sense, educational institutions have an important role to play in preparing individuals for the new international economy. Emphasis in secondary education on language learning and a renewed vigour in business schools to adopt a wider European perspective (to include links with industry at a Europe-wide level) will also better prepare individuals for the challenges ahead and aid the development of necessary skills for cross-cultural management on a Europe-wide scale. At business school level, this means not just the bland internationalization of courses (in which all too frequently international elements are 'tacked on' to existing course provision) but an integrated approach which prepares managers along a number of dimensions:

- foreign language aptitude

- exposure to tutors and students from other cultures

- exchange programmes which permit individuals to study in a foreign country

- knowledge-based courses which provide a review of key management issues (and not just theoretical models and constructs)

CASE STUDY 10.2 **Cross-cultural effectiveness targeted by automations firm**

Rockwell Automation, the fast-growing US automation group with subsidiaries in nineteen countries, recently turned to a UK-based business school, Ashridge, to help develop an international management programme. The group needed to develop talented staff with management potential and to equip new and existing managers with core business skills and the international expertise necessary in a global company. The major aim of the programme was to make managers more culturally aware. The programme leader Jean Vanhoegaerden remarked 'The US (head office) did not understand the European division – marketing and distribution, for instance, operate very differently in the US and in Europe – and the Europeans complained'. 'We encouraged US managers to spend a week in the European division and vice-versa. The programme helped work out cross-cultural difficulties and focused on developing a more international approach.' Vanhoegaerden believes that, in a global world, 'managers need above all else speed, transparency and an understanding and respect for cultural differences. However respect does not mean adapting to another culture, but knowing where your limits are and understanding the strengths and weaknesses of your own culture'.

Source: Financial Times, Business Education Section, 3 April 2000

- texts and case studies which reflect the experiences of business in other countries
- transnational experience of educational provision in other countries.

Again, within the company, providing opportunities to work in (or with people from) other member states is required so that individuals attain the experiential elements required for the development of good European managers. Project groups and cross-cultural team work, coupled with longer stays in a foreign location, are essential. So too are well-defined career paths which incorporate job rotation for attaining European exposure. Failure of expatriate managers (and their early return to their domestic base) is thought to be attributable to a variety of factors, including inadequate training and preparation in working with foreign personnel, a lack of experience of working in foreign environments, and ethnocentric attitudes.

Cultural diversity and competitive advantage

Porter (1990) developed a model to explain the competitive advantage of different nations. While, in the past, advantages were assumed to result from comparative advantage in factors of production, growing evidence in the world economy that factors of production are mobile, means that these give only transitory advantages and do not support long-term competitive advantage. Porter therefore focused on four key aspects of national environments which support the development of different national advantage. These are depicted in Figure 10.14. While culture is not explicitly included in the model, it is assumed that cultural differences work through the four key variables.

Each country within the EU boasts a different set of conditions (factor, demand, competitive and relationship) which dictates its comparative advantage *vis-à-vis*

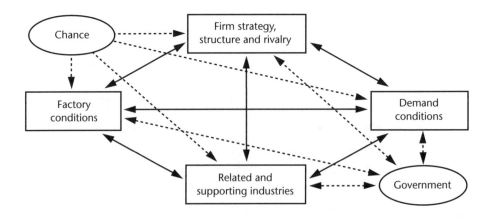

Figure 10.14 The determinants of national competitive advantage
Source: Based on Porter (1990)

other member states. In essence, it means that various nations offer up different locational advantages and disadvantages. European firms, which have the freedom to reorganize their businesses across the member states, are therefore well placed to tap into the advantages (many of which are culturally determined) of the various EU nations. From this point of view, European firms have the ability to strengthen their Europe-wide (and international) competitive advantage as a result of cultural diversity. But how can they achieve this? Relating back to Chapter 8, much issue was made of the growing importance of flexibility, and, without wishing to labour the point, it is important to reiterate this in relation to cross-cultural management. Flexible organizations have the potential to maximize benefits from different business practices and national economic conditions through a variety of means:

1. Locating businesses in markets where factor conditions are favourable leading to cost advantages and efficiency.

2. Operating in non-domestic markets where demand conditions are more favourable and profit potential apparent. This critically involves the identification of common patterns of demand and submarkets which are likely to cut across national boundaries.

3. The development of relationships with suppliers can improve the quality and efficiency of inbound logistics. Europe-wide sourcing facilitates this process. Companies can build relationships with suppliers in other member states which show a high propensity for co-operation and long-term relationship management.

4. Joint ventures, strategic alliances and mergers allow firms to internalize not only the knowledge and learning of organizations from other member states (and thus potentially benefit from their comparative advantages) but also new business practices.

At this level, then, the recommendation for firms managing across cultures in Europe is this:

1. Cultural difference should not be viewed as an inhibitor of competitive advantage but a facilitator.

2. Having established critical success factors in its industry, the firm must look at national cultures and economic conditions across Europe and identify areas of national advantage.

3. Having identified areas of strength, firms must devolve ways of tapping into these strengths.

4. Identify commonality in demand conditions between markets as a means of ensuring maximum coverage for common products and brands.

5. Be prepared to be flexible and adaptive, but don't lose sight of Europe-wide objectives. In other words, adapt where it is essential to do so, but standardize wherever possible.

The last point is likely to be difficult to achieve for European firms which have traditionally viewed Europe as a series of discrete markets which require separate treatment. As alluded to in Chapter 8, high levels of decentralization have characterized the Europe-wide activities of many firms which, in the past, viewed this as the most appropriate way of dealing with foreign market differences. Despite this, as firms are moving more towards networked structures, with subsidiary managers coming together to voice their concerns, they are finding that common problems and opportunities exist across a large number of markets and that there is real potential for standardization (particularly in cross-market niches).

Whether or not then European culture becomes more homogeneous, by developing a flexible approach to European strategic management and by looking to manage diversity, firms can turn differences into competitive advantage. However, there is some concern that, in the current environment, firms showing the greatest aptitude for this approach to pan-European management are the Japanese and Americans who are therefore outcompeting Europeans on their own soil. Here, too, however, change within Europe opens up new potential for cultural learning. Exposure to Japanese management practices, through either competing against them or working with them, has resulted in a worldwide move towards the adoption of some of the factors which have arguably led to the Japanese 'miracle' in the second half of the twentieth century.

Bridging the culture gap – the adoption of Japanese business practices

While this chapter is on European business culture, value can be added with a review of Japanese management practices. The meteoric success of Japan in the world economy in recent years has led many businesses to ask, what makes the Japanese so successful? Much has been written about the success of Japan in recent years, researchers looking for clues as to why the Japanese have been able to outperform their Western counterparts. Much of this research has focused on cultural differences between Western and Japanese management practices which are depicted in Table 10.8. For the sake of convenience, 'Western' management practices are grouped together, although, as has already been demonstrated, distinct differences do exist on a country-by-country basis. Nevertheless, it is possible to make certain generalizations at a generic level.

Oliver and Wilkinson (1992) identify four groupings of factors characteristic of Japanese industry:

1. manufacturing methods including: total quality control, quality circles, in-process controls such as statistical process control, just-in-time (JIT) delivery and management systems and continuous improvement – 'kaizan';

2. organizational structures and systems (including management accounting), which do not simply inform but force improvements, R&D led by powerful susha (project leaders), and flatter organizational structures;

3. personnel practices (including lifetime employment, longer working hours and commitment to consultation and improvement);

4. wider social, political and economic conditions (incorporating enterprise unions, buyer–seller relationships, government support, and economic structures including an integral banking system).

All of these reflect how different cultural norms in Japan have impacted on the way in which the Japanese do business. In terms of manufacturing techniques, for example, while the systems employed are not unique to Japan, many of them being introduced with US aid packages and technology transfer deals after the Second World War (particularly quality control techniques), they were enthusiastically implemented by Japanese managers after being adapted to suit the Japanese cultural preference for group and teamworking. Thus, it is not the systems in themselves which have offered great scope for 'good practice' but the way in which they have been adopted into the culture.

Table 10.8 Japanese-style management versus Western-style management

Japanese style	Western style
Organizational principles	
1. The firm viewed as a collective body; total devotion of the individual to the firm.	1. Functionalist organization of individuals as specialists.
2. Human-centred, not functionalist-centred, organization.	2. Co-operative work system based on a thoroughgoing division of labour; subdivision and standardization of jobs.
3. Stress on co-operative teamwork.	3. Pyramid-shaped bureaucracy.
4. Indeterminate job description and job standing (authority and responsibility); generalist oriented.	4. Clearly defined job description and job standing (authority and responsibility).
5. Japanese style adaptation of modern bureaucracy.	5. Employment of contract (give and take commercial exchange).
Decision-making and communication	
1. Collective decision-making (bottom-up consensus type decision-making as seen in the *ringi* system).	1. Top-down decision-making and one-way orders (no consideration given to opinions at the lower echelons).
2. Verbal and non-verbal communication (*nemawashi* or behind the scenes manoeuvres; information transmitted by implicit understanding).	2. Autocratic authority at the top; expanded power of the bureaucracy.
3. Collective work performance system (common room system; total membership participation and planning).	3. Individual responsibility and competition (fair-play principles).
4. Exemption from responsibility (seat of authority is obscure; no one takes responsibility).	4. Strong owner consciousness (the company President is also a hired hand).
5. Separation of ownership and management (no real power in officers' meetings and general stockholders' meetings).	5. Legal armament by lawyers (legal specialists).
6. Japan Inc. (collusive relationships of government, business and labour).	

Japanese style	Western style

Personnel system–labour management

Japanese style

1. Life-long employment (no lay-offs but there is flexibility by means of part-time and temporary employees).
2. Seniority-based promotion system (evaluations for promotions are quite comprehensive; they stress not just work results but incentive and effort as well and also reflect capability).
3. Seniority wage system (stress is placed not just on compensation for labour but on overall exhibition of ability); stress on fringe and welfare benefits.
4. Extensive employee training and education.
5. Enterprise labour unions; co-operation between labour and management.

Western style

1. Employment of people only at times when needed; layoffs in bad times.
2. Wages are job compensation according to competency (efficiency system) with no relationship to age and seniority.
3. Seniority system at times of promotion and layoffs.
4. Labour unions are functionally organized by craft and job type; unions safeguard the individual's life and rights.
5. Much tension between labour–management relations.

Human relation and values

Japanese style

1. Groupism (the group comes first; value on the group; the individual is devoted heart and soul to the group) mutual dependence.
2. Concurrence of the firm's goal and the individual's life goal (devotion to the group; prestige, sense of security, and morale pursuant to participation; co-prosperity idea; love of company spirit).
3. Stress on harmony in human relations (emphasis on feelings and motives, warm human relations, mutual consent of all members and linking of hearts).
4. Egalitarianism in substance (little chance for class discrimination; small earning differentials).
5. Strong desire for the elevation of quality and efficiency.

Western style

1. Individualism (ultimate value on the individual; devotion and loyalty to the group are weak).
2. To the individual the firm is nothing more than a means to obtain wages and to the firm the individual is a piece of machinery, a tool.
3. Human relations in the workplace are simply artificial relations for work purposes; relations cease outside of the company.
4. Egalitarian in form (strong class consciousness, competition for equal opportunity).
5. Purpose of life resides in the family and leisure, strong community consciousness.

Source: Based on Mirza (1984).

Japanese manufacturing techniques

Japanese manufacturing techniques constitute the most tangible elements of the Japanese business system. They are essentially concerned with quality and efficiency and the improvement of competitiveness and thus it is unsurprising that it is these, more than any other aspects of Japanese management, which are now being adopted by Western firms. Table 10.9 outlines the nature and scope of the most commonly followed techniques–methods in this respect, many of which have been alluded to in earlier chapters (see Chapter 6 on quality circles and Chapter 8 on JIT). Given the limited scope of this chapter, analysis of all of these techniques

Table 10.9. Japanese manufacturing techniques

Manufacturing technique	Overview
Total quality control	The de-specializing of the business function. Responsibility for quality remains in its 'natural' place, namely where production is performed. It incorporates all business functions with the aim being customer satisfaction both internal to the organization (downstream business units) and external to the company (intermediaries and final customers).
Quality circles	These are small groups, usually between five and ten people who meet voluntarily to try to find ways to improve quality and productivity. Members are trained in statistical analysis and problem solving techniques.
Statistical process control (SPC)	This system is used to assist in the control of production processes in order to achieve less variation in output and ensure quality. SPC involves operators periodically sampling their own production not with a view to accepting or rejecting it, but in order to produce a chart of how the process itself is behaving. In addition to reducing scrap and reworking costs, minimizing variation in components can significantly improve product performance.
Just-in-time (JIT) production	'The JIT idea is simple: produce and deliver finished goods just in time to be sold, sub-assemblies just in time to be assembled into finished goods, fabricated parts just in time to go into the sub-assemblies and purchased materials just in time to be transformed into fabricated parts' (Schonberger, 1982). The system requires predictable and planned demand, or production flexibility to cater for changes in demand.
Kanban production system	This system involves containers for holding stock and cards for initiating production. This means that the amount of stock in the system can be varied by altering the number of cards in the system. In this way materials are pulled through the production process according to the demand for final assembly rather than pushed through by an inflexible production plan.
Flexible working	In Japanese firms this includes team working (or cellular manufacturing). This is facilitated by multi-skilled workers who can be rotated between jobs. The system simplifies workflow, allowing workers to be moved to alleviate bottlenecks and ensure a continuous flow of production.

(on an individual basis) is impossible. What is clear, however, is that a total quality approach provides their underpinning, directed as they are to achieving improvements in each stage of the design and production process. It is this concept of 'total quality' that we can usefully discuss.

Total quality (and TQM)

The ideas associated with 'total quality' are a primary characteristic of Japanese manufacturing. More than their European and American counterparts, Japanese manufacturers have seen quality as the responsibility of everybody in the workforce and have viewed quality to be central to manufacturing and service provision. In a genuine sense, the global trend towards integrating quality considerations into all levels of industrial activity begins with the emergence of modern Japan as a powerful manufacturing force. At the same time, in some European companies, there has been a backward tendency to assume that the concept of total quality is something peculiarly Japanese and related to cultural and other factors which cannot be translated into the Western context. Such a view represents an inherent misunderstanding of the theory behind total quality and of how to introduce proper quality management systems. Indeed, while total quality is a theme which finds natural expression in Japanese culture (given its group orientism, and high notions of duty and responsibility), the total quality approach (and total quality management (TQM) system) is easily implemented in a Western context given an adjustment of attitudes, the commitment of senior managers, effective leadership and teamwork.

The theory behind a total quality management system is that, as quality improves, costs actually fall through lower failure and appraisal costs and less waste. TQM is much more than ensuring product or service quality, it is a system of dealing with quality at every stage of the production process, both internally and externally. While the force behind a TQM system has to come from senior management, the responsibility for quality itself belongs to everybody in the organization. The TQM system requires that every single part of the organization is integrated and must be able to work together. This is exactly the ethos which is needed for an environmental management system to be successful; the push must come from the top but everyone has a role (see Chapter 11). The main elements of the system are:

1. Teamwork: this is central to many parts of the TQM system where workers have to feel they are part of an organization. In addition, teams of workers will often be brought together into problem-solving groups, quality circles (as discussed in Chapter 6) and quality improvement teams.

2. Commitment: to be successful TQM needs to be truly company wide and therefore commitment is required at the top from the chief executive as well as from the workforce. Middle management has an important role to play in not only grasping the concepts themselves but also explaining them to the people for whom they are responsible.

3. Communications: poor communications can result in organizational problems, information being lost and gaps occurring in the system. A good flow of accurate information, instructions and feedback is vital in maintaining the cohesion needed by the system.

4. Organization: a cohesive system needs to be an organized one with clear channels of responsibility and clearly defined reporting procedures. Quality-related errors can be quickly rectified if an efficient organizational structure is in place.

5. Control and monitoring: the TQM system will not remove the need to monitor processes and sample outputs, neither will it simply control itself. But many organizations use after-the-fact controls, causing managers to take a reactive rather than a proactive position. The TQM systems needs a more anticipative style of control.

6. Planning: processes need to be planned carefully if they are to be efficient. This

usually requires recording activities, stages and decisions in a form which is communicable to all. A clearly defined process reduces the scope for error and provides the basis of an analysis into possible improvements.

7. Inventory control system: it is in the storage of raw materials, components or the finished product that quality can diminish. The keeping of stocks is also physically expensive and can lead to cash flow problems. An inventory control system is therefore required to keep stocks to a minimum, while ensuring that supplies never dry up. One such system is the just-in-time system.

A breakdown in any part of the TQM system can lead to organizational gaps where wastage may occur or quality be overlooked. Errors have a habit of multiplying, and failure to meet the requirements of one part of the organization creates problems elsewhere. This means that managers must plan strategically both externally and internally and that internal strategic planning has to involve everyone in the workplace. TQM is an approach aimed at improving the effectiveness and flexibility of business as a whole and is aimed at eliminating wasted effort as well as physical waste. Gains follow by involving everyone in the process of improvement and by improving the effectiveness of work so that results are achieved in less time and at less cost.

Returning to an earlier theme, central to the TQM approach is a need for a change in the attitude and culture prevailing within many organizations (corporate culture). Organizations have to move away from the acceptance of defects and mistakes as if they were just part of life. Divisional, competitive structures within organizations need to be broken down and replaced with committed, co-operative relationships between all employees, who should see themselves as working towards the same goal. Linked with attitude change is the need to create a climate of continuous improvement. Organizations need to ensure that they have information about quality at all times, so that they understand what is happening within any particular process. This moves the culture of the company away from checking whether a particular product or process is working effectively, after the event, to ensuring that one understands and identifies any quality problems early in the process, seeking continuously to improve performance. It therefore requires everybody, at every level in the organization, to understand and implement their own responsibilities for the quality management process. It is perhaps these challenges that question the ability of many Western firms to introduce and to implement a total quality approach. The experience to date, however, is that it is those firms which adopt such systems that are achieving a competitive edge.

Organizational structures

Organizational structures are, arguably, more ephemeral and difficult to replicate. They are reflective of family values and the country's national identity. It is often assumed that Japanese organizations are flat, with management being by consensus. This is rather misleading. Many Japanese organizations exhibit hierarchical characteristics, with decision-making coming from the top. Although there is great talk of a 'bottom-up' approach to management (the *ringi* system) this is more about consultation and involvement than lower-level decision making. There is a strong belief that workers have the potential to improve the quality of their work and thus they are encouraged to participate in problem-solving, usually through the formation of teams. Teamwork is essentially the hallmark of the Japanese organization. It not only involves bringing people together to solve common problems and work on group activities but manifests itself in common goals and commitment by every individual to the company's welfare.

Teamwork is also fundamental to flexible manufacturing and TQM. As increased global competition is placing more emphasis on local responsiveness, market segmentation, differentiation and product quality, firms need to develop more flexible manufacturing systems and quality programmes to respond to the new demands. Part of the teamwork ethos prepares individuals for a variety of functions within the workplace. Through cross-training, workers can stand in for absent co-workers and respond quickly to changes in models and production runs. Used in conjunction with flexible manufacturing technology (computer-aided design and manufacture), firms employing a teamwork ethos have the potential to change product models more than a dozen times a day. Similarly, teamwork enables TQM initiatives by providing a forum for problem-solving and continuous improvement. It is unsurprising then, that many Western firms, keen to pursue TQM principles, are moving towards team development and management (see Chapter 11). However, for many of them, introducing these techniques is proving difficult because it cuts across cultural norms. Many Western firms (as was highlighted earlier) are based on an individualistic rather than collective culture, which means that teamwork is anathema to the underlying work ethic. Teams challenge individual power and authority and thus their introduction fuels resistance. However, suggesting that differences centre on a clear distinction between collectivism and individualism is over-simplistic. Personal leadership in Japan is regarded highly, and many leading Japanese companies have attained their position in world markets as a result of strong leadership. Equally, many Western firms have pursued a policy of co-operation and teamwork for many years and, while they have not considered this to be directly akin to Japanese-style management, the effects are markedly similar. It is also wrong to assume that individualism is not conducive to good business practice. The benefits of individualism have been well proven in Western organizations. The notion of entrepreneurial spirit is not only welcomed, it is actively encouraged as the tendency for individuals to compete against each other frequently gives rise to the development of new ideas. In the commercial organization this means new products and technologies which have a positive impact on the national economy.

Nevertheless, individualism has its drawbacks. First, it tends to promote mobility between organizations as employees attempt to build impressive work records and move up the management ladder at a faster rate than their peers. This produces managers with broad general management experience but limited knowledge and understanding of the workings of an individual company. Nevertheless, mobility can mean that Western managers are exposed to a wide array of differing business practices as they move between organizations. This mirrors the situation in Japan, to some extent, although here mobility tends to be controlled within organizations by senior managers rather than at the personal level. Second, it dilutes continuity in management with new personnel frequently replacing old and constantly moving business departments in a different direction. This can be unsettling to the workforce and overall morale with concomitant adverse effects on productivity. Finally, individualism may make it difficult to build co-operation both within and without the company. With co-operation between business departments and between organizations becoming an increasingly important feature of global business activity, there is a case for concern regarding Western managers' ability to adapt from a competitive to a co-operative mentality.

In Chapter 8, much emphasis was placed on the competitive success of Japanese firms accruing from the close business relationships developed with suppliers. Although inter-firm collaborations in Japan are centred on the keiretsu (linked group) business system, which is a product of Japan's historical development, the basic elements of the system are being replicated by Japanese firms within the EU through collaborations with local firms, but, more importantly, with Japanese suppliers who have followed the lead of the major producers and located production within the EU. The success of these linked groups (based on mutual interdependence and trust) is prompting many EU firms to find new ways of working with their suppliers. Technical and business collaborations between suppliers and buyers for problem-solving and the mutual development of components and inputs are becoming more prevalent within the EU as firms seek to capitalize on established business links to enhance competitive advantage. These linkages have, in turn, led to the development of JIT systems.

Planning timeframes

The idea that the Japanese take a longer perspective in planning was alluded to earlier. Management accounting procedures differ radically from those typically found in Western organizations. Systems are based more on products and market share than profit. This leads to activity-based costing programmes rather than cost-plus, and permits greater flexibility to adapt to changes in the external environment. However, it is possible to over-emphasize the long-termism of the Japanese economy:

> A far-sighted Japan and a myopic America make a tidy contrast, but one with little basis in fact. By and large, Japanese managers are at least as much obsessed with short-term results as their American counterparts. ... They have arrived where they are today, not by rigidly adhering to predetermined long-range strategies, but by paying scrupulous attention to performance on a monthly or even weekly basis – performance measured not against a three- or five-year plan, but against budget, against return on sales, against competitor performance. (Ohmae, 1982, pp. 2–3)

Thus it is more the difference in approach to measuring profits rather than profit concerns themselves which distinguish between Japanese and Western firms. Whereas Western firms tend to concentrate on return on investment (ROI), Japanese organizations concentrate on return on sales (ROS).

Communication and employee involvement

Japanese personnel practices centre on co-operation, not mere compliance. The concept of collectivism, which starts in the family, and is mirrored in businesses, relies on mutual interdependence and loyalty. Groups are based on strict hierarchical models based on seniority systems in which individuals respect and look up to their elders. Loyalty is promoted through involvement and consultation. Loyalty brings with it a sense of belonging, a common purpose and high levels of motivation and commitment. In Japan, this is also facilitated by life-long employment (although this is no longer guaranteed in many Japanese firms) which gives individuals a sense of security and heightens their commitment to the organization. Japanese companies see their workforce as an asset. Core workers are protected and nurtured and, although they go through tough recruitment and selection procedures, in return they enjoy secure contracts and attractive remuneration packages. Nevertheless, profit-linked bonus schemes can result in broad differentials in pay between boom and slump periods.

Traditionally, many Western organizations have shown a limited propensity to involve employees in decision-making. The main exceptions to this are provided by the Nordic countries and Rhenish countries. Recent and draft EU legislation is attempting to redress this situation and to strengthen management–worker consultation (see Chapter 6) but much resistance has been displayed by Western firms in the adoption of employee involvement despite the apparent quality and productivity pay-outs. Arguably, employee involvement is not so much to empower the workforce to take action against management but to provide an environment in which employees are encouraged to take a greater interest in the long-term success of the organization. Nevertheless, a shift to this way of thinking necessitates cultural change in a number of European societies (especially in the UK) and shrugging off individualistic tendencies in favour of a more collective approach to management. The cultural barrier argument again seems to hold some sway. Examples of successful employee involvement within the EU suggest an approach somewhat different to that employed by the Japanese. The German systems of worker participation rely on the involvement of workers in decision-making, which acts contrary to the intentions of the Japanese approach. Whereas the Japanese are concerned with employees playing a part in identifying and solving problems on the production line to reduce the number of defective goods produced, the German system is geared more towards real empowerment, giving workers a voice in company-wide decisions. Teams are more loosely supervised and workers actively encouraged to work under their own initiative. In essence, then, the Germany system, by empowering employees in this way, is combining both the benefits of co-operation and teamwork with individualism and entrepreneurship – adapting systems to suit local cultural conditions.

Training and development

Japanese companies stress life-long learning and multi-skilling as central to the development of their workers. As the demands on firms in Europe are changing and increasingly requiring more flexible manufacturing and work practices, teamwork and multi-skilling are essential if firms are to remain competitive. This means training the workforce in a variety of skills so that they can react quickly to changes in models and production runs. Harnessing the knowledge and expertise of in-house managers can reduce the cost of such training considerably. The Commission's efforts to improve EU training and its commitment to life-long learning clearly reflect the recognition that without systems in place to improve the skills of workers the EU is likely to be beset by problems of skills shortage and structural unemployment. Lessons from Japan are clear: improve the skills of the workforce or run the risk of losing the competitive battle. In the current European environment, however, high levels of unemployment and business rationalization act against the development of employee commitment, raising some doubts about successful development of vocational training programmes, at least in the short term.

Wider economic considerations

The term Japan Inc. has often been used to describe the interrelated nature of Japanese industry, society and government. The Japanese keiretsu groups, broad-based conglomerates which stem from the activities of large wealthy industrial families, have produced a marketplace dominated by large conglomerates with complex cross-shareholdings and directorships. Each keiretsu involves a wide array of disparate industries including manufacturing organizations, banking institutions, trading companies and service firms. There is, therefore, great potential for synergy within the keiretsu groups as skills and resources can be drawn from a wide pool of industrial and commercial activity. The twenty-two existing groups account for a substantial proportion of the economy, are extremely influential, and constitute the international face of Japan. However, this is not the full picture: outside the keiretsu groups the economy boasts a very high proportion of small firms and family firms which make up half of the employment in Japan. They enjoy long-term relationships with the keiretsu groups although they are vulnerable and tend to suffer in periods of economic down-turn. As these firms are subcontractors and suppliers to the major economic groups, they are a significant feature of the total Japanese business system. A key feature of the keiretsu group is the integral nature of the banking sector. With banks being part of the conglomerate, tied in to the successes of the group, Japanese firms tend to enjoy more favourable banking rates than their economic counterparts. In addition, the keiretsus have strong links with powerful state bureaucracies which involve joint decision-making and consultation. This gives the main economic groups a leading voice in industrial policy and development which ensures political policy takes into account the needs of industry and commerce.

In Europe, banks remain removed from industry and an instrument of government economic policy. Although German banks have formed close links with some of the larger German MNEs and with the Mittelstand, this kind of relationship development tends to be the exception rather than the norm in the EU. Unlike their Japanese counterparts, EU banks have little incentive to offer low-cost capital loans, firms providing a major source of income on loans granted. Without some provision being made for redressing the situation it is arguable that Japanese firms will always be able to reap the benefits of their integrative system and exploit the greater competitive advantages so offered.

The lessons to be learned

Important lessons are being learned by multinational managers as they are exposed to the different business practices utilized in other countries of the world. In terms of Japanization, Graham (1988) identified three levels of business practice permeation into Western economies:

> *direct Japanization* – Japanese companies setting up operations in the West, training workforces and establishing links with local suppliers;
>
> *mediated Japanization* – the attempt by Western firms to emulate Japanese business practices in the belief that they may improve the competitive standing of their organizations;
>
> *permeated Japanization* – the adoption of similar strategies and investment patterns, including government support programmes.

Although the focus in this section has been on differences in Japanese versus Western management practices, this picture can be regarded more broadly. The three mechanisms outlined above serve as the conduits for learning and change in business practices on a global scale. Firms are now looking beyond the systems and structures developed in their own marketplace and towards global best practice. They are adopting systems and techniques from a variety of organizations – either their competitors or their partners – to improve their standing in European (and world) markets. From this point of view it is difficult not to argue that multinational firms are changing culturally. While their behaviour may be partly attributable to national characteristics in their domestic market, this can no longer be seen as the only driving force behind corporate culture and management practices. Managing across cultures in the context of the EU is therefore about not only looking at different national markets, or European companies, but looking at global business cultures and managerial practices and learning how other organizations are solving problems and facing up to the new strategic challenges being posed by global environmental change. In this way, firms can draw on a wide pool of experience and proven behaviour as a means of deriving ways of improving their competitive position.

Research on Japanese management and prescriptions for its adoption in the West have tended to highlight the difficulties rather than the opportunities and have often tried to find mechanism for 'transfer' of techniques, rather than focus on learning opportunities. Their conclusions have frequently centred on the fact that it is impossible to replicate Japanese management practices as they rely on subtle ambiguities of culture, different ways of thinking (which often means they cannot be precisely defined) and an acceptance of constant dynamism of processes (Fry, 1991). Some have also tended to implicitly assume that everything about Japanese management is better than anything the West can offer. This is clearly not the case. Rather, many Japanese firms, through incorporating effective business techniques into their culture, have been able to perform to very high standards. The message then is that European firms may have a lot to learn, both from each other and their international competitors or collaborators. The Japanese have never been frightened of learning from the West. Their business practices are continually evolving, and often draw on Western input. Peters and Waterman's best selling book *In Search of Excellence* (1982), which describes the strategies employed by the most successful US Corporations, sold 50,000 copies in two days of being launched in Japan, and Ohmae (1982) reports Japanese managers remarking on similarities between their companies and the 'excellent' ones in the USA.

The challenge, then is to adopt 'best practice', regardless of its source. Successful firms from individual countries do not have a monopoly over best practice: they have simply derived a good fit between efficient business techniques and company culture. This means adapting systems and techniques to fit existing company values and norms. Even the Nissan business operation in the UK is not solely based on Japanese-style techniques, being a combination of the best of Japanese and British strengths to create a harmonious and productive working environment. Differences lie in approach rather than practice. IBM, for example, which for many years pursued strategies which have now been labelled 'Japanese', was described by Basset (1986) as following strategies 'exactly the opposite of the Japanese method'. This conclusion was drawn on the basis of IBM's promotion of individualism rather than collectivism, which seemed to be in stark contrast to the Japanese ethic. However, the underlying intent of their strategic programme was improved efficiency and quality, and while they employed different means to the same ends, it is possible to argue that while processes may differ, ultimate outcomes are the same. Thus, while there may be some validity in the statement 'Japanese and American management is 95 per cent the same and differs in all important respects' (Takeo Fujisawa, co-founder of the Honda Motor Company), it is important not to lose sight of the fact the differences matter far less than the opportunity for learning.

Conclusion

Cultural differences pertinent to managers within the EU cover a wide array of factors blanketing the state of intellectual development of the people and the state of commercial development of the nation. As culture is learned and not innate, there appears to be no reason why managers cannot embrace the challenge of learning about foreign cultures and their implications for doing business in other member states. Although it is easy to reject the study of something as non-specific as cultural difference, failure to address the issue can be costly. If advertising campaigns, business strategies and business meetings do not cater for these differences and thus offend or antagonize individuals or institutions, or if they fail to convey the desired messages or break local laws, then the cost to the firm can be enormous. Lost sales, failure to secure a contract, fines and lost opportunities can all arise as a result of business being conducted without due attention to the local cultural environment. These central points – established throughout the chapter – are brought home in our final case study on EuroDisney (Case Study 10.3).

Equally, while cultural differences may be regarded as a barrier to the achievement of a truly harmonized single market, they do not act as a barrier to doing business abroad. By adapting to local cultural conditions firms can operate successfully across the member states of Europe. Indeed, it is possible to argue that the diver-

---

CASE STUDY 10.3 EuroDisney- an American in Paris

Insensitivity to cultural differences was one of the many problems that afflicted the launch of Disney's European theme-park operations in France in 1992. From the beginning, Disney's executives had found unexpected difficulties in negotiating with French officials and in understanding an anti-American outcry in many quarters of French society. As reported in the *Daily Telegraph* (13 April 1997), 'The park opened to howls from the guardians of French culture. Why go to look at artificial castles, asked some, when there are hundreds of real ones a few hours from Paris?' Shortly after opening, the park also became a symbol of protest. French farmers angry with US demands in Uruguay Round trade talks expressed their disaffection for mooted subsidy cuts by blockading the park's entrance. If Disney couldn't control things going on outside of its gates, it could have done a much better job on the inside. An initial policy of not selling alcohol in its Paris park had to be hastily abandoned after widespread customer dissatisfaction. Wine and beer were introduced into some of the park's restaurants in 1993. Restaurant provision was also found to be inadequate, with a shortage of tables at preferred eating times. Further, assumptions that French visitors would want continental-style breakfasts and French-style table service were proved to be entirely false. Far from desiring a Frenchification of the Disney concept (something French people were inclined to resent), visitors wanted self-service and American-style snacks. A high level of staff turnover was also seen to reflect a clash of employment and training cultures, with Disney trying to use the same teamwork models used successfully at home.

To its cost, the company also found that the French (and other Europeans) were less inclined to stay for more than one or two days. Disney had invested heavily in theme-park hotels on the assumption that people would desire to stay for longer breaks. Hotel rates had to be considerably reduced with a decision made in 1995 to cut prices by 20%. Similarly, day tickets were initially introduced at around FFr250 (more than £30). Low visit rates in the first years of operation, suggested that Europeans would not pay such prices for a theme-park excursion. Ticket prices have since been cut to FFr195 – about £22. Disney was also led to question its very choice of France for its first European theme-park. In 1994, only 40% of the park's visitors were French and less than 10 million visitors came through the gate. The original name, EuroDisney, was changed to Disneyland Paris to strengthen the park's local–French identity. Following its renaming, price cuts and a much needed refinancing package, operator EuroDisney finally began to record annual profits (before financial changes). The company is now busy reducing its cumulative debts, estimated at £1.6 billion by the end of 1997. Its second Parisian park, provisionally called Disney Studios, is due to open in 2002. EuroDisney had originally expected to have two theme parks with 21 million visitors by 1996. Currently, its one park attracts around 12 million visitors a year. US Entertainment giant Walt Disney owns 39% of EuroDisney.

gence of cultures across Europe actually offers EU firms an advantage over their international competitors as it permits scope to identify national strengths and weaknesses and develop strategies which tap into these critical resources. Equally, exposure to different cultures provides opportunities for learning new ways of doing business and improving company performance. The rich cultural mix of Europe needs to be regarded as an asset and not a barrier to improving Europe's position in the world economy.

Obviously, operating across cultures requires firms to adjust their strategic thinking. While, in the past, firms believed that mass decentralization of decision-making to subsidiaries in the various member states of Europe allowed more effective management at the local level, it is important to develop structures which, while sympathetic to market differences, concern themselves more with similarities and commonalties. One of the biggest hurdles ahead for most firms will be changed thinking: a new view of what Europe has to offer and how this can be tapped for competitive success. Firms must show a willingness to learn and develop within a Europe-wide context; greater flexibility in management structures and business practices; and should look to new recruitment and training practices which provide scope for the development of European managers. Overriding these issues are changes which are taking place on a global scale which are re-shaping business practices within the context of international competitive advantage. It is, therefore, not possible to assume that cultural change in the future, either for the individual or the firm, will merely be a product of changes taking place within the confines of the Single Market. To this extent, it is important for firms to keep one eye on developments in the rest of the world when they are planning for future success within their own backyard.

Review questions for Chapter 10

1. What is culture?

2. Clarify some of the most important ways in which cultures differ.

3. What are the limitations of concentrating only on cultural differences?

4. What is the usefulness of identifying cultural clusters across different member states?

5. Describe the difference between high-context and low-context cultures.

6. What would you suggest are the main challenges likely to be encountered by UK and German managers when dealing with each other? Refer back to Case Study 10.1.

7. With reference to the bipolar dimensions advanced by Hofstede, compare and contrast the cultures of two other European countries and their effects on business practice.

8. What common perceptions do you hold about other nationalities in the EU?

9. Why might it be dangerous for you to assume that your perceptions of other cultures are adequate to conduct business in foreign markets?

10. Why would it be wrong to suggest that corporate culture is simply a reflection of national cultural identity?

11. In what way might European firms be able to turn cultural diversity into competitive advantage?

12. What are some of the qualities desirable in an international manager?

13. Evaluate your own skills qualities. If you are weak on any of the dimensions necessary for being an international manager, how would you attempt to overcome these difficulties?

14. What do we mean by intercultural effectivenesss? Why is it important to European international businesspeople?

15. How much can be learnt from Japanese culture and management practices?

Web guide

The Web of Culture (a useful starting point for those seeking a better understanding of different national cultures) @ http://www.webofculture.com

Cultural Tips for Doing Business Abroad (a guide published by Getting Through Customs) @ http://www.getcustoms.com/omnibus/dba.html

Trompenaars Hampden-Turner Intercultural Management Consulting (some limited free material) @ http://www.7d-culture.com/

See also

CIA World Factbook @ http://www.odci.gov/cia/publications/factbook/au.html

The Library of Congress Country Studies @ http://lcweb2.loc.gov/frd/cs/cshome.html

References

Albert, M. (1991) *Capitalism Against Capitalism*, Whurr Publishers.

Basset, P. (1986) *Strike Free: New Industrial Relations in Britain*, Macmillan.

Crawshaw, R. and Spieser, P. (1997) The cultural and economic context, in Crawshaw, R. (ed.), *The European Business Environment: France*, Thomson Business Press.

Daniels, J.D. and Radebaugh, L.H. (1995) *International Business: Environments and Operations*, 7th edition, Addison-Wesley.

Fry, E. (1991) Subtlety and the art of Japanese management, *Business Credit*, October.

Hall, E.T. (1973) *The Silent Language*, Doubleday.

Hall, E.T. (1976) *Beyond Culture*, Doubleday.

Hall, E.T. and Reed Hall, M. (1995) *Understanding Cultural Differences*, Intercultural Press.

Hannagan, T. (1995) *Management Concepts and Practices*, Pitman Publishing.

Hill, C.W. (2000) *International Business: Competing in the Global Marketplace*, 3rd edition, McGraw-Hill.

Hoeklin, L. (1995) *Managing Cultural Differences: Strategies for Competitive Advantage*, Addison-Wesley.

Hofstede, G. (1980) *Culture's Consequences: International Differences in Work-Related Values*, Sage.

Hofstede, G. (1983) National cultures in four dimensions: a research theory of cultural differences among nations, *International Studies of Management and Organization*, **13**.

Hofstede, G. (1986) Cultural difference in teaching and learning, *International Journal of Intercultural Relations*, **10**, 301–20.

Hofstede, G. (1991) *Cultures and Organizations: Software of the Mind*, McGraw-Hill.

Hofstede, G. (1995) Managerial values: the business of international business in culture, Jackson, T. (ed.), *Cross-Cultural Management*, Butterworth-Heinemann.

Kroebe, R. and Kluckhohn, F. (1952) *Culture*, Vintage Books.

Lachman, R., Nedd, A. and Hinings, N. (1995) Analysing cross-national management and organisations: a theoretical framework, in Jackson, T. (ed.) *Cross-Cultural Management*, Butterworth-Heinemann.

Lane, W. , DiStefano, J. and Maznevski, M. L. (1997) *International Management Behaviour*, 3rd edition, Blackwell.

Lee, J.A. (1966) Cultural analysis in overseas operations, *Harvard Business Review*, March–April, 106–14.

Mirza, H. (1984) Can-should Japanese management practices be exported overseas?, *The Business Graduate*, January.

Mole, J. (1992) *Mind Your Manners: Culture Clash in the European Single Market*, The Industrial Society.

Murdock, G.P. (1945) The common denominator of cultures, in Linton, R. (ed.), *The Science of Man in the World Crisis*, Columbia University Press.

Ohmae, K. (1982) *Mind of the Strategist: Art of Japanese Business*, McGraw-Hill.

Oliver, A. and Wilkinson, S. (1992) *The Japanisation of British Industry: New Developments in the 1990s*, 2nd edition, Blackwell.

Peters, T. and Waterman, R. (1982) *In Search of Excellence*, Harper and Row.

Porter, M.E. (1990) *Competitive Advantage of Nations*, Macmillan.

Porter, M.E. (1992) A note on culture and competitive advantage: response to van den Bosch and van Prooijen, *European Management Journal*, **10**(2), 178.

Ricks, D.A. (1997) *Blunders in International Business*, Barnes and Noble.

Robock, S.H. and Simmonds, K. (1989) *International Business and Multinational Enterprises*, Irwin.

Rogers, E.M. (1962) *The Diffusion of Innovations*, Free Press.

Rohrlich, P.E. (1987) Economic culture and foreign policy: the cognitive analysis of economic policy-making, *International Organization*, **41**(1).

Ronen, S. and Shenkar, O. (1985) Clustering countries on attitudinal dimensions: a review and synthesis, *Academy of Management Journal*, September.

Thurrow, L. (1992) *Head To Head: The Coming Economic Battles Among Japan, Europe and America*, William Morrow.

Tijmstra, S. and Casler, K. (1992) Management learning for Europe, *European Management Journal*, **10**(1), 30–8.

Trompenaars, F. (1993) *Riding the Waves of Culture: Understanding Cultural Diversity in Business*, The Economist Books.

Trompenaars, F. and Hampden-Turner, C. (1997) *Riding the Waves of Culture: Understanding Cultural Diversity in Business*, 2nd edition, Nicholas Brealey.

van Dijck, J. (1995) Transnational management in an evolving European context, in Jackson, T. (ed.), *Cross-Cultural Management*, Butterworth-Heinemann.

VanderMerwe, S. (1993) A framework for constructing European networks, *European Management Journal*, **11**(1).

Wills, S. and Barham, K. (1994) Being an international manager, *European Management Journal*, **12**(1), 49–58.

The greening of European business: environmental policies and management

Introduction

Since the 1960s, there has been a growing interest in the environment, or more specifically in the damage being done to the environment, in Europe and North America. The process of European integration has brought the transnational nature of the environmental problem to the forefront. The hole in the ozone layer and global warming are the results of not one country's action but those of many. Acid rain, which is polluting rivers and lakes and damaging forests, often emanates from one country and is deposited in another. European integration therefore offers an opportunity for transnational co-operation and this has been reflected in a multitude of European Union environmental regulations. Much more legislation is planned for the decades ahead and a large amount of this will affect the way in which every business is run. Perhaps more importantly, many of the more recent initiatives on the environment emanating from the European Union, have been market driven and are voluntary. These are dealt with in detail towards the end of this chapter, but collectively their impact is to demand that businesses take on more responsibility for environmental damage and approach environmental management in a more proactive way.

Everything which consumers, companies and other institutions do will have some impact on the environment. Even substances which, in their final form, are environmentally benign may have been unfriendly in their manufacture especially if that manufacture was energy greedy. They may have been produced using non-renewable resources and may also pose problems after they have been used and come to be disposed of. If we take what is commonly called a 'cradle-to-the-grave' view of products, where we examine their environmental impact through their life-cycle from raw material usage to disposal, then there are few, if any, products which will not have some negative impact on the environment. The key question is therefore not how we completely eliminate environmental damage but how we reduce it over time and how we achieve a state of balance such that the amount of environmental damage done is reparable and therefore sustainable. It is generally accepted that the world cannot go on using the resources of the planet at the present rate. But there is a free rider problem at work. Everyone thinks that there should be something done, but many people just assume that everyone else will do it and, since their individual impact is minute, it will not matter to the environment. The trouble is that when too many people or firms think in that way then nothing is ever achieved. The world has scarce resources and only limited capacity to deal with the pollution caused through production and consumption. The ability to deal with that pollution is also being reduced as we strive for further economic growth. One way in which this is happening is that forests, which help to control the amount of carbon dioxide in the atmosphere, are being cleared.

One thing is clear: industry, particularly in the developed world, must take into clearer account the costs of its operations for the natural environment. In the past, few companies have counted the costs of the pollution which they discharged into the atmosphere, and many have been ignorant or abusive of environmental legislation. This has contributed to serious ecological problems – high levels of factory emissions, a depleting ozone layer, poor air and water quality, and accelerating volumes of waste. However, as individuals have collectively exercised their environmental conscience (as customers, employees, investors and voters), so corporate actors have come under new and greater pressures. Governments across Europe (and the Brussels Commission) have all been pushed to implement more stringent environmental legislation and to establish laws aimed at forcing companies to comply with certain standards and to tax firms which pollute. Voluntary efforts by industry and corporations have also been expected given that there are good economic reasons to do so. Analysis of corporate responses to environmental challenges suggests that major opportunities for competitive advantage can come from process and product improvements and from a marked trend towards 'green consumerism'.

Industry can respond in many ways. Less energy consumption and more efficient use of resources are obvious targets for improvement and should not conflict with industry's aims since their attainment can actually reduce costs. Firms can also take steps to ensure that their products are less harmful to the environment and to green their production and distribution strategies (creating a basis for competitive advantage). Businesses can also audit their environmental performance, systematically assessing all of their environmental impacts. Perhaps above all, they can adopt a precautionary approach to managing their ecological impacts and contribute to the reshaping of customer behaviour.

Such steps are examined at the heart of this chapter. Throughout, analysis is directed to the many ways in which business organizations are integrating environmental considerations into their strategies and are responding to the green agenda. While the condition of the continent's environment (and its environmental legislation) are necessarily addressed, it is unit-level issues and the various elements of a corporate environmental management strategy which are given central treatment here. Thus, the chapter should contribute well to the ongoing address of strategic issues for European managers in Part II of this book.

The natural environment: the European situation

As a major part of the industrialized world, economic activity in Europe is responsible for much of the environmental damage facing the planet. Human activities have resulted in the introduction of numerous chemical contaminants into the global environment, many of which are manmade and have no natural sources. Contamination of the environment has reached global proportions with trace metal and organic pollutants being detected in even the remotest parts of the northern hemisphere. Issues such as climate change and ozone layer depletion emphasize the global scope of the impact of environmental degradation. There is insufficient room for a full review of environmental pollution in this section but an analysis of selected statistics concerning atmospheric pollution and waste is able to paint a broad picture from a (west) European perspective. A reminder is given of the efforts made in Chapter 7 (on CEE transition) to characterize the many environmental problems afflicting former Communist economies in Europe. In many respects the CEECs share similar environmental problems to EU states but 'dirtier' energy sources and established production techniques contribute to higher volumes of plant and factory emissions. The reader may like to return to this section in order to gain a wider overview of the state of Europe's natural environment.

Atmospheric pollution: the greenhouse effect

The naturally occurring abundance of greenhouse gases such as water vapour, carbon dioxide, methane, chlorofluorocarbons and nitrous oxide exerts a warming effect on the Earth by absorbing radiation emitted by the Earth's surface. Continuing increases in concentrations of greenhouse gases due to human activities are therefore warming the atmosphere and leading to global climate change. Carbon dioxide or CO_2 emissions are a primary contributor to the enhanced greenhouse effect. Atmospheric concentrations of carbon dioxide are increasing globally but concentrations are higher in the northern hemisphere (including Europe) owing to a greater density of industry and energy generation and to high-level transport emissions.

In the EU, carbon dioxide emissions fell about 1% between 1990 and 1996 albeit with some considerable variation between the member states. This fall has been due to a combination of low economic growth and increases in energy efficiency. Initially, the EU aims to stabilize CO_2 emissions (by 2000) at 1990 levels. It then aims to reduce emissions of CO_2 (and five other greenhouse gases) so as to meet its obligations under the 'Kyoto Protocol' of April 1998. This agreement was concluded under the auspices of the United Nations Forum on Climatic Change and followed on from the Kyoto Summit on climatic change staged in December 1997. The Protocol commits the EU to achieving an 8% reduction in greenhouse gas emissions at agreed points between 2008 and 2012. Again, a baseline for reductions is provided by recorded levels for 1990. However, in its recent report, '*Environment in the European Union at the turn of the century*', the European Environment Agency (EEA), signals that EU-15 total greenhouse gas emissions are projected to increase *(not fall)* by some 6% over this reference period. In early 2000, the European Commission was suggesting an increase of some 8%. The main culprit is identified as the massive increase in transport-related emissions which, the EEA concludes, are unlikely to be reversed. Transport-related emissions are already responsible for over one-quarter of all CO_2 emissions compared with just 19% in 1985. They are projected to account for one-third of all emissions by 2010 (European Environment Agency, 1999). The EEA notes that, since 1980, the number of air passengers has doubled, the number of kilometres travelled per person per year in passenger cars has jumped by 60% and that freight traffic has increased by three-quarters. The number of kilometres driven by motorists in the EU alone led to a 12% increase in emissions of CO_2 from road transport between 1990 and 1995. Thus, while the combustion of

Table 11.1 Carbon dioxide emissions from fossil fuel combustion, 1995

Country	Total emissions (million tonnes)	Per capita emissions (tonnes per head)
EUR-15	3,047.6	8.1
Austria	56.7	7.1
Belgium	111.3	11.0
Denmark	59.9	11.5
Finland	56.4	11.1
France	347.5	6.0
Germany	848.9	10.4
Greece	78.2	7.5
Ireland	31.9	8.9
Italy	405.1	7.1
Luxembourg	8.7	21.4
Netherlands	170.9	11.1
Spain	238.1	6.1
Portugal	47.9	4.1
Sweden	53.6	6.1
United Kingdom	532.3	9.1

Source: Eurostat, 1997

fossil fuels for energy production is still the single biggest source of greenhouse gas emissions (see Table 11.1), the main driving force for increasing CO_2 emissions now comes from the transport sector.

The hole in the ozone layer

The ozone layer in the stratosphere provides protection from harmful solar ultraviolet (UV) radiation. Manmade ozone depletion is caused by the mass use and emission of chlorofluorocarbons (CFCs) and other ozone-depleting substances (ODSs). This has led to an increase in harmful ultraviolet radiation and the incidence of radiation-induced skin cancer. Ozone depletion is estimated to be greatest over the western parts of Europe where chlorofluorocarbons have been commonly used in refrigerators and aerosol propellants. In these same countries, other ODSs have also been used extensively, for example as coolant, foam and cleaning agents.

Production and consumption of ODSs are falling sharply, in part because of a ban on the EU-based production of chlorofluorocarbons. However, despite a significant fall in the consumption and atmospheric concentration of CFCs (see Figure 11.1), the consumption and atmospheric concentration of other ODSs, including hydrochlorofluorocarbons (HCFCs), is on the increase. For example, with the ban on CFCs, HCFCs are being more widely used in refrigerators, foams and solvents. The EU remains several years away from a complete ban on the production and consumption of HCFCs and of other ozone-depleting substances.

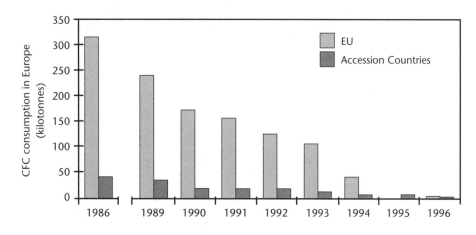

Figure 11.1 CFC consumption in Europe, 1986–96
Source: European Environment Agency (1999)

Urban air pollutants

The main effects of air pollution are felt in acidification (acid rain), in the eutrophication of soils and waters, in ozone depletion and in poorer urban air quality (contributing to urban smogs and various health problems). The main causes are the usage of fossil fuels for power generation and transport, which leads to man-made emissions of sulphur dioxide (SO_2) and nitrogen oxides (NO_x). Agricultural practice contributes to harmful emissions of ammonia (NH_3), while volatile organic compound emissions (VOC emissions) follow from solvent and chemical use in industry and households. The use of heavy metals (such as lead) and of persistent organic pollutants (POPs) also contributes to the bioaccumulation of toxic substances (European Environment Agency, 1999).

Table 11.2 shows national emission rates for sulphur dioxide (SO_2) and nitrogen oxide (NO_x) expressed on a per capita basis. The table shows that there are significant differences in emissions within Europe, relating to differing means of energy generation and to variations in transport usage–policies. It is interesting to see that Sweden produces very little sulphur dioxide despite suffering heavily from the acidification of its waters and forests. This highlights the transboundary nature of air pollution, which can be generated in one country and felt in several others (see also Chapter 7). The table also highlights the extremely high levels of SO_2 and NO_x emissions in the US compared with those of the EU states. In fact, while US emission levels have remained stubbornly high, SO_2 emissions in the EU have been falling steadily. The EEA estimates a 40% fall in EU-15 SO_2 emissions between 1980 and 1996, with aggregate European levels falling by nearly 50% (see Figure 11.2). EU reduction efforts have been governed by the principles and targets of the UN–ECE Convention on Long-Range Transboundary Air Pollution (CLRTAP) and by the EU's Fifth Environmental Action Programme, EAP5 (see later). Through EAP5, the EU has set a number of air emissions reduction targets which are designed to realize and, in certain cases, to surpass the targets set under the CLRTAP.

Table 11.2. Per capita SO_2 and NO_x emissions (latest available year)

Country	Sulphur dioxide (kg/cap)	Nitrogen oxides (kg/cap)
Austria	7.1	21.2
Belgium	23.7	32.9
Denmark	20.7	47.0
Finland	19.5	50.6
France	16.2	29.1
Germany (West only)	17.9	22.0
Greece	48.2	35.1
Ireland	45.1	33.9
Italy	23.1	30.9
Luxembourg	14.3	47.5
Netherlands	8.0	28.5
Portugal	36.2	37.6
Spain	49.1	31.7
Sweden	10.3	38.1
United Kingdom	34.5	35.0
USA	69.0	79.9
Japan	7.3	11.3

Source: OECD Environmental Data Compendium, 1999 edition © OECD, 1999

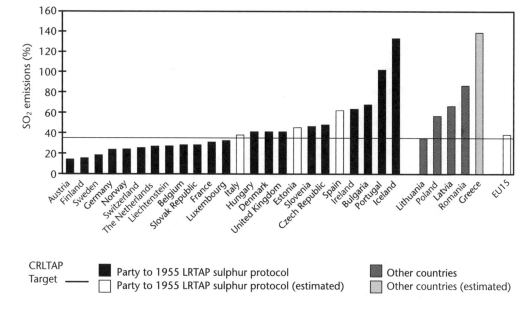

Figure 11.2 Percentage reduction in sulphur dioxide (SO$_2$) emissions 1980–96 (EU and other European states)
Source: European Environment Agency (1999)

On current projections, EU emissions reductions between 1990 and 2010 should approximate 70% for sulphur dioxide and 45% for nitrogen oxides (see Table 11.3). While this suggests good progress, it remains the case that European ecosystems are badly affected by these organic pollutants and that the continent's cities are blighted by smog every summer. According to the EEA (1999):

> Projections for 2010 suggest that, despite the projected emission reductions, areas of the EU and (especially) the Accession Countries will continue to be affected by acid and nitrogen deposition above the level defined as 'critical load'. Ecosystems in the EU still receive 7% acid deposition and 39% nitrogen deposition above their critical loads.

Table 11.3. Projected emission reductions in Europe (ktonnes)

Pollutant	EU15			Accession countries		
	1990	2010	Reduction	1990	2010	Reduction
SO$_2$	16,300	4,800	71%	10,300	4,300	59%
NO$_x$	13,200	7,300	45%	3,500	2,600	27%
NH$_3$	3,600	2,900	19%	1,400	1,390	1%
VOC	14,000	7,200	49%	2,600	2,300	10%

Source: European Commission, 1999

Wastes

Population growth, increasing urbanization, industrialization and rising standards of living have all contributed to an increase in the amount of waste generated in the EU countries. In 1995, the total amount of waste generated in the EU-15 (excluding agricultural waste) was estimated to be 1.3 billion tonnes (or 3.5 tonnes per capita). These figures show a 10% increase in total waste production between 1990 and 1995. Very shortly, annual waste levels will be approximating 2 billion tonnes, with gains from recycling measures outweighed by an increase in economic activity and total waste production (European Environment Agency, 1999). Countries are faced not only with massive volumes of waste but also with the challenges related to hazardous waste materials. Each year, the Community generates around 40 million tonnes of hazardous waste. Wastes, which arise from virtually all human activities, can be broadly classified with respect to their source. The major categories include 'municipal wastes', 'industrial', 'agricultural', 'sewage' and 'nuclear' wastes. Municipal wastes, levels for which are shown in Table 11.4, include household and public wastes. Industrial wastes encompass a very wide range of materials, a proportion of which are hazardous. As such, these wastes often require special treatment and disposal. The main industrial sectors producing hazardous waste are the chemical sector, engineering sector, and mineral and metal processing industries. High volumes of nuclear waste (50,000 m^3 annually) are generated within the EU energy sector.

An efficient way to cut down the volume of waste is to reduce the use of pack-

Table 11.4 Municipal waste generation (latest available year)

Country	Municipal waste (kg/per capita)
Austria	510
Belgium	480
Denmark	560
Finland	410
France	590
Germany (West only)	460
Greece	370
Ireland	530
Italy	460
Luxembourg	460
Netherlands	560
Portugal	380
Spain	390
Sweden	360
United Kingdom	480
USA	720
Japan	400

Source: OECD Environmental Data Compendium, 1999 edition © OECD, 1999

aging and to recycle paper, cardboard, plastic, aluminium tins, and glass. Levels of recycling in the member states range from 28% to 53% for paper and cardboard (EU average: 49.6%) and between 20% and 76% for glass (European Parliament, 1999). These figures highlight extreme variations in performance between the member states. Overall, about one-third of all types of packaging for soft drinks, mineral water, beer and wine, is being re-used. Again the re-use rates of different member states vary significantly. Denmark re-uses almost 100% of beer packaging but the equivalent rates for Italy and the United Kingdom are below 20%.

Counting the costs of the environment

The use of the market mechanism to distribute goods and services in the West, with its consequent stress on property rights, has contributed to the environmental degradation which we have experienced. Much of the environment (particularly the air and atmosphere) is treated as a free good since no individual owns it and there are no assigned property rights to it. Firms and consumers have therefore made excessive uses of environmental resources both as an input and as a source of output (or sink). This can be illustrated in Figure 11.3.

Suppose that a firm produces a good and in the process of doing so it pollutes the air around it. Traditionally, and ignoring legislation which might or might not exist, the firm can do this freely since no one owns the air. Assume that the demand for the product is D_1 and the production and marketing costs of the firm imply that it is willing to sell along a supply curve given by S_1. Essentially, S_1 is drawn based on only the private costs of the firm, that is those which it must pay in a monetary form. But the pollution imposed on the local community imposes a cost on them and on society as a whole. If the firm was required to internalize those costs, either by paying a tax to pollute based on an estimate of the social cost that that pollution imposed (the tax might subsequently be used to clean up the pollution) or by the

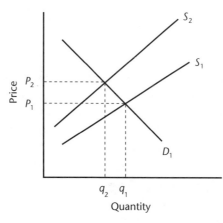

Figure 11.3 Using the market mechanism to deal with environmental damage

use of legislation banning the pollution (meaning that the firm would have to invest in a new non-polluting process), then its own costs would rise. The firm's willingness to supply at any particular price would be reduced and S_1 would shift backwards to S_2. The equilibrium in the market would shift from p_1q_1 to p_2q_2. Thus less of the good would be produced at a higher price.

The premise on which EU and member states' environmental legislation has largely been based is the 'polluter pays principle'. In other words this is a notion that public money should not be used in clearing up or avoiding pollution but, as described above, that polluters themselves should face those costs. From a welfare point of view the difference between a firm compensating a local community for the pollution it creates and the community paying the firm not to pollute is purely distributional. But from an ethical perspective it is often argued that the polluter pays principle is superior.

We might extend the sort of analysis described by Figure 11.3 to the economy as a whole. Since most processes will impose at least some negative impact on the environment, the fact that the environment has not been properly costed and treated as a free good over time has meant that we have produced too many goods. Moreover, we might hypothesize that mass production techniques, which have enabled firms to produce more and more goods and to charge lower prices, have been particularly damaging. Indeed this is largely confirmed by evidence. The implication which then arises is that Western economies have developed using a particular model and in a way that has caused significant and often irreparable damage to the environment. It is further argued that that sort of development is not sustainable into the future and it is the concept of sustainable development to which we now turn.

Sustainable development

The belief which lies behind the concept of sustainable development is that there is a trade-off between continuous economic growth and the sustainability of the environment. Over time, growth causes pollution and atmospheric damage. The concept of sustainable development stresses the interdependence between economic growth and environmental quality. It is possible to make development and environmental protection compatible by following sustainable strategies and by not developing the particular areas of economic activity that are most damaging to the environment. The concept was popularized by the 1987 Brundtland Commission Report and has been echoed in subsequent declarations, for example those following the UN Earth Summits in Rio (1992) and Kyoto (1997).

The Brundtland Report

The Brundtland Report was commissioned by the United Nations to examine long-term environmental strategies. The Report argued that economic development and environmental protection could be made compatible, defining sustainable development as 'development that meets the needs of the present without compromising the ability of future generations to meet their own needs'. Its central argument was that the environment should be valued as an integral part of the economic process and not treated as a free good. It argued that the environmental stock has to be protected and that this implies minimal use of non-renewable resources and minimal emission of pollutants. The Report suggests that lifestyles be adopted that are within the planet's ecological means and that intensified efforts be directed towards energy conservation, resource regeneration and environmental preservation. In its detail, the Report argues that society, businesses and individuals must operate on a modified time scale. It notes that while companies commonly operate under competitive pressures to achieve short-terms gains, long-term environmental protection is often compromised. To ensure that longer-term, intergenerational considerations are observed, longer planning horizons need to be adopted. The Report also deals with Third World development issues (arguing broadly for campaigns against poverty and Third World debt). It warns that while developing countries want to grow rapidly to achieve the same standards of living as those in the West, such development (if modelled on past experiences) would cause a major environmental disaster. For example, bringing developing countries' energy use up to the level of the developing world's would mean an increase in consumption by a factor of five. Using present energy generation methods, the planet could not cope with the impact of sulphur dioxide and carbon dioxide emissions and the acidification and global warming of the environment which would be consequential. Critics of the ecologically sustainable development (ESD) concept have seized on the lack of answers to this essential puzzle and to the vague prescriptions on partnership development.

The stark warning of the Brundtland Report is that established approaches to economic development are unsustainable and will lead to exhaustion of the world's finite stock of natural resources. The industrialized world has already used much of the planet's ecological capital and non-renewable resources are being depleted. Moreover, renewable resources such as soil, water and the atmosphere are being degraded by a form of economic development that, in time, will undermine the very foundations of that development. In short, mass consumption is not possible indefinitely and efforts must be directed to achieving growth which is environmentally and socially sustainable. The challenge, therefore, is how to work towards ecologically sustainable development and how to ensure that governments, corporations and individuals deal with, and overcome, the many obstacles preventing sustainability.

The corporate response to sustainable development

While governments are adopting many instruments to promote ecology-sensitive development (e.g. polluter taxes), if the goals of sustainability are to be achieved, then industry itself must be encouraged to embrace the sustainability principle. Firms have an important role to play in the development of substitutes for non-renewable resources and of innovations which reduce waste and use energy more efficiently. Companies must seek to address these demands and to meet the challenge of producing higher levels of output while using lower levels of inputs. In doing so, they should recognize not only that it is ethical to be environmentally friendly but that there are good economic reasons to do so. For example, those companies that achieve high standards of environmental performance may benefit from related cost savings and establish marketplace advantages over their rivals (more of this later). While organizations will define their own environmental policies, the general principles of such policies may be embodied within the International Chamber of Commerce Business Charter for Sustainable Development:

1. Corporate priority – to recognize environmental management as among the highest corporate priorities and as a key determinant to sustainable development; to establish policies, programmes and practices for conducting operations in an environmentally sound manner.

2. Integrated management – to integrate these policies, programmes and practices fully into each business as an essential element of management in all its functions.

3. Process of improvement – to continue to improve corporate policies, programmes and environmental performance, taking into account technical developments, scientific understanding, consumer needs and community expectations, with legal regulations as a starting point, and to apply the same environmental criteria internationally.

4. Employee education – to educate, train and motivate employees to conduct their activities in an environmentally responsible manner.

5. Prior assessment – to assess environmental impacts before starting a new activity or project and before decommissioning a facility or leaving a site.

6. Products and services – to develop and provide products and services that have no undue environmental impact and are safe in their intended use, that are efficient in their consumption of energy and natural resources and that can be recycled, re-used, or disposed of safely.

7. Customer advice – to advise, and where relevant educate, customers, distributors and the public in the safe use, transportation, storage and disposal of products provided, and to apply similar considerations to the provision of services.

8. Facilities and operations – to develop, design and operate facilities and conduct activities taking into consideration the efficient use of energy and raw materials, the sustainable use of renewable resources, the minimization of adverse environmental impact and waste generation, and the safe and responsible disposal of residual wastes.

9. Research – to conduct or support research on the environmental impacts of raw materials, products, processes, emissions and wastes associated with the enterprise and on the means of minimizing such adverse impacts.

10. Precautionary approach – to modify the manufacture, marketing or use of products or services, to the conduct of activities, consistent with scientific and technical understanding, to prevent serious or irreversible environmental degradation.

11. Contractors and suppliers – to promote the adoption of these principles by contractors acting on behalf of the enterprise, encouraging and, where appropriate, requiring improvements in their practices to make them consistent with those of the enterprise, and to encourage the wider adoption of these principles by suppliers.

12. Emergency preparedness – to develop and maintain, where appropriate hazards exist, emergency preparedness plans in conjunction with the emergency services, relevant authorities and the local community, recognizing potential cross-boundary impacts.

13. Transfer of technology – to contribute to the transfer of environmentally sound technology and management methods throughout the industrial and public sectors.

14. Contributing to the common effort – to contribute to the development of public policy and to business, governmental and intergovernmental programmes and educational initiatives that will enhance environmental awareness and protection.

15. Openness to concerns – to foster openness and dialogue with employees and the public, anticipating and responding to their concerns about the potential hazards and impacts of operations, products, wastes or services, including those of transboundary or global significance.

16. Compliance and reporting – to measure environmental performance; to conduct regular environmental audits and assessments of compliance with company requirements and these principles, and periodically to provide appropriate information to the Board of Directors, shareholders, employees, the authorities and the public.

It is clear of course, that many organizations and their managers will make little attempt to act on these principles. The prioritization of short-term needs, entrenched attitudes and disregard for environmental concerns will often combine to leave businesses at the bottom of the environmental learning curve. Equally, there is always an incentive for profit-maximizing firms seeking short-term rewards to opt out and to become a free rider (assuming that everyone else will be environmentally conscious). However, regulatory controls are increasingly plugging the gaps which allow this to happen and firms attempting to hide their illegal pollution are now subject to severe penalties. At the same time, many businesses are recognizing that it is not only responsible to be environmentally friendly but also a source of gain. Integrating environmental considerations into management, design and production can contribute to cost reductions (e.g. through the recycling and reuse of materials) and to competitive advantage in the marketplace. Shrivastava (1995) highlights the cases of Toshiba and Hitachi, both of whom have gained competitive advantage in the worldwide battery industry through the design of acid-free and renewable batteries. In similar vein, Howard (1999) notes the success of German firm Siemens in developing and marketing electronic products based on salvaged components. Managers at DuPont (the US chemicals company) also found that costs were reduced when production processes were redesigned to be more environmentally sound. These cases highlight that major opportunities can come from learning new behaviour and from moving up 'the environmental learning curve'.

Corporate environmental management

As we have stressed, companies are beginning to realize that environmental issues need to be addressed for a number of reasons, including consumer pressure, quality considerations and a surge in environmental legislation. Some organizations are developing solutions to particular threats or regulatory changes but others (such as Sony, 3M, BT and Unilever) are evaluating all of their environmental impacts and are introducing sophisticated environmental management strategies (see Welford, 1994). In doing so, they are establishing themselves as proactive rather than reactive firms and are taking an approach to the environment which may be characterized as 'strategic' (see Howard, 1999). But how can firms increase their efforts and integrate environmental considerations more fully into their business strategies? Over the following pages we address this question, exploring the various elements of corporate environmental management. For extended study, the reader may turn to a number of titles, including the work of Roome (1992), Wheeler (1992), Shrivastava (1995), Hutchinson (1996), Bansal and Howard (1997), Welford and Gouldson (1993) and Welford (1994, 1995, 1996a, 1996b).

In thinking about environmental management there are a number of questions which companies should initially ask themselves:

1. Is the company meeting its existing environmental commitments?
2. Is the company adhering to environmental legislation and what will be the impact on the firm as environmental legislation becomes more stringent?
3. Is concern for the environment integral to each company operation?
4. Do managers and workers see environmental improvement as a goal and in what ways are personnel being encouraged to be more involved?
5. Does the company have the capacity to evaluate the environmental impact of its processes and products including packaging and distribution channels?
6. Are there new product opportunities which the company could exploit which would have less of an environmentally negative impact?
7. How vulnerable is the company to environmental changes such as climate change?

8. What financial and organizational constraints are there which might prevent environmental improvement taking place?

9. How are the company's competitors placed in terms of environmental accountability and can the environmental performance of the firm be turned to a competitive advantage?

10. Does the company have a systematic approach to management which can be used to integrate environmental issues across the organization?

The answers to these questions provide the firm with the basis of a strategic plan for the environment. An environmental policy can be developed from these questions and it can be circulated to company personnel, suppliers and vendors, and the public. This policy sets out the context for future action. There is no single model and the policy will reflect a company's structure, location, industrial sector and business culture. If such a document is published then it is important that the plan is adhered to, thereby providing an all-important environmental ethos around which the company must operate.

All aspects of a company's operations, from accounting and purchasing to product design, manufacture, sales, marketing, distribution and the use and disposal of the product, will have an impact on the environment and the environmental policy should recognize this. The policy needs to be comprehensive and detailed but it should not contain statements or targets which the firm cannot hope to achieve. This will do more harm than good if exposed. The content of any policy will vary from firm to firm and be influenced by the activities of that organization. However, there are some general principles which can be applied to the content of the policy statement:

1. Adopt and aim to apply the principles of sustainable development which meet the needs of the present, without compromising the abilities of future generations to meet their own needs.

2. Strive to adopt the highest available environmental standards in all site locations and all countries and meet or exceed all applicable regulations.

3. Adopt a total 'cradle-to-grave' environmental assessment and accept responsibility for all products and services, the raw materials you use and the disposal of the product after use.

4. Aim to minimize the use of all materials, supplies and energy and, wherever possible, use renewable or recyclable materials and components.

5. Minimize waste produced in all parts of the business, aim for waste-free processes and where waste is produced avoid the use of terminal waste treatment dealing with it, as far as possible, at source.

6. Render any unavoidable wastes harmless and dispose of them in a way which has least impact on the environment.

7. Expect high environmental standards from all parties involved in the business including suppliers, contractors and vendors and put pressure on these groups to improve their environmental performance in line with your own.

8. Be committed to improving relations with the local community and the public at large and where necessary introduce education and liaison programmes.

9. Adopt an environmentally sound transport strategy and assess the general infrastructure of the company.

10. Assess, on a continuous basis, the environmental impact of all operations and procedures via an environmental audit.

11. Assist in developing solutions to environmental problems and support the development of external environmental initiatives.

12. Preserve nature, protect ecological habitats and create conservation schemes.

13. Accept strict liability for environmental damage, not blaming others for environmental damage, accidents and incidents.

Environmental policies should identify key performance areas and form a sound basis for setting corporate objectives. They need to be detailed enough to demonstrate that the commitment of the company goes beyond lip-service. A clearly defined environmental policy should be implementable, practical and relate to the areas in which the company wishes to improve its environmental performance. In particular, when designing an environmental policy, the organization needs to think hard about how it is going to quantify its objectives and measure its environmental performance.

For a policy to be implemented, personnel with special responsibilities for environmental performance will have to be found. Many companies in Europe have found that the best way to achieve this, in the short run, is to appoint a main board environment director. This person will be there to champion the environment and will need some very important personal skills as well as legitimacy. Such legitimacy is often achieved by the publication of the firm's environmental policy. There are three very clear roles which an environmental director can take on:

1. Taking a strategic view: promoting minimal environmental impact from products and processes and developing an integrated and comprehensive approach.

2. Raising the profile of the environment: co-ordinating educational effort within the company, developing partnerships with customers, other companies (particularly suppliers), environmental pressure groups, legislators, the EU and national government.

3. Putting policy into practice: the establishment of company monitoring systems and environmental audits, the establishment of environmental improvement plans, involving all personnel and making them accountable and responsible for the environmental performance of their business, and taking anticipatory action which is central to good environmental performance.

The initial stage in the implementation of an environmental approach at a firm level must be for a firm to establish exactly how well or how badly it is performing environmentally. An increasingly common way of achieving this is to have the firm environmentally audited.

Eco-auditing

Environmental audits ('green' or 'eco' audits) are tools that companies use to identify their full range of environmental impacts and to evaluate their operations' compliance with company policies and legal obligations. Audits measure how well organizations, management and equipment are performing with the aim of helping to safeguard the environment or in terms of 'environmental performance'. They serve as a means to identify opportunities to save money, to reduce waste and to achieve other forms of value. Management information is generated which can be used in the control and improvement of practices.

There is no set methodology for carrying out an audit and audits may be adapted in scope and application to suit the needs of any particular business. There are also a variety of strategies for auditing, from self-reporting exercises (based on various check-lists) to independent external audits that measure the full range of a company's environmental impacts. Examinations are often conducted with reference to company goals, industry benchmarks and to international environmental management standards such as ISO 14001. The first environmental audits can be traced back to the USA, where US corporations adopted this methodology during the 1970s in response to their domestic liability laws. Such audits, which are now common among US industry, are growing in importance in Europe. In fact, in industries such as chemicals and pharmaceuticals (which are low on reputation), firms are not only taking a systematic approach to environmental auditing but are prioritizing environmental standards certificates such as EMAS and ISO 14001. Certification can be used to demonstrate 'good' environmental credentials to consumers and governments and as an advantage over rivals in the marketplace.

Breaking this down, we can see that the key objectives of an environmental audit are as follows:

- to determine the extent to which environmental management systems in a company are performing adequately;
- to verify compliance with local, national and European environmental legislation;
- to facilitate certification by external standards agencies;
- to verify compliance with a company's own stated corporate policy;
- to develop and promulgate internal procedures needed to achieve the organization's environmental objectives;
- to minimize human exposure to risks from the environment and ensure adequate health and safety provision;
- to identify and assess risk resulting from environmental failure;
- to assess the impact on the local environment of a particular plant or process by means of air, water and soil sampling;
- to advise a company on environmental improvements it can make.

There are a number of benefits to firms in having an environmental audit undertaken. These include assurances that legislation is being adhered to and the consequent prevention of fines and litigation, an improved public image (which can be built into a public relations campaign) and a reduction in costs (particularly in the area of energy usage and waste minimization). Other gains include an improvement in environmental awareness at all levels of the firm and an improvement in overall quality. On the other hand, there are some potential disbenefits of the audit. These include the initial costs of the audit and the cost of compliance with it. It is also vital that management sees that the recommendations of the environmental auditor are adhered to, otherwise an audit report could be incriminating in a court case or insurance claim.

Environmental audit stages

All environmental audits involve gathering information, analysing that information, making objective judgements based on evidence and a knowledge of the industry and of relevant environmental legislation and standards. There is also the need to report the results of the audit to senior management with recommendations and possible strategies for the implementation of the findings. This all needs considerable preparatory work as well as follow-up time in order that the findings are accurate and comprehensive. Ideally, therefore there need to be three clear stages to an audit (see Figure 11.4).

The first, the pre-audit stage, will aim to minimize the time spent at the site and to maximize the audit team's productivity and will involve:

1. Planning the nature and scope of the audit and providing a framework for setting goals and objectives, developing strategies for their achievement and specifying accountability for accomplishing the work and scheduling the audit process.

2. Selecting members of the audit team and allocating resources to the strategies and policies determined in step 1 above. The audit team will consist of people not only chosen for their expertise in environmental matters but also having knowledge of the industry in which a company operates. An assignment of audit responsibilities should be made according to the competencies and experience of the team.

3. Getting to know the industry and company to be audited. A useful strategy here is to use pre-survey questionnaires submitted to management in order for the audit team to familiarize themselves with the type of installation, the site and the location. It will also focus the minds of management on what will be required of them during the audit.

4. Questionnaires may also be sent to a representative sample of the workforce (to be filled out in confidence), asking about key issues such as communications, planning, health and safety and working conditions.

The second stage is the on-site audit itself. This will include:

5. An inspection of records kept by the company, certificates of compliance, discharge consents, waste licences etc.

6. The examination of inspection and maintenance programmes and the company's own policy on what to do in the event of spills and other accidents. Auditors will have to assess the soundness of the facility's internal controls and assess the risks associated with the failure of those controls. Such controls will include management procedures and the equipment and engineering controls that affect environmental performance.

7. Examining lines of management and responsibility, competence of personnel and systems of authorization. There needs to be a working understanding of the facility's internal management system and of its effectiveness.

8. A confidential interview of selected staff at all levels of operation with a view to collecting information, particularly in the area of the effectiveness of systems and waste management.

9. A physical inspection of the plant, working practices, office management systems and surrounding areas including a check on safety equipment, verifying the company's own sampling and monitoring procedures, investigating energy management systems and where necessary taking samples of waste, liquids, soil, air and noise.

The final stage of the audit will involve:

10. Confirming that there is sufficient evidence on which to base and justify a set of findings and evaluating the audit information and observations. Such evaluation will involve the audit team meeting to discuss all facets of the environmental audit.

11. Reporting the audit findings in written form and in discussion with the management of the audited company. This entails a formal review of the audit findings to avoid misinterpretation and discussion about how to improve the environmental performance of the firm based on the audit report. Management is thus provided with information about compliance status and recommendations regarding action which should be taken.

12. This will often result in the development of an action plan to address deficiencies. This will include assigning responsibilities for corrective action, determining potential solutions and establishing timetables. Recommendations for the next audit may also be made.

The environmental audit is more likely to be successful if the general ethos of the firm is supportive to the success of the programme and the welfare of the company. To this extent it is useful to consider some key characteristics which will provide the foundation for a successful programme. These factors will include:

(a) comprehensive support for the programme throughout management and particularly by senior management;

(b) acceptance that an auditing programme is for the benefit of management rather than a tool of individual performance assessment and is a function which, in time, will improve management effectiveness;

(c) the recognition that useful information will come out of the audit programme and that information needs to be shared and acted on;

(d) the commitment to considering the comments and suggestions at each level of the organization's management and workforce and encouraging responsible participation;

(e) a commitment to establishing systems for managing and following up on results;

(f) clearly defined roles and responsibilities and clear operational systems;

(g) the recognition of an integrated approach where the auditing system is linked to a wider management system.

Much stress needs to be placed on the idea that audits should be seen by management as a positive help rather than a threatening or hostile exercise. The company must create a culture, led by its main board directors, which recognizes the positive benefits of the audit and sees it as good day-to-day management practice. Management must feel that they own the audit and even though some external expertise may be used, it is an activity which is promoted and driven internally rather than externally.

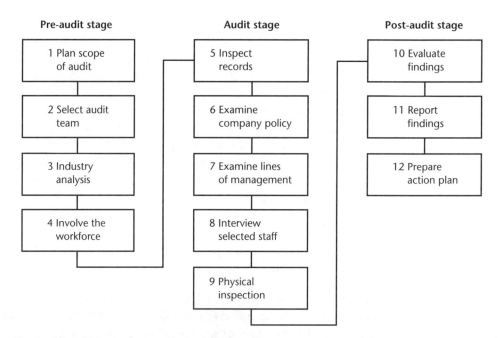

Figure 11.4 Stages of an environmental audit

Environmental auditing in Europe

In the Netherlands, the concept of environmental auditing has been known since 1984, although Dutch subsidiaries of American-owned firms had used the technique before then. The Confederation of Dutch Industries promotes environmental management within companies, encouraging interaction between government and industry and providing guidelines. In the early 1990s, environmental auditing in the Netherlands was largely confined to the largest of corporations but good practice by large, successful firms has been emulated by many small and medium-sized firms. In Norway, factories are required to establish and maintain an internal environmental control system, supervised by a government agency. Environmental auditing is not legally required but a number of companies practise environmental auditing on a voluntary basis. Within the Norwegian company Norsk Hydro, every major installation is audited once every two years, lasting between three and five days in each case. In the UK, where again environmental auditing is not legally required, the number of companies voluntarily operating audit programmes continues to increase. In a 1997 survey by accountants KPMG, it was shown that 79% of the FTSE-100 firms produced a formal environmental report based on some form of environmental audit (see Harris, 1998, p. 335). However, it is only a minority of firms – less than 2% of all large and medium-sized firms in the UK – that back their internal assessments with an external audit. As in other EU states, the trend towards environmental auditing has been encouraged by:

■ increased public scrutiny,

■ more stringent national and supranational (EU) environmental regulations,

■ the emergence of international environmental management standards (e.g. ISO 14001),

■ EU schemes and initiatives such as EMAS (see Box 11.1), and

■ the reduced availability of pollution insurance.

BOX 11.1

EMAS – the EU eco-management and audit scheme

At the end of 1991, the Commission approved a proposal for a Council regulation to establish an EU eco-management and audit scheme which would be open for voluntary participation by industrial companies. The scheme (EMAS) was established by EC Regulation 1836/93, and came into operation in April 1995. Its objective is to promote improvements in the environmental performance of industry by encouraging companies to:

■ establish and implement environmental protection schemes,

■ comply with legislative requirements,

■ carry out regular, systematic and objective evaluations of the environmental performance of these systems, and

■ provide information about environmental performance to the public.

The scheme applies to manufacturing sites and those engaged in waste disposal, recycling, mining and power generation. In order to get a site (and its name) on the EMAS register, a company has to:

■ define an environmental policy, based on an overall review of the environmental impacts of its activities,

■ set targets for achievement within a set time,

- put into place plans and systems to achieve these targets and include provisions for their constant monitoring,
- complete periodic environmental audits, covering all activities at the site(s) concerned,
- report audit findings to the public in an external environment statement,
- have these findings verified by a third party, and
- set new targets for further progress and repeat the procedure (see Figure 11.5).

The public environmental statement, and its validation by accredited environmental verifiers, is fundamental to the eco-management and audit scheme. If the statement is not an accurate and fair description of the site's activities, environmental management systems etc., then it will not be validated. The scheme highlights the need for a continuous cycle of improvement. A serious lapse in environmental standards will result in the removal of a site (company name) from the register. Inclusion on this Europe-wide register provides a strong signal to the public, regulators etc. that the company is committed to high standards of environmental performance. A graphic symbol can be used by companies to publicize and promote their involvement in the scheme. The European Commission estimates that nearly 3,000 sites are now registered under the scheme. Participating companies include Canon, SGS-Thomson, ICI, Novartis, National Power (UK) and BP.

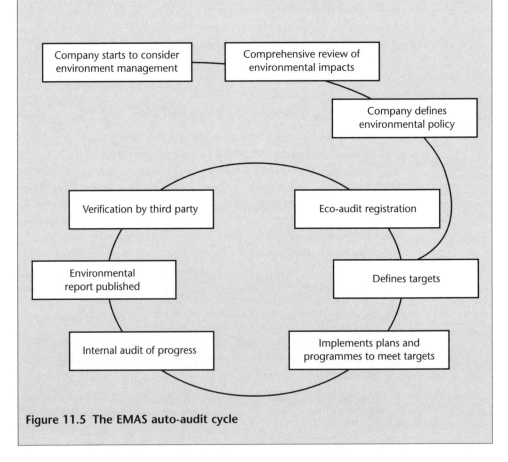

Figure 11.5 The EMAS auto-audit cycle

Environmental management systems and TQEM

An environmental management system (EMS) is a formalized set of procedures, which aim to guide an organization on how to control its impacts on the environment. Systems can be certified against International Environmental Management Standard ISO 14001. There have to be good reasons for instituting an EMS and they need to be thoroughly explained and discussed with everyone in the firm, including workers, shareholders and customers. The trend towards environmental management systems is explained by several factors including:

- the desire to take a holistic approach to environmental management,
- the need to ensure compliance with burgeoning environmental legislation,
- public relations advantages,
- reductions in the use of resources (and the targeting of cost savings),
- the demonstration of environmental commitment to influential stakeholders, and
- commitment to ecologically sustainable business practices.

Whether or not an environmental management system is ultimately successful may depend, in part, on factors outside the control of the firm. But, apart from the existence of a growing legislatory framework aimed at directing firms, the most significant determinants of success will be commitment, careful planning and the development of a responsible culture. Reward and recognition provide the incentives to maintain the EMS culture, that is reward directly related to performance for the workforce and recognition by customers, shareholders, pressure groups and regulatory authorities for the company as a whole. This can help managers and workers to develop a sense of pride in their company which in turn feeds back into commitment.

It should be noted that there are some very strong links between the idea of systematized environmental management and the principles of total quality management (TQM). In earlier chapters it was seen how the adoption of a TQM system can help a firm to achieve improvements in quality, to minimize defects during production, and to eliminate unnecessary costs and waste. The concept of *total quality environmental management (TQEM)* is a natural extension of the TQM philosophy. In TQEM, environmental improvements are sought in the production, design and quality of goods and services, with environmental damage treated as a quality defect.

Shrivastava (1995) provides an interesting analysis of TQEM, characterizing it as 'a total systems perspective'. On the input side, he explains, TQEM encourages efficiency 'by reducing use of energy and virgin materials through product redesign ... by making greater use of renewable materials ... and by developing ecologically sensitive purchasing policies and inventory-management systems'. Highlight is made of Tetrapak (the Swedish company), which has innovated packaging technologies to use recycled and recyclable materials and moved to energy-saving production. In the throughput process notes Shrivastava, focus is on 'improving the

515

efficiency of production, minimizing wastes, and reducing costs'. An effort is made 'to eliminate emissions, effluents, and accidents' with a long-term goal of zero pollution. On the output side is added an emphasis on sustainable product choice and design which can provide a strong basis for competitive advantage.

CASE STUDY 11.1 **German chemical firm tops global list**

The Düsseldorf firm Henkel has gained a reputation as the world's greenest chemical company. In a recent survey by the independent Hamburg Environment Institute, Germany (HUI) – http://www.hamburger-umweltinst.org/Top50.htm – the company was found to have the best environmental credentials out of the world's fifty largest chemical and pharmaceutical companies. In 1993, Henkel identified environmental leadership as a key strategic aim. Today, the company has a sophisticated environmental management system, certified under ISO 14001 and EMAS, the EU Environmental Management Scheme. The company has placed great emphasis on internal eco-audits and on developing new, responsible processes. In 1998, it was the world's largest processor of oil and grease from renewable raw materials. Public pressure has made the chemical industry one of the leading industries in Europe in terms of improved production process. However, in a recent interview, Henkel boss Winkel pointed out that Henkel was not a firm that would jeopardize profit or shareholder interest for the sake of environmental aims. In this sense, Henkel is well aligned with the other chemical companies who, for all their recent initiatives, remain far from the goal of sustainability.

Life-cycle assessment

Among its many emphases, TQEM seeks to minimize the life-cycle costs of products and services. Product design managers are increasingly examining ways in which the life-cycle costs of a product (loss of environmental quality, disposal costs etc.) can be minimized. In other words, they are looking to create an enclosed resource loop where product and product waste can be recycled. Natural ecosystems operate in a similar fashion so that the waste from one process feeds into another as a nutrient. Traditional environmentally damaging production and consumption works more in a linear way such that inputs and outputs are not connected and possible environmental improvements are missed. One alternative is cradle-to-grave management where companies have to recognize their wider responsibility and manage the entire life-cycle of their products.

Many companies are recognizing their responsibility in this area in terms of what has been termed product stewardship. This involves:

1. Examining the design of a product and considering how efficient it is.

2. Considering the energy sources, raw materials and components used in the product.

3. Deciding whether they might be substituted by alternatives which are more environmentally friendly.

4. Examining the production process itself and considering whether a more energy efficient and less polluting process innovation might be found.

CASE STUDY 11.2 The Body Shop International

Background

The Body Shop was founded in March 1976, when Anita Roddick opened her first shop in Brighton. Before 1976, working for the United Nations, she had travelled around the world and met people from a number of different cultures. Observing how people treated their skins and hair, she learned that certain things cleansed, polished and protected the skin without having to be formulated into a cream or shampoo. When she started The Body Shop, Anita Roddick aimed to utilize these raw ingredients such as plants, herbs and roots in products which would be acceptable to consumers. Only six years later she was described by the International Chamber of Commerce as 'the inventor of sustainable retailing' (Williams and Goliike, 1982).

The first shop was basic and initially sold only fifteen lines. They were packed in different sizes to fill up the shelves and to give the customer an opportunity to try a product without buying a large bottle – a principle which remains today. A refill service operated which allowed customers to refill their empty bottles instead of throwing them away. Although this was clearly an environmentally friendly strategy, it was also initially implemented to cut down the costs of packaging.

Today, The Body Shop's principal activities are to formulate, manufacture and retail products which are primarily associated with cleansing, polishing and protecting the skin and hair. In FY 1997–98, worldwide retail sales were in excess of £600 million. The underlying aims are to conduct that business ethically, with a minimum of hype and to promote health rather than glamour. Naturally based, close-to-source ingredients are used wherever possible and ingredients and final products are not tested on animals (Wheeler, 1992). Packaging is kept to a minimum and refill services are offered in all shops. Packaging, in the form of plastic bottles, can be returned to shops and is recycled into The Body Shop's carrier bags. The Body Shop's full range now contains over 400 products. The organization trades in forty-seven countries with over 1500 outlets. Senior management in the organization is committed to the encouragement of positive change and environmental strategies are at the centre of the Body Shop's approach to business. The aim is to establish a new work ethic that will enable business to thrive without causing adverse damage to the environment, at both the local and the global level. There is an emphasis placed on not selling products which have an adverse effect on sustainability, that is those which consume a disproportionate amount of energy during manufacture or disposal, generate excessive wastes, use ingredients from threatened habitats, which are obtained by cruelty or which adversely affect other countries, especially in the developing countries (Welford, 1994).

It is claimed that the company is not a major polluter or a major user of energy and raw materials. Manufacturing at its principal site, Watersmead, in West Sussex, produces no airborne emissions and only 23 m³ of waste water per day. Progressively, greater use has been of wind and solar energy sources at this site. Energy consumption by the entire UK operation (including distribution and retail outlets) is responsible for only 0.003% of total UK emissions of CO_2 (around 18,000 tonnes per annum), and the use of plastics in packaging is well below corporate averages (Wheeler, 1992).

The organization has been so successful in raising the profile of the environment both within and external to the business that it is endlessly cited as being the leading business, worldwide, in this field. When, in 1995, the company published three independently verified reports on the company's environmental, animal protection and social–ethical performance, it was hailed as a global leader by the UNEP (United Nations Environmental Programme). Even though the organization itself would argue that there is still more to be achieved, this extended case study examines the practices and systems which have enabled The Body Shop to reach this leading position.

Commitment and policy

One of the most apparent characteristics of The Body Shop is its commitment to environmental and social excellence. This is often attributed to Anita Roddick herself and, while many of the principles are hers, the truth is that commitment in the organization exists not only at board level but throughout the whole organization. Everybody is encouraged to contribute to environmental improvement. The ultimate aim of The Body Shop is to include environmental issues in every area of its operations but, at the same time, the organization rejects environmental opportunism which has often paralleled the green marketing strategies of more cynical firms. At first, The Body Shop did not commit itself to a formal strategy or programme of environmental improvements. Action was taken when environmental problems were identified. This approach tended to increase employee involvement and reduce bureaucracy. However, with the continued growth of the organization, it has been necessary to move to a more systematic approach, setting targets and planning for environmental improvement.

The overriding factor for The Body Shop is the perception of a moral obligation to drive towards sustainability in business (Roddick, 1991). It is impossible to measure progress towards this ideal without a detailed policy statement followed by a systematic process of data gathering and public reporting. Hence, auditing activities are considered absolutely essential to the company's long-term mission to become a truly sustainable operation. In other words, aiming to replace as many of the planet's resources as are utilized. That fundamental aim translates into a wish to play a full part in handing on a safer and more equitable world to future generations. The fundamental basis of this goal is a commitment to the broader concept of sustainable development. It is the strong belief of The Body Shop that the moral burden of achieving sustainability in business should become the principal driving force behind business in the future.

Environmental management and environmental auditing

The only real way to achieve the environmental improvement is to take a systematic approach to achieving its aims through an appropriate management structure and to periodically assess or audit progress, measuring the extent to which targets and basic objectives are being met. For that reason environmental auditing has a very high profile at The Body Shop. Since 1991, the Body Shop has carried out environmental auditing in line with the EU eco-management and audit scheme (then in draft form), laying out a report on its environmental performance (the so-called 'Green Book'). On the main site, it involves all staff and managers in continuous data collection, frequent reviews of priorities and targets (on a department by department basis), and an annual process of public reporting of results. The process extends to all retail outlets and franchise operations. All UK shops, for example, are given an 'eco-audit' checklist covering their most important environmental issues. Auditing for sustainability, introduced since 1993, has emphasized the need for continuous improvements in key areas like waste minimization, re-use and recycling, product life-cycle assessment, and the use of renewable resources. In 1995, the company introduced an independently verified audit of its own performance promises on social and environmental issues. Its follow-up report in 1997 scooped the UNEP's top award for social and environmental reporting.

In parallel with its efforts at environmental auditing, The Body Shop has put in place holistic management systems capable of achieving targets and adhering to environmental policy. The Body Shop maintains a very decentralized system of environmental management. A corporate team of Environment, Health and Safety (EHS) specialists acts as a central resource for networks of environmental 'advisers' and co-ordinators in headquarters departments, subsidiaries, retail outlets and international markets. Environmental advisers and co-ordinators are usually part-time, fulfilling their role in environmental communications and auditing alongside normal duties. Efforts are supplemented by training programmes on environmental improvement for Shop Environmental Advisers (SEAs).

5. Re-examining the disposal of the product and the waste from its production in terms of recycling and returning the used materials to the production cycle after use and

6. Reconsidering the after-sales service and packaging of the product and ensuring that adequate information is provided for its safe and energy efficient use and environmentally friendly disposal of waste caused by consumption of the product.

It is relatively easy for firms to target their internal systems and to adopt a life-cycle environmental management system. The part of cradle-to-grave management which is probably hardest to achieve is the return of materials from the consumer waste stream. For example, only a small percentage of consumer used plastic is recycled in the EU owing to a lack of an effective collection infrastructure combined with underdeveloped markets for recycled plastics. One solution is for companies to take action and to construct their own recycling infrastructure.

The European Union and the environment

Throughout the preceding analysis we have alluded to the important role played by the European Union in shaping and regulating the environmental behaviour of firms. At this point in our analysis we attempt to bring together the different threads and forms of EU action on the environment and to establish the key principles of EU environmental policy. In this sense, the section should provide a useful complement to the numerous EU policy profiles featuring in the first half of our book.

Although there was no mention of environmental policy in the original EEC Treaty, the EU has developed a substantial body of environmental law to protect against water, air and noise pollution, and to control risks related to chemicals, biotechnology and nuclear energy within the Union. As early as 1972, heads of state recognized that it was necessary to implement a common policy on the environment and, by 1985, over 100 environmental instruments had been enacted. Since the Single European Act introduced a new Treaty Title on 'the environment' in 1987, the member states have been committed to concerted action in this area. At the end of 1998, 528 items of Community legislation relating to environmental protection were in force: 200 directives, 92 regulations and 236 decisions (European Parliament, 1999). Many of these have been designed to give effect to the objectives of Environmental Action Programmes that have run sequentially since the first programme was launched in 1973. The most recent of these, the Fifth Environmental Action Programme (1993–2000), is currently promoting sustainable development 'at all levels of society and in harmony with international objectives'.

Principles of EU policy

The (first) EU environmental action programme (which ran from 1973 to 1976), set out a number of principles which have formed the basis of environmental action in the EU ever since:

1. Prevention is better than cure.
2. Environmental effects should be taken into account at the earliest possible stage in decision-making.
3. Exploitation of nature and natural resources which causes significant damage to the ecological balance must be avoided.
4. Scientific knowledge should be improved to enable action to be taken.
5. The polluter should pay for preventing and eliminating environmental nuisance (the polluter pays principle).
6. Activities in one member state should not cause environmental deterioration in another.
7. Environmental policies of member states must take account of the interests of developing countries.
8. The EU and member states should act together in international organizations and also in promoting international environmental policy.
9. Education of citizens is necessary as the protection of the environment is a matter for everyone.
10. The principle of action at the appropriate level; for each type of pollution it is necessary to establish the level of action which is best suited for achieving the protection required, be it local, regional, national, EU wide or international.
11. National environmental policies must be co-ordinated within the EU without impinging on progress at the national level. It is intended that implementation of the action programme and gathering of environmental information by the proposed European Environment Agency will secure this.

These principles were reaffirmed by the Single European Act and by the Maastricht and Amsterdam Treaties. Between them, these Treaties have given most of those principles a clear and legal basis. The Single European Act, which gave the Community explicit powers in the environmental field for the first time in 1987, established that Community action was to be based on the principles of prevention, rectifying pollution at source, and 'the polluter pays'. The Act also demanded the incorporation of environmental protection requirements into other Community policies (see Articles 130r–t of the SEA). The TEU and Treaty of Amsterdam confirm that Community environment policy rests on these principles and on that of 'precaution'. This new precautionary principle establishes that the absence of full scientific certainty about the causes of an environmental problem should not be used to justify delays in the introduction of measures believed necessary to prevent further environmental degradation.

Legal basis

In legal terms, the basis for Community environment policy now rests with Articles

174 – 176 of the consolidated EC Treaty. Article 6 (3c) of the Treaty also mentions the need to integrate protection of the environment in all Community sectoral policies. These and other isolated provisions empower the Community to act in protection of the Community environment in accordance with the subsidiarity principle. In short, the Union will tackle environmental problems only when it can deal with them more effectively than national or regional government. It may be noted here that the Treaties also provide for qualified majority voting on most environmental matters with the exception of those of a fiscal nature. Since the ratification of the Amsterdam Treaty, the co-decision procedure (see Chapter 2) has also been extended to all environmental matters, strengthening the role of the European Parliament in environmental legislation. Indeed, it is somewhat ironic that, since this innovation, an institution which has previously championed green law-making has adopted a much more conservative approach to environmental policy. This follows the centre–right's victory in the 1999 European Parliament elections (Harding, 2000).

EU environmental legislation

The body of secondary environmental legislation is vast, boasting over 500 legislative items. A review of these provisions is beyond the scope of this chapter. Below, we provide highlight of some of the more significant directives and Council regulations under two broad headings: *'pollution prevention and control'* and *'horizontal measures'*. The horizontal measures are those which govern practice and environmental management across sectors and which do not relate specifically to the prevention, management and control of waste, air, water or noise pollution.

EU legislation: horizontal measures

The Directive on Environmental Impact Assessments (85/337), as modified by Directive 97/11, requires government to inform the general public of its plans for large-scale developments such as road construction projects, plans for power stations or incineration plants. The Directive also demands the use of environmental impact assessments (EIAs) for plans to deforest large areas of land.

Council Regulation 1210/90 establishes an EU environmental watchdog in the form of the European Environment Agency and a European environment information and observation network. It defines the Agency as a central Community body providing objective information for the drawing up and implementation of effective environmental protection policies (European Parliament, 1999). In the first part of this chapter we reflected on some of the recent findings of the EEA which has produced a series of 'state of the environment' reports, beginning with the so-called Dobris Assessment in 1995. Recently, the EEA has warned the EU member states that rising emissions of greenhouse gases are threatening to undermine the EU's legally binding commitment (under the Kyoto Protocol) to reduce carbon dioxide emissions by 8% by 2010. The Regulation establishes that the EEA must 'supply the technical, scientific, and economic information required for laying down, preparing and implementing measures and laws related to environmental protection; develop forecasting techniques to enable appropriate preventive measures to be taken in good time; and ensure that European environmental data are incorporated into international environmental programmes, such as those of the United Nations and its agencies'.

Council Regulation 880/92 on a Community eco-label award scheme allows manufacturers or importers of a product to apply for an eco-label or Community mark. Applications are made to the competent body in the member state in which they manufacture or first market the product or import it from a third country (European Parliament, 1999). The eco-label is a symbol of product quality and its award is linked to specific criteria laid down for individual product groups (see Box 11.2).

Council Regulation 1836/93 allows for the voluntary participation of industrial companies in a *Community eco-audit system*. Companies which, in addition to complying with current law, make a commitment to continuously improving their environmental protection measures can draw attention to their advanced level of environmental protection by using a standard EU mark. An examination of this scheme was provided at an earlier stage in this chapter.

BOX 11.2

The European Union eco-labelling scheme

The objectives of the EU's eco-labelling Regulation (880/92) are to promote products with a reduced environmental impact during their entire life-cycles and to provide better information to consumers on the environmental impacts of products. These must not be achieved at the expense of compromising product or workers' safety or significantly affecting the properties which make the product fit for use. The EU scheme is designed to reduce confusion by providing an authoritative and independent label to identify those goods, with the lowest environmental impact in a particular product group. That is not to suggest that those products are environmentally benign, but simply that their environmental performance is superior to those products in the same group which do not have a label. The scheme should also encourage the production and sale of more environmentally responsible products and so lessen the impact of consumption on the environment.

The label should affect all businesses along a supply chain even if some suppliers cannot use the label themselves. This is because suppliers will have to provide detailed information about their own components and their manufacturing process, in order that the suppliers of the end-product can apply to use the eco-label, on the basis of a life-cycle assessment. Thus, in time, the label may become a minimum standard, specified by an increasing number of buyers, who practise green procurement policies.

All products, excluding food, drink and pharmaceuticals, are potentially eligible for an eco-label if they meet these objectives and are in conformity with the EU's health, safety and environmental requirements. Products including substances or preparations classified as 'dangerous' under EU legislation will also be barred from receiving an eco-label along with any product manufactured by a process likely to cause significant direct harm to humans or the environment. The scheme applies directly to all member states and is EU wide. It is a voluntary scheme and self-financing. As it assesses individual products and their manufacturing processes, multi-product firms will have to make multiple applications if they would wish all of their products to have eco-labels. The scheme is not restricted to domestic made goods.

BOX 11.2

Environmental fields	Product life-cycle				
	Pre-production	Production	Distribution	Utilization	Disposal
Waste relevance					
Soil pollution and degradation					
Water contamination					
Air contamination					
Noise					
Consumption of energy					
Consumption of natural resources					
Effects on ecosystems					

Figure 11.6 European Union eco-labelling scheme indicative assessment matrix

The criteria for the award of an EU eco-label are ever tightening, such that, on application for the renewal of an eco-label, producers cannot assume that, just because their environmental performance has remained unchanged, it will be awarded the label again. Judgement of the products must be made on the basis of a cradle-to-grave analysis or life-cycle assessment (LCA). The assessment matrix in Figure 11.6 must be used in setting criteria for the award of an eco-label. This will require account to be taken, where relevant, of a product group's soil, water, air and noise pollution impacts, waste generation, energy and resource consumption and effects on eco-systems. These impacts must be assessed in the pre-production, production, distribution, use and disposal stages. The criteria established for the award of an eco-label within a product group must be precise, clear and objective so that they can be applied consistently by the national bodies which award the eco-labels. National competent bodies are independent and neutral. They are made up of representatives from industry, government, environment pressure groups and consumer groups and the body has to reflect the full range of social interests. These bodies act as a kind of jury and assess the environmental performance of the product by reference to the agreed general principles and specific environmental criteria for each product group.

The use of an eco-label is not necessarily open to any product. The first step is to get a particular product group accepted as suitable for the award of a label. It may be the case that a particularly polluting group of products will not be open to such an award. Requests for the establishment of new product groups may come from consumers or industry itself and are addressed to the competent body in the member state. The competent body if it so wishes can ask the Commission to submit a proposal to its regulatory committee. In any event the Commission will consult with interest groups and take advice from a range of sources. If it is decided that a particular product group will be open to the award of an eco-label then this will be announced in the Official Journal of the EU.

Following applications from manufacturers or importers of a particular product for the award ▶

BOX 11.2 of an eco-label, the national competent body has to notify the Commission of its decision relating to the award of an eco-label, enclosing full and summary results of the assessment. The Commission will then notify other member states and they usually have thirty days to make reasoned objections to the recommendations. If there are no objections the award proceeds and a contract to use the label for a specified time period is drawn up. Lists of products able to use the eco-label are published. In the case of any objections and disagreement the Commission acting through its advisory or regulatory body of national experts will make the final decision. This procedure is summarized in Figure 11.7. Companies applying for an eco-label have to pay a fee to cover administration costs and a fee is also charged for the use of the label if awarded. Companies which succeed with their applications can only use the eco-label in advertising the specific products for which it was awarded.

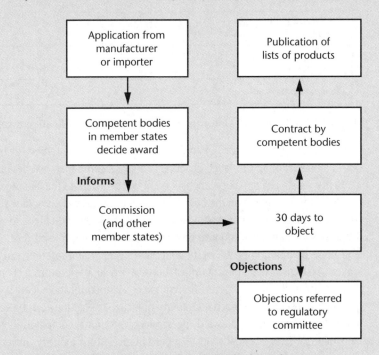

Figure 11.7 Award of EU eco-label to individual products

The whole process of LCA used in the eco-label assessment process is fiercely controversial. The key issue here is the degree of scrutiny to which companies are expected to subject their products. To undertake a complete LCA with accurate assessment of all the environmental impacts of a product would be very expensive and time consuming and like environmental impacts cannot be guaranteed to be 100% accurate because of a lack of scientific knowledge in many areas. On the other hand, anything short of this sort of approach is open to criticism and might easily be destroyed by competitors or interest groups which were not involved in the process. In time the LCA will need a much more focused definition if it is to be successfully implemented and form the long-term criteria for the award of eco-labels. It is clear from the EU eco-labelling Regulation that a full life-cycle assessment is not actually needed. Products must be able to satisfy the criteria laid out for each product group and therefore any application for an eco-label need only to address these key areas and show that there is no additional significant harm done by the manufacturing process. This has led many environmentalists to criticize the EU scheme on the basis that only a piecemeal LCA is needed. Indeed many have gone as far to suggest that this is not true life-cycle assessment and that all the Regulation demands is that firms jump through some predetermined hoops.

Companies which are keen to identify their more environmentally friendly products within their marketing strategy will be aided by the EU's eco-labelling scheme which is able to confer a recognized accreditation for a particular product. The scheme sits alongside, and does not replace, existing national schemes such as Germany's Blue Angel eco-label. This is probably the world's best-established programme. Launched in 1978 by the German government, by the mid-1990s, it had over 4,000 products carrying the label. The organizers of the scheme claim that 80% of German households are aware of the scheme and it receives widespread support from manufacturers. Many firms are aware that they cannot be without the Blue Angel award because the public sector, and many large German companies, will make every attempt to only buy products which carry the label. The same cannot be said for the EU scheme. To date, few products have received the award, public recognition is poor and support from manufacturers is uneven. Arguably, because the award criteria are not selective enough, the incentive for companies to market new products and to apply for the label is not great.

EU legislation: pollution prevention and control

Several directives have been passed to prevent and to control air, water, soil and noise pollution. The EU has also established a legal framework for the management of wastes and chemical substances. Again, a comprehensive summary is impossible here and our brief presentation is limited to a selection of measures.

Air quality

The Community has adopted directives to reduce traffic pollution, setting maximum emission limits for motor vehicles and other sources of atmospheric pollution. *Directive 91/441* (concerning passenger vehicles) as amended by Directive 94/12, regulates exhaust and evaporative emissions. Other directives exist to limit emissions from large combustion plants (particularly power stations) and from factories. The Commission has also set the member states a series of targets for emissions reductions, discussed in the first part of this chapter. In a paper entitled 'Climate change – towards an EU post-Kyoto strategy' (COM(98)0353), the Commission has proposed measures to reduce emissions of six greenhouse gases by 8% on 1990 levels by set points between 2008 and 2012. Taking 1990 as the reference year, it also aims to reduce annual emissions of SO_2 by 71% by the year 2010. A full range of reduction targets (schedules) was presented earlier in Table 11.3.

Noise

EU measures have also targeted the problem of noise pollution. Noise emission levels have been established for motorcycles, cars, tractors, lawn-mowers, construction equipment and civil aircraft.

Water

Several directives have been passed to protect the status and quality of surface and underground water, bathing water, tap water and aquatic environments. There is also a Directive (91/271) imposing a basic requirement that waste water treatment plants be provided for all towns with more than 15,000 inhabitants. Among its various water measures, the Community's 'Blue Flag' initiative has particular profile. Under this initiative, a blue flag (EU endorsement) is awarded to beaches and ports meeting certain criteria such as cleanliness, rescue and sanitary facilities (European Parliament, 1999).

Waste and chemicals

In legal terms, the *Framework Waste Directive 75/442/EEC* (as amended by Council Directive 91/156/EEC) sets out the framework for waste management in the European Union (EU). *Directive 78/319* supplements Directive 75/442 with regard to the *disposal of toxic and dangerous waste*. In essence, this Directive requires member states to store and treat dangerous substances in specialized facilities. This is backed by the *Waste Shipment Regulation (no. 259/93)* on the supervision and control of shipments of waste within, into and out of the European Union. In 1997, this regulation was amended so as to ban EU states from exporting most forms of hazardous waste to developing countries (see Council Regulation 120/97). For many years, a number of EU countries have been moving dangerous wastes to developing nations for treatment and disposal. In most cases, these nations have had neither the resources nor the knowledge to do this safely.

Recovery and recycling of packaging waste

Directive 94/62/EC is concerned specifically with recovery and recycling. Within five years, member states are expected to meet a target of 50% for the recovery of packaging wastes and to attain a recycling rate of 25% across all packaging materials. The performance of the member states was discussed in the first part of the chapter. The only material for which the averge national recycling rate is below that of the 25% target is plastic.

The evolution of EU policy-making

The integration of the environmental dimension in all major policy areas is now a central concern of the EU institutions. While it has taken the member states some time to appreciate the point, it is clear that environmental protection targets can only be achieved by involving those policy areas causing environmental deterioration. As explained in interview by Jimenez Beltran, the Director of the European Environment Agency:

> If you comply with the waste-water treatment directive and ignore agriculture then the run-off waste from agriculture will neutralise part of the advantages you get from treating the water. (Eur-Op News, 1999)

Such integration is not easy. For example, with rising transport emissions, a 'green' policy would be to build fewer roads and to incentivize the use of public transport systems. However, development needs in many parts of Europe (including the Southern countries covered by the Cohesion Fund) 'require' transport network development, including the building of more roads. Such tensions often pit Commission Directorates against one another (e.g. the environment versus the transport directorate) and lead to tensions within the Council of Ministers.

The EU is also moving away from a traditional command-and-control approach and is developing a range of policy instruments designed to prevent as well as to punish pollution. The use of a broad range of policy instruments is a central theme of the Fifth Environmental Action Programme (1992–2000). This Programme has emphasized the concept of sustainable development, objectifying:

- efforts directed towards the maintanence of the overall quality of life;
- continuing access to natural resources;
- the avoidance of lasting environmental damage; and
- sustainable development which meets the needs of the present without compromising the ability of future generations to meet their own needs.

Tools of future policy are likely to include:

- legislation to set environmental standards;
- environmental charges designed to avoid pollution (e.g. energy taxes);
- market-based instruments such as tradeable pollution permits;
- voluntary schemes to encourage the production and use of environmentally friendly products and processes;
- horizontal support measures (information, education, research etc.); and
- financial support measures (funds) directed towards the promotion of sustainable development.

Alongside more traditional instruments, it is to be hoped that the application of economic market based instruments and voluntary agreements such as the eco-labelling and EMAS schemes may encourage change in all sectors of industry and society. However, problems have been experienced with regard to common agreement between the member states on energy taxation, and the eco-label and EMAS schemes have yet to achieve wide coverage. Proposals for tradeable pollution permits (which the Commission says can help the EU to meet its Kyoto commitments) are also at an early stage and are likely to provoke heated discussion between member governments and between the EU and environmental groups (see Case Study 11.3).

The implementation and enforcement of environmental legislation

For all its present (and future) innovations, little environmental benefit will be felt unless the EU ensures better implementation and enforcement of existing (and

---

CASE STUDY 11.3 Commission looks to emissions trading

The European Commission will tomorrow endorse controversial proposals to allow companies to buy and sell permits to pollute, helping the European Union to cut a bill of up to €20 billion to meet internationally agreed targets.

Its scheme is part of an EU effort to cut emissions of greenhouse gases including carbon dioxide by 8% between 1990 and 2012 following an international agreement in Kyoto in 1997.

The Commission will warn tomorrow that 'without a reinforcement of current policy measures', emissions will increase by up to 8% rather than fall by that amount. Transport emissions of carbon dioxide would rise 40%. The EU executive will say the EU needs all the tools possible to meet its Kyoto commitments and that emissions trading will be an 'integral part' of its strategy.

Its endorsement of emissions trading will disappoint some environmentalists who fear the practice will be used by countries including the US to buy their way out of reducing indigenous pollution. The EU has traditionally been highly sceptical about emissions trading and insists that industrialized countries should put in place domestic policies rather than buy pollution permits, as the 'main means of action' to meet targets.

Emissions trading is a scheme whereby companies are allocated allowances for polluting; those that reduce their emissions by more than their allowances can sell their surplus to others less able to reach their targets. Supporters argue that the trading does not undermine the environmental objective since the overall amount is fixed.

International emissions trading is scheduled to start in 2008 but in a green paper the Commission says there is a good case for a 'limited' EU scheme from 2005.

This would start with carbon dioxide, the most easily and accurately monitored of the greenhouse gases, and should be limited to certain industries.

While there is no formal recommendation on which industries to include, the green paper suggests a range of 'fixed point sources' – electricity and heat production, iron and steel, refining, chemicals, glass, pottery and building materials and paper and printing – as the 'most suited'.

Together these account for about 45% of all carbon dioxide emissions. According to the Commission, the annual costs of meeting the Kyoto targets could reach €20 billion if member states allocated 'burden sharing' targets uniformly to all sectors without allowing trading.

In a separate analysis using more optimistic figures, it estimates that costs could be cut by a third if all sectors were allowed to trade emissions.

The EU has already allocated emission cutting targets to individual countries but the Commission argues a community approach is needed on emissions trading to ensure that competition is not distorted.

Source: Financial Times, 7 March 2000

future) eco-legislation. To date, massive difficulties have been encountered in the incorporation of EU legislation into national law. In 1997 alone, the Commission referred thirty-seven cases to the European Court of Justice. A real problem here is that most environmental measures take the form of directives, rather than regulations. Directives are not immediately actionable and must be transposed into national law by national authorities. Given that environmental directives often involve substantial costs of compliance by public authorities and/or by commercial entities, the incentives to do this quickly (if at all) are not always clear. The Commission proposes a number of measures to rectify the situation, including stricter reporting requirements, name-and-shame seminars and heavier sanctions for non-compliance.

Realizing that environmental policy is of little use unless enforced, the EU's new Environment Commissioner, Margot Wallstrom, has given increased emphasis to the improved enforcement of existing legislation, indicating that the pace of new legislative action will be slowed. To some extent, this should allow governments and industry to take stock of the rapid increase in environmental legislation over recent years and to focus on achieving compliance with existing legislation. However, there are many pieces of environmental legislation in the EU policy pipeline which are awaiting final adoption, many of which will have fundamental implications for business (see Case Study 11.4). At the same time, as governments play catch-up and comply more fully with existing EU legislation, businesses in various EU states will face new demands. In the meantime, the delay between the release of Community legislation and its subsequent implementation in member states offers vital time for planning for those companies who monitor the development of European environmental policy in order to avoid the costs and exploit the opportunities which are undoubtedly generated.

CASE STUDY 11.4 **Directive rings time on car metal scrap**

European Union motor manufacturers face an environmental clean-up bill of up to €25 billion after the European parliament backed laws forcing the industry to take back redundant cars and pay the bulk of the costs.

Motorists will be entitled to have discarded cars towed away free from 2006 under a directive that also sets targets for how much of each vehicle should be recycled.

Margot Wallstrom, EU environment commissioner, said the parliament had approved 'trail-blazing legislation' which would cut hazardous waste and help bring about a European single market.

The measures are among the most stringent in the world for end-of-life vehicles. The Commission is planning similar laws for consumer electronics.

Parliament firmly rejected amendments that would have shared the take-back costs between the industry and consumers, agreeing with the 'common position' of member state governments that industry pay all or a significant part of the costs.

MEPs also rejected carmakers' appeals they should escape the costs of taking back cars already on the road.

Acea, the car industry association, estimates that the so-called 'retroactive' costs amount to €25 billion, while the Commission says that is a gross exaggeration.

By forcing the industry to take back cars, the EU hopes to reduce the dumping of cars that have no value.

Under the legislation, manufacturers will have to start recycling 80% of the weight of vehicles by 2006 rising to 85% in 2015. Classic or vintage cars are not included in the scope of the directive.

Source: Financial Times, 4 February 2000

The EU view of the future of environmental policy and its interface with industrial development is clear. With some 376 million inhabitants, the EU is the largest trading bloc in the world and is therefore in a critical position to take the lead in moving towards sustainability. The Commission accepts that tighter environmental policy will impact on the costs of industry; however, increasingly a high level of environmental protection has become not only a policy objective of its own but

529

also a precondition of industrial expansion. In this respect, a new impetus towards a better integration of policies aiming at consolidating industrial competitiveness and at achieving a high level of protection of the environment is necessary in order to make the two objectives fully mutually supportive. Again, these views are given substance within the Fifth Environmental Action Programme. The EU shares the view that urgent action is needed for environmental protection and that many of the great environmental struggles will be won or lost during this decade. Further, it states that achieving sustainability will demand practical and political commitment over an extended period and that the EU as the largest trading bloc in the world must exercise its responsibility and commit itself to that goal.

The strategic significance of the EU's views cannot be overstated. By taking a long-term EU-wide perspective and accepting that industrial competitiveness is enhanced by tight environmental legislation, the policy framework within which all European companies must participate will reflect these views. Some companies, some regions and some nations will benefit. If the views of the EU are correct, the economic prospects of the EU as a whole will benefit and the environment will certainly benefit. However, at the company level realizing these benefits will not be automatic; strategic planning and proactive responses to the changing policy climate are imperative if success is to be secured. Information must be gathered, its implications assessed, and the necessary action taken in a systematic and integrated way.

Tackling environmental problems always requires a concerted and co-operative effort and, in the EU, success will depend on the extent to which member states are politically committed to the environmental philosophy and the extent to which they are willing to co-operate and to pursue concerted action. There will be those, therefore, who will argue that the attainment of an effective and concerted environmental policy in Europe will require political and economic union. However the EU and national governments legislate over environmental protection and police offenders, significant environmental improvement will only be attained with the co-operation and commitment of producers. There is therefore a need for firms to institute the sort of environmental management practices examined at the heart of this chapter.

Conclusion

Environmental considerations are likely to form an integral part of future commercial normality. Already, businesses are thinking and acting in terms of environmental management and competitive advantages are being achieved through the initiation of organizational change. Many businesses are developing new environmentally friendly products and production processes and are busy institutionalizing 'green' values. Several factors are contributing to this trend – growing consumer awareness, the rise of environmental pressure groups, a surge in national and international environmental legislation, quality considerations, and the desire to reduce costs. Firms which do not take action on the environmental front are in danger of losing markets.

In the future, European businesses will have to be comprehensive in assessing how to comply with 'green regulation'. Polluters will find themselves exposed and punished, with governments seeking to make the polluter pay. Challenges (and opportunities) will also extend from the further development of international environmental management standards and, at EU level, from the development of voluntary schemes such as the eco-management and audit scheme (EMAS) and the EU's eco-labelling scheme. Voluntary standards are likely to become the norm, increasingly written into contracts. European firms will need to think carefully about how they are going to move towards meeting the requirements of such standards. The role of the EU will continue to develop. Each of the major Treaty revisions has extended its powers and its scope for environmental action. Business managers must monitor the development of EU policies, especially as the EU modifies its traditional command-and-control approach and widens its membership.

Review questions for Chapter 11

1. What is meant by ecologically sustainable development?

2. Do you consider that a sustainable development model of economic development is possible?

3. What role can corporations play in achieving ecological sustainability?

4. Why should firms integrate environmental considerations into their business and management practices?

5. What key steps can they take?

6. What are the objectives of an environmental audit?

7. How does the EU eco-management and auditing scheme operate?

8. How does the EU eco-label scheme operate?

9. Explain the relationship between TQM and TQEM.

10. In what ways does cradle-to-grave management mimic natural ecosystems? Why might this be of benefit to the planet?

11. Outline the ways in which The Body Shop manages its business so as to promote the concept of sustainable development.

12. How is the commitment to environmental achievement achieved at The Body Shop?

13. What are the main objectives of EU environment policy? What are the basic principles underlying this policy?

14. What sort of steps are being taken within the European Union to control pollution?

15. In what sense is the EU's environment policy undergoing a transformation?

Web guide

European Commission: Environmental Directorate @
http://europa.eu.int/comm/environment/index_en.htm

European Environment Agency (EEA), Copenhagen @ http://www.eea.eu.int

United Nations Economic Commission for Europe (UN–ECE) Environment and Human Settlements Division @ http://www.unece.org/env/

EUBusinessNews (Environment) @ http://www.eubusiness.com/environ/index.htm

References

Bansal, P. and Howard, E. (1997) *Business and the Natural Environment*, Butterworth-Heinemann.

Eur-Op News (1999) *Our way of life threatens the environment*, April, 1–7.

European Environment Agency (1999) *Environment in the European Union at the Turn of the Century*, EEA.

European Parliament (1999) Environment policy: general principles, *European Parliament Fact Sheets*, 4.9.1.

Harding, G. (2000) Union struggles to fulfil pledge to put green issues at heart of policy-making, *European Voice*, 15 February.

Harris, N. (1999) *European Business*, 2nd edition, Macmillan.

Howard, E. (1999) Keeping ahead of the green regulators, in *Mastering Global Business*, Financial Times Management.

Hutchinson, C. (1996) Integrating environment policy in business strategy, *Long Range Planning*, **29**(1).

Roddick, A. (1991) In search of the sustainable business, *Ecodecision*, **7**.

Roome, N. (1992) Developing environmental management strategies, *Business Strategy and the Environment*, **1**(1).

Shrivastava, P. (1995) The role of corporations in achieving ecological sustainability, *Academy of Management Review*, **20**(4), 936–50.

Welford, R. (1994) *Cases in Environmental Management and Business Strategy*, Pitman.

Welford, R. (1995) *Environmental Strategy and Sustainable Development: The Corporate Challenge for the 21st Century*, Routledge.

Welford, R. (1996a) *Corporate Environmental Management*, Earthscan.

Welford, R. (1996b) *The Earthscan Reader in Business and the Environment*, Earthscan.

Welford, R. and Gouldson, A. (1993) *Environmental Management and Business Strategy*, Pitman.

Wheeler, D. (1992) Environmental management as an opportunity for sustainability in business – economic forces as a constraint, *Business Strategy and the Environment*, **1**(4), 37–40.

Williams, J.O. and Goliike, U. (1982) From ideas to action, business and sustainable development, *ICC Report on the Greening of Enterprise*, International Chamber of Commerce, London.

12 European business: competing in the global marketplace

Central themes

- Globalization
- World trade and investment
- The Common Commercial Policy
- EU market access
- Foreign market access
- International business strategies
- Gaining global competitiveness
- The global competitiveness of European firms

Introduction

For many years the fragmented nature of Europe – consisting of a number of relatively small, highly distinct national markets – was believed to be one of the major causes of poor competitive performance among European firms. The barriers to operating on a pan-European scale, often restricting firms to domestic market operations, hampered the development of large firms and the realization of economies of scale. With the removal of barriers and with the arrival of a 'single' European currency, the scope for expanding across Europe has heightened along with the potential for EU firms to secure and to develop their position within international markets. In short, the wider market which the EU has now become, although not always fully exploited, offers new potential for European companies to expand and to raise their stature within European and global markets. Not only has the European Single Market developed into an economic reality but the integration and liberalization of European markets have taken place during a period of profound change in the global political economy. Most critically, a process of 'globalization', which has been driven by various forces, has taken character and form in the internationalization of production and competition and in the emergence of global-scale markets and undertakings. Most industries are now worldwide in their scope, and many have adopted or refined an 'international' form and competitive strategy (allowing for the definitional ambiguities that surround this term).

In the present chapter, our aim is to provide an overview of such trends and to demonstrate their effects on European firms and markets. In the first part of the chapter, our aims our divided between providing a conceptual approach to the phenomenon of globalization and an account of the expansion (and liberalization) of international trade and investment (including developments in EU trade policy). Study is focused on the environmental forces, structures and institutions that characterize the global political economy and which contextualize the international business activities of European firms. Having examined the causes and expressions of globalization, progression is made to a study of the competitive challenges and opportunities presented by globalization and of the organizational and strategic responses of European business to increased global economic interdependence. Thus, while the chapter extends our analysis of the structure and strategy of European business, it combines macro- and micro-level analysis so as to assess the position of Europe (and European business) in the new world economy.

Globalization and the new world economy

Throughout this work we have concentrated on the integration of markets (and industry) in Europe and on the effects of an increasingly interdependent European economy. In a true sense, these trends are a part of that wider process of globalization resulting in a system of integrated (and more open) global markets. Companies and managers in Europe, must understand these processes (and their relationship) and anticipate the effects of globalization on their organizations and business environments. As Govindarajan and Gupta stress:

> The opening of borders to trade, investment and technology transfers not only creates market opportunities for companies but also enables competitors from abroad to enter their home markets (creating competitive threats). As competition intensifies, it fuels the race among competitors to serve globalizing customers, to capture economies of scale, to exploit the cost-reducing or quality-enhancing potential of optimal locations and to tap technological advancements wherever they may occur.... Companies will need to adapt to this changing landscape and those that choose to move first will have a better chance of turning these changes into competitive advantage. (Govindarajan and Gupta, 1999a, p. 9)

So what then do we mean by globalization and how do we understand its nature and effects?

The globalization phenomenon

In recent years, globalization has become a key theme in nearly every discussion of international business and strategy. Although few have agreed on an appropriate

535

definition, most have recognized a trend towards the development of global brands and products and towards the internationalization of markets and enterprise. In the 1980s, writing in the management field reflected on new 'global' competitive landscapes and on the growth of global organizations integrating business units and processes into unified corporate structures. Kenichi Ohmae (1989), for example, spoke of the challenges of managing in 'a borderless world', identifying the growth of global commercial operations and of new value systems which emphasized 'seeing and thinking on a global basis'. Ohmae suggested that the idea of national products, firms, technologies or industries would become increasingly fictitious and that products, firms and markets would become increasingly global. A quick sweep of companies and competition around the world adds support to this view. Companies in petroleum, electronics, pharmaceuticals and consumer goods, for example, are thinking and acting globally. In many cases, multinational enterprises (MNEs) are executing integrated strategies on a worldwide basis. At a different level, Theodore Levitt (1983) advanced a thesis of growing similarities between certain groups of consumers within global markets, provoking a debate around the question of the desirability of standardizing products and services for international market segments. Since this seminal work, a number of commentators have stressed the relative homogeneity of consumer tastes in specific markets (e.g. consumer electronics) and the trend towards standardization of products and services.

Today, globalization is a word firmly established in our vocabularies and, despite the absence of a universal definition, is a term which has come to have meaning (and descriptive power) at various levels. At the highest level (economic globalization), globalization refers to the international integration of product and capital markets and to the development and integration of international production and service networks. At the industry level, a global industry is defined 'as an industry in which a firm's competitive position in one country is significantly affected by its position in other countries or vice versa'. In this regard, the global industry 'is not merely a collection of domestic industries but a series of linked domestic industries in which the rivals compete against each other on a truly worldwide basis' (Porter, 1986, p. 18). At the business level, globalization is manifest in the 'functional integration of firms' value-added activities across national boundaries' (Makhija et al., 1997) and 'in the evidence of substantial (intra-firm) flows of capital, goods and know how' (Govindarajan and Gupta, 1999a). Thus the automotive vehicles industry is a good example of a global economic sector and General Motors of a highly globalized company. Notions of global culture and/or consumerism may also be advanced, suggestive of processes of convergence and/or homogenization encouraged by increased rates of travel and by a trend towards global media communications.

The preceding statements hint at the many drivers of globalization. While globalization is driven by a complex of forces, among the most important contributory factors underlying the globalization of business and economic activity are the decline in global trade and investment barriers and the heightened mobility of international capital. The decline in barriers to the free flow of goods, services and capital is addressed (and evidenced) in some detail as the chapter develops. It is clear, however, that, as trade expands, nations and markets are brought closer together and that the production of goods and services becomes ever more specialized. Countries are drawn to specialize in the production of specific products (those that they can produce most efficiently) and to import many other goods and services. The lowering of investment and capital barriers also facilitates a new international division of labour and a process of industrial relocation, with firms able to move their capital around world markets and to (re-)locate value creation activities to optimal locations. Most popular accounts of globalization also describe how dramatic technological advances, especially in information processing, communications, production and transportation technologies, are rapidly integrating the global economy (see for example Friedman, 1999). Many commentators highlight how the process of globalization itself accelerates the development and rate of change of various technologies (Aggarwal, 1999). Quite clearly, technological advance has been key in providing for higher levels of cross-border communications and for faster knowledge transfer. The Internet, for example, along with the adoption of technologies such as video conferencing and electronic mail, has made worldwide communication faster and cheaper. These technologies build on the contributions of satellite and wireless technologies to a modern revolution in telecommunications which has reduced the relative costs of international communication and which assists the co-ordination of dispersed business operations. Technology innovations have also led to an avalanche of new products and to changes in the methods and modes of production. Global companies have proved able to transfer innovations, technologies and processes between markets with greater speed and efficiency, with innovations in transport technologies leading to a reduction in the real costs of international transportation. Technological development has also created new forms of business and enterprise (electronic commerce), challenging traditional business structures and distribution channels. These trends lie at the core of a phenomenon which encompasses the globalization of business practices and the marketing of many worldwide standardized products to relatively homogenous consumers in different countries.

Perspectives on globalization

The idea of globalization has spread among industrialists, politicians and technocrats who find themselves involved in the internationalization of economic activities or in determining the conditions under which firms and other economic actors may operate across national borders. As suggested by Roberts (1998) '[t]he idea of globalization has also spread among those who travel, use computer technology and information resources such as electronic mail and the Internet ... [and for whom] the world is held to be shrinking'. It is clear, however, that the phenomenon of globalization promotes strong and divided opinion. In the neo-liberal view, globalization is a triumph for the market and holds out the prospect of progress through the breaking down of all manner of barriers to the cross-border flows of goods, services, people, ideas, money and technology. In particular, the elimination of trade (and investment) restrictions between countries promotes country specialization in certain products and industries. The theory of comparative advantage asserts that under free-market conditions countries specialize in the production of goods and services which can be manufactured at a comparatively lower cost than in other countries rather than attempt to produce all goods and services domestically. This promotes trade and welfare. A more radical view is that globalization is a process directed towards making the rich richer and the poor poorer. MNEs and capitalist institutions such as the World Bank, International Monetary Fund and World Trade Organization are identified as the agents of a process designed to serve the interests of global capital and to benefit big companies. Critics of globalization also charge that globalization undermines national sovereignty, curtailing the ability of individual governments to carry out autonomous economic policies and to implement effective national regulation. In particular, developing nations (their societies and environments) are seen as vulnerable to the power and demands of the more advanced states and of powerful global institutions. Equally, as globalization allows companies to move production from market to market with less and less impediment, so it also encourages countries to compete for investment by lowering their standards and by conceding to each whim and requirement of investing firms. The result is more tax breaks for the investors, less tax revenue for the host(s) and a greater repatriation of profits. At a different level, globalization may also be associated with a cutback in indigenous jobs in developed markets and with their relocation in low-wage countries (see Bloch, 1998). One consequence of globalization is that countries that lack decent labour and/or environmental standards are allowed to compete for investment with those that offer higher standards.

A debate has also been played out as to whether or not there is a real distinction between the concepts of 'globalization' and 'internationalization'. There is a great deal of conceptual and definitional ambiguity concerning the distinction between these two terms, which are often used interchangeably. While this debate is hardly settled, those subscribing to the concept of globalization believe that globalization is a process marked by the emergence of autonomous global economic structures (e.g. transnational product and capital markets) and by a trend towards multiple levels of economic governance (national, regional, international etc.) in the context of an open 'global' economy. In this view, the power and economic significance of the nation-state is declining, with a shift in power and influence to international institutions and to transnational actors such as MNEs and international banks. Globalization is thus regarded as a more advanced and complex form of internationalization which implies that international markets are increasingly autonomous from states and which emphasizes the role of non-state actors in the development of international economic activity. By contrast, in 'the international economy', the principal entities are held to be national-states, with economic activity dominated by that between national actors.

The distinction between 'international' and 'global' can also be established by direct reference to the structure and organization of enterprise in an open international economy. At this level, companies engaged in cross-border activities can be seen to follow either international (multidomestic) or global strategies, adopting suitable organizational structures. As considered in Chapter 8, multidomestic (or multilocal) companies have attempted to become insiders in a range of geographic markets by building or acquiring business operations in each and by adjusting products and practices in accordance with local conditions. Companies such as Shell and Unilever took this approach to international business and organization for many years before beginning to refashion their strategies and organizations in the late 1980s. 'Global' companies such as Sony and Coca Cola have, by contrast, aimed to create and to exploit global markets for specific products. In essence, these corporations produce standardized products for sale around the world so that they can reap the maximum benefits of (global) economies of scale and integrate their business units on a worldwide basis.

Europe, trade and the global economy

It should be clear to the reader that a primary engine of the globalization of business and markets has been the progressive growth in international trade. Trade in goods and services has grown more rapidly than the world economy since the Second World War, with significant change in the types of product traded and in the forms of cross-border trade. Over the last twenty years, trade in commercial services and intermediate products has boomed and we have seen dramatic growth in intra-firm trade, reflecting the internationalization of production. In global terms, world trade flows have increased fourteen-fold since 1950 – exceeding US $6,000 billion for the first time in 1995. This is compared with a five-fold increase in global production. Between 1985 and 1996, the ratio of trade to world gross domestic product rose three times faster than in the preceding decade and nearly twice as fast as in the 1960s. The volume of world merchandise exports grew by 9.5% in 1997 alone, the second highest rate recorded in more than two decades.

Trade itself allows countries to specialize in economic activity which best allows them to utilize their relative strengths, abilities, resources and expertise. Trade means lower prices and wider choice for consumers. Trade provides a means of sharing ideas, know-how and technology across borders, and enables efficient companies to increase sales and expand production. Our understanding of international trade (and its advantages) extends primarily from a body of theoretical contributions falling within a liberal tradition of international trade theory. This body of theory encompasses the work of Adam Smith, David Ricardo and Heckscher and Ohlin and is given brief review below.

Theories of international trade

The classical economist David Ricardo was the first to advance a coherent theory of international trade. In his book *The Principles of Political Economy and Taxation* (1817), Ricardo uses a simplified two-country, two-product model to explain how a country exports to another, or by implication to the rest of the world, the commodity in which her labour force is relatively more productive. Critically, labour is identified as the sole factor of production. Ricardo's model also assumes, improbably, that markets are characterized by perfect competition and that there are no barriers to trade such as tariffs or non-tariffs.

The Heckscher–Ohlin hypothesis replaces Ricardo's assumption of a single factor of production (labour) with the identification of two key factors of production (capital and labour). This theory of factor proportions states that a country will have a comparative advantage in goods that require a relatively large input of factors of production that are relatively cheap in that country, deriving from a relatively plentiful supply. Its comparative disadvantage comes therefore in goods that require a relatively large input of factors of production that are relatively scarce and costly. As such, the Hecksher–Ohlin hypothesis stands on two key notions:

1. that different commodities use factors in different proportions, and
2. that different countries are endowed with factors of production in different proportions.

This leads to a basic conclusion that countries should specialize in the goods which use intensively the factor of production which they have in abundance. This 'factor proportions' argument maintains the assumptions of perfect market conditions and the simplistic two country–two good dimension characterizing the earlier work of David Ricardo. Thus, while a significant advance on the Ricardian hypothesis, it remains open to serious criticism on the basis of real-world conditions which include imperfect market conditions, barriers to trade, and trade between countries in the same goods. The model also assumes conditions of factor immobility between countries, and products are treated as homogenous (there is no product differentiation).

While these theories form much of the case for free trade, they are clearly limited in their ability to account for the modern realities of trade and commerce. It is unsurprising, therefore, that trade theory has continued to evolve (within a liberal tradition) in response to modern developments in international trade. Neo-factor proportions theorizing, for example, has brought the role of scale economies and technology gaps (Posner) into the basis of international trading patterns. Product cycle theory (Vernon) introduces the notion that a product and its methods of manufacture may go through stages of maturation (introduction, growth, maturity and decline), with countries first developing new products and then, as products fall victim to mass production and manufacture within lower-cost economies, moving on to new products. This provides us with a theory of shifting comparative advantages in production and export across countries and explains how eventually, products may be exported to the country of their innovation. Trade theory has developed too under the influences of intra-industry trade models – intra-industry trade concerning the exchange of similar or slightly differentiated goods between countries producing similar products. Linder's overlapping product-ranges theory, for example, provides us with an account of such realities rooted in terms of market segmentation, product sophistication and the preferences of consumers. Focus is on the demand side and not simply on the production or supply side. This work has not only been instrumental in extending trade theory beyond cost considerations but has also helped to explain intra-industry trade (e.g. in motor vehicles) between comparably developed economies (e.g. France and Germany).

Porter's theory of national competitive advantage has also been influential in explaining why particular countries excel in the production and export of certain products. For Porter (1990), factor endowments are significant in a country's ability to compete in a given industry but other key attributes include demand conditions at home (which should be favourable and should pressure firms to produce innovative and high-quality products), the presence or absence of supplier and related industries that are internationally competitive (which should be plentiful), and the state of domestic rivalry (which must be sufficient to prompt innovative strategies). Where these attributes/conditions converge to constitute *'the diamond'*, competitive advantage will result.

Another American academic, Paul Krugman (1996) has focused on trade under imperfect competitive conditions and on 'strategic trade'. Krugman's work suggests that countries may export certain products simply because they have a firm that was an early entrant into an industry that will support only a small number of players owing to substantial economies of scale (e.g. commercial aircraft design and production). Thus countries may lead in the production–export of certain goods not because they are better endowed but because they were first movers and enjoy economies of scale that deter subsequent market entry. This theory is allied to the controversial argument that a government may increase the chances of its domestic firms becoming first movers in high-rent or 'strategic' sectors through such practices as export subsidization and strategic import protection (strategic trade policy).

If the protection and promotion of first-mover advantages can legitimize forms of protectionism, what are the other conditions under which protectionism may be justified? Certain industries may also be considered as so 'strategic' that defence can be justified on the grounds of importance to the national economy. Such industries may require special government policies to nurture and support them given high levels of R&D investment. Such arguments have sometimes been used to defend protectionism in such industries as aerospace and semiconductors. Governments have also legitimized their protectionism in terms of retaliation for the protectionist policies of others. Accusations and counter-accusations of protectionism have underlain the proliferation of non-tariff barriers in the modern era, barriers which have come to complement tariffs (or import taxes) as an important means of border protection (see Box 12.1). Porter (1990) argues that protection only works under three conditions. The first is intense domestic rivalry, which acts as a surrogate to international competition and stimulates efficiency. The second is the development of competitive advantages in the domestic market which can be transferred and sustained internationally. Finally, success (and legitimacy) depends on protection being implemented for a limited period as, in all cases, protectionism serves to delay competitiveness. One circumstance in which it may play a positive role is in preventing infant domestic industries from being undermined by international competition at an early stage of their development (the infant industry argument).

However, while a case can be made for protectionism under specific circumstances, it is clear that protectionism in whatever form imposes hurdles to business and detracts from the benefits of free trade.

BOX 12.1

Tariffs and non-tariff barriers

Tariffs and non-tariff barriers (NTBs), while offering home producers some protection from international competition, hamper the process of international trade and lead to a reduction in the stream of benefits extending from free international exchange.

Tariffs are taxes imposed on imports of commodities or services. Non-tariff barriers are obstacles to trade other than tariffs and can involve a variety of restraints including:

■ national–regional controls on trade such as import quotas, anti-dumping duties, certificates of origin, voluntary export restraints and government imposed restrictions on the purchase of imports;

■ other national–regional controls such as health and safety regulations, technical and product standards, domestic subsidies, customs clearance procedures and patent laws.

While the restrictions in the latter group may be designed to protect the well-being of the nation or economic group, like those in the first category they may limit the inflow of trade.

The institutional framework of international trade

Central to the landscape of post-war international trade has been the General Agreement on Tariffs and Trade (GATT). The GATT, and its successor institution the World Trade Organization, has played a pivotal role in the promotion of worldwide tariff reductions and in the progressive elimination of quotas and other non-tariff barriers. Under the auspices of these institutions, we have witnessed the conclusion of a series of landmark agreements (designed to promote freer trade) and the institutionalization of global co-operation towards an open, rules-based multilateral trading system. The General Agreement on Tariffs and Trade was formed in 1948 as a means of promoting the expansion of international trade and of establishing 'ground rules' for post-war commerce. Since this time it has been the major international forum for international trade negotiations (and dispute settlement), acquiring a membership of over 140 nations. Since its inception, the GATT has adopted a number of basic principles, that of non-discrimination being the most fundamental. This principle is implemented in the form of the most-favoured nation clause (MFN), which dictates that countries should apply their lowest tariff to all importers. The GATT has generally regarded tariffs as the only legal instrument of protection and has looked to eliminate or to tariffy other forms of market protection. One notable outcome of the last GATT round (Uruguay 1986–93) was the transition from a standing General Agreement on Tariffs and Trade into a new and fully institutionalized World Trade Organization. Thus, the WTO supersedes the GATT in its efforts to promote more global co-operation on trade issues and provides the central point of reference for trade disputes in the early twenty-first century.

Throughout its existence, the institution has attempted to bring clarity and transparency to international trade rules and to facilitate the negotiation of reciprocal tariff reductions among GATT signatories. Each of the three major GATT Rounds (Kennedy, 1964–67; Tokyo, 1973–79; and Uruguay, 1986–93) led to reductions of more than 30% in the tariffs between industrialized countries and to significant reductions in the tariff rates faced and applied by developing economies. The Tokyo Round was also significant for its attack on non-tariff barriers (such as quotas) though did little to prevent the spread of NTB ('new') protectionism in the early 1980s. The Uruguay Round continued the assault on NTBs and targeted new protectionist measures such as voluntary export restraints (VERs). In this eighth round of multilateral trade talks, the GATT also extended its concerns to new issue areas and incorporated ground-breaking deals on trade-related aspects of intellectual property rights (TRIPS), trade in services (GATS) and trade-related investment measures (TRIMS). Furthermore, in two heavily protected sectors (agriculture and textiles), the round was 'the first serious attempt to turn back the protectionist tide that had been running for more than a generation' (see Croome, 1996, p. 106). This 'liberalization' of trade and of world markets has presented multiple challenges to European firms and economies, some of which we explore in succeeding sections.

Open market policies and European business

For many years, domestic producers in Europe hid behind a panoply of protections. While it is beyond the scope of the present chapter to fully characterize the extensive Euro-protectionism of the 1970s and early 1980s, it is to be noted that throughout this period, tariff barriers in Europe were maintained at relatively high levels and that national import quotas and other quantitative restrictions were widely used, most prominently in such sensitive sectors as automotives, steel, textiles and consumer electronics. The number of known voluntary export restraint agreements increased five-fold between 1970 and 1980 and the number of anti-dumping measures in force in the EU shot up from 5 in 1973 to 187 by 1984 (see Hanson, 1998). In an era marked by declining levels of (EU) output and rising levels of unemployment, the idea of external market liberalization was anathema to a majority of Community governments who feared even higher levels of mass unemployment as a consequence of market opening. In many circles, moves to open up to foreign competition were viewed as 'a direct threat to the social and political peace that the post-war welfare state had achieved' (see Hanson, 1998, p. 58). A defensive European trade policy was further manifest in an ambivalent attitude towards international trading rules and dispute settlement (the GATT regime) and in terms of restrictive bilateral trade agreements.

Despite the internal liberalization facilitated by the Internal Market Programme (IMP), the EU had engaged in little external trade liberalization prior to 1990. Negotiations on the Single European Act focused strictly on internal trade barriers and in the run-up to 1992 there was evidence of more stringent EU rules on dumping and on product origin. Strict terms on reciprocity and discrimination against particular goods also fuelled the fear that Europe was becoming a protectionist 'fortress'. The Japanese, in particular, had good cause to shout unfair discrimination in the light of their being singled out as a target for restrictive European trade policies. Action against many of their industrial exports, particularly in high-technology sectors, suggested that the new Europe was not going to be any more liberal in its external dealings than the old one and that the Europeans would resist further encroachment by competitive foreign imports (see also Chapter 3).

Today, EU interests are still defended in multilateral trade talks, and tariffs (often high ones) continue to impede the import of many agricultural and industrial items into EU markets. We also see residual quantitative restrictions and a genuine enthusiasm for contingency measures of protectionism such as anti-dumping actions. Despite this, the Brussels Commission has genuinely succeeded in directing EU trade policy along a more liberal path and, while the EU is hardly a paragon of virtue, its trade policies and outlook are hardly recognizable from those that characterized the 1970s and 1980s. The EU has been rolling back quantitative restrictions (in even the most sensitive of fields) and has been busy reducing tariffs to historically low levels. The high tariffs and extensive import restrictions characteristic of the 1970s and early 1980s have been dramatically slashed and a restrictive trade policy has been largely abandoned. The EU executive and a majority of member states have even shown a moderate enthusiasm for the GATT (now WTO). New objectives such as reciprocal market opening and transparent trade rules, have been pursued through the GATT–WTO framework and the EU has generally backed a strengthening of the multilateral trading system. At the Ministerial Conference of the WTO held in May 1998 in Geneva, the EU states confirmed their support for comprehensive WTO negotiations starting in 2000. The EU views such negotiations as a way forward to multilateral liberalization and as a means of further casting multilateral rules to the Community's advantage. These efforts to liberalize EU market access and the acceptance of internationally determined schedules for reductions in tariffs (and other forms of market protection) thus represent a sea-change both in EU trade policy and in the business environment of European firms. In particular, the EU's endorsement of liberalization agreements (both at regional and multilateral levels) and a relaxation of border defences has exposed European business to new sources of competitive pressure. In many sectors, Europe has come to look less like a 'fortress' and more like an 'open market' with high rates of inward investment and import penetration.

The explanation of these changes is highly complex. At one level, fears of industrial defeat in domestic markets and of higher unemployment (dominant in the 1970s) have been replaced by a realization that shielding Europe from the rest of the world is damaging to the efficiency and global competitiveness of European business. Since the mid-1980s, the European Commission, or more precisely its external trade directorate, has also been successful in persuading member governments that liberalization of the internal EU market should be matched by the implementation of a more liberal and transparent external trade policy. In various communications, the Commission has promoted the complementarity between internal efforts at market liberalization and those directed at a strengthening of the multilateral trade system. The centralization of EU trade policy has also limited the scope for national actors to protect local markets. In particular, national import quotas have been made impossible to enforce (see subsequently). Relatedly, Community leaders have modified their view of the GATT 'as a potential impediment to their own freedom of action' (Howell *et al.*, 1992, p. 424). EU trade officials have come to view the GATT (now WTO) as an important constraint on the unilateral actions of its main rivals (principally the US) and as a vehicle for the pursuit of key EU objectives. Among key EU objectives we may count improved access to overseas markets and new global trade rules in such areas as services, intellectual property and electronic commerce. Of course the EU has faced external demands for policy reform from the US and Japan (its principal rivals), from the GATT and from regional partners (such as Poland and Hungary) looking for improved market access. It would be wrong, however, to remove from the explanation of changes in EU trade policy the evidence of failing protectionist policies at home and the impetus provided towards liberalization by the factors cited above.

How is the EU opening its markets?

The EU has been opening its markets to foreign competitors in a number of ways. On one front, the EU has been exempting many trading partners (e.g. Poland and the Czech Republic) from all tariff applications on industrial items, extending a variety of trading privileges through preferential trade deals. Over the period of the early to mid-1990s, the EU has consolidated and expanded a network of free trade, association and other preferential agreements linking the EU with nearly all regional trading partners on preferential terms. These efforts have resulted in a series of (graduated) trading privileges for countries trading with the EU and, in many cases, for those aspiring to future EU membership. Principal here are:

- a European Economic Area (EEA) Agreement (extending the SEM to Norway, Iceland and Liechtenstein),

- an evolving Euro-Mediterranean economic area (the EMEA), and

- an emergent free trade zone with 'associate' EU members in Central and Eastern Europe.

The EU has also sealed a customs union agreement with Turkey and has promoted improved trade links (and a reduction in trading obstacles) with a number of former Soviet Republics under new Partnership and Co-operation Agreements (PCAs). These agreements are non-preferential (extending MFN treatment to countries still outside of the WTO), but are nonetheless characterized by a reduction of mutual tariffs and quantitative restrictions over varying timetables.

Beyond this, the EU has also been meeting demanding (multilateral) tariff reduction schedules agreed under the Uruguay Round negotiations and detailed in the WTO Marrakesh Agreement of April 1994. Reviews of EU trade policy by the WTO's Trade Policy Review Body (TPRB) suggest that the main consequences of the

Average tariff rates by HS Chapter (%)

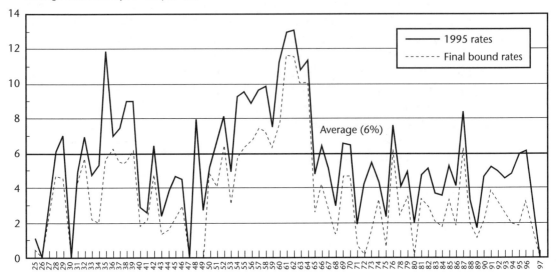

HS Chapter

Chapter	Description	Chapter	Description	Chapter	Description
25	Salt; sulphur; earths and stone, etc.	48	Paper and paperboard, etc.	72	Iron and steel
26	Ores, slag and ash	49	Printed books, newspapers, pictures, etc.	73	Articles of iron and steel
27	Mineral fuels, mineral oils, etc.			74	Copper and articles thereof
28	Inorganic chemicals; organic or inorganic compounds of precious metals, etc.	50	Silk	75	Nickel and articles thereof
		51	Wool; fine or coarse animal hair, etc.	76	Aluminium etc.
				78	Lead and articles thereof
29	Organic chemicals	52	Cotton	79	Zinc and articles thereof
30	Pharmaceutical products	53	Other vegetable textile fibres	80	Tin and articles thereof
31	Fertilizers	54	Man-made filaments	81	Other base metals, etc.
32	Tanning or dyeing extracts, etc.	55	Man-made staple fibres	82	Tools, implements, cutlery, spoons and forks, etc.
33	Essential oils and resinoids; perfumery, cosmetic or toilet preparations	56	Wadding, felt and non-wovens; special yarns; twine, cordage, etc.	83	Miscellaneous articles of base metal
		57	Carpets; other textile floor coverings		
34	Soap, organic surface-active agents, washing preparations, etc.	58	Special woven fabrics; lace, etc.	84	Nuclear reactors, boilers, machinery, etc.
35	Albuminoidal substances; modified starches; glues, etc.	59	Impregnated, coated, covered or laminated textile fabrics, etc.	85	Electrical machinery and equipment, etc.
36	Explosives; pyrotechnic products; matches, etc.	60	Knitted or crocheted fabrics	86	Railway or tramway locomotives, etc.
37	Photographic or cinematographic goods	61	Articles of apparel and clothing accessories, knitted or crocheted	87	Vehicles other than railway or tramway rolling-stock, etc.
38	Miscellaneous chemical products	62	Articles of apparel and clothing accessories, not knitted, etc.	88	Aircraft, spacecraft, etc.
39	Plastics and articles thereof	63	Other made-up textile articles: sets, worn clothing, etc.	89	Ships, boats, etc.
40	Rubber and articles thereof			90	Optical, photographic, etc. apparatus
41	Raw hides and skins and leather	64	Footwear, gaiters, etc.		
42	Articles of leather, etc.	65	Headgear and parts thereof	91	Clocks and watches, etc.
43	Furskins and artificial fur; manufactures thereof	66	Umbrellas, walking-sticks, etc.	92	Musical instruments, etc.
		67	Prepared feathers and down, etc.	93	Arms and ammunition, etc.
44	Wood and articles of wood, etc.	68	Articles of stone, plaster, etc.	94	Furniture, bedding, etc.
45	Cork and articles of cork	69	Ceramic products	95	Toys, games, etc.
46	Manufactures of straw, of esparto, etc.	70	Glass and glassware	96	Miscellaneous manuf. articles
47	Pulp of wood or of other fibrous cellulosic material	71	Natural or cultured pearls, precious or semi-precious stones, precious metals, etc.	97	Works of art, antiques, etc.

Figure 12.1 Tariffs on manufactured products (EU-12 only), 1995 and 2000

Note: In the Uruguay Round negotiations, certain items in chapters 25–9 were classified as 'agricultural' products.
Source: World Trade Organization

Uruguay Round will be an average reduction in MFN average tariffs on industrial imports into the European Union of around 37%. This fall is measured in terms of the effect of agreed tariff reduction schedules covering the period 1995 and 2001. By 2001, the EU's final unweighted MFN average tariff on industrial products should be reduced to just 3.7% with the bulk of duty rates on fully manufactured goods standing at between 3% and 10%. The highest EU tariffs are set to apply for textiles, clothing, motor vehicles and consumer electronics. Many goods, especially raw materials and semi-manufactures, will enter the European Union duty free along with the majority of items in such areas as pharmaceuticals, furniture, soaps and detergents. It is interesting to note here that on completion of the Community's customs union in 1968, its unweighted average tariff on industrial products stood at 10.4%.

Figure 12.1 provides an indication both of 1995 rates for select industrial prod-ucts–lines and of expected (and bound) rates for the year 2000. Given that these fig-ures are based on most-favoured nation tariffs and do not reflect the operation of the Community's various preferential agreements, in actuality many imports do not attract these 'nominal' rates. A number of the EU's external trading partners now qualify for zero tariff duties under the terms of free trade area agreements or other designs for preferential treatment. It may be noted here that tariffs for agricultural products (not represented in Figure 12.1 or in preceding data) have traditionally been among the highest of tariff rates applied by the EU countries. While the Uruguay Round establishes a schedule for reductions in EU (and international) agri-cultural tariffs, market access commitments in agriculture involve the tariffication of variable levies contributing to a pattern of peak tariffs on meat, dairy products, cereals and tobacco. In 1995, EU agricultural tariffs averaged just over 25%. Average rates are now below 20%.

The fall in EU tariffs has also been accompanied by a reduction in the number (and protectionist effect) of various non-tariff barriers. As such, the domestic protection of European industry has been further weakened. While the EU has maintained its right to use anti-dumping actions (in cases of dumping) and retains other safeguards against injurious imports, it has been phasing out most of its 'quotas' or quantitative restrictions. Most of the EU's recent trade deals have provided for a reduction in (or elimination of) quantitative restrictions, and restrictions previously maintained by member states have generally disappeared without substitute. Voluntary export restraint agreements such as the 'car consensus' with Japan (which capped Japanese car exports into the EU until 1999) have also lapsed without replacement.

Despite the conditionality of these concessions (changes to EU quotas and tariffs are generally made conditional on reciprocal efforts at market opening), moves to open EU markets have not always found support. For some, including many domes-tic producer groups, fears of higher import penetration and cheap competition (in home markets) have come to dominate. Very often, the enthusiasm for improved foreign market access and for a strengthening of international trade rules has been tempered by such concern. The case of textiles and apparel (see Case Study 12.1) illustrates the tensions and uncertainties created by the process of international trade liberalization. Here, we see the opportunities presented to EU firms (and

CASE STUDY 12.1 Trade liberalization and EU textiles

As with many other sectors, since the mid-1980s the EU has moved on textiles and apparel from a defensive neo-protectionist policy to a more pragmatic policy stance. This has been characterized by a qualified liberalism and has seen the promotion of progressive market liberalization on a quid pro quo basis. By the mid-1990s, the EU had dramatically relaxed the terms of its textiles trade with a raft of trading partners. Despite a steady growth in the number of exporters to European markets and in the volume of their exports, individual deals with partner economies in Europe signalled 'free' EU market access in textiles and clothing by the end of 1998. Agreements with Turkey and other developing economies resulted in new trade concessions and fewer quantitative restrictions on textiles and clothing imports from developing suppliers. In 1993, the EU also signed a ground-breaking multilateral Agreement on Textiles and Clothing (ATC) which scheduled the termination of a restrictive international textiles regime, the so-called MFA (Multi-Fibre Arrangement). Like other WTO members, the EU has thus committed to terminating all quantitative restrictions on the import of textiles and apparel by 1 January 2005. In the Marrakesh Agreement of 1994, which finally sealed the market access commitments attaching to the ATC, the EU also 'signed up' to a significant cut in tariffs in nearly all product categories. Tariff cuts (at an average 30% for textiles and 12% for clothing) will be applied incrementally over a ten-year transitional period (culminating in 2005) at an effective rate of 1/10 per annum. All tariffs will be bound.

By 1997, the EU market for textiles and clothing products had never been more open with a market penetration ratio of almost 50%. Average applied tariffs on raw materials (2% ad valorem), yarns (6%), fabrics (11%) and clothing (13%) were down (and falling), with the prospect of further cuts under agreed schedules. The European Union was by now also meeting its obligations under the WTO Agreement on Textiles and Clothing to phase-out quantitative restrictions previously maintained under bilateral MFA agreements. It was also accepting record levels of imports from Central and Eastern Europe and Turkey following the conclusion of bilateral trading agreements. Many of these imports were by now free of tariffs and quantitative restrictions under terms of preference.

Today, therefore, while European consumers are enjoying a wider, and frequently cheaper, range of imported clothing and fabrics, EU producers are having to adjust to a new environment marked by escalating imports, freer (if regulated) EU market access for overseas producers, and eroding protections. Textiles and clothing producers throughout the EU are facing up not only to an intensification of competition in domestic and overseas markets but to a future free from quota protections and state paternalism. Already, while some EU textiles and clothing companies are taking advantage of improved foreign market access and a stronger legal framework for the protection of their designs and trademarks, others, including many smaller and domestically oriented firms, are losing market share (and contracts) to cheap importers from Turkey, Eastern Europe, North Africa and the Far East. Critically, employment in the EU textiles and clothing industries has collapsed from a point of 4 million in 1983 to just 2.4 million in 1996. The number of enterprises has fallen to just 115,000. Although the EU remains the largest world consumer market for textile and clothing products, the share of that market held by domestic firms continues to fall with an escalating import penetration rate.

While EU exporters of silk, linen, wool and branded goods are benefiting from the opening up of previously protected markets in the US, Latin America and the Far East, the majority of EU firms are struggling to defend home markets and to exploit the new opportunities presented by international (sectoral) liberalization. For example, the German textiles industry is far ahead of Portugese industry in terms of its modern production plants, export orientation and formidably efficient outward-processing facilities. Larger German textiles producers, like their Italian counterparts, are better positioned to compete in international markets and to achieve sales of branded apparel and high-quality textiles at the top end of textiles and apparel markets. International production networks, flexible production systems, heavy investment in technology (e.g. CAD and CAM) and advanced design skills give some of these firms a basis for competing in the European and global marketplace. The majority of EU enterprises simply lack these attributes. Improved protection for designs, models, trademarks, logos and patents (achieved in return for market opening agreements) suggests an improvement in international trading conditions for those EU businesses able to survive.

consumers) by international market opening but also evidence of the new competitive pressures created by market opening.

The tensions and trade-offs associated with these processes echo those surrounding argument over the creation of a Single European Market. On the one side, successful producers have larger markets and consumers have wider choice. On the other, increased trade and competition equates with greater competitive threat and for many sectors (and regions) this will result in painful processes of industrial adjustment. While there is limited opportunity here to rehearse the debate over the merits of free trade (and market liberalization), it is clear that the benefits of open markets arise from increased competition, which in turn stimulates enterprise efficiency and boosts competitiveness, stimulating growth and investment. The alternative, where firms hide behind import barriers, creates inefficiency for business and reduced choice (and quality) for consumers. However, while the European Union's single market programme and international liberalization may result in similar effects (and may even be considered as being mutually supportive), greater openness in the global trading system places additional demands on EU policy as it does on European firms. The Community must now meet its responsibilities not only to ensure open (and fair) market conditions within the Single Market but also to ensure that European firms are able to compete in external markets on fair and equal terms with other businesses. Where necessary, it must also look to provide protection for Community firms when operating (or seeking to operate) in third markets. In turn, undertakings or businesses within the EU must take the necessary steps in terms of strategies for investment, financing, sourcing and production etc., so as to meet the competitive challenges presented by market opening. Surviving in the waters of global competition is no easy job. The EU may be expected to play a supporting role in fostering (and smoothing) change and in creating the conditions for business development and innovation, but it can no longer be expected to provide a shelter from the forces of competition or to support inefficient enterprises.

These observations invite a further address of the challenges inherent in framing and executing a common European trade policy. The succeeding section highlights the main features of the EU's external trade policies and its strategy for improving the access of European business to third-country markets. Among the many EU policies contributing to the competitive environment of European firms, the EU's common commercial policy represents an important case and one addressed weakly in the first half of our text.

The principles and foundations of EU trade policy

From the outset of post-war European economic integration, the corollary to a process of regional market integration has been commonality in external trading relations and the construction of a common trading regime. The Common Market concept suggests not only the freedom of movement of goods, services, capital and labour (the foundations of the Internal Market), but also a common external tariff and the adoption of a common external policy. Without common tariffs, third countries would tend to export to the lowest tariff member and then re-export the goods within the common market area. Without a common external policy, common market members would be weakened in their ability to manage common commercial interests and market distortions would arise from fragmented efforts at market defence. Since its inception, the EC–EU has built upon the early achievement of a common external tariff (CET) to establish a system or network of common trade instruments and initiatives. In seeking to pursue their interest in 'open' international exchange (Article 131, ex Article 110) and in unified principles and measures to protect trade, the member states have progressively invested the Commission of the European Communities – the executive arm of EU trade policy – with a range of common trade policy powers and instruments. These 'powers' are akin to those of the most powerful state policy-makers in the contemporary global economy. In practice, the European Community has full responsibility for multilateral trade policy and for external negotiations (covering trade in goods and services). The Community also manages EU trade policies on a sectoral basis (i.e. textiles, footwear, steel and ship-building) and is responsible for the management of 'common instruments' (i.e. anti-dumping rules and safeguards). In recent years, the EU has also been empowered by the member states to take action in support of EU business where companies and industries confront illegal trade barriers in the markets of third countries. This provides the EU with a complement to its trade policy powers matching that of Section 301 in the US Trade Act.

The 'competence' of the European Community in the field of external trade and economic relations rests centrally with Article 133. This Article (better known by its previous numbering, Article 113) establishes a common commercial policy based on uniform principles, the conclusion of tariff and trade agreements, and broader trade-related measures. Under this article, the Commission is empowered to make recommendations on overall trade policy to the national representatives of the Council of Ministers and will conduct policy and related negotiations under mandate from the Council. Its provisions have been supported by a number of further articles relating to the establishment of the CET, aid for exports, and the structure of Community action in international fora. The substance if not the interpretation of these Treaty foundations has remained unchanged since the Rome Treaty. Community authority in this realm is further extended under Article 300 (ex Article 228) on the negotiation of trade and tariff accords with non-members and by Article 310 (ex. Article 238) concering association with non-members. These Treaty articles ensure that the Community has wide-ranging ability to conclude bilateral and regional trade agreements as well as to conduct multilateral commercial negotiations on behalf of the member states. A number of legal rulings, including a 1994 decision by the European Court of Justice, have served to clarify the legal and technical boundaries of the Community's competence in this field. Although exclusive competence in the trade of goods and agriculture is firmly established under EC law, the competence of the EC to sign multilateral codes on behalf of the member states in certain aspects of trade is not yet fully established. As a consequence, in negotiations and policy relating to some commercial services and to intellectual property, competence is shared between the member states and Community institutions. While significant, this does not prevent the European Commission from acting as sole negotiator in these new issue areas.

Instruments of EU trade policy

The 'tool-kit' of the Common Commercial Policy rests with an array of trade policy instruments. The main instruments to be identified are the common customs tariff (CCT), anti-dumping rules, quotas, safeguard measures, rules of origin and content requirements, surveillance measures, and a (foreign) trade barriers regulation. In the sections below, we provide a brief overview of some of these instruments which are described and evaluated in much greater depth in a number of works (see Hine, 1985; Murphy, 1990; Marasceau, 1993; O'Keefe and Emiliou, 1996). It should be noted that alongside its management of tariff-based, quantitative, and legal trade tools, the Commission administers (internal) policies – i.e. on the environment, competition and consumer protection – that can be employed to shape the terms of international competition. Each of these areas of Community policy-making promulgates rules and regulations which have a direct effect on trade and trading freedoms. Current EU rules in areas such as banking, insurance and air transport also contain reciprocity provisions which can be used in the absence of bilateral access commitments or multilateral obligations.

The common customs tariff

The establishment of a CCT by the harmonization of differing tariff levels across the individual member states was one of the most visible elements of the Community's progress towards an effective customs union. As each new member state accedes to the Union, it too must adopt the Union's common customs tariff. This does not suggest a single unified tariff for all goods whatever their identity, but a unified rate applying to all member states for particular classes of goods and services such as motor vehicles, VCRs, carpets and plastics. Imports of some of these goods attract relatively high tariffs while others attract no duty at all. All imports into the Community are subject to duty rates defined in the EU's harmonized tariff schedule. Revenues from the imposition of the CCT form part of the Union's own resources. It should be emphasized that, although tariff barriers to the EU market have steadily fallen, the application of tariffs on imported goods remains an integral aspect of the EU's system of market protection in many sectors. The reader is again directed to the detail of Figure 12.1 which provides for a presentation of the EU's current MFN tariffs on a range of industrial imports.

Quantitative restrictions

Quantitative restrictions (QRs) (generally in the form of import quotas) have played a significant part in the Community's historical attempts to limit imports and to protect domestic producers. Although such restrictions have generally been confined to 'sensitive sectors' and/or to parties falling outside of the GATT, QRs have had a major effect in a number of industrial markets (e.g. textiles, consumer electronics and motor vehicles). National restrictions, traditionally invoked under *ex* Article 115 of the Rome Treaty, can no longer be enforced since the abolition of goods controls at internal EU borders. This has resulted in the abandonment of most QRs or their replacement with communitized (EU-wide) quotas. Prominent examples of Community quotas are the Common Market Organization for Bananas and the new quota regimes for canned sardines and tuna. In addition, Community measures have replaced national restrictions on specified consumer products from China (e.g. toys and bicycles) and on iron and steel categories from Mongolia, Vietnam and members of the Commonwealth of Independent States (CIS). The Community is widely viewed as seeking to move away from the device of quantitative restrictions, which run counter to the GATT–WTO principle of non-discrimination. Agreements have provided for the phasing-out of all such restrictions between WTO members.

(Import) surveillance

Community law also provides for import surveillance. Member states can request that the Commission monitors imports into a particular Union economy where these are causing difficulties for indigenous industry. In cases of urgency (and injurious imports), the Commission can impose short-term quantitative restrictions. These will be revoked unless supported or extended by formal Council decision. Over the last decade, the Community has held under surveillance VHS imports from Korea, textiles and clothing from the Mediterranean basin, a range of engineering machinery and electronic products from Japan, apple imports from Chile and shoe imports from Taiwan. As Murphy (1990, p. 56) observes, '... the initiation of surveillance procedures, as with anti-dumping procedures, may encourage third countries to voluntarily curb exports of the product in question to the EC'. This brings us directly to the community's use of trade defence instruments beginning with anti-dumping actions.

Anti-dumping action (and duties)

'Dumping' takes place when exporters sell their products in an overseas market at a lower price than in their own market or below the cost of production plus a reasonable mark-up (see Box 12.2). Where the EU is able to demonstrate that such dumping has taken place on its markets and has caused material injury to domestic industry, it is entitled to take 'anti-dumping' measures (typically by imposing additional duties). In accordance with GATT codes, the imposition of both provisional and definitive duties is contingent on the establishment of 'dumping' and of 'material' injury caused thereby. Provisional duties may hold for a maximum of six months and can become definitive only after majority vote in the Council. Definitive duties lapse after a maximum 'sunset' period of five years. While duties are often imposed on products 'dumped' on the EU market, reports prepared by the Community and the GATT–WTO Secratariat have suggested that exporter price undertakings – a binding commitment to raise export prices so as to alleviate injury suffered from dumped exports – are increasingly secured by the Community as an alternative outcome of anti-dumping procedures. The high frequency of such undertakings as a way to end proceedings reflects exporter interest in price increases as distinct from the payment of anti-dumping duties. Ultimately, any exporter to the EU who thinks that he or she might be accused of dumping has a strong incentive to raise prices or to modify competitive practice, in order to avoid anti-dumping duties.

At present, Community officials view anti-dumping law, among wider safeguard actions, as a vital tool of common commercial policy and the EU remains one of the most frequent users of anti-dumping remedies amongst the community of WTO members. At the end of 1994, the EU maintained over 150 separate measures involving provisional or definitive duties. Examples included definitive duties at between 60% and 96% on imported broadcasting camera systems (from Japan) and

---

BOX 12.2 | **Dumping – a primer**

Various definitions of dumping exist, many of which refer to the exporting of goods at prices below the cost of production. Other definitions, however, focus on the fact that dumping is the charging of different prices in various markets without these differences being supported by variances in costs. These two definitions are clearly very different: the former concerns prices which are set below cost, the latter prices which are lower than those in other markets, specifically the domestic market. Indeed, Penrose (1990, p. 181) asserts 'It does not necessarily, or even usually, mean that sales are made "below cost" in order to drive out competition'.

Although pricing below cost suggests anti-competitive behaviour, charging different prices in different markets is less obviously 'unfair'. There are good reasons why a firm cannot standardize prices on a global scale:

- competitive conditions differ on a market-by-market basis, which often makes local adaptation a prerequisite of competitive success. Different costs of factor inputs, different levels of local competition and differences in the price elasticity of demand for goods between countries prevent firms establishing common market prices.

- a higher degree of intra-industry trade between divisions of multinational firms distorts the assessment of prices. Efficiencies of internalized business functions arising from both horizontal and vertical integration make it difficult to determine what may or may not be deemed a 'fair' competitive price.

50% duties on ferro-silicon imports from China and South Africa. A survey of EU anti-dumping action around the period of the mid-1990s also highlights the imposition of special duties on colour television receivers from Malaysia, on ammonium nitrate imports from Russia and Lithuania, and on photocopiers from Japan. It should be noted that anti-dumping legislation (and the threat of anti-dumping action) is particularly relevant to firms from less developed countries wherein a Catch-22 situation often arises. Competitive advantage for firms from less developed countries centres on their low-cost production which is reflected in low prices in export markets. However, by exploiting their low-cost base, firms run the risk of being reported in export markets for 'unfair' pricing and dumping. While promoting exports is essential to less developed countries improving their economic performance, in some cases they may be prevented from utilizing their comparative advantage in the most effective way.

Accusations have been frequently levelled against the EU that its rules and methods for determining the existence of dumping are unfair and lack transparency. Critically, the EU, like other nations, shows a propensity for calculating export prices and domestic prices (in the exporter's market) in such a way as to exaggerate the differential. Under the GATT code, dumping must be determined on the basis of conclusions drawn from fair comparisons of the export price and the domestic price in the exporting market. Amongst its many 'tricks', the EC determines a domestic sale price ('the reference price') not as a simple average of actual prices charged but with low-priced sales in the home market thrown out on the basis that they are unprofitable. Not only will the reference price be higher but EC methodology calculates the export price by chopping off the excess over the reference price of all actual export prices. It is also common for the EU to deduct more overhead on the export side of its calculations.

Local content requirements and rules of origin

Legislation against the import of certain goods is complicated by the fact that it is often difficult to establish rules of origin. If, for example, an anti-dumping duty has been levied on a particular US product, the question to be answered is what makes the product American? Adjudging a good to be American simply because it emanates from a US manufacturing plant may be misleading. The good may have been assembled in the USA from components manufactured elsewhere. In 1968, the EU's definition of origin was established as being the place where the good underwent its last major transformation. Even this, however, is open to a degree of different interpretation and therefore more specific rulings have been established on an industry-by-industry basis, many of which include stipulations of the extent of local content – that is the amount of component input sourced from local manufacturers. Specific local content requirements have been set (as an outcome of anti-dumping investigations) in manufactures including televisions, radios, photocopiers and semiconductors. There is also an effective (although not legally binding) 80% local content requirement for Japanese cars produced in EU plants. The EU has suggested that it will only treat those vehicles satisfying this requirement as 'European production' and this has led to major local content commitments by

Japanese car firms in the EU. Integrated circuits are also required to be *diffused* (etched onto blank silicon wafers) in Europe to be regarded as 'European'. Not dissimilarly, the EU's Public Procurement Directive establishes, for governments and local authorities, the right to insist of non-EU companies at least 50% local supplies and equipment in completing the job. There are also non-binding European content requirements for television programme stations in the EU under the 1989 EC directive on 'Television Without Frontiers' discussed at greater length in Chapter 9.

The imposition of stiff local content rules addresses the issue of *screwdriver* plants. Such plants have sometimes been set up in the EU (and in associated territories) by Japanese and US firms looking to side-step EU market access barriers. Under the guise of local manufacturing centres, such plants involve minimal value adding and may be regarded as 'windows' to free imports rather than centres for manufacture. In this context, it is interesting to note that local content requirements have been made central to the many bilateral trading agreements recently concluded with European partner economies. Under the Europe Agreements, for example, the EU has come to stipulate that, in order to qualify for tariff-free access to the EU, East–Central European manufactured exports must have at least 60% local or EU content.

Japanese firms have responded positively to local content rules. Toyota agreed to reach 60% local content by August 1993 at its UK plant and attained the prescribed 80% mark by August 1995. The local content commitments by Japanese firms in the EU also tend to be higher than corresponding amounts in the USA. For example, in the production of television sets in the USA, Japanese firms source only 28% of their components locally, while in Europe this figure is 70%.

The Trade Barriers Regulation (and the EU's market access strategy)

The EU is now also equipped with a different type of trade policy instrument. The EU's New Trade Barriers Regulation (which came into effect on 1 January 1995) empowers the EU to take action against illicit commercial practices in third-country markets, where such practices adversely affect the market access of EU companies. If bilateral talks fail to resolve the problem and/or if WTO dispute settlement procedures do not result in corrective action, then the EU may take recourse to retaliatory measures including the suspension or withdrawal of trade concessions, increased customs duties on the offending party's exports, and/or the introduction of quantitative (import) restrictions. Between January 1995 and January 2000, the TBR has been invoked in twelve separate cases. One case has concerned the problem of discriminatory taxation (additional VAT and advance payment of income tax) on imports of finished leather into Argentina. Another has concerned excessive administrative requirements and discriminatory taxation on the importation of cognac in Brazil. A wide range of trade barriers or obstacles to trade are covered by the TBR. Practices forbidden by WTO rules are naturally included but the regulation (TBR) also stretches to those measures which are not forbidden under WTO agreements but which are nonetheless considered harmful.

The TBR is a key component of the EU's 'new market access strategy', the aim of which is to improve market access for EU firms in third countries by identifying and removing as many illicit trade barriers as possible. The strategy itself it supported by a market access database launched on the Internet in November 1996. This database identifies all of the major obstacles facing EU exporters in the EU's major export markets. At time of writing, the database lists over 1,000 'barriers' as reported by EU exporters, producer groups and trade associations. The inclusion of a problem in the database has generally proved sufficient to initiate a dialogue with the country concerned leading to an acceptable compromise. Where such a dialogue has failed to develop and/or where amicable solutions have proved elusive, cases have been brought under the Trade Barriers Regulation and/or recourse made to the consultation and dispute settlement mechanisms of the WTO.

External relations and the EU's hierarchy of trading preferences

The EU enjoys trading relations with nearly 200 countries, including those like China who remain outside of the structure of the WTO. A characteristic of these relationships is the extent to which the EU treats certain trading partners preferentially and thereby deviates from the basic MFN principle of the WTO. In effect, the EU countries have five types of trade relationship:

1. within the EU customs union itself, international trading relationships which are free from tariffs and from other impediments;

2. with fellow WTO members (on the basis of mutual most-favoured nation treatment);

3. with fellow WTO members (on the basis of preferential terms and agreements);

4. with countries which are not party to the WTO (based on non-preferential agreements);

5. with countries which are not party to the WTO (based on preferential terms).

Discounting the first category of relationships which are not the subject of external EU trade, trade ties with the US and Japan (among a small number of industrialized economies) come under the second category of MFN treatment. Trade ties with other European economies and with most developing economies fall principally into the third category of preferential conditions, although some of the developing markets that receive preferential treatment from the EU remain outside of the WTO framework.

The meaning of this is that the vast majority of the Union's trading partners qualify for some form of preferential treatment. As a consequence, the EU can be said to discriminate in favour of certain countries and to operate a hierarchy of trading preferences. Concerning this hierarchy, it is clear that the EU has tended to group countries under common agreements or to extend a rough equivalence of treatment through like bilateral agreements. It is also clear that the EU does not always expect (or demand) reciprocal concessions from those trading partners to which it extends trading privileges. For example, one-way (non-reciprocal) preferences are extended to a number of developing economies and to former European colonies under the EU's Generalized System of Preferences (GSP) and the EC–ACP Partnership (see subsequently).

EU external trading relations: the preferential agreements

Below, we explore some of the EU's main preferential agreements. Analysis highlights a complex of free trade, association and other preferential agreements concluded by the EU and some of its major trading partners.

The European Economic Area Agreement: Norway, Liechtenstein and Iceland

At the head of the EU's hierarchy of trading preferences are the three parties still outside of the EU that are signatories to the European Economic Area (EEA) Agreement – Norway, Iceland and Liechtenstein. The EEA Agreement was concluded in 1994 between the then EU-12 and six of the seven countries constituting the membership of EFTA in 1994 (Norway, Iceland, Liechtenstein, Austria, Sweden and Finland). Alone amongst the EFTA countries, Switzerland refused to ratify the EEA Agreement. In practical terms, the EEA establishes the mutual application of the four freedoms of the Single European Market as laid down by the Treaty of Rome – the freedom of movement of goods, services, persons and capital. As a consequence, and although special arrangements are established for agriculture, fisheries and transport, the EEA is effectively an enlarged single market and has added services to the industrial goods free trade area established by the 1972–73 free trade agreements between the EC and EFTA. With the accession of new EU members from the ranks of the EEA membership and with the refusal of Switzerland to join the EEA, there may be some doubt over the long-term survival of the EEA as a distinctive economic area. Nonetheless, successive EEA Councils have concluded with affirmation of the agreement's value and functionability. It appears that the EEA will continue to exist and to govern relations with Norway and Iceland in particular.

Customs Union Agreements: Turkey, Malta and Cyprus

The EU is in the process of developing customs union arrangements with three applicant countries – Turkey, Malta and Cyprus. It is to be recalled that, under a customs union, tariffs and quotas are eliminated on trade between members and that they apply a common external tariff on those imports covered under the terms of the customs union agreement. Turkey and the EU formed a customs union on 1 January 1996. The agreement covers industrial and processed agricultural goods. Textiles and agricultural trade are covered by special protocols removing most quota restrictions on Turkish imports. As a part of this customs union, Turkey has adopted the EU's Common External Tariff on most products. As a result, Turkey's tariffs for third countries have generally been lowered. Cyprus and Malta have also made progress towards customs unions with the EU. A customs union between Cyprus and the EU should be completed by the year 2003 and with Malta by 2004. These unions will involve the elimination of all tariffs and quantitative restrictions on all manufactured goods and on a number of agricultural products. Such steps are generally seen as a precursor to the full integration of these countries into the EU.

European Association Agreements: Bulgaria, the Czech Republic, Estonia, Hungary, Latvia, Lithuania, Poland, Romania, Slovakia and Slovenia

Ten European Association Agreements ('Europe Agreements') concluded by the EU member states and reforming CEECs have served to create the beginnings of a free trade area joining the European Union to much of Central and Eastern Europe. The core of these agreements – in commercial terms at least – is the creation of a series of industrial free trade areas, all of which should be in place by the year 2004. Duty and quota free access to the EU market is already in place for industrial items. Residual EU restrictions on steel, coal and textiles imports were removed in 1999. The EAs also provide for some concessions on agricultural trade and for the progressive elimination of barriers to commercial services trade. The fuller content (and lineage) of these agreements is covered in Chapter 7.

Euro-Mediterranean Association Agreements: Algeria, Egypt, Israel, Jordan, Lebanon, Morocco, Palestine, Syria and Tunisia

Somewhat behind the development of the Europe Agreements (and more limited in scope), the EU is making progress towards a series of new association agreements with nine economies in the Mediterranean basin. For a number of years, the EU has extended a series of trading privileges to these states, which have generally benefited from non-reciprocal free access to the EU market for most industrial products and for some raw materials and agricultural products. In Israel's case, trade co-operation was enhanced by conclusion of a special Co-operation Agreement in 1975. The effort now is to upgrade and (to some extent) to harmonize these privileges as a part of a structured effort to create a more cohesive and open Euro-Mediterranean Economic Area (EMEA). Bilateral Association Agreements are to be joined by a series of multilateral activities in the political–security, economic–financial and social–cultural fields. Each of these agreements will provide for a reciprocal free trade area in industrial goods (by 2010) with special arrangements governing trade in agricultural products, fisheries, textiles and clothing.

The Barcelona Declaration of November 1995 states that the association agreements concluded with the Community should be followed by similar agreements on free trade and co-operation among the Mediterranean countries themselves, including Turkey, Malta and Cyprus. The conclusion of such agreements between the twelve 'Med' economies should result in a Euro-Mediterranean FTA of at least twenty-seven countries. The creation of such a vast free trade area will be supported by multi-party efforts to promote private investment in the Mediterranean basin, to develop the region's economic and social infrastructure and to establish suitable regulatory systems. This forms a part of a wide-reaching Euro-Mediterranean Partnership based on political and security dialogue, economic, financial and commercial co-operation, and partnership in cultural, social and human affairs.

ACP–EC Partnership Agreement: seventy-one developing economies

The ACP–EC Partnership Agreement applies to seventy-one developing countries from Africa, the Pacific and the Caribbean region. The Agreement provides non-reciprocal tariff-free access to almost all ACP products on the EU market. For a number of agricultural products, border charges apply but at reductions on standard MFN tariffs. The ACP–EC Agreement builds on the successive Lomé Conventions which have regulated trade between the ACP countries and the EU for nearly thirty years. While Lomé I–IV have promoted the economic growth of the ACP states, their present level of development requires the continuation of preferential treatment.

The Generalized System of Preferences: 145 developing economies

The GSP scheme has long seen the EU grant, without any formal agreement and without any involved reciprocity, a series of generalized duty reductions for imports originating from developing economies. The granting of these reductions (renewed multi-annually) has been to the benefit of over 100 developing countries. Under the present arrangements, tariff reductions vary depending on the type and sensitivity of the product. For very sensitive products (such as textiles and certain agricultural products) the preferential duties are as much as 85% of the CCT duty normally applied. For semisensitive products, the modulated preferential duty will be 35% of the CCT. Many imports are completely exempt from customs duty. In principle, all countries covered by the scheme face the same tariff rate on each product line irrespective of their relative competitiveness or level of development. However, special concessions apply to a small number the 'least advanced' of the developing countries such as Bangladesh, Yemen and Nepal. These countries have complete exemption from duty for industrial products and admission of a wide range of agricultural products under zero-duty rates. It should be noted that when a GSP beneficiary's exports exceed 25% of EU imports in specified sectors, then its GSP benefits will be withdrawn.

EU external trading relations: Japan and the US

It should be clear then that the EU has only a small number of purely MFN suppliers. However, the largest share of imports by value into the EU enters under non-preferential conditions. This reflects the status of countries such as the United States and Japan among the EU's most important trading partners. Relations with these countries are amongst the most important of the EU's external ties. EU–US relations are currently dominated by proposals for a New Transatlantic Marketplace (NTM). An outline of a plan is in place which would see the elimination of mutual industrial tariffs by the year 2010 and the establishment of an EU–US free trade area in services. The NTM plan is being realized under the auspices of a Transatlantic Economic Partnership (TEP) agreed between the EU and US in London in May 1998. The NTM proposal has been carefully designed to be compatible with all multilateral commitments such that the elimination of industrial tariffs by 2010 must be multilateralized. The proposal for bilateral free trade in services is not dependent on multilateral agreement to completely liberalize global services trade. Rather, the proposals are intended to achieve a bilateral platform for free trade which would set an example for others. In the context of the WTO, the EU and the US have also worked together to conclude the Information Technology Agreement, the Basic Telecommunication Services Agreement and the Financial Services Agreement. These agreements build on the GATS deal secured under the Uruguay Round and liberalize large portions of international trade in services. Despite such co-operation, EU–US relations have always been characterized by dispute over trade questions. In recent years, argument has surrounded the extraterritorial effects of US trade legislation (e.g. the Helms-Burton Act on Cuba), aerospace subsidies, hormone-treated beef and genetically modified food products.

The relationship between Japan and the EU has historically been more difficult. An imbalance of trade (in favour of Japan), EU controls on Japanese imports and innumerable obstacles faced by European firms wishing to export to Japan have all been at the heart of longstanding tensions. Although market access remains a thorny issue, bilateral co-operation has developed on multilateral trade issues and the EU and Japan have strengthened a bilateral dialogue on trade and investment barriers. Subsequent sections add a statistical profile to this trading relationship and that with the United States.

Member states' trade

The importance of international trade from a European perspective cannot be overstated. The European Commission estimates that between 10 and 12 million jobs depend directly on exports which, in turn, provide 9% of the Union's wealth. The European Union is itself the world's largest trade grouping. Even discounting internal trade between the member states, it is responsible for approximately one-fifth of world trade in merchandise goods (see Table 12.1) and over one-quarter of international services transactions.

The trade of member states is dominated (in value terms) by merchandise trade consisting of trade in raw materials, energy and manufactured goods. In 1998, according to the Eurostat-Comext database, the EU's export trade in merchandise goods (excluding intra-EU exports) totalled €731.58 billion. The EU's largest (individual) export markets were the USA (22% share of EU total), Switzerland (7.8%), Japan (4.3%), Poland (3.8%), Norway (3.4%), Turkey (3.0%), Russia (2.9%) and China (2.4%). In the same year (1998), the EU countries imported €712.37 billion worth of goods, establishing a merchandise trade surplus of just under €20 billion. The biggest exporters to the EU were the USA (21.3% of EU total), Japan (9.2%), Switzerland (6.9%), China (5.9%), Norway (4.1%), Russia (3.2%), Taiwan (2.6%) and Poland (2.3%).

In recent years, the EU's external trade performance has steadily improved. A peak ECU 49 billion surplus in 1997 concluded five successive years of positive trade performance. Between 1988 and 1992, the EU recorded major trade deficits, with a low of ECU 70.2 billion in 1991. This improvement in external trade performance can be explained by a number of factors including the real depreciation of many EU

Table 12.1 Leading exporters and importers in world merchandise trade (excluding intra-EU trade), 1998

World exports				World imports		
Rank	Share (%)	Value ($bn) 1998	Country/Grouping	Rank	Share (%)	Value ($bn) 1998
1	20.3	813.8	European Union	2	19.1	801.4
2	17.0	683.0	USA	1	22.5	944.6
3	9.7	388.0	Japan	3	6.7	280.5
4	5.3	214.3	Canada	4	4.9	205.0
5	4.6	183.8	China	6	3.3	140.2
6	4.3	174.1	Hong Kong	5	4.5	188.7
7	3.3	133.2	Korea	10	2.2	93.3
8	2.9	117.5	Mexico	7	3.1	128.9
9	2.7	109.9	Taiwan	8	2.5	104.2
10	2.7	109.8	Singapore	9	2.4	101.5

Source: World Trade Organization.

currencies, relatively weak domestic demand (causing exports to rise faster than imports), high-productivity growth and the opening up of new export markets (e.g. Russia, China and the CEE markets). A narrowing in the EU's trade surplus in 1998 reflected the economic and financial crises that beset the Asian markets during this year.

Table 12.2 disaggregates the merchandise trade performance of the EU states providing a ranking of individual (national) exporters and incorporating intra-EU exports. The list includes seven of the EU-15 and compares their individual (national) performance with other producer-exporters over the last twenty years. It is interesting to note that the top six countries have not changed their ranking throughout this time but that newly industrialized countries such as China, Singapore, Mexico and Malaysia have made dramatic trade gains.

Trade in services is of major importance to the EU economies. The EU is the world leader in this field and a list of the world's top ten commercial services exporters features no less than seven EU states (see Table 12.3). Together, the EU states are responsible for 45% of all global services transactions, a figure which falls to 26% if intra-EU trade is stripped out. By comparison, and as can be seen in Table 12.3, the United States' share is just 18% and Japan's just 4% (based on WTO estimates for 1998). The EU's capabilities in this field reflect the maturity of its leading economies (each of which has a developed service sector) and the openness of EU markets. Its domestic services market is one of the most integrated and lightly regulated in the world. It is unsurprising, therefore, that the EU has been a driving force behind the efforts to realize an open global market in services including computer and information activities, finance and insurance, transport and telecommunications. Development on the General Agreement on Trade in Services (GATS), which established a set of basic rules and obligations regarding world trade in services, is

Table 12.2 Leading exporters in world merchandise trade 1979, 1989 and 1998

Rank				1998
1979	1989	1998	Exporters	Value ($bn)
1	1	1	USA	683.0
2	2	2	*Germany*	539.7
3	3	3	Japan	388.0
4	4	4	*France*	307.0
5	5	5	*United Kingdom*	272.7
6	6	6	*Italy*	240.9
10	7	7	Canada	214.3
8	9	8	*Netherlands*	198.2
34	14	9	China	183.8
27	11	10	Hong Kong	174.1
11	10	11	*Belgium-Luxembourg*	171.7
29	13	12	Korea	133.2
37	20	13	Mexico	117.5
22	12	14	Taiwan	109.9
32	17	15	Singapore	109.8

Source: World Trade Organization

crucial to the long-term interests (and growth) of many EU businesses. Accordingly, the EU has been a major influence in the conclusion of post-Uruguay agreements in the fields of telecommunications, information technologies and financial services. These agreements mean that WTO rules will apply to over 90% of global trade in telecommunications, IT, banking and insurance, with significant progress towards tariff reductions.

The EU's competitive advantage now rests heavily with a number of commercial services (transport services, travel services, financial and business services especially) and with a number of high value added and high-skill manufactures such as chem-

Table 12.3 Leading exporters in commercial services, 1998

Rank	Share (%)	Value ($bn) 1998	Exporter
1	18.1	233.6	USA
2	7.7	99.5	*United Kingdom*
3	6.1	78.6	*France*
4	5.9	75.7	*Germany*
5	5.4	70.1	*Italy*
6	4.7	60.8	Japan
7	3.7	48.3	*Netherlands*
8	3.7	48.0	*Spain*
9	2.7	34.7	*Belgium-Luxembourg*
10	2.6	34.2	Hong Kong

Source: World Trade Organization

icals, aircraft, cars and machinery. In several commercial services, machinery and transport equipment markets, chemicals, pharmaceuticals, food and beverages, the EU maintains a healthy trade surplus. Each country holds a presence in most sectors but is relatively specialized. Among the four large EU states, the UK is relatively specialised in financial services, telecommunications, fuels, chemicals, printing and publishing. Germany's strengths rest with engineering, chemicals, plastics and metals, industrial and transport equipment (including motor vehicle production). France's comparative advantage rests primarily with the food and beverages sector, machinery and transportation equipment, chemicals and glass. It is also a major exporter of wheat and dairy products. Italy specializes in cement and clay products, clothing and textiles, production machinery, motor vehicles and food products. Each country retains a presence in most industrial sectors but specializes in narrow product categories within each industry and with concentrations on high value added segments. Elsewhere in the EU, other patterns of trade specialization include the Netherlands in electrical machinery, refining and industrial chemicals, Belgium in iron and steel, Portugal in textiles, Spain in leather goods, Ireland in food, and Sweden in wood products, paper and furniture. The EU runs a significant trade deficit in raw materials, agricultural produce, energy, textiles and clothing.

The emergence of regional trade blocs

The growth and consolidation of the EU as a regional trade grouping must be observed in terms of a trend towards 'regionalized' economic unification in the new global economy. In this view, the EU bloc is seen as just one (albeit perhaps the most important) of a number of regional economic groupings (REGs) including the North American Free Trade Agreement (NAFTA), MERCOSUR and ASEAN. Various economic groupings and the degree of economic integration pertaining to each group in 1999 are shown in Table 12.4. The levels and forms of economic integration have been characterized in Chapter 3. It may be recalled that a *free trade area (FTA)* sees a group of countries agree to removal all trade barriers – tariffs, quotas and non-tariff barriers. Each country retains discretion in establishing trade barriers with non-members. The next stage of integration is a *customs union* in which as well as adhering to the removal of all trade barriers, members have a common external policy on international trade with non-members. *Common markets* are those which, along with the removal of trade barriers and the adoption of a common external policy, also feature additional provisions to encourage trade and integration through the free mobility of factors of production. Finally, an *economic union* is formed when the individual member countries agree to forgo unilateral control over economic-decision-making and policy. Characteristically this involves a unified monetary system, a common fiscal and monetary policy, and a unified international trade policy. With the realization of a single currency in Europe, the development of the EU from a common market to an economic union has been brought much closer.

Liberalization of trade between countries within these blocs promotes trade (trade creation) and supports efficient patterns of specialization. Conversely, the expansion of trade within the bloc may potentially take place at the expense of

Table 12.4 Major regional economic groupings (REGs), 1999.

Group	Type	Members	Population (million)	GDP (PPP) $bn
MERCOSUR	Customs union	Argentina Brazil Paraguay Uruguay	217	1,457
Association of South East Asian Nations (ASEAN)	Free Trade Area	Brunei Indonesia Malaysia Singapore Philippines Thailand Cambodia Laos Myanmar Vietnam	500	1,759
European Union (EU)	Common Market	Austria Belgium Denmark Finland France Germany Greece Ireland Italy Luxembourg The Netherlands Portugal Spain Sweden UK	376	7,752
North American Free Trade Agreement (NAFTA)	Free Trade Area	Canada Mexico USA	403.9	9,214

Note: GDP and population figures calculated from national statistical entries. Population figures, latest available estimate. GDP figures, estimates for 1998. GDP dollar estimates for all countries are derived from purchasing power parity (PPP) calculations rather than from conversions at official currency exchange rates.
Source: CIA World Factbook 1999

trade with non-member countries (trade diversion). The balance between these effects determines to what extent the creation of a grouping is beneficial to its members and to world welfare. Many observers have concluded that, on balance, the creation of the EU has had a beneficial effect on world welfare. Trade creation effects have been apparent within the EU but, perhaps more significantly, the creation of the single market has also catalysed inward trade from non-EU members. Although a degree of trade diversion has been apparent (for example, the adverse effects felt by the Caribbean sugar industry following the UK's entry into the EEC in 1973) its extent has been limited by a lowering of tariffs (through GATT) and through preferential trade deals with former colonies and non-EU member regions. Despite this, the enlargement of the Union and the expansion of the EU's preferential network of free-trade agreements, which continues, is bound to give some concern to MFN trading partners in relation to potential trade diversion.

The global Triad

The growing trend towards the development of economic unions is having a powerful effect on the shape of international trade and investment. Ohmae (1985) argues that the economic world is now dominated by three major markets – Japan, the US and EU – each of whom he saw as dominating a regional economic theatre. Ohmae labelled these markets 'the Triad'. Any assessment of international trade and investment data would support this conclusion. Japan, the US and the EU account for 47% of all world merchanise exports (excluding intra-EU trade flows) and for three-quarters of the world's accumulated stock of FDI. In 1997, 50.5% of inward FDI flows went to the Triad economies who were responsible for 75.5% of all outward FDI in the world economy (see Table 12.5).

Over 75% of production and sales in automotives, chemicals, petrochemicals,

Table 12.5 Regional distribution of FDI flows, 1994–97 (percentage shares)

Region–country	Inflows				Outflows			
	1994	1995	1996	1997	1994	1995	1996	1997
Developed countries	58.2	63.9	57.9	58.2	85.0	86.9	85.1	84.8
Western Europe	32.3	37.1	29.6	28.7	47.0	49.4	50.6	46.2
European Union	29.5	35.3	27.4	27.0	42.4	45.2	45.3	42.4
Other Western Europe	2.8	1.8	2.2	1.7	4.6	4.3	5.3	3.7
United States	18.6	17.7	22.6	22.7	25.8	26.1	22.5	27.0
Japan	0.4	–	0.1	0.8	6.4	6.4	7.0	6.1
Developing countries	39.3	31.9	38.5	37.2	15.0	12.9	14.8	14.4
Africa	2.3	1.6	1.4	1.2	0.2	0.2	0.1	0.3
Latin America and the Caribbean	11.8	9.6	13.0	14.0	1.8	0.7	0.7	2.1
Developing Europe	0.2	0.1	0.3	0.2	–	–	–	0.1
Asia	25.0	20.3	23.7	21.7	12.9	12.1	14.0	12.0
West Asia	0.6	-0.2	0.1	0.5	0.4	0.2	0.3	0.1
Central Asia	0.4	0.5	0.6	0.7	–	–	–	–
South, East and South-East Asia	24.0	20.1	23.0	20.6	12.5	11.9	14.2	11.8
The Pacific	–	0.2	0.1	0.1	–	–	–	–
Central and Eastern Europe	2.4	4.3	3.7	4.6	0.1	0.1	0.2	0.8
World	100	100	100	100	100	100	100	100

Source: World Investment Report 1999 (UNCTAD/WIR, 1999)

steel and other major industrial sectors takes place inside the Triad. There is no doubt that these economies dominate the global economy and anchor dynamic regional markets.

Considering the volumes of trade and investment now concentrated in the Triad it is unsurprising that such concentration of economic activity is changing the strategic focus of many multinational enterprises. Most MNEs focus attention on attaining a global balance in their business activities but interest in diverse international portfolios must now be balanced with the 'need' for competitive positioning in the three Triad markets. Part of the reasoning for this is gaining access to the largest industrial and consumer markets in the world as well as benefiting from regionally initiated R&D programmes either internal to the firm or through government initiatives. For smaller firms from the developed world, the challenges are no less significant. Concentration on consolidating business or securing a broader position in the home region rather than attempting to expand on a global scale may theoretically be the most attractive option. This permits exploitation of the advantages being offered by greater integration in home regions and will generally entail less risk. Nevertheless, links with non-bloc members and the potential rewards of business in other markets may encourage many companies to look outside of their regions. This reinforces the need for openness between the trading blocs.

A characteristic of the Triad is the high level of trade and investment conducted across and between the members. Figure 12.2 gives some indication of the intra-Triad trade flows for 1998 (merchandise trade only). The US shows a trade deficit with both the EU and Japan (which has led to much of the US's concerns over access to European and Japanese markets). While the EU enjoys a small trade surplus with the US, it continues to run a sizeable deficit with Japan.

Tables 12.6 and 12.7 highlight the direct investment stocks and flows linking the EU with Japan and the US. The data highlight the scale of the investment relationships between these partners, cumulative stocks of cross-investment and recent (annual) FDI flows. There are relatively few restrictions on inward investment in the US and EU. Although investment barriers in Japan have long been a

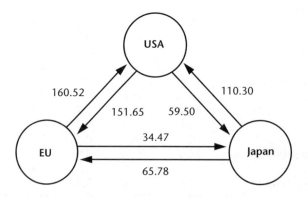

Figure 12.2 Intra-Triad merchandise flows, 1998 (in billion Euros)
Source: EuroStat-Comext; UN-Comtrade

Table 12.6 EU foreign direct investment with the United States (billion Euros)

	1995	1996	1997		1995	1996	1997
Inflows	28,579	25,152	27,753	Outflows	31,616	28,160	53,583
Share of EU total	*67.8*	*64.3*	*59.1*	*Share of EU total*	*52.0*	*39.9*	*45.7*
Inward stocks	189,310	210,585	270,100	Outward stocks	207,181	232,967	298,167
US share on total EU				*US share on total EU*			
inward stocks	*51.3*	*49.9*	*53.9*	*outward stocks*	*43.9*	*42.9*	*45.3*

Source: European Commission, 1999

Table 12.7. EU foreign direct investment with Japan (billion Euros)

	1995	1996	1997		1995	1996	1997
Inflows	944	324	2,371	Outflows	1,243	2,507	1,137
Share of EU total	*2.2*	*0.8*	*5.0*	*Share of EU total*	*2.0*	*3.6*	*1.0*
Inward stocks	28,160	31,915	35,334	Outward stocks	11,047	12,062	12,005
Japan share on total				*Japan share on total*			
EU inward stocks	*7.7*	*7.6*	*7.1*	*EU outward stocks*	*2.3*	*2.2*	*1.8*

Source: European Commission, 1999

problem for many Western firms, Japan is opening up to foreign investment and tackling many of the legal impediments to inward investment. Increasing foreign investments is now evident in Japan's banking, manufacturing, and telecom industries.

The data in Table 12.6 highlight a stock of cross-investment between Europe and the US exceeding €500 billion. This is the world's largest investment relationship. The inward stock of US investment in the EU had reached €210 billion by the end of 1996, a major share of all US FDI assets abroad (€620 billion). The creation of the Single Market clearly had a marked impact on levels of US business activity within the EU. For American (and Canadian) firms, penetration of this vast and integrating market was increasingly seen as essential to a company's competitive position in the European and global marketplace. As with Japan, fears that Europe would become a 'fortress' following the establishment of the Single European Market were also a reason why American investment increased in the region around the period of the IMP. A more recent stimulus has been provided by the moves towards European Monetary Union. Present levels of US investment represent approximately one-half of total EU inward investment stocks. Key investors include Ford, General Motors, IBM and Hewlett Packard. Traditionally, much of the investment activity of these and other firms has been concentrated in a small number of EU countries (France, Germany, the Netherlands and the UK).

European companies are the number one international investors in forty-one US states, and rank number two in the remaining nine states (http://www.eabc.org/). EU investment in the US is valued at €298 billion (1997) with the US garnering 45% of the EU's total outward investment in 1997. European Union statistics show that annual outward investment flows into the US economy are rising dramatically.

Although Japanese investment in Europe remains relatively low compared with US levels (just 7% of total EU inward investment stocks), levels have grown significantly since the 1970s. In the 1980s, external restrictions imposed on Japanese exports encouraged many Japanese firms to invest inside the EU. Rather than face external barriers, technology companies such as Sony and Hitachi decided to locate their production within the EU and to bypass the barriers altogether. Increasingly, direct investment was seen as a means not only of servicing local markets and of building global networks (a traditional view amongst pioneering investors) but of avoiding European trade barriers. Europe's Internal Market Programme (and fear of exclusion from SEM benefits) provided a further catalyst to Japanese investment in the late 1980s and early 1990s. Throughout this period, the stock of Japanese investment in the EU increased dramatically as Japanese firms positioned themselves to exploit insider advantages and as vertically integrated investment took off. By 1993 (and the completion of the SEM), the inward stock of Japanese investment in the EU exceeded ECU 20 billion. Over a ten-year period, the proportion of Japanese outward direct investment flows going to Europe had more than doubled. By the end of 1996, the inward stock of Japanese investment in the EU market had reached €31.9 billion, a significant proportion of all Japanese FDI assets abroad (€206 billion).

While Japanese investment has been controversial (raising fears over the plight of domestic manufacturers), it has generally been welcomed. FDI creates new jobs, enhances the capital stock or production capacity of host countries and offers a higher tax revenue for host governments. Throughout the EU, areas with high unemployment and declining industries have been bolstered by major industrial investments by Japanese firms. This is particular true of UK regions such as the North-East, Wales and the Midlands, all of which have benefited from major investment projects. For example, the Nissan plant in the North-East of England and the Toyota plant in the Midlands have provided direct and indirect employment opportunities (and altered status) for two ailing UK regions. Add to this the contribution of Japanese exports to the UK's weak balance of trade figures, and it is clear why Britain not only accepts Japanese investment but actively encourages it.

The growth in FDI

The explosion in foreign direct investment has deepened the internationalization of the world economy. The sheer volume of foreign direct investment has mushroomed from an annual amount of some $30 billion in 1975 to $640 billion in 1998 (UNCTAD, 1999, PR2820). Such figures make it clear that, by simply concentrating on international trade flows, the changing shape of the global economy cannot be fully captured. There is no doubt that the developed countries continue to dominate the FDI scene. These countries have more than two-thirds of the world's inward FDI stock and 90% of the world's outside FDI stock (UNCTAD, 1998, p. 8). Analysis has already attested to the leadership role in global FDI played by European, Japanese and American investors. It is clear, however, that many developing countries are making efforts to create favourable conditions for FDI, changing investment regulatory regimes and taking steps to liberalize industries such as telecommunications, energy and banking (UNCTAD, 1998, p. 12). In this respect China and the Latin American countries have succeeded in attracting record levels of inward FDI. Investment incentives have also been strengthened in many countries as multiple states look to compete for FDI. Recent statistics suggest that developing countries are now attracting nearly 40% of annual inward FDI flows. Developing countries now host a third of global inward FDI stock.

European business: competing in the global marketplace

The global presence of European business

A profile of the world's largest 200 corporations shows that many corporations in Europe have established a strong competitive position in the new global economy. Of the world's 200 biggest non-financial corporations (as measured by global turnover) seventy-six are currently located in Western Europe (sixty-eight in the EU). Germany (twenty-three), France (nineteen), the UK (thirteen), Switzerland (six), the Netherlands (six) and Italy (five) provide a base to many of these firms. By comparison, the US provides headquarters to seventy-four of these corporations and Japan forty-one (source: *Le Monde Diplomatique*, December 1999). By an alternative measure, a number of the world's top corporations as measured by market capitalization – Deutsche Telekom, Nokia and Royal Dutch/Shell – are 'European' firms. Table 12.8 provides a global list and ranking by total revenue. Although the presence of European firms in this league table is hardly overwhelming, DaimlerChrysler, Royal Dutch/Shell Group, AXA, BP Amoco and VW all make the list. Nestlé, Royal Dutch/Shell, BP, BMW, Deutsche Bank, L'Oreal, SAP and Nokia are also among the world's most respected companies based on surveys published by *Forbes Magazine* and the *Financial Times*. Attributes that characterize these firms include strong leadership, quality of products and services, strong and consistent profit performance, and globalized activities.

At an industry level, banking and insurance, chemicals, pharmaceuticals, electrical engineering, IT, telecoms, food and beverages, metals, motor vehicles and financial services have emerged as Europe's strongest business sectors. Global indus-

Table 12.8 World's top twenty corporations by global revenue (2000)

Search Rank	Company	Revenues ($m)
1	General Motors	176,558.00
2	Wal-Mart Stores	166,809.00
3	Exxon Mobil	163,881.00
4	Ford Motor	162,558.00
5	Daimler-Chrysler	159,985.67
6	Mitsui	118,555.21
7	Mitsubishi	117,765.64
8	Toyota Motor	111,670.92
9	General Electric	115,630.00
10	Itochu	109,068.87
11	Royal Dutch/Shell Group	105,366.00
12	Sumitomo	95,701.61
13	Nippon Telegraph & Telephone	93,591.68
14	Marubeni	91,807.42
15	AXA	87,645.72
16	Intl. Business Machines	87,548.00
17	BP Amoco	83,566.00
18	Citigroup	82,005.00
19	Volkswagen	80,072.74
20	Nippon Life Insurance	78,515.14

Source: Fortune Magazine

try top tens for these sectors include some of Europe's largest and most successful corporations.

European success stories are easy to find. Nokia (Finland) is now the world's largest manufacturer of mobile phone handsets, challenged hard by Sweden's Ericsson group. Its rise to prominence in the mobile telecommunications market is considered in Case Study 12.2. Vodafone AirTouch, formed from the merger at the beginning of 1999 of Vodafone of the UK and AirTouch of the US, has now become the world's largest telecoms company. German software company SAP (studied in Chapter 4) is outperforming all comers in the global market for business software. These are just a number of 'European' firms achieving success in globalized industries. As commented by Barnard (1998):

> Europe has closed the gap with the US in other important sectors, such as automobiles, aerospace, energy, and financial services. A series of transatlantic deals [like the Vodafone–AirTouch merger], including Daimler Benz's purchase of Chrysler and BP's of Amoco, is evidence of a more muscular corporate Europe.

This observation highlights the prominent part played by European business in increased worldwide M&A activity. The United Nations Trade and Development Conference reports (UNCTAD, 1999, pp. 18–19):

CASE STUDY 12.2 Nokia leads in mobile phone market

It is the biggest company in one of the world's fastest-growing industries. Not only is Nokia selling three of every ten mobile handsets being made – it overtook Motorola last year to become the world's biggest mobile phone maker – but its market share is rising fast.

The dramatic success gives the Finnish group, led by chief executive Jorma Ollila, an obvious claim to membership of any league ranking the world's most respected companies. According to one of the respondents to the FT/PwC survey, the company has quite simply 'changed the future'.

Success has happened in less than a decade. Moreover, it has happened in a country, on Europe's outer fringes, which has a population of just 5 million and where the traditional industry – pulp and paper – is anything but high tech. Luck has played a part too: nobody quite realized a decade ago that the mobile phone would move so quickly from being an expensive status symbol to a popular mass-market product. The group's decision to concentrate on the GSM segment was also a fortuitous one, because GSM has become the *de facto* world standard.

Back in 1992, shortly after Mr Ollila took over as chief executive, he wrote down the four phrases which he saw as the key to the group's future. They were 'telecom-orientated', 'global', 'focus' and 'value-added'.

Nobody can say he did not stick to his own brief. Focus meant turning a Nokia from a sprawling conglomerate, with a promising mobile business, into a dedicated mobile phone company. Out went much of 'the baggage' – chemicals, tyres, cables and television-set manufacturing were among the businesses offloaded during the early 1990s.

On the telecommunication side, the company has succeeded in establishing a strong brand that is recognized throughout the world. There may even have been an initial benefit from some customers thinking it was a Japanese company. In fact, the name comes from a town in southern Finland.

The group has outstripped its rivals, Motorola and Ericsson, because it has allied engineering excellence with great marketing flair. Analysts say that it has usually produced more fashionable, reliable and user-friendly handsets than its competitors.

Moreover, it has kept at the forefront of innovation, shortening product cycles, and launching new models just when the margins on old ones are starting to dive. It has a consistent record of increasing volumes by more than enough to offset falling prices. In 1999, sales growth will be more than 40%.

Also, the company has been able to manage its growth – staff numbers have grown from 25,000 in 1993 to 44,000 today – and bureaucracy has not been allowed to stifle the culture of innovation.

If success is measured by market capitalization, Nokia can have few equals. In January 1994, it was worth just €3.5 billion. In mid-November 1999, the figure had risen to €142 billion. The company is Europe's fifth largest and singlehandedly accounts for more than 50% of the Helsinki stock exchange and a substantial chunk of Finnish GDP growth.

Analysts, not surprisingly, are fulsome in their praise. 'Nokia has a 30% and growing share of the handsets market and more than 60% of the profit in the sector. It is incredibly efficient, with the best products, the best brand and the best logistics', says Lauri Rosendahl, analyst at Aros Securities in Helsinki.

So far, the company has defied predictions that its rivals will catch up. So far, it has managed growth. And so far, the US Internet giants have stayed out of the mobile arena. But even more advanced technologies are on their way, rivals are snapping at its heels and living up to the market's high-placed expectations will be an ever more daunting challenge.

Source: Financial Times, 7 December 1999

571

Table 12.9 The ten largest cross-border M&A deals in 1998

Deal	Value ($bn)
British Petroleum (United Kingdom) – Amoco Corp. (United States)	55.0
Daimler-Benz AG (Germany) – Chrysler Corp. (United States)	40.5
ZENECA Group PLC (United Kingdom) – Astra AB (Sweden)	31.8
Hoechst AG (Germany) – Rhône-Poulenc SA (France)	21.2
Scottish Power PLC (United Kingdom) – Pacific Corp. (United States)	12.6
Total SA (France) – Petrofina SA (Belgium)	11.5
Universal Studios (United States) – PolyGram NV (Netherlands)	10.3
Deutsche Bank AG (Germany) – Bankers Trust NY Corp. (United States)	9.1
Northern Telecom Ltd (Canada) – Bay Networks Inc. (United States)	9.0
Texas Utilities Co. (United States) – Energy Group PLC (United Kingdom)	8.8

Source: UNCTAD World Investment Report: 1999 (UNCTAD/WIR, 1999)

> The number and value of total cross-border M&As has increased dramatically in recent years, with the absolute value of all cross-border M&A sales and purchases amounting to $544 billion in 1998 ... In 1998, there were 89 'mega' cross-border M&A deals, each with more than $1 billion in transaction value, compared to 35 such deals in 1995, 45 in 1996 and 58 in 1997.

Nine of the ten largest cross-border deals in 1998 involved at least one European party (see Table 12.9). Many of these transactions highlight the rapid growth of European MNEs and aggressive expansion strategies.

For all this 'flexing of corporate muscle', it is clear, however, that many of Europe's leading companies remain rooted to their home markets. Measures of foreign assets, sales and employment in the overall activities of European MNEs evidence a continuing bias to home (and neighbouring European) environments. Highly transnationalized companies such as Nestlé, Unilever, Philips Electronics, Glaxo-Wellcome, Electrolux, and Cable and Wireless (with a high ratio of foreign to total assets and sales) provide some exception to this rule but European sales and assets still dominate. Of course such measures provide only a partial view of the engagement of European firms in global markets but the extent to which many European MNEs are regional rather than global giants should be noted, not least as their performance may suffer more dramatically with a downturn in just one regional economy. Excitement over the involvement of European firms in 'mega' M&A deals must also be tempered by realization that consolidation with other firms is often viewed as the only way to maintain a footing in competitive markets. In industries such as oil, telecommunications and utilities, European firms have tended to conclude cross-border M&As as a means of defence. While such deals provide a way to improve the competitiveness of many businesses in France, Britain etc., they also exposes the weakness of even large 'national players' in increasingly globalized markets. There are also a number of weaknesses within European industry which may hinder the competitiveness of European business in the face of global competition and their ability to internationalize (European Commission, IP/99/33):

- Specialization remains underdeveloped in sectors with high growth and highly differentiated products.

- European enterprises form relatively few alliances in advanced technology areas.

- The level of R&D spending in terms of EU GDP is still below that of its principal global economic partners.

- The EU suffers from relatively high production, capital and labour costs.

- European enterprises put very few joint research projects in place.

- Small companies do not easily become medium-size enterprises and medium-sized companies find it even more difficult to become large, world-scale actors.

Globalization as opportunity

Whatever the threats (and the barriers to success), globalization must be seen as an opportunity for European business to seize. In particular, through competing in international markets and through building global presence, European firms can secure huge rewards. Govindarajan and Gupta (1999b) detail four main opportunities that a global presence offers:

1. *Increased market share.* Global presence means being present in multiple countries. This creates clear opportunities to expand the market. In particular, by operating inside of foreign market environments and by acquiring knowledge of local needs and tastes, firms can maximize their local market responsiveness, adapting products, services and processes etc. Of course, firms may sometimes achieve global success by offering standard products across countries but local adaptation of products will expand the market by capturing those customers whose needs are better met by tailored products (1999b, p. 43).

2. *Economies of global scale.* A primary effect of building global presence is that companies enjoy a larger scale of operations. This can create cost savings and larger revenues provided that the company systematically converts larger scale into economies of scale. Exploiting economies of scale can result in the distribution of fixed costs over larger volume, a reduction in capital and operating costs per unit, an increase in purchasing power over suppliers and the creation of critical mass in selected activities (1999b, p. 44).

3. *Location economies.* Through global presence firms can exploit location economies, locating value creation activities (production, marketing, distribution etc.) in optimal locations. By tapping the optimal locations for each activity, companies can enhance their performance (developing centres of excellence), and reduce their costs and exposure to political and currency risks (1999b, pp. 44–5).

4. *Greater knowledge.* Every subsidiary or foreign business unit acquires unique knowledge. Global companies, where suitably configured, can benefit from multidirectional knowledge transfers, aggregating and incorporating new ideas and information from many different sources (1999b, pp. 45–6).

Of course, attaining global presence (and more importantly, turning that presence into global competitive advantage) requires a company to have developed some form of international capability and expertise. In many cases, this competence will have been developed in the regional marketplace following initial efforts at international expansion. In the following section, we step back to consider the basic features of internationalization and some of the incentives for firms to internationalize their business activities–strategies.

The internationalization process

We may define internationalization as the process of increasing involvement in international operations. A variety of external stimuli can push and pull a company along the path of internationalizing their operations, some of which we highlight below:

- adverse domestic market conditions such as growing competition, declining sales, market saturation or recession;
- overproduction or excess capacity compelling the company to sell the product abroad or face wasting resources;
- the existence of overseas markets (and rents);
- the desire to diversify risk and therefore decrease the company's dependency on any one market;
- the prospect of increasing production in order to achieve economies of scale;
- the attempt to lower cost factors of production (i.e. wages) and/or to access natural resources;
- favourable developments in exchange rates, so as to make it cheaper to export and/or to invest abroad;
- scope for profitable partnerships and collaborations with entities in foreign markets.

Additional stimuli relate to the internal environment of the firm. For example, the information, experience and perceptions of management will profoundly influence the extent to which a company may develop an international strategy and the form and direction of that strategy itself. Managers with previous experience of international operations or with a clear view of competition and opportunities in international markets are more likely to prompt the domestically oriented firm to re-examine its position and to internationalize.

It should be recognized that firms can develop presence in international markets (and the means of servicing those markets) through a variety of strategies – exporting, franchising, joint ventures, alliances, licensing, subsidiary operations and cross-border acquisitions to name but a few. These methods of initiating and undertaking business in and across foreign environments have been profiled elsewhere in this book and further outline is avoided here. However, international stages theory provides an important perspective on foreign expansion as yet unaddressed. According to this theory (see Johanson and Vahlne, 1977), the internationalization of the firm typically follows a logical and sequential process with an enterprise developing in foreign markets on an incremental basis. The enterprise passes from one stage to another – i.e. from exporting via the use of a foreign agent, to a sales subsidiary, to the establishment of a foreign production subsidiary – as it acquires more and more international experience. Progressively, the enterprise involves itself in deeper foreign market engagements and heavier resource commitments.

International stages theory is supported by many studies which have shown both small and large enterprises passing through distinct and gradual stages during the development of their international business operations. However, there is no conclusive evidence to suggest that all firms do (or should) follow this path and the international stages theory is clearly deterministic. The internationalization process is not necessarily sequential and, as discussed in Chapter 8, firms may simultaneously employ different market entry strategies (exporting, joint ventures, direct investments etc.) at the same time in the same country. Each process of internationalization will be unique and will be conditioned by the specific objectives, attributes and opportunities confronting the organization.

Forms of international strategy and organization

There are also different approaches to being international, some of which were alluded to in Chapter 8. Bartlett and Ghoshal (1989) have differentiated between four basic strategies and organizational characteristics, each involving different configurations of assets and a unique role for overseas operations. Some of these forms (i.e. the global) are suited only to organizations that undertake business across many national frontiers. Nonetheless, an examination of the four basic forms advanced here provides a useful insight into how businesses may structure themselves as international operators and direct their strategies:

International exporter – firms whose direct presence in foreign markets is limited to sales and marketing. There are no country-based production points/subsidiaries, just sales and marketing affiliates. This international strategy (form) enables a domestic firm to become international quickly and with little capital investment.

Multinational (multidomestic) – firms pursuing a multinational or 'multidomestic' strategy focus on local responsiveness, extensively customizing both their product offering and their marketing strategy in individual foreign market environments. Each country is treated as an independent market and nationally responsive strategies are pursued through semi-autonomous subsidiaries dedicated to meeting local demands and conditions. This strategy/form works best when conditions are diverse among countries and where buyers insist on highly customized products.

Global – centralized companies producing standardized products for sale around the world. Global firms think in terms of creating products for a world market and manufacturing them on a global scale so that they can reap the economies of scale. Subsidiaries are tightly controlled and are required to implement parent company strategies. Business and functional strategies are integrated across different countries so that the business achieves worldwide leverage through the integration of business units and processes. This strategy and form works best when great similarities in products and buyer requirements exist among countries and where competitive conditions across internal markets are linked.

Transnational – the transnational represents a truly global enterprise combining the best aspects of global and multidomestic forms. Competences and resources are dispersed and integrated into an interdependent network of worldwide operations in which the concept of the corporate centre has reduced meaning and in which many of a company's value-added activities take place outside of the 'home country'. The transnational model is often seen as an attempt to capture global specialization and scale advantages and to maximize local responsiveness.

Recently, the organization and strategies of multinational enterprises have begun converging around the global–local, or 'transnational' model, 'combining the best aspects of each approach' (Bryan and Fraser, 1999). The trend reflects the new shape of the global economy/competition which requires growth on a scale never before envisioned and the pursuit of simultaneous targets: local market adaptation; economies of scope; location optimization; and economies of global scale.

Conclusion

The creation of the Single European Market is one of the most spectacular attempts at promoting economic integration the world has ever seen. At each stage of its development the world has been able to see the opportunities and threats posed by changing legislation and policy and in response, establish codes of practice for reacting to and living with, this union of countries. It is partly the public nature of the developments and partly the economic interdependence of countries in the developed world which have seen proposed responses run the gamut from reactionary moves to regional integration (see NAFTA) to increased levels of foreign direct investment. Although there remain doubts about how the Single Market integrates with the broader world economy, fears of a 'fortress Europe' have slowly dissipated. Today, the EU is recognized less as a protectionist bloc and more as a rejuventated and outward-looking trading area.

Asian and American firms are keen to establish a presence in this market as one of the three major economic centres now dominating the world economy. For many, presence in the EU market is critical to the development and success of global business strategies. For indigenous European firms, the new European market provides massive opportunities, albeit opportunities increasingly shared by rivals from outside of Europe. Nonetheless, enormous scope for market development lies outside of Europe (in the Americas, Asia and the rest of the developing world) and most large businesses are looking to pursue some form of global strategy. The challenges in this process are enormous, but with a truly global strategy, European firms can gain competitive advantage and sustain that advantage through innovation and learning.

Review questions for Chapter 12

1. What do you understand by the term 'globalization'?

2. In what ways does 'globalization' impinge on European markets and Industry?

3. What are some of the drivers of globalization?

4. What are some of the advantages (and consequences) of 'free' trade in an open world economy?

5. Are the arguments put forward to support the practice of protectionism in any way justifiable?

6. What are the future prospects for the new World Trade Organization given the changing patterns of world business?

7. What recommendations would you make to countries which are currently not part of the major world economic groupings?

8. How far would you consider the EU 'a protectionist trade bloc'?

9. In what ways are EU markets opening up to foreign competition and Investment?

10. How significant are the investment and trade relationships between the EU, US and Japan?

11. How might we measure the success of European firms in the global marketplace?

12. What are some of the attributes of Europe's most successful firms?

13. How might (European) firms build a global presence?

14. How can companies turn global presence into global competitive advantage?

15. What do we mean by an integrated global business strategy?

Web guide

International business information and research

GRA Research Hotlinks (links for international business research) @
http://www.grai.com/links.htm

About.com: Global business (examination of international business trends and a
gateway to hundreds of links) @
http://globalbusiness.about.com/money/globalbusiness/

International organizations

International Monetary Fund @ http://www.imf.org/

The World Trade Organization (WTO) @ http://www.wto.org/

United Nations Conference on Trade and Development (UNCTAD) @
http://www.unctad.org/en/enhome.htm

Business data and rankings

Forbes International 800 (Forbes magazine rankings of the world's top 800 companies)
@ http://www.forbes.com/Forbes 500

FT 500 (*Financial Times* rankings of the world's top 500 companies) @
http://www.ft.com/FT500/

Global 500 (*Fortune Magazine* rankings of the world's top 500 corporations) @
http://www.fortune.com/fortune/global500/

References

Aggarwal, R. (1999) Technology and globalization as mutual reinforcers in business:
reorienting strategic thinking for the new millennium, *Management International
Review*, 15 July, 83.

Barnard, B. (1999) High-tech titans – European firms unveiling 21st century products,
EUROPE Magazine, 382.

Bartlett, C.A. and Ghoshal, S. (1989) *Managing Across Borders*, Hutchinson.

Bloch, B. (1998) Globalisation's assault on the labour market: a German perspective,
European Business Review, **98**(1).

Bryan, L.L. and Fraser, J.N. (1999) Getting to global, *The McKinsey Quarterly*, Autumn, 68.

Croome, J. (1996) *Reshaping the World Trading System: A History of the Uruguay Round*,
World Trade Organization.

Friedman, T.L. (1999) *The Lexus and the Olive Tree – Understanding Globalization*, McGraw-Hill.

Govindarajan, V. and Gupta, A.K. (1999a) Setting a course for the new global landscape, *Mastering Global Business*, Financial Times/Pitman Publishing, 5–11.

Govindarajan, V. and Gupta, A.K. (1999b) Turning global presence into global competitive advantage, *Mastering Global Business*, Financial Times/Pitman Publishing, 42–8.

Hanson, B.T. (1998) What happened to Fortress Europe? External trade policy liberalization in the European Union, *International Organization*, **52**(1), 55–85.

Hine, R.C. (1985) *The Political Economy of European Trade: An Introduction to the Trade Policies of the EEC*, Wheatsheaf.

Howell, T.R., Wolff, B.L., Bartlett, B.L. and Gadbaw, R.M. (eds) (1992) *Conflict Among Nations: Trade Policies in the 1990s*, Westview Press.

Johanson, J. and Vahlne, J. (1977) The internationalisation process of the firm: a model of knowledge development on increasing foreign commitments, *Journal of International Business Studies*, Spring–Summer, 23–32.

Krugman, P. (1996) *Strategic Trade policy and the New International Economics,* MIT Press.

Levitt, T. (1983) The globalization of markets, *Harvard Business Review*, **61**, May–June, 92–102.

Makhija, M.V., Kim, K. and Williamson, S.D. (1997) Measuring globalization of industries using a national industry approach, *Journal of International Business Studies*, **28**(4), 679–709.

Maresceau, M. (ed.) (1993) *The European Community's Commercial Policy After 1992*, Martinus Nijhoff.

Murphy, A. (1990) *The European Community and the International Trading System*, Vol. I, *Completing the Uruguay Round of the GATT*, Centre for European Policy Studies.

Ohmae, K. (1985) *Triad Power: the Coming Shape of Global Competition*, Free Press.

Ohmae, K. (1989) Managing in a borderless world, *Harvard Business Review*, May–June, 152–61.

O'Keefe, D. and Emiliou, N. (eds) (1996) *The EU and World Trade Law*, Wiley.

Penrose, E. (1990) Dumping – unfair competition and multinational corporations, *Japan in the World Economy*, **2**, 181–7.

Porter, M.E. (1986) *Competition in Global Industries*, Harvard Business School Press.

Porter, M.E. (1990) *The Competitive Advantage of Nations*, Macmillan.

Roberts, S. (1998) Economic globalization: a break from the past?, *International Review of Applied Economics*, **12**(2), 311–15.

UNCTAD (1998) *World Investment Report 1998. Trends and determinants.*

UNCTAD (1999) *World Investment Report 1999. FDI and the Challenge of Development.*

Index